ARE WE LIVING IN THE DAYS OF THE GREAT TRIBULATION, AT THE TIME OF THE END, DURING THE FULFILLMENT OF THE PROPHECIES OF REVELATION AND DANIEL?

An Exercise in Accepting the Reality of the Way Things Actually Are

by Miner T. Perkins III (2023)

Copyright © 2024 by Miner Perkins III
All Right Reserved by the Author

Front Cover Designed and Created by John Perkins
<u>Front Cover Photo</u>: Захоплений в бою ворожий танк T-72 used from **Mil.gov.ua** under license CC BY 4.0 – Deed Attribution 4.0 International (edges cropped from original)
https://creativecommons.org/licenses/by/4.0/deed.en

W.O.W! Publishing
Scottsbluff, NE
ISBN: 978-0-9914985-5-0

CONTENTS

End Time Prophecy Myths that are Not Found Anywhere in Scripture – Page 3

How to Know if the Prophecies of the Time of the End and Great Tribulation are Happening, and that Yahuweh/Yehovah's Coming to the Earth is Not Far Away – Page 35

The Prophecies that Need to be Either Already Fulfilled or in Process of Fulfillment in Order for it to be the Time of the Great Tribulation at the Time of the End Right Before Yeshua Returns – Page 49

Table of Contents – Page 51

There is one thing that has been consistent throughout history, man has never been able to fully understand or comprehend or accurately interpret any of Yahuweh/Yehovah's prophecies before they happen. And in most cases, people reject the fulfillment of Yahuweh/Yehovah's prophecies when they do happen, because they happen in ways that are different from how people wanted them to happen or imagined them to happen in their own understanding.

At Yahuweh/Yehovah's first coming to the earth, when he came to Abraham in the form of a man, and gave him the prophecy about making Abraham into a great nation in covenant with him through the miraculous birth of a male child through his wife Sarah, they did not understand the prophecy and tried to figure out a way they could fulfill it themselves without any miracle involved. That is how Ishmael was born.

Yahuweh/Yehovah also gave prophecies to Abraham about his future generations through Isaac, and when Yahuweh/Yehovah fulfilled those prophecies at his second coming to the earth, to bring the nation of Israel out of Egypt and meet him on Mount Sinai, the people fought Yahuweh/Yehovah all the way through the fulfillment of the prophecies. And ultimately the entire generation, except for Joshua and Caleb, rejected the way that Yahuweh/Yehovah fulfilled the prophecy of taking them out of bondage in Egypt to make them into the nation of Israel in their own land. The entire generation rebelled against Yahuweh/Yehovah and told him that they wanted to go back to Egypt to have him redo the fulfillment of the prophecy in a different way that was according to how they wanted it to happen, so that they could stay in the world and love the comforts of the world in slavery, and not have to do anything hard like fighting to take over a new land. No one was able to figure out ahead of time the way that Yahuweh/Yehovah would fulfill the prophecies to Abraham about making Isaac into a great nation Israel, and then be miraculously pulled out of bondage and take the land Yahuweh/Yehovah had promised to them through war and fighting. And almost everyone rejected the fulfillment of the prophecies when they came, when they found out that it was going to be hard and they would have to sacrifice their lives to follow Yahuweh/Yehovah.

Then when Yahuweh/Yehovah came in his third coming to the earth as Yeshua, the Messiah, born as a man, to fulfill his prophecies again, which he had spoken to the prophets for hundreds of years before, once again he fulfilled the prophecies in ways that no one had understood or expected before they happened. And once again the majority of the people rejected the way Yahuweh/Yehovah fulfilled his prophecies, because it was too different from how they had imagined the prophecies would be fulfilled in their imaginations.

As Yahuweh/Yehovah is now in process of returning again in his fourth coming to the earth, to end the world, it is happening the same way all over again as the three times before. The prophecies are being fulfilled in ways that no one was able to understand or expect or imagine before they happened, and the majority of the people on the earth are rejecting those fulfillments of the prophecies as they happen. This is the pattern of Yahuweh/Yehovah's prophecies and their fulfillments that has happened all through history.

The sad thing is how so many people miss out on getting to know Yahuweh/Yehovah more deeply as he fulfills his prophecies his way, according to who he is as a person. The whole purpose of all prophecy that Yahuweh/Yehovah gives to man is for man to know him in its fulfillment. Yahuweh/Yehovah's thoughts and ways are higher than our thoughts and ways (Isaiah 55:6-11), to translate it more literally Isaiah records that Yahuweh/Yehovah's plans and plots from his thoughts are higher than man's plans and plots that come from his thinking. And Yahuweh/Yehovah wants everyone to know him and understand him (Jeremiah 9:23-24; Jeremiah 31:34), to understand his ways, which are eternal life (Isaiah 58:1-2; John 14:6).

Instead of knowing Yahuweh/Yehovah for themselves, most just argue among each other about the correct interpretation of Yahuweh/Yehovah's prophecies and the correct way his prophecies should be fulfilled. And when they see the fulfillment of prophecy in front of them, most argue among each other if it is a true fulfillment or not, like the people in Yeshua's day arguing if he, as a man from Galil, is really the Messiah, since the Messiah should be born in Beyth Lechem Ephrathah (Bethlehem) (John 7:40-53). None of them bothered searching out the truth and actually knowing Yahuweh/Yehovah for themselves, and knowing for themselves through investigation if the prophecies had really been fulfilled, because they were too busy arguing with each other about whether or not the prophecies were really fulfilled or not.

Let us lay aside all of the arguing about how the prophecies of the Time of the End and the Great Tribulation are supposed to be fulfilled, and instead know Yahuweh/Yehovah and humbly investigate if the prophecies are actually being fulfilled now, at this present moment, according to just Yahuweh/Yehovah's own words which are written down in Scripture. And let us all remove the vain imaginations that we each have in our own minds and thoughts about how the End Time prophecies of Great Tribulation and Yeshua's Return should be fulfilled, and see what the actual words are that are written down in Scripture that need to happen in order for each prophecy to be fulfilled.

End Time Prophecy Myths that are Not Found Anywhere in Scripture:

A myth can sound very logical in the imagination of the mind, until it is brought into reality, and then often times a myth is found to be impossible in reality, historically or physically. A myth about a prophecy can also sound very logical, that it could happen that way in the future, until you know the reality of who Yahuweh/Yehovah is and how he does things, and then you can recognize him and his signature in the true fulfillment of the prophecy when it does happen in reality.

An unfulfilled prophecy deals with the unseen realm of the future that has not yet entered into our reality in the present, whereas a fulfilled prophecy deals with the very tangible and real realm of the past that is recorded and preserved in our present reality. Unfulfilled prophecies in the future are not something that are tangible and real to us yet in the present, but prophecies that have already happened and have been fulfilled are very real and concrete. Fulfilled prophecies are solid and can be seen very easily exactly how they were fulfilled in every detail, but when dealing with a prophecy that has not yet happened, in order to try to understand it, the mind has to imagine it, and make up ideas of what it might mean and how it might happen, to try to think about the prophecy abstractly in a non-real way in the mind. That is what makes it tricky to try to study and teach ideas about a prophecy that has not yet been fulfilled, because everyone thinks about it in a different way in their mind, since there is no concrete and solid way to see how it actually will happen in reality.

In the mind, people make up fiction stories, stories that are myths and legends, that never have happened in the past and never will happen in the future. The fiction stories are fun to think about, as long as they are not treated as reality, as being real in the real world. The trouble with prophecies that have not yet happened, and are still in the future, is that when people are using their imaginations of what they might mean, they automatically as a part of the natural thinking process, begin to create imaginary ways of fulfillment for the prophecies, in the same way that they process a fictional story, which then turns into creating myths and legends about the prophecies.

It is easier, and more fun, for people to process and think about myths and legends about things and people. People generally even prefer the legends about historical people and things that happened in reality in the past, because they are easier to think about and accept than reality oftentimes. After a while, people stop reading the historical records of the truth about people and words spoken in the past, and only the myths and legends are told and retold, to the point that people do not even know what the original words are anymore, only the myths about the words. Everybody knows the story about George Washington cutting down the cherry tree and saying he cannot tell a lie, but the whole story about George Washington and the cherry tree is actually a lie. It never happened; it is only a myth or legend about George Washington. The historical records of the person Robin Hood are completely lost, so that there is no way to even know what the reality was of who he was and what he did; only the myth and legend of Robin Hood has survived in an ancient minstrel song. People make up myths and legends about everybody and everything, past, present, and future.

A natural thing that Yahuweh/Yehovah created people to do is to be able to play make believe, and imagine things being able to happen that are not real, in real life. There is nothing wrong with playing make believe and making up fictional tales as long as it is not treated as reality and the truth of something that really happened or will happen or is happening.

Yahuweh/Yehovah's unfulfilled prophecies about the Time of the End, and the Great Tribulation, and His Coming to Rule the Earth in Scripture have not been immune from people, in their imaginations through hundreds of years, creating myths and legends about the prophecies and how they will be fulfilled. And it has come to the point where in many cases the myths now take precedence over the actual words of the prophecies themselves, and even when people read the words of the prophecies, it is difficult to remove the myths from the mind to see what is really written there in Scripture. [I know, because it has taken me many decades to be able to break free from the myths and just see the words of the prophecies in Scripture all on their own without adding any imagination to them.]

But this is no different from what happened when Yeshua came as the Messiah, God (Yahuweh/Yehovah) Himself. There were so many myths about the Messianic prophecies that had been created in the Pharisee (Rabbinic Orthodox) religious system, that most could no longer see the original words of the prophecies and the fulfillment of those words right in front of them. The interesting thing is that most of the myths about the End Times today were not created until the 1800's. It is a common saying in the modern world today that every Christian generation for the last 2,000 years has believed that their generation would be the one to see the return of Yeshua, and that the prophecies of his return and the end of the world were happening in their generation and lifetimes, and they have all turned out to be wrong. The truth is that the majority of Christians and majority of generations of Christian believers through recorded history never believed that Yeshua was returning in their lifetime or that they would see his return in their generation.

In fact there are only two eras in Christian history in which Christians believed that Yeshua's return would be imminent and soon, and that the prophecies of his return were being fulfilled in their lifetimes: the era of the Early Church from the early 300's to the early 600's, and the era that we are in now that began in the early 1800's. And it is interesting that it is also from these two eras that the majority of the myths about prophecies in Scripture were created. The writings in the New Testament in the 1st century C.E. show that the followers of Yeshua at that time certainly believed he was returning very soon, but they also understood that it might not be in their lifetimes or their generation by the end of the century. The writings of the early Christians in the 2nd to 3rd centuries C.E. shows that the Christians at that time still mostly believed the same way as the 1st century believers concerning the return of Yeshua.

It was not until around the early 300's that things began to change, when the Christians of that time began to try to calculate the years from creation using the erroneous Greek Septuagint translation of the Old Testament, instead of using the original Hebrew. It was the errors found in the counting of years from the Greek Septuagint that led them to believe that Yeshua would be returning sometime around the years 500 C.E. to 600 C.E. by various calculations. This together with the fact that the Western Roman Empire was collapsing in the 400's, led many Christians to believe at that time that Yeshua was returning imminently in their day and lifetime, in their generation, and that the Anti-Christ Beast Kingdom with its Horns would be rising up at any moment in place of the fallen Roman Empire. This belief continued for about 300 years from the early 300's to the early 600's, culminating with Pope Gregory I, the Great proclaiming from surviving records of letters he wrote that the world would be ending at any moment with the fulfillment of the prophecies and the return of Yeshua.

That 300 year era of Christians believing that Yeshua's return was coming soon and imminently in their lifetimes ended with the death of Pope Gregory in 604 C.E. (together with the strengthening of Europe in the early 700's through Charles Martel and the Carolingian Dynasty that later founded the Holy Roman Empire through Charlemagne). For about 1,200 years after 604, until the early 1800's, there was almost no generation of Christians who believed that Yeshua was returning in their lifetimes or that the prophecies of his return were happening in their lifetimes. There was only a brief moment just before the year 1000 C.E. when there was a short lived frenzy of a couple of decades when Christians once again thought that Yeshua might be returning and the world would end in about the year 1000. But this was only a leftover incident that was part of the earlier era in the 300's to 600's, using the exact same Christian writings with the exact same erroneous calculations from the Greek Septuagint that had caused the earlier frenzy in the 500's. The short frenzy in the few decades before the year 1000 disappeared as quickly as it came, and there are few reliable sources from that time to know the extent of what really happened, because during that time the official teachings of the Church were that Yeshua was <u>not</u> returning at that time. All of what is written about that time comes from later, less reliable histories and sources that might have only been later myths and legends creating hype about something that never actually happened.

Outside of this one moment before the year 1000, there was no other time recorded between the 600's to the 1800's when there was a generation of Christians believing that Yeshua was returning imminently in their generation or that the prophecies of his return were being fulfilled in their time. There were lots of accusations made during that time claiming different people or institutions were Anti-Christs or fulfillments of the Beasts and Horns in Daniel and Revelation, but no belief that fulfillments of Beasts and Horns in prophecy meant that Yeshua was actually about to return in their lifetimes. All of the teachings during that time taught that there were certain prerequisites that had to happen first before any of the real End Time prophecies specifically of Yeshua's Return could happen, such as that the Jews had to return to the land of Israel and become a nation first, or that the Holy Roman Empire had to collapse first. Thus during this timeframe in recorded history no one was expecting Yeshua's Return imminently in their day or lifetimes.

There were of course always some individuals who believed this way, as evidenced in the 1600's where there are records of some individual Christians (mostly Anabaptists) who had ideas that the world might end soon and Yeshua might be returning soon, because of comets seen at that time and other various reasons; or records of political cult offshoots of Christianity that believed in the return of Yeshua in their lifetime, like the Fifth Monarchists in the 1600's. But there is no record of any major denominations or mainstream Christian religious groups during those times that seriously taught or believed as an entire denomination that Yeshua was returning in their lifetime or in their generation. Christians generally believed that his return would happen in a later generation in the future, and most of the time would outcast any Christians who believed otherwise that Yeshua might come at any moment or in their generation. Most Christians who are recorded giving predictions about when Yeshua would return during this time from about 600 to 1800, such as Martin Luther, Christopher Columbus, Pope Innocent III, Sir Isaac Newton, or John Wesley, predicted dates or ranges of dates of his return that would happen after they would have already died, because the belief was so prevalent among most Christians during that time that Yeshua would not return in their lifetimes.

Then suddenly in the late 1700's to early 1800's everything changed, and everybody started shifting to talking about, studying, and teaching about End Time prophecy as something that was coming soon that people needed to prepare for. It was a new movement that birthed many new denominations solely based upon End Time prophecy teaching, and everybody started talking about the End Times, and once again examining if any of the prophecies specifically of Yeshua's imminent return were being fulfilled in their lifetime. It was this explosion of interest in prophecy again that caused most of the myths about End Time prophecy to be created. Most of the myths about End Time prophecy did not exist prior to the 1800's, which can be seen in the various Christian literature written during that time and around the turn of the 20th century, with many people trying to figure out where all of these different new teachings about prophecy had come from, such as where the idea had come from that the Anti-Christ would confirm a covenant for 7 years. That was a brand new idea in the late 1800's which no one had ever thought of prior to that, along with the idea of a 7 year tribulation and a pre-tribulation rapture, which did not begin to circulate until about the 1830's.[1]

In order not to stumble and fall over the myths about the prophecies of the Time of the End and the Great Tribulation, here is a list of some of the major myths concerning End Time prophecy, and the verses in Scripture that show the truth of what the prophecies actually say. There are many well-meaning prophecy teachers and scholars who have taught these myths for over a hundred years, or even over a thousand years in some cases, totally trusting in these myths as true and trustworthy. But when these myths are examined against the actual words in Scripture everyone will find for themselves that these myths are not there.

Myth 1. There will be a Dictator Called the Anti-Christ who Rules Over a Global Empire (One World Government) and is Worshipped as a god.

Truth. Most people are shocked to learn that there is not one single prophecy about the Anti-Christ (Anti-Messiah) in all of Scripture. For someone who is so important in prophecy teachings and commentaries, one would think there would be at least one prophecy about this Anti-Christ person, but there is not even one. The Anti-Christ (Anti-Messiah) is not mentioned once in the entire book of Revelation, nor is he ever mentioned once by Yeshua in any of the Gospels, nor is he mentioned once in the entire Old Testament.

The Anti-Christs (Anti-Messiahs) are only mentioned by John three times in his first and second letters (**1 John 2:18-25, 1 John 4:1-6, and 2 John 1:7**). And John does not record any prophecies at all about these Anti-Christs, only explaining that they are already there in his present time and will be coming in the future.

---

[1] John Nelson Darby (1800-1882) is the one credited with being the first to create and teach the theology of the pre-tribulation rapture still taught today, in about the year 1830, and was also probably the first to teach the idea of a 7 year timeframe of tribulation. He is also known as the father of the theologies of Dispensationalism and Futurism. Johann Georg Ferdinand Müller (1805-1898), known more widely by his English name George Müller, in the end had to separate from John Darby and Darby's theologies. Müller all his life continued to believe, as Christians through history up to that time believed, in the post-tribulation rapture.

And he describes the Anti-Christs as: 1. Believers in Yeshua that go out from the midst of the believers in Yeshua falsely claiming to be sent by Yeshua's Apostles (Emissaries); 2. Anyone who denies that Yeshua is the Messiah; 3. Anyone who denies the Father and the Son; 4. Any demonic spirit that denies Yeshua Messiah came in the flesh; 5. Any human being that denies Yeshua Messiah came in the flesh; 6. Anyone that leads others astray, teaching them that Yeshua Messiah did not come in the flesh.

This is all that John teaches about the Anti-Christs, who are false prophets leading people astray about who Yeshua was, either claiming that Yeshua was just a man like everyone else, and not the Messiah, or claiming that Yeshua as the Messiah was never a physical man inside of a physical body walking on the earth. There is nothing about the Anti-Christs ever becoming a dictator ruler of a global empire and there is nothing about the Anti-Christs ever being worshipped as gods. This is all that is recorded in Scripture about the Anti-Christs; anything beyond this is only speculation and theory.

Over time the myth of the Anti-Christ was created by combining these verses in 1 and 2 John (which contain no actual future prophecies about the Anti-Christ), with:

The Beast Out of the Sea in **Revelation 13, 16, 19** (and the Scarlet Beast Out of the Pit of the Deep in 17)
The Little Horn in **Daniel 7 – 8**
The Man of Lawlessness/Sin in **2 Thessalonians 2**
Antiochus IV Epiphanes in **Daniel 11** (Already fulfilled in the 1 and 2 Books of Maccabees)
The King of Babel, Helel in **Isaiah 14**
The Prince of Tyre in **Ezekiel 28**
Gog of the Land of Magog in **Ezekiel 38 – 39**

All of the above prophecies were arbitrarily combined together to create a mythical Anti-Christ person. He was considered to be the Beast Out of the Sea in Revelation 13 so that he could become a powerful world leader, and he was considered to be the Little Horn in Daniel 7 so that he could be a deceptive villain, deceiving the world and the set-apart ones (saints), overcoming them. He was called the Man of Lawlessness/Sin in 2 Thessalonians so that he could be worshipped as a god as the head of a religious cult, sitting on the throne of Yahuweh/Yehovah, and by becoming the Man of Lawlessness/Sin he had to at the same time become the King of Babel in Isaiah 14 and the Prince of Tyre in Ezekiel 28, because they both also sit on the throne of Yahuweh/Yehovah in the last days too. And then he was called Gog in Ezekiel 38 so that he could become the great military leader, leading the world to attack and destroy Israel and Jerusalem during or at the end of the Great Tribulation. And through the process Daniel 11 got thrown into the mix, and even in some cases people have combined the physical object of the Disgusting Idol (Abomination) Desolating in Daniel 11 – 12 and Matthew 24 and Mark 13 into the Anti-Christ person, making the Abomination object into the person of the Anti-Christ, a person who does not even exist in the prophecies in Scripture.

When one actually reads each of these prophecies, about these different entities and persons who are in positions of authority when Yeshua returns at the Time of the End, it becomes clear that each of them is a different person; they cannot all be combined together into one person. The Little Horn in Daniel 7 cannot be the Beast Out of the Sea in Revelation 13, because in Daniel 7 the Little Horn is a separate person and entity that comes out of the exact same Beast Out of the Sea that is described in Revelation 13. There is no way that one single person can be both the Little Horn and the Beast Out of the Sea at the same time, because they are two different entities according to Daniel 7. The Little Horn is never even mentioned in Revelation. And the Little Horn cannot be the Man of Lawlessness/Sin that Sha'ul (Paul) writes about in 2 Thessalonians, because the Little Horn never once is worshipped as a god in the prophecies about him in Daniel 7 and 8, and he never once sits on any thrones claiming to be a god or Yahuweh/Yehovah, and he is never once called a man of lawlessness/sin or a son of destruction/perdition. Even though he exalts himself as high as the Prince of the host, it never actually says that he is worshipped by other people as the Prince of the host (God) in Daniel 8:11.

There is further study about this later on, but anyone who reads each of these verses for themselves will see that all of these entities cannot be combined together into one single person, even if they might do similar things. Just because the King of Babel, called Helel, sits on the throne of Yahuweh/Yehovah in the heavens, trying to be like him, and the Prince of Tyre in Lebanon also sits on the throne of Yahuweh/Yehovah at the same time, does not mean that the King of Babel and the Prince of Tyre are the same person. They do lots of different thing from each other as well, but both of their cities end up destroyed in the end.

Also, just because the Little Horn causes some of the stars to fall out of the sky in the exact same way that the Dragon in Revelation 12 causes 1/3 of the stars to fall out of the sky, does not mean that the Little Horn and the Dragon are the same person. The Dragon is the Serpent of old in the garden, haSatan (the Adversary), and the Little Horn is a king or ruler who is a physical person on the earth. They do the same thing, but they are not the same person or entity. The Little Horn has a mouth speaking great things, and the Beast Out of the Sea has a mouth speaking great things and blasphemies, but the Little Horn is a horn that comes out of the Beast Out of the Sea and cannot be the same entity as the Beast Out of the Sea. They are two different entities that have one thing in common of speaking great, powerful words with a mouth.

Anyone who reads each of these prophecies for themselves will see that there are many different ruling persons and government entities who are doing similar things all at the same time during the Great Tribulation before Yeshua returns, not one, single, individual person called an Anti-Christ fulfilling all of the prophecies and doing everything all by himself. There is no indication in the actual written words in Scripture (using only the literal and exact words that are written down) that all of these prophecies are about the same person or entity, nor that they have anything to do with the Anti-Christs that John speaks about in his letters.

Myth 2. An Anti-Christ Ruler Confirms a 7 Year Peace Covenant with the Israeli Government in Jerusalem, Then Breaks that Covenant in the Middle of the 7 Years.

Truth. For this myth the prophecies of **Isaiah 28:1-22** and **Daniel 9:24-27** were combined together, even though there is no indication in the two prophecies that these two covenants are even remotely related to each other. One of them is a new covenant made by Jerusalem with death and the grave in Isaiah 28, and the other is a covenant that is already in existence that is made stronger for a One Seven or one week span of time in

Daniel 9. The Isaiah 28 covenant is a bad one with death, but there is no indication that the Daniel 9 covenant is a bad one in any way.

This myth of a 7 year confirmation of a covenant by an Anti-Christ was first created because of ignoring basic language grammar rules in the Hebrew prophecy of Daniel 9:24-27. And a person does not even have to know Hebrew to see the obvious grammar error that was made to twist the Daniel prophecy in 9:27 into being about an Anti-Christ/Anti-Messiah instead of being about the true Messiah/Anointed One who is cut off and has nothing. Daniel 9:27 begins, "And He shall strengthen a covenant for many for one week." Most English translations use the word "confirm" instead of "strengthen," but the Hebrew word here "Gavar גָּבַר" more accurately means to prevail or strengthen or make stronger in victory. This already exposes the error of one part of the myth that an Anti-Christ breaks the covenant in the middle of the week, because this person is strengthening a covenant for an entire week or 1 seven, not breaking it at any time during that week. This covenant spoken of in Daniel 9:27 is a covenant that is never broken at any time, because it is made stronger so that it cannot be broken.

The question is, who does the pronoun "He" refer to? In the previous sentence there are only two subjects in the sentence: the first is Messiah, "And after the sixty-two sevens (weeks) Messiah is cut off and has nothing for himself." The second is the people, "And the people, of a prince coming, shall destroy the city and the set-apart place." Messiah is a singular person who should be referred to with the singular noun "He" and the people are a plural group of more than one person who should be referred to with the plural noun "they." Messiah and the people are the only two subjects in the previous sentences that the "He" can refer to, so obviously "He" has to refer to Messiah (the anointed prince) who is cut off and has nothing for himself, he is the one who strengthens the previously made covenant for many for one week and stops the sacrifices in the middle of the week, as part of that strengthening and prevailing of the covenant.

In the myth, the "He" in Daniel 9:27 is changed to no longer refer to the whole subject of the prophecy, Messiah, Anointed One, but instead to refer to this prince that does not even participate in the prophecy or do anything in the prophecy, because he is not the subject of the sentence. It is the people who are the subject, not this prince. In any grammar in any language, the pronoun "He" in the following sentence has to refer to the main subject person in the previous sentences, not to a person listed in a prepositional phrase describing a subject in the sentence.

The final error creating the myth came from an imperfect English translation of the final sentence of Daniel 9:27. It should read this way: "And upon a wing of disgusting idols (abominations) shall be one desolating, and until the complete destruction and what is decided is poured out upon the desolating." This is a more literal, exact translation of what the Hebrew actually says. But the English translators, to try to make the sentence flow better in English, used the pronoun "he" in the sentence, so that it sounds like the same person in the previous sentences who is strengthening the covenant and stopping the sacrifices is also desolating or laying waste with abominations (disgusting objects of idolatry) that are on a wing. Almost all English translations have written something like, "And upon the wing of disgusting idols (abominations) *he shall* make desolate."

The pronoun "he" does not technically exist there in the original Hebrew words. What is written there is "shiqqutsim meshomem שִׁקּוּצִים מְשֹׁמֵם" which means "abominations desolating" or "abominations, shall be one desolating" or "abominations, shall be one making desolate." The word "meshomem" is the Piel Participle (adjective verb) describing the noun "shiqqutsim" or "abominations." This means that the Hebrew word action verb written here for "desolate" is written in the Hebrew form where it becomes an adjective describing the noun next to it, in English requiring "ing" to be put at the end of the word, so that it becomes "desolating." Often in Hebrew participle phrases as this one, the pronoun "he" is left out entirely, making it implied that there is "one" desolating, but not a definite "he" who is desolating.[2] So this sentence is referring to another person, another "one," not previously mentioned in the prophecy, and is not referring to the "He" or Messiah previous in the prophecy. The one desolating is a different person from the one strengthening the covenant for one week and then stopping the sacrifices and offerings in the middle of the week.

The one strengthening the covenant in Daniel 9 can only refer to the true Messiah Yeshua who strengthened his already made covenant for many people, for a week, by stopping animal sacrifices in the middle of the week through becoming the eternal Passover Lamb sacrifice for sin for all time. The one strengthening the covenant cannot be any Anti-Christ/Anti-Messiah or False Messiah or Little Horn or Beast Out of the Sea or anything like that.

Myth 3. The Covenant with Death made by the Israeli Government in Jerusalem is Made for a 7 Year Span of Time.

Truth. Because of the aforementioned myth about Daniel 9 being about a one week or one seven strengthening of a covenant, one week representing seven years, the **Isaiah 28:1-22** prophecy is now automatically associated with being a 7 year covenant with death. But this too is a myth, because the Isaiah 28 covenant with death that the government in Jerusalem makes is not associated with any set span of time. Anyone reading the prophecy for themselves can see this very obvious fact, the Isaiah 28 covenant prophecy could last for any number of days, months, or years, there are no limitations on it.

---

[2] Wilhelm Gesenius (translated by A. E. Cowley), *Gesenius' Hebrew Grammar, as Edited and Enlarged by the Late E. Kautzsch* (Oxford: Clarendon Press, 1910) 116.5.Rem.3, pg. 360 [It should be noted that this exact same Piel Participle phrase "hashshiqquts meshomem הַשִּׁקּוּץ מְשֹׁמֵם" is later translated as "abomination desolating" or "abomination of desolation" or "abomination causing desolation/making desolate" in all translations in Daniel 11:31, leaving out any pronoun "he" or "one" entirely, the only difference here being that it is purely in just the singular case, without any plural.]

Myth 4. There will be a Temple or Tent/Tabernacle Built on the Temple Mount with Animal Sacrifices Resuming Before the Disgusting Idol (Abomination) Desolating can be Set-Up and Before the Great Tribulation can Begin.

Truth. One would think that with all of the importance placed on the rebuilding of a new temple (usually called a Third Temple) in End Time prophecy teaching and study that there would be at least one prophecy about a new third temple being built. And yet there is not one prophecy anywhere in Scripture about another temple being rebuilt on this earth ever again, especially not one before Yeshua returns at the end of the Great Tribulation. All of the prophecies about the rebuilding of the Temple into the Second Temple, after the destruction of the First Temple, have already been fulfilled, and no prophecies were ever given in the Old Testament or the New Testament about another Temple ever being rebuilt again after the Second one was destroyed. Yet this is a very old prophecy myth about a new temple that has been around for a long time.

If there are no prophecies about another Temple that will ever be rebuilt again, where does the idea of a new Third Temple come from? The primary source is the prophecy of Yeshua about a disgusting idol (abomination) desolating being placed at the set-apart place in **Matthew 24:15-22** and **Mark 13:14-20**, which is the sign that The End and the Great Tribulation have begun. Yeshua is referring to the prophecies in **Daniel 11:1-45** and **Daniel 12:1-12** about a disgusting idol (abomination) desolating that is placed at the set-apart place, and he is giving interpretation and understanding to these Daniel prophecies in connection with the Great Tribulation that comes right before his return.

Daniel chapter 11 was already fulfilled during the time of the Seleucid and Ptolemy divisions of the Greek Empire, and by Antiochus Epiphanes, recorded in the events of the first and second books of Maccabees. The Festival of Hanukkah is a remembrance of this fulfillment of the Daniel 11 prophecies. But Daniel chapter 12 was never fulfilled at that time, only chapter 11. This means that the disgusting idol (abomination) desolating in chapter 11 was fulfilled, but the disgusting idol (abomination) desolating in chapter 12 was never fulfilled, the one that lasts for 1,290 days connected with Great Tribulation for the nation of Israel. This is why Matthew adds the note in chapter 24 for the reader to understand, since the prophecy was already partially fulfilled a couple hundred years before Yeshua's teaching about the Great Tribulation and his return.

In Daniel 11 and 12 the two main elements of the prophecies about the disgusting idol desolating are that it is placed at "the set-apart place" (sanctuary or holy place) and "the continual" is removed. Most translations erroneously have "daily sacrifices" written instead of "the continual" which gives a false impression that daily sacrifices have to be happening at a Temple or Tabernacle structure in order for this prophecy to be fulfilled. But in the original Hebrew it says that "the continual" is removed, which can refer to any of the continual duties done at the set-apart place, including the lighting of the menorah, the renewing of the showbread, the incense renewed in the golden altar, or the sacrifices of the animals for the sin offerings on the brazen altar.

From the prophecy of the disgusting idol desolating in Daniel, connected with Yeshua's words that this event in Daniel begins the Great Tribulation, it sounds like there must be first a Temple building or Tabernacle structure in place with a set-apart place (holy place) inside it, and with the continual operations of the set-apart place happening in order for the Great Tribulation to begin and this prophecy to be fulfilled. But here are the serious problems with this possible theoretical interpretation of the prophecy:

1. The first problem is that there is no prophecy in Scripture that indicates that Yahuweh/Yehovah ever wants another Temple or Tabernacle/Tent to be built again in Jerusalem after the destruction of the Second Temple by the Romans. The indications that Yahuweh/Yehovah gives are all the opposite, that he never wants another physical building or tent structure to be built anywhere again. In the New Jerusalem in the New Heavens and New Earth there is no more Temple, because Yahuweh/Yehovah himself is the Temple, in **Revelation 21:22**. And this concept is also spoken of by Yahuweh/Yehovah in **Isaiah 66:1-2**, repeated in **Acts 7:48-50**, that he does not dwell in Temples and does not need them. This is part of the prophecy of the New Heavens and New Earth in Isaiah 65, that Yahuweh/Yehovah does not need a physical building anywhere in order to have a set-apart place for him to dwell in, nor does he have any desire for one to be built.

Since there is no prophecy in Scripture about another Temple or Tabernacle/Tent ever being built as a physical set-apart place in Jerusalem or anywhere else, the only way that another Temple could be built is if Yahuweh/Yehovah gave a prophetic word now, today, in the present time, to the Christians of the world to go and build a Third Temple themselves. Otherwise to build another Temple or Tabernacle/Tent in Jerusalem would be disobedience against Yahuweh/Yehovah, doing something that goes against his will and is not according to his command.

2. The second problem is that there is no prophecy in Scripture that indicates that Yahuweh/Yehovah ever wants the continual Temple services of sacrifices and offerings and the incense and showbread and menorah to ever be implemented or started up ever again either. Yahuweh/Yehovah is the one who stopped the sacrifices and offerings already himself, according to the **Daniel 9:27** prophecy, and there is no prophecy in Scripture that says that he ever wants them to be started up again after he has completed and finished them himself, as the sacrifice of the Passover Lamb Yeshua. **Hebrews 9:1 – 10:31** explains how those shadow pictures of the animal sacrifices and other continual services of the set-apart place are completed and finished and there is no need for them to come back again. Without any prophecy or command from Yahuweh/Yehovah himself in Scripture to bring back the sacrifices of animals, anyone who does so without a direct command from Yahuweh/Yehovah is in disobedience and sin against him, as Samuel says in **1 Samuel 13:1-14** and **1 Samuel 15:18-26**. To do any kinds of sacrifices or offerings to Yahuweh/Yehovah without his command is disobedience and sin against him, and King Saul lost his kingdom because of disobedient sacrificing to Yahuweh/Yehovah.

This means that if a Temple or Tabernacle set-apart place is built in Jerusalem without a new command from Yahuweh/Yehovah first (since no such command exists in Scripture), it is disobedience and rebellion against Yahuweh/Yehovah, and therefore can never even be considered set-apart (holy), and can never be the fulfillment of the prophecy of the set-apart place in Matthew/Mark and Daniel. And if the animal sacrifices are resumed in Jerusalem without a new, direct command from Yahuweh/Yehovah himself to bring them back again, the animal sacrifices that anyone would do in Jerusalem or on or around the Temple Mount would be disobedience and rebellion and sin against Yahuweh/Yehovah, and therefore could never be a set-apart (holy) continual thing that could fulfill the Matthew/Mark and Daniel prophecy of it being removed.

Any Temple or Tabernacle and sacrifices done at the Temple Mount become an abomination themselves, when they are done in disobedience against Yahuweh/Yehovah, and if the bringing back of the sacrifices to Jerusalem or the Temple Mount were truly a set-apart (holy) thing to do, then it is the Christians, the believers in Yeshua, who should be the ones bringing them back, not the Jews who do not believe in Yeshua as the Messiah. And yet there are no Christians who are willing to do it themselves, because they know that it is wrong, that it goes against the will of Yahuweh/Yehovah to bring them back again. So they expect the non-believing Jews to do it for them, but the Orthodox and Religious Jews of today do not even obey the commands of Yahuweh/Yehovah in properly carrying out the sacrifices. Instead they follow the commands of men (**Isaiah 29:13**), in the Talmud, which is in direct rebellion and disobedience against the commands of Yahuweh/Yehovah written down in his Torah of Moses. The Talmud has completely changed many of Yahuweh/Yehovah's commands on animal sacrifices and other duties at the set-apart place. Any sacrifices they do will be disobedient ones like King Saul's sacrifices.

Since Yeshua's sacrifice as the Lamb, it has changed things so that the Matthew/Mark and Daniel prophecy about the set-apart place and the continual cannot be fulfilled in the same way that it happened in the days of Antiochus Epiphanes and the Maccabees. In this prophecy there is not even a mention of a physical Temple or Tabernacle/Tent structure that is in existence when the prophecy is fulfilled, just a set-apart place (holy place); so there is no requirement in this prophecy for a physical building or structure to be made before the disgusting idol desolating is placed at a place that is set-apart. And the prophecy only speaks of "the continual" being taken away, in such a way that it does not even have to mean that there are any sacrifices happening at all to be taken away. There is no requirement for a Temple to be built or sacrifices to happen first before this prophecy is fulfilled.

Yeshua himself begins in Matthew 24 by saying to his disciples that the current Temple, the Second Temple, that they were viewing, would be completely destroyed without a single stone left on another stone. And yet through the entire teaching he gives about the Last Days and the Great Tribulation and his return, he never once mentions that the Temple, after it is destroyed, would ever be rebuilt again. This was the perfect opportunity for Yeshua to give a prophecy about a Third Temple being built, and yet he never once mentions that another Temple would ever be built again after the Second one was destroyed. Obviously the prophecy that Yeshua gives about the disgusting idol standing at the set-apart place has nothing to do with a physical Temple being built or in existence at the time of its fulfillment.

If there is no requirement in the Matthew/Mark and Daniel prophecies for a Temple or sacrifices to be put in place before the disgusting idol desolating is placed, or before the Great Tribulation begins, then are there any other prophecies that indicate a Temple is in existence during the Great Tribulation? The only other two prophecies are **Revelation 11:1-2** and **2 Thessalonians 2:3-8**. In both of these prophecies there is no way to know if the Greek wording used is referring to a Temple structure like the First and Second Temples, or to a Tabernacle structure like what was built by the children of Israel in the wilderness. In Revelation 11 there is a Temple or Tabernacle mentioned that is measured by John, and then the outer court is given over to the nations or gentiles. The important detail here is that John not only measures the Temple or Tabernacle, but also measures the worshippers inside of this Temple or Tabernacle.

Why would John need to measure the people themselves who are inside of this Temple/Tabernacle? It certainly could not be for tailoring purposes for making clothing for them. There is nothing in this prophecy that says that an actual physical Temple or Tabernacle structure has been, or will be, rebuilt again. The only reason to measure the people who are worshipping inside of the Temple/Tabernacle is because it is a Temple building that is built out of people instead of physical stones or leather and cloth sheets. The worshippers of Yahuweh/Yehovah are the Temple/Tabernacle of Yahuweh/Yehovah that he dwells in and with. It is the people that are the building material of this Temple/Tabernacle in Revelation 11, existing wherever Yahuweh/Yehovah's people are on the earth, including his people who are believers in Yeshua living in Jerusalem. This is not a prophecy about a physical Temple/Tabernacle in Jerusalem, but one about the true believers and followers of Yahuweh/Yehovah existing as the true Temple/Tabernacle where he dwells with them, as he builds all of his people together into one nation or city of people.

As for 2 Thessalonians 2, the Temple/Tabernacle mentioned here is where a man of lawlessness/sin is supposed to sit like God in God's Temple/Tabernacle, trying to portray himself as God. It was Paul who wrote this, and Paul knew full well from his own writings that it is the bodies, and the body, of the believers that are now the Temple/Tabernacle of God in **1 Corinthians 3:16-17**, **1 Corinthians 6:19-20**, and **1 Corinthians 12:12-27**. If Paul himself recognized that it is the bodies of the believers in Yeshua who have now become the set-apart Temple/Tabernacle Dwelling Place of the Spirit of Yahuweh/Yehovah, then could he have meant any other Temple/Tabernacle in his writings about such a Temple/Tabernacle in 2 Thessalonians 2? It is in Yahuweh/Yehovah's Temple/Tabernacle built of his own people, those who are believers in Yeshua, that this Man of Lawlessness/Sin sits and tries to portray himself as the one true God Yahuweh/Yehovah, trying to deceive the true believers in Yeshua to follow after false gods and false worship.

So there is no indication in Revelation 11 or 2 Thessalonians 2 that either of these Temple/Tabernacles have to be physical structures existing during the Great Tribulation, and all of the evidence in both cases points to the fact that they are speaking of the believers in Yeshua themselves who are the Temple/Tabernacle of Yahuweh/Yehovah on the earth during the Great Tribulation, his set-apart Dwelling Place.

Are there any other prophecies that indicate that a physical Tabernacle or Tent will be built in Jerusalem before or during the Great Tribulation, before Yeshua returns? The only other possible prophecy remaining is **Amos 9:11-12**, which is repeated in Acts 15:13-18, speaking of the Booth of David that has fallen down and is rebuilt again, so that the nations (gentiles) will seek Yahuweh/Yehovah and be brought into his nation Israel. While this is a prophecy that has not yet been completely fulfilled, there is still no indication that this Booth of David is referring to a physical Tabernacle or Tent like the Tabernacle in the wilderness being rebuilt or set up again, because the Hebrew words for Tabernacle (Mishkan) and Tent (Ohel) are not even written in this prophecy. It is the Hebrew word Booth (Sukkah) in reference to the Booths (Sukkoth) that are built during Yahuweh/Yehovah's Festival of Sukkoth. The indications are that this prophecy will not be fulfilled until Yahuweh/Yehovah has come at the end of the Great Tribulation to fulfill the Festival of Sukkoth, by making his Sukkah or Booth with men, as in **Revelation 21:3**.

These are the only prophecies about possible Temples or Tabernacles or resuming of sacrifices that are about the Great Tribulation and Yeshua's Return, and none of them have any requirements or indications of a physical building or tent structure being built in order for them to be fulfilled, nor do any of them have any requirements that there has to be any of the "continuals" of the priestly duties and services come back in a physical form in Jerusalem for the prophecies to be fulfilled. The only prophecy about an actual described Temple and sacrifices that has not yet been fulfilled is **Ezekiel 40:1 – 48:35**, and according to **Revelation 21:10 – 22:2** this Temple exists in the New Jerusalem in the New Heavens and New Earth, with the exact same descriptions of the composition of the city of Jerusalem in both.

And the key here is that in Revelation 21 John specifically says that there is no Temple at all in the New Jerusalem where the Temple of Ezekiel is located, because Yahuweh/Yehovah himself, and the Lamb, is the only Temple. This sounds like a contradiction, but its meaning is clear; the only way this can be possible for the Ezekiel Temple to be in the New Jerusalem is that Yahuweh/Yehovah never intended it to be built as a physical Temple, but for it to be a shadow picture and symbol of him as the true Temple, the only one who has always been the only true Temple/Tabernacle/Set-Apart Place, dwelling with his people everywhere at all times.

Myth 5. A Person Who Refuses to Take the Mark of the Beast Out of the Sea is Beheaded or Killed in Some Way.

Truth. This myth causes many to stumble over their thinking of what to watch for with the Mark of the Beast Out of the Sea and what it looks like. The people who have believed and taught this myth have been well meaning and have thought it correct, but this is not what is actually written down in Scripture. The reality is that Revelation is the only book that gives any prophecies about the Mark, in **Revelation 13:16-18**, **Revelation 14:9-11**, **Revelation 16:1**-2, and **Revelation 20:4**, and there is nowhere in Revelation that says that a person who refuses to take the Mark is beheaded or even killed or attacked in any way. In Revelation 13 and 14 there is no mention of anyone who is killed or hurt in any way for refusing to take the Mark of the Beast Out of the Sea. The only consequence for those not taking the Mark is that they are unable to buy or sell, in the literal Greek they are unable to buy or sell specifically in the physical marketplace. And that is the only consequence for them. They are not killed by anyone, or even caused to be killed by anyone, because there is nothing written in this prophecy about the Mark of the Beast Out of the Sea that says that anyone dyes or is killed for refusing the Mark.

If this is the case, that no one is killed for refusing to take the Mark, where does the myth come from? It is Revelation 20:4, which says that there are people who are beheaded for their witness to Yeshua and the Word of God, and that is the only reason that Revelation gives for their beheading. There is no other reason for which they are beheaded other than their witness to Yeshua and the Word of God. It then continues on in a list of the people who sat on thrones of judgment:

1. Those who were beheaded for their witness to Yeshua and the Word of God.
2. Those who did not worship the Beast.
3. Those who did not worship its Image.
4. Those who did not receive its Mark upon their foreheads or upon their hands.

There is no mention of anybody else being beheaded for refusing to worship the Beast Out of the Sea, or its Image, or receiving its Mark. The myth inadvertently tried to move the word "beheaded" out of its place in the sentence, and multiplied it into the next section of the list, attempting to change the Scriptures to mean and read: those who *were beheaded for* not worshipping the Beast, nor its Image, and *were beheaded for* not receiving its Mark. But of course this is not what Revelation 20:4 says, and to say that a person is beheaded for refusing the Mark would require actually changing the very words of Scripture, adding in words that are not there. Therefore according to Scripture there is no prophecy about anyone being beheaded or killed for refusing to take the Mark of the Beast Out of the Sea.

There is no one who is forced against their will to get the Mark of the Beast Out of the Sea; people are only "caused/made" or convinced into getting it. If people were forced to get the Mark, then the Greek word for "forced," "βία Bia" or "βιάζω Biazo" should be used here instead of the word "ποιέω Poieo" which means "caused/made." The word here "made" means in the sense of constructing or building something, not "making" in the sense of force. So there is no one who is "forced" by physical means of attack or violence to receive the Mark, only "caused or convinced" into it by preventing people from being able to buy or sell without it.

Myth 6. It is Impossible for a Person to be Deceived into Taking the Mark of the Beast Out of the Sea, because an Obvious Oath of Allegiance or Visible Act of Worship to a Single, Dictator Anti-Christ Person, or to a Tyrannical Government, or to a Religious Cult, will be Required at the Same Time as Taking the Mark.

Truth. This is an odd myth that has been taught and believed for an unknown period of time, that it is impossible for a person to be deceived into taking the Mark. The whole purpose of the Beast Out of the Earth that causes people to take the Mark of the Beast Out of the Sea is to lead astray everyone dwelling on the earth in **Revelation 13:14-18**. And in these verses of Revelation, as well as in **Revelation 14:9-11**, **Revelation 16:1-2**, and **Revelation 20:4**, there is no mention of anyone being required to have to first take any oaths of allegiance or make any outward acts of worship to the Beast Out of the Sea, or its Image, in order to be allowed to take its Mark upon their hand or forehead.

The reason that Yeshua warns in **Mathew 24:21-26** about the false prophets and false messiahs being able to deceive even the Chosen during the Great Tribulation is because it is possible for a person, even a Christian believer, to be deceived at that time. And if it is possible for even the Chosen to be deceived during the Great Tribulation, that means that any person, believer or non-believer, is able to be deceived into taking the Mark of the Beast Out of the Sea without even knowing that it is the Mark. There is no requirement in the prophecy about an obvious, outward sign of worship or allegiance being made towards any one single person, or government, or religion, because taking the Mark is simply an economical thing to do, to have access to buying and selling. The prophecy does not say that it is a religious mark, just an economic regulatory mark for operating in the marketplace. Yeshua gives the warning to the believers during the Great Tribulation, because it is possible for anyone to be deceived at that time, and he does not want any of his people to be deceived.

Myth 7. A Christian can take the Mark of the Beast Out of the Sea without Losing Their Salvation and Eternal Life.

Truth. The only thing we know for certain from the prophecies about the Mark of the Beast Out of the Sea is from **Revelation 14:9-11**, that anyone who worships the Beast Out of the Sea, or its Image, or received its Mark drinks of the wine of the wrath of God and is tortured with fire and sulphur. This is anyone, including Christians who are believers in Yeshua, who receive the Mark upon their forehead or hand. The ones being tortured with fire and sulphur are not the ones who are entering into eternal life together with Yeshua in Revelation 20. Perhaps there is a chance for someone to repent of taking the Mark of the Beast Out of the Sea, and repent of worshipping the Beast, but there is nothing about this in the prophecies in Scripture, so there is no way to know for certain that a person can even repent and return back into eternal life and salvation with Yeshua. It is best not to play with fire and sulphur by testing Yahuweh/Yehovah with taking any mark upon the hand or forehead that is used for access to buying or selling.

Myth 8. The Little Horn is Worshipped as a god at the Head of a Political/Religious Cult.

Truth. Since the prophecies about the Little Horn in **Daniel 7:7-8, 19-26** and **Daniel 8:1-27** were combined with the prophecy about the Man of Lawlessness/Sin in 2 Thessalonians and the prophecy about the Beast Out of the Sea in Revelation, it created a myth that the Little Horn is the leader of a religious/political cult and has followers worshipping him as a god, or even worshipping him as Yahuweh/Yehovah himself or a false messiah, calling himself Yeshua. The Man of Lawlessness/Sin raises himself above all that is worshipped and sits like Yahuweh/Yehovah in his Temple/Dwelling Place, declaring himself to be Yahuweh/Yehovah the true God, and the Beast Out of the Sea is worshipped by people.

On the other hand according to what is written about the Little Horn in Daniel:

1. There is no record the Little Horn declares himself to be Yahuweh/Yehovah or Yeshua or the true God of Israel, or that he ever sits in the Temple/Tabernacle/Dwelling Place/Set-Apart Place of Yahuweh/Yehovah as a god.

2. There is no record that the Little Horn is ever considered to be a god by anyone, or that he is ever worshipped as a god by anyone.

Daniel **8:10-11** is the closest that the Little Horn ever comes to trying to be god-like, by going up into the heavens to take some of the stars down to trample and exalt himself above "the Prince of the Host" which probably is referring to Yahuweh/Yehovah. But even here in exalting himself above Yahuweh/Yehovah there is nothing about him trying to deceive people into thinking that he himself is the God of Israel, Yeshua or Yahuweh/Yehovah, or that he is worshipped or considered to be a god by anyone.

Only the Beast Out of the Sea and its Image in Revelation 13:1-15 are worshipped, but the Little Horn that comes out of the Beast Out of the Sea is not worshipped, and neither are the Ten Horns that come out of the Beast Out of the Sea. The Little Horn is leading a rebellion against Yahuweh/Yehovah to try to overcome him, but there is nothing about him being considered a god or worshipped as a god.

Myth 9. The Little Horn will be a World Dictator Ruling Over a Global Empire and Conquering Other Nations in Conquest.

Truth. Once again because of the combining of the Little Horn with the Beast Out of the Sea in Revelation and the Anti-Christs in 1 John, it has created the myth that the Little Horn is somehow a big, powerful ruler or dictator, either with control over the whole world, or an entire region of the world such as Europe or the Middle East. But when looking at the reality of the Little Horn in **Daniel 7:7-8, 19-26** and **Daniel 8:1-27**, the only prophecies that actually talk about the Little Horn, he is a little king who is an insignificant ruler in the world compared to all of the big horns and rulers in the Beast Out of the Sea world of the Time of the End. The Little Horn has only small, limited power in a region of the world, unable to really conquer anybody, let alone the whole world. The only ones the Little Horn is really successful in conquering are the Set-Apart Ones (Saints), Yahuweh/Yehovah's set-apart people, by wearing them out or wearing them down for a Time, Times, and Half a Time.

Additionally, the Little Horn is only able to subdue or humble, not completely conquer, three of the Ten Horns. The other seven horns he is unable to even influence, and may not even have any contact with them at all. His only power that he has according to **Daniel 8:24** does not even come from his own power, but from somebody or something else that is not mentioned. The primary power of the Little Horn is that Yahuweh/Yehovah allows him to prosper and be successful in prevailing against, destroying, and wearing out his set-apart people. As for the rest of the world, only three kings or horns are humbled by him (under his influence or control in some way), and concerning the rest of the kings/horns of the world there is no mention that the Little Horn is ever in contact with them or has any power or control over them.

And according to **Revelation 17:12-13** the Ten Horns on the Beast Out of the Sea do not even have any authority or power in the Beast Out of the Sea system of governing except for one single, short hour at the very end before Yeshua returns. And then the Ten Horns, including the three horns or kings that are humbled by the Little Horn, give all of their power and authority to the Beast Out of the Sea. This means that the three horns that are humbled by the Little Horn, in the end give all of their power and authority to the Beast Out of the Sea instead of to the Little Horn, leaving the Little Horn with nobody under its control in the end. The Little Horn is a small, little king or ruler with little influence or power over the world and the nations in the world. The primary power that Yahuweh/Yehovah allows the Little Horn to have is his ability to destroy and deceive Yahuweh/Yehovah's own set-apart people, to wear them out and prevail over them.

Myth 10. The Beast Out of the Sea will be a Single Man Dictator Ruling Over a Global Empire and Forcing People to Worship an Image of Him and Taking a Mark of Him on Their Hand or Forehead.

Truth. This myth comes from **Revelation 13:18**, which says, "let him calculate the number of the beast, for it is the number of man, and its number is six-hundred sixty six." The problem is that in Greek and Hebrew there is no indefinite article "a" that exists. So this prophecy could be translated two different ways as "the number of man," meaning the number of the beast is the number of all mankind, or "the number of a man," meaning the number of the beast is the number of a particular, individual man. Both are valid possibilities, but if this were speaking of a particular, single man, then it should say "the number *of the name* of a man" since in the previous sentence it is the number of the name of the beast that is mentioned.

If John in his writing was wanting to make sure that no one would incorrectly think that the number six hundred and sixty-six was the number of a single, individual man or the name of a particular, individual man, then he would make sure to say that the number of the beast is the "number of man" instead of the "number *of the name* of a man," which is exactly what he did. In the verse right before he says that people have an option to buy and sell if they have the "number of the name of the beast," then in the next verse when talking about man, he drops the word "name" so that it is only the "number of the beast" in order to avoid people thinking incorrectly that the number of the name of the beast was the number of the name of a particular man.

This clarifies the sentence to make it crystal clear that the number of the beast, and the number of the name of the beast, is the number for all of mankind, six hundred and sixty-six. This number is the number representing all of mankind, created on the 6th day, and the number of the name of the Beast Out of the Sea represents all of mankind in that number six hundred and sixty-six, and it is not the number of the name of a single or particular man. From the evidence of the way John wrote the sentence, using a language that does not contain the indefinite article "a" like English has, he used the context of the sentence to clarify so that no one would misunderstand and think that he was saying the number of the beast was the number of the name of an individual man, but instead clearly stating that it is the number of men in general.

Nowhere else in Revelation does it mention the Beast Out of the Sea being just one person or man, with ten more kings or men (horns), and a little king or man (horn), ruling out of one man. The Beast Out of the Sea is a rule divided up among many men and governments (horns). In **Revelation 16:10** when the Fifth Bowl of Wrath is poured out in the throne of the Beast, its reign became darkened, and "they gnawed their tongues," referring to the Beast Out of the Sea as plural, multiple people "they" instead of a singular person. It is referring to all of the people "they" of the entire kingdom or reign of the Beast Out of the Sea, who had worshipped the Beast and taken its Mark, who had sores upon them from the First Bowl of Wrath. It is all of the people who worship and follow the Beast Out of the Sea who make up the Beast Out of the Sea, all of mankind bowing to its systems of governing; they are all the Beast Out of the Sea, not any one man who is ruling on his own. And this means that the Image of the Beast Out of the Sea and the Mark of the Beast Out of the Sea are not the Image or Mark of any single man or ruler called an Anti-Christ, but instead the Image and Mark of all the people of the Beast Out of the Sea, all of mankind who are part of the Beast.

Unfortunately the myth of the Anti-Christ that has changed the wording of Revelation to transform the Beast Out of the Sea into a single man being worshipped and giving out a mark of himself for buying and selling has blinded people's vision from being able to see what the Beast Out of the Sea really is, as a governing and control/authority system. And it has caused everyone to be watching for a Mark that people receive from an individual man, instead of a Mark that is received from the society of mankind; and an Image that is worshipped of a single man, instead of the Image of mankind that is worshipped, worshipping the images of mankind in the Beast system as gods. But unfortunately, according to the words of Scripture in Revelation, it is a myth that the Mark of the Beast Out of the Sea will be the Mark of a single man, a single Anti-Christ ruler. And this myth causes people to stumble and fall thinking that the Mark of the Beast Out of the Sea prophecy will not be the real thing, or be the true fulfillment, unless it comes from just one man/ruler, convincing people to become part of his political/religious cult.

Myth 11. The Beast Out of the Sea Government System will be an Empire (One World Government) Ruling Over Every Nation, Tribe, and Tongue on the Earth with No Nations Outside of Its Control.

Truth. This myth thankfully most are realizing more and more that it is not true according to Scripture. The reason for the myth is **Revelation 13:5-7** where it says that the Beast Out of the Sea has "authority given to it over every tribe and tongue and nation." This word "authority" is interpreted to mean ruling, governmental power and authority to control every single nation and tribe and language in the world. But there are two things in Revelation that show this is not what it is actually saying.

The first is in Revelation 13 itself, a few sentences earlier where John says that the Beast Out of the Sea is given authority to blaspheme and speak greatly, of great matters or words, for 42 months. The Beast Out of the Sea is only given authority to do these two things for those 42 months, just blaspheme Yahuweh/Yehovah and his Set-Apart Ones (Saints), and speak great big words and matters with its mouth. This is the authority that it has been given to do over all of the nations and tribes and languages of the earth for 42 months, not the authority to rule over all of the nations and tribes and languages.

The second is in **Revelation 16:12-14**, where it says that the Beast Out of the Sea has to go and convince the other kings of the other nations in the entire world to join with it in attacking Israel. The Beast Out of the Sea has to convince other kings and nations to gather against Israel, because there are many nations and kings across the earth that are not under the control or power or rule of the Beast. In other words, the Beast Out of the Sea does not rule over all the nations and people of the earth; it only has the authority to influence every nation and tribe and language on the earth to blaspheme against Yahuweh/Yehovah and his Name and Tent and entities living in the heavens, and to influence them to join in its rebellion against Yahuweh/Yehovah and follow its example. The Beast Out of the Sea only has the authority to convince all those dwelling on the earth to worship it and its Image and even possibly to receive its Mark, but not all the earth is under its direct rule.

Myth 12. The Beast Out of the Sea with the Ten Horns and the Beast Out of the Earth with the Two Horns Kill People who Stand Against Them, or Disagree with Them, or Refuse to Worship Them.

Truth. In prophecy teachings and studies the Beast Out of the Sea and the Beast Out of the Earth are pictured and imagined as being very violent and oppressive governmental and religious regimes that kill anybody that resists them, or refuse to obey them or worship them. The reality is that this idea and concept is not actually written anywhere in any of the prophecies in Revelation about the Beast Out of the Sea or the Beast Out of the Earth. There is never one time in all of **Revelation 13:1-18** that the Beast Out of the Sea or the Beast Out of the Earth ever kill anyone or even indirectly cause anyone to be killed. It is only the talking IMAGE of the Beast Out of the Sea that indirectly causes people to be killed who refuse to worship the talking IMAGE of the Beast Out of the Sea.

The Beast Out of the Sea never kills anyone, or even is given authority to kill anyone. It is only given the authority to speak with its mouth, to say great words and to speak blasphemies against Yahuweh/Yehovah and to fight with and overcome the Set-Apart Ones (Saints). There is nothing about the Beast Out of the Sea specifically killing the Set-Apart Ones, only overcoming them in its fighting with them. And there is nothing here in Revelation 13 that indicates that overcoming the Set-Apart Ones means to physically kill them. And the Beast Out of the Earth only leads the whole world astray into worshipping the Beast Out of the Sea and receiving its Mark. But it does not directly or indirectly kill anyone in the actual words written in the prophecy.

In all of **Revelation 16:1-16** about the Beast Out of the Sea and in all of **Revelation 17:1-18** about the Scarlet Beast Out of the Pit of the Deep (which is probably the same Beast as the Beast Out of the Sea) there is nothing about the Beast ever killing anyone, until the very end when Yeshua returns and the Beast Out of the Sea convinces the Kings/Sovereigns of the world to gather in Israel for war and battle (Joel 3 and Zechariah 14). And even here in Revelation 16 there is no mention of the Beast Out of the Sea ever actually killing anybody, just gathering them to kill people in battle. In Revelation 17 the Ten Horns that are on the Beast Out of the Sea probably kill people when they destroy the Prostitute Woman, the city of Mystery Babel, but the Beast Out of the Sea itself is not killing people. And there is nothing about the Ten Horns killing anybody either before they destroy the city Babel. It is only at the very end when Yeshua returns that they kill those people who do not escape, when they destroy Babel in war and battle.

And even in **Revelation 20:4** there is nothing about the Beast Out of the Sea killing people or beheading them. There are believers in Yeshua who are beheaded for their witness to Yeshua during the Great Tribulation, but even here in Revelation 20 there is nothing that says that it is the Beast Out of the Sea or even the Scarlet Beast Out of the Pit of the Deep that is beheading them.

The only time in the entire book of Revelation that a Beast actually does any kind of killing is in **Revelation 11:7-8**, where it says that the Beast Out of the Pit of the Deep, which is probably the Scarlet Beast Out of the Pit of the Deep in Revelation 17, kills the Two Witnesses. This is the only time that a Beast in Revelation kills, and as is shown later on in the section about the Two Witnesses, according to Scripture the Beast Out of the Sea may not even be killing physical people with bodies of flesh in this instance either when it is killing the Two Witnesses.

The Fourth Beast in **Daniel 7:7, 19, 23** is a very ferocious Beast that came out of the sea with the others, that tramples and devours all the earth, and destroys the three Beasts that came before it. But the Beast Out of the Sea in Revelation 13 only represents the final Fourth Beast in Daniel 7 at the very end of its reign and existence, when all of the four Beasts in Daniel have been combined together into one single Beast that has come out of the sea, with all of the heads and horns of all of the four Beasts combined together into a decentralized rule of many nations and governments broken apart and weak.

The Beast Out of the Sea in Revelation is representing the Fourth Beast in Daniel long after it has finished trampling and devouring the other three beasts into itself. It is a time when the Beast Out of the Sea is being ruled by many kings, of which there are Ten Horns and a Little Horn who have power over governments and nations within it. And by that time at the end of the rule of the Beast Out of the Sea, when the Ten Horns and Little Horn are in power right before Yeshua returns and destroys all of the Beasts (Kingdoms and Reigns of men) forever, according to both Daniel and Revelation the Beast Out of the Sea is not doing anymore execution style killing or direct murder of people who stand against it.

The Beast Out of the Sea and the Horns are only fighting against, prevailing against, wearing out, and overcoming the Set-Apart Ones, but doing so in ways that does not involve directly killing them. And certainly there are still believers in Yeshua who are being physically killed and beheaded during the Great Tribulation for their witness in Yeshua, but there is nothing written in the prophecies in Daniel or Revelation that indicate it is the Beast Out of the Sea or the Beast Out of the Earth that is doing that. Only the Image of the Beast and the Prostitute Woman, the city of Mystery Babel, are specifically recorded as actually killing people, especially killing believers in Yeshua in the case of Babel.

Therefore the truth in Scripture is that the way the Beast Out of the Sea and Little Horn overcome and wear out the Set-Apart Ones is not specifically stated, but there is nothing written there about them physically killing anybody, including the Set-Apart Ones. But the only thing that the Beast Out of the Sea and Ten Horns and Little Horn have authority to do for a Time, Times, and Half a Time or 42 Months is to speak with their mouths with great words that people would listen to and be influenced by, and to speak blasphemies against Yahuweh/Yehovah and everything that is set-apart to him, including his people. From the context of

Daniel 7:20-21 and **Revelation 13:5-7** the way the Beast Out of the Sea and Little Horn overcome the Set-Apart Ones, the believers in Yeshua, is with the words of their mouths. Because both are given the authority to speak great things with their mouths, and then instantly, right after they start speaking with their mouths, they start fighting with and prevailing against and overcoming the Set-Apart Ones, the believers in Yeshua.

Myth 13. The Time of the Great Tribulation will be the Worst Time and the Worst Tribulation that There has Ever been on the Earth.

Truth. This myth has come from skimming over words and not paying attention to the precise words of Yeshua in **Matthew 24:21** and **Mark 13:19**, (which we all are guilty of doing from time to time in life) where he says, "For then shall be great trouble (tribulation) which has not been from the creation of the world until now, and as such shall not be." The word "Trouble" or "Tribulation" is clearly the subject of this sentence, and the word "Great" is the adjective of "Trouble/Tribulation", describing the type of Trouble/Tribulation. Yeshua is clearly saying that there shall be a time of Trouble/Tribulation that has not been from the creation of the world up to the present, and shall not be again in the future after it happens. It is a Trouble/Tribulation that has never been before, never happened before, and will never be or happen again afterwards.

The only way that Yeshua could be saying that the Great Tribulation is a time of greater tribulation/trouble than there has ever been on the earth is if he had switched the word "Great" to become the subject of the sentence, saying that there will be great trouble/tribulation that is greater than any other time from the creation of the world to now, and will never be greater again. But instead Yeshua says that there will be a time of Great Trouble/Tribulation which has not ever even happened before or after that time. It is a new kind of Trouble/Tribulation that has never happened or been in existence before, and will never be in existence or happen again afterwards. It is not the greatness of the tribulation that has never happened before; it is the type of tribulation itself that has never happened before.

The Great Tribulation is not a time of Greater Tribulation than there has ever been on the earth before, since creation, it is a time of a brand new Great Tribulation that has never been on the earth before, since creation. It is not the time of the worst tribulation there has ever been, but instead a time of a unique tribulation that has never been before, until that time. And because of that unique time of new tribulation that has never existed before, the days have to be reduced or shortened, because otherwise no flesh would still be saved after that unique tribulation/trouble had played out to its completion.

In Matthew and Mark Yeshua is referring to the prophecy of the time of tribulation/trouble in **Daniel 12:1-2**, in which Daniel's people, the people of Israel, will go through a time of tribulation/trouble such as has never been in existence since Israel was a nation. But Yeshua expands the concept of this unique tribulation/trouble, adding understanding to this prophecy that it does not apply just to the nation of Israel, but during that time it will be the entire world that will go through that unique tribulation/trouble with Israel. And here in Daniel the words of this messenger (angel) are still in agreement with Yeshua's words in Matthew and

Mark that it is a time of a unique tribulation/trouble that has not been on the earth before, not the worst tribulation/trouble that there has ever been.

Myth 14. When the Disgusting Idol (Abomination) Desolating is Set-Up, the Thing that Everyone is Supposed to Flee from in Jerusalem and Judea is War or Physical Violence and the Destruction of the City of Jerusalem.

Truth. This myth started from Yeshua's prophecy about the destruction of Jerusalem in **Luke 21:20-24** being combined with Yeshua's prophecy about the Disgusting Idol (Abomination) Desolating being set up at the set-apart place in **Matthew 24:15-26** and **Mark 13:14-23**. In Matthew/Mark Yeshua is giving a prophecy about the Disgusting Idol Desolating set up at the set-apart place, but the city of Jerusalem he never mentions once. In Luke 21 Yeshua is giving a prophecy about the city of Jerusalem being surrounded by armies and then destroyed.

In both cases everyone in Judea needs to flee to the mountains, but in Matthew/Mark they are supposed to flee to the mountains when they see the Disgusting Idol Desolating set up, and in Luke 21 they are supposed to flee when they see the city of Jerusalem surrounded by armies. In Matthew/Mark Yeshua is prophesying about Great Trouble/Tribulation that has never been before and will never be again, but in Luke 21 Yeshua is prophesying about Great Trouble/Tribulation on the earth in general with wrath upon the Jewish people specifically, days of vengeance that fulfill all that has been written, as the city of Jerusalem is destroyed. And the key difference between the two prophecies is that after Jerusalem is destroyed in Luke 21, Yeshua says that Jerusalem will be "trodden underfoot by the nations, until the times of the nations are fulfilled."

Because both prophecies have the people of Judea needing to flee to the mountains, and the part that it is not good to be pregnant or nursing during that flight, it makes them sound like they are about the same event. But **Luke 17:26-32** holds the answer, in which Yeshua prophesies again the exact same prophecy about fleeing, except that this time it is everybody in the entire world who needs to flee during his coming at the end of the Great Tribulation. In Matthew 24 and Mark 13 Yeshua talks about people needing to flee at the start of the Great Tribulation and in Luke 17 he talks about people needing to flee in the exact same way at the end of the Great Tribulation, and just because he uses the exact same words it does not mean that these two prophecies are the same event.

In the same way Luke 21 sounds exactly the same in the fleeing, but every single other word in the prophecy is completely different from Matthew 24 and Mark 13, because they are two different prophecies about two different events. When Jerusalem is destroyed in Luke 21, there is nothing at all about any Disgusting Idol (Abomination) Desolating being set up, or anything about the set-apart place either. Also, after Jerusalem is destroyed the city of Jerusalem is trodden and trampled under the feet of the nations (gentiles) from that time onward until the times of the nations are fulfilled. In Matthew 24 and Mark 13 there is nothing about the city of Jerusalem being destroyed or the nations suddenly taking control over the city and trampling it down.

The Jews of the tribes of the southern kingdom of Yehudah (Judea) controlled Jerusalem and owned the city in its entirety until the Romans destroyed it in the 1st century C.E. And since that time the nations have always owned and walked in and controlled all or some of Jerusalem. There has not been a time since Jerusalem was destroyed by the Romans that the nations have not been trampling the city of Jerusalem under their feet. And according to Yeshua they will continue to do so until the times of the nations have been fulfilled. This means that this prophecy in Luke 21 about the destruction of Jerusalem was already fulfilled when the Romans destroyed the city.

Yeshua says that once that destruction happens, there will not be a time ever again when the city of Jerusalem is not being trodden down by the nations, owning or controlling at least part of the city, until the times of the nations are fulfilled. And according to Revelation 11:2 that time of the nations trampling the set-apart city Jerusalem, which is part of the times of the nations, will continue all the way until Yeshua returns at the end of the Great Tribulation. So the Luke 21 prophecy cannot be the same prophecy about the Disgusting Idol Desolating in Matthew 24 and Mark 13 that happens at the beginning of the Great Tribulation. It would never work anyways for the city of Jerusalem to be destroyed at the beginning of the Great Tribulation, because then the prophecy of Jerusalem's destruction at the end of the Great Tribulation in Zechariah 14 and Joel 3, when Yahuweh/Yehovah comes to stand on the Mount of Olives and rule as king from Jerusalem. It would be impossible for the city of Jerusalem to be completely rebuilt in just 3.5 years after being destroyed at the beginning of the Great Tribulation, just to be destroyed again at the end.

Therefore, since Luke 21 is a different prophecy, the prophecy Yeshua gives in Matthew 24 and Mark 13 does not have anything about destruction of cities or violence as being the reason for everyone needing to flee to the mountains in Judea. There is in fact no specific reason at all that Yeshua gives for needing to flee to the mountains, except one, to flee from the Disgusting Idol Desolating itself in order to avoid the unique Great Tribulation/Trouble that has begun. Yeshua does not say that this unique Great Tribulation is physical violence or war or destruction in Judea or Jerusalem. He does not give any precise descriptions of it, only that people need to flee from the Disgusting Idol Desolating when they see it at the set-apart place.

Myth 15. During the Great Tribulation Conditions will be so Horrible on the Earth that All Normal Life will Stop, with No Hope for Life to Continue on the Earth for Even One More Generation, Making it Obvious to Everybody on the Earth, Both Christians and Non-Christians, that the World and All Life on Earth is About to End at Any Moment.

Truth. Over the last 1,900 years people have created more and more of a mythical fantasy about the Great Tribulation being a time of such horrible disaster and destruction that all life on earth will end before Yeshua can even return at the end of the Great Tribulation, and he will be returning to an empty and lifeless planet without anything on it. Everyone forgets that Yeshua says the days of the Great Tribulation will be reduced or shortened, so that he returns and ends the world himself before all life on the planet is destroyed and ended (**Matthew 24:15-26**; **Mark 13:14-23**). But even during the time of the Great Tribulation, before Yeshua returns, the reality of how Yeshua himself describes the Great Tribulation is exactly opposite of how everyone has taught and imagined in the make believe, imaginations of their own minds for centuries.

In **Matthew 24:37-39** and **Luke 17:26-32** Yeshua says that his coming, after the tribulation of those days, at the end of the Great Tribulation, will be like the coming of the flood in the days of Noah, and the coming of the fire in the days of Lot. All the people of the earth during those times were eating, drinking, marrying and being given in marriage (being fruitful and multiplying), buying, selling, planting, and building right up to the very day and moment when the flood came and destroyed all life on earth, or the fire came and destroyed all life in the cites of Sodom and Gomorrah. This is Yeshua's description of the very end of the Great Tribulation, on the day of his return, everybody on the earth will be continuing their normal, everyday lives of eating, drinking, marrying and having children, buying and selling, planting and building.

And in the surviving manuscript copies of the original Hebrew Gospel of Matthew, Yeshua says that they are "being fruitful and multiplying" [3] instead of the Greek translation "marrying and being given in marriage," quoting from Genesis 1:28 where Yahuweh/Yehovah commands the man and woman to "be fruitful and multiply." This means that normal life is going on so much so, that people are even still have children all the way up to the very last day of the Great Tribulation when Yeshua returns. Life at the end of the Great Tribulation is so normal, that there is not even any concern by anyone that life on the earth is going to end anytime soon, or any indications that the world is going to end or that Yeshua will return in the lifetimes of the current generations living on the earth during the Great Tribulation.

The famines during the Great Tribulation are not enough to prevent people to continue eating and drinking like they have always done, and the wars and conflicts are not bad enough to prevent people from continuing to marry and have children, and the natural disasters are not bad enough to prevent people from continuing to plant their food and build their structures of houses and buildings, and the economic disasters are not enough to prevent everyone from continuing to buy and to sell as they have always done for thousands of years. Yeshua's description of the Great Tribulation is exactly the opposite of how it has been taught and imagined over the centuries, with him returning to a world that is going on very normal in its everyday life, completely unaware that Yeshua is about to return at any moment to end the world.

The description of the days of Noah in **Genesis 6:1 – 7:24** and the days of Lot in **Genesis 19:1-38** are exactly as Yeshua describes. Before the flood everyone continued on with their normal, everyday lives, without any signs or evidence that the world would end at any time in the future. Noah had to believe Yahuweh/Yehovah entirely by faith when he said that he would destroy the world in a flood. The only thing unusual at the time of Noah was that earth was so filled with man's sin, that everybody on the earth only did evil continuously, without any commands or Torah of Yahuweh/Yehovah given to follow yet to be able to keep from sin. Mankind was destroying itself in evil, but everyone continued on with their normal, everyday

---

[3] See Appendix: Hebrew Matthew Chapter 24

lives without a thought of the world ending, and the day of the end of the world came as a complete surprise to them.

Likewise, with Sodom and Gomorrah and the cities of the plain, they were all continuing with their everyday, normal lives, without any sign or evidence that their cities would be destroyed and they would all die the next day. Lot's sons-in law and daughters refused to even believe him that they needed to flee the city, because they did not believe that in the morning it would be completely destroyed. Lot even had a hard time believing it, and the two messengers had to pull him out of the city by the hand. Life was so completely normal the day right before the cities were destroyed, there was no indication at all that they were about to end forever the next morning.

That is how Yeshua describes the Great Tribulation, as being normal, everyday life happening throughout the entire 3.5 years of the unique Great Tribulation, even up to the day right before he returns. And his coming in the clouds as the Son of Adam to end the world will be a complete surprise to everyone, except for those faithful and righteous servants like Noah who are listening to him and believing him when he says he is coming to end the world of man. The only real difference that will be happening on the earth during the Great Tribulation from times before it is that the evil is so common and prevalent and uncontrolled that Yahuweh/Yehovah is forced to have to end the world in order to end the evil, as with the days of Noah and Lot.

In **Matthew 24:42-51** Yeshua describes the Great Tribulation as a time when his unfaithful and wicked servants (the unfaithful Christians and believers in Yeshua) are having parties and having a good time enjoying the pleasures of the world, and loving the world. The wicked servants who are followers of Yeshua do not even have any inkling that the world is about to end or that he is about to return, because life is so good for them at the end of the Great Tribulation. It is the same in **Matthew 22:1-14** and **Luke 14:15-24**, where those Christians who are invited to the wedding are so busy with their planting in their fields and buying and selling in their businesses, so busy living their normal, everyday lives in the world, that they are too busy to even come to the wedding when Yeshua returns. They do not even see that it is time to leave the world and prepare their wedding garments of righteousness to be ready for Yeshua's imminent return at the end of the Great Tribulation, because life in the world is so good for them during the Great Tribulation, and they are too busy getting married in the world, and working the fields of their Christian ministries, and too busy making money during the Great Tribulation.

And in **Matthew 25:1-13** life is so normal during the Great Tribulation that both the righteous and unrighteous believers in Yeshua fall asleep. But the difference is that the righteous believers in Yeshua believe him that he is returning, and they prepare themselves with the oil they need to wait out the Great Tribulation for his return at the end of it. Yeshua's words and descriptions about the Great Tribulation are consistent over and over again throughout his teachings of his return, that the time of Great Tribulation/Trouble he is talking about is a time of very normal life happening on the earth, without any indications or signs that the world is about to end. The end of the world comes suddenly and unexpectedly to everyone at the end of the Great Tribulation, to the point that even the day right before Yeshua returns to end the world of man, no one will even know that it is about to end, except for the righteous servants and followers of Yeshua who watch for his coming (such as watching for the signs and fulfillments of prophecies Yeshua said to watch for) and believe him when he says he is about to return.

There are certainly trials and troubles and tribulations and persecution of Christians and rampant, uncontrolled evil across the earth, with birth pains all over during the Great Tribulation. But none of these things are happening in such a way to an extreme that would indicate to anyone that the world is about to end tomorrow, or that Yeshua is about to return, the very next day, even the day before his coming at the end of the Great Tribulation. The world has always had lots of bad things happening in it, and in the past the world has always gotten through them without ending, so most are not going to believe that simply because bad things are happening on the earth again, like all of the times before in the past, that it means the world is actually going to end in their lifetime.

Myth 16. Babel (Babylon) is Only One Single City on the Earth that has Control Over All the Rulers and All the Nations of the Earth.

Truth. This myth has come about from prophecy studies and teachings only focusing on what **Revelation 17:1 – 18:24** says about the last days Babel (Babylon) and not paying attention to what Jeremiah and Isaiah have to say about it. The first clue that the city Babel or Mystery Babel that is destroyed in Revelation 17 to 18 is not just a single city somewhere on the earth is in the fact that John in his description of the destruction of Babel actually paraphrases and quotes from the prophecy of the destruction of the city of Tyre (Tsor), Lebanon in **Ezekiel 26:1 – 28:26**. This prophecy in Ezekiel about the complete destruction of the city of Tyre has never been fulfilled so far to this day since Ezekiel wrote the prophecy almost 2,400 years ago.

If John is writing a prophecy about the destruction of a city called Babel, then why does he use Ezekiel's descriptions of the destruction of Tyre in writing about Babel being destroyed, instead of using the prophecies in Jeremiah and Isaiah that are also about the destruction of Babel? Obviously there is something more to this prophecy that just a single city somewhere on the earth being destroyed, if the city of Tyre, Lebanon is described to be destroyed in the exact same way.

It is Jeremiah's prophecy about the destruction of Babel that holds part of the answer. Ever since Jeremiah wrote the prophecy about the city of Babel being destroyed, the prophecy has never been fulfilled. The physical city of Babel that used to exist, in what is now modern day Iraq, was never completely destroyed in all of its time of existing. It slowly became a suburb over the years, and eventually an abandoned ghost town, until it just ceased to exist without ever being destroyed. Some have thought that because the physical city of Babel ceased to exist without ever being destroyed, then it must have to be rebuilt again into a physical city again to fulfill the prophecy.

Jeremiah 51:7 is a primary piece of the puzzle of what the mystery of the city of Babel is. In this verse it is revealed that Babel is a golden cup in the hand of Yahuweh/Yehovah, making all of the earth drunk, and that the nations of all the earth have drunk the wine of Babel, ingesting the city of Babel inside of their nations. Right here in this prophecy from Jeremiah it clearly says that all of the nations across the earth have the city or cities of Babel inside of them. Even in Jeremiah's prophecy we can see that the prophecy is not about the physically located city of Babel that existed in Jeremiah's day; it is really about the concept and philosophy of the city of Babel in **Genesis 11:1-9**. It is all the nations of the earth taking in Babel inside of them and joining together again as one great "city" of people covering the entire earth and every nation.

Isaiah 14:16-17, 21-22 confirms this prophecy in Jeremiah, saying the same thing. This Isaiah prophecy is about the destruction of the King of Babel and why he has to be destroyed. It is because Babel has destroyed the cities of the world, making the world a wilderness, in order to fill the entire world with cities. And Yahuweh/Yehovah has to destroy Babel because otherwise it will "fill the face of the world with cities." Babel destroys in order to replace the cities with Babel cities, like the type of city of Babel in Genesis 11, the type of city that Yahuweh/Yehovah had to confuse the mouths and languages of the people in order to stop them.

All the nations of the world have ingested Babel into their cities, transforming all of the cities of the world into Babel. This is why in **Revelation 17:1-6, 18** and **Revelation 18:2-3, 6-10** it says that the prostitute woman, Mystery Babel, is sitting as a queen with sovereignty over all the rulers of the earth and all the inhabitants of the earth have ingested Babel inside of themselves. By the time of the fulfillment of the prophecies of Revelation during the Great Tribulation, and by the time of Yeshua's coming at the end of the Great Tribulation, all the cities of the earth have become the city of Mystery Babel, which is the same city and tower of Babel in Genesis 11 come back again in its fullness as it was after the flood when Yahuweh/Yehovah had to stop the people of the earth from building it. And the description of Babel being destroyed in Revelation 18 and Jeremiah 50 – 51 is describing all of the cities of the earth being destroyed at the end of the Great Tribulation when Yeshua comes in the clouds.

Babel is all of the cities of the earth in every nation, as the centers of power that are essential for every king and ruler in every nation to be able to govern over their people. All the rulers of the earth and all of the nations of the earth rely on Babel for their power to be able to rule and govern and bring all of the world together as one "city" of people. It is not only one single city in one single, physical location that has power as a ruler over all of the nations and kings of the earth; it is all of the cities. Since all of the nations of the earth have ingested Babel, the cup of the wrath of Yahuweh/Yehovah, into their nations, all of the nations of the earth have to be destroyed in the wrath of Yahuweh/Yehovah when Babel is destroyed at his coming.

Myth 17. There is a Seven Year Period of Time Called "The Tribulation".

Truth. The 7 Year Tribulation is such a common by-word of End Time prophecy that one would think there would be at least one verse in Scripture talking about it. There is no way to even know where this myth comes from, because there is nowhere in Scripture that even vaguely suggests or implies any 7 year period of special tribulation. The myth may have come from the earlier discussed myth about a 7 year covenant that is confirmed by a mythical Anti-Christ figure that does not exist in any prophecies in Scripture either, which does not make any sense, because there is nothing in the Daniel 9 prophecy about any tribulation associated with the covenant that is strengthened by the Messiah for one week. The only prophecy that places an amount of time on the Great Tribulation that Yeshua speaks of in Matthew 24 and Mark 13, that begins with the placing of the Disgusting Idol (Abomination) Desolating, is in **Daniel 12:1-12**. It says that the time of tribulation that begins with the placing of the Disgusting Idol Desolating lasts for a Time, Times, and Half a Time, which the messenger (angel) goes on to explain means that it lasts for 1,290 days, plus an extra 45 days that lasts to 1,335 days. 1,290 days is 3.5 years, and then everything is made right again at the end of 3.5 years.

Therefore "The Tribulation," according to Scripture, only lasts for about 3.5 years, and there is no 7 year period of special tribulation that happens in prophecy. Before the 3.5 years of Great Tribulation there is only the usual everyday tribulation that has gone on for thousands of years, which Yeshua has promised that all those who believe in him and follow him will experience (Matthew 10:16-29, Matthew 13:21).

Myth 18. There has to be a Big, End Time Revival/Harvest of Yahuweh/Yehovah Pouring Out His Spirit on All Flesh Across the Earth Before the Great Tribulation can Begin.

Truth. This is a very new myth that has only started within the last few decades, so it is not as widespread as the older myths. The prophecies in Scripture say the exact opposite, that the final Revival and Harvesting of the people of the earth into Yahuweh/Yehovah's kingdom and reign does not happen until during the end of the Great Tribulation in **Revelation 14:14-20**. When the Son of Adam (Yeshua) appears in the clouds at his coming, then he takes the sickle and harvests all of the wheat at the very end of the Great Tribulation. From Yeshua's prophecy in **Matthew 24:29-31** and **Mark 13:24-27** we know that he comes in the clouds at the very end of the Great Tribulation, after the tribulation of those days is finished; and from Yeshua's parable in **Matthew 13:24-43** we know that the wheat are the righteous believers in Yeshua who are harvested out of the earth into his nation/family/kingdom in the final revival at his coming.

The wheat are those on the earth who are harvested into eternal life, to be with Yahuweh/Yehovah in eternity in the New Heavens and New Earth. And that harvesting of people from the earth into eternal life through revival and Yahuweh/Yehovah pouring out his Spirit is not completed and finished until the exact moment of his coming in the clouds at the end of the Great Tribulation.

Joel 2:28-31 is also in perfect agreement with this, where it says that Yahuweh/Yehovah pours out his Spirit on all flesh before the Great and Terrible Day of Yahuweh/Yehovah. When is the Day of Yahuweh/Yehovah? According to **Joel 3:1-2, 14** the Day of Yahuweh/Yehovah is when he gathers all of the nations in Israel for war against Jerusalem, when he comes at the very end of the Great Tribulation. According to **Zechariah 14:1-9** the Day comes for Yahuweh/Yehovah when he tangibly comes to be the king of the entire earth at the end of the Great Tribulation, at his gathering of all the nations to battle against Jerusalem. According to **Revelation 16:12-16** the Great Day of Yahuweh/Yehovah happens when the Beast Out of the Sea gathers all of the nations together for Yahuweh/Yehovah, to do battle in Israel at his coming like a thief in the night. And according to **Isaiah 13:6-9** the Day of Yahuweh/Yehovah is the day he completely destroyed all the earth, turning it into a waste land with all of the sinners killed from the earth at the end of the Great Tribulation.

The Day of Yahuweh/Yehovah is clearly the day of his coming to judge and harvest the earth, both the wheat harvest and the grape harvest of the righteous and the wicked, and according to Joel 2 Yahuweh/Yehovah pours out his Spirit on all flesh in his final revival/outpouring right before that day at the end of the Great Tribulation, which is still during the Great Tribulation.

The Creation of Myths and Legends About How the Prophecies in Scripture will be Fulfilled Prevents People from Seeing the Fulfillments of Prophecy in Reality, when the Myths and Legends are Taken as Facts in Greater Authority than the Original Words of Yahuweh/ Yehovah in Scripture.

There is nothing wrong with playing pretend and make believe with the imagination of the mind, creating fictional stories about things that never happened in reality or people that never existed. Yahuweh/Yehovah created the imagination for being able to play as a child or to dream up plans of things to do in reality. It is fun to imagine all of the infinite possibilities of how Yahuweh/Yehovah's prophecies might be fulfilled in the future. But when the actual fulfillment of a prophecy comes in reality, in the present, then the imagination of the mind must be put away in order to be able to recognize it and understand it when it happens. Holding on to the imagination and pretend make believe in the mind about a prophecy prevents a person from accepting the real way the prophecy is fulfilled in reality. Reality is different from imagination, because it is a concrete, physical world that is outside of the control of our desires and wishes, outside of the control of the make believe in the mind. And it is a very good thing that Yahuweh/Yehovah created reality to be that way, as something outside of ourselves and outside of the desires and imaginations of the mind and heart.

Yahuweh/Yehovah always speaks his words of prophecy as the reality of the way things actually are in real life, not according to fantasies or imaginations. The reality of what happens in the future, in real life, is never the same as what we imagine in our minds, in fantasies and make believe. They are separated by a very clear dividing line of reality. And when Yahuweh/Yehovah's prophecies happen in real life, in reality, it is very important to let go of all past imagination in the mind about that prophecy in order to see it and recognize that it is happening, and most importantly not to reject the fulfillment of the prophecy when it happens. The myths and imaginations and theories of prophecy from the past have to be let go of to accept the reality of the present, when the prophecies of the future enter into the present, and have become reality that everyone can see and experience for real, without any imagination.

At the present time a whole myth and legend has been created around the prophecies in Scripture about an Anti-Christ person (who does not even exist in prophecy) coming to rule over the world as a supreme dictator ruler, with absolute power and authority over everybody and everything, and elevating himself as a god with everyone worshipping him in some form of a religious cult, with a name that calculates to the number six hundred and sixty-six. And this Anti-Christ figure is fulfilling all of the prophecies in the End Times single handedly, without anybody else involved, including forcing people to take a special Mark upon their hands showing that he owns them, and making people worship a talking Image of himself. And then making a seven year peace covenant between Israel and their neighboring countries, allowing the Jews to build a Third Temple and start sacrifices again; then in the middle of the seven years coming into Jerusalem and destroying the Third Temple and stopping the sacrifices again, while claiming to be the God of Israel, who stops the animal sacrifices again, even though he already finished them before and did not need to have them resume again only to stop them again.

It is always easier for people to process stories that have just one, single mastermind villain running an evil empire with lots of minions. That is why throughout the fictional stories in novels and movies and every medium there is the arch-nemesis, villain character that has to be destroyed by the good guy. And then as soon as the one villain leader is dead, then all of the world is happy again, with no more evil. It is the same with the creation of the Anti-Christ mythical, villain, mastermind character in Scriptural prophecy. The reality in Scripture is that there are many bad guys across the world, some working together and others working separately on their own, to destroy Yahuweh/Yehovah's people on the earth in completely different ways, and to rebel against Yahuweh/Yehovah and his commands and instructions.

There is a king who is the Little Horn, and there are another ten kings who are the Ten Horns, and there Seven Heads that are another seven kingdoms or reigns, and they all make up the Beast Out of the Sea of People, and then there are another Two Horns that are leading the world astray, that come from the Beast Out of the Earth, and a Dragon that has another Seven Heads and Ten Horns that are ruling in the spiritual realm, helping the Beast Out of the Sea to have its power and authority, and then a prostitute woman called Mystery Babel the Great that is ruling over the rulers of the Beast Out of the Sea and its Horns, that is eventually destroyed by the Ten Horns, and Mystery Babel the Great is riding on a Scarlet Beast Out of the Pit of the Deep with another Seven Heads and Ten Horns that may or may not be the same beast as the Beast Out of the Sea, and then there is a Messenger Out of the Pit of the Deep with a horde of Locusts that are together hurting people across the earth with their stingers, and finally in the end there is all of the kings and all of the nations of the earth that are going to war against the city of Jerusalem, with lots of false prophets and false messiahs all over the place, each doing their own, separate deceptions.

The list goes on and on in the Time of the End prophecies of all of the different players and bad guys, hordes of them that are not even connected to each other sometimes, or in any kind of alliance or coordination. There are so many that it is impossible to keep track of them all, because in reality there are billions of people at the end who are all the enemies of Yahuweh/Yehovah in rebellion against him and in friendship with the world (James 4:4), all of whom unfortunately refuse to repent (Revelation 9:20-21) and have to die in Yahuweh/Yehovah's kindness of judgment as with Sodom and Gomorrah and days of Noah in the flood. Reality is so much more complex and deep to understand, so it is no wonder that all of the dozens of different people and governing systems and entities in prophecy were all combined into one single man called an Anti-Christ, so that there is only one evil arch-villain that has to be destroyed to make the whole world happy again, instead of billions of people who will sadly die and be thrown into the lake of fire because of their refusal to repent and stop their rebellion against truth and reality and the person who Yahuweh/Yehovah is in reality.

The book of Revelation is the only book of prophecy that has the warning to not add to the words or take away from the words written in it (Revelation 22:18-19), because it is the one book of prophecy that has had more prophecy myths created about it than any other book of prophecy in Scripture. It is the one book of prophecy in Scripture that people have added their own ideas to or taken away words from what it actually says more than any other book of prophecy to create whole fictional legends about how the future will happen at the time of Yeshua's coming. It is because everyone thinks that they need to understand the book of Revelation when they read it, which is not important at all. The really vitally important part of the book of Revelation is simply for the warnings in it on how to walk through the Great Tribulation without falling for the deceptions of that time. There is no need to understand the book at all in order to be able to learn word for word the warnings in the book in order to be able to recognize them happening in the real world when they happen. Understanding of prophecy is not necessary to be able to know it when one sees it in real life.

When you know Yahuweh/Yehovah for yourself, truly know who he is, then prophecy begins to make sense when it is fulfilled in reality. And one thing about Yahuweh/Yehovah, about who he really is, is that free will is very important to him according to how he created the world and reality in the first place in Genesis. It is so important to Yahuweh/Yehovah for people to accept him exactly as he is without using any manipulation or control over people. And this is why he always sets up every choice for people to choose life or death, to accept him or reject him, with a way for a person to reject him if they want to, and to reject reality in the process. This is what delusions are all about, if that is the make believe, imaginary world a person wants instead of reality and life with Yahuweh/Yehovah.

This is why Yahuweh/Yehovah always makes sure that the fulfillments of his prophecies in Scripture happen in such a way that a person can come up with a logical sounding reason, in the imaginations of their own mind, to reject the fulfillment of the prophecy, and reject the person of Yahuweh/Yehovah in the process. This is what has happened throughout history, because even the entire nation of the children of Israel, except a few dozen people, rejected Yahuweh/Yehovah's fulfillment of the prophecies to take them out of Egypt and bring them to their own land in Canaan. And he even did massive plagues with water turned to blood, and frogs, and flies, and huge natural disasters of hail with fire, and thick darkness over the land, and killing every single male first-born child in the entire nation of Egypt. Then to top it all off he parted an entire sea right down the middle so that the people could walk across on dry land, and then all of the people to thank Yahuweh/Yehovah decided to reject the prophecy fulfillment that had just happened, and go back to Egypt to wait for a better fulfillment more to their liking. They even built an idol of an imaginary false god to worship, because they liked their imagination of prophecy better than the reality of Yahuweh/Yehovah, and then they refused to even go into the land of Canaan to fight and create their own nation.

Even with those massive miracles, almost the whole nation of Israel rejected Yahuweh/Yehovah and his fulfillment of his prophecies in reality. And it happened again with Yeshua, and it will happen again now as he returns to fulfill his prophecies again. Even when Yahuweh/Yehovah fulfills his prophecies in the biggest, most massive miracles he always does so in such a way that anybody can choose to reject the fulfillment of that prophecy if they want to, and reject him in the process if they choose to harden their hearts against him and turn away from him completely in rebellion, to live their own lives their own way in their man made religion. This is who he is and this is the only way that he can know that a person is accepting him and wanting to be with him for who he really is as a person, not because they want his power for themselves, or the stuff he can give them.

How to Know if the Prophecies of the Time of the End and Great Tribulation are Happening, and that Yahuweh/Yehovah's Coming to the Earth is Not Far Away:

1. **Theory Versus Reality – All Theory is No Longer Relevant When Reality Happens and All Arguments Over the Theories of How a Prophecy will be Fulfilled No Longer Matter in the Reality of Fulfillment**: A theory is simply playing pretend with the imagination of the mind to try to think about possible ways something might happen in reality, from trying to predict the way the physical universe works scientifically to trying to predict how an event will happen in the future. As soon as reality happens and is observed for how it happens in real life, all theories become irrelevant and of no importance.

It is the same way with the prophecies in Scripture about future events which have not yet happened and cannot yet be observed in the reality of the present and past. While the prophecy is still coming in the future, people can only come up with theories about what will happen, and how the prophecy will take place, theories which are simply imaginations in the mind. A theory is nothing more than imagination like playing make believe in the mind. As soon as the prophecy becomes a reality in the present, then all of those imaginations of the mind about the prophecy, all of the theories about how the prophecy might happen, become irrelevant and of no importance in the reality of the fulfillment of the prophecy in real life and in the real world.

This means that in order to truly be able to examine an event in the present moment, or in records and witness accounts of a past moment, as to whether it is a fulfillment of a prophecy in Scripture happening in real life, all previous imaginations about that prophecy have to be removed from the mind and let go of. All previous theories and thoughts and ideas and preconceptions and interpretations about every prophecy have to be removed from the mind and let go of as irrelevant when examining events happening in the real world, in reality, as to whether or not they are a fulfillment of prophecy. All previous expectations and desires and wishes and beliefs about each and every prophecy have to come to an end and be let go of in order to know for certain if a prophecy has really been fulfilled or not, because we can believe something all that we want or desire something all that we want, but those beliefs and those desires do not make something true, just by believing.

Only the truth is true, and no beliefs or desires can ever change that reality of the way things actually are. That is why it is important to believe the truth and not believe lies, because believing a lie can never make that lie true. And all past commentaries and teachings that have ever been written or orally taught about how the prophecies will be fulfilled in the future (specifically and especially the ones that try to predict <u>how</u> the prophecies will be fulfilled before they have happened) all become irrelevant in the reality of the fulfillment of prophecy in real life, because every commentary and teaching about prophecy, no matter how inspired, are still only theories and beliefs and preconceived ideas and desires and wishes and interpretations. All commentaries and teachings about prophecy are still only playing pretend make believe in the imagination of the mind about how the prophecies might happen in the future. The imaginations of the mind cannot predict what will actually happen in reality, or how it will happen. Sometimes a person can come close to getting a few details right here and there in their imagining of a possible way the future might happen, but it will never be entirely or perfectly right or accurate enough to rely upon more than the words themselves in Scripture.

The one and only thing that matters in determining and investigating if an event in the present moment or a past moment is a fulfillment of prophecy is through the Words in the prophecy itself, and only the Words. The Words written down in the prophecies in Scripture are the only thing that matter, and those Words have to be examined in complete purity without any previous imaginations, ideas, thoughts, theories, preconceptions, beliefs, desires, wishes, commentaries, or teachings of men mixing as impurities with those Words, blinding the eyes and ears and heart from seeing a fulfillment of prophecy. And it is also important to remember never to argue about whether an event that has happened in reality, in the present or past, is really a fulfillment of a prophecy in Scripture or not, because arguing, just like believing, does not change reality. Either the event being examined in reality is a fulfillment of prophecy, or it is not. It is one or the other, and arguing about it is not going to change one way or the other. It is more important to truthfully and honestly examine each event in reality to find out for certain if it is a fulfillment or not a fulfillment.

Arguments are only the theories that people have held onto from past imaginations and ideas of the mind about how a prophecy might be fulfilled in the future. Arguments become completely irrelevant and of no importance in the present moment of reality, when a prophecy is actually fulfilled and observable in real life, and is no longer in the theoretical world of the imagination.

One of the most complete examples of why theories and imaginations and arguments and beliefs and commentaries and teachings become irrelevant when a prophecy is fulfilled in reality is in **John 7:1-53**:

Arguing and Grumbling about prophecy are of no value in the reality of fulfillment of prophecy:
Verses **7:12** and **7:40-43**: There were many in the crowd who grumbled and argued about Yeshua when he came. In one argument some said that Yeshua is good and others said that he is not, because he is leading the crowd astray. And in another argument the crowd argued and became divided over whether or not the Messiah can come from Galil, because the prophecies in Scripture say he must be a descendant of David born in Beyth Lechem (Bethlehem). And they were so busy arguing about whether or not Yeshua could be the fulfillment of the prophecies about the Messiah, none of them ever investigated to find out the truth, if Yeshua was really the fulfillment of the prophecies or not. None of them bothered to find out where Yeshua was born, because they were too busy arguing about all of their theories of how the prophecies should be fulfilled. Arguing and grumbling about prophecy is a waste of time that distracts from finding out the truth about whether or not a prophecy has actually been fulfilled in reality, in the real world.

Past Theories and Imaginations and Thoughts and Ideas and Interpretations and Preconceptions about how prophecy will be fulfilled are of no value in the reality of the fulfillment of prophecy:
Verses **7:25-27** and **7:40-42**: There were diverse theories and imaginations and ideas and interpretations that people had come up with about how the prophecies of the Messiah would be fulfilled at the time when Yeshua came. Some thought that the Messiah could only be the true Messiah if no one knows where he came from, and others thought that the Messiah has to come only from Bethlehem as a descendant of David, and nowhere else except from Bethlehem only, without there being any other places that he has come from at the same time as Bethlehem (such as Galil). Both of these theories and imaginations of the mind turned out to be

wrong and irrelevant in the reality of the fulfillment of the prophecy. The one theory, that the Messiah has to come from a place where no one knows where he has come from turned out to be wrong, and the other theory that the Messiah can only come from Bethlehem without being from any other places simultaneously, such as Galil, also turned out to be wrong. But because the people held onto the theories and interpretations that had come from the imaginations of their own minds, they denied reality and rejected the fulfillment of prophecy that was happening right in front of them.

Verses **7:40-42** and **7:50-52**: From the theories and interpretations from the imaginations of the minds of the people during Yeshua's coming, they thought that it was impossible for any prophet or Messiah to come from Galil. And this theory and idea stopped many people from accepting or recognizing that Yeshua was the fulfillment of the prophecy. All of the theories and imaginations and interpretations that the people had come up with about the prophecies of the Messiah and how they should be fulfilled blinded everyone from seeing the reality of the fulfillment of prophecy right in front of their own eyes, because their imaginations of pretend make believe about how the prophecies would be fulfilled turned out to be wrong. But they still held onto their wrong theories, denying reality, denying the fulfillment of the prophecies, and denying Yeshua, the God of Israel and Creator of the universe himself in the process. The people at the time did not interpret the prophecy of Isaiah 9:1 about Galil of the nations to have anything to do with the Messiah, and their theoretical, imaginary interpretations of this prophecy prevented them from seeing that it is prophesied in 9:6 that the Child that would be born as a ruler from the throne of David, the same child that would be born in Bethlehem, would actually come from Galil of the nations after his birth. All of their theories and imaginations about how the prophecies would be fulfilled became irrelevant in the reality of the fulfillment in real life.

Past Beliefs and Desires and Wishes about how prophecy will be fulfilled are of no value in the reality of the fulfillment of prophecy:

Verses **7:31** and **7:45-48**: Everything that everyone had believed about the prophecies in Scripture and all of the ways that they wanted and desired the prophecies to be fulfilled, became irrelevant when the reality of fulfillment came, and they had to choose to either believe in the reality of the way they were fulfilled in real life or not believe in reality. There were many in the crowd who did believe that Yeshua was the fulfillment of the prophecies of the Messiah. But from the rulers and Pharisees (which was a religious denomination consisting of tens of thousands of followers) at that time there were virtually none who believed that Yeshua was the Messiah. This is because they still believed in their imaginary, pretend, make believe theories about how the prophecies would be fulfilled, even after the reality of fulfillment happened. They could not see that their beliefs in those past doctrines and theories about how the prophecies might be fulfilled were all wrong, because man cannot predict how the future will happen with perfect accuracy from the imagination of his mind, even when he has the words of Yahuweh/Yehovah in a prophecy to reveal his plan for the future. Their beliefs in an imaginary world of prophecy theory that does not exist in the real world prevented them from believing in the reality of the fulfillment of prophecy in real life.

Past Teachings and Commentaries about how prophecy will be fulfilled are of no value in the reality of the fulfillment of prophecy:

Verses **7:45-49**: The Pharisees (consisting of tens of thousands of people, not just the leaders of the denomination), and even other religious denominations at that time such as the Sadducees and Essenes, had put together all of their theories and beliefs from the imaginations of their minds into teachings and commentaries, as have the many Christian denominations today. The teachings and commentaries about how the unfulfilled prophecies in Scripture should be fulfilled in the future, according to the many, various, pretend, make believe theories that people have <u>played</u> out from their minds through almost 2,000 years are even more vast and diverse than the number of different teachings and commentaries that were available during Yeshua's time on the earth. The Pharisees at that time said that those of the crowd listening to Yeshua and believing in him were accursed because they did not know the Torah (the Five Books of Moses called the Law in Greek). It was those considered to be unlearned in Scripture who were believing in Yeshua and following him; those who were unlearned in the teachings of the religious denominations at that time, such as the Pharisees.

The Pharisees were in a crisis, because all of their teachings and commentaries about Scripture and the prophecies in Scripture had suddenly become irrelevant in the reality of the fulfillment of the prophecies with Yeshua coming as the real Messiah. The Messiah was no longer a theoretical concept that could be controlled and manipulated in the non-existent world of the imagination. The Messiah was real, in front of them, and the prophecies were happening real, in front of them. And all that they had held onto as important for so many generations was suddenly unimportant in the reality of Yeshua walking on the earth, fulfilling the Scriptures in different ways from their teachings and commentaries.

The only way they could hold onto their irrelevant teachings about Scripture was to belittle the people who believed in the reality of prophecy in front of them, that they were ignorant of the true meanings of Scripture, meaning ignorant of the Pharisees' imaginary interpretations of Scripture they had come up with from their minds. Any teachings and commentaries that have been made prior to the fulfillment of prophecies in Scripture, that try to predict how the prophecies will be fulfilled in the future, are still only untested theories that have not gone through the testing fire of reality and real life, of the way things actually are or actually will be. When the fulfillment of prophecy comes, all of the past teachings and commentaries about the prophecies have to be let go of in order to accept reality and not reject Yahuweh/Yehovah and the reality of him in the process. Only the exact words of the prophecies in Scripture matter, none of the teachings or beliefs or imaginations or theories or interpretations of those prophecies.

In Christianity today there are even more teachings and commentaries about unfulfilled prophecies in Scripture to contend with than the Jews living in Israel had to deal with when Yeshua came before. But Yahuweh/Yehovah loves all of his little children as they play pretend make believe about how his prophecies might happen in the future, as they try to imagine them with imagination, and write down their play, make believe scenarios of prophecy as teachings and commentaries. His ways and thoughts are far above our own, and we are compared to him like little children who have been so cute, as believers in Yeshua, playing with our little toys and playing pretend ways of how we think that Yahuweh/Yehovah's prophecies might be fulfilled in the future, like children making up pretend stories about things we read or study or experience in life.

But as we grow up and mature in our walk with Yahuweh/Yehovah we have to let go of those old imaginations of playing about the prophecies and accept the reality of how they really happen, when they do actually happen in real life. This is the only way to know Yahuweh/Yehovah, by accepting the reality of who he is in his fulfillment of his prophecies in reality. When we are still immature we cry and throw tantrums and argue like little children about how we want the prophecies to be fulfilled our way. But to be truly humble as a child means to grow and mature as a child, and then we accept reality even when it is not the way we want it to be. All that matters is that the prophecies are how Yahuweh/Yehovah wants them to be, and that his will is done. As children we do not care if our playing pretend turns out to be different from what happens in the real world; we just accept the way reality is, and how the real world actually works in real life.

2. Prophecies are NOT for Predicting How the Future will Happen – They are for Revealing Who Yahuweh/Yehovah is and His Plan In the Present Moments When They Happen: It is only possible to recognize and understand a prophecy happening by revelation from Yahuweh/Yehovah, specifically revelation from him about who he is and his ways of doing things. It is really a revelation from Yahuweh/Yehovah about himself that brings understanding, and especially the ability to see and recognize, when a prophecy is being fulfilled in the present. And the only way that that revelation of the prophecy happening in reality can be a pure revelation is by removing all of our self-imagination and self-thought and self-interpretation from our ideas of how we think a fulfillment of that prophecy should look like.

Yahuweh/Yehovah gives his prophecies about the future in order to reveal who he is and help people to come to know him better for who he really is, while revealing his plans and purposes:

Verses **Isaiah 45:1-13**: Using Yahuweh/Yehovah's prophecies to predict how the future will happen will always fail, because on purpose Yahuweh/Yehovah leaves out a lot of important specific details from the majority of his prophecies in Scripture, such as the exact names of all of the people who will be involved in the prophecies, and all of the specific actions they will take to cause the prophecies to happen in a chronological order of events, and specific dates of when the prophecies will be fulfilled that are not veiled in countings of days and months, or specific weather conditions or positioning of the sun or moon (if it is day time or night time) when the prophecy happens. Most of the details that are needed to successfully predict how the future will happen are mostly missing from Yahuweh/Yehovah's prophecies. The only things present in the prophecies are general ideas of what Yahuweh/Yehovah's goals and plans are for the future, in order to reveal himself at the time that he does those things in the future.

On a few rare occasions Yahuweh/Yehovah does give some very specific details in his prophecies, but even in those cases there is not enough details in order to know ahead of time exactly how the future will happen or even all of what will happen. Isaiah 45 is one of those rare examples where Yahuweh/Yehovah reveals the exact name of a person in the future who will be a fulfillment of his prophecy, when he names Koresh כורש as the name of the man who would one day in the future release the Jewish captives and be the one to rebuild the city of Jerusalem after it had been destroyed. It turned out that the first ruler from Babylon of the Persian Empire was named Koresh in Ancient Hebrew (pronounced as Cyrus in the modern Latinized English and Kurush in Ancient Persian).

Even in this case there was no one who knew before the prophecy was fulfilled if the name Koresh was prophesying the literal name of the coming person who would rebuild Jerusalem, or if it was a symbolic title name. This was not known until Koresh the Great became the fulfillment of the man in the prophecy. There are indications in the prophecy that Koresh would be a king, but there are many important details left out, without any mention about him being a gentile king who was not even an Israelite or Jewish, and nothing about him being the ruler of the Persian Empire. But once the prophecy is fulfilled, there is no doubt about its fulfillment, because it is so precisely accurate in the details that are provided. There are only enough details in order to know when the prophecy is fulfilled, not enough to know how it will happen until after it has happened.

The more important thing about this prophecy is that Yahuweh/Yehovah is revealing himself and his plan, so that when Koresh becomes a mighty ruler and releases the captive Jews to go back to Jerusalem and orders the rebuilding of the city of Jerusalem, everyone will know that Yahuweh/Yehovah himself is the one who put Koresh into his position of power to the point that Yahuweh/Yehovah is even the one who gave him his name before he was born, even though Koresh never knew him. And even more importantly Yahuweh/Yehovah is revealing in the prophecy that he is the one who actually brought about the return of the Jews and the rebuilding of Jerusalem for his purposes and plans, even before they had been taken into captivity yet. Koresh had no power whatsoever to do anything; it is Yahuweh/Yehovah who has the real power, calling Koresh for Yahuweh/Yehovah's purpose even before he existed. This was Yahuweh/Yehovah revealing himself to all the nations of the world through all of time, from the rising of the sun to its setting, that there is no other God but Yahuweh/Yehovah alone.

Verses **1 Samuel 3:1-10**: When Yahuweh/Yehovah first spoke to Samuel in 1 Samuel 3 it is recorded that Samuel did not yet know Yahuweh/Yehovah, because the word of Yahuweh/Yehovah had not yet been revealed to him. Yahuweh/Yehovah then began to reveal his words to him, speaking prophecies to him, so that Samuel would then know him. Samuel, and others, come to know Yahuweh/Yehovah from the words he speaks, especially the words of his prophecies. The very first words that Yahuweh/Yehovah spoke to Samuel after calling his name "Shemu'el" was to give him a personal prophecy about Eli, who Samuel served under in the Tabernacle. A personal prophecy is a little different from the general prophecies found in Scripture, because it is directed at the life of a specific person instead of for nations and the world, but the principle is still the same that he reveals himself, for others to know him, through the words of the prophecies he speaks.

At the very beginning of the prophecy Yahuweh/Yehovah spoke to Samuel, he says that, even though it is a personal prophecy for Eli and Eli's sons, both ears of everyone in Israel will tingle when they hear it. It is a prophecy for everyone to hear and come to know Yahuweh/Yehovah better through it when he causes it to happen. Then everyone can understand how Yahuweh/Yehovah does not allow the sin in his house of set-apart people to continue, and eventually will judge it and end it. Then Samuel could know Yahuweh/Yehovah through the words of the prophecy he spoke to Samuel, and anyone else could also know him who heard the prophecy as well. When the event prophesied takes place, in this case the death of the two sons of Eli in one day, then everyone would know that it was Yahuweh/Yehovah doing what he said he would do, and why he did it. Yahuweh/Yehovah's prophecies are for revealing who he is to his people, and revealing the purpose and plan he has behind why he does what he does.

Verses **Isaiah 55:8-11**: In these verses of Isaiah pretty much 100% of translations translate this passage as Yahuweh/Yehovah saying, "For My thoughts are not your thoughts." But the Hebrew word used here "מַחֲשָׁבָה machashavah" does not simply mean just the word "thought" on its own. It specifically means thoughts that are "devices" or "plans." It is the planning type of thinking that is referred to here, so that it is specifically Yahuweh/Yehovah's plans that are not the plans of man. He comes up with plans in his thinking that are much higher and beyond the plans of man, and it is when he speaks his words in prophecy, going forth from his mouth, his words do not return empty, but instead accomplish the plan that he has thought about. His plans are accomplished in the fulfillments of his prophecies, and then it reveals himself and his plans, his thinking, when the prophecy is fulfilled.

The purpose of Yahuweh/Yehovah speaking his prophecies is to accomplish his purpose and plan on the earth, taking his thoughts and then making those thoughts and plans in his mind come true in reality. And when they comes true, in fulfillment of the prophecy he has spoken, then everyone can know him and his thoughts and plans better than before the prophecy was fulfilled. Yahuweh/Yehovah's prophecies are revelations about himself and who he is, not revelations about predictions of how the future will happen. Yahuweh/Yehovah has to reveal his plans to his people, because they are so far above and higher than the thinking and planning of man, we cannot even figure out what Yahuweh/Yehovah is doing without his explaining it to us.

Another part of Yahuweh/Yehovah's purpose in his prophecies is for them to be a public witness about himself to the world, for anyone and everyone to have a chance to know him and accept him and believe in him:

Verses **Revelation 19:10**: The witness of Yeshua is the Spirit of prophecy, because prophecy is for the purpose of being a public witness about Yeshua, revealing to the world the witness of who Yahuweh/Yehovah really is. And anyone can come to know Yahuweh/Yehovah if they want to. No one is prevented from knowing him, except when they themselves prevent their own selves from knowing him by rejecting him.

Truly recognizing and understanding the fulfillment of a prophecy comes by revelation from Yahuweh/Yehovah, which is part of his revealing understanding about who he is:

Verses **Matthew 16:13-23**: While still in the midst of the fulfillment of the prophecies Yahuweh/Yehovah has to reveal the fulfillment of prophecies to people, as with Peter when he revealed to him that Yeshua is the Messiah, the Son of God. Everyone else who tried to figure out what Yahuweh/Yehovah was doing from their own understanding thought that Yeshua was John the Immerser, or Elijah or Jeremiah come back from the dead. But they missed the revelation of who Yeshua really was when they tried to figure it out for themselves. It is listening to Yahuweh/Yehovah in humility with a circumcised heart that allows a person to recognize what Yahuweh/Yehovah is doing on the earth, because they are focused on knowing him instead of trying to predict the future.

Even Peter in his revelation from Yahuweh/Yehovah about who Yeshua is did not always listen and humble himself. Shortly after this moment he tried to convince Yeshua that Yeshua, as the Messiah, had made a mistake in what he was saying, and that he was not really going to be killed. Then Yeshua had to tell Peter that he was an adversary (a satan in Hebrew) who had to get behind him and reminded him in a paraphrase from Isaiah 55:8-11 that Peter's thoughts are not God's thoughts, that he was thinking with the thoughts of men that are not the thoughts or plans of Yahuweh/Yehovah. As Yahuweh/Yehovah reveals his fulfillments of prophecies to us, we have to remember to never use our own thoughts, imaginations, plans, and desires in our minds to interpret those fulfillments, because Yahuweh/Yehovah has a much higher and smarter plan than we do that he is working on. We can trust his will and trust his plan, especially when he fulfills his prophecies in completely different ways from what we expected, such as with the followers of Yeshua who never expected the Messiah Yeshua to be killed as a fulfillment of prophecy.

There will always be some details of the fulfillments of prophecies that will not be fully understood until after Yahuweh/Yehovah comes and is walking and dwelling on the earth with mankind, explaining directly from his own mouth how all of the prophecies were fulfilled:

Verses **Luke 24:14-48**: After all of the prophecies are finished and completed, then everyone can finally understand and recognize them all, but only once again by Yahuweh/Yehovah explaining it all. All of his followers missed all of the fulfillments of prophecy that were happening right in front of their eyes, as Yeshua was killed as the blameless sin sacrifice. It was not until after it was all done and completed that Yeshua walked with two of the disciples to Emmaus, and then later appeared to the disciples in Jerusalem, and opened their minds to understanding the prophecies in Scripture for the first time. It was Yeshua who explained to them all of the prophecies that had just been fulfilled right in front of them, which they had all missed completely.

And the reason that it took them all so long to finally recognize and understand all of the prophecies that had been fulfilled was because they had been slow of heart to believe in all of the words written in the prophecies in Scripture. They did not believe the words of Yahuweh/Yehovah's prophecies in Scripture, and they did not believe the fulfillments of Yahuweh/Yehovah's prophecies. They did not believe it and they rejected it, until they were finally able to open their hearts up to Yahuweh/Yehovah and believe him, instead of believing in their thoughts and imaginations about the prophecies. They believed their own thoughts about the prophecies instead of believing in the actual words written in the prophecies. Then they were finally able to accept the fulfillments that had happened word for word to the actual words written in Scripture, instead of believing in the myths about the prophecies that people had come up with at that time from the imaginations of their hearts.

3. **Only the Exact Words Written in the Prophecy Matter – As Long as the Exact Words in the Prophecy Happen, They are Fulfilled, Even if Other Events Happen in Conjunction with the Prophecy that are Not Written in the Prophecy**: Only the exact words written in each prophecy can be used to determine fulfillment of each prophecy, by examining every word in a prophecy to determine if each word in the prophecy has happened in a present or past moment event. No theories or imaginations or desires or wishes or teachings about the prophecies can be used to accurately determine if a prophecy has been fulfilled in reality. All of those things are irrelevant compared to the original words written in the prophecy. It is still possible for other events to happen in connection with the prophecy that are not written down in the prophecy, without stopping the prophecy from being fulfilled, as long as the exact words in the prophecy have happened in some way in the real world, in tangible reality. Also, context around each prophecy is irrelevant in its fulfillment, because on purpose Yahuweh/Yehovah the majority of the time gives his prophecies through the prophets in a non-chronological order of events, with many different events placed side by side in the prophecies that happen at different times spread apart, not simultaneous.

Each word in a prophecy has to be fulfilled and happen in detail, but does not have to be fulfilled in context with the other words and prophecies around it:

Verses **Jeremiah 31:15** and **Matthew 2:16-18**: The prophecy in Jeremiah 31 is a very straightforward prophecy about all of the tribes of Israel coming back together to live in the land of Israel again. Almost the entire prophecy is about this subject, and that there is a new covenant that Yahuweh/Yehovah will make with all of the tribes of Israel in which he puts his Torah (Five Books of Moses) inside of all of his nation of people, writing his Torah on their hearts. This is a prophecy that to this day has never been completely fulfilled, only partially. If verse 15 in this prophecy were to be fulfilled in context, then it should be all about all of the tribes of Israel coming together again as one nation under the new covenant that Yahuweh/Yehovah brought through Yeshua. But instead the fulfillment of verse 15 happened all by itself, without any of the other verses around it being fulfilled at the same time.

This prophecy of a single sentence is about a place or town called Ramah, and it refers to Rachel, the wife of Jacob, weeping for her children, because they are no more. Rachel's children were Joseph and Benjamin, who obviously did not die while Rachel was still alive. After Rachel died, according to Genesis 35:19 and 48:7 she was buried along the way to the little village of Ephrathah, at the location of where the town of Beyth Lechem (Bethlehem) was located. She was buried in Bethlehem, within the borders of the tribe of Yehudah (Judah), but on the southern border of the tribe of Binyamin (Benjamin), the inheritance of her descendants or children through Benjamin. And the town of Ramah was located a little father north from Bethlehem, towards the northern border of the tribe of Benjamin, a town of her descendants or children. Ramah is where Deborah lived and where Samuel lived, and the mention of Ramah is what connects Rachel, buried in Bethlehem, with her children or descendants of the tribe of Benjamin, Ramah being a primary city representing the tribe of Benjamin.

There are two separate locations given in the prophecy, Ramah and Bethlehem, and one would think that the prophecy would be fulfilled inside of the town of Ramah. But instead it happened right where Rachel was buried in Bethlehem, when Herod gave the order for all male children two and under to be killed, as he tried to kill the true king of Israel, Yeshua, who was born in Bethlehem. Many of those children killed there in Bethlehem may have even been literal descendants or children of Rachel through Benjamin, right on the border of the tribe of Benjamin. And the order was given by Herod from the city of Yerushalayim (Jerusalem), which was also located within the borders of the tribe of Benjamin. The order included killing the male children in the border areas around Bethlehem, which included a larger area around at least the southern city of Jerusalem than just the town of Bethlehem itself.

And the way the prophecy was fulfilled was, poetically, by the people in Ramah hearing the voice of Rachel where she was buried in Bethlehem, crying for her children. The prophecy is saying that the cries of the mothers over their dead children by where Rachel is buried in Bethlehem are so loud, that even the people living in Ramah, far to the north in the tribal borders of Benjamin, are able to hear their cries. The events of the children killed close to Yeshua's birth in Bethlehem fulfilled every word of this prophecy in Jeremiah 31:15 exactly, word for word.

But in this fulfillment of this prophecy of a single sentence, there was no restoration that happened to bring all of the tribes of Israel back together again as one nation physically living in the land of Israel, as the rest of the prophecy states. To this day that part of the prophecy has still never been fulfilled. But this one single sentence within the prophecy was fulfilled completely out of context from the rest of the prophecy around it. This is the way that Yahuweh/Yehovah gives his prophecies, outside of the boundaries of time, so that one part of a prophecy can be fulfilled at one time in history, and other parts of the prophecy fulfilled at other times in history. This does not mean that Jeremiah 31:15 was not fulfilled, simply because it happened out of context from the rest of the prophecy.

Verses **Hosea 11:1** and **Matthew 2:13-15**: The prophecy of Hosea 11 is all about Ephrayim and the northern tribes of Israel turning away from Yahuweh/Yehovah and then having to come under judgement because of it, exiled out of their land into Egypt and Syria, then the promise of returning them from those places. But once again when Yeshua became the fulfillment of this prophecy, of a half of a sentence in verse 1, it had nothing to do with the tribes of Israel returning to become a unified nation again in the land of Israel. The prophecy begins with Yahuweh/Yehovah remembering the past when he loved the nation of Israel when they were a child born, and then he calls his son out of Egypt, which was the nation of Israel in the past. And yet this sentence about the past became a prophecy about the future at the same time, that the Messiah, the son of Yahuweh/Yehovah, would also come out of Egypt like the children of Israel before him.

This prophecy becomes a dual layer prophecy about both the nation of Israel as the child of Yahuweh/Yehovah and the Messiah, the son, of Yahuweh/Yehovah. And when Yeshua became the fulfillment of this prophecy as the son who returned to Israel after his flight to Egypt, it was fulfilled completely out of context, having nothing to do with the exile of Ephrayim and the northern tribes of Israel into Egypt as judgement, and then being returned back to Israel again, restoring the nation with all of the tribes. It is its own little prophecy of a single sentence, of a half-sentence, that is separate from the other prophecy connected to it. Its fulfillment out of context with the rest of the prophecy around it does not stop this prophecy from being fulfilled in the events of Yeshua's birth.

Other events can happen in connection with the fulfillment of prophecy that are not written down in the prophecy itself without preventing the prophecy from being a true fulfillment:

Verses **Isaiah 40:3-11** and **Matthew 3:1-17**: There can also be other events happening in connection to a prophecy around it, that are not actually written down in the prophecy itself, and this does not prevent the prophecy from being fulfilled. John the Immerser fulfilled Isaiah 40 as the voice that was crying in the wilderness, preparing the way of Yahuweh/Yehovah himself, so that the esteem of Yahuweh/Yehovah would be revealed, for all flesh together to be able see it. But John the Immerser also did some things that are not found in the Isaiah 40 prophecy, or any prophecy in Scripture. He wore camel fur skins with a leather belt for clothing and ate the honey and locusts he found in the wilderness.

There is nowhere in the Isaiah 40 prophecy that says that the person who is the voice in the wilderness would be wearing camel fur or eating honey and locust, living wild out in the wilderness. Also, there is nowhere in the Isaiah 40 prophecy that says that the person who is the voice in the wilderness would immerse the Messiah in water out in the wilderness. These details that John the Immerser did are not found anywhere in the Isaiah 40 prophecy, or in any prophecy in Scripture. Just because John the Immerser did other things connected with the Isaiah 40 prophecy that are not written down in the prophecy does not mean that he cannot be the fulfillment of the Isaiah 40 prophecy. He was still the fulfillment of verses 3 through 8, preparing the way for the one who would come bringing Good News to places around Israel.

Every word of this prophecy beginning from verse 3 through 11 were fulfilled at that time, and other events happening in conjunction with the fulfillment of the prophecy that are not mentioned anywhere in any prophecies in Scripture does not stop that fulfillment. All that matters are the exact words of the prophecy being fulfilled, even when there are other important and interwoven events that happen simultaneous with the fulfillment of the prophecy. There is nothing in this Isaiah 40 prophecy about the person who is the voice in the wilderness being beheaded either like John the Immerser was beheaded, but the exact words of the prophecy were already fulfilled, and just because the prophecy does not mention the voice crying in the wilderness later being beheaded, it does not mean that the prophecy was not fulfilled when the "voice" John the Immerser was beheaded after its fulfillment.

Verses **Matthew 14:15-33**: It is the same with Yeshua, when he multiplied the bread and fish to feed the more than five thousand people, or when he walked on water. There are no prophecies anywhere in Scripture about the Messiah multiplying food for people to be able to eat, or about the Messiah walking on top of water across a lake in the middle of a storm. These were extra events without any prophecies written down about them, but simply because Yeshua did these extra miracles that were not prophesied about beforehand in Scripture, he still did do the other miracles and acts that were prophesied about for the Messiah to do in Isaiah and Zechariah and the other books of the prophets, and Psalms. Yeshua still fulfilled the exact words in the other prophecies about the Messiah who would come; and just because he did extra things that were not prophesied about ahead of time does not mean that suddenly he cannot be the Messiah or cannot be the fulfillment of the prophecies of the Messiah which he did do. Oftentimes there are extra events that happen that are intricately connected with the fulfillment of a prophecy, but were not prophesied about or written down in any of the prophecies beforehand.

4. **Yeshua, Not Paul, was the First One to Prophesy About a "Catching Away" at the End of the Great Tribulation when the Messengers will Gather All of the Chosen from the Four Winds (in the Air), from One End of the Heavens (Sky) to the Other End of the Heavens (Sky), from Where the Chosen are Floating in the Sky to be Taken to Meet Yeshua in the Clouds at His Coming, After the Tribulation of Those Days [Matthew 24:26-31]**: Everybody places the rapture either sometime before the 3.5 years of Great Tribulation has even started or at the end when it is done, and everybody is in agreement that there is nowhere in Scripture that says that the rapture happens in the midst of or during the 3.5 years of Great Tribulation. Therefore, when examining the fulfillment of prophecies concerning the Great Tribulation, there is no reason to talk about or discuss the pre-tribulation rapture, because either the pre-tribulation rapture already happened and you have already been Left Behind without even realizing it, or there was no pre-tribulation rapture, and the "Catching Away" into the air to be gathered up by the messengers to meet Yeshua in the clouds is still coming in the future after the 3.5 years of Great Tribulation are finished. That is the unchangeable reality of the situation if the prophecies concerning the Great Tribulation, before Yeshua's return, are really happening.

Everyone always talks about how Paul was the first one and only one to have a prophecy about the "rapture," more accurately called the "catching away." This is primarily to support the pre-tribulation rapture idea that there are no <u>elect</u> or <u>chosen</u> left on the earth during the Great Tribulation. Because of this most either ignore or do not even know about the fact that it was Yeshua who was the first to prophesy about the "catching away" or rapture idea in Matthew 24:31, when he says that the messengers will gather together the <u>elect</u>, the <u>chosen</u>, from the four winds, from one end of the sky to the other end of the sky. Yeshua says that the chosen, his followers and believers, will be gathered from one end of the heavens to the other end of the heavens, gathered together from the sky itself where they are floating in the wind and in the air above the earth, in order to be brought to Yeshua to meet him in the clouds.

It was Yeshua who first prophesied about the chosen being gathered from the air in the heavens (in the sky) to him by the messengers, at the sound of the trumpet at his coming at the end of the Great Tribulation; and the only way that anyone could be gathered from the sky is if they were already floating in the sky, after having been "caught up" there. If anyone were to acknowledge that it was Yeshua who first prophesied about the catching away of the chosen into the air to be with him in the clouds, then they would also have to acknowledge that the "catching away" or "rapture" does not happen until Yeshua comes at the end of the 3.5 years of Great Tribulation, "after the tribulation of those days."

5. Everyone, Even the Chosen, are Either Already Fallen into One Kind of Deception or Another, or are in Danger of It During These Times – No One is Exempt from the Possibility of being Deceived, but Even the Deceived Yahuweh/Yehovah Uses to Fulfill Prophecies as in the Case of the Pharisee Sanhedrin that Sent Yeshua to His Death so that He could become the Passover Lamb Sacrifice to Take Away the Sins of the World [Matthew 26:57-68]: There were three main religious sects of Judaism who were followers of Yahuweh/Yehovah at the time of Yeshua's coming in the 1st century C.E. These were the Perushim (Pharisees), the Tsadeqim (Sadducees), and the Isiyim (Essenes). At that time, before Yeshua began his ministry, these were the only primary religious denominations in Judaism, and most Jews belonged to these three religious denominations. They were all considered true believers in the God of Israel, Yahuweh/Yehovah, at that time, with differences in beliefs of practice and doctrine concerning Scripture. From surviving records in Scripture they certainly fought one another to at least some extent as to whose beliefs and interpretations of Scripture and prophecy were more correct and true to the words of Scripture. The majority of the early followers of Yeshua were once members of these three different denominations, the majority of them being Perushim (Pharisees).

After Yeshua started his ministry he began pulling everyone out of these three denominations to follow him into the new container (the new wineskin) in Matthew 9:17, causing people to return back to the pure words in Scripture, to obey and teach the Torah (Five Books of Moses called the Law in Greek) according to only the actual words written there, nothing added and nothing subtracted, in Matthew 5:17-20. He began teaching that people had to be even more righteous than the Perushim (Pharisees) in order to enter into the reign (kingdom) of the heavens, in other words saying that the practices and interpretations of Scripture of the Perushim and other religious denominations of followers of Yahuweh/Yehovah at that time were inadequate as the old container (the old wineskin) for entering into his reign and kingdom.

With Yeshua's coming Yahuweh/Yehovah had brought another step for people to make a choice about if they wanted to come closer to him and know him more deeply than before, or not. And the only way to take that step closer to him was to leave the old manmade religious denominations and go with him into the new container. What had just been errors in belief in the denominations beforehand turned into deceptions for any of those who refused to leave their old manmade religious denominations. Those who refused to leave the old container in order to follow Yahuweh/Yehovah into the new container, who refused to stay with him as he revealed himself more and fulfilled more of his plan for saving the people he created on the earth to have a chance at eternal life with him, fell into the deceptions of their denominations and doctrines and interpretations of Scripture and manmade religious beliefs, their commands and traditions of men that are in disobedience against the commands of Yahuweh/Yehovah in Scripture (Matthew 15:1-9; Isaiah 29:13).

After Yeshua came and led the people away out of the various denominations to continue following Yahuweh/Yehovah more closely than they had before, those who decided to stay behind in the old denominations had to then deny and reject Yeshua as the Messiah in order to be able to hold onto their old doctrines and traditions and commands of men. And the only way they could deny and reject Yeshua was to deny and reject the truth itself and reality, which meant they had to give themselves over to believing the deceptions of their hearts.

Even in spite of being deceived and following after the deceptions, Yahuweh/Yehovah still used them to fulfill his prophecies, by causing many of them from among the Perushim to be the ones to capture Yeshua and condemn him to death, and then convince the Roman rulers in Jerusalem to kill Yeshua. Just because a person is deceived or in the midst of a deception where they are believing in religious lies and are turning away from Yahuweh/Yehovah, it does not mean that they cannot still be used by Yahuweh/Yehovah as part of a fulfillment of prophecy. Even when a person in deception is part of a fulfillment of prophecy, this does not prevent that fulfillment from happening, nor does it create a reason to throw out that fulfillment of prophecy as false.

It is the same with Judas who betrayed Yeshua. Just because he was deceived into betraying Yeshua, the deception that Judas was under, and the sin of his heart that he was in the midst of, did not prevent him from still taking part in fulfilling the prophecies of Yahuweh/Yehovah in Scripture. So even when there is someone who is in deception, and even possibly turning away from Yahuweh/Yehovah in sin, taking part in the fulfillment of a prophecy, it does not mean that that prophecy cannot be fulfilled anymore, and its fulfillment has to be thrown out. Everyone who takes part in Yahuweh/Yehovah's fulfillments of prophecy all through Scripture is a sinner, in varying degrees of righteousness or wickedness in their hearts, in the process of being cleansed from sin or choosing rebellion against Yahuweh/Yehovah.

6. There is No Such Thing as a False or Deceptive Fulfillment of Yahuweh/Yehovah's Prophecies When the Prophecy has Truly Happened in Real Life in Every Detail, Word for Word to What is Written in Scripture: There is nowhere in all of Scripture that Yahuweh/Yehovah warns that at some point in the future one of his prophecies will happen and be fulfilled in a false way, or in a way that is against his will. There is never once that he says that his prophecies will accidently be fulfilled the wrong way, in a different way than he intended, or that people in their own flesh will fulfill one of his prophecies in a false way that is not the correct way. He is strong enough and big enough as the only God in existence, as the creator of the heavens and the earth and all the universe, to make sure that his prophecies are only fulfilled his way when they happen, and that they only happen in his timing for when he decides to do them.

He does not ever once say in all of Scripture or recorded history that if we see any of his prophecies fulfilled, that we have to be careful, because it might be a false fulfillment done as a deception by the demonic or by men or false prophets. The false prophets and false messiahs will give prophecies that come true, which are deceptions Yahuweh/Yehovah sends as tests for the hearts of his people to see if they truly want to follow him or not. And it is even he himself who empowers those false prophets to give prophecies that come true in order to test the hearts of his people in Deuteronomy 13:1-5. But those prophecies that are given by false prophets are not Yahuweh/Yehovah's prophecies. The prophecies that Yahuweh/Yehovah himself has given, recorded through the many books in Scripture, are all true prophecies, and Yahuweh/Yehovah never says that any of his true prophecies will ever be fulfilled in a false or incorrect way that is outside of his will, and certainly never in a deceptive way that would lead people astray from the truth. When Yahuweh/Yehovah's true prophecies have truly been fulfilled word for word in reality, in real life, then it is his true fulfillment always.

The Prophecies that Need to be Either Already Fulfilled or in Process of Fulfillment in Order for it to be the Time of the Great Tribulation at the Time of the End Right Before Yeshua Returns:

Now as we are examining and investigating if any of the Time of the End, Great Tribulation prophecies are being fulfilled today, **we are dealing with the realm of reality in the real world, not the realm of theory or fantasy or imagination or interpretation in the make believe world of playing pretend about the future in the mind.** We are not examining theories of possible ways the prophecies might or might not happen in the future, but instead examining reality, and if any of the prophecies are happening in the real world, in real life, according to the exact words that are written in Scripture. Are the exact words in the prophecies in Scripture happening in real life according to just the words written there without the involvement of any added imaginations or theories or fantasies or interpretations about the Scriptural prophecies.

This means that if the exact words of a prophecy are happening in real life, and they are happening in a different way from how anyone had previously imagined or interpreted or thought or believed or wanted that prophecy to happen, all of those previous thoughts or interpretations or imaginations or theories about that prophecy must be put aside to accept the reality of how it is happening in real life. This is what it means to completely believe in and follow Yahuweh/Yehovah, to accept the reality of how he is doing things in real life and fulfilling his prophecies in real life, even when it is not the way we think he should be doing things or the way we want him to be doing things.

And this is the key, to know Yahuweh/Yehovah for yourself, because then you can know and recognize for yourself when he is causing his prophecies to happen in the reality of real life and not miss them. If the words of a prophecy are not happening word for word to the exact words that are written in the prophecy, then it is not happening. But if the words are happening exactly word for word in the prophecy, then you will clearly see Yahuweh/Yehovah himself in the fulfillment, and know him better, and come closer to him through that recognition of the prophecy fulfillment. And when you accept his fulfillment of prophecy in reality, you will also be accepting him and not denying reality and rejecting him in the process, as many did when Yeshua came, rejecting their own God of Israel, the one and only God Yahuweh/Yehovah come in the flesh (Deuteronomy 6:4-5, John 14:9-11, John 17:11), in order to hold onto the imaginary fulfillments of the prophecies they had invented in playing pretend in their minds.

When Yeshua came the first time everyone was watching for their own theories or imaginations or fantasies or beliefs or desires about the prophecies to happen, instead of watching for the words of the prophecies themselves to happen. That is the stumbling block that we want to avoid now today and in the future, to not make the same mistake again of watching for theories about prophecies to happen instead of watching for the actual words of the prophecies to happen. Unfortunately though, most are again watching for the theories people have come up with about the prophecies (the myths and legends) instead of the reality of the words of prophecy, and many will be disappointed once again when Yahuweh/Yehovah does his prophecies completely differently from how anyone thought he would in the expectations of their theories.

Read all of the verses of the prophecies for yourself. They are all completely listed out in the following sections of examinations and investigations so that anyone can read all of the exact words of each prophecy for themselves, preferably in many multiple translations, or preferably in the original language if possible, since no translation is perfectly accurate to the original words and all translations are filled with errors. Not one translation in existence contains all of the perfect, inerrant, original words of Yahuweh/Yehovah without errors in many various places. Only the original languages of Yahuweh/Yehovah's words in Scripture are the perfect words without error that can be completely relied upon.

In this investigation we will be primarily looking at only the prophecies that have requirements written within them in some form or another showing that they have to be in process of happening or already fulfilled sometime before Yeshua returns at the end of the Great Tribulation. There is no need to look at or investigate the other prophecies dealing with the moment of Yeshua's coming or the events after he comes as he rules and reigns and creates a new heavens and new earth, since we will be with him at that time and he will be able to explain all of those prophecies to us directly from his own mouth as he does them. So there is no need to speculate or theorize about how those prophecies will happen in the future, since they will happen however Yahuweh/Yehovah wants them to happen, as he does with all of his prophecies. This is only an investigation of the concrete world in reality in the present, to see if any of the prophecies from before Yahuweh/Yehovah's coming are happening now, in reality and not in theory.

There are many different opinions about which prophecies have to be fulfilled first before Yeshua can return, but the prophecies examined in this book in the following list are the only ones that have a requirement specifically written down, either in the actual prophecy itself, or in a corresponding prophecy about the same time period, that shows that the prophecy has to be happening before Yeshua's coming in the clouds at the end of the 3.5 years of Great Tribulation. These are prophecies that include wording in them that say they happen "before the Day of Yahuweh/Yehovah," or have indications that they happen during the "Great Tribulation" described by Yeshua in Matthew 24, all of which of these Great Tribulation prophecy events happen before the "Coming of the Son of Adam (Yeshua)" in the clouds. Also any prophecies that specifically happen before the sounding of the "Shofar" or the "Seventh Trumpet" or the "Last Trumpet" (Matthew 24:31, 1 Corinthians 15:51-52, 1 Thessalonians 4:16, Revelation 11:15-19) all of which are references to Yeshua's coming in the clouds at the end of the Great Tribulation.

And also any prophecies that clearly happen before Yahuweh/Yehovah comes down to earth and "His feet stand on the Mount of Olives," to set up his rule over mankind from his throne in Jerusalem in Zechariah 14 and Joel 3. These include prophecies about the southern tribes of Judah becoming a nation in Israel again with Jerusalem as their capital before, since the Jews are living in Jerusalem as a nation together at the time of the fulfillment of the prophecies of Zechariah 14 and Joel 3.

But there is no reason to write about or examine the signs of the "Birth Pain" prophecies Yeshua gives in Matthew 24, Mark 13, and Luke 21 (which are also mentioned in Isaiah 13), because these are simple signs of wars between nations and reigns, along with famines and earthquakes happening around the world, and strong persecution of believers in Yeshua, which should be obvious to everyone as they watch these things happening, currently and historically. Most of these things have always been on the earth since the

Global Flood at the time of Noah, and will always be on the earth until the end of the world of man, but with increasing intensity and frequency as Yeshua's coming nears.

TABLE OF CONTENTS

The following is a list of the primary prophecies that need to be either already fulfilled or in process of fulfillment before Yeshua's Return at the end of the Great Tribulation, which will be examined and investigated in this book:

Before the 3.5 Years of Great Tribulation:

1. The Birth of the Natural Israel into a Nation Again with Jerusalem as Its Capital – **Page 55**
2. Psalms 83 Armies Attack Israel (War for Independence 1948-1949 and Six Day War 1967) – **Page 69**
3. Zechariah 12 Armies Attack Israel and Israel Retakes and Lifts the Siege of Jerusalem (Six Day War 1967) – **Page 71**
4. Joel 1 – 2 Army of Locusts Invades and Attacks Israel (Yom Kippur War 1973) – **Page 73**

Before or at the Beginning of the 3.5 Years of Great Tribulation:

5. The First through Fifth Seals (The Four Horsemen) – **Page 81**
6. The 144,000 Sealed from the 12 Tribes of Israel – **Page 86**
7. The Transgression Desolating (2,300 Evening and Morning) – **Page 90**
8. The Finishing of the Proclaiming of the Good News Witness of Yeshua to All Nations – **Page 93**

During the 3.5 Years of Great Tribulation (A Time, Times, and Half a Time):

9. The Disgusting Idol (Abomination) Desolating (1,290 Days) – **Page 99**
10. The Outer Court and City of Jerusalem Trampled by the Gentiles (42 Months) – **Page 115**
11. The Two Witnesses (1,260 Days) and the Removal of the Oil and Light of the Word and Commands of the Witness of Yahuweh/Yehovah (3.5 Days) – **Page 118**
12. The Dragon and the Woman in the Wilderness Who Birthed the Male Child (1,260 Days) – **Page 141**
13. The Beast Out of the Sea with Authority to Blaspheme Yahuweh/Yehovah (42 Months) – **Page 153**
14. Mystery Babel on the Scarlet Beast Out of the Pit of the Deep and the Seven Heads that are Seven Mountains – **Page 166**
15. The Ten Horns – **Page 177**
16. The Little Horn – **Page 182**
17. The Beast Out of the Earth and the Image of the Beast Out of the Sea – **Page 205**
18. The Mark of the Beast Out of the Sea – **Page 216**
19. The Deceiving of the Elect (the Chosen) and Their Refining – **Page 233**
20. The Shepherds (Pastors/Religious Leaders) Removed to Make Way for Only One Shepherd, Yeshua, to Shepherd His People – **Page 252**
21. The Final Great Harvest of All the Earth and Yahuweh/Yehovah Pouring Out His Spirit on All Flesh – **Page 255**

22. The Days of Noah and Lot and the Great Tribulation Trouble for a Time, Times, and Half a Time – **Page 269**
23. The Roaring Sea of People – **Page 292**
24. The Covenant with Death and the Grave – **Page 296**

During or at the End of the 3.5 Years of Great Tribulation:
25. The Sixth through Seventh Seals and the First through Fourth Trumpets – **Page 303**

The rest of these following prophecies are not fulfilled until around the time of the end of the Great Tribulation when Yeshua is coming in the clouds, or much, much later after his coming; and therefore there is no need to examine or discuss these prophecies in this book, since Yeshua himself will be there tangibly with us to explain all of these prophecies to us as he does them:

At the End of and After the 3.5 Years of Great Tribulation:
1. The Fifth through Seventh Trumpets (The Three Woes)
2. The First through Seventh Bowls of Wrath
3. The Nations Gather into the Joel 3, Zechariah 14, and Revelation 16:12-16 Armies for War Against Israel and Jerusalem (Possibly Including the Gog of Magog Ezekiel 38 – 39, Revelation 19, and Revelation 20:7-9 Alliance)
4. The Resurrection and Catching Away Gathering to the Son of Adam in the Clouds at His Coming (Finishing the Harvest)
5. The Wedding of the Lamb
6. Yahuweh/Yehovah Comes Down to Earth, Stands on the Mount of Olives, and Reigns from Jerusalem
7. Yahuweh/Yehovah's Nation Israel is Made One in His Hand (Made Up of All Those Who will Live with Him in Eternity in the New Heavens and New Earth, Both Jew and Gentile Believers)
8. Possibly the Gog of Magog Alliance of Ezekiel 38 – 39, Revelation 19, and Revelation 20:7-9 Attacks Jerusalem at the End of the One Thousand Year Reign
9. Yahuweh/Yehovah Creates the New Heavens and New Earth for All of His People to Dwell in Together with Him After the One Thousand Year Reign is Finished (Taking into Account that in Yahuweh/Yehovah's Sight, a Thousand Years are Like Yesterday)

Explanatory on Gog of Magog: Even though most watch for the prophecy of the Gog of the Land of Magog war against Israel to happen before Yeshua has returned, or even before the 3.5 years of Great Tribulation have begun, Revelation 20:7-9 clearly says that Gog of Magog coalition does not attack Israel and Jerusalem until after the one thousand years have ended, well after Yeshua has already come and the Great Tribulation is long over. Also, Revelation 19 contains quotes and paraphrases directly from Ezekiel 38 and 39 in its descriptions of Yeshua coming onto the earth riding on the white horse and destroying all of his enemies who have come to battle against him. So both places in Revelation that reference Ezekiel 38-39 have this prophecy of Gog of the Land of Magog happening after Yeshua has returned.

This is the only prophecy about a war in Scripture that clearly says that it will happen after Yeshua's coming in the clouds. The other prophecies in Joel 3 and Zechariah 14 clearly say that they happen at the time of Yeshua's coming, but neither of them are prophesied with the same precision of timing and certainty of their taking place <u>after</u> Yeshua has already come to earth, as is prophesied with the Gog of the Land of Magog prophecy. Unfortunately this Gog of the Land of Magog prophecy is the only prophecy about war that anyone ever watches for to happen, even though it is the only prophecy about war in Scripture that clearly and precisely says that it does not happen until after Yeshua returns at the end of the Great Tribulation, at around the time of the Wedding of the Lamb, or perhaps not even for a thousand years after. That is what Revelation says, which means there is no requirement in Scripture that the Gog of the Land of Magog coalition attack on Israel has to happen before Yeshua comes.

<u>Explanatory on the Fifth through Seventh Trumpets</u>: The eagle in Revelation 8:13 clearly says, "Woe, woe, woe," three times, and that these three woes that he has spoken specifically refer to the remaining blasts of the three trumpets from the three messengers that are to come next. The eagle clearly says that the remaining three trumpets, which are the fifth, sixth, and seventh trumpets, are each a woe. Then in Revelation 9:12 it clearly says again that the events of the fifth trumpet of the fifth messenger is the first woe that is past, with two more woes that are still coming. Immediately after saying that the first woe is finished and two more woes are coming, the sixth trumpet of the sixth messenger sounds.

And then in Revelation 11:14, when it says that the second woe is past and the third woe is coming speedily, immediately after the seventh messenger sounds the seventh trumpet, and the events of the seventh trumpet are the third woe. There is no doubt at all in the wording of Revelation that the fifth trumpet events are the first woe, and the seventh trumpet events are the third woe, happening immediately after the second woe is past, and that the events of the sixth trumpet are the second woe, happening immediately after the first woe is past. Revelation 9:12 and 11:14 are in perfect agreement and harmony with what the Eagle says in 8:13, that the remaining three trumpets, referring to the fifth, sixth, and seventh trumpets, are each of them one of three woes. This is according to what the exact words of Revelation say.

It is important to understand that each of the last three trumpets are the three woes, because it explains their approximate timing in relation to the Great Tribulation. The Seventh Trumpet is clearly the coming of Yeshua to reign on the earth and make his dwelling place with men, as he comes in the clouds at the sound of the shofar or trumpet blast. This Seventh Trumpet, which is also the Third Woe, is at the end of the Great Tribulation, after the 3.5 days of the Two Witnesses' dead bodies have lain in the street. And since the Sixth Trumpet is the Second Woe, it means that the events of the sounding of the Sixth Trumpet take place right at the end of the Great Tribulation also, because the Second Woe events of the Sixth Trumpet are not happening and being completed until right before the sounding of the Seventh Trumpet, until right before Yeshua returns. The Sixth Trumpet events of 1/3 of mankind being killed in a world war do not happen until right at the moment of Yeshua's coming or within days or weeks right before, at the very end of the Great Tribulation.

So the Sixth and Seventh Trumpet prophecy events do not take place until the very end of the Great Tribulation. And this means that the Fifth Trumpet event of the locust creatures and messenger named

Abaddon coming out of the pit of the deep does not happen until shortly before the Sixth Trumpet, meaning that it happens within about at least five months (Revelation 9:10) before Yeshua comes at the end of the Great Tribulation, placing it also very close to the end of the Great Tribulation. According to Revelation the Three Woes of the Fifth and Sixth and Seventh Trumpets do not happen until the end of the Great Tribulation, and therefore are some of the very last prophecies and signs to watch for to take place at around the time of Yeshua's coming in the clouds.

Unfortunately most prophecy teaching has ignored Revelation 8:13 that clearly says the last three trumpets are the three woes, in order to create a myth that all of the trumpets and seals, except for the Seventh Trumpet, happen before the 3.5 years of Great Tribulation have even started yet. But Revelation says just the opposite, that at least the last three trumpets from the Fifth through the Seventh do not happen until the very end of the Great Tribulation, and the other trumpets and seals do not have any specific timing given for them to happen, except that they could happen at any time during the Great Tribulation or before it. Unfortunately everyone forgets that even the entire New Testament was written by Jews with a Hebrew writing mindset, and in Hebrew writing it is customary when talking about a large subject over a span of time to write about the overview of events first, then go back and start over from the beginning of the events, filling in details, such as in Genesis 1 through 3.

Moses wrote about all of the days of creation first, and wrote about the overview of everything in the creation of the man and the woman, then went back to fill in the details about the creation of the man and the woman, starting over from the point where nothing living had been created yet on the dry land, both plants and animals, and then showing the details of the creation of the living things. In the same way John shows the large overview of events of the Great Tribulation with all of the Seals and Trumpets, leading up to the Sixth Trumpet at the end of the Great Tribulation, then goes back in time to the beginning of the Great Tribulation to fill in the details with the events of Jerusalem and the Two Witnesses. And then finally he writes about the finish of the Great Tribulation with the Seventh Trumpet at Yeshua's coming, then goes back in time to the beginning of the Great Tribulation again to fill in more details about the Woman in the Wilderness and the Dragon and the Beast Out of the Sea, then writes about the end of the Great Tribulation again with Yeshua's coming in the clouds at the sounding of the Seventh Trumpet and the events of the Seven Bowls of Wrath after the Great Tribulation is ended. Then he goes back to the beginning and even before the Great Tribulation again to explain about the Woman Whore who is Mystery Babel the Great on the Scarlet Beast Out of the Pit of the Deep, then goes forward again to the end of the Great Tribulation with the destruction of the city Mystery Babel the Great, and once again for a third time John writes about Yeshua's coming at the end of the Great Tribulation, with the Marriage of the Lamb and his riding out onto the earth itself this time to destroy all his enemies who have come to fight against him.

Four times John writes about the events of the Great Tribulation up to Yeshua's coming, and then goes back and starts all over again with new details. But except for the last three trumpets, from the Fifth to the Seventh, that have to happen at the end of the Great Tribulation, there are no requirements or revelations of timing given for the other First through Fourth Trumpets and the First through Seventh Seals, which could happen at any time during the 3.5 years of Great Tribulation, or before.

Section 1. **The Birth of the Natural Israel into a Nation Again with Jerusalem as Its Capital:**

The Prophecy of the Nation Israel Physically Born into Existence Again in One Day:
Isaiah 66:7-11

Prophecy Fulfillment of Verses **Isaiah 66:7-9** – There are many prophecies about the time of the Great Tribulation which refer to the tribes of the southern kingdom of Yehudah (Judah) coming back to the physical land of Israel to be living there during that time, and also when Yeshua comes as the Son of Adam in the clouds. This Isaiah prophecy is the one that specifically describes the nation of Israel coming back into existence again in preparation for Yahuweh/Yehovah's coming to the earth at the Time of the End and the Great Tribulation. And a specific sign is given in the prophecy to know that it is Yahuweh/Yehovah himself who brings back the nation of Israel into physical existence in the land of Israel, when we see it happen. That sign is that there will not even be any long period of time of laboring or pain beforehand of birthing the nation into existence, as is the case with all nations through history that take time to become a nation. Instead at the very moment of the beginning of laboring, the nation of Israel would be born at once, brought forth in one day.

On the evening of Friday May 14, 1948, before sunset, the nation of Israel was declared a nation at a secret meeting in Tel Aviv. Eleven minutes later President Harry Truman representing the United States of America officially recognized the State of Israel, and a few hours later at midnight the new State of Israel officially came into existence with the ending of the British Mandate in Palestine, so that by the morning of Saturday May 15, 1948, less than a day or 24 hours later, the nation of Israel was completely born into existence, after having not existed as a nation for 1,812 years before that day. The day before no nation of Israel existed at all, and then the next day, in less than 24 hours, suddenly the nation of Israel was born into existence, and was fighting its War for Independence after it had already come into existence instead of before. At that moment this prophecy in Isaiah 66 was fulfilled, and all of the world could see that it was Yahuweh/Yehovah himself who brought about the fulfillment of this prophecy, doing it exactly as he said he would do in a single day, bringing the nation of Israel back into existence in their own land according to his timing, and not the timing of man.

Prophecy Fulfillment of Verses **Isaiah 66:10-11** – Jerusalem (Zion) brought forth her children, the Jews of the southern kingdom Yehudah, including the tribes of Yehudah (Judah), Binyamin (Benjamin), and Levi (Levi), into a nation again in their homeland around Jerusalem. And the physical land and city of Jerusalem afterwards became like a mother to her children, the Jewish people, living within her, providing a place of refuge and comfort for them to live in after the Holocaust.

The Prophecies of the Tribes of Israel Physically Returning to the Land of Israel to become a Nation Again:

Isaiah 43:1-13

Isaiah 52:1-10

Jeremiah 16:14-18; 23:7-8

Ezekiel 36:1-38

Ezekiel 37:1-14

Zechariah 10:1-3

Prophecy Fulfillment of Verses **Ezekiel 36:1-38** – Mark Twain witnessed in 1867 how the land of Israel had become a completely barren wasteland and wilderness with nothing growing in it. He wrote, "Of all the lands there are for dismal scenery, I think Palestine must be the prince. The hills are barren, they are dull of color, they are unpicturesque in shape. The valleys are unsightly deserts fringed with feeble vegetation that has an expression about it of being sorrowful and despondent. … It is a hopeless, dreary, heart-broken land. Small shreds and patches of it must be very beautiful in the full flush of spring, however, and all the more beautiful by contrast with the far-reaching desolation that surrounds them on every side. … Palestine sits in sackcloth and ashes. … Nazareth is forlorn; … Jericho the accursed, lies a moldering ruin, … Bethlehem and Bethany, in their poverty and their humiliation, have nothing about them now to remind one that they once knew the high honor of the Saviour's presence; the hallowed spot where the shepherds watched their flocks by night, and where the angels sang Peace on earth, good will to men, is untenanted by any living creature, and unblessed by any feature that is pleasant to the eye. Renowned Jerusalem itself, the stateliest name in history, has lost all its ancient grandeur, and is become a pauper village; … The noted Sea of Galilee, where Roman fleets once rode at anchor and the disciples of the Saviour sailed in their ships, was long ago deserted by the devotees of war and commerce, and its borders are a silent wilderness; Capernaum is a shapeless ruin; Magdala is the home of beggared Arabs; Bethsaida and Chorazin have vanished from the earth, and the 'desert places' round about them where thousands of men once listened to the Saviour's voice and ate the miraculous bread, sleep in the hush of a solitude that is inhabited only be birds of prey and skulking foxes. Palestine is desolate and unlovely. And why should it be otherwise? Can the *curse* of the Deity beautify a land?"[4]

Mark Twain also wrote concerning the area around Jerusalem, "The further we went the hotter the sun got, and the more rocky and bare, repulsive and dreary the landscape became. There could not have been more fragments of stone strewn broadcast over this part of the world, if every ten square feet of the land had been occupied by a separate and distinct stone-cutter's establishment for an age. There was hardly a tree or shrub anywhere. Even the olive and the cactus, those fast friends of worthless soil, had almost deserted the country. No landscape exists that is more tiresome to the eye than that which bounds the approaches to Jerusalem."[5]

By the year 1867 and the subsequent decades afterward the land of Israel had become a completely barren wasteland and wilderness. And this was prophesied to happen in Ezekiel 36:1-6, that the land of Israel would be possessed by the gentile nations around Israel, especially those of the nation of Edom, located in northern

---

[4] Mark Twain, *The Innocents Abroad* (Hartford, Connecticut: The American Publishing Company, 1869), pgs. 606-608
[5] Mark Twain, *The Innocents Abroad* (Hartford, Connecticut: The American Publishing Company, 1869), pgs. 324-325

Jordan, giving the land of Israel to themselves as their own possession. And it was Jordanian Bedouins who lived in much of the area of Israel in the 1800's and even today there are still millions of Jordanians who live in the West Bank, calling themselves Palestinians, even though they are really the descendants of Edom in Jordan. And in the prophecy Yahuweh/Yehovah describes how there would be a time when all of the cities of Israel would be forsaken, and the cities together with the deserted ruins and the mountains, hills, rivers, and valleys would be a mockery to the rest of the nations around, as Mark Twain described them as being more dismal for scenery than any other nation in the world. The land of Israel bore the shame of all the nations.

But then moving on into verses 36:7-15 and 33-38 Yahuweh/Yehovah promises to one day bring back the house of Israel to dwell in the land of Israel, increasing them on the land again. And the cities would be rebuilt and inhabited once again, with the mountains bearing fruit with living trees again, and the land that had laid waste as a ruin be tilled and farmed again, to the point that people would talk about how the barren wasteland of Israel had turned into a garden of Eden and the destroyed cities that lay waste are now inhabited.

The most important key in this prophecy is that when we see the land of Israel that had lain as a desert waste land for many centuries, all the way up to the point when Mark Twain witnessed it, rebuilt and filled with plants bearing fruit and farms growing food and the land full of descendants of Israel once again, after it had been possessed by the nations around them for many centuries, we know that it was Yahuweh/Yehovah himself who rebuilt the destroyed cities and filled them with people and replanted the desolate land that had lain waste. He says it himself in the prophecy, that he himself is the one who did it, when we see it happen as we have seen since that time of Mark Twain the Jews descended from Israel return to the land of Israel, and rebuild the cities, and replant the land with farms, so that it looks like a garden of Eden now today compared with the wilderness wasteland that Mark Twain described in 1867.

Already in 1891 when William Blackstone wrote the Blackstone Memorial petition to President Benjamin Harrison, the land of Israel was beginning to grow life on it again and become fertile once more, as he said at that time, "Does not Palestine as rightfully belong to the Jews? It is said that rains are increasing and there are evidences that the land is recovering its ancient fertility. If they could have autonomy in government the Jews of the world would rally to transport and establish their suffering brethren in their time-honored-habitation. For over seventeen centuries they have patiently waited for such an opportunity. They have not become agriculturists elsewhere because they believed they were mere sojourners in the various nations, and were yet to return to Palestine and till their own land."[6]

Now today there are at least seven million Jews living in Israel today, one of the highest population totals they have ever had in their history as a nation, and the land is filled with vegetation all over as they till their own land and grow their own food once more as they did 1,800 years before their return.

Also, in verses 36:16-24 and 30-32 Yahuweh/Yehovah goes back through the history of why he had to remove the house of Israel from the land in the first place, because of their sin and rebellion against him, causing him to have to pour out his wrath on them. But then he explains that when we see him return the descendants of Israel back to the land to live there again, he is not doing it for their sake, for the sake of the

---

[6] *Blackstone Memorial*, William Blackstone (March 5, 1891) Collection 540, Papers of William Blackstone, Box 6, Folder 9; Wheaton College, Wheaton

Israelis he has brought back. He has brought them back for his own sake and for his own name, so that his own set-apart name is not profaned among the nations anymore. He says that the house of Israel that he brings back to the land of Israel from the nations where he scattered them should blush and be ashamed as they come back, because they do not deserve to be brought back to the land to become a nation again on account of their sin and rebellion against him. But it is for the purpose of the nations of the world seeing Yahuweh/Yehovah bring them back himself and make them into a nation in the land of Israel again, that he does it as a witness about himself for all the world to see him through his fulfillment of his prophecy.

All of these verses in Ezekiel 36 are now in fulfillment in our day, all of them happening exactly word for word according to the words written down in Scripture. And the final part of this prophecy that is happening now, among a remnant of Israel, is verses 36:25-29, which has deeper implications than just for the physical descendants of Israel. As Yahuweh/Yehovah has brought back the physical nation of Israel into existence again, not all of the natural descendants of Israel are going to return back to him to worship him and serve him and become part of his nation Israel that will go on into eternity in the new heavens and new earth, through acceptance of Yeshua as the true Messiah.

But after the land of Israel came into existence again there has been a large remnant that has grown of believers in Yeshua among the descendants of Israel around the world and even in the land of Israel itself. Yahuweh/Yehovah has been sprinkling clean water on them and has been giving his Jewish people a new heart, removing the heart of stone that had been there within the majority of them as a people for nearly 1,800 years of resisting and rejecting their own Messiah Yeshua. And many have returned back to Yahuweh/Yehovah through Yeshua to be made clean and be filled with the Spirit of Yahuweh/Yehovah again, returning to do the precepts and judgements of Yahuweh/Yehovah in his Torah, breaking free from the commands of men in the Talmud, which are in rebellion against Yahuweh/Yehovah. And the gentile believers in Yeshua who have come into Yahuweh/Yehovah's spiritual nation Israel have been experiencing this same cleansing and returning back to Yahuweh/Yehovah in the purity of his ways and his precepts and his judgements in Scripture.

Prophecy Fulfillment of Verses **Ezekiel 37:1-14** – This prophecy continues more detail from the Ezekiel 36 prophecy, that Yahuweh/Yehovah would bring the house of Israel back into the land of Israel in the same way as bringing old dry bones of people back to life from their burial tombs, restoring all of the living parts of the human body back again to life from the dead. And the physical descendants of Israel have been as a nation as though they were dead among the gentile nations of the world, completely out of existence as a nation for 1,812 years. Then when Israel came back into existence as a nation after such a long time, it was as though they were brought back to life from the dead.

And as part of this prophecy, once again Yahuweh/Yehovah promises, as in Ezekiel 36, to be spiritually restoring the physical descendants of Israel back to him, by putting his Spirit into them and bringing them back to life in following him again, which ultimately is through Yeshua as shown later on in another prophecy. Not all of the natural born descendants of Israel will choose to follow Yahuweh/Yehovah and return to him again, as many will continue to follow their false gods in the Talmud that turn people away from following Yahuweh/Yehovah in his written Torah (in the Five Books of Moses), but there are still some who were promised by Yahuweh/Yehovah in Ezekiel 36 and 37 to return to him and be filled with his Spirit to live again with him, which we are now living in the fulfillment of today as many Jews in Israel and in the world have returned back to him through Yeshua.

Prophecy Fulfillment of Verses **Isaiah 43:1-13** – In this prophecy Yahuweh/Yehovah explains how he is the creator of the nation of Jacob, also called Israel, the one who formed the nation into existence. The nation of Israel belongs to him, because he has called the nation by name; he is the Set-Apart One and Savior of Israel, and his nation he has created over the years is precious to him, and he loves Israel his nation of people. Because of this he will bring back the descendants of Israel into the land of the nation again. He says that he will bring the descendants of Israel from the east, from the countries of Asia, and from the west, from the countries of North America and South America, which has happened across the last hundred years.

Many Jews have returned to the land of Israel from the east since 1948 from the Asian nations of Iraq and Iran and Afghanistan and Turkmenistan and Uzbekistan and China and India, where they had been living in Jewish communities for hundreds of years, and in some cases for nearly 2,000 years. And they have also returned to Israel from the west, from countries in North Africa such as Morocco and Algeria, from ancient Jewish communities over a thousand years old and more, as well as from North America and South America, from Jewish communities in the United States that began in the early 1600's, and from Jewish communities in Central and South America that began in the early 1500's.

But the key part of this prophecy is how specific Yahuweh/Yehovah brings back his people from the north and from the south. Yahuweh/Yehovah says to the north, "Give them up," and to the south, "Do not hold them back." After Israel became a nation in 1948 all of the Jews living to the east and to the west of Israel were freely able to return to the land, but not the Jews still living in the north, in Russia and Ukraine, or in the south, in Ethiopia. The Jews in the north were not being given up by the Soviet Union that controlled Russia and Ukraine at that time, and the Jews living in Ethiopia were being held back by the Ethiopian government.

Then suddenly everything changed in the 1980's when Yahuweh/Yehovah commanded the Soviet Union to give the Jews up they were preventing from leaving, and in 1989 General Secretary Mikhail Gorbachev began to relax the emigration restrictions from the Soviet Union, allowing Jews to begin leaving the country. Eventually Yahuweh/Yehovah collapsed the Soviet Union, which dissolved on December 26, 1991 and the laws of emigration were completely changed, allowing a flood of Jews in Russia and Ukraine to begin moving to Israel. From 1989-2006 about 1,000,000 Jews emigrated to Israel from former Soviet Union controlled countries, and the north was forced to "give them up."

Also, Yahuweh/Yehovah commanded Ethiopia to not hold the Jews back any longer, and beginning with Operation Moses from November 21, 1984 to January 5, 1985, Ethiopian Jews began to be airlifted out of Ethiopia to Israel, after having been in exile in Ethiopia for possibly as long as 2,400 years since the days of the destruction of the First Temple at the time of Jeremiah. Continuing with Operation Joshua on March 22, 1985, Operation Solomon on May 24-25, 1991, and Operation Dove's Wings from November 14, 2010 to February 2, 2022, almost every Ethiopian Jew has now moved to Israel, numbering in the tens of thousands. The south in the end was unable to hold them back, and the Jews living even in the south of Israel were able to return to the land of Israel to form into a nation again.

And Yahuweh/Yehovah says that he is the one who does this, when we see the Jews returning to Israel from every direction of the compass, and even those from the north and south that are prevented from returning are released to go back home to their land. But Yahuweh/Yehovah says that as he brings them back, they will be a blind people with eyes, and deaf people with ears. As they are returning they will be completely blind and deaf to Yahuweh/Yehovah, even though they have eyes to see and ears to hear; they will be totally blind and deaf to what Yahuweh/Yehovah is doing for them in creating them into a nation again, to the point as we see today that most of them do not follow him or believe in him or live according to his ways in Scripture.

As Yahuweh/Yehovah is bringing back the Jewish people to become a nation in the land of Israel again, he also says in this prophecy that he will assemble all of the nations, and gather the peoples, as witnesses of what he is doing in creating the nation of Israel again by bringing back the descendants of Israel back to the land to be a nation again. Yahuweh/Yehovah says that the nations he assembles together are his witnesses and the ones he has chosen to be his servant, in order to reveal to the nations of the world that he is Yahuweh/Yehovah and there are none others beside him. He is the only God, there were none that existed before him and there are none after him, and all the nations of the world would bear witness that Yahuweh/Yehovah is the only God in existence.

This prophecy has also been fulfilled, as all of the nations and peoples of the world were assembled into the United Nations General Assembly and have witnessed in the gatherings over and over again, with resolution after resolution, as Yahuweh/Yehovah has formed the nation of Israel into existence again from nothing, bringing the Jews back from every corner of the earth. And the General Assembly of the Nations of the world were even there to witness the beginnings of Israel coming into existence again with the *United Nations Partition Plan for Palestine, Resolution 181* passed on November 29, 1947.

All the nations of the world have assembled together exactly as Yahuweh/Yehovah prophesied as witnesses to the return of Israel into a nation again, and even serving Yahuweh/Yehovah by helping in bringing back the nation of Israel into existence, though certainly without any knowledge they were helping Yahuweh/Yehovah at the time, or else they would have certainly fought hard to ensure that Israel did not become a nation again. But even as the Nations gathered together in the General Assembly have fought against Israel and tried to destroy the nation at every turn since 1947, they have failed over and over again, once again witnessing how Yahuweh/Yehovah is God and they are unable to defeat him or prevent him from doing what he says he will do in prophecy. All of this prophecy in Isaiah 43:1-13 has now been fulfilled word for word, in exact detail to every word, during the last hundred years, even including in the prophecy the future participation of the United Nations General Assembly in the return of Israel to become a nation again.

Prophecy Fulfillment of Verses **Isaiah 52:1-10** – This prophecy of Isaiah is all about the city of Jerusalem being awoken back to life and being clothed again in garments of splendor, in preparation for the day when the uncircumcised and unclean no longer enter into the city. And Jerusalem shakes itself off from the dust, rising up out of the dust of the ground to sit above the ground once more, released from its bondage and captivity under the ground. This prophecy has been in fulfillment since Israel reclaimed all of the old city of Jerusalem as its capital, restoring and rebuilding the city to what it once was, before it had fallen into ruins during the 1700's to 1800's. But additionally, the ancient city of Jerusalem, the old City of David, that had lain buried underground for thousands of years, under the dust of the earth, has risen up literally out of the dust, shaking off the dust to sit above ground again, through the archeological excavations that have been done during the last few decades. The archeologists have removed all of the dust from around the ancient, buried portions of the original city of Jerusalem as it existed at the time of David and Solomon, and have cleaned all of the dust off of it to reveal the city in its ancient splendor once more, exactly as Yahuweh/Yehovah described it would happen.

As part of this prophecy about Jerusalem, there is also Yahuweh/Yehovah talking about how his people, Israel, have been sold off to the nations, as they left Israel to live in other nations like Egypt and Syria. And in their captivity they were under harsh rule from the gentile rulers over them, causing Yahuweh/Yehovah's name to be despised continually all day long. This is why Yahuweh/Yehovah begins to reveal himself and his name to his people in Israel, by restoring and redeeming Jerusalem, so that eyes of all the nations can see what he is doing on the earth. And at the same time that Jerusalem is being restored as a city, it is a sign that the Good News, the Gospel, of Yeshua is being brought and proclaimed throughout the mountains of Israel, bringing salvation to the Jewish people once again. And this has all been fulfilled now, as the Good News of Yeshua is proclaimed throughout Israel now today, and many Jews have come to believe in the Good News of Yeshua.

It is even more so than just the Good News of Yeshua though that comes to Israel, it is the Good News of his return, as he comes to reign and rule over Israel. That is the most important part of this prophecy, that as we see the city of Jerusalem restored and brought back from the dust of the ground, and we see the Good News of Yeshua proclaimed in the nation, these are signs of the watchmen, to lift up their voices, shouting with joy, because they see Yahuweh/Yehovah himself returning to Zion, to dwell in Jerusalem. It is the sign for all those who are believes in Yeshua to see in the distance, that Yahuweh/Yehovah is coming, he is returning once more to come tangibly to the earth, and this time to dwell in and reign from Zion in Jerusalem. The eyes of all the nations and the ends of all the earth are a witness to seeing that Yahuweh/Yehovah is coming, now that he has fulfilled this prophecy as he said he would do, of restoring the city of Jerusalem back from the dust of the earth.

Prophecy Fulfillment of Verses **Jeremiah 16:14-18; 23:7-8** – In this prophecy Yahuweh/Yehovah is explaining very precisely that there would come a day when there would be literally a second exodus or a repeat of the exodus of the children of Israel leaving Egypt. But when it repeats, instead of people saying that Yahuweh/Yehovah brought the children of Israel from the land of Egypt, they will be saying that Yahuweh/Yehovah has brought the children of Israel out of the land of the north and from all of the lands around the world where he had driven them away to. And in this prophecy Yahuweh/Yehovah himself promises that he will bring back the children of Israel into their land in Israel that he had given to their fathers.

The key part of this prophecy is that when there is a repeat of a second exodus of the children of Israel back into the land of Israel, Yahuweh/Yehovah will be supernaturally bringing them back in large numbers primarily from the north of Israel, and then from other lands around the world after he has brought them back from the north. Before the Holocaust and the birth of the nation of Israel in the 1940's, the majority of remaining Jews and Jewish communities lived north of Israel in Europe, from France to western Russia. And the largest concentration of Jews lived in Poland, almost directly north of Israel.

In the prophecy Yahuweh/Yehovah first begins to fish for his people to return to the land of Israel, by sending fishermen to begin fishing out some of the Jews to begin returning to Israel. And these fishermen at the beginning were mostly Christians. The earliest fishing to bring back the Jews into the land of Israel was the Blackstone Memorial written by William Blackstone and presented as a petition to President Benjamin Harrison on March 5, 1891. In the Blackstone Memorial petition he wrote, "What shall be done for the Russian Jews? It is both unwise and useless to undertake to dictate to Russia concerning her internal affairs. The Jews have lived as foreigners in her dominions for centuries and she fully believes that they are a burden upon her resources and prejudicial to the wellfare of her peasant population, and will not allow them to remain. She is determined that they must go. … Why not give Palestine back to them again? According to God's distribution of nations it is their home, an inalienable possession from which they were expelled by force. Under their cultivation it was a remarkably fruitful land sustaining millions of Israelites who industrially tilled its hillsides and valleys. They were agriculturists and producers as well as a nation of great commercial importance – the center of civilization and religion. … We believe this is an appropriate time for all nations and especially the Christian nations of Europe to show kindness to Israel. A million of exiles, by their terrible suffering, are piteously appealing to our sympathy, justice, and humanity. Let us now restore to them the land of which they were so cruelly despoiled by our Roman ancestors."

As the Christians in America and Europe began to fish for the Jews, to bring them back to Israel, there were Jews who began fishing for other Jews as well, starting the Zionist movement. The First Zionist Congress met in Basel, Switzerland on August 29-31, 1897 where they created the "Basel Program" for legally creating a nation of Israel for the Jews once again in the land of Israel. The Basel Program stated as follows:

English Translation: "Zionism aims at establishing for the Jewish people a publicly and legally assured home in Palestine. For the attainment of this purpose, the Congress considers the following means serviceable: 1. The promotion of the settlement of Jewish agriculturists, artisans, and tradesmen in Palestine. 2. The federation of all Jews into local or general groups, according to the laws of the various countries. 3. The strengthening of the Jewish feeling and consciousness. 4. Preparatory steps toward obtaining the consent of the government, where necessary, for the achievement of the Zionist purpose." [7]

The fishing had started a movement of Jews returning as settlers to their land in Israel, which continued throughout the early 1900's, bringing very small numbers of Jews back into Israel to live there again. There were always a very small minority of Jews that had been living in Israel ever since the nation ceased to exist

---

[7] Original German: "Der Zionismus erstrebt für das jüdische Volk die Schaffung einer (öffentlich-)rechtlich gesicherten Heimstätte in Palästina. Zur Erreichung dieses Ziels nimmt der Congress folgende Mittel in Aussicht: I. Die zweckdienliche Förderung der Besiedlung Palästinas mit jüdischen Ackerbauern, Handwerkern und Gewerbetreibenden. II. Die Gliederung und Zusammenfassung der gesammten Judenschaft durch geeignete örtliche und allgemeine Veranstaltungen nach den Landesgesetzen. III. Die Stärkung des jüdischen Volksgefühls und Volksbewusstseins. IV. Vorbereitende Schritte zur Erlangung der Regierungszustimmung, die nötig sind, um das Ziel des Zionismus zu erreichen."

at the time of the Bar Kokhva Revolt. But for over a thousand years before 1891 there had not been any serious movements among the Jews around the world to even try or attempt to return back to Israel to become a nation again. They were all content in the nations where they were living for the most part, except during times of persecution when they had to flee to other nations, but for the most part there was no desire among the Jewish population around the world to actually try to return to Israel. This fishing by the fishermen started a small movement to return in very small numbers.

After the United Kingdom of the British Empire had taken control of the land of Israel in 1917 during fighting against the Ottoman Empire in World War I, England began to control the land instead of the Ottoman Turks. At that time there was the Balfour Declaration of November 2, 1917, which was a letter addressed to Lord Rothschild from the Foreign Secretary Arthur James Balfour, stating, "His Majesty's Government view with favour the establishment in Palestine of a national home for the Jewish people, and will use their best endeavours to facilitate the achievement of this object, it being clearly understood that nothing shall be done which may prejudice the civil and religious rights of existing non-Jewish communities in Palestine, or the rights and political status enjoyed by Jews in any other country."

This declaration continued the fishing to bring more Jews back to Israel, as the British government, after the Balfour Declaration, allowed larger numbers of Jews to immigrate into Israel each year during the 1920's and 1930's. But for all of the fishing that Yahuweh/Yehovah did, there were very few Jews who responded to him, and most decided to stay where they lived in the gentile nations. The Rabbis at that time even taught and convinced the Jews in Europe to stay where they were, because they said that it was not time to go live in Israel yet or for the nation of Israel to exist again yet.

But this was part of the fulfillment of the prophecy in Jeremiah 16:14-15 and 23:7-8, because Yahuweh/Yehovah said that it would be like a repeat of the first exodus from Egypt, except it would be from the nations of the north instead of from Egypt. And exactly the same way that the generation of the children of Israel who left Egypt rebelled against Yahuweh/Yehovah and refused to enter the land of Israel and take it for their own land and nation, the generation of Jews before the Holocaust were also rebellious and stubborn against Yahuweh/Yehovah, refusing to go into the land of Israel and take it back again for their land. And this is why then after Yahuweh/Yehovah had sent the fishermen to fish for his people, he then sent for hunters, the Nazis, to hunt them out of every hole and hiding place, from every mountain and hill, in Europe, in the land of the north. And then the Jews of Europe entered into the time of the Holocaust beginning in spring 1942.

In the same way that the children of Israel refused to enter the land of Israel and take the land in war and battle, because they feared the inhabitants, the children of Israel before the Holocaust refused to go back to the land of Israel and take it back through war, because they did not trust in Yahuweh/Yehovah to be with them in battle. And when the children of Israel who had left Egypt refused to go in and take the land that Yahuweh/Yehovah had promised them, Yahuweh/Yehovah let that entire older generation die, refusing to let them even go into the land at all. In the wilderness Yahuweh/Yehovah took his time in letting them die over a 40 year period of time, cutting off all of the adults that had left Egypt, so that only the children were left alive, with their children.

In the same way that Yahuweh/Yehovah let all of the older generations of the children of Israel who refused to go into the land to take it as their nation die for their disobedience, he also let all of the older generations of Jews in the land of the north in Europe die in the Holocaust for their disobedience and refusal to go take the land of Israel and make a nation there again. Yahuweh/Yehovah allowed the Nazis to kill the older generations of Jews in Europe instead of old age as with the first exodus out of Egypt, but he did not allow all of the children of Israel to die in the Holocaust. There are thousands of supernatural testimonies about how he saved and protected one or two children from every single Jewish family group and family line in Europe, saving the younger generation as he had done the first time that he brought the children of Israel out of Egypt. And it was the young generations of teenagers and young adults in their twenties and thirties from the land of the north from Europe who had survived the Holocaust who flooded into Israel and took back the land through very costly but supernatural wars in 1948-1949 and 1967.

This happened because of verses 16:17-18 in the prophecy, that Yahuweh/Yehovah saw all of the crookedness and sin of the Jewish people in rebellion against him, in the same way that the generation that had left Egypt was in sin and rebellion against him. He says that he sees it all and none of it is hidden from him, and because of their sin, and their defilement that they had done to his land in Israel in the past, he brought double repayment for their crookedness, cleansing and refining his Jewish people in the fires of the Holocaust first, before their mass exodus return out of the land of the north in Europe like a flood into Israel, by the millions ultimately. And now this prophecy has been fulfilled in every detail of every exact word.

Prophecy Fulfillment of Verses **Zechariah 10:1-3** – This prophecy begins with telling people to ask Yahuweh/Yehovah for rain in the time of the latter rain, because he is the one who makes storm clouds. In Israel there are two times and forms of rain in the seasonal cycle. The land of Israel does not experience four seasons, because of their climate. They only experience two seasons known as the rainy season in winter and the dry season in summer. And because of this, even though they are in the northern hemisphere, their agricultural climate is opposite, like that in the southern hemisphere, with the planting and growing season from about October to February, in the middle of winter, and the harvesting season in about March to June in the spring and early summer. This is the way it has always been since the ancient times in Scripture when Moses first wrote about how to keep the times of planting and harvest connected with Yahuweh/Yehovah's appointed times or festivals in Leviticus 23, as well as the instructions on keeping the Sabbath or Shemitah years.

And since ancient times, all throughout Scripture, the Israelis have described the rainy season in Israel with two terms, the former rain and the latter rain. There is no rain at all in Israel during the dry season, but when the rainy season comes, it begins with the former rain, with smaller amounts of rain, beginning in about October usually. Then in about January the heavy, bigger rainfalls come, which are called the latter rain. Deuteronomy 11:14 and Jeremiah 5:24 and many other places in Scripture describe this cycle of rain. This prophecy in Zechariah 10:1 begins with a prophecy about the latter rain of Yahuweh/Yehovah, that in the physical realm begins in about the beginning of January. Hosea 6:3 reveals that the former and latter rain in Israel also have another spiritual meaning, that they prophetically also refer to Yahuweh/Yehovah himself coming to his people, pouring himself out upon his people, like the former rain and the latter rain.

This prophecy in Zechariah 10:1 begins with a dual prophecy, about the literal latter rain in Israel, but also spiritually, asking Yahuweh/Yehovah to bring the latter rain outpouring of himself onto the earth. And in the case of this prophecy, to be poured out as showers of rain for the plants of the field for everyone. On December 28, 2017, at the literal time of when the physical latter rain begins to rain in Israel, the Agricultural Minister of Israel gathered thousands of Orthodox Jews together to pray for rain at the Western Wall in Jerusalem, and specifically to pray for rain for "everyone," as it says in this Zechariah 10 prophecy. They came together at the literal time of the latter rain to ask Yahuweh/Yehovah to bring literal rain on Israel, and on everyone, because they were in a drought at that time, needing rain. There was no expectancy of any significant amounts of rain in the weather forecast at that time, for the season, but only seven days later on January 2, 2018 the storm clouds gathered and a flood of rain showers came in answer to the prayers the week before, as a sign of the beginning of the fulfillment of this prophecy in Zechariah 10. This was a big event showing that the "time of Yahuweh/Yehovah's latter rain" outpouring had come and begun in fulfillment of the prophecies about the latter rain in Scripture.

But the physical rain coming in fulfillment of this prophecy was only the sign that Yahuweh/Yehovah had begun to pour himself out, his Spirit, on everyone, not just the Jewish people, but on everyone on the earth. And the sign given in the next verses of the prophecy, in 2-3, that he is pouring himself out like rain, with the latter rain, which is an even bigger portion of himself than in the former rain that started on the Festival of Weeks (Pentecost) in Acts 2:1-41, was that he would begin dealing with all of the idols and deceptions in his people, especially dealing with the shepherds (religious leaders) who have led the people astray into the falsehoods. Yahuweh/Yehovah begins to visit his flock of people, and the outward sign of this is his cleaning house, with his wrath against the shepherds to deal with them, because the people, like sheep, have been left without a true shepherd to keep them from wandering astray.

After this event in December 2017 to January 2018, Yahuweh/Yehovah began dealing with the Rabbis, the shepherds, leading astray his flock of Israel, beginning to expose many of them in various kinds of scandals of sin they were involved in, and exposing the witchcraft of divination and deceitful dreams in Orthodox Judaism. On April 30, 2021 there were at least 45 killed in the Lag B'Omer festival stampede at the tomb of a 2nd century Rabbi Shimon bar Yochai. This festival is actually based in witchcraft, with pagan gentile origins, all about worshipping the dead as gods, and coloring Easter eggs like a pagan Easter celebration. Yahuweh/Yehovah began dealing with the Orthodox Jews about their Pagan holidays that are in rebellion and sin against him. Additionally there was COVID that went heavily through the Ultra-Orthodox Jewish communities in Israel, preventing them from doing their normal religious meetings, separating the flock of people in Judah from their Rabbi shepherds, with many Rabbis even killed by COVID as they tried to go on with their normal religious meetings. This is Yahuweh/Yehovah's love and kindness, to deal with the sins and falsehoods in the midst of his people, to turn back as many in repentance as possible, and it all is happening exactly as he prophesied in this Zechariah prophecy, as Yahuweh/Yehovah began to deal with the shepherds and the straying flock in Israel. And this is what the Orthodox Jews and Rabbis (shepherds) at the Western Wall gathering prayed for Yahuweh/Yehovah to do for them when they asked him for the Rain at the time of the Latter Rain, to deal with their sin and falsehood.

In these first few verses Yahuweh/Yehovah is only visiting the house of Judah, which is the southern kingdom of tribes of the Jews who live in Israel today. But as Yahuweh/Yehovah deals with the house of Judah that are living in Israel today and pours out his Spirit on everyone, both Jews and Gentiles, like the Latter Rain in fulfillment of this first part of the prophecy, it means that the rest of the prophecy fulfillment is on its way, with the return of all of the other ten northern tribes of Israel that are still scattered around the world, which are poetically referred to as Ephrayim (Ephraim) and Yoseph (Joseph) in this prophecy.

But now the question is, if all of the prophecies about the return of the two southern kingdom tribes of Yehudah (Judah) have already happened and been fulfilled in continuing fulfillment today, which also include the tribes of Binyamin (Benjamin) and part of Levi, then what about the prophecies about the ten northern tribes of Yisra'el (Israel) returning to the land of Israel, which include Ephrayim (Ephraim) and Menashsheh (Manassas), both together representing the tribe of Yoseph (Joseph), and Zevulun (Zebulun), Naphtali, Shim'on (Simeon), Re'uven (Reuben), Yissakar (Isachar), Dan, Gad, and Asher (with part of Levi)?

At the Time When Yahuweh/Yehovah Gathers the Nations Together to War Against Jerusalem, at the Time of His Coming to the Earth to Rule from Jerusalem, Only the Southern Tribes of the Nation State of Yehudah have Returned to the Land of Israel and have Control of Jerusalem:

Joel 3:1-6

Word for Word Prophecy Examination of Unfulfilled Verses **Joel 3:1-9** – At the time when Yahuweh/Yehovah comes to the earth to rule from Jerusalem, when he gathers together all the nations to come for battle against Israel and Jerusalem at the end of the Great Tribulation, he has only turned back the captivity of Judah and the city of Jerusalem. Only the tribes of the southern kingdom of Judah have returned to the land of Israel at that time, and they have control of the city of Jerusalem. But there is no mention of any of the other ten tribes of the northern kingdom of Israel who have returned yet at the time of Yahuweh/Yehovah's coming at the end of the Great Tribulation.

In order for the prophecies of the Great Tribulation to be fulfilled, only the southern kingdom tribes of Judah are required to be present and living as a nation in the land of Israel with Jerusalem as their capital. There is no requirement anywhere in the prophecies in Scripture for the other tribes to have returned yet, when Yahuweh/Yehovah gathers together all of the nations of the world to war and battle against the nation of Israel and Jerusalem, in order to bring the final judgement upon the nations.

The Other Ten Northern Tribes of Israel Called Symbolically Ephrayim or Yoseph or Yaʻaqov (Jacob) do Not Return to the Land of Israel to become Part of the Nation of Israel Until Yeshua Returns and Brings Them Back Through Him, as Believers in Him:

Isaiah 49:1-26

Word for Word Prophecy Examination of Partially Unfulfilled Verses **Isaiah 49:1-26** – This prophecy was already fulfilled by Yeshua coming as the Messiah in the first few verses 1-5. It is Yeshua who is the child in the womb of his mother, whose name Yahuweh/Yehovah has caused to be remembered for thousands of years. He kept Yeshua hidden during the early years of his life, but prepared him like a sword or spear as the Messiah, the servant of Yahuweh/Yehovah. Yeshua was formed from the womb to come as the suffering servant Messiah, the child born to rule Israel as a descendant of David in other prophecies of Isaiah. There is no doubt that Yeshua as the Messiah from the line of David is the servant and child spoken of here in the first five verses.

But when he came at first, Israel was not yet gathered to him, though that is part of his plan and purpose. When he returns he will be fulfilling the rest of this prophecy, beginning in verse 6 and on through the end of the prophecy. The Messiah Yeshua, who is the servant, when he returns will be raising up all of the tribes of Israel and personally bringing them back to the land of Israel, as a light to the nations and Yahuweh/Yehovah's deliverance to all the earth. In verse 8 it is Yeshua who has been given by Yahuweh/Yehovah as a covenant of the people, to go out to all those who are living in darkness, including all of the tribes of Israel, and bring them back from the nations.

This is when all of the other ten northern tribes of Israel return to the land of Israel, from the north and from the west, from the Sinim (which is the ancient Hebrew name for the country of China) when they come as believers in Yeshua, gathered by him at his coming. All of the prophecies in Scripture about the ten northern tribes returning to live in the land of Israel cannot be completely fulfilled until after Yeshua comes and is reigning as the descendant of David over the land of Israel. Only those of the tribes of Israel who believe in Yeshua as the Messiah, gathered by him personally, and who recognize Yeshua to be their king ruling over them, will return to the land of Israel to live under his reign and rule.

The southern kingdom tribes of Judah in the prophecies return before Yeshua comes as the Messiah to rule over them, but the northern kingdom tribes of Israel, poetically called Ephrayim or Joseph or Jacob, do not return except through Yeshua, as believers in Yeshua who have made him their king, as in Jeremiah 30:9 where the descendant of David is their king when they have returned to the land of Israel. And also in Ezekiel 37:24 when all of the tribes of Israel are joined together as one stick and one nation in the hand of Yahuweh/Yehovah, with the descendant of Yahuweh/Yehovah's servant David as their king.

There is no requirement in the prophecies for the ten northern kingdom tribes to return to Israel before Yeshua comes in the clouds at the end of the Great Tribulation, only for the two southern kingdom tribes to be living in the land with Jerusalem as their capital. Therefore verses 49:6-26 are not completely fulfilled until after Yeshua returns, with no requirement that they have to be fulfilled beforehand. But verses 49:22-23 have started to be fulfilled in many ways, as the southern tribes of Judah have returned to the land of Israel to become a nation again with the help of gentiles and nations around them. During the last 130 years many gentiles have helped Jews be able to get to Israel in many various ways, either helping them through the Holocaust, or helping them financially, or helping them physically to take them into Israel. Even rulers of nations helped through the years to open up ways for Jews to be able to get back to Israel to live there, such as with the Balfour Declaration, and during the years after the Holocaust, with the President of America recognizing Israel as a nation.

At the Same Time Yahuweh/Yehovah Restores the Tribes of Israel Back to Their Land in Israel, He Also Brings Gentiles and Israelites Together into His Spiritual Nation Israel:
Isaiah 56:1-8

Prophecy Fulfillment of Verses **Isaiah 56:1-8** – At the same time that Yahuweh/Yehovah brings together all of the tribes of Israel into one nation through Yeshua, at his coming, he is also bringing in all of the gentile believers in Yeshua as one nation together with Israel. This prophecy in Isaiah 56 has been in process of fulfillment for nearly 2,000 years, ever since Yeshua came and started to build his House of Prayer for all nations upon the foundation of Kepha (Peter), in Matthew 16:18 who was the first to begin to take the Good News of Yeshua to the gentiles. In the original Hebrew Gospel of Matthew Yeshua said to Kepha, "And I say to you that you are a stone, and I shall build upon you My House of Prayer, and the gates of Gehinnom[8] shall not be able to endure against you,"[9] in reference to this prophecy in Isaiah 56 about the House of Prayer of Yahuweh/Yehovah that is for all of the nations of the world to be able to come into his nation Israel and make Yahuweh/Yehovah their God whom they serve. It has taken 2,000 years, but now there are peoples from all the nations of the earth who have entered into and hold onto Yahuweh/Yehovah's covenant, not separated from Yahuweh/Yehovah's people, but instead joined together in them, with a place and a name given to them in Yahuweh/Yehovah's House that is better than that of sons and daughters.

And when we see the outcasts of Israel being gathered together back to Yahuweh/Yehovah as in 56:8, we know that the gathering of gentiles from the nations into Yahuweh/Yehovah's covenant and people is also at its time of completion, as this prophecy nears its complete fulfillment and finish of the harvest of believers in Yeshua from the nations, built together as one house and one nation.

Conclusion – All of the prophecies that needed to be fulfilled in regard to the southern kingdom tribes of Judah to be a nation in the land of Israel again with Jerusalem as its capital are completed and fulfilled today, so that there are no other prophecies specifically concerning the nation of Israel that are still in need of being fulfilled before the 3.5 years of Great Tribulation can begin.

---

[8] Valley of Hinnom (Gehenna)
[9] "ואני אומר לך שאתה אבן ואני אבנה עליך בית תפלתי ושערי גהינם לא יוכלו נגדך" *Even Bochan*, Shem Tov (1696 C.E. copy) Add. Ms. 26964; British Library, London. [Hebrew word pun between "stone" (even אבן) and "build" (evneh אבנה) in this verse.]

Section 2. **Psalms 83 Armies Attack Israel (War for Independence 1948-1949 and Six Day War 1967):**

The Prophecy of the Nations of Edom, Moʻav, ʼAmmon (Jordan); ʼAmaleq (Egypt and Jordan); Yishmeʻelim, Hagrim (Saudi Arabia); Geval, Tsor (Lebanon); Ashshur (Syria and Iraq); and Pelesheth (Philistia in the Gaza Strip) Attack Israel Together at the Same Time, Fulfilled in 1948 and 1967:

Psalms 83:1-18

Prophecy Fulfillment of Verses **Psalms 83:1-18** – According to this prophecy most likely written by Asaph, there is a coalition and alliance of nations and cities and tribal groups that come together to attack and attempt to completely destroy Israel. The nations and cities are listed in the prophecy as:

1. Edom אֱדוֹם, Moʻav מוֹאָב and ʼAmmon עַמּוֹן = Modern Day Jordan
2. ʼAmaleq עֲמָלֵק = Modern Day Egypt and Jordan (land in south Israel mostly under Egypt control in 1948)
3. Yishmeʻelim יִשְׁמְעֵאלִים and Hagrim הַגְרִים = Modern Day Saudi Arabia
4. Geval גְּבָל and Tsor צוֹר = Modern Day Lebanon
5. Ashshur אַשּׁוּר = Modern Day Syria and Iraq
6. Pelesheth פְּלָשֶׁת = Modern Day Gaza Strip (which was under the control of Egypt in 1948 through 1967)

On May 15, 1948 Israel was attacked by the nations of Jordan, Saudi Arabia, Lebanon, Syria, Iraq, and Egypt (through the area of the Gaza Strip), from all of the lands and territories listed in this prophecy. And the reason they had for attacking Israel was in order to "wipe them out as a nation" exactly as the prophecy says, in order that the name of Yisraʼel (Israel) would no longer be remembered. These nations conspired together, and came together into a covenant alliance against Yahuweh/Yehovah. They wanted to take possession of the land belonging to God in Israel for themselves, exactly as was prophesied they would try to do.

But even though they all came against Israel together at the same time, they lost the Israel War for Independence in 1948-1949 after about 11 months of fighting, until about March 10, 1949. And their combined armies were turned away in shame as Yahuweh/Yehovah consumed them and pursued them, turning them away. Later in the Six Day War on June 5-10, 1967 this prophecy was fulfilled into its completion, when these same nations began gathering together again to attack Israel, and Israel preempted their invasion with their own offensive that wiped out their forces and drove them completely out of the land of Israel, retaking Jerusalem.

Yahuweh/Yehovah intervened supernaturally and drove away all of this coalition of nations from Israel's borders, consuming them like a fire, pursuing them with a whirlwind, frightening them away with his storm, so that the gentile nations would know Yahuweh/Yehovah, and that they would seek him and know that he is the only one who is the Master, the Most High, over all the earth. There are many recorded eye witness accounts from Arabs and members of the armies in the fighting listed in Psalms 83 that spoke of seeing supernatural beings like messengers or the hand of Yahuweh/Yehovah standing in the sky or close behind the

Israeli army, driving them away in fear for their lives, and other similar supernatural events of Yahuweh/Yehovah fighting for Israel. After these two wars this prophecy was finished and completed, allowing Israel to come into existence again with Jerusalem as its capital, in preparation for the prophecies of the Time of the End and the Great Tribulation to eventually be fulfilled.

Section 3. Zechariah 12 Armies Attack Israel and Israel Retakes and Lifts the Siege of Jerusalem (Six Day War 1967):

The Prophecy of Jerusalem Under Siege as Yahuweh/Yehovah Makes the City of Jerusalem a Cup of Reeling and a Heavy Stone to all the Nations and Yahuweh/Yehovah Supernaturally Saves Jerusalem and the Jewish People of Yehudah (Judah), as They Consume All of the Nations Around Them and Retake the City of Jerusalem as Their Own Again in 1967:

Zechariah 12:1-8

Prophecy Fulfillment of Verses **Zechariah 12:1-8** – During the 1948-1949 Israel War for Independence, Israel lost control of the old city of Jerusalem, and only barely held onto the western part of the city, by securing a small corridor to the city famously known as the "Burma Road." The Israeli army built the Burma Road in the midst of the fighting of the war, through impassable desert, only barely making the road operational enough in time before the first UN ceasefire of the war on June 11, 1948, in order to ensure the corridor to Jerusalem would remain under Israeli control under the UN designated ceasefire lines. Israel was never able during the war in 1948-1949 to take control of the rest of Jerusalem, or to take any of the rest of the land around Jerusalem except for this corridor linking Jerusalem with the rest of the nation of Israel.

Because of this situation, the city of Jerusalem was almost completely surrounded by Jordan controlled territory in the West Bank, and was essentially under siege, under the constant threat of being attacked from all sides at any time, up until 1967. This is exactly as was prophesied in Zechariah 12 in verse 2, that the city of Jerusalem would be under siege, as part of Yahuweh/Yehovah making the city of Jerusalem into a cup of trembling/drunkenness/reeling to the peoples all around the city and he makes the city of Jerusalem a very heavy stone, for all the peoples of the earth, so that anyone who tries to lift it is injured severely.

Then during the Six Day War on June 5-10, 1967 Israel was able to lift the siege of Jerusalem and recapture the city for the first time in nearly 1,900 years, so that the city of Jerusalem once again was able to dwell in her own place in fulfillment of verse 12:6. Also, in fulfillment of verses 12:6-7, Yahuweh/Yehovah made the leaders of Judah, of the Jewish nation in Israel, like a fire pot and torch of fire, as the nation of Israel consumed all of the nations around them in just 6 days, in lightning fire speed, on both the right and the left, retaking all of the territory around Jerusalem up to the Jordan River, as well as the Golan Heights in Syria, as well as the entire Sinai Peninsula (literally on the right of the nation and the left of the nation). And before this in the 1948-1949 War of Independence Yahuweh/Yehovah had saved the tents of Judah first, before then later saving the city of Jerusalem in 1967, in order that the esteem/glory/comeliness of the house of David and inhabitants in Jerusalem would not be greater than that of the Jewish nation, Judah. Even to this day the city of Jerusalem, even though it is the capital, is not greater in appearance or wealth than the other cities of Israel. It is even lowlier in appearance than many of the other cities in the nation.

And in fulfillment of verses 12:4-5 and 8, Yahuweh/Yehovah during the Six Day War made the inhabitants of Jerusalem a great strength to the nation of Israel and their leaders, shielding the inhabitants, and making even the feeble and weak in that day like David, and the house of David like the messenger of

Yahuweh/Yehovah going before them, driving out the Jordanian nation and peoples from the land and completely retaking the city. Everyone in Jerusalem and the nation were made strong in Yahuweh/Yehovah at that time to be able to supernaturally drive out all of the nations from the land around them. And Israel moved so quickly in their attack that everything was in chaos for their enemies, bewilderment and panic and madness, for both horses and riders.

It was because of the fulfillment of the verses in 12:4-8 that then brought about the fulfillment of verses 12:2-3. Before the Six Day War in 1967 Israel did not have control of the Old City of Jerusalem, or of the ground of the original city of Jerusalem, now known in excavations as the City of David. After the Six Day War suddenly Israel was in complete control of the entire city of Jerusalem, and this event is what Yahuweh/Yehovah brought about in order to make his city into a cup of drunkenness or reeling for the nations around Israel, as well as a heavy stone that all of the nations of the world would get injured in trying to move, causing all of the nations of the world to turn against the city of Jerusalem, because the Jews of Judah were in control of it again. From 1967 onwards the city of Jerusalem has been the catalyst that has caused all of the nations of the world to gather together again and again in the United Nations General Assembly against the nation of Israel and against the city of Jerusalem that is under their control and the location of their government. By the time of the Yom Kippur War in 1973 every nation in the world had turned against Israel, except America, which was the only country who helped them at that time, and even today countries who claim to be friends of Israel still continually vote against them in the UN dozens and hundreds of times every year.

The fulfillment of this prophecy in Zechariah 12:1-8 in the Six Day War in 1967 is what has now set up the conditions of all of the nations turning and gathering against Jerusalem and the nation of Israel, as they have tried over and over again to divide the city and lift it like a heavy stone, to solve the problem of the Israel-Palestinian conflict over the city. And after decades of trying to solve this problem, no nation has come up with a solution, and any nation that tries, especially America, only gets severely injured over and over again, in many different ways such as militarily or politically. The city of Jerusalem has become the major problem of the world that no one has ever been able to solve, and this prophecy fulfillment in Zechariah 12 has now set up the conditions for the future fulfillment of the prophecy in Zechariah 14 and Joel 3, which will happen when Yahuweh/Yehovah comes to rule over the earth from Jerusalem at the end of the Great Tribulation.

Conclusion: All of the conditions and prophecies that need to be fulfilled in regard to the city of Jerusalem coming back under the control of the tribes of the southern kingdom of Judah have happened and are in place, so that there are no other requirements in terms of these prophecies that need to happen before the Great Tribulation can begin. In terms of the prophecies particularly about Jerusalem, everything is in place for the 3.5 years of Great Tribulation to be able to happen whenever Yahuweh/Yehovah is ready to begin it.

Section 4. **Joel 1 – 2 Army of Locusts Invades and Attacks Israel (Yom Kippur War 1973):**

The Prophecy of the Darkest Time in Israel's History When They are Almost Wiped Out of Existence by an Army Stronger than Any Army that Israel has Ever Faced in its History Up to that Point Since Ancient Times, and will Not Face Again for Several Generations Afterwards, but Yahuweh/Yehovah Supernaturally Saves the Nation and Afterwards Pours Out His Spirit on Israel in Revival [Fulfilled by the Syrian Army in the Yom Kippur War of 1973, which was One of the Most Advanced Armies that had Ever Fought A War in the History of the World Up to that Time Due to Their being Equipped by the "Northerner" Russia, Combined with the Egyptian Army, and had the Opportunity to Completely Annihilate and Conquer the Nation of Israel in Less Than 48 Hours in the Initial Invasion]:

Joel 1:1 – 2:27

Prophecy Fulfillment of Verses **Joel 1:1 – 2:27** – This prophecy about an invading army attacking Israel has six basic parts to it that have to be fulfilled together at the same time or same event, which are examined below. The description that Joel uses of the men in the army being like locusts is a common Hebrew expression from that time period when Joel was written. Jeremiah also poetically describes armies of men and horses as being like locusts in Jeremiah 51:14 and 27, but they are not literal locusts. This army in Joel is clearly an army of regular men, but they are given poetical descriptions that they devour and consume like locusts, and have shredding teeth like lions, as well as appearing to be like horses, in their swiftness and speed as they run and overrun enemy defensive positions in battle. Also, Lance Lambert was an eye witness who was in Israel at the time of the Yom Kippur War, who spoke to many Israelis, including soldiers on the front lines, and some of these accounts from his book *Israel: A Secret Documentary* are used in the following examinations of the Joel 1 – 2 prophecy. The following organizes the different elements of the prophecy that have to be fulfilled together.

1. Joel 1:1-6; 2:2-3, 4-10 – *Yahuweh/Yehovah sends an innumerably large army to attack and invade Israel that is consuming like locusts, with strength like the teeth of lions, looking like swift horses, that is so strong that there has never been an army like it that has attacked Israel in all of its history in the past and there will not be one to attack Israel again in the future for at least several generations; This army is unstoppable, as they smash through any obstacles or buildings or defending forces that are in their way, not breaking ranks even as they fall dead marching forward*: The first part of this prophecy is that there is a large and very strong army that Yahuweh/Yehovah sends to invade his land and nation Israel. They are Yahuweh/Yehovah's great army that invades into his land according to the verses in the prophecy. This army has to be unlike anything that Israel has ever fought in its 3,500 years of history, according to verse 2:2, and that Israel would not encounter such an army again for at least three generations according to verses 1:2-3 and 2:2. The Syrian army, together with the Egyptian army, had just been equipped by Russia prior to the Yom Kippur War, so that they had the most advanced weapons available to them at that time, even some of the newest weapons that had never been tested in war before. They had the most advanced anti-tank and anti-air

weapons the Soviet Union had produced, and the Syrian army were equipped with the latest technology, including night vision, something that not even one western-made Israeli tank had at that time.

The Syrian army was the most technologically advanced army that had ever invaded Israel up to that point in its entire 3,500 years as a nation, and one of the most advanced armies in the world at that time, because of Russia's armament of their military in the months before the Yom Kippur War started. And the Egyptian also was not far behind the Syrian army in its advanced weaponry capabilities supplied by Russia. On October 6, 1973, on the Day of Atonement or Yom Kippur, the Syrian and Egyptian armies began their initial surprise attack and invasion of Israel. The Syrian army poured into Israel with 1,200 tanks along a tiny 20 mile front line in the Golan Heights, an army of tanks larger than the combined British and French armies at that time.[10] Israel only had about 70 to 180 tanks along the Golan Heights frontline, defending against 1,200 tanks that came in waves, quickly overwhelming and overpowering the Israelis.

Israel's losses were enormous in the initial attack of Syrian armor and men, with every single Israeli soldier dead in most of those units defending the Golan Heights lines within the first few hours of the invasion. Entire Israeli units and companies of men were completely wiped out with none left alive, and because of the Israeli policy to let all of the men from the same villages and communities serve together, whole communities and villages in Israel lost every single drafted man of fighting age who lived there. The Syrian and Egyptian anti-air weapons from Russia were so advanced that Israel had three out of five of their jets in the air shot down during the first few days of the war,[11] losing hundreds.

Israel's defenses at the Hermon Fortress in the Golan and the Bar-Lev line in the Sinai Peninsula had been thought at the time to be invincible defenses, but the Syrian and Egyptian armies overran and completely destroyed these defensive fortifications and lines within just a few hours.[12] In only five hours the Egyptian tank brigades had smashed through and overrun the Bar-Lev line, leaving no Israeli resistance between them and the heart of southern Israel. Likewise, in a matter of a few hours by sunset of the initial attack the Syrian army had annihilated the Israeli defense line and Hermon Fortress fortifications in the Golan. At that time all that stood between the Syrian forces and the heart of northern Israel were 2 tanks and 10 Israeli infantry.[13] By that night the Syrian army could have taken Tiberias, and been in position to start pushing towards Tel Aviv with no serious resistance stopping them. The Egyptian forces could have been inside southern Israel by morning.

In exact fulfillment of this prophecy in verses 1:3 and 2:2, the Syrian army, together with the Egyptian army, were the greatest army that Israel had ever fought up to that time in their 3,500 year history, and Israel has not fought such a great army since, now 50 years later after at least two or three more generations have been born. The generation that was alive at that time in 1973 is now able to tell their children, their grandchildren, and their great-grandchildren about the Yom Kippur War as is described in the prophecy, and how there has never again been another invasion and attack on Israel like that one. Even in the past generations in the last 3,500 years when Israel has been destroyed by conquering armies like the Babylonians

---

[10] Lance Lambert, *Israel: A Secret Documentary* (Wheaton, Illinois: Tyndale House Publishers, Inc., 1975), pg. 13
[11] Lance Lambert, *Israel: A Secret Documentary* (Wheaton, Illinois: Tyndale House Publishers, Inc., 1975), pg. 14
[12] Lance Lambert, *Israel: A Secret Documentary* (Wheaton, Illinois: Tyndale House Publishers, Inc., 1975), pg. 14
[13] Lance Lambert, *Israel: A Secret Documentary* (Wheaton, Illinois: Tyndale House Publishers, Inc., 1975), pg. 15

or Romans, it took many years for them to be defeated, but the Syrian army, together with the Egyptian army, were in the position on the first day of the attack to defeat and destroy the nation of Israel in a matter of only days instead of years, with weapons and equipment far more advanced and powerful than any army had attacked Israel with up to that point in 3,500 years of history.

And the Syrian army, together with the Egyptian army, moved ever forward with nothing able to stop them or stand in their way, smashing through and overrunning any defensive structures or buildings or fortifications, exactly as is described in verses 2:7-9, rushing and running very swiftly like horses with incredible speed fulfilling verses 2:4-5 and 7 and 9. And from them there was no escape, especially on the Syrian attack side of the battle, as the Syrian army wiped out and killed every last Israeli soldier in the front lines they encountered, leaving none alive, none that escaped them, in verse 2:3. The invading army of Syria and Egypt also had teeth like lions, ripping through the Israeli defense lines, with enormous sized armies that were greater and more advanced than in the previous wars of Israel's modern history, as in verse 1:6. And the earth would have been literally trembling and shaking from the massive number of tanks coming from the Syrian side into Israel on such a small front line of only 20 miles width, in fulfillment of verse 2:10.

This was also the first time in Israel's modern history that they were afraid they might lose the war and be destroyed as a nation, as can be seen in Prime Minister Golda Meir's statement after the war, "For the first time in our twenty-five year history we thought we might have lost,"[14] in fulfillment of verse 2:6 with the flushed faces of fear from the invading army. At one point in the middle of the two week war the Israeli army was about to run out of ammunition, and the Golda Meir government were preparing to flee the country and set up an Israeli government in exile, while Golda herself was thinking of committing suicide, because it was so certain that the nation of Israel was going to be lost during the midst of the Yom Kippur War. The Yom Kippur War fulfills every part of these verses about the army that attacks Israel in the Joel 1 – 2 prophecy.

2. Joel 1:7-12, 16-20; 2:3 – *This army destroys farms and farmland, including wheat and barley fields, vineyards, and orchards of various kinds of fruit trees, with fire, and this fire consumes in front of them where they are attacking, turning a garden of Eden into a wasteland behind them*: Another element to this prophecy is the destructive fire that goes in front of the invading army, destroying specifically farm land and fruit producing crops and grain. During the Yom Kippur War there were a significant amount of both Israeli and Druze orchards of fruit bearing trees destroyed in the fires caused by the invading Syrian army in the Golan Heights, along with wild trees from the fields.[15] The fires burned before the Syrian army, turning areas of crop land and farm land into wastelands where they had once been like a garden of Eden in the wilderness, exactly as the prophecy describes in the above verses. The farm and crop land was destroyed and the farmers lost their crops fulfilling the words of the prophecy, taking away from the tithe that Yahuweh/Yehovah would have had in crops from these farms if it had been in ancient times with Israel practicing the tithes and offerings. The Yom Kippur War fulfills this part of the prophecy as well, with destruction by fire of farmland and fields and forests in Israel.

---

[14] Lance Lambert, *Israel: A Secret Documentary* (Wheaton, Illinois: Tyndale House Publishers, Inc., 1975), pg. 9
[15] Martin Gilbert, *The Routledge Atlas of the Arab-Israeli Conflict: Seventh Edition* (11 New Fetter Lane, London EC4P 4EE: Routledge, 2002), pg. 90

3. *Joel 1:13-15; 2:1-2, 11-18 – The inhabitants of Israel and Yahuweh/Yehovah's people are assembled together at the sound of the alarm of the shofar, in mourning and fasting and prayer in crying out to Yahuweh/Yehovah and turning back to him in repentance with all of their hearts, to ask him to spare his people and the nation of Israel from destruction, which causes the previously <u>unstoppable</u> army invading Israel to be <u>stopped</u> by Yahuweh/Yehovah as he saves the nation of Israel from annihilation*: The Yom Kippur War invasion came on the day of Yahuweh/Yehovah's festival of Yom Kippur, the Day of Atonement, when the entire nation of Israel was shut down and already assembled together with fasting and prayer, as it says in the prophecy in verses 1:13-14 and 2:12 and 15. And there were in fact an unusually high number of Israeli men who were in prayer and fasting in synagogues that particular Yom Kippur when Syria and Egypt launched their surprise attack. Naomi Shemer wrote a song during the war called "Lu Yehi" לו יהי in which she describes the war as it was ongoing. She wrote in her song, "What is the sound that I hear, The cry of the shophar ... If only could be heard among all these, A prayer from my mouth." [16] She was describing the exact words of the prophecy in Joel during the Yom Kippur War, to sound the cry of the Shofar and gather together the people of Israel to prayer, in fulfillment of verses 2:1 and 15. The people of Israel assembled in mourning, fasting, and weeping like never before in their modern history during the Yom Kippur War, and they even had their very first national call to repentance that went out from one of the head Rabbis at that time, in fulfillment of verses 2:12-13 to turn back the hearts of the people of Israel to Yahuweh/Yehovah.

But even more so, the Christians in Israel and around the world at that time assembled together in prayer and intercession for the nation of Israel. Lance Lambert happened to be there in Israel at the time when the Yom Kippur War started. He describes the sound of the air raid sirens as they started wailing at 2:10 PM and again at 2:20 PM in Jerusalem,[17] warning of the starting invasion of the land of Israel, in fulfillment of verse 2:1, like the sound of the shofar sounding the alarm on Yahuweh/Yehovah's set-apart mountain Zion in Jerusalem. And Lance Lambert, together with Colonel Orde Dobbie and many other Christians in Jerusalem, gathered together[18] in fulfillment this prophecy in verses 1:13-14 and 2:15-18 to pray for the salvation of Israel, both spiritually and physically. Samuel Howells, son of Rees Howells, together with the Bible College of Wales were also interceding for Israel at that time, as well as Kitty Morgan and Gladys Thomas from within Israel.[19]

There was a large assembly of Christian believers in Yeshua who Yahuweh/Yehovah assembled and gathered together in prayer for his land and nation Israel, that the nation of Israel might be spared in fulfillment of the prophecy in Joel 2:17-18. And Yahuweh/Yehovah answered these prayers in fulfillment of the prophecy, turning around the war and supernaturally stopping the unstoppable invading army of Syria and Egypt. On the first night of the invasion, all that stood in the way between the Syrian army and victory over Israel in the north were 2 tanks and 10 Israeli soldiers, and yet they suddenly stopped their advance for no reason. They had Israel defeated and could have been inside of Tiberias before darkness had fallen, and yet

---

[16] מה קול ענות אני שומע קול שופר ... לו תישמע בתוך כל אלה גם תפילה אחת מפי
[17] Lance Lambert, *Israel: A Secret Documentary* (Wheaton, Illinois: Tyndale House Publishers, Inc., 1975), pgs. 7, 12
[18] Lance Lambert, *Israel: A Secret Documentary* (Wheaton, Illinois: Tyndale House Publishers, Inc., 1975), pgs. 21-24
[19] Lance Lambert, *Israel: A Secret Documentary* (Wheaton, Illinois: Tyndale House Publishers, Inc., 1975), pg. 27

they just stopped. An Israeli captain who was there and witnessed them stopping suddenly for no reason reported seeing in the sky above the Syrian army a large, gray hand that was pushing down on the Syrians, appearing to be holding them back.[20] It was the hand of Yahuweh/Yehovah supernaturally stopping the Syrians from moving any farther, stopping the unstoppable army in Joel 1 – 2 in fulfillment of the prophecy.

The same happened with the Egyptian army, which could have moved on to the Mitla Pass and beyond that first night of the invasion. There were no Israeli defenses or units in their way, nothing stopping them from charging straight across the Sinai Peninsula that night, but they suddenly just stopped their advance for no reason.[21] Israel experienced their greatest miracles from Yahuweh/Yehovah during the Yom Kippur War, saving them from certain destruction, in fulfillment of the prophecy, sparing his people Israel. In the Golan in the middle of the two week war, tank battalion commander Avigdor Kahalani led a charge of only 5 Israeli tanks against the hundreds of Syrian tanks that had come across the border, causing the Syrian tank brigades to turn their tails and run in fear from 5 tanks, even though they had hundreds and completely outnumbered them.

Israel almost ran out of ammunition and would have had to stop fighting and surrender, the ammunition supply situation was so dire. And yet President Richard Nixon stepped in and personally saw to it that Israel received the largest air drop of military supplies since World War II. But the supplies from America almost did not reach Israel in time, because every NATO country decided to side with the Arabs in the Yom Kippur War against Israel, refusing to allow any of the American planes with supplies for Israel to land on their territory. It was Portugal that finally opened up their air fields, allowing the American planes to get through just in time with their ammunition supplies.[22] The Israeli soldiers at the front lines were actually down to their very last magazine, firing their final bullets, just at the exact moment that the American ammunition supplies got to them at the front lines.

Without these supplies from Richard Nixon and America Israel would have lost the Yom Kippur War and ceased to exist as a nation again. And the reason that Richard Nixon gave for why he sent the military arms and ammunition supplies to Israel was because his mother had told him over and over again when he was a child that one day he would be in a position to help the Jewish people, and when that time came, he must help them. In the end Israel drove out and annihilated the Syrian and Egyptian armies, according to the fulfillment of this prophecy in Joel of driving out the invading army and being spared by Yahuweh/Yehovah. Syria was pushed back to the gates of Damascus and the Israel army was only 50 miles away from Cairo and the Nile River at the end. Every part of these verses in Joel about the assembling of the people in mourning and prayer, asking for Yahuweh/Yehovah's salvation for Israel, the sounding of the alarm of the shofar in Jerusalem, and Yahuweh/Yehovah supernaturally intervening to stop the unstoppable army from being able to destroy the nation of Israel all happened and were fulfilled exactly in the Yom Kippur War.

4. Joel 1:15; 2:1-2, 10-11 – *The attack by the invading army, and the alarm of the shofar that goes out from Jerusalem because of it, are a sign that the Day of Yahuweh/Yehovah (at his coming in Joel 3) is near,*

---

[20] Lance Lambert, *Israel: A Secret Documentary* (Wheaton, Illinois: Tyndale House Publishers, Inc., 1975), pgs. 15-16
[21] Lance Lambert, *Israel: A Secret Documentary* (Wheaton, Illinois: Tyndale House Publishers, Inc., 1975), pg. 15
[22] Lance Lambert, *Israel: A Secret Documentary* (Wheaton, Illinois: Tyndale House Publishers, Inc., 1975), pg. 17

but it is not going to happen yet, even though the sun, moon, and stars are darkened during the time of this invading army similar to when Joel 3 happens at the end of the Great Tribulation: With the sounding of the siren alarm mentioned before in Jerusalem, it is a sign that the Day of Yahuweh/Yehovah is near, but that it does not happen yet at that time. The events happening in the Joel 1 – 2 war are similar to the events of Joel 3, but they are only a preparation for Joel 3, a preparation for the Day of Yahuweh/Yehovah that is coming soon at the Battle of Har Megiddon (Armageddon) in Revelation 16 and 19 and Joel 3 and Zechariah 14. The sun, moon and stars are darkened in this war in Joel 1 – 2 in the same way that they are darkened at the final war that happens at Yahuweh/Yehovah's coming in Joel 3, so it is similar, but the Joel 1 – 2 war happens before the Joel 3 war, with a time of peace and restoration in between them.

The sun, moon, and stars being darkened in the Joel prophecy is a way of saying that both the day and the night are dark, without light coming from the sky at either time of day. Naomi Shemer once again writing about the Yom Kippur War as it happened described in her song "Lu Yehi" the darkness in the sky over Israel at that time, during the day and the night, saying, "There is still a white sail on the horizon, Opposite a dark and heavy cloud," [23] showing the day to be dark with black clouds. And then at night, "And if suddenly rising from the darkness, Over our heads the light of a star shines," [24] referring to that during the Yom Kippur War the Israelis would have liked to have seen even the light of one single star because the darkness was so great, in fulfillment of this prophecy in verse 2:10.

The Joel prophecy in chapters 1 and 2 are the Battle of Har Megiddon and the end of the world of man almost happening, but stopped from happening yet, because the Day of Yahuweh/Yehovah is near but not yet, until later in Joel 3. The Joel 1 – 2 prophecy is a small taste of the Day of Yahuweh/Yehovah and the Battle of Har Megiddon, without it happening in its fullness yet, which is exactly what the Yom Kippur War was. Israel as a nation was almost destroyed and removed from existence once again, and Israel was even in direct fighting and war against Russia at that time, sinking and shooting down Russian controlled warships and fighter jets. A nuclear world war and a gathering of the nations to battle at Har Megiddon (Mount Megiddon) in Israel almost happened during the Yom Kippur War. When Russia saw that Syria and Egypt had been defeated by Israel, they became furious, especially with the Russian operated military assets that Israel had destroyed in the process. Russia was actually preparing a nuclear strike on Israel and an invasion of their paratroopers directly into the land of Israel itself. They even told America at the time that that was what they were going to do, as they put their paratroopers on alert in readiness for the invasion, and moved one of their nuclear missile equipped warships into the port in Alexandria, Egypt[25] in readiness for a nuclear strike on Israel if needed.

The world almost ended in the Battle of Har Megiddon and a world nuclear war at that moment of the Yom Kippur War, if it had not been for President Richard Nixon raising the Defcon level and signaling to Russia that America was ready to fight a nuclear war with them if they were to invade or attack Israel in any

---

[23] עוד יש מפרש לבן באופק מול ענן שחור כבד
[24] ואם פתאום יזרח מאופל על ראשנו אור כוכב
[25] Lance Lambert, *Israel: A Secret Documentary* (Wheaton, Illinois: Tyndale House Publishers, Inc., 1975), pg. 26

way, which surprised Russia and made them back down. A Nuclear World War III and the Day of Yahuweh/Yehovah almost happened, but did not happen yet, in exact fulfillment of the Joel 1 – 2 prophecy.

5. Joel 2:20-21 – *The Northerner who came against Israel is removed back far away from Israel to where the Northerner was from, far away from Israel, because Yahuweh/Yehovah has supernaturally removed them, acting mightily against them*: In Joel 2:20 the prophecy speaks about the "Northerner." It does not say anything about an army from the north, or a people from the north. It simply says the "Northerner" is removed from Israel, and driven back far away to a deserted land, that is sparsely inhabited, and dry, that has a sea to the east of it and to the west of it. It was Russia from the exact north of Israel that was really behind the entire Yom Kippur War. It was Russia who armed and equipped the Egyptian and Syrian armies to become such a strong and unstoppable force, among the most advanced armies in the world at the time, in order to wage a proxy war against Israel and America through them. And it was Russia who reportedly told Syria and Egypt to do the surprise attack against Israel on the Day of Atonement, on Yom Kippur. It was also Russian spy satellites that provided Syria and Egypt with all of the intelligence on Israeli forces they needed to be able to carry out their surprise attack. The Russian army trained the Syrian and Egyptian armies so that they would be better fighters than in the previous wars with Israel.

It was the Northerner, Russia, who was behind the whole war, and after the Yom Kippur War defeat Yahuweh/Yehovah removed the Northerner, Russia, from Israel, so that they have never bothered Israel or been involved in any war against them again, for all of these 50 years later. The Northerner, Russia, was taken back to their land in the north, far away from Israel, where they sit with the Black Sea and Baltic Sea to their west, and the Bering Sea and Chuckchi Sea to their east, facing toward the eastern sea, toward America, the only nation standing in their way stopping them from destroying Israel. And Russia sat there with the stench and smell of their failure, because Yahuweh/Yehovah is the one who ultimately defeated them and took them away from Israel, fulfilling verses 2:20-21 exactly word for word to the prophecy.

6. Joel 2:19, 22-26 – *There is a revival in Israel that begins after the great and mighty army is defeated by Yahuweh/Yehovah, as he pours out his Spirit like rain on Israel, and restores the land from the destruction the army has caused, so that the nation of Israel lives in peace without fear of another such invading army again for at least several generations, no longer a reproach to other nations*: After the army that comes against Israel in the Yom Kippur War is defeated and removed, Yahuweh/Yehovah takes the nation of Israel through a time of restoration where the nation sits in relative peace and prosperity for a time, with the nation rebuilt from all of the damage done. And this is exactly what happened after the Yom Kippur War, in exact fulfillment of the prophecy.

For 50 years now Israel has never been severely attacked or hurt again like in the Yom Kippur War or the wars before that. The wars that Israel has fought since 1973 have been mostly outside of its borders with Lebanon, or only small wars and Intifadas with the Palestinians, the terrorist bombings and rocket barrages being the worst parts of these wars. But over the years since the Yom Kippur War they have been restored and grown into greater prosperity and comfort for the last 50 years, with the nation becoming agriculturally and economically restored, in fulfillment of verses 2:22-27. And the nation of Israel has no longer been a reproach to the nations during the last 50 years either, in fulfillment of 2:19.

But more importantly, Yahuweh/Yehovah promises to send his rain, which from Hosea 6 is referring to himself being poured out on the nation of Israel, turning the Jews in Israel back to him. And the Yom Kippur War was the start of the revival in Israel that has caused many Jews in Israel to believe in Yeshua and turn back to Yahuweh/Yehovah through Yeshua. There was a Messianic Jew in the Israeli army during the Yom Kippur War named Haim, and during and after the war other Israeli soldiers would seek him out from all over the army to hear him read the Hebrew Scriptures and talk about Yahuweh/Yehovah, and the prophecies being fulfilled in their time.[26] At that time of the war most Jews were secular and Atheist, not believing in any God or anything spiritual, but the miracle of Yahuweh/Yehovah intervening to save Israel in the Yom Kippur War turned many Jews back to seeking after Yahuweh/Yehovah, the God of Israel, once again. The different soldiers and units were even fighting over Haim, wanting him to be in their group so that they could hear the Scriptures and learn about Yahuweh/Yehovah.

Ever since the Yom Kippur War there has been revival in Israel, bringing Jews back to Yeshua, the God of Israel, in greater and greater numbers. Before the Yom Kippur War there was only a small number of Messianic Jews in Israel, and now today that number has grown into the hundreds of thousands, in fulfillment of this prophecy in Joel 2:23, as Yahuweh/Yehovah has rained down himself, raining down to Israel as the "Teacher unto Righteousness" הַמּוֹרֶה לִצְדָקָה as it literally says in the Hebrew of 2:23. Even Prime Minister Golda Meir, who had been an Atheist before the war, changed to an Agnostic afterwards and began to believe in the existence of the God of Israel in later years.

Conclusion: Every word of this prophecy of Joel 1:1 through 2:27 was fulfilled word for word during and after the Yom Kippur War, preparing the way for the rest of the Joel prophecies in 2:28 and beyond to be fulfilled. All of the requirements of fulfillment in the Joel prophecies that have to happen before the Great Tribulation have already been fulfilled, leaving nothing left in these particular Joel prophecies that are required to happen before Yahuweh/Yehovah can pour out his Spirit on all flesh with the signs of the sun turned to darkness and the moon to blood. The Joel 2:28 prophecy is free to happen at any time, now that we are "after this," after the events of Joel 1:1 through 2:27. And there is nothing else that has to happen with this Joel 1:1 – 2:27 prophecy before the Great Tribulation can happen. Therefore the Great Tribulation can also happen without any other Scriptural requirements from this particular prophecy in Joel preventing it from happening either.

---

[26] Lance Lambert, *Israel: A Secret Documentary* (Wheaton, Illinois: Tyndale House Publishers, Inc., 1975), pgs. 46-47

Section 5. **The First through Fifth Seals (The Four Horsemen):**

The Four Horsemen/Charioteers Prophecies with the Opening of the First Four Seals:
Zechariah 6:1-8
Revelation 6:1-8

Prophecy Fulfillment of Verses **Zechariah 6:1-8** – This prophecy is about "four spirits of the heavens" who go out from the presence of "the Master of all the earth" which is Yahuweh/Yehovah. These four spirits are riding chariots pulled by four sets of horses of four different colors, and they ride out from between two mountains of brass/bronze. The metal brass/bronze is a manmade alloy metal that does not naturally exist in nature. This means that these four spirits in the spiritual dimensions are riding out from between two physical mountains in the natural realm that are made by human hands out of human formed and made metal.

Today there are numerous mountains on the earth made out of human created alloy metals that do not exist in nature called "sky scrapers." They are made out of steel and lots of glass most of the time, mountains of metal that to Zechariah in his day seeing them in a vision of the future he certainly would have described as mountains of brass/bronze, with how shiny the skyscrapers look from a distance because of the glass having a mirrored effect, just like the mirrored shine on the surface of brass/bronze. These chariot riders that are four spirits, after leaving the presence of Yahuweh/Yehovah in the heavens where they have presented themselves to him, go to these two manmade mountains on the earth, and ride out from there in different directions.

This prophecy in Zechariah 6:1-8 was fulfilled on September 11, 2001 when the two Twin Towers or manmade mountains of the World Trade Center in New York City were hit by the two terrorist hijacked planes, causing these two Twin Towers to collapse into two literal mountain piles of rubble of manmade metals and materials. From between these two manmade mountains, these four spirits in the spiritual dimensions rode out in fulfillment of this prophecy:

1. The spirit driven by the <u>black</u> horses going to <u>the land of the north,</u>
2. The spirit driven by the <u>white</u> horses going out after the black horses to <u>the land of the north,</u>
3. The spirit driven by the <u>speckled/spotted</u> (sprinkled with hail) horses going out to <u>the land of the south,</u>
4. The spirit driven by the <u>red</u> horses going out to <u>walk to and fro on the earth.</u>

There is no more detail given in this prophecy in Zechariah about what the four spirits do driven by the four teams of horses of four different colors when they get to their destinations. The only other thing is that the two spirits driven by the black and white horses that went into the land of the north give rest to Yahuweh/Yehovah's Spirit there in the land of the north.

Prophecy Fulfillment of Verses **Revelation 6:1-8** – Once again in this prophecy in Revelation 6 there are four spirits or spiritual beings in the heavens who have been before Yahuweh/Yehovah, the Master of all the earth, in the heavens, and once again these four spirits are riding four different horses of four different colors as with the four spirits in Zechariah 6. These four spiritual beings in the heavens ride out from

Yahuweh/Yehovah, from his presence in the heavens, in exactly the same way as the four spirits ride out from Yahuweh/Yehovah in Zechariah 6, and with four different horse colors once again as in Zechariah 6.

1. The rider on the white horse goes out with a bow and crown, conquering and to conquer,
2. The rider on the red horse goes out with a great sword, to take peace from the earth and cause the people to kill each other,
3. The rider on the black horse goes out with a pair of scales, for determining staple food (wheat and barley) prices in a bad economy and causing things like oil and wine to become a precious commodity,
4. The rider named Death on the pale green horse goes out with the grave, and has authority over ¼ of the earth surface to kill with sword, famine, death, and the beasts of the earth.

On September 11, 2001 the first four seals were opened as Yahuweh/Yehovah sent out these four spirits, with their four different colored horses, from himself in the heavens down to the two manmade mountains of the World Trade Center Twin Towers, collapsed into rubble, for them to ride out from there across the earth. In Zechariah 6 the prophecy reveals where these four spirits ride out to, and in Revelation 6 the prophecy reveals what each of them is doing. Each of the colors of white, red, and black correspond to each other, and the other horses in the Hebrew of Zechariah 6 are described as "barod" בָּרֹד, which literally means to be spotted in the sense of sprinkled with hail. But in the prophecy of Zechariah 6 it does not reveal what the color of these spotted horses looks like. The color of this spotted horse is not revealed until Revelation 6, with the Greek word "chloros" χλωρός, meaning green as with a green plant, or a pale green color as when someone is feeling sick and might vomit.

The four things that each of these four spirit beings from the heavens are carrying with them are: 1. a bow and crown for conquering (representing governments and rulers with crowns hunting with a bow for power through conquering), 2. a great sword for taking away peace and causing people to kill each other (representing militaries of nations fighting wars), 3. a pair of scales for weight measurements for measuring out food against money value in a bad economy (representing economic recessions and depressions), and 4. is Death with the grave causing people to die from various things such as war with the sword, hunger from lack of food in famine, and causing death earlier than usual from the natural causes of old age, and death from animal attacks (representing an increase in death in general for certain areas of the earth).

After the September 11 attack on the World Trade Center, it was these four things that went out from that event, from the midst of the ruins of the destroyed manmade mountains of metal. Since that time there has not been a moment of peace on the earth, with continuous war and fighting and people killing each other, sometimes almost daily with terrorist attacks. America invaded Afghanistan in a war that lasted 20 years and which America lost in the end, as well as invading Iraq and losing that war too. The invasion of Iraq opened up the way for ISIS to gain control of parts of Syria and Iraq for a time. The Middle East collapsed in the Arab Spring in 2011, bringing Civil War to Libya, Egypt, Yemen, and Syria. The Yemen war has spilled over into Saudi Arabia, including them in the war, and in Syria the fighting has brought in Turkish involvement in the fighting. Israel has been in constant conflict with the Palestinians. Ethiopia has been in its own Civil War. Russia invaded Georgia and then later in 2014 started an invasion of Ukraine that has lasted for 9 years now this year. And currently this spring all of the nations of the world are posturing and preparing for a World War between the East and the West, between Asia and Europe and North America. War has been "to-ing and fro-ing" all across every part of the earth.

The world economies have been in constant turmoil in one place or another, especially in the northern hemisphere in the land of the north. There was the Great Recession that was really a depression beginning in 2008, and the economies have never fully recovered, still under turmoil of ups and downs around the world. And also during the last more than twenty years since September 11 all of the major world leaders with crowns, the rulers of the world and people with power through wealth, who have been trying to hunt for more power by going out to conquer other nations, with conquering, have primarily been in the northern hemisphere as well, in the land of the north, in Russia and China and Iran and Turkey and North Korea and in the European Union and NATO countries and in the United States of America and the various Islamic Terrorist Groups (such as Al-Qaeda and ISIS) primarily based in central Asia and the northern Middle Eastern countries. Since the September 11 attacks it has been America with its NATO allies who have been doing the most conquering in search of power in the Middle East, until Russia's full invasion of Ukraine in 2022. But all of the major famines and starvation have been experienced in the southern hemisphere, in the land of the south, primarily in Africa and the extreme southern parts of Asia and the Middle East. Some of the worst famine droughts in world history are currently ongoing in eastern Africa. This is where the main deaths occur from animal attacks as well, and they have had their own sets of bloody wars in central and southern Africa that have been mostly isolated from the wars going on in the rest of the world. The things brought from the rider Death are more isolated across a small area of the earth, across ¼ of the earth, than the other three riders.

But these four things of conquest, war, economic depression, and death by various means are four things that have always been on the earth in tandem together since the time of the Tower of Babel when Yahuweh/Yehovah confused the languages and created separate nation states. These four things have been happening in every place and every nation on earth in cycles since that time around 4,500 years ago, with people wanting to conquer other people and rule over them as kings, with their crowns, and nations waring against other nations, and economies of countries or regions falling apart and going through depressions, and people dying from famine and war and animals and natural causes of old age or disease. If these four things that come with the four riders are all common things that have always been on the earth for at least around 4,500 years, and always will be on the earth until it ends, then why is there a prophecy about them?

They are the final cycle of these four things on the earth. When these four spirits rode out with their horses across the earth they were representing the chain of events that would happen from the catalyst of the September 11 terrorist attack. And as they went out across the earth in fulfillment of this prophecy, to the north and the south and to-ing and fro-ing across the earth, it was the sign that from that moment of September 11, 2001 these four things of conquest, war, economic depression, and death in its various forms are not going to be stopping or letting up ever again until Yeshua returns, only increasing in frequency and intensity as the final birth pains that Yeshua spoke of in Matthew 24 and Mark 13 up to the moment that

Yeshua ends the world. As the events in the first four seals continue to happen and increase on the earth into stronger birth pains than have been seen before in the past, we are watching these prophecies in Zechariah 6:1-8 and Revelation 6:1-8 continue to happen and be fulfilled across the earth.

The Fifth Seal Prophecy:
Revelation 6:9-11

Prophecy Fulfillment of Verses **Revelation 6:9-11** – Here in this Fifth Seal prophecy together with Revelation 17:6 and 20:4, as well as Matthew 24:9, is a description of the martyrs, those who have been killed/slain for their witness about Yeshua, and for the Word of God in Scripture. It is those who are killed for witnessing to their belief in Yeshua and his followers, and also killed for their following and obeying and living the Word of God in Scripture, the entire Word of Yahuweh/Yehovah everywhere that his words are recorded in all of Scripture from Genesis to Revelation. John sees under the sacrificial altar (in the spiritual realm) the "beings" or souls who have been killed for their witness and for standing strong on the Word of Yahuweh/Yehovah in Scripture.

And they are asking Yahuweh/Yehovah how much longer they have to wait until he judges those who are dwelling on the earth, avenging their blood upon them. And they are told they have to wait a little longer, until the number is complete of all those who have to be killed as martyrs as they were. This is all a conversation that happens in the heavens, in the spiritual realm, where nobody in the physical universe can hear the conversation when it happens or see it happening in the physical realm. So then what are the signs that can be seen in the physical realm showing the fulfillment of the Fifth Seal?

Ever since Stephen was martyred at the hands of the Pharisees for his witness about Yeshua, in the early 1st Century C.E., there have been an estimated millions of martyrs through the centuries, perhaps as many as 70 million, although only Yahuweh/Yehovah knows the true number of martyrs through history. And this is excluding those killed in wars between Christian denominations and Christian government nations in Europe, since both sides were killing each other, which has nothing to do with martyrdom, or the various wars between Christian and Islamic nations that also had nothing to do with martyrdom according to the description of martyrdom in Matthew 24 and Revelation 6 and 17 and 20.

During the 20th Century there were an estimated 15 million to 45 million people martyred for their witness to Yeshua, and for their belief in the Scriptures, the Old and New Testaments, the most in any single century since Stephen, the first martyr, was killed for his witness to Yeshua in the 1st Century. And depending upon how high the number of martyrs really was in the 20th Century, there may have been more killed for their witness to Yeshua in the 20th century than in all of the rest of the centuries before that combined together since the time of Stephen.

Now by the end of the deadly 20th Century in terms of martyrdom, after so many people have been killed for their witness to Yeshua for so many long years, this is certainly a time in history when one would expect those who have been martyred through history to be asking how much longer they have to wait for Yahuweh/Yehovah to bring justice in avenging their blood, after almost 2,000 years and tens of millions of martyrs. The killing of Christians for their belief and witness in Yeshua certainly has never stopped in the last 2,000 years up to the present time, and with persecution of Christians staying as strong as ever around the world this year, there are no signs that the martyrdom of believers in Yeshua will ever stop in the future until Yeshua returns. So this is a very reasonable time in history, in the context of today, for the martyrs who have already been killed to be asking Yahuweh/Yehovah, how long is this going to go on before he avenges their deaths.

Another key part of this prophecy is that it is the "blood" of the martyrs that they are asking Yahuweh/Yehovah to avenge. In 2014 the Islamic State of Iraq and the Levant (ISIL or ISIS) came quickly into power as a nation state in portions of Iraq and Syria, as well as other allied groups operating in Africa, and central and southern Asia, including the island nations of south Asia. Throughout 2014 and 2015 ISIS killed many believers in Yeshua for their witness to Yeshua and for their belief in the Scriptures, including entire Christian families. [ISIS killings of Christians have continued even up to the present time, with some of the most recent being in Mozambique in 2020 to 2021.] The unusual thing about the martyrdom of Christians by ISIS during 2014 to 2015 was that this was the first time in history that these killings of Christians (and of other religious groups or western political affiliation) were broadcast live to the whole world to see on television and their computers.

This broadcasting of the murders of Christians caused international attention through all forms of media about the Christian martyrs and persecution of Christians on a scale that had never been seen before in history. The attention of the world was suddenly focused on the martyrs killed for their witness to Yeshua, which is exactly what happens when the Fifth Seal is opened in the heavens. When the Fifth Seal is opened there is a sudden pause to focus on the martyrs who have been slain for their witness they held about Yeshua and the Scriptures. It is only a momentary pause, but for a short time there is a focus brought onto the martyrs and a discussion about how much longer this is going to go on before Yahuweh/Yehovah brings justice and avenges their blood on the earth. This momentary pause and worldwide focus and discussion in various media on the martyrs happened in 2014 to 2015, as the Fifth Seal was opened and this prophecy was fulfilled at that time.

And because of the live video of the executions of Christians, everyone in the world could specifically see the blood of the martyrs being spilled out for their holding onto their witness to Yeshua. In Libya the blood of the Christian martyrs from Egypt turned the sea to blood red as the executions were carried out on the beach. As everyone could see the blood of the martyrs on television and internet around the world, the question was how much longer will it be until Yahuweh/Yehovah avenges that blood of the martyrs? And the answer comes to the martyrs in the heavens to rest a while longer in their sleep, until the complete number of other believers in Yeshua had been killed for their holding onto their witness about Yeshua, even unto death. Only a little while longer until Yahuweh/Yehovah will bring justice and vengeance on all those who had murdered and slain believers in Yeshua for their witness to Yeshua through history, and vengeance on those dwelling on the earth (which comes with the Seven Bowls of Wrath in the future).

Section 6. The 144,000 Sealed from the 12 Tribes of Israel:

The 144,000 are Only First-Fruits (the First Born) and the Seal that They Receive on Their Foreheads is the Name of Yahuweh/Yehovah, the Same Seal the High Priest is Commanded to Wear on His Forehead:

Exodus 28:36-38

Revelation 14:1-5

Word for Word Prophecy Examination of Unfulfilled Verses **Revelation 14:1-5** with **Exodus 28:36-38** – Even though the prophecy about the 144,000 in Revelation 14 will not be fulfilled until after Yeshua, the Lamb, returns, it provides an important description of the seal that is on the foreheads of the 144,000. The seal that is upon the foreheads of the 144,000 has the Name of the Lamb Yeshua's Father, the Name of Yahuweh/Yehovah יהוה written upon the seal that is upon their foreheads. In Exodus 28:36-38 the High Priest is also commanded to wear a seal upon his forehead that also has the name of Yahuweh/Yehovah written on it. Here in verse 28:36 the Hebrew word "Chotham" חֹתָם meaning "seal" is very clearly used, describing the exact same kind of object and seal that is upon the foreheads of the 144,000 sealed from the 12 tribes of Israel.

And more than that the instructions for the High Priest seal upon the forehead gives more detail of exactly what the spiritual seal on the foreheads of the 144,000 looks like, made of a plate of gold with a blue cord around it to hold it in place on the forehead. And the Hebrew words written on the seal are "qodesh laYHWH" קֹדֶשׁ לַיהוה, which translates as "Set-Apartness unto YHWH" or in most translations, "Holiness unto the LORD." This physical seal worn by the High Priest that says "Set-Apartness unto Yahuweh/Yehovah" fits the same description as the spiritual seal that is worn by the 144,000 in the prophecies in Revelation.

Also, the 144,000 are first-fruits or the first born. These 144,000 from the 12 tribes of Israel are the first to be sealed with the name of Yahuweh/Yehovah on their foreheads, and these men and women are the first born male child, given to Yahuweh/Yehovah as the first-fruits according to his instructions and commands in the Torah. But eventually everyone who is a believer in Yeshua receives this same seal with the name of Yahuweh/Yehovah written on it.

Eventually All of Yahuweh/Yehovah's People Receive the Same Seal of the 144,000 on Their Foreheads of the Name of Yahuweh/Yehovah:

Revelation 22:3-4

Word for Word Prophecy Examination of Unfulfilled Verses **Revelation 22:3-4** – This prophecy will not be completely fulfilled until the New Heavens and New Earth, but it does give further details about the seal on the forehead of the 144,000, that eventually everyone who is a believer in Yeshua, a servant of Yahuweh/Yehovah, will have the name of Yahuweh/Yehovah written on their foreheads with this exact same seal as the 144,000. It says in this prophecy that the servants of God will have his name upon their foreheads, all of his servants. And his name is Yahuweh/Yehovah. It begins with the 144,000 as the first-fruits or firstborn, but eventually everyone who is a follower and servant of Yahuweh/Yehovah will have the same seal containing his name on their foreheads, the seal that makes them "set-apart unto Yahuweh/Yehovah," made clean and set-apart, completely belonging to Yahuweh/Yehovah and washed clean in the blood of the Lamb.

The Prophecy of the 144,000 Sealed from the 12 Tribes of Israel:
Revelation 7:1-8

Prophecy Fulfillment of Verses **Revelation 7:1-8** – In 2018 there was an Egyptian Christian man living in Egypt who had a dream about the upcoming Onething Conference that would be held by the International House of Prayer in Kansas City. In the dream he saw the word "Holiness to the LORD" written over/above the Onething Conference gathering upcoming later that year and in the dream Yahuweh/Yehovah instructed him to make a seal of gold fashioned after the same seal worn by the High Priest in Exodus 28:36, and to design it himself from the description in the verse. Yahuweh/Yehovah instructed this Egyptian man to write the words "Holiness to the Lord" in English and in Hebrew (קדש ליהוה) and in Arabic on the seal plate of pure gold. Then on the back of the seal he was to write the names of two nations from North America (U.S. and Canada), three nations from Asia (China, Korea, and Japan), three nations from Europe (U.K., Germany, and France), and the three nations from the highway of holiness in Isaiah 19 (Egypt, Israel, and Syria). He carried out these instructions, making this golden seal to be worn upon the forehead, with a blue ribbon attached as is instructed in Exodus 28:36 and brought this seal with him to Kansas City for the gathering at the Kansas City Convention Center.

What this Egyptian believer in Yeshua did not know is that decades before in 1990 Yahuweh/Yehovah had also given Paul Cain a vision and word that he instructed Paul Cain to go to Kansas City to deliver to Mike Bickle. The vision was of an auditorium with the words "Holiness to the LORD" written on a banner over it, like the dream that the Egyptian believer in Yeshua had, in a place where thousands of young people were gathered. In the vision Paul Cain was shown specific details about the auditorium to be able to identify it and while he was visiting Mike Bickle, Mike was called away on an errand to sign a contract for renting the Kansas City Convention Center. Paul Cain decided to go along and was shocked to find that the Kansas City Convention Center was the place he had seen in the vision with the banner "Holiness to the LORD" written over it, the same place where the International House of Prayer were about to hold their very last Onething Conference in 2018, never to use that building again for their gatherings.

This Onething Conference in 2018 was also different, because it was actually not the traditional Onething Conference as before. This year Egyptian born David Damien was attending with a large group of Chinese Christians from China as part of the gathering. On the night of December 28, 2018 the Egyptian man presented the seal he had made according to the dream to Mike Bickle and the International House of Prayer, and then on the next day, on December 29, 2018 of the gathering, the Chinese Christians and many believers in Yeshua from many countries were on the stage together. Then some of the Chinese leadership who were there representing the Christians of China took the gold seal with the name of Yahuweh/Yehovah written on it in Hebrew קדש ליהוה and placed the seal upon the forehead of Mike Bickle. At that same moment, as Mike Bickle was wearing the seal upon his forehead, David Damien spoke a word from Yahuweh/Yehovah he received, in which Yahuweh/Yehovah said, "I am releasing before the world puts the chip in your hand and your forehead. I am marking my chosen ones, because the time has come for the enemy to do what he wants. And I am going to go ahead of him, and I am going to mark my chosen ones. I don't need chips. With my fire of the Holy Spirit I will write on every forehead "Holiness unto the LORD."

All of these events were in fulfillment of Revelation 7:1-8, fulfilling every detail of the prophecy. The seal that the Egyptian man made is the seal upon the forehead of the High Priest with the name of Yahuweh/Yehovah on it, "Set-Apartness unto YHWH," which is the same spiritual seal that the 144,000 of the 12 tribes of Israel are given by Yahuweh/Yehovah upon their foreheads. It was this seal of gold that Yahuweh/Yehovah had instructed this Christian man from Egypt to make that was the representative and symbolic seal of the 144,000 as the sign in the natural realm that on December 29, 2018 Yahuweh/Yehovah had begun sealing the foreheads of the 144,000 believers in Yeshua who are natural descendants from the 12 tribes of Israel all across the world. This is why there were representative nations from all over the world written on the seal, showing that natural descendants of all of the 12 tribes of Israel were being sealed with this spiritual seal on their foreheads from Yahuweh/Yehovah at that time, setting them apart unto Yahuweh/Yehovah in fulfillment of verses 7:3-8.

The Egyptian Christian who made the seal according to Yahuweh/Yehovah's instructions, and the Chinese Christians who placed the seal upon the forehead of Mike Bickle, even came from the east to Kansas City, from the rising of the sun, as a sign of the fulfillment of verse 7:2 where the messenger with the spiritual seal of the 144,000 came from the rising of the sun, from the east, holding the seal in his hands. The physical seal with the name of Yahuweh/Yehovah written upon it in Hebrew, representing in the natural realm the spiritual seal of the 144,000 actually was brought from the east, from the rising of the sun, showing that this prophecy was now in fulfillment in the spiritual realm.

There is no way at this point to know for certain who on the earth is a natural descendant of all of the 12 tribes of Israel. The southern kingdom tribes from Judah are known, from the tribes of Yehudah, Binyamin, and part of Levi, but the other tribes are not as well known. There is a lot of evidence supporting many groups across Asia as being descendants of the northern kingdom tribes of Israel, but one thing that is known absolutely for certain from Isaiah 49:12 is that there are descendants of the 12 tribes of Israel who are living in the nation of Sinim, which is the ancient Hebrew name for the nation of China, who return to Israel as believers in Yeshua at his coming. And it was the Chinese Christians specifically who came to be part of this unplanned event of the shadow picture sign of the seal of Yahuweh/Yehovah being placed on the foreheads of believers. China is one country that we know from Scripture absolutely for certain that there are descendants of the 12 tribes of Israel living in it today, who do not even know that they are descended from the 12 tribes.

From Zechariah 10:7-10 there are also two other nations specifically mentioned that have descendants of the 10 northern tribes of Israel, poetically called Ephrayim in the prophecy, living in them today, who will eventually return to the land of Israel, from the nations of Egypt and Syria. And there were also Christians present and a part of the event specifically from Egypt as well as China, two of the nations that are mentioned in prophecy as having descendants of the 12 tribes of Israel living in them at the time of Yeshua's return, these two nations having people from them who believe in and follow Yeshua when he comes, but who might not yet know at the time of his coming that they are descended from the 12 tribes. There is no way to know who at the gathering on December 29 might be actual descendants of the tribes of Israel, but it is no mistake that there were Chinese and Egyptian Christians present there and participating, two of the nations in prophecy that are specifically mentioned as having descendants of the 12 tribes of Israel living in them in the last days, representing that the time of the fulfillment of the prophecy of the sealing of the 144,000 from "all" of the tribes of Israel had begun.

And Mike Bickle[27] was only the prophetic symbol representation that the seal was beginning to be placed upon the foreheads of the 144,000 as the first fruits of the sealing, in the same way that the High Priest Yehoshua son of Yehotsadaq in Zechariah 6:11-12 was only the prophetic symbol of prophecy, not the one himself who is the fulfillment of that prophecy. Yehoshua the High Priest was only a prophetic symbol of prophecy, and was not the fulfillment of that prophecy himself, as Mike Bickle with the seal upon his forehead was only the symbol of the prophecy of the spiritual seal of the 144,000 being fulfilled, not the personal fulfillment of it himself.

The word that David Damien gave during the event of the sealing upon the forehead also matches with Scripture, that after the 144,000 believers in Yeshua from all of the tribes of Israel are sealed upon their foreheads, then all believers in Yeshua receive this same seal of "Set-Apartness unto Yahuweh/Yehovah" upon their foreheads according to Revelation 22:3-4, as Yahuweh/Yehovah is writing his name "Holiness unto the LORD" "קדש ליהוה" upon the foreheads of all those who follow him through Yeshua. In Revelation 7:3 it says that the forehead seal (that has the name of Yahuweh/Yehovah written on it) is for the "servants of God" and then later in Revelation 22:3-4 the name of Yahuweh/Yehovah written upon the foreheads of the people is for "His servants." Before the four messengers holding back the four winds in verse 7:1 have sounded their first four trumpets in verses 8:6-12, the servants of Yahuweh/Yehovah have been sealed with the spiritual golden seal of Yahwueh/Yehovah, as he is writing "Set-Apartness unto Yahuweh/Yehovah" on their foreheads, beginning with the first-fruits of the 144,000 from all of the tribes of Israel. And this prophecy has now happened and been fulfilled in its every detail, word for word to what Yahuweh/Yehovah said he would do with his seal for the foreheads of his servants.

---

[27] Unfortunately at the point of the writing of this book the situation of sexual abuse allegations against Mike Bickle is unresolved and there is no way to write a complete summary about it. We only know at this time that as more and more evidence comes out in e-mails and dozens of eye witness, first-hand testimonies, including confessions by Mike Bickle himself, the evidence continues to confirm that Mike Bickle did commit all of the sexual and spiritual abuse he is alleged to have done. It is also clear that this alleged abuse went on for decades involving multiple women. Even if it comes out as a result of all of this that Mike Bickle might be at the extreme level of a Judas betrayer or a manipulative wolf disguised as a sheep it does not change anything concerning the fulfillment of the prophecies, as Judas Iscariot was also involved in the fulfillment of many prophecies throughout Yeshua's ministry, in his closest inner circle. And throughout the above described events Mike Bickle mostly resisted and fought against everything that took place, trying to get control of the narrative of what was happening and change it into what he wanted it to be whenever he had the chance instead of accepting the reality of what was really happening, acting mostly as a bystander throughout the most important, key parts of the events. During these events Mike Bickle also went out of his way to try to stop and control the narrative of Lou Engle's amazing repentence and public confession he did, trying to stop and prevent any public repentence of sin at that time. (The shepherds have to be judged just prior to Yeshua's return in Ezekial 34.)

Section 7. **The Transgression Desolating (2,300 Evening and Morning):**

The Transgression Desolating Prophecy:
Daniel 8:11-14

Prophecy Fulfillment of Verses **Daniel 8:11-14** – This prophecy about a Little Horn in Daniel 8 sounds like it could be referring to Antiochus IV Epiphanes, king of the Seleucid Division of the Greek Empire, coming out of one of the four horns of the four divisions of the Greek Empire, during the time of the Maccabees. However, the interesting thing is that nowhere in the first or second books of Maccabees, nor anywhere in the surviving histories about the Greek Empire from that time, is there any record of any of this prophecy about a Little Horn in Daniel 8:9-14 or 8:23-25 having happened or been fulfilled in any way at that time. No transgression desolating happened against the foundation of the set-apart place at the Temple Mount in Jerusalem for a span of 2,300 evening morning (2,300 evenings and mornings or 2,300 literal days where the sun rises and sets a literal 2,300 times, which cannot be symbolic of other countings of time such as weeks, months, or years) in the ancient recorded history of Israel since the time when Daniel received this prophecy up until the destruction of Jerusalem and the Second Temple and the exile of Judah by the Romans in the 1st to 2nd Centuries C.E.

The prophecy talks about the ram with two horns representing Media and Persia of the Persian Empire, being destroyed by the male goat with one horn from the west, Yavan, the Greek Empire under Alexander the Great conquering the Persian Empire. And then the Greek Empire broke apart into four different horns or divisions under four different kings and kingdoms, including the Seleucid, Ptolemy, Attalid, and Antigonid. That part of the prophecy happened during the time of the ancient Persian and Greek Empires, but then the part about the Little Horn coming from one of the four horns never happened, and the part of the Transgression Desolating at the foundation of the set-apart place also never happened. Daniel 8:1-8 and 8:18-22 happened at that time, but there are no records of any of the rest of the prophecy happening in history. Antiochus came close to fulfilling this prophecy during the time of the Maccabees, but it never actually happened in any of the surviving records of that time or in the books of the Maccabees.

There are two primary differences between this prophecy in Daniel 8 and the prophecies in Daniel 11 and 12. The first is that the Daniel 8 prophecy is about a "transgression desolating" instead of an "abomination (disgusting object of idolatry) desolating" and the second is that the counting of days in Daniel 12 is 1,290 plus 45 instead of the 2,300 evenings and mornings in Daniel 8. The literal Hebrew in Daniel 8:14 says, "For two thousand three hundred evening morning," literally in Hebrew "evening morning," "erev boqer" עֶרֶב בֹּקֶר. There is also a third, small difference between them, in that Daniel 8 is specifically about the foundation of the set-apart place being attacked (the foundation of the set-apart place being what is known as the Temple Mount today, with the Western Wall of the foundation being the place where Orthodox Jews gather for prayer). This is something which is not mentioned at all as happening in connection with Daniel 11 or 12.

The Temple Mount in Jerusalem is today under the control of the Jerusalem Waqf, run by Palestinians but under the authority and funding of the Jordanian Monarchy. The Israeli government still has the ultimate authority over the ground of the Temple Mount itself, since the Temple Mount sits on the land of the nation of Israel, governed by Israeli law. In 1999 the Jerusalem Waqf started illegal renovations in the foundation of the Temple Mount in preparation to build another mosque. The dirt removed from the Temple Mount was taken in dump truck loads to a trash dump site, which archaeologists later discovered and searched through, finding thousands of artifacts from the First and Second Temples, from the set-apart place, that had stood on the site of the Temple Mount thousands of years ago. All of these thousands of artifacts are what archaeologically establish the fact that the First and Second Temples were built upon the Temple Mount and that they were not located anywhere else in the city of Jerusalem except on the Temple Mount. In 2004 the Israeli High Court of Justice banned the Jerusalem Waqf from removing any more of the dirt or ground from the Temple Mount. For many years after 2004 nothing more happened with this incident.

Then during the night of June 13, 2018 through the early morning of June 14, 2018, from sunset to sunrise or from evening to morning, in fulfillment of the exact time frame described in Daniel 8:14 of "evening morning," a large host or army of people, of over 1,000 Palestinians, in fulfillment of verse 8:12 converged onto the Temple Mount during the end of Ramadan. (The Hebrew in 8:12 literally says, "And a host shall be given over against the continual," but many translations add words about the Little Horn into this sentence that do not exist there in the original Hebrew. This host is separate from the Little Horn, not necessarily in direct association or contact with it in the prophecy.

The host or army of people came secretly at night, while no Jews were allowed on the Temple Mount still during the Ramadan festival, and began to remove more dirt from the Temple Mount, from the foundation of the set-apart place, throwing the foundation of the set-apart place down to the ground in fulfillment of 8:11. The Jerusalem Waqf had tried to remove this dirt for all of the years before since 2004, but had not succeeded. This time when it acted it succeeded and prospered in fulfillment of 8:12. It was also throwing the truth to the ground, the truth that the First and Second Temples, that the set-apart place of Yahuweh/Yehovah, had once stood on that ground of the Temple Mount. They were trying to destroy the evidence of this truth, removing the dirt filled with many artifacts of the set-apart place, and destroying them in the process. Archaeologists looking at the sight a few days later estimated that most of the artifacts in that area of dirt where they were digging and removing artifacts were destroyed by the Palestinians that night.

These remains and artifacts giving evidence of the set-apart place had been there continually in the foundation of the set-apart place for thousands of years, until they were removed that night. The literal Hebrew in 8:11 says, "It throws away the continual from Him." The Palestinian workers with shovels and other digging tools literally threw away these remains of the set-apart place from Yahuweh/Yehovah, destroying them and throwing them in a trash dump that still no one knows where they ended up. These set-apart remains of the set-apart place had been there continually in the foundation of the set-apart place for thousands of years, and then suddenly those continual things of the set-apart place were thrown away and destroyed, in fulfillment of 8:11. There were also ancient building structures of stone work from the First or

Second Temple time periods that they threw down and destroyed, breaking up all of the stone blocks and tiles and pillars into dust.

And the actions of this host of Palestinians was not only a transgression against Yahuweh/Yehovah, to attempt to remove the truth about him and his set-apart place that had stood on the Temple Mount, but literally a transgression against the law and court ruling of the Israeli High Court in 2004. It was because of this transgression, in fulfillment of 8:12, that this host of Palestinians went against and opposed the continual, both the continual foundation of the set-apart place and the continual set-apart remains of the set-apart place speaking the truth of its existence on that location, which the host of Palestinians tried to remove and destroy. And this transgression of the Jerusalem Waqf and the host of Palestinians against the Israeli High Court, and against Yahuweh/Yehovah ultimately, caused desolation, a transgression of desolation, to the foundation of the set-apart place and the continual remains and evidence of the set-apart place there, in fulfillment of 8:13. In this act during the night of June 13-14 the host of Palestinians and Jerusalem Waqf also trampled, literally trampled, the set-apart place under their feet, causing great destruction, as well as figuratively trampling the host of the Israeli people under their feet by violating the law of the land from the ruling of the Israeli High Court, and trampling the Jewish people under their feet by despising them and trying to remove any evidence of their having lived in the land of Israel before the Palestinians were there.

As to who was really behind this event of desolation, at this point there is no way to know. The Jerusalem Waqf is in control of the Temple Mount and gives orders in administration over that land, but ultimately the Jordanian Government and Jordanian Monarchy are in a higher authority in control of the Jerusalem Waqf, and there is no way to know at this point where the orders came from or who instigated this attack to the foundation of the set-apart place in the middle of the night. Even though this event fulfilled every word, precisely and exactly, in this Daniel 8:11-14 prophecy, there is still more that needs to be investigated and examined concerning this event and its prophecy connections, which unfortunately cannot be done at this point. Because what the Palestinians and Jerusalem Waqf were doing under the cover of darkness on the Temple Mount was illegal, they are not going to be openly talking about it or revealing everything that happened and what they did for fear of prosecution and criminal charges. The only reason we know anything at all about what happened is because a few of the Palestinian workers that night recorded video that they uploaded to social media. And the Israeli police with so many other things to deal with are certainly not going to be motivated to thoroughly investigate this incident and bring to light all that happened and who the people were that were involved, or what they were even trying to accomplish ultimately.

Unfortunately, because it was all done in secret under the cover of darkness, from evening to morning, there is no way to know at this point everything that happened, until Yahuweh/Yehovah decides it is time to uncover and reveal the rest of the missing details. [There is more on the Little Horn connections with the Daniel 8 prophecy later on.]

Section 8. The Finishing of the Proclaiming of the Good News Witness of Yeshua to All Nations:

The Prophecy of the Good News Taught in All the World as a Witness About Yeshua at the Time When the End Comes:

Matthew 24:14   Mark 13:10

Revelation 14:6-7

Prophecy Fulfillment of Verses **Matthew 24:14** and **Mark 13:10** – The key, primary part of this prophecy that has to be fulfilled is "all the nations." When the Good News of Yeshua has been proclaimed and taught in all of the world, to "all the nations," as a witness about Yeshua, then this prophecy has been fulfilled and the end can come. Yeshua does not say that the Good News has to be proclaimed or taught in every language in existence, nor that the Scriptures have to be translated into every language in existence, nor that the Good News has to be taught to every single tribe or family on the planet. Yeshua does not even say that every single person on the earth has to hear the Good News taught to them before this prophecy can be fulfilled. The only things that has to happen for this prophecy to be fulfilled is that every nation on the earth has had the Good News of Yeshua proclaimed and taught within its borders at some point in history, with a witness about Yeshua and the Good News being available to the people to hear if they want to in every nation on the earth.

Even about 100 years ago in the early 1900's there were still some nations in the Pacific Islands and in the deep Amazon jungles of South America that had not yet heard the Good News taught to them. But now today there is not a single nation left anywhere on the earth that has not had the Good News taught and proclaimed inside of that nation during the last 100 years. Even 400 years ago there were all of the Native American nations on the North and South American continents who had not heard or been taught the witness of the Good News yet. One of the primary reasons that the Congregationalist Pilgrims came to America on the *Mayflower* in 1620 was to bring the Good News of Yeshua to the nations of peoples living in the North America regions of the world.

William Bradford even stated this himself in his book *Of Plimoth Plantation*, of which his original autograph manuscript of the book still exists today. He wrote as one of their reasons for leaving Leiden to start a colony in the new world was, – [note: y^e is a 17th century abbreviation for the word "the"] – "Lastly (and which was not least) a great hope, & inward zeall they had of laying some good foundation (or at least to make some way therunto) for ye propagating & advancing ye gospell of ye kingdom of Christ in those remote parts of ye world; yea though they should be but even as stepping-stones unto others for ye performing of so great a work. These, & some other like reasons, moved them to undertake this resolution of their removall; the which they afterward prosecuted with so great difficulties, as by the sequell will appeare." [28] Because of the undertaking of the Pilgrims and other Christian outcasts of Europe who followed them to colonize in America, all of the Native American nations of North and South America have heard the Good News of

---

[28] *Of Plimoth Plantation*, William Bradford (1630-1650) ocn137336369, folio 16; State Library of Massachusetts, Boston.

Yeshua, even in spite of all of the later European emigrants who tried to force Pagan European culture on them, which has nothing to do with Christianity or the Good News. There is nowhere left on the entire North and South American continents where the Good News is not available to anyone who wants to seek after it and find it, when only 400 to 500 years ago there was nothing taught of the Good News at all in any of the western hemisphere.

In later years after the time of the Pilgrims and the New England missionaries who went to the Native American nations, William Carey pioneered bringing the Good News to India, Dr. David Livingstone pioneered taking the Good News to the heart of Africa, and James Hudson Taylor pioneered taking the Good News to China. The Good News first began to arrive in Japan in 1549 but the real witnessing of the Good News in Japan began after World War II, with the American military presence in the nation and the close relationship that came about between Japan and America after the war.

Anyone can go through the list of 197 nations, and there is not a single nation on the list that does not have living inside of that country, either believers in Yeshua and his Good News living in that nation, or people who have heard about the Good News of Yeshua and know all about him, but have rejected him and chosen not to believe in him. Even in the persecuted nations like North Korea and Iran there are millions of Christians. North Korea, together with South Korea, was the most Christian nation in Asia before the Communist takeover of the country. Saudi Arabia and the Arabian Peninsula countries in the heart of Islam still have some Christians living in their borders, and most Muslims have heard about Yeshua and have knowledge <u>about</u> the Good News, even if they choose not to believe or follow it or search deeper to know Yeshua and his Good News more. In Muslim countries it is not illegal to know about Yeshua and the Good News, because he is written about in the Quran. It is only illegal to like Yeshua and choose to follow him, and to believe in the Good News.

The simple Good News of Yeshua, recorded in the Books of the Good News (Gospels) is known and taught all throughout the earth, and anyone in the world has the opportunity to get past all of the manmade Christian religious traditions in all of the denominations to get to the pure truth of what the original words of the Good News of Yeshua are if they want to. Anyone who wants to seek after Yeshua can now find him without anything stopping them anywhere in the world. All those who have not yet heard the Good News or know about Yeshua have access in every nation where they live in the world to hear the Good News and be taught about it if they want to. Every Muslim in every Muslim nation has heard about Yeshua and knows about him even if they might still reject the truth about who he really was or decide not to believe in him; or decide to believe in him and suffer persecution from other Muslims in those nations. The Good News of Yeshua is available to everyone now who wants to hear it on the earth. It is mission accomplished; the Good News has now been taught and proclaimed as a witness about Yeshua across "all the nations," every single literal nation that exists on the earth.

Psalms 98:3 literally reads, "All the ends of the earth have seen the Yeshua of our God." The name Yeshua <u>ישוע</u>, meaning "salvation," is literally written in the Hebrew of this verse " ראו כל אפסי ארץ את <u>ישועת</u> אלהינו." And in the original Hebrew Gospel of Matthew, Yeshua makes a connection here to this verse in the way that he talks in Matthew 24:14, saying, "And this Good News shall be taught in all the ends of the earth for a witness about Me across all the nations. And then the end comes…"²⁹ In the original Hebrew Yeshua says that the Good News would one day be taught "in all the ends of the earth for a witness about Me," when "all the ends of the earth have seen the Yeshua/salvation of our God" in Psalms 98:3. There are people through history who have believed in Yeshua and experienced the salvation of Yahuweh/Yehovah through him in every nation on earth now, in all the ends of the earth to the farthest extreme edges of civilization.

The other interesting thing in the original Hebrew is that Yeshua says that the Good News would be taught "across all the nations," instead of "to all the nations" as in the Greek translation. The Hebrew here says, "al kol hagoyim" "על כל הגוים," which is translated literally as "upon all the nations" or "above all the nations" or "across all the nations." The way that Yeshua worded his sentence in the original Hebrew that he spoke it in was prophesying about our time today in the last few decades since the early 1900's when the Good News would actually be proclaimed and taught literally "above" all the nations of the earth, through the radio and television airwaves, then later through satellite television and wireless internet. The Good News is literally being taught in the air constantly "above" all the nations for anyone with a device able to communicate with the different airwaves to pick it up and hear it. We are living at the time when this prophecy is completed and finished in every detail, completely fulfilled with nothing preventing the end from coming with the Disgusting Idol (Abomination) Desolating.

Prophecy Fulfillment of Verses **Revelation 14:6-7** – This prophecy in Revelation also describes the days that we are living in today, with a messenger flying in mid-heaven above the earth, in the space where satellites orbit the earth, holding onto and announcing the Good News to everyone on the earth, to every nation and tribe and tongue and people. From the air and space in orbit above the earth the Good News is now literally being announced to the world below, available to absolutely everyone now in every nation and in every tribe. There are only about a dozen small tribes about the size of small families left on the earth that have not been contacted from the outside world and have no access to the Good News. All other tribes on the earth have access to hear the Good News if they want to at any time. And this is during the 3.5 years of Great Tribulation, after the end has already come with the Disgusting Idol (Abomination) Desolating, that this messenger is flying in mid-heaven announcing the Good News of Yeshua and at the exact same time warning everyone on the earth that the "hour of His judgement" has come.

This is in the final hours of the Great Tribulation as Yahuweh/Yehovah's judgement is about to come on the earth showing that, even though the time of the "proclaiming" and "teaching" of the Good News to all nations is completed already now, there will still be some "announcing" of the Good News from the air waves and satellites all the way up to the very end of the Great Tribulation and the day of Yeshua's return at that time, to bring judgement on the earth. Even though there are currently today about 7,150 recognized official languages in use on the earth, the actual number of languages that most people in the world are able to understand and speak is much smaller in the dozens or scores. Most people in the world are able to communicate in just a few languages, including such languages as English, Spanish, Portuguese, French,

---

²⁹ See Appendix: Hebrew Matthew Chapter 24

Arabic, German, Italian, Russian, Mandarin Chinese, Hindi Indian, Farsi Persian, Turkish, Malay, Korean, Japanese, Fula, Swahili, and Afrikaans.

There are fewer and fewer people left on the earth who are unable to communicate in at least one of these aforementioned languages, which means that the Good News of Yeshua being communicated to everyone in every tongue or language that they can understand is growing less and less all of the time. The Good News of Yeshua is being broadcast or "announced" from the air, literally from the mid-heaven, in almost every language now on the earth that people on the earth are able to communicate in and understand, in fulfillment of this prophecy. And this prophecy in Revelation 14 is about a messenger in the spiritual realm announcing the Good News during the Great Tribulation, showing that at the time when the proclaiming and teaching of the Good News to all the nations is completed and finished by men and women on the earth, in fulfillment of Matthew 24, Yeshua is still witnessing his Good News in the spiritual realm to the people on the earth, through spiritual means.

Even in the nations where there are no missionaries or physical people able to go and teach the Good News, Yeshua is showing up to the people in those nations in dreams and visions and spreading his Good News himself without any Christians or believers even having to go to those nations, especially in the Muslim and Buddhist/Hindu nations across central and south Asia. Verse 14:6 is certainly in its time of fulfillment now, and verse 14:7 is coming on its way, as the warning of Yahuweh/Yehovah's judgement of the earth comes nearer and nearer to the time of his coming. This is a good time to fear/respect Yahuweh/Yehovah and turn to him in repentance before the hour of his judgement has arrived at the end of the Great Tribulation.

Mockers Come in the Last Days Who Refuse to Believe in the Scriptures or the Coming of Yeshua, Simultaneously with the Same Timeframe of the Fulfillment of the Prophecy About the Good News of Yeshua being Taught to All the Nations:

2 Peter 3:1-7

Prophecy Fulfillment of Verses **2 Peter 3:1-7** – Peter warned that in the last days, at the time of Yeshua's return, there would be mockers who would come, mocking about how Yeshua has still not returned like he promised, and that the world has continued on normally like it always has for many generations. This is at the time when the teaching of the Good News to all the nations is completed, there are still those who do not believe in Yeshua and mock how he still has not come back, mocking how there are no signs happening in the world to show that he would even be coming back soon. The teaching and proclaiming the Good News to all the nations on earth has nothing to do with everybody believing the Good News or even large numbers of people believing in the Good News of Yeshua.

Even up to the very end of this world of man, at Yeshua's coming, when the world will be destroyed in fire in the same way it was once destroyed in the flood, there will still be people who deny that the flood that destroyed the world ever happened, and who will never believe that Yahuweh/Yehovah will be destroying the world again in fire. The teaching of the Good News to all the nations was only ever for the purpose of being a witness about Yeshua himself, and that his words and prophecies are true. It is only for the purpose of the witness about Yeshua that the Good News has been taught to all the nations and all the ends of the earth, not for the purpose of making every single person on the earth into a believer in Yeshua. Only those who want to follow him will follow him, and that is all that matters. This prophecy about mockers who deny that the flood ever happened, and who believe that the world can go on forever as it always has without having to worry about Yeshua coming to judge the world one day, is certainly also being fulfilled and happening today at the same time that the proclaiming and teaching of the Good News to all the nations is now completed and fulfilled.

At the Same Time when the Teaching of the Good News to the World is Finished, All Those Who are Not Killed by the Judgment Plagues at the Time of the End Still Refuse to Repent and Believe in the Good News of Yeshua:

Revelation 9:20-21

Word for Word Prophecy Examination of Unfulfilled Verses **Revelation 9:20-21** – By the time of the end of the Great Tribulation, during the Sixth Trumpet, which has not yet happened, there is hardly anyone left on the earth who is willing to repent and change their ways, to turn back to Yahuweh/Yehovah anymore. In spite of all of the judgements and plagues on the earth, there is nothing anymore that causes the people on the earth to turn away in repentance from their idols and sins. No one wants to change their hearts anymore, because their hearts are hardened to do what they want to do, and they do not want righteousness or the ways of Yahuweh/Yehovah. This is also in process of happening simultaneously with the fulfillment of the proclaiming the Good News to all the nations. As another sign that that time is finished now of taking the Good News to all the nations, more and more people on the earth everyday are turning farther and farther away from Yahuweh/Yehovah and his Good News, going deeper into sin and rebellion against him, and refusing more and more to repent.

The time of the traditional revivals/awakenings of the last 3,500 years is coming to an end simply because there is almost no one left on the earth who wants to repent of their sin anymore or change their lives to be obedient to Yahuweh/Yehovah's way of life in his Torah instruction, including Christians who do not want to repent and change their lives to believe in Yeshua. Even most Christians today are living unrepentant lives of sin and want nothing to do with Scripture or the Commands and Words of the God of Israel in Scripture. All they want is their imaginary false gods of the world and culture today that will give them whatever they selfishly want, and they have no desire to repent and give up their will for Yahuweh/Yehovah's will to be done. The repentance on the earth is rapidly disappearing as is prophesied in Revelation 9, as we move very rapidly closer and closer to the time of the Sixth Trumpet at the end of the Great Tribulation, when the harvest of the wheat of the earth is complete and there are no other people on the earth who want Yeshua or the Good News anymore. Even though this prophecy is not completely fulfilled yet, it is very quickly getting to the point of fulfillment as it is happening right now for the first time on a global scale in the world today, right at the same time that the Good News of Yeshua has been proclaimed to all the nations as a witness about him.

Not All of the Cities of Israel will have Heard the Good News of Yeshua Before the Son of Adam (Yeshua) Comes at the End of the Great Tribulation:

Matthew 10:23

Matthew 24:27-31

Word for Word Prophecy Examination of Unfulfilled Verses **Matthew 10:23** and **Matthew 24:27-31** – In Matthew 10 Yeshua slipped in a little prophecy about his coming. As is shown in Matthew 24, whenever he talks about the coming of the Son of Adam, he is talking about his own coming at the end of the Great Tribulation in the future, and here in Matthew 10 he has put a little prophecy into his words, telling his disciples (at that present time and his disciples in the future) that they will not even be able to go through all of the cities of Israel proclaiming the coming of the "reign of the heavens" before he comes as the Son of Adam in the future.

Yeshua is letting us know that there will be some cities and towns and villages on the earth, even in Israel, that will not have had any physical person go into them and proclaim the Good News and the reign of the heavens before he comes, even though the Good News will have been sitting around available for the people to read in books or hear on the radio or watch on television or the internet. There will be some people who will have never heard the Good News at the time of his coming, even though the Good News will have been broadcast across all the nations of the earth so that everyone alive at that time has had the opportunity to hear it if they want to seek and find it where it is available in their nation. In order for the prophecy of the Good News being taught to all the nations to be fulfilled there is no requirement that every single human being on the earth has to have heard the Good News before the end can come and the Great Tribulation happen. The only requirement is that it is available in all the nations, but the Good News of Yeshua will not be proclaimed in every single city or village on the earth before Yeshua, the Son of Adam, comes.

Section 9. **The Disgusting Idol (Abomination) Desolating (1,290 Days):**

The Antiochus IV Epiphanes Disgusting Idol (Abomination) Desolating Prophecy Already Fulfilled at the Time of the Maccabees Revolt:

Daniel 11:1-45

Prophecy Fulfillment of Verses **Daniel 11:1-45** – Anyone can go look for themselves to see all of the details of how this prophecy in Daniel chapter 11 was fulfilled over a period of time spanning about 325 years during the days of the Persian and Greek empires, but here is a summary of the fulfillment. Everything following is recorded in the histories of the Greek Empire that were written at that time by various Greek historians, as well as in the First and Second Books of Maccabees.

Daniel 11:1-2 – This prophecy begins with the days of the king of the Persian Empire known as **Darius I the Great**. He was the first of the Persian kings of the empire to invade Greece, but his invasion attempt failed. This is the starting point of the prophecy, when the prophecy was written while Darius I was still alive. After his death the prophecy says there are three more kings of Persia and then a fourth king who is richer than the previous ones, who stirs up the governing rulership of Greece with his power and riches. The four kings that came after Darius I, who continued to fight against Greece, were:

1. **Xerxes I** – Continued his father's invasion of Greece and burned the city of Athens along with many of the Athenian temples of the city in 480 B.C.E.
2. **Artaxerxes I** – Continued to fight against Greece
_ Xerxes II reigned for 45 days and was not involved with Greece, nor is listed in the ancient king lists
_ Sogdinius reigned for 6 months and was not involved with Greece, nor is listed in the ancient king lists
3. **Darius II** – Continued to fight against Greece
4. **Artaxerxes II** – Was forced to fight against Greece because of his younger brother trying to take the throne from him with a Greek hired mercenary army; he was also very wealthy, known for his many expensive building projects and wealthy enough to afford having 350 wives and many children

It was because of the wars of these four Persian kings with Greece, from Xerxes I to Artaxerxes II, that they stirred up the Greeks against the Persian Empire.

Daniel 11:3-4 – This part of the prophecy is referring to **Alexander the Great** who came from Greece/Macedonia, Yavan in Hebrew, and conquered the Persian Empire by about 330 B.C.E. After his death the empire was divided up into four parts, to the four winds of the heavens, but it was not divided by his descendants, nor did he have any descendants that continued to reign. His rule was uprooted and divided among others, fulfilling the prophecy exactly that Daniel had written down hundreds of years before, becoming the four separate kingdoms of Seleucid, Ptolemy, Antigonid, and Attalid.

Daniel 11:5-6 – For the rest of this prophecy in Daniel, the "king of the South" refers to the Ptolemy Kingdom of Greece based in Egypt in the south, and the "king of the North" refers to the Seleucid Kingdom of Greece in the north, based in Babylon in Iraq and stretching from Turkey and Lebanon to Persia (Iran). **Berenice Phernophorus**, daughter of the king of the South, **Ptolemy II Philadelphus**, was given in marriage to the king of the North, **Antiochus II Theos**, in about 252 B.C.E. as part of a peace agreement between their two kingdoms (Ptolemy and Seleucid). But this daughter did not keep her hold on power and she was kicked out by her husband Antiochus II Theos after the death of her father Ptolemy II Philadelphus in 246 B.C.E., as he went back to his first wife.

Daniel 11:7-19 – These next verses in the prophecy refer to the wars between Ptolemy in the south and Seleucid in the north over the next years, especially focusing on the war between **Antiochus III the Great** of Seleucid and **Ptolemy IV Philopater** in 219 to 217 B.C.E. Ptolemy IV in the south defeated Antiochus III in the end, despite the initial success of Antiochus III in taking land from the Ptolemy Empire, exactly as was prophesied by Yahuweh/Yehovah in Daniel. Even though Ptolemy IV was able to defeat Antiochus III, there was a revolt within Egypt against him, as was prophesied, in 206 to 204 B.C.E., with the city of Thebes and other places in Egypt being captured by the rebels for a time. Antiochus III and Ptolemy IV fought each other along the Mediterranean coast with the nation of Judah caught in the middle, but in the end Antiochus III, the king of the North, failed to conquer or defeat the Ptolemy Empire.

Daniel 11:20 – This part of the prophecy is referring to Antiochus III's son and successor of the Seleucid Empire, **Seleucus IV Philopater**, who tried to get taxes out of the wealth of the Second Temple and the city of Jerusalem, but failed to do so.

Daniel 11:21-45 – The rest of this prophecy is all about the king of the North, **Antiochus IV Epiphanes**, the son of Antiochus III and brother of Seleucus IV. As the prophecy in Daniel said would happen, the reign of the Seleucid Empire was given to the son of Seleucus IV after his death, and it was not given to Antiochus IV. But later, exactly as the prophecy in Daniel 11 states, Antiochus IV took away the reign from his nephew peaceably and through flattery and deceit. Antiochus IV took the reign away from his nephew while his nephew Antiochus was still alive, and eventually probably executed him. After this he went peacefully through the nation of Judah, as he built his power and army, and then turned against the Ptolemy Empire in the south.

Exactly as prophesied, at first Antiochus IV was successful in his conquest of the Ptolemy Empire, making it all the way into the heart of Egypt (Mitsrayim), gaining many riches in plunder from there, with Put (Libya) and Kush (Sudan) at his steps. But ships came from Kittim (ancient Hebrew name for Italy and the sea faring island and coastal areas of the northern Mediterranean) and told Antiochus IV that they would ally with the Ptolemy Empire against him if he did not leave Egypt. At this point Antiochus IV lost heart to continue his campaign and returned home, with great rage back through the land of Judah, where he sacked the city of Jerusalem and set up the "Disgusting Idol (Abomination) Desolating" or "Appalling Abomination" at the set-apart place in the Second Temple in about 167 B.C.E. But he came into the city of Jerusalem by flatteries and trickery and enacted laws against the Jewish people to prevent them from practicing the true worship of Yahuweh/Yehovah in Scripture. The time of this "Abomination" of Greek idolatry lasted for three years to 164 B.C.E. according to the records in Maccabees, fulfilling the prophecy in Daniel 11, but not the prophecy of 1,290 days in Daniel 12.

The nations of Edom, Mo'av, and 'Ammon, which make up modern day Jordan, escaped from Antiochus IV and never came under his control or attack, but the nation of Egypt he was able to reach. He left Judah when there were disturbing reports that came to him from the north and the east, from the north-east, about Mithradates I of Parthia attacking the Seleucid Empire in Afghanistan in 167 B.C.E. He rode out to fight against him as is said in the prophecy, and then after defeating Mithradates I, as he returned home he pitched his tents between the seas, the Caspian Sea and the Persian Gulf, in Isfahan, Persia (Iran). And there in 164 B.C.E. he came to his end with no one to help him, from a parasite or intestinal illness, as he was on his way to Jerusalem, to the set-apart mountain where the set-apart place sits, intending to deal with the very successful Maccabean revolt that had retaken Jerusalem for their own and removed the abominations at the set-apart place. The Festival of Hanukkah came from these events that fulfilled Daniel 11.

Conclusion: All of Daniel chapter 11 was fulfilled previously in history, up to the time of Antiochus IV Epiphanes. But none of Daniel chapter 12 was fulfilled at that time. The First Book of Maccabees even records the exact dates of when the Disgusting Idol (Abomination) Desolating was in existence at the set-apart place, and it only adds up to exactly 3 years, not the 1,290 days or 3.5 years of the prophecy in Daniel 12. The Abomination in Daniel 11 happened at that time, but the Abomination in Daniel 12 never happened in ancient history, indicating that these are two entirely different and separate prophecies about two entirely different and separate "Disgusting Idol (Abomination) Desolating" events in Daniel 11 and Daniel 12.

Shadow Picture / Type of the Disgusting Idol (Abomination) Desolating:
Exodus 32:1-35
Examination of Verses **Exodus 32:1-35** – When Daniel 11 was fulfilled at the time of the Maccabees, it became a shadow picture of what a Disgusting Idol Desolating at a set-apart place looks like. The events of the past that are connected with fulfillments of Yahuweh/Yehovah's prophecies or events he is involved in become shadow pictures of future events and fulfillments of prophecies. The future fulfillments never happen exactly the same way as the past shadow pictures, but the shadow pictures do become a pattern to help understand future fulfillments of prophecies when they happen in the present.

Another such shadow picture of a Disgusting Idol Desolating at a set-apart place like the one Yeshua talks about in Matthew 24 is in Exodus 32, when the children of Israel create a Disgusting Idol Desolating, the golden calf idol, and place it at the base of Yahuweh/Yehovah's set-apart place on Mount Sinai. The main elements in this shadow picture are:

1. Exodus 32:1-4, 19 – The children of Israel themselves create a physical object idol to worship as the image of the God Yahuweh/Yehovah, the God of Israel, but it is really an image of a false, Pagan Egyptian god. They say that they are worshipping Yahuweh/Yehovah, but are not actually doing so in reality. The people placed this idol of a golden calf in their camp at the base of Mount Sinai, at the foot of the mountain of Yahuweh/Yehovah, Mount Sinai, at the edge of the set-apart place.

2. Exodus 32:5-6 – The children of Israel say they are making a festival to Yahuweh/Yehovah, a festival which he has not commanded or given any instruction about, a festival or appointed time of worshipping Yahuweh/Yehovah that was made up by man on the basis of worshipping false gods and not created by Yahuweh/Yehovah himself.

3. Exodus 32:6, 17-19, 25 – The children of Israel were playing and dancing and singing with music, having a good time with the festival that they had created for themselves, setting up an abominable idol at the base of the set-apart place of Yahuweh/Yehovah. They did not recognize that they were doing anything evil or wrong, because they were doing their idol worship for Yahuweh/Yehovah, the God of Israel.

4. Exodus 32:1-4, 22-24, 35 – Aharon (Aaron), the brother of Mosheh (Moses), was the one who made the golden calf idol, the Disgusting Idol Desolating placed at the set-apart place. Even some of the chosen (elect) were deceived by this worship of false gods and idols, because it appeared that they were doing this for the true God Yahuweh/Yehovah.

5. Exodus 32:7-14, 26-34 – The children of Israel discovered that what they were doing was wrong and a sin against Yahuweh/Yehovah and his covenant, as Yahuweh/Yehovah's wrath and judgement came on them. They did not understand how serious this idol worship was, and that this sin would cause their names to be blotted out of Yahuweh/Yehovah's book of life, and he had to teach them the seriousness of idolatry as a shadow picture recorded for all future generations to understand the weight and gravity of worshipping false gods and idols and saying that Yahuweh/Yehovah is the one being worshipped.

This same shadow picture is in the fulfillment of Daniel 11 recorded in the First and Second Books of Maccabees, where it is the Jews themselves who bring in the worship of false, Pagan, Greek gods, welcoming Antiochus IV Epiphanes into Jerusalem with his new laws to replace the true worship of Yahuweh/Yehovah in Scripture with a false worship of him based on Greek culture and religion. The true worship of Yahuweh/Yehovah was almost lost at that time, as any copies of the Hebrew Scriptures in the Tanak (Old Testament) were ordered to be destroyed, and there was an attempt by Antiochus IV and the Jews who were with him to completely erase all record of Scripture and of Yahuweh/Yehovah.

If Antiochus IV had succeeded at that time, by the time Yeshua came to the earth 150 years later, there would have been no Scriptures or records of the prophecies in Scripture left in existence for him to fulfill. There would have been nobody left on the earth who even knew the truth about Yahuweh/Yehovah or his covenant or his prophecies or his existence, because all of the records in the books of Scripture would have been wiped out and ceased to exist from the earth and from among the Jewish people. Yahuweh/Yehovah miraculously saved his Scriptures and the truth about himself and worship of him at that time through the Maccabean revolt that defeated the armies of all of the nations around them, including the armies of a vast empire, with an inferior number of men. The Maccabees family was certainly not completely clean and set-apart themselves in their following of Yahuweh/Yehovah, which is why the books about them are not included in Scripture, but Yahuweh/Yehovah still used them to save the true record of his prophecies and commands in Scripture for future generations to know him, and so that the records of the prophecies would still be in existence for the coming of Yeshua to fulfill them 150 years later.

Everyone always looks at the physical danger to the physical body that comes from the Disgusting Idol Desolating, because of persecution against those who still follow and adhere to the truth in the Scriptures. But the real danger that is revealed in the shadow pictures of Exodus 32 and the fulfillment of Daniel 11 recorded in Maccabees is the spiritual danger of the Disgusting Idol Desolating. In both shadow pictures the large majority of the nation of Israel went after the spiritual deception of the Disgusting Idol Desolating. Only a very small minority stood against the Disgusting Idol Desolating at the set-apart place in the records of both instances, because most believed in the deception. It is the spiritual danger of losing eternal life and salvation from the Disgusting Idol Desolating that is the far more dangerous thing to flee from than any physical harm to the body.

The Sacrifices and Offerings were Already Completed by the Sacrifice of the Lamb Yeshua, and therefore cannot be the Continual that is Removed; Only Yahuweh/Yehovah Himself Forgives and Takes Away People's Sin, Not Sacrificed Animals:

Exodus 32:30-34   Exodus 34:8-9

Jeremiah 31:31-34

Jeremiah 33:7-8

Daniel 9:24-27

Hosea 6:4-6

Psalms 103:1-3

Mark 2:5-12

John 1:29-30

Hebrews 9:1 – 10:31

Examination of Verses **Jeremiah 31:31-34** and **Daniel 9:24-27** and **John 1:29-30** and **Hebrews 9:1 – 10:31** and **Hosea 6:4-7** – In Daniel 9:24-27 the anointed one, Messiah, is prophesied to cease sacrifices and offerings as part of the strengthening of Yahuweh/Yehovah's covenant that is for many people (those who accept it). And in Jeremiah 31:31-34 this covenant that is strengthened is also renewed and made new by Yahuweh/Yehovah, so that he himself forgives the crookednesses and sins of his nation Israel. This was through Yeshua as the Lamb sacrifice for sin, as John the Immerser declared of Yeshua in John 1:29-30, "See, the Lamb of God who takes away the sins of the world." This is further explained in detail in Hebrews 9:1 – 10:31 that through Yeshua as the High Priest (through the order of Malkitsedeq), Yahuweh/Yehovah is able to forgive our sins through the cleansing blood and sacrifice of the Passover Lamb Yeshua.

This means that the sacrifices of animals are complete and not needed in order for Yahuweh/Yehovah to forgive us through the blood of the sacrificed animals. This is why Yeshua, as the Messiah or anointed one fulfilling Daniel 9 causes the sacrifices and offerings to cease, because he has become the complete and final sacrifice and offering for the forgiveness and cleansing of sin. This is a basic concept that every believer in Yeshua should know about and already understand that the sacrifices of animals is completed and made final now through Yeshua by Yahuweh/Yehovah's own prophecy and instruction in Daniel 9. In Hosea 6:4-7

Yahuweh/Yehovah himself also says that he does not delight in sacrifices, but instead he delights in kindness, and he delights in people knowing him more than in the offerings they bring.

Yahuweh/Yehovah does not like having the animal sacrifices in place, and would rather that people be kind to each other, without sin, so that there is no reason to do the animal sacrifices ever again. This is why he strengthened his covenant with Israel, making it new through Yeshua, so that all those who accept that covenant can be made clean without continuous animal sacrifices, which were only ever the shadow picture of Yeshua in the first place. He would rather that everyone know him and follow his ways of eternal life instead of sinning and requiring continuous saving from death, transgressing his covenant like Adam. There is nowhere in prophecy or in Yahuweh/Yehovah's instructions in Scripture that says he wants to bring back animal sacrifices, nor any command in any prophecy that he has given for the animal sacrifices to be brought back again after the Second Temple was destroyed, nor any prophecy about animal sacrifices being necessary to bring back again after the destruction of the Second Temple in order for people's sins to be forgiven.

Because Yahuweh/Yehovah has already ceased the sacrifices and offerings, and has given no indication in prophecy or Scripture that he ever wants to bring those sacrifices back again, "the continual" spoken of in the unfulfilled prophecy of Daniel 12, that Yeshua refers to in Matthew 24, cannot be the sacrifices and offerings at the set-apart place. "The continual" that is removed that Yeshua refers to from Daniel that is still coming in the future has to be a different "continual" than the sacrifices of animals that took place at the set-apart place up until Yahuweh/Yehovah ceased them with the destruction of the Second Temple.

Examination of Verses **Exodus 32:30-34** and **Exodus 34:8-9** and **Jeremiah 31:34** and **Jeremiah 33:7-8** and **Psalms 103:1-3** and **Mark 2:5-12** – It should be clear as a very basic concept in Scripture that it is only God, Yahuweh/Yehovah himself, who forgives sin, not dead, sacrificed animals that forgive sin. It is Yahuweh/Yehovah, as God, who takes away and forgives people's sins through the death and blood of one who is perfect and innocent and who has never committed any sin. In Exodus 32 and 34 Mosheh (Moses) is asking Yahuweh/Yehovah to forgive the sins of the nation of Israel that they sinned against him, not a dead, sacrificed animal to forgive their sins. And in Jeremiah 31 and 33 Yahuweh/Yehovah himself says that he is the one who will forgive the sins and crookednesses of Israel and cleanse them from it. It is the same in Psalms 103 where it is Yahuweh/Yehovah, not dead, sacrificed animals, who forgives all of our crookednesses.

Even during the time of Yeshua, such as in Mark 2, the Pharisees (Orthodox Rabbinic Jews) recognized that it is only God who forgives sins. They were angry at Yeshua forgiving sins, because they did not want to accept that Yeshua is the God of Israel, Yahuweh/Yehovah, who is the God of Abraham, Isaac, and Jacob, the creator of the heavens and the earth, who is the only one able to forgive sins.

Sacrifices of Animals are Only to be Done when Yahuweh/Yehovah Commands It, in the Exact Way He Commands, Not According to the Commands of Men:

1 Samuel 13:1-14

1 Samuel 15:18-26

Isaiah 29:13

Examination of Verses **1 Samuel 13:1-14** and **1 Samuel 15:18-26** and **Isaiah 29:13** – In 1 Samuel 13 and 15 there is a clear example of when the sacrificing of animals to Yahuweh/Yehovah is a sin and rebellion against him, when it is not done according to his command and instruction. Saul did the sacrifice to Yahuweh/Yehovah on his own, instead of waiting for Samuel to come and do it according to the command of Yahuweh/Yehovah. And because he did the sacrifices to Yahuweh/Yehovah in a disobedient way, that was not according to his command, Saul's family was removed from the throne over Israel. And Samuel said to Saul in 15:22 that it is better to obey Yahuweh/Yehovah than to perform sacrifices of animals to him, or give offerings to him.

It is more important to obey Yahuweh/Yehovah in his commands and his words, than to give offerings and sacrifices to him. And it is especially important to only perform sacrifices to Yahuweh/Yehovah when he says to do them and according to the way he says to do them. He has provided detailed instructions on the way sacrifices of animals are to be done to him in his Torah (the first five books of Moses), and the sacrifices of animals are only to be done in obedience to him. If they are done in any other disobedient way, they are actually a sin and rebellion against Yahuweh/Yehovah, according to Samuel's words in 13 and 15. And the consequences of doing disobedient sacrifices of animals against the will of Yahuweh/Yehovah are severe, to the point that Saul was even cut off from his reign over Israel over this issue.

The sacrifices and offerings were already ceased by Yeshua, the anointed one or Messiah, and they should only be resumed at the direct command of Yahuweh/Yehovah himself. Otherwise, any sacrifices of animals that are done without his express command to resume them again, can never be set-apart (holy), and cannot be the set-apart "continual" prophesied in Daniel 12 and referenced by Yeshua in Matthew 24 and Mark 13. The sacrifices themselves that are <u>not</u> done according to the command or will of Yahuweh/Yehovah become an abomination of rebellion and sin and disobedience against him.

Yahuweh/Yehovah warns in Isaiah 29 about people who say with their mouths that they are obeying and following him, but instead obey and follow commands of men. Obeying a command of men at any time, even when the people say they are doing this command of men for Yahuweh/Yehovah, is not obedience to Yahuweh/Yehovah. And those people do not know Yahuweh/Yehovah, because their hearts are far away from him as they obey the commands of men instead of his commands. In Matthew 15 Yeshua used this prophecy description in Isaiah 29 in reference to the Rabbinic Orthodox Jews (Pharisees) who obey the commands of men instead of the command of Yahuweh/Yehovah in the Torah of Moses. At that time in the 1st Century C.E. the Rabbinic Orthodox Jews had not yet written down their commands of men, and their commands were called the Oral Torah of the Rabbis. It was not until a few hundred years later that those Oral Torah commands were written down into the Talmud, and the Talmud is what the Orthodox Jews follow and obey today, not the Torah of Moses in Scripture.

The Talmud is filled with commands of Rabbis, commands of men, which are contrary and in rebellion against the commands of Yahuweh/Yehovah in his Torah written down in Scripture. The Orthodox Jews follow these commands of men in the Talmud as a higher authority than the word of Yahuweh/Yehovah in Scripture, and even have changed the commands of Yahuweh/Yehovah concerning sacrifices and offerings and the way the priests do the services at the set-apart place, in direct disobedience to Yahuweh/Yehovah. As long as they follow the commands of men in the Talmud, the Orthodox Jews are unable to obey Yahuweh/Yehovah in sacrificing to him according to his commands and instructions, and therefore any sacrifices they do will always be out of disobedience to him and cannot be set-apart. According to Isaiah 29 just the act of obeying the commands of men takes a person's heart far away from Yahuweh/Yehovah, and away from obedience to him.

Orthodox Judaism (Phariseeism) was only just beginning to come into existence at the time of the Maccabees, and had not yet overtaken the set-apart duties of the priests in the sacrifices and offerings at the Second Temple with their commands of men that disobey the commands of Yahuweh/Yehovah. This is why the fulfillment of Daniel 11 worked with "the continual" referring to the sacrifices and offerings and lighting of the menorah and replenishing of the show bread at that time. It was still set-apart because the Levi priests were still carrying out the duties of the set-apart place in strict obedience to Yahuweh/Yehovah's commands in Scripture. Today this is no longer the case, with no one in Christianity or Judaism who follows the commands of Yahuweh/Yehovah in Scripture concerning the "continuals" performed by the priests at the set-apart place. Now today there is no way for "the continual" to refer to the sacrifices and offerings, because there is no one who is either willing or able to do them in perfect obedience to Yahuweh/Yehovah, which means they cannot be set-apart anymore as they were in the time of the Maccabees at the fulfillment of Daniel 11.

The Great Tribulation Disgusting Idol (Abomination) Desolating Prophecies Spoken of by Yeshua that is Fulfilled in the Days Before His Coming:
Daniel 9:27
Daniel 12:1-12
Matthew 24:15, 21-26   Mark 13:14, 19-23

Prophecy Fulfillment of Verses **Matthew 24:15, 21-26** and **Mark 13:14, 19-23** and **Daniel 12:1-12** and **Daniel 9:27** – The reason that Matthew adds the note, "let the reader understand," into Yeshua's prophecy about the Disgusting Idol Desolating in Matthew 24:15 is because part of the Disgusting Idol Desolating prophecy was already fulfilled, the part in Daniel 11, with Antiochus IV Epiphanes. But there was part of the prophecy in Daniel 12 which was not fulfilled at that time, meaning that Daniel 12 still has to be fulfilled, but there is no requirement that Daniel 11 ever has to be fulfilled or happen again. It can happen again in a pattern or shadow picture way, different from how it was fulfilled before, but there is no requirement that Daniel 11 has to happen again.

After sunset on the night of March 23-24, 2021, on the 10th day of the 1st month, the day Yahuweh/Yehovah commands for the choosing of the lamb to be sacrificed four days later at Passover, there was a gathering of Rabbinic Orthodox Jews at the base of the Temple Mount, across the road from the Western Wall, for the sacrificing of a Passover lamb for the nation of Israel. This was the first time since the destruction of the Second Temple almost 2,000 years ago that such a sacrifice had taken place in proximity of the set-apart place at the Temple Mount. There had been other "reenactments" of the Passover sacrifice done much farther away in the vicinity of the city of Jerusalem, but this was the first that was at the Temple Mount itself.

The year before, in the spring of 2020, they had tried to do a lamb sacrifice for Passover in Jerusalem (not in the vicinity of the Temple Mount), but were stopped by the COVID plague that Yahuweh/Yehovah had sent on the land. Yahuweh/Yehovah did not intervene to help the Orthodox Jews to be able to do the sacrifice anyways, in spite of the COVID plague, showing very clearly that it is not his will or desire for the ritual animal sacrifices to continue at the set-apart place in Jerusalem. He very clearly showed the Orthodox Jews that to try to continue with the sacrifices and restarting all of the Temple/Tabernacle duties of the set-apart place would be disobedience to him. Over and over again through the last 100 years Yahuweh/Yehovah has supernaturally intervened to help the Jews return to the land of Israel and become a nation again and have their capital Jerusalem back under their control. At the same time he has also over and over again supernaturally intervened to stop the Jews from getting control of the Temple Mount again and being able to rebuild a Third Temple or Tabernacle on the Temple Mount, showing clearly that it is not his will for a physical set-apart place to be rebuilt there again, nor for the sacrifices and offerings to resume there at a set-apart place again.

This sign in 2020 was again very clear that Yahuweh/Yehovah was using COVID to stop the Orthodox Jews from being able to do the Passover animal sacrifice that year, because he does not want it to continue. If the Passover sacrifice they were trying to do was truly obedient to Yahuweh/Yehovah and in his will, he would have made sure it went ahead no matter what stood in the way, removing all obstacles as he did in bringing the nation of Israel into existence again with Jerusalem as their capital in 1948 and 1967. The following year in 2021 after Yahuweh/Yehovah had stopped the Temple Organization from doing the lamb sacrifice for Passover in 2020, they continued with the sacrifice anyways without any express command directly from the mouth of Yahuweh/Yehovah to restart the sacrifices, showing that they were moving forward in their own will and desire against the will of Yahuweh/Yehovah, which is unfortunately disobedience.

The Temple Organization Headquarters set up a tent at the foot of the Temple Mount set-apart place, and the word used in the writing on the tent to describe it was the Hebrew word "Miqdash" מקדש, which means "set-apart place," with an image of a Third Temple pictured on the face of the tent. They did not use the Hebrew word "Heykal" היכל, meaning temple, to describe this tent, but instead "set-apart place," as it is written in Daniel 9 and 12 and in Matthew 24 (in the original Hebrew). The writing on the face of the tent said in Hebrew, "Mitqadmim lamiqdash" מתקדמים למקדש, meaning "Advancing to the set-apart place."

For the sacrificing of the Passover lamb they used the sacrificial altar that had already been built and partially used in the past, which is made from crushed gravel that is formed into bricks in violation of the command of Yahuweh/Yehovah in Deuteronomy 27:5-6 to only sacrifice animals on altars with whole stones that have not been cut or formed by human hands in any way. This is because they were following the commands of men in the Talmud, the commands of the Rabbis, who say it is alright to violate the command of Yahuweh/Yehovah and disobey him in this way of forming bricks for the sacrificial altar. This was further evidence of the disobedience of this Passover lamb "reenactment" sacrifice, because it was done on an altar built in a disobedient way in violation of Yahuweh/Yehovah's commands in the Hebrew Scriptures.

In the past the animal sacrifices had only been considered reenactments, but that year on March 23-24, 2021 was different, because a week before on March 17, 2021 the Chief Rabbi of Jerusalem Aryeh Stern had made a new ruling making it a requirement for the Passover sacrifice to be performed by and for the Jewish people as a nation from that year onward. This was in spite of the absence of a Temple building or red heifer, and in spite of the fact that the sacrifice is required to be performed on the Temple Mount, which no Jews are allowed access to for performing such a sacrifice. This ruling made the Passover sacrifice that year more real and more urgent that they were needing to perform a real Passover sacrifice for the nation of Israel that was not only a reenactment, but in part, according to the ruling, to help bring an end to the COVID plague on the land of Israel.

This means that this event of the Passover sacrifice at a miqdash "set-apart place" tent at the foot of the Temple Mount was the first time that this was done on the backing of a command of men, the command of the Chief Rabbi of Jerusalem saying that it is time to bring back the Passover lamb sacrifices, not by the command of Yahuweh/Yehovah. This time it was a clear choice that the Orthodox Jews participating in this event were making to obey the commands of men, and disobedience to the commands of Yahuweh/Yehovah regarding his sacrifices and set-apart place duties of the priests. It was the choice to follow men in the Passover sacrifice and turn away from Yahuweh/Yehovah.

They did not even perform the Passover sacrifice on the correct day according to Yahuweh/Yehovah's instruction of the "Mo'ed" מוֹעֵד or "appointed time" of the Passover sacrifice on the 14th day of the 1st month in Leviticus 23, on the day of Pesach (Passover). Instead they changed Yahuweh/Yehovah's appointed times (which is what the Little Horn is supposed to also be doing in Daniel 7:24-25), changing the day of the Passover sacrifice to a completely different day (on the 10th day of the 1st month) in direct defiance and disobedience against the command of Yahuweh/Yehovah in his written Torah in Scripture. Each step of the way the Orthodox Jews in trying to bring back the animal sacrifices are doing so in obedience to the commands of men, the commands of the Rabbis, raising them to a higher authority over Yahuweh/Yehovah, to the position of gods worshipped above the God of Israel Yahuweh/Yehovah. This makes the Passover sacrifice done at the foot of the Temple Mount an act of obedience and worship of the Rabbis, turning them into false gods above the God of Israel in disobedience and rejection of the God of Israel, Yahuweh/Yehovah. This is the exact opposite of something that is set-apart to Yahuweh/Yehovah; it becomes idolatry and worship of false gods, worshipping men as gods.

Also, the fact that there was a command and requirement from the Chief Rabbi of Jerusalem backing the event of the sacrifice of the Passover lamb that year confirmed the intent of the Orthodox Jews to reject the Passover Lamb Yeshua who died for the cleansing and covering and forgiveness of sin once and for all. It was a very clear rejection of the Messiah Yeshua as the Passover Lamb sin offering who died on the day of Passover, on the 14th day of the 1st month, as the eternal sacrifice in the new covenant of Jeremiah 31 with the nation of Israel so that Yahuweh/Yehovah is able to forgive our crookedness and remember our sins no more. The lamb that was sacrificed in this event at the base of the Temple Mount had a wooden pole/stake run through it and stood up/lifted up for the crowd to see. That physical, literal lamb was what they very clearly chose to have their sins forgiven by instead of the Lamb and Messiah Yeshua, rejecting Yahuweh/Yehovah's forgiveness of sin to follow the commands of men instead.

By choosing to make this physical, dead lamb into the object of redemption and forgiveness of sin in place of the Lamb Yeshua, who is Yahuweh/Yehovah's way to redemption and forgiveness of sin, the people made a clear choice that had not been there before in previous Passover sacrifice "reenactments" to turn that physical lamb into an idol to be worshipped in place of the God of Israel Yeshua. They rejected Yahuweh/Yehovah's way of forgiveness of sins through the Lamb Yeshua to try to make Yahuweh/Yehovah forgive their sins through their own way that they wanted, through the death of a physical lamb like it had been before Yeshua came, rejecting Yeshua and substituting a physical lamb in his place to be worshipped in his place. An animal sacrifice done in obedience to Yahuweh/Yehovah is clean and set-apart and good, but any sacrifices done in disobedience to Yahuweh/Yehovah, following after the words of men as gods in place of Yahuweh/Yehovah, even with clean animals, becomes sin and rebellion according to Samuel, even turning into idolatry and worship of false gods.

The Hebrew word "Shiqquts" שִׁקּוּץ used in the book of Daniel that is generally translated as "abomination" literally means "abominable thing" or "detestable thing" or "disgusting thing" and is always used in reference to idols and objects of idolatry throughout Scripture. It is literally an "abominable idol" or "detestable idol" or "disgusting idol" that is being referred to in Daniel 9 and Daniel 12 and by Yeshua in Mathew 24 and Mark 13. Therefore in the Hebrew of Daniel and Matthew, when adding the participle word "Shomem" or "Meshomem" to "Shiqquts" it becomes literally an "Appalling Disgusting Idol" or a "Shocking Disgusting Idol" or a "Desolating Disgusting Idol." And sadly there is nothing more shocking or appalling or desolating than a sacrificial lamb that is supposed to be set-apart to Yahuweh/Yehovah being used as an idol in disobedience and rebellion against him, and rejection of his way of forgiveness through Yeshua, in fulfillment of Matthew 24:15, Mark 13:14, Daniel 9:27 and Daniel 12:11.

This physical sacrificial lamb was made into, and set-up as, an idol on the "wing" or "edge" of the set-apart place on the Temple Mount, at the base of the set-apart mountain, in fulfillment of Daniel 9:27 that says the "Disgusting Idols Desolating" or "Appalling Disgusting Idols" are upon the wing or edge. This was also playing out the shadow picture of the golden calf idol that the children of Israel placed at the foot of the set-apart mountain of Mount Sinai, at Yahuweh/Yehovah's heavenly set-apart place at the top of the mountain. This event of sacrificing a Passover lamb at this location has continued on the 10th day of the 1st month each year since, in fulfillment of Daniel 9:27 that says there are plural, multiple, Disgusting Idols Desolating, and

Daniel 12:11-12 that says the Disgusting Idol Desolating continues for a certain amount of time of at least 1,290 days.

At the event the people were playing music and singing in revelry and joy at the base of the Temple Mount in the same way the children of Israel sang and played music with the golden calf at the base of Mount Sinai. And they said that they were doing this festival of the Passover sacrifice to Yahuweh/Yehovah, this festival that they had made up on the 10th day of the 1st month in violation of the command of Yahuweh/Yehovah to keep the feast on the 14th day of the 1st month. They themselves at the event at that time said they were fulfilling a Rabbinic prophecy about making up a new festival holiday on that date that did not exist before. They changed Yahuweh/Yehovah's appointed times and changed the festival into their own manmade festival, but said they were doing it to Yahuweh/Yehovah in the same way the children of Israel made up a festival and said they were doing it to Yahuweh/Yehovah at the base of Mount Sinai, doing their idol worship at the base of the set-apart place on the Temple Mount in the name of Yahuweh/Yehovah in the same way the children of Israel did at the base of the set-apart place on Mount Sinai.

It is the spiritual deception and spiritual destruction of the Disgusting Idol Desolating that is far more dangerous than any bodily harm or physical destruction, and this Passover sacrifice event was and still is very spiritually deceiving. But it is only the sign and symbol for the deadlier spiritual deceptions that were beginning at that time, which Yeshua warned to flee from (discussed further on). Turning a physical lamb into an "Appalling Abominable Idol" was the result of a complete rejection of Yeshua as the Messiah and Passover Lamb, raising that physical lamb into the position of a god above Yahuweh/Yehovah, saying that man's way of sacrifice for the removing of sin is above Yahuweh/Yehovah's way of removing sin for eternal life. But it was only the sign of many Jews in Israel (and many Christians around the world) turning away from Yahuweh/Yehovah in a very concrete and real way in the deceptions that came at that time.

Yeshua says that the Disgusting Idol Desolating is the sign that a unique Great Tribulation has begun (discussed in the beginning of the book). The only description that Yeshua gives in Matthew and Mark about this time of a unique Great Tribulation (that has not happened on the earth before and will never happen again) is that there will be at that time false messiahs and false prophets and people claiming to be Yeshua returned to the earth who lead people astray and deceive people, even to the point that it is possible for the chosen (the elect) to be deceived. This is the only description that Yeshua gives about the unique Great Tribulation on the earth after the spiritual deception of the Disgusting Idol Desolating is in place, that it will be possible for absolutely anyone on the earth to be deceived at that time by the spiritual deceptions, even those who are chosen, the choice believers in Yeshua who are close to him and devoted to following him completely, giving up everything to follow him. That is some really extreme and unique Great Tribulation. To put this in perspective, at the time of the Disgusting Idol Desolating of the golden calf most of the nation of Israel was deceived, up to the point of even Aaron being deceived. But during the Great Tribulation of deception after the placing of the Disgusting Idol Desolating, it is possible for even Moses, who talked with Yahuweh/Yehovah face to face, to be deceived.

It is this spiritual deception and spiritual destruction that is the only description Yeshua gives as a warning about what the Great Tribulation is on the earth, the Great Trouble, to the point that he has to reduce or shorten the days of the Great Tribulation of spiritual deception or else there would be no flesh left on the earth that would be saved, under the salvation of Yeshua. That is why it is encouraging that Yahuweh/Yehovah will shorten or reduce the days down of the Great Tribulation, so that will not happen to the point that no flesh would be saved.

This event of a Disgusting Idol Desolating was the sign for Israel entering that time of spiritual deception and destruction. Only a few months before, Israel entered into the very deceptive Abraham Accords (discussed in detail later on) which many Christians also fell into the deception over. And only a few weeks before this the very deceptive Mark of the Beast Out of the Sea (that had nothing to do with vaccines as shown later on in the book) was released in Israel, which was so deceptive that almost every Jew in Israel literally possessed it upon their right hand and even now most Christians deny or ignore or are oblivious that it ever happened. That is a deception on a level that has never before been seen on the earth, where almost all Christians and believers in Yeshua, even among the chosen (elect), were blind to it because it did not happen according to their imaginations.

At that time in the spring of 2021 it was the beginning of the most spiritually dire time in all of the history of the nation of Israel going back to Abraham, in fulfillment of Daniel 12:1, as almost the entire nation turned to the Beast Out of the Sea and the Beast Out of the Earth to save them from Yahuweh/Yehovah's COVID plague by taking the Mark of the Beast Out of the Sea and worshipping the Beast Out of the Sea, just so that they did not have to turn in repentance to Yahuweh/Yehovah and give up the world to follow him, and keep doing their normal life (discussed in detail later on). There has never been a more disastrous time in the history of Israel than starting at the time of this Disgusting Idol Desolating event when almost the entire nation turned away from Yahuweh/Yehovah to take a Mark that according to Revelation 14 causes a person to be burned in sulphur and fire eternally.

Only a few days after this Disgusting Idol Desolating event, on the night of April 14-15, 2021 there was a celebration event for Israel's Independence Day on Mount Hertzel where there were very strange Pagan worship abominations and idolatry that were used as part of the ceremony, and through much of the ceremony there were songs of worship of mankind as gods, boasting of defeating Yahuweh/Yehovah's COVID plague with man's ability and ingenuity, worshipping the Beast Out of the Sea which is made up of mankind and the sea of people, the worship of mankind as gods. That time in the spring of 2021 was only the beginning of the spiritual deception and destruction of the nation of Israel, and it was only the sign of the even greater spiritual deceptions and destruction that began to attack and take down believers in Yeshua around the world, more of which is discussed in greater detail later on in other sections.

At this March 23-24 event, there was a seven branch menorah inside of the "Miqdash" set-apart place tent used in the event. The priests descended from Levi performing the ceremonies tried to light the lamp, which is supposed to be burning as a "continual" in the set-apart place according to Yahuweh/Yehovah's instructions in Exodus and Leviticus. But they were only able to light the lamp in the middle of the menorah. The other six lamps kept being blown out by the wind, showing the fulfillment of "the continual" being taken away from man on the earth, the number six being the number of man, created on the sixth day, in fulfillment of Daniel 12:11. Only the central branch remained with light, the light of Yahuweh/Yehovah remaining continually with him, but removed from the world of man as the time of the Great Tribulation spiritual deceptions had begun, with the light of Yahuweh/Yehovah and his truth removed from the world for the time of the deceptions.

The "continual" being taken away and removed is Yahuweh/Yehovah leaving the old container of the manmade religious structures in the Church to move to the new structure of his nation in the new heavens and new earth, like when he left the old Temple structure and eventually destroyed it, never allowing another Temple or Tabernacle to be built again to resume the old container. All those who are trying to stay in the old container (the old wineskin) are in greater danger of the spiritual deceptions and Disgusting Idols Desolating in the Church now at this time, because the continual light of Yahuweh/Yehovah that had been there is now gone and removed, taken away, into the new container. Those believers in Yeshua (virgins) who stored up extra oil with them in their containers will be able to weather through the deceptions, because they have the oil and continual light of Yahuweh/Yehovah with them, but those who rely on merchants (physical locations and physical people) for their oil to light their lamps will be lost without the continual light of Yahuweh/Yehovah there in those physical locations and people available to them anymore, and will miss the bridegroom when he comes at midnight.

All of "the continual" things inside of the set-apart place with the menorah, show bread, bronze incense, and ark of the covenant are shadow pictures of the person of Yahuweh/Yehovah himself, and when man brings in an unclean Disgusting Idol Desolating into his set-apart place, he has to remove his dwelling place from that place (Ezekiel 8:5-6). He is still always everywhere, but he cannot be in that place in a form of being able to commune with him anymore. Yahuweh/Yehovah is still continual, but the removal of "the continual" is the shadow picture of Yahuweh/Yehovah removing himself from the lives of the people who want the Disgusting Idol Desolating and the spiritual deception and destruction it brings in their lives. And that is "the continual" that was removed on March 23-24.

Yeshua Says in Matthew and Mark for Those in Yehudah (Judea) to Flee When They See the Disgusting Idol (Abomination) Desolating at the Set-apart Place at the Beginning of the Great Tribulation, but in Luke Yeshua Says in General for Everyone to Flee at the Time of His Coming at the End of the Great Tribulation:
Matthew 24:16-26   Mark 13:14-23
Luke 17:28-32
Word for Word Prophecy Examination of Partially Unfulfilled Verses **Luke 17:28-32** – In this prophecy in Luke Yeshua uses the exact same words describing how to flee in Matthew and Mark, except that he uses them to describe fleeing at his coming like the days of Noah and Lot at the end of the Great Tribulation. This shows that the entire time of the Great Tribulation is a time to be ready to flee in multiple places around the world for different reasons. In this case in Luke it is to flee Yahuweh/Yehovah's destruction and judgement of cities and the world at his coming. In Matthew and Mark it is specifically those who are living in Yehudah (Judea or Judah around the area of Jerusalem) who are supposed to flee, but in Luke it is all the world in general that should flee.

Prophecy Fulfillment of Verses **Matthew 24:16-26** and **Mark 13:14-23** – As already discussed, the real thing that Yeshua says to flee from in Matthew 24 and Mark 13 is the Disgusting Idol Desolating itself, to flee from the spiritual danger that has begun on the earth that could deceive even the chosen (elect) which could even cause them to lose their salvation in Yeshua in order to chase after the world and the Beast Out of the Sea. There are multiple things to flee from for different reasons. In this prophecy in Matthew 24 and Mark 13 those who were living in the region of Yehudah (Judea) in central Israel around Jerusalem and were paying attention to the Disgusting Idol Desolating that happened, if they fled to the mountains as Yeshua instructed they were safe from the civil war rioting and violence that started in the region of Yehudah on April 23, 2021. The violence took place across that region and across Israel between Jews and Arabs for weeks on a scale not seen since the 1948 War for Independence, with the police unable to control it and the widespread destruction. The violence that started in Jerusalem on that day has continued indefinitely to the present time, still flaring up consistently over and over again with riots and terrorist attacks.

That day also started a trend of increasing terrorist attacks in the Yehudah and surrounding region in Israel, to the point that it is the most violence that Israel has seen in terrorist attacks since the first few years of the Second Intifada, except this time unlike then Israel cannot simply build another wall to stop the attacks like before. There was also the most serious rocket attacks that Israel had come under from the Gaza Strip ever beginning on May 12, 2021, with destruction even in Tel Aviv and Jerusalem. Those who listened to Yeshua's warning and got to the mountains were safe from all of this physical violence in fulfillment of Matthew 24:17-20 and Mark 13:15-18.

But more importantly, in fulfillment of these verses, those who listened to Yeshua and fled to the mountains or wilderness areas at that time were safe from the spiritual deceptions and destruction that had begun in Israel at that time. This includes the very deceptive Mark of the Beast Out of the Sea that had nothing to do with vaccines had begun (discussed in detail later on), but was only implemented and imposed in urban areas. Anyone who listened to and obeyed Yeshua was safe from this spiritual deception, even if they did not recognize it at the time, because anyone living in a wilderness mountain area was safe from having to worry about using the Mark of the Beast Out of the Sea at all. Those in Israel who did not listen to Yeshua to get to a safe place in the mountains or wilderness areas were in grave danger of their eternal lives being lost by taking the deceptive Mark of the Beast Out of the Sea, especially if they did not recognize it happening word for word in fulfilment of the prophecy in Revelation 13 (discussed in detail later on).

Those who are believers in Yeshua living in Israel who listened to him and escaped to the mountains were also safe from the spiritual deceptions and desolations that had started around that time, including the Abraham Accords and other deceptions discussed in more detail in a later section. But the most dangerous of all of the deceptions was the Mark of the Beast Out of the Sea and the worship of the Beast Out of the Sea and the Image of the Beast Out of the Sea that had started in Israel at that time, which were only concentrated in the cities and urban areas, but much more sparse in the wilderness mountain areas. Yeshua warned that the Great Tribulation his people needed to flee from was the deceptions from false messiahs and false prophets that are so great even the Chosen are able to be deceived by them and be in danger of losing their eternal lives. That is why there is the hope that he will reduce the days for the sake of the chosen (the elect) so that not all of them will be lost.

And the fulfillment of Yeshua's warning for a person to pray their flight would not be on the "day of Sabbath" [30] in Matthew 24:20 is explained at that time as well, because the Sabbath day is a day when the whole nation of Israel shuts down in a lockdown, including festival Sabbath days as well as the weekly Sabbath. But at that time for a year the whole nation of Israel had been shut down in a continuous Sabbath lockdown every day for weeks on end because of COVID. The whole nation was in lockdown at around that time, so Yeshua was saying to pray that your flight at that time not be during a lockdown, shutdown of the nation as with COVID, because it makes it very difficult to get out of the cities while they are in a daily Sabbath lockdown with police preventing people from going places on the streets.

---

[30] See Appendix: Hebrew Matthew Chapter 24

Section 10. **The Outer Court and City of Jerusalem Trampled by the Gentiles (42 Months):**

The Temple/Tabernacle Measurement and Gentiles Trampling Outer Court and Jerusalem Prophecy:
Revelation 11:1-2

Prophecy Fulfillment of Verses **Revelation 11:1-2** – This prophecy only talks about the gentiles, the nations, trampling the physical structure of the set-apart city Jerusalem. The people inside of Jerusalem are not trampled down upon by the feet of the nations. It is only the physical city itself which is being trampled. On April 23, 2021 the riots by the gentile nations of the Palestinians began in the set-apart city Jerusalem, as they attacked the physical city itself, such as buildings and vehicles, but not the people inside of the city, in fulfillment of verse 11:2. This rioting trampling down of the city of Jerusalem brought widespread destruction, and has continued to flare up and happen again and again up to the present time. Buildings and vehicles were set on fire and firework rockets were used to shoot at buildings in the city. The physical city itself, not the people, was trampled under the feet of the gentiles.

The measuring of the Temple/Dwelling Place together with the worshippers inside of it shows that the Temple/Dwelling Place in this prophecy is referring to the spiritual body of believers in Yeshua, both Jew and Gentile, being measured at the same time as the gentiles are trampling the city of Jerusalem. The physical sign of the trampling of Jerusalem shows the spiritual part of this prophecy happening also in the spiritual measuring of the spiritual Temple made up of the believers in Yeshua around the world. As in Matthew 7:1-2 Yeshua explains that a measure of a person has to do with judging them according to a standard. This measuring in verse 11:1 is not the measure of man but instead the measure and standard of Yahuweh/Yehovah, upon his people to measure them according to his standards. No man or woman can measure up to Yahuweh/Yehovah's standards on their own, without his help as Yeshua, which is why he brings in the refining to purify and mold his people into his standard of eternal life. The measuring of the believers in Yeshua is the preparation for bringing the refining fires of Great Tribulation to get the believers in Yeshua on the earth ready to meet him when he comes (discussed in greater detail later on).

References to the Gentiles Trampling the Set-Apart City Jerusalem Prophecy (that Shows the Gentiles are Already Trampling Jerusalem Long Before the 42 Months Begin, Continuously for Thousands of Years Before):
Genesis 48:13-19
Luke 21:20-24
Romans 11:1-25

Examination of Verses **Genesis 48:13-19** and **Luke 21:20-24** and **Romans 11:1-25** – In Luke 21:20-24 Yeshua says that the gentiles, the nations, will be trampling the city of Jerusalem under their feet all the way until the "time of the nations is fulfilled" or reaches its fullness. This trampling of the city of Jerusalem by the nations has been ongoing for nearly 1,900 years already, and the prophecy in Revelation 11:2 is to let everyone know that that trampling continues all the way until Yeshua returns. It is in order to know that the time of the fullness of the nations does not come until the end of the Great Tribulation when Yeshua returns. Yeshua in Luke 21:24 is quoting from Genesis 48:19 in which Jacob is giving the prophecy about the descendants of his grandson Ephrayim one day becoming the "fullness of the nations."

This is why the tribe of Ehprayim is usually the one poetically used to refer to the ten northern tribes of Israel, because it is when all of the tribes of Israel return as believers in the Messiah Yeshua (from Isaiah 49) that the physical descendants will become the "fullness of the nations" in fulfillment of this prophecy and the nations will no longer trample the city of Jerusalem under their feet, because the nations who will be in Jerusalem will be believers in Yeshua themselves, as one nation Israel with all of the tribes of Israel. Paul also refers to this prophecy in Romans 11, explaining how some Jews as natural branches leave the faith in Yahuweh/Yehovah by rejecting Yeshua as their Messiah, while gentiles of the nations come as grafted in branches into the nation of Israel by faith in Yahuweh/Yehovah through Yeshua.

The <u>Individual</u> <u>Bodies</u> of the Believers in Yeshua, and the <u>Corporate</u> <u>Body</u> of Believers in Yeshua, are now the Set-apart Temple of Yahuweh/Yehovah:

Matthew 27:39-40   Mark 15:29-30

John 2:19-22

1 Corinthians 3:16-17

1 Corinthians 6:19-20

1 Corinthians 12:12-27

Examination of Verses **Matthew 27:39-40** and **Mark 15:29-30** and **John 2:19-22** and **1 Corinthians 3:16-17** and **1 Corinthians 6:19-20** and **1 Corinthians 12:12-27** – Most believers in Yeshua should be familiar with and understand the concept that the literal, physical body of Yeshua in Matthew 27, Mark 15 and John 2 is the Temple/Tabernacle/Dwelling Place and set-apart place of Yahuweh/Yehovah that was destroyed or killed and then raised back up to life again in exactly 3 days and 3 nights. Paul explains in 1 Corinthians 3 and 6 that each literal, physical body of every believer in Yeshua is also the Temple/Dwelling Place of the Spirit of Yahuweh/Yehovah, set-apart to him. And in 1 Corinthians 12 he takes the concept further in explaining how all the believers in Yeshua together make up one symbolic body or Temple of believers for Yahuweh/Yehovah to dwell in as his set-apart place.

This is the Temple or set-apart place that is the more important place where, beginning in the spring of 2021, believers in Yeshua around the world began bringing in Disgusting Idols Desolating in a new way, with all of the more serious spiritual deceptions that began (discussed in more detail later on). This is why there was the need at the same time for the measuring of the believers in Yeshua who are his Temple in Revelation 11:1, to begin the refining process of the body/Temple of believers in Great Tribulation, to clean out the Disgusting Idols Desolating of strong spiritual deception being brought in and exposed among believers all over the world.

Yahuweh/Yehovah's Goal is for There to be No More Physical Building Temples, Only the Person of Yahuweh/Yehovah Himself Dwelling Together with Man to be the Only Temple (It is Man, Not Yahuweh/Yehovah, Who is Always Wanting to Build a Physical Temple):

2 Samuel 7:1-17

Isaiah 66:1-2

Acts 7:44-50

Revelation 21:22

Examination of Verses **2 Samuel 7:1-17** and **Isaiah 66:1-2** and **Acts 7:44-50** and **Revelation 21:22** – In 2 Samuel 7 Yahuweh/Yehovah explains how he has never asked at any time for a permanent house or temple structure to be built for him. It was David, not Yahuweh/Yehovah, who wanted to build a physical house for him, but Yahuweh/Yehovah has always been busy building his spiritual house of his people and a physical house is something he has never asked for or desired or wanted. In Isaiah 66 Yahuweh/Yehovah repeats the same concept again, that he has no need for a physical house or temple to live in on the earth, because he is God. In Acts 7 Stephan quotes from this verse in Isaiah 66 and paraphrases from 2 Samuel 7 saying the same thing, that Yahuweh/Yehovah does not dwell in manmade physical buildings or temples and he has no need for them.

Eventually in Revelation 21:22 John sees that in the New Jerusalem in the New Heavens and New Earth there is no more physical Temple building of any kind, because Yahuweh/Yehovah himself is the only Temple. He himself as his own person is the only Temple that he needs for himself and wherever he is, he is his Temple, everywhere simultaneously in all existence. It is only man who wants another physical Third Temple or Tabernacle/Tent structure to be built again on the Temple Mount or somewhere in Jerusalem. But Yahuweh/Yehovah all through Scripture and prophecy has never requested or wanted or prophesied another physical Temple or Tabernacle/Tent structure to be built ever again, because he has no need for it and does not live in physical houses of any kind of material. This is why there is no prophesy about another Temple or Tabernacle/ Tent being built in Jerusalem ever again.

And the only unfulfilled prophesy about a Temple in Ezekiel 40 – 48 is so enormous it would never fit inside of the city of Jerusalem, nor within the region around Jerusalem. In Revelation 21 – 22 it is clearly shown in the quotes and paraphrases from Ezekiel that this Temple in Ezekiel exists in the New Jerusalem in the New Heavens and New Earth, as discussed at the beginning, where there is no Temple but Yahuweh/Yehovah himself. A permanent physical Third Temple or Tabernacle/Tent structure rebuilt in Jerusalem is one thing that is absolutely not required to happen in any prophecies in Scripture, and is not required to be in existence during the time of the 3.5 years of Great Tribulation before Yeshua's Return.

Section 11. The Two Witnesses (1,260 Days) and the Removal of the Oil and Light of the Word and Commands of the Witness of Yahuweh/Yehovah (3.5 Days):

Shadow Pictures / Types of Two Witnesses:
    Genesis 18:1 – 19:29
    Exodus 6:26 – 15:21
    Matthew 17:1-13   Mark 9:2-13   Luke 9:28-36

Examination of Verses **Genesis 18:1 – 19:29** – The first example of a time of two witnesses in history are the two messengers (angels) that went to the city of Sodom to witness the evil in the city before its destruction. In this shadow picture of the Two Witnesses, the two who went to act as a witness in the city were two spiritual beings, two messengers. And they went into the city to bring Lot and his family, those who would come, out of the city before it was destroyed. These two messengers are the same two messengers who came with Yahuweh/Yehovah to visit Abraham at his tent and dine with him, while Yahuweh/Yehovah gave Abraham the prophecy about the coming birth of Isaac.

Examination of Verses **Exodus 6:26 – 15:21** – The second shadow picture of Two Witnesses recorded in history is that of Moses and Aaron, two men called by Yahuweh/Yehovah to go to the Pharaoh of Egypt and speak his words to Pharaoh. Then through Moses and Aaron, Yahuweh/Yehovah showed Pharaoh and all of the nation of Egypt that he was the one bringing the plagues upon them in destruction of their empire, and that he is the only true God. In this circumstance it was two living men on the earth, the brothers Moses and Aaron, who acted as the two witnesses in Egypt instead of two messengers as with Sodom and Gomorrah and the other cities of the plain.

Examination of Verses **Matthew 17:1-13** and **Mark 9:2-13** and **Luke 9:28-36** – In the third shadow picture of the Two Witnesses it was Moses again, except Elijah was with him instead of Aaron. This time it was Moses come back from the dead and Elijah who was "raptured" by the chariot into the heavens and never died, two men who had lived in the past and were either dead or caught up into the heavens, come back to life momentarily on the earth, witnessing what Yeshua was about to do as the sacrificial Lamb for the forgiveness and removal of sin.

These are three entirely different ways that Yahuweh/Yehovah has had Two Witnesses on the earth witnessing to the events of what he was doing at each time he came in an interactive form walking on the earth, first with Abraham, then at the time of the Exodus at Mount Sinai, and finally as Yeshua, born of a virgin woman in the physical body of a man as the Messiah. Each time that two witnesses have come, Yahuweh/Yehovah has used the two witnesses in such completely different ways and in entirely unexpected and different forms, there is no way to say that the final fourth set of Two Witnesses in Revelation 11 will come in the same form or way as any of the previous three sets of Two Witnesses. The final set of Two Witnesses can be similar to the previous sets, in the pattern of the previous ones, but they do not have to be the same as any of the others.

References in the Two Witnesses Prophecy:

Zechariah 4:1-14

Prophecy Fulfillment of Verses **Zechariah 4:1-14** – In Revelation 11 as John talks about the Two Witnesses he says that those Two Witnesses are the "two olive trees and two menorah" that are standing before the Master of all the earth. These two olive trees and the seven branch menorah are in the prophecy of Zechariah 4, in which Zechariah is woken up from his sleep and shown these objects in a vision. The two olive trees are standing over a seven branch gold menorah, pouring oil through spouts into the seven lamps on the menorah. The messenger explains to Zechariah that the seven branch menorah with seven lamps is the seven eyes of Yahuweh/Yehovah searching diligently throughout the earth. And the two olive trees standing over the menorah are literally in the original Hebrew "sheney beney hayitshar ha'omdim 'al adon kol ha'arets" "שְׁנֵי בְנֵי הַיִּצְהָר הָעֹמְדִים עַל אֲדוֹן כָּל הָאָרֶץ" "two sons of oil standing over the Master of all the earth."

The Hebrew word " 'al " "עַל" only ever means "upon" or "above" or "over" or "across" or "on high" or "because" and never "beside" as this is often mistranslated in this verse. It can sometimes mean "by," but only in the sense of literally "leaning over" someone or something close by. It is because these are trees, which obviously stand over or "lean over" the things that they are next to, that this word " 'al " "עַל" is used here by Zechariah. And the fact that these two trees that are the two sons of oil are "standing over" Yahuweh/Yehovah, the Master of all the earth, is simply showing that Yahuweh/Yehovah himself is the menorah that Zechariah sees positioned directly under the branches of these two olive trees or sons of oil, as they are leaning over the seven eyes of Yahuweh/Yehovah of the seven lamps of the menorah. The original Hebrew here clearly shows that the seven branch menorah can only be Yahuweh/Yehovah himself and his seven eyes. And yet according to Revelation 11:4 the Two Witnesses are supposed to be multiplied into two of this one seven branch menorah, which is Yahuweh/Yehovah himself.

This whole prophecy was already fulfilled at the time of Zerubbavel and the building of the Second Temple, but the parts of this prophecy about the menorah representing the seven eyes of Yahuweh/Yehovah and the two olive trees that are the two sons of oil go beyond the time of Zechariah and Zerubbavel. They are revelations about the person of Yahuweh/Yehovah and how he does things. So these particular parts of the prophecy go beyond the time of the fulfillment of the building of the Second Temple. When John writes that the Two Witnesses are these two olive trees and two of this single menorah that is the seven eyes of Yahuweh/Yehovah, he is saying that the Two Witnesses were already around at the time of Zechariah when he saw this vision and this prophecy was fulfilled at the building of the Second Temple. John is saying that the Two Witnesses are these two olive trees and the menorah representing Yahuweh/Yehovah himself, through his eyes that have always been continuously around since at least the time of Zechariah, and they are not something or somebody that suddenly is new on the earth since the time of Zechariah. The Two Witnesses were there at the building of the Second Temple and they have always been around since at least that time all the way through to when they are doing their 1,260 days of prophesying.

The Seven Branch Menorah in Zechariah with the Seven Eyes of Yahuweh/Yehovah that Search Diligently Throughout All the Earth is the Same Seven Branch Menorah in Revelation Sitting at the Throne of Yahuweh/Yehovah with the Seven Spirits of Yahuweh/Yehovah, which are the Same Seven Eyes of the Slain Lamb Yeshua that are Sent Out Into All the Earth:

Zechariah 4:1-14

Revelation 4:5

Revelation 5:5-6

Examination of Verses **Zechariah 4:1-14** and **Revelation 4:5** and **Revelation 5:5-6** – John actually clearly knew what he was saying when he said that the Two Witnesses are the menorah from Zechariah 4. In Revelation 4:5 John wrote about seeing the seven branch menorah with seven lamps on it that Zechariah saw. John describes the seven eyes of Yahuweh/Yehovah in the seven lamp menorah as the seven Spirits of Yahuweh/Yehovah. Then later in Revelation 5:5-6 John describes seeing the seven eyes, except that the seven eyes of Yahuweh/Yehovah from the menorah are on the Lamb Yeshua, the exact same seven eyes that search diligently through the earth. John says that the seven eyes on the Lamb Yeshua are the same seven Spirits of Yahuweh/Yehovah represented in the menorah, and that these seven eyes that are simultaneously the seven Spirits of Yahuweh/Yehovah are sent out into all the earth, in the exact same way that the seven eyes of Yahuweh/Yehovah search throughout all the earth in Zechariah 4.

John very clearly connects all of these things together with the seven lamp menorah in Zechariah 4, with the seven Spirits of Yahuweh/Yehovah and the seven eyes of Yahuweh/Yehovah being the exact same thing, searching through the earth. These seven Spirits that are seven eyes are clearly connected to the menorah that John sees, the exact same menorah in Zechariah 4, but the only difference is that there is the additional revelation that the seven eyes of Yahuweh/Yehovah from the menorah are also on the Lamb Yeshua.

When John says that the Two Witnesses are the two menorah from Zechariah 4 he is clearly saying without any confusion that these Two Witnesses are Yahuweh/Yehovah and Yeshua himself. No man can be the seven eyes or seven Spirits of Yahuweh/Yehovah and Yeshua, and no spiritual being or messenger can be the seven eyes or seven Spirits of Yahuweh/Yehovah and Yeshua. Only Yahuweh/Yehovah can be himself and no other can take his place, as he says over and over in Isaiah. John knew exactly what he was writing when he said that the Two Witnesses are the two menorahs, because he had just seen for himself in the throne room of Yahuweh/Yehovah in the heavens what these menorahs represent. The only way that the Two Witnesses can be the menorah from Zechariah 4 as John writes is if the Two Witnesses are God himself, Yahuweh/Yehovah and Yeshua himself, or his words and attributes that come from him. But John clearly says in his writing about the Two Witnesses that they cannot be men, living or come back from the dead, or messengers or spiritual beings. Even Moses and Elijah or Enoch and Elijah come back from the dead are not God and therefore cannot take the place of Yahuweh/Yehovah and Yeshua as the one true God. Only God himself can be God and represent God. Only Yahuweh/Yehovah is God and no one else can be his seven eyes or his seven Spirits except himself.

Yahuweh/Yehovah as the Father and Yeshua as the Son are Two Witnesses of Himself:

John 8:17-19

Examination of Verses **John 8:17-19** – In John 8 Yeshua references the commands in the Torah that there have to be at least two witnesses in any legal matter before a person can be condemned of a crime. And then he says that he himself is one witness, and that the Father Yahuweh/Yehovah who sent him is a second witness, so that Yahuweh/Yehovah and Yeshua together are two witnesses of himself. Then the people he was talking to ask him where his father is. And Yeshua says to them that if they had known him, they would have known his Father also, and the only way that is possible is if Yeshua is the Father. Continuously through the book of John, John who is the same author of Revelation reveals through Yeshua's own words, that Yeshua the Son and the Father Yahuweh/Yehovah are one, such as in John 14:6-12. Yeshua says that those who know him know the Father Yahuweh/Yehovah, and those who see him have seen the Father Yahuweh/Yehovah. The only way this is possible for those who have seen Yeshua to have also seen the Father Yahuweh/Yehovah would be if Yeshua is the Father Yahuweh/Yehovah.

There is no other possible way to see Yeshua and see the Father Yahuweh/Yehovah unless they are both the same person. Yeshua said it himself here in John 8 and John 14 that he is the "I Am" Yahuweh/Yehovah (Exodus 3:14), the Father, who existed before Abraham came to be, because Yeshua and Yahuweh/Yehovah are one. John knew exactly what he was writing in Revelation 11 when he was writing about the Two Witnesses, because he also wrote down Yeshua's words in John 8 where Yeshua says that he and Yahuweh/Yehovah are the Two Witnesses of himself.

The Prophecies of the Birth of the Messiah Also Clearly Indicated the Messiah Would be God, Yahuweh/Yehovah Himself in the Body of a Man, but Before Yeshua Came Everyone was Still Expecting the Messiah to be Just a Man:

Isaiah 7:10-16

Micah 5:1-4

Word for Word Prophecy Examination of Fulfilled Verses **Isaiah 7:10-16** and **Micah 5:1-4** – In Isaiah 7 it was prophesied that a virgin woman would give birth to a son whose name would be called 'Immanu el עִמָּנוּ אֵל, which means when translated literally "God is with us." This should have been obvious that this prophecy is saying that this baby that is born is God himself, Yahuweh/Yehovah, but it is also shown again in Micah 5. The ruler who comes forth from Beyth Lechem Ephrathah came forth from ancient times, from everlasting. The one prophesied to be born in Bethlehem is prophesied to have always existed from everlasting before he is even born there, which could only mean that God, Yahuweh/Yehovah himself the one true God, is the true Messiah to be born from Bethlehem.

All of the words were right there in the prophecies about the Messiah that it would be God himself coming in the body of a man to dwell with mankind on the earth, which was fulfilled with Yeshua, the Messiah, Yahuweh/Yehovah. But from surviving records of the time before and during Yeshua's coming no one had figured out yet that the Messiah in the prophecies was God himself, Yahuweh/Yehovah himself, the God of

Abraham, Isaac, and Jacob, even though it clearly says it in Isaiah and Micah. All of us through the history of Christianity have been the same way with the Two Witnesses, not realizing all this time that John clearly writes in this prophecy in Revelation 11 that the Two Witnesses are Yahuweh/Yehovah and Yeshua himself, and especially his words.

Fire from the Mouth and Word of Yahuweh/Yehovah:
> Deuteronomy 4:10-36
>
> Isaiah 30:27-30
>
> Jeremiah 5:13-14
>
> Jeremiah 23:29
>
> Psalms 18:6-13

Examination of Verses **Deuteronomy 4:10-36** and **Isaiah 30:27-30** and **Jeremiah 5:13-14** and **Jeremiah 23:29** and **Psalms 18:6-13** – John shows again in Revelation 11:5 that the Two Witnesses can only be Yahuweh/Yehovah himself, or Yahuweh/Yehovah's words. He says that the Two Witnesses send fire out from their mouths to consume their enemies, which is something that only God himself, Yahuweh/Yehovah himself, does according to Scripture, or Yahuweh/Yehovah's words. In Psalms 18 smoke comes out of the nostrils of Yahuweh/Yehovah and a consuming fire goes out from his mouth. And he sends out his voice, which turns into coals of fire. In Isaiah 30 Yahuweh/Yehovah's tongue is burning like a devouring fire, with lips of rage, and his breath is like a stream that flows over, as he sifts the nations of the earth with a sieve of falsehood.

In Jeremiah 5 it is the words of Yahuweh/Yehovah that become a fire in the mouth of Jeremiah, so that the words of Yahuweh/Yehovah devour the people who hear them from Jeremiah's mouth. It is not Jeremiah that shoots fire out of his mouth to consume the people around him; it is the words of Yahuweh/Yehovah that are the fire consuming the people, as Jeremiah speaks the words of Yahuweh/Yehovah. Yahuweh/Yehovah repeats this same concept again in Jeremiah 23 when he says that his Word is like a fire. Also in Deuteronomy 4 Moses describes the words of Yahuweh/Yehovah as he spoke them audibly for all of the children of Israel to hear at Mount Sinai, saying that they all heard Yahuweh/Yehovah's words coming out from the midst of the literal fire that was consuming Mount Sinai, the Ten Words or the Ten Commands spoken by Yahuweh/Yehovah coming out from the fire.

John describing the Two Witnesses with fire coming out of their mouths again shows that the Two Witnesses have to either be Yahuweh/Yehovah and Yeshua himself, or the Two Witnesses have to be the words of Yahuweh/Yehovah. Because the messenger says to John, "My Two Witnesses," in Revelation 11:3, indicating that these two witnesses are Yahuweh/Yehovah's Two Witnesses, this shows that the Two Witnesses are simultaneously both the seven eyes and seven Spirits of Yahuweh/Yehovah of the menorah, and also the words of Yahuweh/Yehovah that come from his mouth. Yahuweh/Yehovah's words are his Two Witnesses. (This is also shown in the two olive trees that are the two sons of oil, discussed further on.)

The Words from the Mouth of Yahuweh/Yehovah Kill People:

Hosea 6:5

Examination of Verses **Hosea 6:5** – In Hosea 6:5 Yahuweh/Yehovah says, "I have killed them by the words of My mouth." This shows how it is the words from the mouth of Yahuweh/Yehovah himself that kills people, not the prophets who speak those words. It is the words of Yahuweh/Yehovah that come from his own mouth that kill the people wishing to harm his Two Witnesses in Revelation 11:5, his Two Witnesses being the words of his mouth.

Commands About Two Witnesses:

Numbers 35:30

Deuteronomy 17:6-7

Deuteronomy 19:15

Examination of Verses **Numbers 35:30** and **Deuteronomy 17:6-7** and **Deuteronomy 19:15** – The principle of two witnesses is part of Yahuweh/Yehovah's legal system, that no one can be condemned of a crime or especially executed for a crime unless there are at least two witnesses who clearly saw that crime committed beyond any doubt. And another command that is part of the commands about two witnesses is part of the Ten Commands, that no one bear false witness against their neighbor, or against their "another." And Yeshua answered the question about who a person's neighbor is; our neighbor is every single person who lives on the entire earth.

For the legal proceedings of judgment and mercy upon the people on the earth Yahuweh/Yehovah always has at least two witnesses in various forms at each time to witness the crimes being done that need to be judged, or witness the repentance that holds back the judgment, or to witness the sacrificial death of an innocent in place of the guilty party, as with the Lamb Yeshua.

Two Stone Tablets of the Witness with the Ten Commands in the Ark of the Witness:

Exodus 25:10-23

Exodus 31:18 – 32:19

Exodus 34:1-29

Deuteronomy 4:9-13

Deuteronomy 5:15-22

Deuteronomy 10:1-5

Examination of Verses **Exodus 25:10-23** and **Exodus 31:18 – 32:19** and **Exodus 34:1-29** and **Deuteronomy 4:9-13** and **Deuteronomy 5:15-22** and **Deuteronomy 10:1-5** – In Exodus 25 Yahuweh/Yehovah had Moses build the ark of the covenant for the express purpose of putting "the Witness" into it which Yahuweh/Yehovah would give to Moses. This is why the ark of the covenant is called the "ark of the Witness" in Exodus 31, because it was made for the purpose of holding and preserving "the Witness" inside of it. This Witness turned out to be the stone tablets of the Ten Commands or Ten Words carved into the stone by the hand of Yahuweh/Yehovah himself, according to Exodus 32. It is also in Exodus 32 that is the first time they are called, "the Two tablets of the Witness." These first two tablets Moses broke when he threw them at the base of Mount Sinai in his anger at the children of Israel for building the golden calf idol, but he cut two more stone tablets and in Exodus 34 Yahuweh/Yehovah rewrote the Ten Words of the covenant onto these two new tablets of stone. And once again they are called "the Two tablets of the Witness."

These Two tablets of stone that are a Witness were then put into the ark of the covenant or ark of the witness by Moses, in order to preserve these Two tablets of the Witness to this day on the earth. These two stone tablets with the writing of the Ten Words or Ten Commands from Yahuweh/Yehovah in his own hand are Two Witnesses of his words. His words upon these Two tablets of stone are Two Witnesses to the world of the way that Yahuweh/Yehovah instructs people to live and have life, so that they do not die or have death (Deuteronomy 30:19-20). These tablets of stone with the Ten Words of Yahuweh/Yehovah written upon them are Two Witnesses about Yahwueh/Yehovah and his true way to live and have life, and at the same time bearing witness to Yahuweh/Yehovah as Two Witnesses against those on the earth who violate and break these Ten Words.

The Stone that Hears the Words of Yahuweh/Yehovah that He Speaks to Mankind, and Then Witnesses Against Mankind When They Disobey His Words:
Joshua 24:24-27

Examination of Verses **Joshua 24:24-27** – After Israel had entered the land of Canaan and become a nation, Joshua made a covenant with the people of Israel to serve Yahuweh/Yehovah and obey him, according to his commands in the Torah. And he took the "Book of the Torah of God," which was probably the original Torah scroll written in the hand of Moses, and wrote some words in it about the covenant the people of Israel made that day to serve and obey Yahuweh/Yehovah. He then picked up a large stone and set this stone by the set-apart place, the Tabernacle, of Yahuweh/Yehovah, and he said that that stone had heard all the words of Yahuweh/Yehovah that he had spoken to them, and the stone itself was a witness against the people of Israel if they had lied in their hearts and anyone breaks the covenant with Yahuweh/Yehovah.

The literal Two stone tablets of the Witness are also stones that heard the words of Yahuweh/Yehovah, and had the Ten Words of Yahuweh/Yehovah even written upon them. And they are also Two Witnesses against all those on the earth who do not keep the covenant of Yahuweh/Yehovah, or who do not obey his commands, which disobedience without repentance and the sacrificial offering of the blood of Yeshua to clean and cover that sin, leads to the verdict or judgment of death. This verse in Joshua shows the principle of how the Two stone tablets of the Witness are Two Witnesses, bearing the Witness of the Words of Yahuweh/Yehovah upon them.

The Words of Yahuweh/Yehovah Written on a Tablet or Inscribed on a Scroll are a Witness Forever:

Isaiah 30:6-8

Examination of Verses **Isaiah 30:6-8** – Isaiah 30 shows how the words of Yahuweh/Yehovah that are written down in a tablet of stone or metal or on a scroll or any material are a witness forever. All of the written words of Yahuweh/Yehovah are a witness to him and about him, which he preserves on the earth as a witness to the world.

The Witness of the Word of Yahuweh/Yehovah in the Torah of Mosheh and the Scriptures:

John 5:31-47

Examination of Verses **John 5:31-47** – Yeshua says that the Scriptures of Yahuweh/Yehovah are all a witness, specifically in this case about Yeshua. And also that the Torah of Moses, all of the writings of Moses in the Five Books of Moses, is a Witness about Yeshua, because Moses wrote about Yeshua. Then Yeshua says that it is impossible to be able to believe him unless a person first believes what Moses wrote in the Torah, since Moses wrote about Yeshua in the Torah. All of the words of Yahuweh/Yehovah in Scripture are a Witness about him.

The Witness of the Word of Yahuweh/Yehovah in the Torah of Mosheh (Bound Up, Sealed, and Hidden):

Isaiah 8:11-22

Examination of Verses **Isaiah 8:11-22** – In this prophecy in Isaiah 8 Yahuweh/Yehovah says to bind up and seal the Witness of the Torah (the Five Books of Moses). This once again shows an example of how the commands and words of Yahuweh/Yehovah written in the Torah are a witness, while at the same time showing how there are times when Yahuweh/Yehovah seals and binds up this Witness, removing this Witness and himself from the people when they turn as a nation into evil and wickedness in rebellion against him, in order to bring the consequences and judgment of their sin upon them. By sealing up his Witness so that the people cannot see it or hear it, they stumble and fall into the desires of their hearts, the desires for sin, destroying themselves with their own darkness and evil they have brought upon themselves. There are times when Yahuweh/Yehovah hides his Witness and himself from people when they are determined in their rebellion and are hardened in their unrepentance, but the Witness of Yahuweh/Yehovah's Words is still there, even though it is hidden from them, still witnessing against them.

Yeshua, as God Yahuweh/Yehovah in the Flesh, is Called a Prophet by Mosheh in One of the Prophecies About Him in the Torah, the Prophet Who Everyone Must Listen to and Obey (The Words of Yahuweh/Yehovah Throughout Scripture are Also All Prophecies that are Prophesying):

    Deuteronomy 18:15-19

    Acts 3:13-26

Examination of Verses **Deuteronomy 18:15-19** and **Acts 3:13-26** – Peter explains in Acts 3 that one of the places that Moses wrote about Yeshua was in the prophecy about a Prophet that Yahuweh/Yehovah would raise up like Moses himself, and that everyone must listen to and obey that Prophet, Yeshua. This is one place where Yeshua in prophecy is called a prophet, in the same way the Two Witnesses in Revelation 11 are called prophets. And Yeshua is God, Yahuweh/Yehovah, which means that Yahuweh/Yehovah himself as God is also called a prophet in this prophecy. The Two Witnesses are called prophets, and Yahuweh/Yehovah is the true, original prophet, the one who is truly prophesying with his words. There is no true prophet in Scripture speaking the true words of Yahuweh/Yehovah who is truly a prophet themselves, because it is not their own words they are speaking. It is Yahuweh/Yehovah's words that are true prophecy, and his words through all of Scripture are prophesying, as the Two Witnesses do in Revelation 11. Yahuweh/Yehovah's words are the original and true words that are actually prophesying through all of time, continuously, especially those written down as a Witness.

The Oil of the Light and Word of Yahuweh/Yehovah:

    Exodus 25:6, 31-40

    Zechariah 4:1-14

    Psalms 119:105

Examination of Verses **Exodus 25:6, 31-40** and **Zechariah 4:1-14** and **Psalms 119:105** – It should be obvious from Exodus 25 that oil is used as the fuel source for the flame of light in ancient lamps. The oil is the fuel that provides the fire to burn and make light in the seven branch menorah used in the set-apart place. And that is what the two sons of oil, the two olive trees, in Zechariah 4 are, the fuel source of oil for the light of the seven lamps on the menorah. Psalms 119 reveals the spiritual significance of the menorah lamps of light in the set-apart place, saying that the Word of Yahuweh/Yehovah is a "lamp" and a "light" for helping people to see where they are going, to walk on their path and see where their feet are stepping.

The word of Yahuweh/Yehovah is a lamp that has light coming out from it, and the only kinds of lamps that can have light coming out from them are those that are fueled, which in ancient times means they have to have oil in them to burn for the light, or else they are useless. The oil, together with the lamp and light, are the Word of Yahuweh/Yehovah. The two olive trees in Zechariah 4 that are the two sons of oil are the Two Witnesses of the Word of Yahuweh/Yehovah. The seven lamp menorah and the two olive trees in Zechariah 4 all together represent Yahuweh/Yehovah himself, especially his seven eyes, and his words which are light to help people to see with their eyes.

The two olive trees are called "two sons of oil" because they are the Word of Yahuweh/Yehovah that he has spoken forth out of himself that act as Two Witnesses in addition to his own witness of seeing everything everywhere at all times with his seven eyes. The olive trees of oil that are sons of oil are Yahuweh/Yehovah's double Witness of his Words on earth for everyone to see and hear, bringing light for those who want to see the way to go without stumbling in the dark. And his Words that are the two sons of oil are the Witness of himself to others while at the same time acting as a Witness against those who do not obey his Words, allowing plagues of judgement to fall on the unrepentant.

Yahuweh/Yehovah himself as God is Two Witnesses and Yahuweh/Yehovah's written and recorded Word is Two Witnesses. The Two Witnesses of the written Word of Yahuweh/Yehovah in the two olive trees that are two sons of oil were there at the time of Zechariah and have always been there since the time of Zechariah, and were there before Zechariah as well. The Two Witnesses in Revelation 11 of the Word of Yahuweh/Yehovah and of Yahuweh/Yehovah himself are nothing new that suddenly appear for 1,260 days, but according to John himself in his writing about the connection to Zechariah 4, were there long before the Great Tribulation begins, since before the days of Zechariah.

The Oil of the Light and Word of Yahuweh/Yehovah (Stopped Flowing at the Time of His Coming):
Matthew 25:1-13

Prophecy Fulfillment of Verses **Matthew 25:1-13** – Since the Two Witnesses in Revelation 11, according to John, are the two olive trees that are the two sons of oil, it should be clear and obvious from the parable of the ten virgins in Matthew 25 that that oil of the Two Witnesses has stopped flowing and is gone during the Great Tribulation. The five wise virgins store up extra oil that they take with them during the Great Tribulation as they wait for the bridegroom to come, because there is no more oil flowing at that time available on hand. The five foolish virgins did not take extra oil with them to wait during the Great Tribulation for the bridegroom to come, and their lights went out because of not having any more oil. This lack of oil for their lights caused the five foolish virgins to have to go to the merchants to buy more oil (since the oil from Yahuweh/Yehovah had stopped flowing as a continuous supply on hand) which caused them to miss the bridegroom when he came at midnight, and not enter into eternal life.

In January 2017 Jerry Pearce claimed that his personal Bible had begun to supernaturally flow with oil, coming directly out of the center of the Bible itself continuously. Three years later on January 10, 2020 he said that the oil had stopped flowing from the Bible and he decided to go and buy oil from a store. There were allegations at the time that he had in fact been buying the oil from a store for the entire three years and was faking the miracle, but no investigation done was ever able to prove one way or the other whether this was a real miracle or a hoax. Either way it does not matter, because Jerry Pearce by going out to buy oil, because of not being able to get that oil from the Word of Yahuweh/Yehovah in the Bible, was still carrying out the prophetic action showing the timing of the beginning of fulfillment of this parable of the ten virgins, when the five foolish ones had to go to the local store or merchant to buy oil, because they had not stored up the oil of the Word of Yahuweh/Yehovah with them.

Whether the Bible had actually been flowing oil and then suddenly stopped, causing Jerry Pearce to go out and buy some oil in his panic, as he claimed, or if he had been buying oil from a local store for the entire three years as was alleged (but so far not proven in any published records or investigation for the general public to view) it was still the prophetic sign that during those three years from 2017 to 2020 the time of Yahuweh/Yehovah removing his oil as in the parable of the ten virgins was beginning. It was the sign that people were not getting the oil of the Word of Yahuweh/Yehovah anymore, and feeling the need to literally go out to the local store and buy oil from a merchant seller instead of getting it directly from Yahuweh/Yehovah himself and his words. And without the oil of Yahuweh/Yehovah, of his Word, then the light goes out.

This same sign was shown again on the night of the Disgusting Idol Desolating event at the foot of the Temple Mount set-apart place. The oil in the six outer branches of the menorah would not light because of the wind blowing them out, from the inside of the enclosed space of the tent. The oil and light are inseparably connected together in all of these prophecies such as in Zechariah 4 and Matthew 25 as representing both attributes of Yahuweh/Yehovah himself and his Word at the same time. The reason the foolish virgins needed more oil was because their lights were going out, as the six lights on the menorah that night kept going out, the lights of man represented in the number six.

By the time of Yeshua's coming as the bridegroom at the end of the Great Tribulation, the oil is completely gone for the foolish virgins who did not keep a store of the oil of Yahuweh/Yehovah on hand with them. And John clearly says in Revelation 11 that the Two Witnesses are the two olive trees in Zechariah 4 that are the two sons of oil, which means the Two Witnesses being made up of the oil also have to be used up and gone at the time of Yeshua's coming at the end of the Great Tribulation. This means that the oil during the Great Tribulation has stopped flowing at that time, the oil of the Two Witnesses of Yahuweh/Yehovah, the oil of the Witness of his Word, has stopped flowing and been sealed up and hidden as in Isaiah 8. And only the wise virgins who stored up this oil of the Two Witnesses of the Word of Yahuweh/Yehovah still have that witness with them so that their lights can still continue to burn and shine.

But those who are cut off from Yahuweh/Yehovah personally and directly to him, those who have relied upon the merchants of oil at the local churches or colleges/schools or religious gatherings as their source of the oil of the Word of Yahuweh/Yehovah, suddenly do not have that source of the real oil of Yahuweh/Yehovah flowing to them anymore through other people and sources, because they do not get it directly from Yahuweh/Yehovah himself. And they have to try to buy that oil to keep their lights burning anywhere in any physical location or from any physical person that they can find it, as they try to keep their light from going out. They have to buy manufactured, imitation oil from a store, from any physical person or place that appears to have oil available to buy from them, but the oil is not the real thing. According to Matthew 25 and Zechariah 4 they do not have the oil of the Two Witnesses (two olive trees that are two sons of oil) of the Word of Yahuweh/Yehovah with them anymore at the time of his coming at the end of the Great Tribulation. The Witness of the Word of Yahuweh/Yehovah is sealed and hidden from them and they will miss the coming of the bridegroom because of it.

It is clear from Matthew 25 that the Two Witnesses, which are the oil according to John, are sealed up and hidden and removed from most of the earth during the Great Tribulation, to the point that they are "killed." The supply of oil from the Two Witnesses of the Word of Yahuweh/Yehovah is cut off during the Great Tribulation and only those wise virgins with the extra oil of the Two Witnesses of the Word of Yahuweh/Yehovah, and of Yahuweh/Yehovah himself, still have that Witness with them, keeping their lights burning to be able to see with through the darkest hour at midnight. All of these things with the five foolish virgins and five wise virgins and their oil we are watching happen today, especially since 2020 and the worldwide COVID plague.

The Beast Coming Up Out of the Pit of the Deep (that Kills the Two Witnesses) Carrying the Prostitute Who is Drunk with the Blood of the Witnesses of Yeshua:

Revelation 17:1-8

Word for Word Prophecy Examination of Verses **Revelation 17:1-8** – It is not the Beast Out of the Sea from Revelation 13 that kills the Two Witnesses; it is the Beast Out of the Pit of the Deep with Mystery Babel the Great upon it in Revelation 17 that kills them. The Beast Out of the Pit of the Deep with the prostitute Mystery Babel riding on it is representing the city of Babel all the way back in Genesis 11, which has always been around in one form or another since then. And Mystery Babel is drunk with the blood of the witnesses of Yeshua, the believers in Yeshua who bear witness to him and are killed for it. Together Mystery Babel and the Scarlet Beast Out of the Pit of the Deep that she rides are the killers of Yahuweh/Yehovah's witnesses in its many different forms. The goal of Mystery Babel and the Scarlet Beast Out of the Pit of the Deep is to remove, kill, and destroy all witness about Yahuweh/Yehovah on the earth, including the Two Witnesses in Revelation 11.

It is the "great city" that the bodies of the Two Witnesses lie in after they are killed, because they are killed by the city Mystery Babel. It is always the cities that are the central places of "killing" Yahuweh/Yehovah's witnesses, removing them from existence to replace the witness of the existence of Yahuweh/Yehovah with the worship of man and his creations. And the only way that mankind can worship themselves as gods is to remove all of the evidence and witness of Yahwueh/Yehovah and his Word and Commands in Scripture, to kill them from society, which is what the idea of the city of Babel from Genesis 11 is all about.

1,260 Days Equals a Time, Times, and Half a Time (1 Plus 2 Plus .5 Equaling 3.5):

Revelation 12:6, 14

Word for Word Prophecy Examination of Verses **Revelation 12:6, 14** – According to Revelation 12 the counting of 1,260 days equals the same as a "Time, Times, and Half a Time." It is the same in Daniel 12 where 1,290 days equal an "Appointed Time, Appointed Times, and a Half." Both are saying the exact same thing in different languages, Hebrew and Greek. It is only the counting of days, either 1,290 days or 1,260 days, that are associated with this time, times, and half a time concept. The prophecies of 42 months are not specifically connected with this mathematical formula. And it is a mathematical formula, taking a time that is 1, and times plural that are 2, and adding a half to them, equaling three and a half or 3.5 in numerical numbers. 1,260 days divided by 30 days equals 42 months; 42 months divided by 12 months equals 3.5 years; 1,260 days divided by 360 days (30 days times 12 months) equals 3.5 years.

Approximately 3.5 years is the total time of 1,260 days and as well as 1,290 days in Daniel 12. The interesting thing about Revelation 11 is that it is the only prophecy with two sets of a "time, times, and half a time" one right after the other. First it is 1,260 days that equals 3.5 years, or a time, times, and half a time of years, and then 3.5 days follow right after, which is a time, times, and half a time of days. The giving of the Two stone tablets of the Witness and the Witness of the Torah of Mosheh was in the year 1495 B.C.E. [According to the records of the dates and numbering of years in Scripture this is the only possible year that the exodus out of Egypt and the camping of the children of Israel at Mount Sinai could have happened, where Moses received the Ten Words written by Yahuweh/Yehovah upon the Two stone tablets of the Witness. All of this I have already thoroughly laid out and shown in *Calculating the Last Seven*, that there is no possibility of the exodus event happening any other year than the year 1495 B.C.E. when going by the record of the Hebrew itself in Scripture and how they counted the year dates they recorded.]

From the year 1495 B.C.E. plus 3,500 years, adds up to the year 2006 C.E. The year 2006 was the completion of exactly three and a half thousand years or 3.5 millennia and the marker will stay at 3.5 millennia for 99 years after 2006 (since 3.6 millennia cannot be mathematically reached until a full 100 years have gone by from that date). 3.5 millennia (3.5 thousand years) is a time, times, and half a time of millennia. The year 1495 B.C.E. was the year that Moses began the writing of the Torah, with the witness of the Word of Yahuweh/Yehovah in it, the very first known time that the words of Yahuweh/Yehovah, his commands and prophecies, were ever written down word for word as he had spoken them as a witness on the earth about himself, and as a witness against the people on the earth who are doing evil in rebellion against his words. As of this time in history today this Witness of the written words and prophecies of Yahuweh/Yehovah has been witnessing on the earth for a total of a time, times, and half a time of millennia or 3.5 thousand years. And the Two Witness of the Ten Words or Ten Commands of Yahuweh/Yehovah, originally written on the Two stone tablets of the Witness, have been giving their witness on the earth for the same amount of time, for a time, times, and half a time of millennia, 3.5 thousand years.

The Two Witnesses Prophecy:

Revelation 11:3-12

Prophecy Fulfillment of Verses **Revelation 11:3-12** – The Two Witnesses are called "my two witnesses" and "two olive trees" and "two menorah" and "two prophets." As discussed earlier Yahuweh/Yehovah himself and his seven eyes, the same seven eyes of the Lamb Yeshua, is the menorah in Zechariah 4, meaning that the two witnesses cannot be men, because men cannot be God. There is never at any time in history or through Scripture that Yahuweh/Yehovah has men or women take his place elevated to a position of godhood with the power of gods. No man can be the seven eyes of Yahuweh/Yehovah, only he himself can be his own eyes.

The "two menorah" represents Yahuweh/Yehovah himself and the "two olive trees" that are the two sons of oil represent the Word of Yahuweh/Yehovah himself. And Yeshua as God himself, Yahuweh/Yehovah, is prophesied by Moses to come as a Prophet, while at the same time Yahuweh/Yehovah throughout Scripture prophesies with his Words, his Word being the true prophetic as well. So the "two prophets" is also showing the person of Yahuweh/Yehovah and Yeshua himself as the true prophet, and the Word of Yahuweh/Yehovah and Yeshua himself, witnessing about himself. The phrase "my two witnesses" indicates that the Two Witnesses are more precisely belonging to Yahuweh/Yehovah, as his Word belongs to him. The Word of Yahuweh/Yehovah is "his two witnesses" belonging to him as a witness about him.

The foundation of the fulfillment of this prophecy in verse 11:3-4 is in the "Two tablets of the Witness," which are the very first known written record of the Word or Command of Yahuweh/Yehovah on the earth, written in his own hand onto two tablets of stone. These two tablets of stone with the Ten Words or Ten Commands of Yahuweh/Yehovah written on them are the foundation of Two Witnesses of his written Word on the earth, recorded into the stone itself in the year 1495 B.C.E. From the two tablets of stone acting as the foundation of the Witness of Yahuweh/Yehovah was built the Torah of Yahuweh/Yehovah written down by Moses, beginning in that same year, which became a total of five volumes of books collected together as one set over the period of 40 years that Moses wrote them down while wandering in the wilderness. All of the Words or Commands/Instructions of Yahuweh/Yehovah were recorded down by Moses word for word from the mouth of Yahuweh/Yehovah as the Witness of Yahuweh/Yehovah, witnessing about him and witnessing against all those on the earth who have violated those Words.

The Witness continued from there with more books with the Word of Yahuweh/Yehovah, but with prophecies instead of commands, which are the two types of witnesses of Yahuweh/Yehovah's written Words that are recorded on the earth, the commands from the Torah and the prophecies from the Prophets. These Two Witnesses of the Word of Yahuweh/Yehovah, especially the foundational Two Witnesses of the two tablets of stone with the Ten Words or Ten Commands written upon them, have been existing as the Witness on the earth for a time, times, and half a time of millennia, for 3.5 thousand years, up to and after the year 2006. As the time of Yeshua's return draws near, and the end of this world of man, that time, times, and half a time of the Two Witnesses of the Word of Yahuweh/Yehovah, of the Two Olive Trees that are Two Sons of Oil, comes to its completion and finish in fulfillment of verse 11:7. When the Word of Yahuweh/Yehovah has ended its time of Witness on the earth, then Yahuweh/Yehovah allows the Scarlet Beast Out of the Pit of the Deep with Mystery Babel the Great upon it to kill that witness of the Word of Yahuweh/Yehovah, his commands/instructions and prophecies, removing it from society, from the cities of the earth, to be thrown out as garbage in the street.

The Word of Yahuweh/Yehovah does not cease to exist, because the body of it remains and is still in existence, but it has been thrown out of the lives of the people themselves, so that they do not live by it anymore, especially in the cities of the earth that have taken in "the great city" Mystery Babel the Great into themselves from Genesis 11, in fulfillment of verse 11:8. The great city Mystery Babel the Great as already discussed at the beginning is prophesied to be in every nation on the earth at the time of the end, as a disease in all of the cities of the earth. And this great city, which is in all of the cities of the earth, is spiritually called Sodom and Egypt and where "the Master was crucified/impaled." These are each of the three shadow picture events in Scripture of Two Witnesses, discussed earlier, at Sodom and in Egypt at the exodus and when Yeshua was crucified in Jerusalem.

Each of these times in history has been a time of people in a city or nation doing evil to others. Throughout history there have been pockets of cities or nations or empires that have transgressed the Word of Yahuweh/Yehovah to the point of their total destruction such as Sodom and Egypt. Those places that have completely turned against Yahuweh/Yehovah in rebellion to his Word never last for very long and one way or another cease to exist or collapse into destruction, as with Sodom and as with Egypt, even to large empires like the Roman Empire or the British Empire. As a city, nation, or empire turns away from Yahuweh/Yehovah, the Two Witnesses of the Word of Yahuweh/Yehovah has been there on the earth for the last 3,500 years to witness against them, and bring the judgments of plagues upon any unrepentant city, nation, or empire, destroying it and causing a halt and stopping of the sin. But upon the repentant city, nation, or empire a halt to the plagues and judgment, bringing mercy upon them instead of destruction.

Yahuweh/Yehovah uses the Witness of his Word to determine whenever he should bring plagues upon any city, whenever and as often as he wishes/determines, plagues of many various kinds through history. And anyone who has tried to destroy or harm the Witness of his Word throughout the earth, he kills them with the fire of the Words of his mouth, as previously shown from examples in Scripture, in fulfillment of verse 11:6. These are anyone through the last 3,500 years who try to wipe out the written Witness of his Word in Scripture on the earth, such as during the time of Antiochus IV Epiphanes, when the written record of the Word of Yahuweh/Yehovah was almost completely wiped out and ceased to exist according to First and Second Maccabees. Whenever there has been anyone or anyplace on the earth that has tried to completely throw out and remove from existence the written Witness of the Word of Yahuweh/Yehovah, especially among the children of Israel themselves during the times when they have turned away from him (through the books of Judges and Kings), Yahuweh/Yehovah has killed those who wished to harm his Witness and prevented them from succeeding, in fulfillment of verse 11:5.

This is the way that it had been for a times, times, and half a time of millennia, for 3,500 years up to 2006. But then in the early to middle 20th Century there began a small shift that grew and grew in society until it began to explode and overtake the world shortly after 2006. There has always been Mystery Babel from Genesis 11 in the cities of the world, trying to take them over and control them with the Babel ideology that is in rebellion against Yahuweh/Yehovah. Wherever Babel is in a city, the witnesses of Yahuweh/Yehovah in his people and his Word have to be removed, because the two are so completely opposite and opposed to each other. The more the people of the cities of the world adopt Babel into their society, the more they have to push out the Witnesses of the Word of Yahuweh/Yehovah and kill or remove those people who bear that witness.

From the early to middle 20th Century to today the world began a rapid shift, led mostly by the United States of America and other western world countries, to adopt in greater fullness and measure the Scarlet

Beast Out of the Pit of the Deep and Mystery Babel the Great into its cities and culture. After 2006 the tide turned and the majority of society in the world began accepting the Scarlet Beast Out of the Pit of the Deep and Mystery Babel completely, throwing out the Two Witnesses of the Word of Yahuweh/Yehovah, of his commands/instructions on how to live, especially the foundational Ten Words originally written on the Two Tablets of the Witness. America was one of the final places in the world at that time that was still holding out against the shift that was happening, but around that time cities across America began taking down the Two Witnesses of the Two Tablets with the Ten Commands of Yahuweh/Yehovah written on them, throwing them out into the street and killing them from their lives.

Since 2006 it has been a rapid and consistent process around the world as people have thrown out morality standards that have existed for thousands of years of recorded history in all societies, and now today, in the name of "freedom" almost all sins in rebellion against the Witness of the Word of Yahuweh/Yehovah in his Torah are either protected by law, or considered a normal part of life, in most countries (such as abortion up to the point of after the baby has already been born; murder in certain circumstances of suffering or old age; stealing in circumstances of rioting where people feel it is their right to steal the things they covet from the wealthy; adultery even among old and aged adults; bearing false witness against others; rape and prostitution in certain circumstances of entertainment; homosexuality to the point of marriage, which is something that has never been done before in thousands of years of recorded history; cross-dressing to the point of physical sex change or gender neutrality; bestiality, etc.; or witchcraft and the worship of Satan and demons normalized in the open as a few examples).

The countries that do still outlaw some of these things still have other problems of unrighteousness and rebellion against the Witness of the Word of Yahuweh/Yehovah, while the culture in most of those countries has changed to the point that the majority of the people still accept these things as they are being normalized among their cultures. And those things which are still outlawed are still being done anyway in the criminal world of mafias and gangs, such as prostitution of children and horrendous murders of many kinds, and governments incapable of stopping it, or do not care to stop it. All of the cities of the world are removing and killing the Two Witnesses of the Word of Yahuweh/Yehovah from their midst, and have succeeded in greater and greater measure since after 2006, in fulfillment of verses 11:7-8.

Ever since Genesis 11 there has been a war between the ideology of Babel and the ways of Yahuweh/Yehovah, and Mystery Babel from Genesis 11 has almost won in killing the Witness of the Word of Yahuweh/Yehovah and his ways and instructions from the cities and towns of the earth. This is the reality of the way things are actually happening; since 2006 there has been a dual process, in fulfillment of verses 11:5-7 of the Two Witnesses of the Word of Yahuweh/Yehovah still there as a witness bringing down the plagues on the earth, while at the same time being fought against by the Scarlet Beast Out of the Pit of the Deep with Mystery Babel, as it has slowly killed the Word of Yahuweh/Yehovah from one city and town in the world after another. Since 2006 we have been in the time when the witness of the Two Witnesses of Yahuweh/Yehovah have been finishing their time of witness, and Yahuweh/Yehovah has allowed the Scarlet Beast Out of the Pit of the Deep to be killing them.

But in fulfillment of verse 11:8 the bodies of the Word of Yahuweh/Yehovah still remain in those cities, in the Bibles and books containing his Word still lying around within the cities. There is simply no one who wants to live by them anymore in their lives, especially most Christians, with new movements of Deconstruction and Acceptance of the 'Other' and Reclaiming Jesus. And they leave the bodies of the Word of Yahuweh/Yehovah visible in the cities of the world. It is not erased or removed completely, only thrown out into the gutter where no one believes in the Witness of the Word of Yahuweh/Yehovah or lives by it anymore.

There are almost no Churches left in the western world today that believe in the Word of Yahuweh/Yehovah, according to polling, but instead believe and teach that all of the commands and words of Yahuweh/Yehovah in Scripture were for those people in Israel who lived in the past, but now today people can live any way they want to according to their own desires of their heart, believing in Jesus as any person or God that they want him to be to fit their lifestyle. And some people around the world are rejoicing and celebrating that the Two Witnesses of the Word of Yahuweh/Yehovah have been killed and they do not have to obey or follow the commands of Yahuweh/Yehovah anymore, in fulfillment of verse 11:9. They think that they have finally broken free of the bondage of the Words of Yahuweh/Yehovah in his Torah, to do whatever they want to in complete freedom. There are many Christians who are so happy to have finally been able in the last few years to break off the bonds of the Words, the Commands, of Yahuweh/Yehovah in Scripture so that they do not have to obey it anymore, as the tidal wave shift in the churches has changed so that most people accept disobedience to the Two Witnesses of the Word of Yahuweh/Yehovah as normal, and there is no longer the stigma from most Christian society. The Two Witnesses of the oil of Yahuweh/Yehovah is currently now only with the five wise virgins and gone from the five foolish virgins.

Revelation 11:9 says that only some, not all, of the people from the various nations and languages and tribes rejoice and celebrate when the Two Witnesses of the two sons of oil of the Word of Yahuweh/Yehovah has been killed. And that is what has been ongoing in the years after 2006 as the Two Witnesses of the Word of Yahuweh/Yehovah are removed from a city or nation more and more, some of the people rejoice and celebrate with parades or parties such as the one recently held at the White House on December 13, 2022. There was much rejoicing and exultation by the people there over the death of the Word of Yahuweh/Yehovah so that they would not have to live by his words anymore. Some, but not all, of the people are rejoicing over seeing the dead bodies of the Word of Yahuweh/Yehovah thrown out of society, because they think that they do not have anything to fear from the plagues of Yahuweh/Yehovah anymore that have come from the Witness of his Word. And Israel has been on the forefront of this movement of removing the Two Witnesses of the Two Tablets of the Witness of Yahuweh/Yehovah and his commands from their nation and lives, with some rejoicing in Israel and Jerusalem as well.

Beginning in the late 1800's the religion of Evolution and worship of man through science began coming up with scientific ways of trying to control the world and the plagues of the world. Through the development of science man came up with a new scientific way of saying that man is in control of the weather, not God, not Yahuweh/Yehovah, through "Global Warming." This idea really started to take over society in 1988, and by 2006 Al Gore released his documentary *An Inconvenient Truth*, and by 2018 the Greta Thunberg protest movement had started over Climate Change. The name Global Warming had to be changed to Climate Change when the world started getting extremely cold and hot at the same time, but the idea that man controls the plagues of the weather, not Yahuweh/Yehovah, has taken over most of the world.

Now today in fulfillment of verse 11:10, even as the plagues of Yahuweh/Yehovah continue on the earth, nobody believes that he is the one doing them anymore, which removes any need for repentance. Most people today believe that man has caused the severe and unusual plagues of the weather on the earth today, of the hurricanes and tornadoes, and extreme hot and cold, and blizzards and fires, and droughts and floods. So they still rejoice over the deaths of the Witness of the Word of Yahuweh/Yehovah, and do not have to worry about those plagues anymore, because if man is god with the power to control the weather plagues (or animal plagues like locusts, such as the hundreds of billions or trillions of locusts across Africa and south Asia a few years ago), then man has the power to stop them without having to change their lives or turn in repentance to Yahuweh/Yehovah anymore.

And man through science has overcome the plagues of most diseases and viruses/bacteria, so that people do not have to fear those kinds of plagues either and can continue in rebellion and sin. Man even thinks that through science he can destroy plagues of asteroids that Yahuweh/Yehovah might send on the earth, with space ships and advanced weapons, so that people do not need to fear being wiped out like the cities of the plain, Sodom and Gomorrah, when fire fell on them from the heavens. Man thinks that they will be able to conquer any plague that Yahuweh/Yehovah sends, so that they can continue unrepentant in their sin this time, unlike in the past, effectively killing the Two Witnesses of the Word of Yahuweh/Yehovah so that those witnesses have no more power over man to hurt or destroy people anymore with plagues.

It is a process of the Witness of the Word of Yahuweh/Yehovah still witnessing while at the same time Yahuweh/Yehovah is allowing the Scarlet Beast Out of the Pit of the Deep to fight with and overcome the Witness of his Word, and ultimately kill it from the hearts of people and society. Both things are happening at the same time, with the final days of the Witness of the Two Witnesses still ongoing while being overcome and killed in different places. That is the reality of what is happening, and why there are two separate sets of a time, times, and half a time associated with the witness for 1,260 days and the killed bodies of the witness lying in the street for 3.5 days. Even as the Two Witnesses of the Word of Yahuweh/Yehovah are being killed and removed from society, the witness still goes on and Yahuweh/Yehovah is still bringing the plagues on the earth in warning of his judgment coming if the world does not turn around in repentance. But no one is listening to the plagues anymore.

Just in the year of 2022 to 2023 the specific plague of Yahuweh/Yehovah withholding rain from the earth during the final 1,260 days of the Witness of his Word has happened all over the world, in fulfillment of verse 11:6. The longest river in China, the Yangtze, almost completely dried up from drought. The longest river in Germany, the Rhine, almost completely dried up from drought. The longest river in France, the Loire, almost completely dried up from drought, along with Lake Montbel. England experienced unprecedented drought that caused wild fires to erupt inside of London. The longest river in Italy, the Po, almost completely dried up from drought. The second longest river in America, the Mississippi, almost completely dried up from drought, along with Lake Mead near Las Vegas and other lakes in that region. The longest rivers in West Asia, the Tigris and Euphrates, almost completely dried up from drought.

The Tigris almost ceased to exist and the Euphrates has places along the river that an army could cross over on foot (Revelation 16:12). In all cases there were places along the rivers where people could cross on foot with dry ground exposed because the water levels were so low. This is not to mention the droughts in places like Texas that had no rain for three months, then received three months of rain in less than 36 hours, causing massive flooding and places like Kenya that have been through three years without rain since 2020, the worst drought that Kenya has ever had in its recorded history. This is one of the specific plagues mentioned in Revelation 11:6, of no rain falling during the final 1,260 days of the prophesying of the Two Witnesses of the Word of Yahuweh/Yehovah on the earth.

The Two Witnesses of the Two Tablets of the Witness of the Word/Command of Yahuweh/Yehovah are still around, still doing their witness and bringing plagues on the earth, but also being removed and overcome and killed in the cities of the earth more and more, as we are reaching the end of the time of their witness. And the Word of Yahuweh/Yehovah is both a witness and a prophecy at the same time, witnessing the violations of the people on the earth of the Word of Yahuweh/Yehovah while at the same time prophesying the consequences of those violations that will come in the forms of warning plagues and eventually the judgment wrath of Yahuweh/Yehovah that comes at the end of the Great Tribulation, when he ends the world of man, the world of the many Beasts of mankind through history and Babel. This time the witness is showing that the whole world has to be destroyed as in the days of Noah and the global flood. As Yeshua said it would be in the parable of the ten virgins in Matthew 25, the oil of the Two Witnesses that are the two olive trees and two sons of oil would be gone (sealed up and hidden) for the world at the time of his coming, but still there with those who are truly following him and have kept a store of the oil of the Two Witnesses with them to keep their lights shining to the end.

Note: The original Two Witnesses of the Two stone tablets of the Witness were placed in the ark of the covenant at the time of Moses and remained with it always. Both the ark of the covenant and the Two tablets of the Witness disappeared from history at the time of Jeremiah, with the last record of them being during that time when Jeremiah talks about that copies of them will never be made again to serve as the original. The only time since then that there has been a witness who has testified to seeing the ark of the covenant and the Two tablets of the Witness is Ron Wyatt, who received documented permission from the Israeli government to do an archaeological dig at the Garden Tomb, and discovered the ark with the two tablets of stone with the Ten Words written on them, buried in a secret chamber directly underneath a crucifixion site where three crosses or stakes had been in the ground next to the Garden Tomb where Yeshua was buried. And if Ron Wyatt is correct about finding them, as it has now turned out he was correct in finding Noah's Ark, and the real Mount Sinai in Arabia, and the true crossing site of the children of Israel across the Red Sea where the Egyptian chariots are still visible today, there they remain in their underground chamber till today, witnessing.

According to Yeshua, John the Immerser was the Elijah Promised to Come in Fulfillment of the Prophecy in Malachi, but There is Still Another Application to This Prophecy Connected to the Time of the Day of Yahuweh/Yehovah:

Malachi 4:1-6

Matthew 11:7-15   Luke 7:24-28

Matthew 17:9-13   Mark 9:9-13

Prophecy Fulfillment of Verses **Malachi 4:1-6** with **Matthew 11:7-15** and **Luke 7:24-28** and **Matthew 17:9-13** and **Mark 9:9-13** – There are two different instances that Yeshua explains how John the Immerser was the Elijah who came in fulfillment of the prophecy in Malachi 4:1-6. The first time is in Matthew 11 and Luke 7 and the second time is in Matthew 17 and Mark 9. Yeshua very clearly says it in Matthew 11, that John the Immerser is Elijah who was promised to come, for those who are willing to accept and believe this, and then alludes to it in Matthew 17, saying that the Elijah that the teachers of the day taught had to come first did already come first, which was John the Immerser. Yeshua also explained that John the Immerser was rejected by the people of that time, even though he was the fulfillment of this prophecy in Malachi 4.

In Matthew 3 and Luke 3 John the Immerser proclaimed paraphrases from the words of Malachi 4:1 and 3, warning the people of the day that would be coming in the future, when there would be no root or branch left from the fire of Yahuweh/Yehovah's day of judgment, burning like a furnace, bringing down all of the trees to be burned in fire that do not produce good fruit. That day is still a future day that has not yet come, which John the Immerser prophesied about from the prophecy of Malachi 4. And at that time Yeshua fulfilled Malachi 4:2, as the Sun of Righteousness that arose with healing in his "wings," in Hebrew "umarpe biknapheha" "וּמַרְפֵּא בִּכְנָפֶיהָ" "and healing in its wings." The original Hebrew Gospel of Matthew even specifically says that Yeshua fulfilled this prophecy, in Matthew 14:36, using the exact same Hebrew word "kanaph" "כָּנָף" in Malachi 4:2, saying, "And the sick turned to Him *that* He consent to allow them to touch upon the wing of His garment; and all who touched it were healed." [31] All those who touched the "kanaph" or the wing of Yeshua's garment were healed of their sicknesses, and then oftentimes, as recorded in the books of the Good News, leaped for joy like calves afterward.

Parts of the Malachi 4 prophecy were fulfilled at the time of Yeshua, and parts are not fulfilled until his return, but were still prophesied about and spoken about at that time when he walked the earth, through John the Immerser. John the Immerser is already the prophet Elijah promised to come before the great Day of Yahuweh/Yehovah, when Yahuweh/Yehovah comes to rule the earth. But in Matthew 11:14 Yeshua makes an interesting statement saying that John the Immerser is the Elijah who will come in the future, in the future tense. This was while John was still alive in chapter 11. Then after John dies, in chapter 17 Yeshua says a double tense statement about the prophecy of Elijah in Malachi 4, first in verse 11 talking about Elijah coming in the future tense, then in verse 12 saying that Elijah already came, referring to John the Immerser. John the Immerser was the Elijah who already came, and yet he is also the Elijah who is still coming in the future

---

[31] "וחלו פניו ירצה לעוזבם יגעו בכנף מעילו וכל אשר נגעו נתרפאו" *Even Bochan*, Shem Tov (16th to 17th century C.E. copy) Ms. Michael 119; Bodleian Library, Oxford.

simultaneously. John the Immerser was part of the fulfillment of Malachi 4:5-6 at that time of Yeshua's coming on the earth, but there is still another fulfilment coming in the future, John the Immerser coming as Elijah again, right before the great and awesome Day of Yahuweh/Yehovah at the end of the Great Tribulation.

Also in Matthew 17:11 Yeshua explains what the prophecy about Elijah means, when it says that Elijah will turn the hearts of the fathers (parents) to the sons (children) and the sons (children) to their fathers (parents). In doing this Elijah is "restoring all," coming first or before in preparation for the coming of Yahuweh/Yehovah on the Day of Yahuweh/Yehovah. Yeshua was explaining all of these things about Elijah and John the Immerser to his disciples in chapter 17, because they had just seen the real Elijah on the mountain, together with the real Moses.

In June 2017 Sadhu Sundar Selvaraj at Yahuweh/Yehovah's instruction gathered his Open Heavens Prophetic Conference on Mount Karmel in Israel, because Yahuweh/Yehovah told him that 2017 was the time for Elijah to appear. From Mount Karmel he did a live broadcast, together with a gathering of about 1,000 people who were there with him in Israel for the conference. During the live broadcast almost all of the 1,000 people at the event saw Elijah descending from the heavens in fire, while at the same time many people who were watching the live broadcast later wrote that they saw Elijah appear in their homes at the same time. There were even some who were not watching the broadcast at all or knew about the broadcast or what Sadhu was doing who later told him they also saw Elijah appear to them on that exact same day.

June 2017 began the time of the prophet Elijah coming first before the great Day of Yahuweh/Yehovah, the time of the prophet Elijah that Yeshua said was still coming in the future that had not yet been fulfilled at that time. June 2017 began the time of the final fulfillment of this prophecy in Malachi 4:5-6, with the time of the restoration of families, turning the hearts of fathers and children back to each other. The reason for this is so that Yahuweh/Yehovah does not have to completely destroy every person with complete destruction on the earth when he comes, because of the people having hardened their hearts to the point of a complete breakdown in the family system that he created from the beginning in Genesis.

Families around the world today are fallen apart because of the culture of rebellion against the Two Witnesses of the Word of Yahuweh/Yehovah in the Torah of Moses, which is why the Torah of Moses needs to be remembered in fulfillment of Malachi 4:4. The family system has been falling apart for over a hundred years, but today it is worse around the world than ever before in terms of the scale and depth of brokenness. Children grow up without a father or a mother more and more because of divorce and homosexual marriages that deny the child from growing up with one of their parents. And many children are abandoned by their parents through adoption or other ways, or are forced to have to give up their children in adoption, or even murdered by their parents through abortion. And many more children are abducted from their parents or sold away by their parents to be slaves and abused all over the world, especially in free nations with democratic governments.

The prophet Elijah comes to hold the line and restore families, and the family system that Yahuweh/Yehovah created, for at least some on the earth so that there does not have to be a complete end to everybody on the earth, in the same way that one family of eight people, through Noah, were saved at the time of the global flood. There will be a remnant of some families saved from the destruction of the earth, when Yahuweh/Yehovah destroys the earth in fire and shaking at his coming (Malachi 4 and Isaiah 24).

It has only been since after 2000 that DNA testing has been available to the public, but at that time only through Y chromosome and mitochondrial testing. And it has only been since after 2010 that autosomal DNA testing has been advanced enough to be available to the general public in a way that people can really use it. This is a unique time in history since 2010 when a person can know with absolute certainty who their parents are, or who any of their genetic family members are. People who do not know who their parents are, or who their father is, can find out with a simple DNA test, and the parents they are looking for do not even have to take that test themselves with autosomal DNA testing. A person only has to match their DNA to distant cousins who have also taken the test, and their genetic parents can be easily traced and found. We are watching a unique time when children are able to find their biological parents and be reunited with them again, with their hearts restored to one another again, or at the very least to know who each other are and know each other exists in order to work through things and deal with things in reality.

This is a unique time in history of literal restoration of families that has never happened before in the history of the world, in fulfillment of Malachi 4:6. Yahuweh/Yehovah created family to be so important, that in creating DNA and the genetics of one generation being born after another, he made it so that each new person born carries the exact fingerprints of DNA and chromosomes from their parents, and from their grandparents and great grandparents before them, so that a person can know with certainty who their parents and family are. It is an amazing creation that is so mathematically precise in its randomness, everyone can find their family even through distant cousins. And everyone can find their ancestry through the Y chromosome and X mitochondrial chromosome back to the one single man and one single woman, Adam and Eve, that everyone on earth is related through as one big family, now proven through DNA. Now more than ever there is a need for a restoration for the hearts of family members, parents and children between the generations, to be restored back to one another, and there is still a small remnant of families left on the earth who are whole or restored and not destroyed as a family yet.

We are living in a time when the Torah of Moses needs to be remembered more than any other time, because almost everyone on the earth, including almost all Jews and Christians, have rejected and forgotten the Torah of Moses in Scripture to follow manmade doctrines and commands of men and imaginations of their own minds or the minds of others they follow. Most Jews in Judaism and most Christians follow oral traditions of manmade religion, and reject the Words of Yahuweh/Yehovah, the Two Witnesses of Oil, in Scripture, especially the Words of Yahuweh/Yehovah that are written in the Witness of the Torah of Moses. And the embodiment of that Witness of the Word of Yahuweh/Yehovah is Yeshua, who is the living Torah of Moses.

Yeshua was the Word of Yahuweh/Yehovah made flesh and born into a physical body as a man according to John 1:1-5 and 14, reaffirmed in Revelation 19:11-13. Yeshua was the living and breathing Witness of the Word of Yahuweh/Yehovah himself on the earth in physical flesh and body, and he was rejected and killed by the people of the city of Jerusalem, his dead body left on the cross or stake structure he was crucified on outside of the Jerusalem gates. This is another reason why there is the mention in Revelation 11:8 of the

Master, Yeshua, who was impaled or crucified. He was a Witness as the living Word of Yahuweh/Yehovah and his Torah on the earth, killed and his body discarded and left by the people, only buried by his own disciples but not by the people of Jerusalem, because they had rejected and thrown out the living Two Stone Tablets of the Witness, or Two Witnesses, of the Word of Yahuweh/Yehovah living among them in the flesh.

It was as Isaiah prophesied in 30:9 of a people rebellious who refuse to hear the Torah of Yahuweh/Yehovah and in 30:11 who try to cause the Set-Apart Ones of Israel, the Witnesses of Yahuweh/Yehovah, to cease and be gone from their midst. Then the dead body of Yeshua as the Witness of the Word of Yahuweh/Yehovah was in the grave for three days and three nights, before a spirit of life entered into that dead body of the Witness of the Word of Yahuweh/Yehovah and he stood up or arose from the dead. It is the same today that the people of the world do not want to hear the Two Witnesses of the Word of Yahuweh/Yehovah and have killed that word in their lives in an attempt to remove it from their midst, but it will be resurrected by to life again and be living in the midst of the people when Yeshua as the Living Word Witness of Yahuweh/Yehovah made flesh returns as the Son of Adam.

The shift is almost complete on the earth now, as everyone is throwing away the Torah of Moses, and the rest of the Words of Yahuweh/Yehovah in Scripture from Genesis to Revelation, into the gutter on the street to follow after men and women, and the laws and commands of men and women, instead, elevating mankind to the position of gods who determine for themselves right and wrong, good and evil, life and death. Remember the oil and light of the Word of Yahuweh/Yehovah and keep that witness stored up with you as the world's lights go dark without the oil Witnesses of the Torah of Moses in their hearts or their lives any longer. Yeshua himself commanded everyone to obey his commands in the Torah of Moses, such as in Matthew 5:17-48, because according to John 1:1-14 Yeshua is the Word of Yahuweh/Yehovah in the Torah of Moses, while simultaneously being the one true God, Yahuweh/Yehovah himself. Obedience to the Words and Commands of Yahuweh/Yehovah is not a salvation issue or a legalism issue; it is a love issue (Matthew 22:34-40; 1 John 2:1 – 5:4).

Section 12. **The Dragon and the Woman in the Wilderness Who Birthed the Male Child (1,260 Days):**

Shadow Picture / Type of the Woman in the Wilderness from the Exodus of Israel Taken Out of Egypt into the Wilderness 3,500 Years or 3.5 Millennia Ago, which is a Time, Times, and Half a Time Ago in Millennia:
Exodus 14:21 – 19:4

Examination of Verses **Exodus 14:21 – 19:4** – John quotes and paraphrases in Revelation 12 from Exodus, concerning the "Woman," because the nation of Israel is the shadow picture prophecy at that time of the Time of the End and Yahuweh/Yehovah's coming. In Exodus 19:4 Yahuweh/Yehovah says that he bore Israel on eagles' wings to himself in the wilderness, in the same way the Woman in Revelation 12:14 is given two wings of an eagle to fly to her place in the wilderness. In Exodus 14:21 Yahuweh/Yehovah divides the Sea of Reeds (eastern branch of the Red Sea) so that Israel is able to walk across on dry ground and escape the army of Pharaoh pursuing them, as the sea closed up again over the army, preventing them from getting across to the other side in the wilderness. In Revelation 12:15-16 the Serpent/Dragon sends a river out of its mouth, instead of an army, to overtake and drown the Woman as she is escaping into the wilderness, but the earth divides and opens up instead of the sea, and swallows up the river so that it cannot reach the Woman, who is safe in the wilderness.

This prophetic shadow picture in Exodus is simple. Yahuweh/Yehovah is taking his people out of the world (Egypt) to go to the New Heavens and New Earth (Promised Land of Israel in Canaan), but the ruling powers of the world, including the demonic powers of the Dragon/Serpent (Pharaoh), do not want to let Yahuweh/Yehovah's people go into the wilderness, out of the slavery and bondage of sin that they have them in, worshipping false gods and following false manmade systems of religion and governance. So as Yahuweh/Yehovah takes his people out of the manmade world systems, the ruling authorities of those systems, especially the demonic ones of the Dragon/Serpent, chase after his people as Pharaoh did, but Yahuweh/Yehovah saves them, bringing them to the place of safety in the wilderness where the world system of man does not exist nor has any power. And through the wilderness a nation (the seed of the Woman) is born into existence. The people and family of Yahuweh/Yehovah (the children of Israel) are already there in the world (Egypt) waiting to become a nation with their own land to live in under the personal rule and governance of Yahuweh/Yehovah and his way of living (the Torah of Moses). But it is through the wilderness that they become birthed into their own nation in their own land in the New Heavens and New Earth (the promised land of Israel in Canaan).

This is why they have to first go into the wilderness, to meet Yahuweh/Yehovah at his coming in the clouds at the end of the Great Tribulation (the clouds above Mount Sinai) at the sounding of the trumpet/shophar blast with lightnings and thunders (as Yahuweh/Yehovah appeared to the children of Israel on Mount Sinai). And Yahuweh/Yehovah supernaturally provides food and water to survive in the wilderness, taking them on the journey to prepare his people to meet him face to face and enter into marriage covenant with him (as he did with the children of Israel on Mount Sinai) then take them to the promised land in the New Heavens and New Earth.

Each of the three prophecies of countings of days (1,260 days or 1,290 days) that are a time, times, and half a time each have their shadow picture taking place in the exact same year of the exodus out of Egypt. The Disgusting Idol Desolating event in Daniel 12 has its shadow picture in the golden calf the children of Israel made at Mount Sinai, and the two witnesses in Revelation 11 have their shadow picture in Moses and Aaron and the plagues that Yahuweh/Yehovah brought on Egypt to destroy that nation through their witness, and the nation of Israel as the woman in Revelation 12 that flees into the wilderness to be protected there from the Dragon or Pharaoh. All of them happened in the same year according to the record of Scripture, in the year 1495 B.C.E. [and they could not have happened in any other year except this year when going by the dates recorded in Scripture as I already extensively proved in *Calculating the Last Seven*], all three of them as of the year 2006 now reaching a completion of a time, times, and half a time of millennia, 3.5 thousand years.

References to the Woman Birthing the Male Child Part of the Prophecy:
Isaiah 7:10-16
Hosea 11:1
Micah 5:1-4
Matthew 1:18 – 2:15

Word for Word Prophecy Examination of Fulfilled Verses **Isaiah 7:10-16** and **Hosea 11:1** and **Micah 5:1-4** and **Matthew 1:18 – 2:15** – There is a dual layer prophecy in Revelation 12 between Yeshua the Male Child and the Seed of the Woman, the newly birthed nation. Hosea 11:1 is an example of this dual layer prophecy, in which Yahuweh/Yehovah refers to the nation of Israel as his Child, who he called out of Egypt as his Son, while in the exact same words he is speaking of Yeshua, his Son who came out of Egypt. In one sentence there is reference to Child and Son, speaking of Yeshua the Messiah and the nation of Israel in one breath. The same is with the prophecy of Revelation 12 in which the Male Child born of the Woman was already fulfilled by Yeshua, but in the same breath is speaking of the Seed born from the Woman, that is Yahuweh/Yehovah's nation born of the Woman Israel.

The Woman in Revelation is simultaneously the nation Israel in Exodus 19 going into the wilderness and the virgin woman Miryam (Mary), prophesied to give birth to a Son, born in Bethlehem, in Isaiah 7 and Micah 5, which is Yeshua the Messiah who shepherds the nations with a rod of iron. And the Male Child is simultaneously Yeshua the Son in Hosea 11 and Yahuweh/Yehovah's nation of Israel in Hosea 11. In Matthew 1 to 2 Yeshua is born from the virgin Miryam in Bethlehem, in fulfillment of Isaiah 7 and Micah 5, and is the Son taken from Egypt in Hosea 11. He is the Male Child in Revelation 12, which was already fulfilled at the time of his coming when he was born of the Woman Miryam, and then later taken up to the heavens after his death and resurrection. But there is still a future fulfillment of Revelation 12 of the Male Child, referring to Yeshua again when he returns to shepherd the nations with a rod of iron in fulfillment of

Psalms 2, simultaneously with Yahuweh/Yehovah's nation of all of his people, the Male Child Seed of the Woman, being born into a complete and whole nation, born from the Woman.

References to the Woman in the Wilderness Part of the Prophecy:
Isaiah 48:20-22
Hosea 2:14-15
Hosea 12:9

Word for Word Prophecy Examination of Partially Fulfilled Verses **Isaiah 48:20-22** and **Hosea 2:14-15** and **Hosea 12:9** – Isaiah 48:20-22 is a prophecy about coming out of Babel, connected with Revelation 18:4 where Yahuweh/Yehovah says to his people to come out of Babel, in order not to share in her plagues. Directly after this prophecy in Isaiah 48 to leave Babel and flee the Kasdim (Chaldeans or Babylonians), there is a prophecy about going into the desert, into the wilderness like the children of Israel in Exodus leaving Egypt, where Yahuweh/Yehovah provides water from the split rock. This prophecy in Isaiah shows the shadow picture of the exodus out of Egypt and the journey in the wilderness are symbol prophecies for the future, except that instead of leaving Egypt, this time Yahuweh/Yehovah's people who are in covenant with him through Yeshua will be leaving Babel, leaving the world of man that exists on this earth, to travel through the wilderness to the New Heavens and New Earth.

This prophecy in Isaiah 48 is partially being fulfilled already now, as Yahuweh/Yehovah has started the process of taking down the world system Babel in the same way he took down Egypt, and the sign of this was when he brought the global COVID plague that completely shut down man's world for a year, all of the cities and systems built by man, on a scale that has never happened before in the entire recorded history of the world since the global flood halted all life on earth temporarily for a year.

Hosea 12:9 is also a future prophecy that has not yet been fulfilled, in which Yahuweh/Yehovah says that he will again make his people live in tents like he did in the wilderness after he brought the children of Israel out of Egypt. He says that as in the days of the "appointed time" or festival, referring to the appointed time in Leviticus 23 of the Festival of Booths/Tabernacles, which is a remembrance of the time Israel dwelt in tents in the wilderness, he will make all of his people dwell in tents in the desert again, in fulfillment of the Festival of Booths/Tabernacles. This again shows how the time in the wilderness and the exodus out of Egypt, commemorated in the festivals of the Day of Trumpets, Day of Atonement, and Festival of Booths, are a shadow picture prophecy of the Time of the End and Yahuweh/Yehovah's coming to end the world of man, the world of Babel, as he ended the empire of Egypt.

Hosea 2:14-15 is also a prophecy that has never been fulfilled in the past, but is beginning to be fulfilled now, where Yahuweh/Yehovah explains why he has to allure his people into the wilderness in the last days, in order to restore the hearts of his people to respond to him as in their youth, and prepare them to become his bride and eventually wife as it talks about in the rest of this prophecy further on. And in that day after the marriage supper of the Lamb (Revelation 19) we will call Yahuweh/Yehovah "My Husband" instead of "My Lord." The wilderness is the preparation to enter into marriage covenant with Yahuweh/Yehovah at the wedding in the wilderness, before entering into the promised land in Israel, in the New Heavens and New Earth. Ever since the COVID plague shutting down the world in the spring of 2020, Yahuweh/Yehovah has been alluring his people to begin leaving Babel (Egypt), leaving this world system of man, to trust in him for provision and follow him into the wilderness, spiritually or physically as each individual case may be.

The Prophecy of the Woman Who Gives Birth to the Male Child and is Taken into the Wilderness, and the Prophecy of the Dragon:
Revelation 12:1-17

Prophecy Fulfillment of Verses **Revelation 12:1-17** – This prophecy was already partially fulfilled with Miryam, the virgin, giving birth to Yeshua, the Male Child and Messiah. With the precise mathematical calculations available to us now of the heavenly bodies and their movements (thanks to Albert Einstein's perfecting of Sir Isaac Newton's astronomical formulas) it is possible to calculate backward (or forward) in time the positions of the stars and planets in the past with perfect accuracy. And now we know that this sign in the heavens of the woman giving birth in Revelation 12 is probably the same sign the star gazers in the East saw announcing the birth of the King of Israel from the tribe of Judah.

Mathematical calculations of the planets and stars now lets us know that in the year 3 B.C.E. the planet Jupiter, known in Hebrew as Tsedeq צדק, meaning "Righteous One" for the only time in human history came into conjunction with the star Regulus, known in Hebrew as Melek מלך, meaning "King." The star Melek is located in the constellation Leo, in Hebrew known as Aryeh אריה, meaning "Lion." Just under the constellation Aryeh is the head of the constellation Virgo, known in Hebrew as Bethulah בתולה, meaning "Virgin." When the planet Tsedeq and star Melek came together in conjunction in the constellation Aryeh, it was announcing the birth of the Righteous King who is the Lion of the tribe of Judah, the Messiah from the lineage of David. And this conjunction happened in the twelfth constellation, the twelve stars positioned directly above the constellation of Bethulah, the Virgin giving birth to the Righteous King and Lion of Judah.

From the best calculations available, this conjunction took place and was visible to the naked eye at sunset and just after sunset on September 11-12, 3 B.C.E. (Julian Calendar), when the sliver of the new moon was positioned in the sky directly next to the constellation of the Virgin Bethulah, under her feet, and the sun light from the sunset was still clothed around her as the constellation was located on the horizon at that time.[32] Since it was during the time of the new moon, when the new moon had just appeared according to the astronomical calculations, we know that this sign happened in the heavens on the Hebrew Calendar date of the 1st day of the 7th month, on the festival of the Day of Trumpets. This sign in the heavens was announcing the imminent birth of the Messiah Yeshua through the virgin Miryam just shortly after that time. But the reason that this already partly fulfilled prophecy sign, in Revelation 12:1-2 and 5, from the time of Yeshua's

---

[32] Astronomical calculations and discovery by Robert Scott Wadsworth, *A Voice Crying in the Heavens* (Oregon City, Oregon: Biblical Astronomy, 1996-1997) [*Biblical Astronomy - A Voice Crying in the Heavens: Celestial Events from the Creation of Adam to the First Appearing of Yeshua Mashiah (Jesus Christ)*]

birth and eventual ascension after his death and resurrection was included by John in Revelation is because there is still another layer of fulfillment that comes at the time of Yeshua's return.

At sunset and during the night of September 21-22, 2017, once again on the 1st day of the 7th month, on Yahuweh/Yehovah's festival of the Day of Trumpets, a sign appeared in the heavens with the sliver of the new moon inside of the constellation of the virgin woman Bethulah, with the setting sun around her. This time the planet Jupiter or Tsedeq, the Righteous One, was together with the moon inside of the constellation, and a collection of planets above its head, beside it in the sky during those few days. The planets in conjunction were Venus, in Hebrew called Nogah נגה, meaning "Brightness" like the sunlight; Mars, in Hebrew called Ma'dim מאדים, meaning "Reddening" in color; and Mercury, in Hebrew called Kokav Chemmah כוכב חמה, meaning "Hot Star." This conjunction of planets and constellations happens about once every 200 years and is not a once in human history event as the alignment that happened on September 11-12, 3 B.C.E., because that primary fulfillment of this verse in 3 B.C.E. was already finished with Yeshua's birth as the Male Child. This is a lesser sign in 2017 that is supposed to be pointing people to the much bigger sign that happened in the heavens at Yeshua's birth, which already was the fulfillment of Revelation 12:1-2.

This time, with this lesser sign in 2017, the moon and the wandering star or planet Tsedeq were within the Virgin Woman Bethulah, in her "womb," during this conjunction, because it is the sign of the coming birth (through the labor pains of the last days) of the nation of the followers of Yeshua, not the birth of the Messiah Yeshua again. In the same way that Israel as a people were inside of Egypt, inside of the world, but had not yet been born into a nation in their own land, the followers of Yeshua have never been taken out of the world, out of Egypt, to be born into a nation living in their own land, in the New Heavens and New Earth ultimately. This modern day sign in the heavens of the Woman Virgin in the heavens is not a sign of Yeshua about to be born, but instead the first-fruits or first-born of the nation of followers of Yeshua about to be born. And this sign is only that the nation of believers in Yeshua is <u>about</u> to be born in the future, but was not yet born at that time.

In Isaiah 66:7 the word "Male Child" is used to refer to the entire nation of the Jewish people being born in a day, so the term "Male Child" can be used to refer to the Messiah Yeshua in Revelation 12, but at the same time in the same breath refer to the entire nation of believers in Yeshua being born as a nation. On May 28, 2020 the "Male Child" or "Seed" of the Woman, referring to the nation of believers in Yeshua, both natural born Israelis and Gentiles as one Israel, was born in fulfillment of Revelation 12:2-3 and 17. On this day of May 28 there was an online gathering, called *The Outpouring*, of many of the same Chinese and Egyptian believers in Yeshua who were at the event of the sealing of the 144,000, including David Damien. This time there were also many Jewish believers from Israel present, including Asher Intrater, but there were also this time believers in Yeshua from Syria present. As already discussed, two of the nations listed in prophecy as specifically having descendants of the northern ten tribes of Israel living in them in the last days and returning to Israel from them are Egypt and China, but there is also one more included in Zechariah 10, which is Syria (Ashshur).

Also, as already discussed, the 144,000 sealed from "all" of the 12 tribes of Israel (all means all in Revelation 7:4) are the first-fruits according to Revelation 14, which means that they are the firstborn Male

Child given over to Yahuweh/Yehovah according to his instruction in Exodus 13:11-16. The prophecy in Isaiah 66 was fulfilled with the birth of the secular nation of Israel only consisting of the Southern Kingdom tribes of Israel, including Yehudah (Judah) and Binyamin (Benjamin) and part of Levi. But the prophecy in Revelation 12 is the birthing of the complete nation of Israel with all of the 12 tribes included in it, which according to Isaiah 49 is not a secular nation, but instead a nation made up of only followers of the Messiah Yeshua, who are literal, physical descendants of all of the 12 tribes of Israel, together with the gentiles of the nations in Isaiah 56 who have entered into the New Covenant of Jeremiah 31 with the House of Israel.

On May 28, 2020 this was the birthing of the 144,000 as the first-fruits and firstborn Male Child (not all of the 144,000 necessarily having to be male) of the complete nation of Israel joined together with believers in Yeshua from all of the tribes of Israel and the gentiles coming together with them as one. [It was only the first-fruits of the birthing, because the complete reality of all of Yahuweh/Yehovah's people living together as one nation in their own land will not be until the New Heavens and New Earth described in Isaiah, Ezekiel, and Revelation.] On May 28 believers in Yeshua gathered together for an all-day online event from all the ends of the earth, from nations across every part of the world from north to south, and from west to Sinim (China). Throughout the event there was much repentance and healing of gentile and Jewish believers coming together as one again after so many years of separation and division since the days of the Book of Acts, repentance for the pride and arrogance that has been on both sides during the last 1,900 years, and the evil of anti-Semitism.

And as everyone came together as One New Man (Ephesians 2), David Damien, without realizing the fullness of what he was saying, spoke the prophetic word of the birth of Yahuweh/Yehovah's complete nation Israel through him in a single day, praying, "Father, you brought us together through the blood on the cross. You brought us together; you adopted us as sons and daughter. And we say, 'Together forever.' You will see the fruit of your labor on the cross from every color and tribe and nation. And that is the joy that you saw, a family, your children coming back to the Father. That is why you came, to restore us to the Father. And you are releasing to us now pieces, because time is short, the hour has come. And the enemy is working very hard to change the seasons and the times, but he doesn't know that that was given to you, O Jesus. You are the only one who can change the seasons and the times. You will not allow the enemy to do what he wants without preparing your body first. And you are doing it by your sovereign hand. Can a nation be born in a day? Can a nation be born in a day? You are birthing us in a day. So we say LORD it's for you. Take joy my King; take joy in what you see. We don't know where to go. Even today we are trying to figure out where to go. What is the next, and we stumble. But you want to show the whole world that it is not by might, not by power, but by your Spirit. We don't know, but our eyes are upon you."

One of the Chinese Christian believers at this online event witnessed to the same thing, of this birthing of the nation of Yahuweh/Yehovah as one nation (a nation in Scripture from Genesis meaning a "family") of believers in Yeshua, saying, "As I have been listening to the family share I feel such a richness of God's presence in this cloud based upper room. I am deeply moved, especially after having heard Paul [Wilber] just share. I feel like God is such an amazing One. As I hear him speak and as I reflect upon what the LORD has been specifically saying to us as the Chinese family, I see how amazing God works. In our last Passover gathering together, especially during the time of when the Egyptians and Arabs showed their love and desire for oneness with the Messianic family, I felt such a fullness of God's presence. And because of what we felt at Passover we had a unique expectation burning in our hearts toward Shavuot this year. We felt that the LORD was going to release something in this Pentecost that has not been experienced before. But we were stirred and gripped in our hearts to stay very focused in seeking his face to be praying. Especially during the last ten days before Pentecost. These last ten days we have canceled many regular things or busyness that we have, and even our young people have decided to stop using their cellphones in these last ten days. Many of us met in small groups, in groups of threes to seek the LORD's face. And during this time of seeking we were regularly directed to focus on the issue of our Jewish brothers and sisters. And the LORD spoke to us through several prophetic dreams he had given to us. As we prayed into these dreams and discern what they meant we felt that the LORD had spoken to us a few things that we had not heard before. The first thing that we felt the LORD was speaking to us clearly about is that in this Pentecost that the one new man that has been described in the book of Ephesians is coming to a fulfillment. Through the prophetic dream that highlights the marriage between Boaz and Ruth, God is saying, 'Yes, this is the time and this is the marriage that he desires.' So again, referring back to what Paul [Wilber] has just shared a while ago, I felt so amazed, because in the past we really did not understand this piece very well. I feel like that God's long time longing and desire for us to become one is coming to a fulfillment. It is like as if he cannot wait any longer, saying that it is time now. No more waiting. And because of that the LORD released much intercession and travailed through us, and in intercession and travail we felt such a burden in our hearts to want to see the Jews, their eyes to be opened. In fact, to see Israel saved has been a generational vision that the LORD has given to us as a Chinese. And in these days of worship and intercession we felt a growing intensity in our hearts to desire to want to bring the Jews home to the Father. So because of that we prayed with much tears before the LORD over this matter. We felt God's heart and his deep desire flow into us and flow out of us in prayer and intercession. We deeply longed to see that the veil that is covering them would be removed and they would enter into salvation. And another thing that we felt clearly was that, soon coming together as one new man, the gentiles and Messianic family, that when this oneness takes place, a lot that has been hindering and blocking the ancient wells will be removed and the ancient wells will start to flow. And that we would see the glory of God manifest, and that we would see the end times harvest take place. So even a while back when we were listening to the ancient sounds being released, my spirit was deeply stirred. I sat there just giving thankfulness to the LORD as I hear what is going on as I can see that the LORD is speaking powerfully and deeply all across his family. We feel so blessed that we can be here in this hour."

During this same event on this day there was a Christian Moabitess woman present, representing like the Moabitess Ruth who married the Jewish man Boaz, the marriage of Jew and Gentile together into covenant through Yeshua, as one family and one nation. On this exact same day on May 28, 2020 on the Mount of Olives in Jerusalem there was a Jewish man, representing the Southern Kingdoms tribes of Judah, and a woman descended from the Northern Kingdom tribes of Israel, represented as Ephrayim in Ezekiel 37, who were married. This was another sign showing that the time of all of the 12 tribes coming together as one nation through Yeshua, as one stick in the hand of Yahuweh/Yehovah in Ezekiel 37, together with all of the gentile believers in Yeshua as one nation under the rule of Yahuweh/Yehovah himself personally, had been born into existence and begun with the birthing of the first-fruits/first-born Male Child of the 144,000 in fulfillment of Revelation 12:2-3 and 17.

Most of Revelation 12 is a prophecy about things happening in the spiritual realm, concerning the Dragon and his messengers with him, and Michael and his messengers with him, and a spiritual war fought in the heavens. Just two days after the May 28, 2020 birthing of the complete nation of Israel in Yeshua, through the 144,000 first-born, in the afternoon of May 30, 2020 (after sunset Israel time on the 7th day of the 3rd month on the day of the Festival of Weeks or Pentecost) a sign of a Dragon appeared in the heavens, showing the Dragon standing before the Woman, waiting to devour her Child/Seed, Yahuweh/Yehovah's complete nation, as it was being born, in fulfillment of Revelation 12:3-4. The sign was of a dragon, called a Crew-Dragon, rising up into the heavens with a fiery-red color coming out of it of literal fire, as the Greek word purros πυρρος, meaning "fire colored" describes. This sign of a dragon in the heavens was seen by the whole world, and was the first time the Space-X Crew-Dragon was manned with a crew in it. The sign of this dragon had also already been appearing in the sky for a couple years before this, ever since after the sign of the Woman in the heavens on September 21-22, 2017, and continued afterward.

This physical, visible sign that was seen was only the sign to show the literal spiritual fulfillment of this prophecy in the spiritual realm, as the Dragon/Serpent and his fallen messengers began their war against Michael and the other messengers of Yahuweh/Yehovah, resulting in the Dragon/Serpent thrown out of the heavens down to earth. It was also the sign of the Dragon/Serpent warring with this new nation that Yahuweh/Yehovah had begun birthing on May 28, trying to prevent it from happening and trying to destroy it in spiritual warfare, as the demonic world tried to overthrow Yahuweh/Yehovah from his throne in the heavens. At the same time while the sign of the Dragon in the heavens happened on May 30, 2020, and during the years before and after, Space-X was also putting falling stars into the heavens, even called stars, the Starlink satellites that are designed to look like falling stars in the heavens and designed to actually be literally falling to the earth continuously until they burn up in the earth atmosphere.

At that same time that everyone saw the sign of the Dragon in the heavens, everyone was watching the sign of the falling stars in the heavens, as people watched these Starlink satellites form lines of stars falling to the earth all over the world, beginning in North America primarily. This was the sign of the Dragon causing 1/3 of the stars in the heavens to fall to the earth with its tail in the spiritual realm, in fulfillment of Revelation 12:4, throwing them down to earth. [These falling stars in Revelation 12 are different stars from the falling stars in the Sixth Seal in Revelation 6.] Yahuweh/Yehovah had brought about the birth and start of his complete nation of Israel that will one day inhabit the New Heavens and New Earth, and the Dragon was there to try to devour and destroy and stop it from happening, in his final war, because he knows his time is short, in verses 12:7-9 and 12-13. All of these literal signs in the physical realm were all symbols of the fulfillment of the prophecies of the literal Dragon/Serpent and his messengers in the spiritual realm.

One of the ways that the Dragon began to war with and go after Yahuweh/Yehovah's newly birthed nation that he began bringing together was by giving his power, throne, and authority to the Beast Out of the Sea to begin the deception of the Mark of the Beast Out of the Sea at around that time, starting in China in the Spring of 2020 and spreading around the entire world, in an attempt to spiritually destroy Yahuweh/Yehovah's people by deceiving them into worshipping the Beast Out of the Sea and taking its Mark, discussed later on. This is when the Dragon/Serpent/Satan began to try to go after the Woman and the Seed of the Woman on the earth in fulfillment of verses 12:13 and 17, as the final spiritual war began to deceive and take down as many believers in Yeshua around the world as possible through increased spiritual attack. It was during that year from 2020 to 2021 that Christians around the world began stumbling and falling in Yahuweh/Yehovah's COVID plague into deceptions of all kinds, as Yahuweh/Yehovah began exposing the world and the people of the world through the sifting process. Yahuweh/Yehovah allowed the deceptions to come as part of the testing, as he began to sift the nations with a sieve of falsehood, putting a bridle into the mouths of the people around the world that would mislead them, as in Isaiah 30:27-28, a cleansing and refining process. All of this is shown in more detail later on.

When one generation births another generation, as with a woman birthing a son, it does not magically change the son in the next generation into a different nation or nationality from the mother and father. The people of Israel descended from Abraham, Isaac, and Jacob were still the people of Israel as they were foreigners and sojourners living in other nations, but they did not become a true nation of people until they had their own land to live in again with their own borders as a people. In the same way the people of Israel stayed Israelis as they sojourned and lived scattered among the nations of the world, living in nations that were not their own. Then when they were born as a nation in a day again in 1948, the birthing meant that they had their own land and borders and government to live as a nation again. The Woman in Revelation 12 and the Seed of the Woman, are the same people, only being born into a nation where they were only a people beforehand.

The Woman and the Seed of the Woman, the Male Child born into a nation, are the same people. They are not magically becoming another people or another nation different from what they were before. The Woman and the Seed of the Woman (the 144,000 first-born/first-fruits) are all part of the same nation and family of people; the difference is that Yahuweh/Yehovah is taking his people who are believers in Yeshua, the Christians, who have been sojourning as foreigners in foreign lands among the nations, to bring them all together as one nation of people in one place, as he did with the Jews in 1948, to live together in their own land under his government. And that land that all of his people will live in together as one, unified nation, with their own borders and physical land to live in, will be the New Heavens and New Earth.

But until Yahuweh/Yehovah takes his people who are being born into one nation into the New Heavens and New Earth, there is still a time on this old earth to get through while the Dragon/Serpent is going after them, to try to destroy them, which is the reason for the Woman, which also represents together with the Seed or Male Child of the Woman, Yahuweh/Yehovah's complete nation of Israel who are in his covenant through the Lamb Yeshua, to have a place in the wilderness to survive away from the Dragon/Serpent until Yahuweh/Yehovah comes.

After sunset on the night of March 28-29, 2021, on the 15th day of the 1st month, the first day of the Festival of Unleavened Bread, Pastor Israel Pochtar and the Messianic congregation of Beit Hallel Israel celebrated the Passover in the wilderness in Israel at a special event called "Passover in the Wilderness." This was the sign, right after the Disgusting Idol (Abomination) Desolating event had taken place and the Mark of the Beast Out of the Sea had just begun in Israel, that it was time at that Passover for the Woman (as shown in the shadow picture of Passover in Exodus) to flee into the wilderness, spiritually or physically as the case may be for each individual, in fulfillment of verses 12:6, and 13-14. It was the time to escape and flee from the spiritual deceptions of the Disgusting Idol (Abomination) Desolating that had begun among Christians and in churches and congregations all over the world. The Beit Hallel Israel congregation went out to the wilderness in Israel to celebrate Passover in a tent, out in the desert, representing the time that the Woman, the people of Yahuweh/Yehovah in covenant with him through Yeshua, have to go through a wilderness time with Yahuweh/Yehovah before reaching the promised land of the New Heavens and New Earth, in the same way as the shadow picture in Exodus.

That Passover in 2021 on March 28-29 was the beginning of that time when Yahuweh/Yehovah began calling people to come out of Egypt, out of the world, made up of the Beast Out of the Sea and Mystery Babel the Great. In the same way that the Israelis were living in slavery in Egypt to the world system of Egypt at that time, the Christians around the world have been living scattered in slavery and bondage to the world systems among the nations for nearly 2,000 years, without a nation to live in that is their own with Yahuweh/Yehovah ruling over them. For 2,000 years Christians have had to live in manmade governments (even if those governments sometimes called themselves Christians, they were still governments created by men) without the government of Yahuweh/Yehovah himself personally ruling over his nation of people. And in the same way it was hard for the children of Israel to leave the world system and go to live in the promised land under Yahuweh/Yehovah's government, it is hard for all of Yahuweh/Yehovah's people in covenant with him through Yeshua today to leave the world systems they have been used to in the nations, to go and live with him in his land under his government in the New Heavens and New Earth. This is why there has to be a transitional wilderness period of time to take the world out of his people and sift them, separating the wheat from the weeds and the sheep from the goats.

This is what the final test of the Beast Out of the Sea and the Beast Out of the Earth and the Image and Mark of the Beast Out of the Sea and the Scarlet Beast Out of the Pit of the Deep with Mystery Babel on it is all about, for Yahuweh/Yehovah to find out who really wants to live in eternity with him under his governance and ways of living, or who would rather have the world, created by man. The world systems of man through the Beast Out of the Sea and Mystery Babel only have control in the urban areas and cities, which are the worlds that are completely manmade and man controlled. But the world systems of man have no power or control in the wilderness, because they depend upon manmade structures and technology to exist, especially in modern times with electricity and machines and computers and advanced building materials for vehicles of many kinds.

In the wilderness the systems of man are unable to operate and function, because it is Yahuweh/Yehovah's created world, where a person can see the truth that Yahuweh/Yehovah is the only source of life and provision for life. The illusion that man has any power or ability to provide life for himself is destroyed in the wilderness. Passover 2020, when COVID spread across the world and caused man's world to be shut down, was the start of Yahuweh/Yehovah calling his people to start leaving the world systems as they are now in the modern world, to trust in him for provision instead of the Beast Out of the Sea and the Beast Out of the Earth and Mystery Babel. And he began the pull on people to start getting them out of the man created world of technology, to the place of safety with him, while still in the midst of Egypt, of the world of the Beast and Babel. There were many around that time who began to feel Yahuweh/Yehovah's pull to cut off from their dependency on manmade technologies and electronics. All those at that time in 2021 who tried to continue to use the modern technologies and interact in the world as normal were caught up into the deceptions of the Dragon through the Beast Out of the Sea, especially its Mark, discussed later on.

Those who did begin fleeing into the wilderness at that time, some of them physically moving to new locations, some cutting off from the technologies in the midst of things, each making the choice in different ways to follow Yahuweh/Yehovah and be ready to leave Egypt, this world system of man, have certainly been pursued by the river the Dragon/Serpent has sent from its mouth, using its mouth to try to convince them to come back into Egypt, because everything is fine and there is no reason to give up the world like Yeshua said to do over and over again. The Dragon/Serpent has sent its river of the sea of people, in the shadow picture Pharaoh's army like a river of people, to try to chase down and stop Yahuweh/Yehovah's people from leaving the world system through various deceptions and false prophets.

The sea of people (Revelation 17) is what make up the Beast Out of the Sea and all of the world systems, and the technologies of man that run those systems. The systems today of man are such that a person cannot even survive or live anymore on the planet without adopting those systems of electricity and government codes and standards of living, dependent upon the system of man to live. It is a constant enticement from the Dragon, sending the need for man's technologies to survive in man's world, to trip up and sweep Yahuweh/Yehovah's people off their feet in a flood, in verse 12:15, and bring them back into the system of man, into the governance of the world of man, the Beast Out of the Sea and Mystery Babel, to stay in slavery and bondage in Egypt. The Serpent/Dragon through history has always used peer pressure from the sea of people to try to deceive or convince Yahuweh/Yehovah's set-apart ones to come back into the world system in Egypt/Babel, and it is an even stronger pull from the stream of the sea of people that the Serpent sends after the Woman today, as Yahuweh/Yehovah is at the same time pulling his people away from Babel and the world to go with him into the wilderness.

The Serpent uses the same lies from his mouth as he did with Israel in the wilderness in Exodus and with Yeshua 40 days in the wilderness, that life is better in his world system, in bondage and slavery in Egypt than in the wilderness with Yahuweh/Yehovah. It is the same lies spewed like a river from his mouth as before, that it is better to stay in slavery in Egypt, in slavery to the world system and governments of man, because there a person can have guaranteed food and nourishment for them as long as they stay under the power and control of man and women ruling over them, and ultimately the Dragon/Serpent over them. The lie is that we have to stay in this world system and use it to survive, instead of depending upon Yahuweh/Yehovah for our life and our needs, and trusting him completely to let us live or die according to his will, because the wilderness exposes that reality of the way things already are, that we are already completely dependent upon him for our every breath and for every moment we are alive. Every believer is working through this choice between the world and Yeshua in their own way (James 4:4), and how much Yahuweh/Yehovah wants them to give up the world to follow him into the wilderness.

As with the shadow picture in the Exodus, Yahuweh/Yehovah uses the plagues of the earth to swallow up the deceptions and sea of people that the Serpent/Dragon sends out of his mouth. Yahuweh/Yehovah uses the plagues to destroy the manmade systems and structures and governments that keep the people in bondage and slavery to the manmade world of sin and rebellion against Yahuweh/Yehovah, breaking the illusion of security and exposing the reality that men and women (and fallen messengers or demons) have no power except what Yahuweh/Yehovah gives to them. As in the shadow picture of the ten plagues Yahuweh/Yehovah brought upon Egypt, we are watching today plagues upon plagues upon plagues of various kinds coming from the earth, swallowing up the sea of people and illusions/deceptions of the Serpent, from earthquakes to droughts, from massive fires to massive floods, hurricanes all over the world and tsunamis, pandemics and highly destructive storms. They are all increasing all of the time, with greater destruction, as Yahuweh/Yehovah is bringing the plagues of the earth onto the world system of Babel in the same way he destroyed Egypt in order to force the Serpent and the systems of man to let his people go into the wilderness with him and be free to finally live according to their choice to follow him and his ways of living. This is the spiritual war that we are watching happening in real life right now across the world, in fulfillment of verse 12:16. The earth right now is literally swallowing up all of the cities and structures and empires and nations built by the sea of people with almost continuous frequency to the point that most of the natural disasters are never fully reported, because there are too many of them happening at once.

Section 13. The Beast Out of the Sea with Authority to Blaspheme Yahuweh/Yehovah (42 Months):

References to the Beast Out of the Sea Prophecy:
Daniel 2:29-45
Daniel 7:2-7, 9-12, 16-19, 23

Prophecy Fulfillment of Verses **Daniel 7:2-7, 9-12, 16-19, 23** and **Daniel 2:29-45** – Yahuweh/Yehovah revealed twice to Daniel in chapters 2 and 7 the future history of the empires of man in the region of Israel, from his time until Yahuweh/Yehovah's coming to end the world of man and set up his eternal reign that will never end. In Daniel 2 Yahuweh/Yehovah reveals the future history (which is now past history for us today) of the region around Israel with a statue/image. It never says explicitly in the text that this image is of a man, but from the description of the image with head, chest, arms, belly, thighs, legs, feet, and toes we know that this image is probably of a man. The other revelation in another dream in Daniel 7 is of Four Beasts with various descriptions about each. We know that these two dreams and revelations are of the exact same four empires or kingdoms, because of Daniel 2:40 and Daniel 7:7 and 23, which both say that the fourth empire or kingdom crushes and breaks in pieces and tramples all of the three empires before it, and also because Yahuweh/Yehovah's eternal reign begins right after the fourth empire in both prophecies. When these two prophecies of the exact same empires are combined together they provide a complete picture of all of the details about them, making it easier to identify all of them.

There have already been many writings about the fulfillments of this prophecy in Daniel, so this is a brief summary. In the interpretation Yahuweh/Yehovah revealed to Daniel of the first dream in Daniel 2, the Babylonian Empire through Nebuchadnezzar is the first of the four empires, the head of gold. This means that the first beast in Daniel 7 is also the Babylonian Empire that looked like a lion with eagle's wings. Then the wings are removed and the lion stands on two feet like a man with a heart of a man. In the archaeological excavations in Iraq many remains of images of lions have been found representing the Babylonian Empire, as well as the Assyrian Empire that existed before it. Sometimes the images and statues of lions have wings, or are of a man standing upright with a lion body and wings. The city of Babylon was at its peak of splendor during the golden reign of Nebuchadnezzar II, and never reached that same height under any of the later empires that ruled from or over that city. Babylon was the fulfillment of Daniel 2:37-38 and 7:4

The second empire in Daniel 2 is the chest and two arms of silver, pictured as a bear with three ribs in its mouth held by its teeth in Daniel 7. The chest with two arms represents the Persian Empire that was formed by two nations uniting together, Persia and Media. They conquered Babylon and remained united throughout their rule over the Persian Empire. It was a lesser empire in splendor represented by silver. The Persian Empire added three more ribs or kingdoms onto the empire as it conquered Babylon: Elam (Susiana), Lydia, and Egypt. The Persian Empire fulfilled Daniel 2:39 and 7:5.

The third empire was the hips of bronze that rules over all the earth and a leopard with four wings and four heads. This was the Greek Empire that very rapidly conquered the Persian Empire through Alexander the

Great, then broke apart into four separate empires or kingdoms very quickly after Alexander's death. It had four heads with four separate capitals and four separate rulers at the same time throughout its entire history. The Greeks used bronze in their military equipment and were stronger than the two previous empires, but not as wealthy and great in splendor. The Greek Empire fulfilled Daniel 2:39 and 7:6.

The final fourth empire is made of two legs of iron that break apart into two feet of iron mixed with clay. This is represented as the fourth beast that has iron teeth and bronze nails. There is no description from Daniel what this fourth beast actually looks like, except for its teeth and nails are made out of metals, not natural teeth or nails like an animal would normally have. Unlike the chest and arms of silver that are two kingdoms united together to form a single empire, the fourth empire is made up of two divided legs of iron that are two separate but twin empires divided against each other, reigning at around the same time. These two divided legs are the Roman Empire and Islamic Empire, which were both strong like iron, crushing the previous empires as they took over in place of them, but never able to overcome or completely destroy each other through hundreds of years of fighting each other. They especially fought each other over the land of Israel, and both tried to conquer each other, but both failed. These two empires making up the fourth beast were different from all the rest, because both became based upon religions as their core system that they functioned by, instead of normal political government, and fought religious wars against each other. The Roman and Islamic Empires are the fulfillment of Daniel 2:40 and 7:7, 19 and 23.

It is important to understand all of these past empires, because the Beast Out of the Sea in Revelation 13 has all of them combined together into it in fractured pieces. This is because of the fulfillment of Daniel 7:11-12 that says that the three previous beasts all have a lengthening of life given to them to still be around at the time of the fourth beast, but without their rule or power. They are part of the fourth beast, but have no power in the fourth beast of the Roman and Islamic Empires. And then all are eventually killed together with the death of the fourth beast.

1. **Babylonian Empire**: Lasted from 605 B.C.E. to 539 B.C.E., from the reign of Nebuchadnezzar II to its conquering by the Persian Empire
2. **Persian Empire**: Lasted from 550 B.C.E. to 330 B.C.E., supported by the two unified nations of (1) Persia and (2) Media
3. **Greek Empire**: Lasted from 330 B.C.E. to 30 B.C.E., in various divisions of the (1) Ptolemy Empire, (2) Seleucid Empire, (3) Antagonid Empire, and (4) Attalid Empire
4-1. **Roman Empire**: Lasted from 27 B.C.E. to 1806 C.E., in various forms and divisions of the (1) Roman Empire reduced down to the Western Roman Empire, (2) Eastern (Byzantine) Roman Empire, and (3) Holy Roman Empire
4-2. **Islamic Empire**: Lasted from 632 C.E. to 1922 C.E., in various forms and divisions of the (1) Rashidun Empire, (2) Umayyad Empire, (3) Abbasid Empire, (4) Fatamid Empire, (5) Ayyubid Empire, (6) Mamluk Empire, and (7) Ottoman Empire

The Roman Empire existed in a total of three empire forms through its history, until it ceased to exist in 1806 with the fall of the Holy Roman Empire to Napoleon Bonaparte. The Islamic Empire existed in a total of seven empire forms through its history, until it finally fell in 1922 at the internal collapse of the Ottoman Empire due to revolution. Three plus seven equals ten as there are ten toes on two feet. These ten versions of the Roman and Islamic Empires are not the final ten horns in Daniel 7 and Revelation 13 and 17, but they still are part of the ten toes, showing how these two empires together are the complete fulfillment of the final fourth beast in Daniel 2 and 7. According to the Daniel 2 prophecy there will never be another empire to emerge ever again now after these Roman and Islamic Empires, only the broken up remains of them will continue to the end, as we see happening today.

Both legs of iron of the Roman and Islamic Empires fell apart over a process of hundreds of years before the end of each, crumbling and broken into the feet of iron mixed with clay. For about a thousand years it was becoming more and more difficult to form empires. Most empires during that time were simply confederations of smaller states coming together under a larger government, but retaining their own borders and smaller governments. The Ottoman Empire was the last true empire to exist, and since 1922 no true empire has been able to exist in spite of many trying. The British Empire by the 20th Century was just a confederation of colonial states around the world, as was the United Soviet Socialist Republic (Soviet Union) made up of many smaller countries with divided borders under a central government control.

Many tried through the last 100 years to recreate an empire again, such as Adolph Hitler and the Nazis, or the Communists in various countries like Russia and China, or elements of the government of the United States of America using the United Nations, or the European Union in Europe, or the Arab League of Nations, or the Islamic terrorist groups trying to bring back the caliphate, but none succeeded, and all have been broken up empires made partly of weakness and partly of strength, divided up among many nations with lots of borders within the empire that fracture easily. We are now at the point of the feet of iron mixed with clay when no one in the world is able to form empires anymore, and instead rely on trying to bring together divided and weak nations, trying to mix the iron and clay together without any success. It is because the seed of man, represented as the clay in the feet, is preventing any empire from being formed again.

Whenever the word "seed" is used in reference to people in the ancient Hebrew and Chaldean cultures, it means the offspring or descendants or children of men. In Genesis 3:15 the word "seed" is used to refer to the descendants of Chavvah (Eve) who will battle with the serpent, crushing its head as it strikes at their heals, as one of the curse consequences of eating from the tree of the knowledge of good and evil. Eventually her "seed" descendant Yeshua will crush the head of the Serpent once and for all. The word "seed" is also used in Genesis 48:4 where Yahuweh/Yehovah says that he will give this land (of Canaan) to the seed of Jacob as an everlasting possession. This is referring to his descendants and children for all generations, the nation of his descendants that were born from him.

At the time when the Roman and Islamic Empires are broken up as the feet and ten toes into iron and clay together, the iron and clay try to mix together, but fail because iron and clay cannot mix. The clay in verse 2:43 is clearly said to be the "seed of men," as man is referred to as being like clay and made out of the dirt of the earth many times through Scripture, but what is the pronoun "they" referring to? It is referring to the iron, "they," who are trying to mix with the clay, and the iron is the broken up remnants of the Roman and Islamic Empires. Those who are in power at the very end all the way up to the toes are trying to bring back the broken up iron together to bring back the Roman and Islamic Empires back to life again, but they fail because the brittle clay of the seed of men keep getting in their way, preventing the iron bits from attaching together again.

The seed of men or descendants of men are the children of the younger generations. We are living in the era of Revolutions, when the people as weak and brittle clay rise up for independence for their countries whenever a dictatorship style government tries to conquer and join together nations into an iron empire again. The people rise up, especially in the younger generations, the seed of the next generation, and overthrow the government or fight for independence from the empire trying to form, because the people do not want empires anymore. They want their own independent states, which causes fractures and borders to form in the empires, keeping the remnants of the Roman and Islamic Empires broken up into independent states that are continuously trying to break apart into smaller and weaker nations all of the time as with Scotland and Catalonia and Kurdistan, and the United Kingdom trying to break from the European Union, and Ukraine fighting for independence from Russia. The broken up remains of the Roman and Islamic Empires, divided among many nations, are the fulfillment of Daniel 2:41-43.

The rulers and powers cannot even bring the two feet together of the Roman and Islamic Empires, which is part of the prophecy that they would always remain divided. For all of the attempts in the last few decades to bring Europe and the Middle East closer together, today they are dividing against each other completely, as the nations of the world decided who to ally with in the current World War that is being prepared. All of Europe, except Hungary, have decided to ally on one side with America, and now all of the Middle East, except so far Turkey and Israel, are one by one deciding to ally with Russia and China against America. Europe and the Middle East, the Roman Empire remnant and Islamic Empire remnant are choosing opposite sides again, against each other.

According to this prophecy in Daniel 2, during the Time of the End of the final kings within this empire, they try to create a new, united empire, a One World Government, but fail. This prophecy says that there will never be a One World Government, or any true empire, to exist ever again from this point on until Yahuweh/Yehovah comes to set up his reign. There will never be a global dictatorship with a single man or government ruling over the entire world, or even over a smaller revived Roman or Islamic Empire. After the final, fourth beast of the Roman and Islamic Empires is broken up, it will never be put back together again according to Daniel 2:42 that specifically says that the toes of the statue are made of iron and clay mixed together. This means that all the way up to the very end when Yahuweh/Yehovah comes there is never again a time when the iron comes together into a complete empire with power and strength ever again, not even in the toes. And after the toes there are no more empires of man. The world today, with rulers and powers in the earth fighting to bring together a global empire, and the seed of men, the children of men in each next generation born fighting back as revolutionaries to break up the global empire into nations with independent governments, is the time of the fulfillment of the prophecy now. There is nothing left to be fulfilled after this moment of fulfillment today; it has been prophesied in Daniel that there is no future One World Government that will ever come after this moment in history, nor anything else of man to ever come after this. The only thing coming in the future now is the stone of Yahuweh/Yehovah crushing all of man's empires and man's world as he sets up his eternal reign.

[This is why Mystery Babel the Great is so important to the final rulers and kings and powers across all of the earth in Revelation 17, because it is their only chance to try to bring all the world together as one, through the reviving of the system of the city and tower of Babel in Genesis 11 (shown later on).]

The Beast Out of the Sea Prophecy:
Revelation 13:1-10

Prophecy Fulfillment of Verses **Revelation 13:1-10** – The fourth beast in Daniel 7 is a mystery beast that is never described by Daniel from what he saw in the dream, except for iron teeth and bronze nails. But John describes it in Revelation 13 according to what he saw, at least according to what it looks like at the very end of the existence of the fourth empire of Rome and Islam as two divided legs. The Beast Out of the Sea that John saw and described in Revelation 13 is a combining of all of the four beasts in Daniel 7.

Four Beasts Out of the Sea of Daniel 7 -
Beast 1: Lion with Two Wings and **One Head**
Beast 2: Bear with Three Ribs in Mouth and **One Head**
Beast 3: Leopard with Four Wings and **Four Heads**
Beast 4: Unknown Beast with Iron Teeth, Bronze Claws, Ten Horns, and **One Head**

Single Beast Out of the Sea of Revelation 13 -
The Leopard Body comes from **Beast 3**
The Bear Feet come from **Beast 2**
The Lion Mouth comes from **Beast 1**
The Ten Horns come from **Beast 4**
The Seven Heads come from Adding Together **Beast 1** and **Beast 2** and **Beast 3** and **Beast 4**

This beast in Revelation 13 is the fulfillment of Daniel 7:11-12 where a lengthening of life was given to the first three beasts to still exist during the time of the fourth beast even though their rule has been taken away from them. At the time of the very end during the Great Tribulation the Babylonian Empire and Persian Empire and Greek Empire still exist within the Roman and Islamic Empires, mixed in with them, but without any authority or power. And this can be seen fulfilled during the last 2,000 years of history as the influences of the Babylonian and Persian and Greek Empires continued within the Roman and Islamic Empires, and throughout civilization and society around the entire world. [This is discussed in greater depth concerning the seven heads that are seven mountains of the Beast Out of the Sea and Scarlet Beast Out of the Pit of the Deep later on.]

The fulfillment of Revelation 13:1-2 can be seen through history up to the present time, as the influences and creations of the Babylonian, Persian, Greek, Roman, and Islamic Empires still run the world today, at least the world that runs on what is generally described as "civilization." These include things like the ideas of scientific invention and city/tower building, and how to govern through democracy/republicanism, and the mail and news and communication systems that run people's daily lives in the modern world, and road/travel systems that keep everyone connected, and philosophy school systems for education and higher learning, and the modern medical system of drugs. This first part is a very important part of the Revelation 13 prophecy, because it explains how during the Great Tribulation the Beast Out of the Sea is nothing new or different that comes into existence suddenly. The Beast Out of the Sea is something that has always been there on the earth for millennia, for thousands of years, and continues to exist for 42 months during the Great Tribulation.

There are three things that are different though for the Beast Out of the Sea in Revelation 13:5-8. The broken up remains of the Babylonian, Persian, Greek, Roman, and Islamic Empires mixed together during the final 42 months: 1. have a mouth with authority to speak great words and blasphemes against Yahuweh/Yehovah for 42 months, 2. have the power to overcome the set-apart ones (saints), and 3. are worshipped. It is important to note that concerning the 42 months the Beast Out of the Sea only has the authority to speak great words and blasphemy against Yahuweh/Yehovah. There is no other authority or power granted to the Beast Out of the Sea in Revelation for that specific amount of time of 42 months.

The fulfillment of the Beast Out of the Sea concerning Revelation 13:1-2 is already complete today, as we see in the broken up remains of the Roman and Islamic Empires in Europe and North Africa and West Asia the amalgamation of parts and pieces of the Babylonian, Persian, Greek, Roman, and Islamic Empires mixed together in the ways that people live and run their lives in the modern world of technology that man has created. The interesting thing is that currently all of the nations of the world across the board without exceptions have either already completely adopted these amalgamated parts and pieces of the Babylonian, Persian, Greek, Roman, and Islamic Empires, or are in process of bringing them into their country in order to rise to the same standard of living as the rest of the world in its modern technology. And most of the time nobody in the nations around the world even know that all of their ways of modern living they are adopting almost all originally came from ideas and inventions and creations of the previous empires continued down the line through history, from Babylon to Islam.

This is partly how Revelation 13:7 is fulfilled now in today's world, as every nation, tribe, and tongue are using some of the Beast Out of the Sea systems of the empires it represents in their daily lives across every part of the world. There is nowhere in the world that does not have some part or influence of these Babylonian, Persian, Greek, Roman, and Islamic Empire invented systems known as "civilization" operating in their societies. It has reached the point now where all of the nations of the world are looking more and more like generic copies and clones of each other as they all try to adopt the most advanced standards of living. Even though the Beast Out of the Sea Empire is now only existing as broken up pieces of divided countries in the former Roman and Islamic Empires, it has authority and influence now in every country in the world as everyone has become dependent on these Beast Out of the Sea old empire systems in order to keep their high standards of living and wealth and luxury and leisure, and even survival in some cases.

Now people are in danger of death if they lose their electricity, which is something new that has never happened on the earth before in recorded history. In the past no one was in danger of dying if they did not have their electricity for their heat or running the cars and trains and planes to take food to people in their grocery stores. Even though most people do not live inside of the borders of the remnants of the Roman and Islamic Beast Out of the Sea Empires, most in the world are trapped into the authority of the Beast Out of the Sea, by being reliant on its systems to live and work in society. According to Daniel 2 there will never again be a true empire that has no internal borders and is not broken up among nations in some way (which is why there are ten horns or ten kings at the end instead of one horn or king ruling, because the Beast Out of the Sea is under the rule of many governments, not a single dictatorship government). The Beast Out of the Sea today of the Roman and Islamic Empires is everywhere in the world with authority and influence, but not power or government to rule everywhere. It is an empire that is broken up by many, many internal borders across the nations, partly strong and partly weak.

The way the world exists today is already the fulfillment and existence of the Beast Out of the Sea across all the world, broken up among many governments and rulers, among many horns. There is nothing new that needs to come into existence or anything more that needs to happen for the Beast Out of the Sea itself, of the Roman and Islamic Empires, to come into any more fulfillment than it already is in today. The question is about the three unique things that happen with the Beast Out of the Sea during the Great Tribulation.

The Beasts or Empires of history are simply the worlds that men create for themselves to live in under a unified system of governance and authority, usually with a single man or woman, or small group of people, as a central power guiding and creating that world that everyone lives in within the empire borders. And from Yeshua's experience of 40 days in the wilderness, the Adversary (haSatan), the Serpent/Dragon or demonic world is always very involved as a spiritual power trying to control the manmade empires and power systems. All through history it has been demonic creatures/beings through images or idols that have been worshipped as gods in the various empires, or imaginary gods from the imaginations of men created in mythologies.

These ancient religions of the world, which were very prevalent in all of the empires, including the later Roman and even Islamic Empires through Islamic mythology, have been generally known by the name or label of Paganism. It was common practice for the rulers and kings of the various empires to be elevated to the status of a god to be worshipped, but each man who ruled was only worshipped as one god among many thousands or hundreds of thousands of gods to be worshipped. The men who ruled the empires were never worshipped as a unique god of any higher authority or more special than any of the many other thousands of gods that everybody already worshipped. What is special about the Beast Out of the Sea in Revelation 13, which is the broken up remains of the four beasts or empires in Daniel 7, is that it is the beast itself, the empire itself and its systems, that is worshipped instead of any particular man or ruler as in the past with the beasts/empires.

Each of the Beasts in history rises up out of the sea of people, coming from the people, from mankind, and are made up of the people. Each Beast/Empire is mankind itself, a world created entirely by man for man to live in, for the sea of people to live in and function in. The Beast Out of the Sea making up all four beasts in history is the final world and system for the sea of people to live in and be, made up of the broken up remnants from all of the previous empires through history. And this is what we see today in fulfillment of Revelation 13:8, as people are worshipping the modern system and world itself that mankind has created, by worshipping the Beast of mankind that has made this world today through invention and man's scientific achievement in technology. The Beast Out of the Sea is the people, it is mankind and the world that man has created out of the remains of all of the previous empires through history. It is a worship of men as gods, through evolution and the religion of evolutionary process, as men lift themselves up to the powers of gods with incredible powers of technology that have never existed on the earth before in recorded history, the powers to destroy life on a massive scale with nuclear weapons or to create life with Artificial Intelligence and genetic engineering.

And in the midst of this is part of the fulfillment of the Dragon giving its authority to the Beast Out of the Sea in Revelation 13:2 and 4, as the Dragon switches over from the traditional deceptions of getting people to worship demons as gods in direct idolatry toward worshipping the Beast Out of the Sea, worshipping mankind, as gods with people worshipping themselves. Then through this worshipping of other people or themselves as gods, the Dragon can deceive people ultimately into still worshipping demons at the same time as worshipping mankind, worshipping both the Dragon and the Beast Out of the Sea simultaneously. The religions around the world and through history of Satan worship and witchcraft are all based upon the worshipping of one's own self as a god entirely focused on selfish, self-gratification without any regard for others, based on gaining power for one's own self as a god to control and manipulate others.

The closest record in history of man creating a world and system for themselves of self-worship is in the building of the city and tower of Babel in Genesis 11, where the reason the people give for building the city is to "make for ourselves a name." The people wanted to collectively build a city to live in so that they could become famous and not have to scatter across the earth. The desire to be famous and known by others is the desire to be lifted up into a position of worship above others, into the position of gods. It is the same old deception throughout history beginning with the Serpent in Genesis 3 that if a person only eats from the fruit of the tree of the knowledge of good and evil, they can "be like God."

The people of the world today have again come together to build cities and towers as with the city of Babel in Genesis 11, and once again the people of the world are wanting to make a name for themselves, to lift themselves up in fame into the position of being worshipped for their accomplishments and deeds. It is men and women who are being worshipped today as they build the Beast Out of the Sea into a great world of technological innovation, defeating diseases; and going up into the heavens into space to colonize; and making everyone's lives supposedly easier (but really only more stressful) with smart cars, smart phones, smart houses; and military improvements with smart bombs that kill people more efficiently with greater power. The world is all about celebrity status and fame with social media, with everyone vying for worship from others, and people in all areas of life being worshipped for their accomplishments from sports to science.

But the worship of the Beast Out of the Sea itself, of the world itself that man has created for themselves to live in, has only recently truly started, during the winter and spring of 2021. The Beast Out of the Sea, made up of the remnants of all of the empires that have existed through history, with authority but not power in all of the nations of the earth, was continuing on as normal as it had since the breaking apart of the Roman and

Islamic Empires. Even though it was broken apart it still continued to exist and run the governments and nations around the world with the same manmade systems of the world of man that had been in place for thousands of years. Then suddenly the COVID plague came and shut down the Beast Out of the Sea across the entire world. It appeared that the head of the Beast Out of the Sea, the final head or empire state of existence of the Beast had received a mortal and deadly wound, and it seemed like the Beast had been killed and shut down permanently by COVID, never to come back to life again, and everybody on the earth were in mourning that they could not continue their normal lives living in the Beast. Then the deadly wound on the head of the Beast Out of the Sea was miraculously healed by mankind with science and technology, and all the earth marveled at the Beast that was, and is not, come back to life again, in fulfillment of Revelation 13:3 and 17:8 and 11.

There is not another time in all of recorded history that the whole earth shut down as it did for the year of the COVID plague, except for the global flood in the days of Noah. But it was only the places where the Beast Out of the Sea was in operation that shut down. Those living in wilderness or rural places without dependency on modern manmade technologies continued on with life as normal, such as in Africa and parts of South America, or the desert areas of Australia. Only the places built on the foundation of the Beast Out of the Sea shut down, as the Beast Out of the Sea itself was the thing that really shut down across the entire world. And when the Beast came back to life, that is when people really started to marvel at the Beast and understand how important the Beast is to them in their daily lives, how much they love the Beast and worship the Beast to live their normal, comfortable lives courtesy of the Beast Out of the Sea.

There is also another layer of prophetic meaning to the seven heads revealed to John in Revelation 17 that is not revealed or talked about in Daniel. The Beast Out of the Sea in Revelation 13:3 and the Scarlet Beast Out of the Pit of the Deep in Revelation 17:8 and 10-11 have seven heads all together. Revelation 17:10 explains that each of these seven heads represent different empires or kings that are representations of empires through history. Six had already gone by up to the time of John, and one was still coming. The interesting thing is that the Scarlet Beast Out of the Pit of the Deep, that is the Beast that was and is not, is an eighth head or empire that is part of the seven heads on the <u>Beast Out of the Sea</u>. The <u>Beast Out of the Sea</u> itself is the seventh head, which is made up of the broken up remains of the Roman and Islamic Empires (together with all of the other empires before that) in the feet of iron and clay in the image of Daniel 2.

The sixth head that existed at the time of John was the Roman Empire, together with the second iron leg of the Islamic Empire that came a short while later. The five heads or five empires that came before John's time, which had already fallen before John was born or wrote the book of Revelation going backward through time in chronological order, were the (1) Greek, (2) Persian, (3) Babylonian, (4) Assyrian, and (5) Egyptian Empires. Of these five empires only the Babylonian, Persian, and Greek Empires are mentioned in the prophecies of Daniel, because Daniel only deals with the empires that were in existence from the time when he was alive until the end of this world and the setting up of Yahuweh/Yehovah's eternal reign. The Assyrian and Egyptian Empires were the extra two empires in existence historically before Daniel was born, bringing the total to five before the time of John.

The Beast Out of the Sea is the final seventh head in existence, existing as the fulfillment of the two feet of iron and clay in Daniel 2 made up of the remnants of all of the previous empires combined together in pieces, and it was the Beast Out of the Sea as the seventh head that was temporarily killed and shut down, appearing to be dead for a year with every single part of normal Beast life made lifeless, from the schools to the medical world, from the governments to the economies and industries. But when the Beast Out of the Sea came back to life again around the world, the Scarlet Beast Out of the Pit of the Deep, that was and is not and yet is, also came back to life again with the Beast Out of the Sea. The Beast Out of the Sea transformed and added another eighth head onto itself, a new head that was the Scarlet Beast Out of the Pit of the Deep ruling with it in its fullness, carrying Mystery Babel the Great. They are really one and the same these two Beasts that are the seventh and eighth heads, because in reality the Scarlet Beast Out of the Pit of the Deep carrying Mystery Babel the Great is the Image of the Beast Out of the Sea, exactly the same as the Beast Out of the Sea, because it is an Image representation of the Beast Out of the Sea (examined in depth later on).

When the Beast Out of the Sea came back to life again everyone on the earth whose names are not written in the Book of Life were greatly relieved and had a new appreciation and thankfulness in worship for the Beast Out of the Sea, with the new realization of how important the Beast Out of the Sea is to them to be able to live their lives of security and comfort. There was a lot of appreciation and worship given to the Beast beginning in the winter and spring of 2021 as it came back to life again and people realized just how much they depended upon the Beast Out of the Sea to be able to live as they do. Over and over again the new COVID vaccines were called a "miracle" by people across the world, and hailed as an amazing achievement of man to miraculously bring back the Beast Out of the Sea to life again.

A miracle by definition is an "act of God" except that the COVID vaccines were praised as a "miracle" of man, of man acting as gods. This caused people around the world to talk about how amazing the world created by man is, that man is able to overcome anything and nothing can destroy the world that man has created, the Beast Out of the Sea that the people of the earth have created as their world to live in. Just like in Revelation 13:4, the world said, who is able to fight with the Beast Out of the Sea, with man's creation and man's invincible world that nothing can stop, that not even God, Yahuweh/Yehovah himself, can stop with a plague like COVID. The COVID shutdown of the world system of the Beast Out of the Sea was a clear moment that Yahuweh/Yehovah created to define the difference between himself and the worship of him, and the Beast Out of the Sea and the worship of man's created world. It was a very precisely defining moment that Yahuweh/Yehovah made so that everyone on the earth living today could make a clear choice in their hearts between him, or the world of the Beast Out of the Sea, to choose which to serve and which to worship.

The majority of the nation of Israel made their choice for the Beast Out of the Sea as was shown in the sign of their Independence Day celebration event on the night of April 14-15, 2021 as they worshipped the Beast Out of the Sea for their salvation from COVID, in gratitude that they did not have to repent and turn back to Yahuweh/Yehovah in order for his plague to be taken away. If the world was ever going to repent and turn back to Yahuweh/Yehovah, the COVID plague was that perfect opportunity for that to happen, but instead of repentance the world went even stronger in their rebellions against Yahuweh/Yehovah, refusing to turn around and change course. Instead the world went for the Beast Out of the Sea, the world that man has created on the earth, to worship and obey that system instead.

On the night of April 14-15 the nation of Israel, as one of the first nations to receive the "miracle" vaccination to bring the Beast Out of the Sea back to life, made a celebration event honoring and worshipping the systems of the Beast Out of the Sea that man has created that had been saved by the miracle vaccines brought to Israel first before any other countries, especially the health care system, that had defeated the COVID plague with man's ability and ingenuity as gods creating miracles. It was a very ceremonial worship service to the Beast Out of the Sea as it came back to life again in Israel, as the nation of Israel made a very clear choice to set up the Beast Out of the Sea empire system as its system to live by and its god to be worshipped and preserved as their way of life, in fulfillment of the worship of man's created world of the Beast Out of the Sea Empire in Revelation 13:8.

There have always been people speaking blasphemies against Yahuweh/Yehovah, trying to dirty or twist or pervert the set-apartness of Yahuweh/Yehovah. But ever since the resurrection of the Beast Out of the Sea fractured empire across the earth after its temporary COVID death, the authority and strength behind the blasphemies against Yahuweh/Yehovah's creation and how he created the man and the woman, and set up the systems of nature, has increased to a new level. There is an empowerment now behind the blasphemies that those in authority and the people in the Beast Out of the Sea have to be able to freely blaspheme Yahuweh/Yehovah and his name and his tent openly in society, accepted as part of the tolerance required in the governing system of the Beast Out of the Sea called democracy, that comes from the surviving fragments of the Greece Beast in Daniel 7.

People speak unclean things (together with unclean actions and appearances) about Yahuweh/Yehovah and the way he created life to be, and against his name Yahuweh/Yehovah or Yeshua/Jesus, with "Pride" and boldness of authority, in fulfillment of verses 13:5-6, to the point where the Beast of the Out of the Sea of People, through their democratic governments in many places in the world, criminally charge anyone who tries to stop the blaspheming against Yahuweh/Yehovah and his set-apart place of his Tent (of truth and righteous judgment rulings in Isaiah 16:5). Even from the governmental level now there is blasphemy against Yahuweh/Yehovah's righteous perfect judgment in determining right and wrong, saying that Yahuweh/Yehovah's judgments on sin and morality are evil, and man's judgments are good and "on the right side of history."

The Beast Out of the Sea has the authority now behind it, emboldening the people to blaspheme against Yahuweh/Yehovah and to overcome the set-apart ones, the believers in Yeshua, so that they cannot be stopped in their blasphemies. But the set-apart ones can be stopped in speaking against those blasphemies, labeling the speech against the blasphemies as hate speech, and the words of blasphemy against Yahuweh/Yehovah as free speech through tolerance of diversity. Ever since the Beast Out of the Sea came back to life after the COVID plague, the people have had greater authority within the Beast of pushing the system and the governments in the system to greater and greater blasphemies against Yahuweh/Yehovah, saying great words of rebellion against him. And there is a greater boldness and authority on those blasphemies as the system of the Beast Out of the Sea has brought protection and strength to speaking blasphemies, speaking uncleanness and profanity about Yahuweh/Yehovah and his set-apart ways in gender and marriage.

Many people on the earth are fed up with the way Yahuweh/Yehovah created things and they want to change it and recreate or evolve nature into what they want it to be, even if it means destroying and bringing down anyone who tries to still live according to the old standards of morality and nature, and bringing down the systems of living that Yahuweh/Yehovah made at creation for people and animals and life to operate in nature. There is a boldness and authority that those profaning and blaspheming Yahuweh/Yehovah have that has not existed before in history, as it is becoming a normal part of society to dress up or create art or write or give speeches that say great words and profanity against Christianity and Yahuweh/Yehovah's morality and set-apartness in Scripture.

And the Christians, the set-apart ones, today are certainly overcome by the Beast Out of the Sea in many various ways. A Christian cannot get much more overcome by the Beast Out of the Sea than by taking its Mark and worshipping it as hundreds of millions of Christians around the world have done since the spring of 2020 when the Mark began in China and the worship began around the world in the winter to spring of 2021, in fulfillment verse 13:7. That is a level of deception from the Beast Out of the Sea of people that has completely overcome most Christians today, still watching for a mythical Anti-Christ who does not exist in any prophecy in Scripture. John gave the warning in verse 13:9 for those who have an ear to hear what he is writing about the Beast Out of the Sea. Yeshua would always say that Hebrew expression whenever he was talking about a hard thing for people to hear, that they would not want to listen to. And that is being fulfilled now today as there are few Christians who want to hear this hard word about what the Beast Out of the Sea and its worship and overcoming of the set-apart ones is really all about. They want to believe in the myths that people have come up with in their collective imagination over the last 2,000 years and they do not want to accept the reality of what this prophecy about the Beast Out of the Sea is really about, as it is happening in real life now.

But that is why the set-apart ones have to endure and keep their belief in Yeshua through these times, in fulfillment of verse 13:10, because eventually in the end everyone will reap what they have sown, and receive the same thing done to them as they do to others. Those who are exiling people and causing them to go into captivity or slavery today will receive the same treatment, as well as those who are killing with weapons today will eventually also die by them. Each person is going through the trials and experiences that Yahuweh/Yehovah has allotted to them during this time on earth, and the set-apart ones have to endure through what Yahuweh/Yehovah has allotted each individual of them to go through as well. In the end when they have endured through the test of the sieve of falsehood and deception (Isaiah 30:28) of who they will serve and follow, the world of men in the Beast Out of the Sea or Yahuweh/Yehovah, and endured through whatever trials Yahuweh/Yehovah wants each set-apart one to go through, including to the point of martyrdom, then they will enter into eternal life with clean white robes, coming out of the refining of the Great Tribulation (Revelation 7:14).

Other Christians have been overcome by giving in and following the culture, throwing out the oil of the Two Witnesses of the Word of Yahuweh/Yehovah to follow, falling away from their belief in Yeshua and

Scripture to follow society and the Beast in the normalization of sin and unrighteousness instead. And other set-apart ones have been overcome by being put in prison or silenced by Beast Out of the Sea laws of governments around the world, as the governments of nations clone each other's laws into their governments to follow the same authority of the Beast Out of the Sea systems. And other believers in Yeshua have been overcome in an even simpler way, by the people in society choosing and deciding that they want sin and their own rebellious way, and pushing out the Christians and Yahuweh/Yehovah's way of life from society because the people just do not want Yahuweh/Yehovah anymore. Over 60% of Americans want legalized abortion now, and even with the overturning of Roe v. Wade, every time a vote has been held on abortion in the country since then, the pro-abortion side always wins with over 60% of the vote, even in the most anti-abortion states. The set-apart ones are overcome by simple popular opinion that is against them. It also means that there is a high percentage of Christians completely overcome in thinking that there is nothing wrong with parents murdering their children.

The Beast Out of the Sea is simply the world that mankind creates for itself to live in, and the Beast Out of the Sea in Revelation 13 is the way that the people of the world want their world that they live in to be at the time of the end of the final fourth beast and the end of all empire beasts of man's created worlds and systems of living. At the end in the world today the people want to keep their national borders breaking up empires into pieces, but they still all want their governments to implement the same laws and authorities from the systems of the larger Beast Out of the Sea empire, from the remains of all of the previous empires combined together, but with a division between east and west, between Europe and Asia, exactly as Daniel 2 and Daniel 7 prophesied in the imagery of the dreams.

The way the world is right now today is already the complete fulfillment of Revelation 13:1-10. There is nothing new that needs to come into existence or anything more that needs to happen to make the prophecy more fulfilled than it already is now. It is complete as it is and there is nothing more to watch for to happen beyond the present moment of fulfillment today. Even though the Beast Out of the Sea has come back to life for a time, Yahuweh/Yehovah has made it clear with his COVID plague shutting down the Beast that his goal from now until his coming is to kill and destroy the Beast Out of the Sea and all of man's empires and worlds of systems of living. Eventually they will all come down with the rock uncut by human hands in Daniel 2 that Yahuweh/Yehovah will use to crush the world and set up his eternal reign. This is the time now at the very end when there will never be another empire or manmade world system of living to exist ever again after this.

Section 14. Mystery Babel on the Scarlet Beast Out of the Pit of the Deep and the Seven Heads that are Seven Mountains:

References to the Mystery Babel Prophecies:
Genesis 11:1-9
Ezekiel 26:1 – 28:26

Examination of Verses **Genesis 11:1-9** with **Ezekiel 26:1 – 28:26** – Mystery Babel the Great in Revelation 17 to 18 is the city of Babel founded in the record of Genesis 11 shortly after the global flood. But it is more than just the physical city, which is why it is a "Mystery" or "Secret" and called "Great" and the mother of the whores and abominations on the earth. It is the city building ideology of Babel that creates cities as places on the earth where all of the whoring and abominations happen on the earth as the central places of sin. It is the collective of people getting together to make bricks and mortar, and together building a city with a tower or towers in it up to the heavens, in order to become famous and be known by a name that creates places on the earth that are entirely manmade without any of Yahuweh/Yehovah's creation on the earth left in them. The cities built or transformed upon the Babel model create worlds that are entirely of man and sin and rebellion against Yahuweh/Yehovah's world and ways of living in Scripture.

This is why Yahuweh/Yehovah confused the language of all the families of the earth as they were building Babel, literally confusing their "lip" in the Hebrew, to divide them and scatter them across the earth. By doing this Yahuweh/Yehovah created nations, with boundaries and borders to prevent everyone on the earth from coming together as one and destroying themselves in their united rebellion against Yahuweh/Yehovah. If he had let them continue as they were going then the whole earth would have been built as one single city stretching out over every place across the earth eventually as the population increased, without any borders or boundaries between people, and everyone concentrated into a completely manmade world in the city. And whenever men and women are completely focused into living in their own world inside of cities, it can be seen through history that eventually everyone spends all of their time sinning and doing evil to one another, and trying to push their way to the top of the pyramid scheme to rule over everyone else as a dictator.

The entire earth would have been just one big city if Yahuweh/Yehovah had not intervened, but instead each nation builds their own cities of Babel that are separated from everyone else's cities with national borders dividing them. And eventually as nations or cultures grow and prosper they build more and bigger cities within their nations, taking on Babel more and more. And the cities become more and more corrupt with less space, requiring more towers to be built and people in smaller spaces, creating gangs and organized crime and places to sin more readily available with all of the wealth. All through history people travel to the cities with Babel in them to participate in the whoring and abominations, because that is where they are easily available, to be able to get drunk in the wine of whoring with the prostitute Babel in Revelation 17. The cities are the places of power where rulers through history have whored with Babel in order to have their power over others and the cities are the places of wealth where people are able to get very rich as merchants and businessmen by only selling their soul to Babel to get wealth from her in the cities.

Much of the description of the destruction of the city of Mystery Babel in Revelation 18 is paraphrased directly out of the prophecy of the destruction of the city of Tyre in Lebanon in Ezekiel 26 through 28. In many cases the descriptions are identical. The prophecy in Ezekiel 26 through 28 is a prophecy that still has not happened at this point. The city of Tyre has never been destroyed at any time in its history, and it still exists today. One might think that if the descriptions are the same then Mystery Babel must be the city of Tyre. But as already discussed Mystery Babel according to Jeremiah has been ingested into all of the nations of the earth, and this is just an example of one city that contains Babel in it. Tyre is one of many cities of Babel on the earth today that have to be destroyed when Yahuweh/Yehovah comes, in order to end the evil system of Babel that started in Genesis 11 once and for all.

If we look back through history the system of the city Babel in Genesis 11 has always been confined to certain cities that are divided from each other by national borders, preventing Mystery Babel from being able to happen in its fullness. But in today's world, just in the last 70 years, the whole world has been coming together again for the first time since Genesis 11 as one single city of Babel. As discussed earlier, the borders of nations and the will of the people in wanting to break up into independent states has prevented the Beast Out of the Sea from bringing together the fragments of iron of the empires like in the old days, to create a single world system with everyone together as one people without borders. The way that the Beast Out of the Sea has found to get around this problem of borders is through the cities, through Mystery Babel, as we are watching all of the cities become generic copies of each other and come together more and more in connectivity of communication and economy, making all of the world into a single city again like in Genesis 11.

This collective building by the people of the world to try to make a single city across all the earth that everyone can be constantly connected into through their smartphones and other technologies and computer devices is the fullness of Mystery Babel come back to life again without national borders preventing Babel from existing as it did in Genesis 11. And it is through this city of Mystery Babel that the world is building on its own with everyone coming together in unity, that the rulers of the world are using this new technology power of Babel to try to rule the world beyond the boundaries of national borders. It is their only last chance to try to bring the world together into a One World Government system, but as already shown in Daniel 2 and 7 it is prophesied to fail and there will never be a true One World Government to ever exist. Only a collective, unified city Babel like the one in Genesis 11, which is very difficult to rule over by any single person, can connect the people of the world together in such a way as removing borders and barriers. It is the last chance to try to make an empire on the earth again, an empire of a global city instead of a single nation ruling over conquered nations as in the past.

This is why we are living in the time when Yahuweh/Yehovah has to destroy Mystery Babel in Revelation 17 to 18, because for the first time in history Mystery Babel is coming back to life in its fullness as in Genesis 11, breaking down the national barriers of language and culture. In order to stop mankind from creating the entire earth into a manmade world of sin and evil, bring about their own destruction as they would have done in Genesis 11, Yeshua has to come and end the world of man and bring the destruction of Babel, to save as many as possible to take into the New Heavens and New Earth. The important key is Genesis 11:4 that gives the reason why the people united to build Babel, so that they could disobey Yahuweh/Yehovah's command to fill the whole earth and subdue it, scattered across the face of the earth. Babel is all about the people uniting in their disobedience against Yahuweh/Yehovah to build a world without him, which is the same thing as building a world without reality or truth.

The Seven Heads of the Beast Out of the Sea are Seven Mountains upon Which the City of Mystery Babel Sits:
    Daniel 7:2-12, 17-23
    Revelation 13:1-2
    Revelation 17:9-11

Prophecy Fulfillment of Verses **Daniel 7:2-12, 17-23** and **Revelation 13:1-2** and **Revelation 17:9-11** – The seven heads of the Beast Out of the Sea are also the seven heads of the Scarlet Beast Out of the Pit of the Deep, upon which the prostitute Mystery Babel sits. Revelation 17 gives two separate but simultaneous meanings for the seven heads. The second meaning in Revelation 17:10-11 of the seven heads representing seven kings of seven empires, plus an eighth head representing the Scarlet Beast Out of the Pit of the Deep, was already previously examined. The first meaning in Revelation 17:9 is that the seven heads are also seven mountains upon which Mystery Babel sits. If we look at Daniel 7, the Four Beasts all together have a total of seven heads. Daniel does not mention anything about the first or second beasts of the lion and bear being completely headless, so it is safe to assume that they each have one head, and no more than one head each since Daniel did not mention them having more than one head as he did with the third beast of the leopard that has four heads. This leaves only one head left for the fourth beast, which Daniel does not give any specific descriptions about, but that John gives more understanding to in his description of the Beast Out of the Sea in Revelation 13.

Looking at these seven heads in history, the first head belongs to the Babylonian Empire, the second head belongs to the Persian Empire, the Greek Empire gets four heads, and the Roman and Islamic Empires get one final head together. Looking at what each of these four sets of empires contributed in history that continued on till today, all of them combined together contributed the seven important elements or mountains into modern society today that are required for the concept of Babel to exist and operate as a city. Everywhere that Babel exists in a city, that city needs these following seven things to be able to function and retain power and control and above all collective unity over the people within the city.

> Head/Mountain 1: Babylon – **Technology/Invention** (The Babylonian Empire is known for being the first empire to start the trend of using its advances in technology to be able to upgrade its military for conquering other nations and using technological invention for its power to rule over its empire; Babylon all the way back to the building of the city and tower of Babel is about invention and advancement of technology, learning and advancing the technology of city building with things like how to make bricks and stick them together with asphalt or mortar for larger and stronger construction)

Head/Mountain 2: Persia – **Diversity of Religion/Culture** (Persia was the first empire to strengthen their rule over the peoples in its empire through the idea of diversity and freedom of religion and local cultures within the empire, so that everyone could still follow their old religious beliefs and customs having unity through diversity)

Head/Mountain 3: Greece – **Philosophy/Education** (Greece is famous for inventing the idea of philosophizing about life and existence, creating the idea of the study of ideas for gaining education and wisdom, which became the basis of the modern education system around the world, especially of universities and colleges)

Head/Mountain 4: Greece – **Pharmacy/Health Care** (The Greeks were the ones who invented Pharmacy, which is the practice of drug sorcery for curing ailments and diseases, the same system of drug Pharmacy in use by the modern health care system today)

Head/Mountain 5: Greece – **Democracy/Politics** (Greece invented the idea of government by democracy, by the rule of the people through election of government, as well as politics, since it is impossible to have politics without some form of democratic or republican government for electing politicians to rule, even if it is just a banana republic)

Head/Mountain 6: Greece – **Entertainment through Sports, Theater, and Novels/Media** (Greece also invented all of the modern entertainment industries through using sports as entertainment with the Olympics, and the invention of theater that is still in use today or translated into the medium of film, And the invention of entertaining story telling written down into the form of novels, such as with the *Odyssey* and *Iliad* being the earliest known true novels preserving mythological stories for the entertainment of audiences)

Head/Mountain 7: Rome/Islam – **Connectivity/Networking through Communication and Travel** (The Roman Empire invented the modern road system that they are famous for, using concrete roads to make travel easier through the empire, as well as inventing the modern structure of books still used today [the codex], and the very first newspapers and modern system of news reporting, and the first official postal service for reliable mail delivery, all of which improve communication and travel, keeping people better connected together; it was also out of the Islamic Empire that the invention of asphalt roads came that kept people better connected through travel on modern roads as with the Roman Empire, as well as the invention of the Arabic Numeral system out of India and Al-Gebra that the entire world uses today to be able to mathematically communicate without any language barriers and make complex mathematical formulas and computer programming that connects the world into an internet network)

Every city modeled after Babel absolutely must have man's technology and invention to be able to build its towers and buildings with greater strength in order to hold everyone close together in a small space. And there absolutely must be a freedom of diversity in religion and culture, with everyone respecting everyone else's beliefs and practices so that everyone can co-exist peacefully without killing one another. Organized and controlled education is also another essential ingredient with schools for all of the children and adults to train them and teach them the proper way to live and work among the collective society. There has to be standardized health care made into an organized institution as well, to keep people healthy and feeling safe and secure in their collective world of Babel. The government system requires politics and democracy to run, so that the collective will of the people is running the society as a decentralized form of government. This way dictators come into power through the will of the majority of the people in society, and whoever is able to control the will of the masses is the one with the power, which is easier said than done. The easiest way to keep the masses under control is through large scale, mass produced entertainment, which is also essential for a city with Mystery Babel to operate, to attract people into the city to live there and to keep everyone happy. Democracy also allows for the collective will of rebellion against Yahuweh/Yehovah and truth in the people to be forced upon everyone in the society of Mystery Babel.

Finally, streamlined roads and networks of communication are absolutely essential to keep everyone constantly connected together, even connecting together cities across long distances, turning the separated cities into one city. And it is also essential to keep everyone alive, by bringing food and water and everyone's needs to them, through a connected economy. Without food a city falls apart and everyone has to return to the wilderness to live as farmers and ranchers, each individual dependent upon Yahuweh/Yehovah's provision from the land he created instead of depending upon the promise of Babel of always having food and needs provided for in the city. Babel has to have all of the people working in unity together in order to function and work, as a collective "us" in Genesis 11. Everyone has to be working together for the same goal of building the city, the world created by men and women in their image. And this brings wealth and happiness for everyone as they can each get what they want from getting drunk from Babel, and the people who want power only have to prostitute themselves with the system of Babel, selling their soul, to rule over it and the people in it. This is certainly all the reality of the cities and most towns around the world today.

Not everything in these seven mountains are bad, but most of them are based in fallen man's ways of rebellion to get power and become gods, and are contrary and in rebellion against Yahuweh/Yehovah's ways in Scripture. There is nothing wrong with entertainment or being connected together across distances as long as it does not become a part of a system of control that leads people away from truth and reality. There is nothing wrong with education as long as it is not a system to teach everyone to become clones of each other and be unable to think for themselves. But there is no religion of Democracy in Yahuweh/Yehovah's world, and there is no Pharmacy either, or eating from the tree of the knowledge of good and evil as in Philosophy, gaining knowledge for power and control instead of for knowing truth and knowing the only person who is truth, Yahuweh/Yehovah himself, the Messiah Yeshua who is the only way, truth, and life.

Now with the internet today, the internet itself is becoming one, single, virtual city where everyone lives and works in an entirely manmade virtual world. Everyone is constantly connected into this city with their smartphones, even in the most rural places of the world. The world has come together as a collective "us" to decide to build a city, a giant city that connects together all of the cities of the world into one virtual city, the city of Mystery Babel that is being built bigger and bigger today. Everyone has the ability of instant contact and communication with everybody everywhere around the world, without language barriers anymore thanks to computer programs that translate all languages for people.

It is all thanks to these seven mountains that are seven heads that come as models from the previous empires of how they functioned as societies that Mystery Babel the Great is able to come back into existence in its fullness in all the cities of the world, mankind coming together to create the whole world into a single city where Yahuweh/Yehovah's ways of life in Scripture are the only things not welcome in it. All other diversity of religion and culture and sin are welcome in Mystery Babel, just not the Witnesses of Yahuweh/Yehovah, because that spoils the world that fallen man and woman make for themselves, and makes people see that they need to be made clean and live a different way according to a standard of perfect righteousness and perfect justice, according to the standard of the God of Israel who created all life on earth to begin with.

The Mystery Babel Prophecies, Describing It and Prophesying Its Destruction:
    Isaiah 13:1-22
    Isaiah 14:17-21
    Isaiah 21:6-10
    Isaiah 48:20-22
    Jeremiah 50:1 – 51:64
    Revelation 14:8
    Revelation 17:1-6, 15, 18
    Revelation 18:1-24

Word for Word Prophecy Examination of Partially Fulfilled and Unfulfilled Verses **Isaiah 13:1-22** and **Isaiah 14:17-21** and **Isaiah 21:6-10** and **Isaiah 48:20-22** and **Jeremiah 50:1 – 51:64** and **Revelation 14:8** and **Revelation 18:1-24** – Even though most of the prophecies about Babel do not happen until after Yeshua returns at the end of the Great Tribulation, when it is destroyed, these prophecies that are not yet fulfilled provide important details describing what Mystery Babel is. From the very first prophecies ever written about Babel in Isaiah, the destruction of Babel has always been inseparably linked to the Time of the End at the Day of Yahuweh/Yehovah when he comes to end the world of man and set up his reign and dwelling place together with men. Isaiah 13 is a prophecy about the very end of this world of man and Yahuweh/Yehovah's coming, but the focus of that prophecy is Babel and its destruction.

Isaiah 13 is about the same time of Yahuweh/Yehovah gathering the nations of the earth into an army for destroying all the earth as is found in Joel 3 and Zechariah 14 and Revelation 16. They are about the same time and the same final war. The same darkening of the sun and moon and stars is also mentioned as in Joel 3. This is when Babel will be destroyed, by the Medes who are an ancient nation that existed in modern day

Iran where the Kurds are now located. Isaiah 14 continues this same prophecy about Babel at the Time of the End when all of the tribes of Israel return together as one nation under Yeshua, and describes the death of the King of Babel, called Helel, the son of the morning. Isaiah 14 gives an important description about Babel, that Babel is all about the destruction of the cities of the earth in order to fill the face of the world with cities. This is the way that Isaiah 14 is actually written, saying that the king of Babel destroyed cities so that his offspring could fill the world with cities. When Babel moves into a city it destroys the old systems of the people who lived there and rebuilds everything into the collective unity system of Genesis 11, where all the world becomes one united city without national borders. Babel is all about city building and filling the whole world with cities that run on the system of rebellion and sin against Yahuweh/Yehovah. But the old cities have to be destroyed first in order to build Babel cities in their place. Isaiah 14:21 explains why Babel has to be destroyed, in order to prevent the whole world from being turned into cities of people coming together in unity in rebellion and disobedience against Yahuweh/Yehovah as they did in Genesis 11.

Revelation 14:8 and 18 are all about the destruction of Mystery Babel at the very end of the world of man, and both quote directly from Isaiah 21:9 and Isaiah 48:20, because all of these prophecies together are about the same event of the destruction of Babel at the end, together with Jeremiah 50 through 51 (quoted in Revelation 18) and Isaiah 13 through 14. Isaiah 48:20-22 together with Revelation 18:4 reveals that Yahuweh/Yehovah's people have to flee and leave Babel this time, instead of Egypt, to escape the plagues that come upon Babel instead of Egypt, as they go into the wilderness to meet Yahuweh/Yehovah in the clouds at the sound of the Shophar above Mount Sinai.

Like Isaiah 13, Jeremiah 51:28 also prophesies that the Medes will destroy Babel, but adds in the additional information that the people from Ararat, Minni, and Ashkenaz in modern day Turkey will join with the Medes, together with many other unnamed nations in Jeremiah 51:27. According to Jeremiah 51:48 at least some of these unnamed nations come from the north, together with the nations listed from modern day Turkey and Iran. Also like Isaiah 13, Babel is destroyed in Jeremiah 50 to 51 at the same time that remnants from all of the 12 tribes of Israel are returning back together again as one nation, at Yeshua's return as he gathers them all together in Isaiah 49. Revelation 17:1 quotes from Jeremiah 51:13, saying that Mystery Babel is the whore, the city of Babel that sits upon many waters. The literal city of Babel that used to exist, but does not exist anymore today, sat on the banks of the many waters in the midst of the Euphrates River and Tigris River in central modern day Iraq near Baghdad, where the rivers begin to form many tributaries.

Revelation 17:15 reveals that these many waters that Mystery Babel sits upon in Revelation 17 and in Jeremiah 51 represent nations and peoples and languages, many of them in the plural form. This verse reveals that Mystery Babel is not a single city physically located in only one location, but is instead sitting upon nations plural, located within many nations of the world simultaneously. Jeremiah 51:7, quoted in Revelation 18:3, is in perfect agreement with this, saying that all of the earth is drunk with Babel, the golden cup in the hand of Yahuweh/Yehovah that he uses to pour out his wrath on the earth. The nations on all of the earth have all ingested and taken in the wine of Babel inside of their nations, and that is why the nations on all of the earth go mad and insane.

In today's world we are watching all of the cities of the earth become clones of each other so that it is harder and harder to tell them apart, because they are all taking in more and more of Babel into them. The world is completely filled with cities of Babel as in Isaiah 14, and all the nations of the earth are filled with cities of Babel sitting over them as in Jeremiah 51 and Revelation 17 to 18. All of the cities of the world in every nation on earth are coming together more and more in unity of rebellion and disobedience and sin against Yahuweh/Yehovah and making all of the nations and peoples and languages one and united as a single city across the national borders, like Babel with its tower in Genesis 11. The cities of the world are filled with towers reaching up into the heavens and Mystery Babel riding on the Scarlet Beast Out of the Pit of the Deep is here in its fullness today. This is why, according to all of the prophecies about the destruction of Babel, that Yahuweh/Yehovah has to come and end the system of Babel once and for all, never to be rebuilt or to exist again. It is simply because of this world that mankind creates for itself that is completely made out of man and woman's rebellion and sin and disobedience against Yahuweh/Yehovah, allowing evil and injustice as everyone fights for power over one another. The whole world turned into a single, giant city of Babel is the only future this world has left for it if Yahuweh/Yehovah does not come to end it and put in place his reign and his world system instead.

Prophecy Fulfillment of Verses **Revelation 17:1-6, 15, 18** – Mystery Babel the Great is the whore sitting upon the many waters of the nations and peoples and languages of the earth. Mystery Babel is sitting everywhere on the earth today where there are people and nations and languages being spoken, in all of the cities in fulfillment of verses 17:1 and 15. Mystery Babel the Great is the mother of the whores and abominations of the earth, and every city in every nation in the world today has become the center of all of the whoring and abominations of sinning and rebellion against Yahuweh/Yehovah today. All of the cities of the world fit this description as the central places where all of the sin goes out from in fulfillment of verse 17:5.

All of the kings of the earth rely upon Mystery Babel, rely upon the cities, for all of their power, which is why they have to whore with Babel in fulfillment of verses 17:2 and 18. The kings and governments of the nations of the earth have to use the seven mountains as the foundation of Babel to have their power to rule and govern over the sea of many waters of people. It is the system that they have to use in order to rule in rebellion against Yahuweh/Yehovah according to their own selfish ways at war against the ways of Yahuweh/Yehovah in Scripture. And Mystery Babel is the one with the real power over all of the kings and governments of the earth, because none of them can rule with power without having cities of power, cities of Babel, in their nations to rule from. They are completely dependent upon their cities of Babel from which they rule, cities of wealth and prestige that give men and women positions of authority. If they tried to rule while living alone in a tent in a remote wilderness from the middle of a corn field or rice paddy everyone would laugh at them and no one would obey them. It is their position in a powerful city, a city of Babel with the strength of united people building a world together, that gives kings and governments their power to rule nations and empires. And the inhabitants of the earth go to whore with Babel, in all of the cities of the world, for all of their wine and pleasure, to get drunk in their sin, in fulfillment of verse 17:2.

The concept of the city of Babel is to remove all of the people out of the wilderness into the city itself, preserving nature and keeping mankind out of Yahuweh/Yehovah's created world in the wilderness. This is why there is the dual situation in Isaiah 14 of making the earth a wilderness and filling it with cities at the same time and this can be seen happening today in fulfillment of verse 17:3. The woman Mystery Babel, upon the Scarlet Beast Out of the Pit of the Deep in the wilderness, is surrounded by wilderness because all of the people are brought within the city, living in the city of united defiance against Yahuweh/Yehovah. More and more those who want rebellion and sin against Yahuweh/Yehovah are gathering into the cities of the world, where the names of blasphemy against Yahuweh/Yehovah are written. All through history the cities have been the central places of man's unification in sin against Yahuweh/Yehovah, and draw people into them for the promise of wealth and power there as it was with Lot when he was attracted to leave the wilderness and live in Sodom.

Mystery Babel is dressed in the fine and expensive clothing and jewelry with the golden cup filled with abominations and her whoring in her hand. All of the cities of the world today are the centers of all of the wealth and finery in fulfillment of verse 17:4, and the sins and abominations are always wrapped in attractive wealth in the cities. The sinning looks so good and seems so good in all of its finery, but it is all really very filthy and unclean in fulfillment of verse 17:4. All the cities in the world are the central places where people go to find all of their wealth and finery and the filthy sin is available right along with it for those who want it. The cities are also the places around the world today where the witnesses of Yeshua are most unwelcome, and where many believers in Yeshua are killed for their witness. The blood of the witnesses of Yeshua is spilled in the cities of the world, both literally and symbolically, through history and especially today. The cities that have become Mystery Babel unified into rebellion against Yahuweh/Yehovah have to push out all those who are true believers in Yeshua, who truly follow the witness of the Word of Yahuweh/Yehovah in Scripture, in fulfillment of verse 17:6.

All through the last 2,000 years of history it has been cities and empires of the world that are based upon the Babel unification model in Genesis 11 that Christians have been martyred in. This is why there is the mention in Jeremiah 51:49 that Babel will be destroyed for the slain of Israel and for the slain of all the earth. All through history Yahuweh/Yehovah's people have been murdered and slain in the cities, and it is because the cities are the places where innocent blood is spilled on a large scale through history, as it was in Sodom and Gomorrah. All of the cities of the world are becoming more and more Babel and more and more guilty of the slaying of innocent blood and the blood of the witnesses of Yeshua every day. Yahuweh/Yehovah will destroy Babel for all of the slain who have ever been slayed on the earth, because Babel is everyone in all of the nations and cities of the earth. That is what Babel from Genesis 11 is all about, to unite everyone in existence together with common cause of disobedience against Yahuweh/Yehovah, in every nation and language and people and tribe, so Babel is not Mystery Babel unless it is everywhere where people are.

The world today of cities has already become exactly what is described in Revelation 17, as well as 18, concerning the cities being the places of power that the kings of the earth depend upon for their power, and the central places where all of the people in them want sin and rebellion against Yahuweh/Yehovah and his Witnesses to be normalized in many forms against his commands in Scripture, whether it be from abortion to prostitution, or worshipping of false gods of selfish gratification in their various forms. And now with the internet there is a virtual city of Mystery Babel that connects everyone no matter where they are on the earth, now available even in remote wildernesses due to satellite technology. Anybody with a smart phone in the most remote deserts with a solar battery charge can still access the great virtual city Mystery Babel, the city of all of the people of the world in constant contact to do all of the things that people would normally do if they were physically together, all of the things that people do in a physical city normally through history. And all sorts of sin and abominations are available at all times through this virtual city.

Mystery Babel is no mystery or secret anymore and it is very much here in existence now today, very real in real life around us. The people of the world have come together to build a global city virtually where they have failed to build Babel physically in the past, and it is a collective city where people in nations all over came together to build the massive internet infrastructure together as the "us" in Genesis 11 without any dictator or single leader directing or controlling it. Now the mad dash among the leaders and kings of the world is for whom among them will overcome all the rest and become the ultimate power and ruler over this new global city of Mystery Babel connecting all the cities and places in the world together like one big city.

Revelation and Daniel are in agreement in their prophecies that in the end no one person is ever able to get control of the vast city of Mystery Babel, because the great city Babel is the one in control of each and every world leader and everybody else. And no one in the end succeeds in bringing back together the broken up remnants of the previous empires to ever be able to form another empire again. No one succeeds in being able to become a single ruler of the Beast Out of the Sea, because all the way up to the very end there are at least ten separate horns or kings or governments that are ruling the Beast Out of the Sea simultaneously, with a decentralized government that has no dictator over it. Today's world is already the complete fulfillment of Mystery Babel in Revelation 17, and there is nothing new that needs to come into existence or anything more that needs to happen to make it more fulfilled than it is today. All that is left is for the great city of Mystery Babel, both in the virtual and physical forms, to be destroyed by Yahuweh/Yehovah through the Ten Horns.

There is nothing wrong or evil with the basic concept of the internet in the same way there is nothing wrong or evil in the basic concept of a city. But when that city or that internet is built by corrupted men and women uniting in sin and rebellion against Yahuweh/Yehovah, then all of the ability for sin in all of those individual people within the city, or within the global city of the internet, combines together into a unified mob with very great power to commit evil and sin to one another on a larger scale. This can be seen through history as the greatest acts of evil come from people in nations joining together in their sin and uniting as a city of people to murder and destroy. It has always been this way as in the record of Sodom when the two messengers went to get Lot out of the city. All through history cities commit great evil as they have the backing of the government and mob of people behind them, committing mass murder or mass theft of property. Even revolutions require a city of people mobbing together and putting in place a new city government to murder and steal everything from the powers that had been in place before them.

Whenever people unite together as a collective mob, a city of people with the same purpose of evil and sin united together, then holocausts and mass murder happen, and the end of all life ultimately. Innocent blood is spilled, including the blood of the Witnesses of Yeshua, along with the removal of all of the Witnesses of Yahuweh/Yehovah. This is why Yahuweh/Yehovah only allows Mystery Babel to exist for so long in the last days, the uniting of all the world together as one city and mob of people, before permanently ending it.

Yahuweh/Yehovah comes to set up his own city of people, based upon unity in righteousness and justice instead. Any city, even an internet city, built upon righteousness and people with pure, clean hearts would be able to exist without needing to be destroyed, if there is no Babel in it, no unification into a global society of people with corrupted hearts wanting sin and evil in rebellion against Yahuweh/Yehovah. The evil is very deceptive in Babel, dressed in its wealth and finery and looking beautiful on the outside, but only filth inside.

Section 15. **The Ten Horns:**

Some of the Geographical Locations of the Ten Horns or Kings that Destroy Babel are Named in Other Prophecies:

Isaiah 13:17-19

Jeremiah 51:26-29, 47-48

Word for Word Prophecy Examination of Unfulfilled Verses **Isaiah 13:17-19** and **Jeremiah 51:26-29, 47-48** – In Revelation 17:16 there is a prophecy that the Ten Horns of the Beast Out of the Sea (and Scarlet Beast Out of the Pit of the Deep) will be the ones to destroy Mystery Babel, the globally united city of Babel on the earth today, virtual and physical, that is in all of the cities of the earth. Revelation 18:21 calls Babel the "great city," and it is in the "great city," which is Babel, that the Two Witnesses of the Word of Yahuweh/Yehovah are currently being destroyed and killed. The Ten Horns are then the ones who destroy and kill the "great city" Babel at the very end, or at least play a major role in Babel's destruction, because of their hatred of the whore of Babel. And it is because they are doing the mind of Yahuweh/Yehovah, what he has given into their hearts to do to destroy Babel.

The Ten Horns are ten kings and the specific geographic locations of some of these ten kings who destroy Babel are given in Isaiah 13 and especially in Jeremiah 51. At least one of these horns comes from the kings of the ancient nation state of Media, which was primarily located in the modern day western-northern parts of Iran. The ancient nation of Minni (Mannaea) listed in Jeremiah 51 was also located in this same northwestern part of Iran. Ararat and Ashkenaz are two more ancient nations listed from which at least one more horn or king is supposed to come from, both of these nation located in modern day Turkey. Ararat was primarily located in what is now modern day eastern Turkey and Ashkenaz in modern central Turkey. At least two of the Ten Horns, two kings of the ten kings that participate in hating and destroying Babel, destroying the modern day Babel system of technology connecting all of the world together as a city, are located in modern day Turkey and modern day Iran.

According to the Jeremiah 51 prophecy there are also many other unlisted and unknown nations that come against Babel to destroy it, to destroy the global city of Mystery Babel that exists in all of the nations and cities of the world today. The locations of these other kings or horns and not revealed in Jeremiah 51, except that there are possibly more nations that come from the north, from the same area around Iran and Turkey, which would possibly include Russia with its nuclear arsenal large enough to destroy almost every city on earth as one of the possible Ten Horns from the north. It should also be noted that the Little Horn in Daniel 7 and 8 does not participate in the destruction of Mystery Babel. Only the Ten Horns destroy Mystery Babel, even to the point of standing up against the plans of the Little Horn itself if they have to in order to destroy Mystery Babel.

The Ten Horns Prophecies:
   Daniel 7:7, 19-20, 24
   Revelation 13:1
   Revelation 17:3, 12-17

Word for Word Prophecy Examination of Partially Fulfilled Verses **Daniel 7:7, 19-20, 24** and **Revelation 13:1** and **Revelation 17:3, 12-17** – The Ten Horns on the Fourth Beast in Daniel 7 are the same Ten Horns that are on the Beast Out of the Sea in Revelation 13, because the Beast Out of the Sea is the final Fourth Beast in Daniel 7 as it looks in its final form at the very end, as already discussed in the descriptions given in both of these prophecies. There are almost no descriptions given of the Ten Horns in the prophecies of Daniel and Revelation, and the Ten Horns do almost nothing of any significance in either of the prophecies. The only description of the Ten Horns in Daniel 7 is in verse 24 that says they are ten kings or ten rulers that come from the reign of the final Fourth Beast. It does not say they are the only rulers or the only kings of this final Fourth Beast; Daniel was only told that they are ten kings that come from or come out of this final Fourth Beast, which is the Beast Out of the Sea in Revelation 13. They are ten kings that are from the broken up remnants of the Roman and Islamic Empires, which are now scattered and present in authority in all of the nations of the earth today.

The only other description of the Ten Horns is in Revelation 17:12-14, that says the Ten Horns are ten kings or rulers who receive positions of authority as kings with the Beast Out of the Sea (or Scarlet Beast Out of the Pit of the Deep) for only one single hour, for a very short time at the very end of the reign of the Beast Out of the Sea. They also are unified in their minds and give their power and authority to the Beast Out of the Sea system that is made up of all of the fragments of the previous empires through history, broken apart into two feet and pieces of iron and clay mixed together scattered into all the nations of the world now today as already shown. For a short time these ten kings give their power to the Beast Out of the Sea to help it exist with its power on the earth and they fight together with the Beast Out of the Sea against the Lamb Yeshua, but are overcome by him in the end. These ten kings, which are not said anywhere to be the only ten kings from the Beast Out of the Sea during its time of existence at the Time of the End, are ten kings that have come out of the Beast Out of the Sea.

They decide for a time to be part of the Beast Out of the Sea kingdom/empire system of ruling and governing and running their nations, using the modern technology and becoming clones of all of the other nations interconnected into the modern world system that is in place today. At first they are part of the interconnected network of today's global economy and internet systems that are bringing all of the world together as a global city of Mystery Babel. But in the end they hate the system, they hate Mystery Babel running their governments and their nations, preventing them from being able to rule as dictators and destroy the global city of Babel connecting together all of the world as one. This is the only significant role that the Ten Horns play in the prophecies of the Great Tribulation and Time of the End, as they come together with one mind to destroy Babel, to destroy this entire modern system of Babel that has taken over the world today, both virtually and physically, making all of the cities clones of each other and keeping everyone on earth constantly connected together in the global city of the internet.

Unfortunately the only thing that all of the Ten Horns do together of any significance to identify them by is to destroy Mystery Babel the Great at the very end of the Great Tribulation, at the time of or after Yeshua's return. So there is no way to know for certain the identities of all of the Ten Horns or ten kings that destroy Babel until after the Great Tribulation is over and the world of man has ended. Simply because the Ten Horns give their power to the Beast Out of the Sea broken empire remnants for it to be able to operate with greater authority in all of the nations around the world in fulfillment of Revelation 13:7, this does not mean that they are the only kings or horns on the earth who are doing the same thing of putting their power and authority behind the Beast Out of the Sea system to keep it going. There is nothing in the prophecy of Revelation 17 or in Daniel 7 that these ten kings are the only kings that come from, or are in control of, the final Fourth Beast, the Beast Out of the Sea remains of the Four Beasts. Nor is there anything in Daniel or Revelation saying that these ten kings are the only kings to be backing up the Beast Out of the Sea with their authority.

We see today that the reality of the fulfillment of these prophecies in Revelation 13 and 17 is that all of the nations and all of the governments and rulers of the world are backing and giving their power and authority to this Beast Out of the Sea global system to keep it operating globally. They are all giving their power and authority letting in the authority of the Beast Out of the Sea to operate the way that the nations of the world live and function in their governments and economies and entertainment and health care systems and education. All of the nations are trying to copy each other to be the same as each other, to have equality in standards of living according to the world that mankind is building for itself across the world from the broken remains of the old empires that came before. The beasts are simply each worlds that mankind builds for itself to live in, and the final world/beast that mankind is building today is made from pieces of all of these previous beasts/worlds/empires that are broken up by national borders.

All of the kings/governments of the world are putting their power behind this global Beast Out of the Sea, which is what allows it to be a standardized world where everybody is cloned with the same living standards, looking alike in clothing and styles and living identical lives with the same schedules of education and work and entertainment choices. This is only possible because all of the kings are doing the same things as the ten kings that are Ten Horns, so there is no way to tell apart the specific ten except when they destroy Babel after the Great Tribulation is over. An interesting observation can be made though in looking at which governments and kings hate the virtual global city of Mystery Babel that unites the world together in a decentralized collective that no dictator or centralized government is able to control or get power over. The kings who hate how their physical cities in their nations are becoming clones of other countries, pushing out their powers over their national cultures and belief systems.

Two such governments and kings are ruling over the nations of Turkey and Iran, exactly in the locations where Jeremiah 51 says they will be located. They hate the global internet city and the global culture that is invading their nations, changing their cultures and ways they have lived for a thousand years, removing the power and control that they once had over the people. They would rather get rid of Mystery Babel that is taking all of their power away, having sovereignty over them as kings as is fulfilled in the prophecy of Revelation 17:18. Another three governments are in China and Russia and North Korea, who try to control the internet and cut it off from their nations, because it erodes away their power in being able to be dictatorships or monarchies like the old days. They are currently fighting against Mystery Babel coming into their nations, because it takes away all of their power and changes the people into a more global culture, making them uncontrollable because everyone is controlled by the peer pressure of the global masses instead of the dictator government of the nation as in the past. The people have become a roaring sea across the earth that no governments can get in control of anymore, with the people rising up and protesting or rioting continuously, empowered by the virtual global city of Mystery Babel through internet and other global communication systems.

This is the reality of what is happening right now in the world, as there are some governments of nations that are getting more and more hateful of the current world order and system of Mystery Babel that is operating the Beast Out of the Sea. At one time all of the kings of the world happily gave their power and authority into the Beast Out of the Sea, bringing Mystery Babel into their nations along with it, in order to bring in the global wealth and technology that it promised for their nations to develop and grow. They deceived themselves into thinking that it would make them more powerful, but instead now all of the kings of the world are slaves to the system with no one able to control it.

There is only one other way to be able to identify three of the Ten Horns, three of the kings, through the Little Horn. Daniel 7:8 says that when the Little Horn comes up, three of the Ten Horns are plucked out by their roots. Then in Daniel 7:20 Daniel describes seeing that these three horns fell before the Little Horn when it rose up. The interpretation of this part of the dream is given in Daniel 7:24 when the messenger explains that this represents the Little Horn humbling or subduing three of the Ten Horns, three of the kings. Literally the Aramaic word used here, "Yehashpil" "יְהַשְׁפִּל" means "he makes low" or "he puts down" three kings. The Little Horn does not defeat them or overcome them or conquer them, only makes three of the kings low. The Little Horn brings three of the kings down in a lowly position under him, so that they bow before him in humility to listen to him and obey him, to be swayed and influenced by him and do what he tells them or advises them to do. And these three kings are seen to be under the Little Horn in position and power and authority, brought down to lowly positions comparatively to the Little Horn.

Unfortunately the prophecy in Daniel 7 does not say that these three horns out of the special grouping of Ten Horns that come from the Beast Out of the Sea are the only kings that the Little Horn makes low or humbles. There are only three out of the Ten Horns, but there is nothing in the prophecy to say that the Little Horn does not humble and make low other kings that are outside of the ten kings. This still makes it difficult to reliably be able to identify these three kings out of the ten kings, or any of the ten kings, until they destroy Babel after the Great Tribulation is over. This is examined in depth with the Little Horn discussion listing out the numerous kings that he has in reality already subdued and humbled and made low, making it difficult to see which three kings are of the Ten Horns. But one prominent king/horn that the Little Horn, Sheikh Mohammed bin Zayed Al Nahyan, recently subdued/humbled was the Turkish government through President Erdogan, corresponding to the geographical location of where at least one of the Ten Horns is located in Jeremiah 51.

Therefore Jeremiah 51 reveals the physical locations of at least a couple of the Ten Horns in the Turkish and Iranian governments, and today in reality there are some kings and governments in that region of the world who are already hating Mystery Babel and wanting more and more to destroy it, but until that day of destruction comes at the end of the Great Tribulation there is no way to know the identities of all of the ten kings yet.

Section 16. **The Little Horn:**

There are No Prophecies in Scripture About the Anti-Christ, and There are No Prophecies in Scripture that Say the Little Horn is the Same Person as an Anti-Christ, nor a Man of Lawlessness/Sin, nor a Son of Destruction/ Perdition, nor the Beast Out of the Sea; the Only Entities Prophesied to be Worshipped as False gods in Scripture are the Dragon, the Beast Out of the Sea and Its Image, and the Man of Lawlessness/Sin, but Not the Little Horn:

1 John 2:18-25; 4:1-5

2 John 1:7

2 Thessalonians 2:3-8

Revelation 13:1-8

Word for Word Prophecy Examination of Partially and Completely Fulfilled Verses **2 Thessalonians 2:3-8** and **Revelation 13:1-8** with **1 John 2:18-25; 4:1-5** and **2 John 1:7** – As already shown at the beginning, there is not one prophecy written in Scripture about the Anti-Christs or any Anti-Christs. John only talks about the Anti-Christs in three very short teachings in his letters of First and Second John, but he gives no prophecy about these Anti-Christs. It is only a warning teaching about the Anti-Christs that are already in existence in his day at the end of the 1st Century C.E. and warns that many more Anti-Christs will continue to come in the future until the very end. He says that it is the way for us to know that we are in the last hour (for the last 2,000 years), because of the Anti-Christs that are on the earth.

In 2 John 1:7 John describes the "many leading astray" as "this one … who is leading astray and the Anti-Christ." Whenever John speaks in the singular about "the Anti-Christ" he is always referring to many people who are leading astray, many people who are the Anti-Christ. The criteria that John gives for a person to be an Anti-Christ are simple: they have to have at one time been Christians or believers in Yeshua, but they leave the body of believers to start false sects and religious groups based on false beliefs. And there are two specific false beliefs that they have to teach and lead others astray with in order to be an Anti-Christ. One is to say that Yeshua was not the Messiah and not the literal Son of the Father Yahuweh/Yehovah in the flesh, but instead just a regular man like all other men who was a prophet or wise person. The other is to say that Yeshua is the Messiah and God, but never came as a man in tangible flesh, in the physical body of a man.

These are the requirements according to John for a person to be labeled an Anti-Christ or Anti-Messiah, someone who is working against the true Messiah Yeshua and who he really is in reality. There is no prophecy anywhere in Scripture about these Anti-Christs, only John's warning teaching that they will be around among the false prophets until the end throughout this entire last hour of the existence of this world, of the last 2,000 years. There is no prophecy about these Anti-Christs in the book of Revelation. John never once mentions any person or entity in the book of Revelation who is at one time a Christian, then breaks away to form a separate denomination religious sect teaching that Yeshua was only a man, or teaching that Yeshua was the Messiah but not a man. There is no prophecy about the Beast Out of the Sea in Revelation 13 ever being a Christian organization of false teachings, leading people astray to follow a false belief in Yeshua.

There is nothing to even remotely connect the Beast Out of the Sea or the Beast Out of the Earth or the Scarlet Beast Out of the Pit of the Deep with Mystery Babel the Great as Anti-Christs in any way. This was a myth created millennia ago to say that any entities in the book of Revelation, especially the Beast Out of the Sea, are in any way connected with the Anti-Christs described in John's letters. John did not prophesy that the Beast Out of the Sea would be a formally Christian organization that creates a religion based upon the belief that Yeshua was just a man, or that Yeshua was the Messiah but never came as a man in physical form. Therefore the Beast Out of the Sea is not an Anti-Christ or the many "the Anti-Christs" that John teaches about, and is something completely separate and different.

Likewise there is nothing in the book of Daniel (or any book of prophecy) that talks about any of the Four Beasts or the Ten Horns or the Little Horn being "set-apart ones" (saints) or believers in Yeshua who leave the Christian faith to start their own "Christian" religious sects based upon the belief that either Yeshua was not the Messiah and just a man, or that Yeshua was the true Messiah but never came as a physical man. So there are no prophecies about any of the entities in Daniel being Anti-Christs, including no prophecy about the Little Horn being an Anti-Christ either. That was a myth added on later to Revelation and Daniel, trying to turn the prophecies about the Beast Out of the Sea in Revelation and the Four Beasts and the Little Horn in Daniel into a single man claiming to be a Christian but leading people astray with false Christian teachings about the Messiah Yeshua, or even claiming to be the Messiah himself.

This is not what is written in prophecy. It was made up in people's imaginations during the last 1,900 years creating a mythical Anti-Christ person that John never wrote about in Scripture. There are no prophecies in Daniel or Revelation about any of the Beasts or Horns, including the Little Horn, ever claiming to be a messiah or a god. The Beast Out of the Sea in Revelation 13 is worshipped, but never claims to be a god or a messiah at any time in the prophecy. The Little Horn is not prophesied to be the Beast Out of the Sea in Revelation with a name numbering six hundred sixty-six, nor is the Little Horn prophesied to be an Anti-Christ in 1 John or 2 John. The Little Horn certainly deceives people and fights against and prevails over the set-apart ones, but there is no mention of the Little Horn being a former set-apart one himself or a former follower of the God of Israel, Yahuweh/Yehovah, who leads astray Christians with false teachings about Yeshua being just a man, or never coming as a man. He certainly can deceive Christians, but he is not prophesied to have to lead astray Christians in the specific way that an Anti-Christ does according to John's short teachings about Anti-Christs.

There is also nothing in Daniel 7 or 8 to connect the Little Horn with the Man of Lawlessness/Sin, Son of Destruction/Perdition that Paul talks about in 2 Thessalonians. There is nothing to connect this Man of Lawlessness/Sin with the Anti-Christs in John's letters either, because an Anti-Christ is not a person who raises themselves up above all that is worshipped, claiming to be a god or the God Yahuweh/Yehovah. This person described as the Man of Lawlessness/Sin in 2 Thessalonians, showing himself to be the God Yahuweh/Yehovah or Yeshua is simply a false messiah, not an Anti-Christ. Anti-Christs do not claim to be God themselves; they lead people astray with false teachings about who Yeshua was. The Dragon and the

Beast Out of the Sea and its Image are not prophesied to claim to be God, Yahuweh/Yehovah, but they are worshipped like gods.

The Man of Lawlessness/Sin is the only one prophesied who will claim to be the God of Israel himself, Yahuweh/Yehovah, and worshipped as a god. This creates a mystery about this prophecy that Paul gives in 2 Thessalonians, because there is no other prophecy anywhere in all of Scripture about a man setting himself up to portray himself as Yahuweh/Yehovah, God, himself. Yeshua prophesies in Matthew and Mark about false messiahs, or people falsely claiming to be the messiah or claiming to be Yeshua himself, but even in those prophecies there is no specific prophesying about these people claiming to be Yahuweh/Yehovah, the God of Israel, himself.

Who then is this unusual Man of Lawlessness/Sin who does not directly correspond to any other prophecy anywhere in Scripture, doing things that no other man or entity is prophesied to do anywhere prophecy, in Daniel or Revelation or Isaiah or Jeremiah or Ezekiel or Psalms or any of the smaller books of prophecy from Hosea to Malachi? The prophecy that Paul gives of the Man of Lawlessness/Sin is a very interesting prophecy mystery, but for certain the Little Horn in Daniel 7 and 8 is not the Man of Lawlessness/Sin that Paul talks about, who sits in the Temple (body of believers) of Yahuweh/Yehovah, portraying himself to be Yahuweh/Yehovah.

Helel, the King of Babel, Together with the Prince of Tyre, are the Only Possible Connections in Prophecy with the Mystery of the Man of Lawlessness/Sin, Son of Destruction/Perdition, Who Raises Himself Above All that is Called God, but None of Them Fit the Descriptions of the Little Horn:

Isaiah 14:1-32

Ezekiel 28:1-26

1 Chronicles 29:23

John 17:12

2 Thessalonians 2:3-8

Word for Word Prophecy Examination of Partially Fulfilled and Unfulfilled Verses **Isaiah 14:1-32** and **Ezekiel 28:1-26** and **2 Thessalonians 2:3-7** with **John 17:12** and **1 Chronicles 29:23** – In 2 Thessalonians 2:5 Paul says that he had already told the assembly of the Thessalonians about this Man of Lawlessness/Sin and "he who restrains" when he was there with them, so since they already know what he is talking about, in verse 2:6 he says that he is not going to write down everything in this prophecy. He says that he already told them the identity of the person who restrains and holds back the Man of Lawlessness/Sin from being revealed, so he is not even going to bother writing down who this restrainer person is.

It is unfortunate that Paul did not write down the entire revelation and prophecy of the Man of Lawlessness/Sin in every detail, leaving out a lot of the most vitally important pieces of information to know what he is talking about. It creates a big mystery since there is no other prophecy about this Man of Lawlessness/Sin anywhere else in Scripture to be able to go look up what he was talking about. He is talking about this really important sign to watch for that will happen first before the Day of Yahuweh/Yehovah at his coming to reign over mankind, but then he does not give all of the details about it in his letter, or explain where he got this idea from of this Man of Lawlessness/Sin that is not prophesied about in any other place in Scripture.

The only other person who is ever called a son of destruction/perdition in Scripture is Judas the betrayer, when Yeshua alludes to Judas in John 17:12 as the only one of his disciples in his care who would be lost, in order for the fulfillment of the prophecies in Scripture. Judas is the only other person called a Son of Destruction/Perdition, but of course this is not a prophecy. It might be that this was a common Hebrew phrase at that time in the 1st Century C.E. that was used for a betrayer or a hateful person who did evil. But this phrase does not help to identify who this Man of Lawlessness/Sin is.

There is a possibility that Paul is talking about Antiochus IV Epiphanes and his past-tense fulfillment of the prophecy in Daniel 11:36-37, in which Antiochus according to what is recorded in the book of First Maccabees tried to raise and exalt himself up above all other gods, to make himself great above them as he tried to force the worship of Greek gods and religion upon the Jews in Judah at that time. This sounds like what Paul is talking about in 2 Thessalonians, except for the problem of Daniel 11:38 in which it says that this man in the prophecy exalting himself above all other gods still gives glory and esteem in worship to a new god of strongholds. This does not sound anything at all like what Paul is talking about.

The other problem is that Antiochus IV Epiphanes in fulfillment of this prophecy in Daniel 11:36-38 raised himself up as a new god above other gods, his own god exalting himself above the God of Israel Yahuweh/Yehovah. In 2 Thessalonians Paul says this Man of Lawlessness/Sin will "show himself that he is God," the same God as the God of the Temple, who is Yahuweh/Yehovah. Paul does not say that this Man of Lawlessness/Sin shows himself to be a new god who is greater than Yahuweh/Yehovah and above him, but instead showing himself that he is the God Yahuweh/Yehovah of the Temple. This is something which is not prophesied to happen in Daniel 11, nor is this something that Antiochus ever did.

Additionally, there is no prophecy in Daniel 11 about a person who is restraining and holding back the "king of the north" from coming to raise himself up as a god above other gods. Nor is there any prophecy in Daniel 11 about this king of the north sitting down in the Temple of Yahuweh/Yehovah claiming to be the God of Israel, and there is no record that Antiochus IV Epiphanes ever sat down in the Temple claiming to be the God of Israel and true ruler of the nation of Israel. If he ever did such a thing that record is now lost, but from records that have survived today we can see that Paul was definitely not talking about Antiochus IV Epiphanes or Daniel 11 in his prophecy of 2 Thessalonians, because the prophecy in Daniel 11 only matches one single phrase in Paul's words "exalts himself above all that is called God or worshipped." There is absolutely nothing else in 2 Thessalonians that corresponds to Daniel 11.

The closest aligning prophecy to Paul's words in 2 Thessalonians is actually the last days prophecy of the King of Babel in Isaiah 14. In Isaiah 14:12 the King of Babel is called the "Son of the Morning" instead of the "Son of Destruction/Perdition," but the other elements are there. The King of Babel raises his throne above the stars of God and above the heights of the clouds, above all which is called God as in 2 Thessalonians. And the King of Babel is the only one prophesied to "sit down" as Paul describes in 2 Thessalonians, sitting down in the Mountain of Appointment on the sides next to the North Star in the heavens. This is the Mountain of Appointment in the heavens as the King of Babel tries to sit in the Temple of God in the heavens. (The Tabernacle Dwelling Place of Yahuweh/Yehovah in the wilderness is often called in Exodus the "Tent of Appointment," often translated as "Tent of Meeting," using the exact same Hebrew word "Mo'ed" "מוֹעֵד" as is found here in Isaiah 14:13 for the Mountain of Appointment.) And the third element is even there in Isaiah 14:14 where he wants to "be like the Most High" or be like God, the true God Yahuweh/Yehovah, to show himself that he is the God Yahuweh/Yehovah, sitting as the God Yahuweh/Yehovah in his throne in the heavens.

The King of Babel is even called a "man" in verse 14:16 showing that this is a man that is being referred to, not a spiritual entity as many have interpreted from the Latin translation of Isaiah 14 that calls him Lucifer instead of the original Hebrew name "Heylel" "הֵילֵל," meaning, "Shining One." The King of Babel is described as a man who goes into the heavens to try to usurp the throne of Yahuweh/Yehovah in his Temple or Mountain of Appointment in the heavens, to become like God as Adam and Eve tried to become like God, like Yahuweh/Yehovah in eating of the fruit of the tree of the knowledge of good and evil. There are only two other men in Scripture who are said to be sitting in the throne of Yahuweh/Yehovah. One of these men was Solomon in 1 Chronicles 29:23 where it says that Solomon actually "sat on the throne of Yahuweh/Yehovah." The other is in Ezekiel 28:2 where the man called the Prince of Tyre says in his heart "I am God, I sit in the seat of God" claiming to be God, to be Yahuweh/Yehovah usurping his throne. And Yahuweh/Yehovah says that he had set this Prince of Tyre or King of Tyre upon the Set-Apart Mountain of God, the place of the Temple.

The descriptions of the King of Tyre all correspond in Ezekiel 28 with the King of Babel in Isaiah 14. This does not mean they are the same person, but it shows that in the last days before Yeshua's return there are many men who are kings like the King of Tyre and King of Babel trying to be God and have power over Babel. The prophecy of the King of Babel is not a prophecy about one single man, but of many men on the earth at the Time of the End who are doing similar things as kings over cities, over the city of Mystery Babel.

It appears that Paul might have combined together Isaiah 14:12-16 with Ezekiel 28:2-16 and Daniel 11:36-37 and Daniel 8:25 (where the Little Horn is skillful with deceit) to create this Man of Lawlessness/Sin in 2 Thessalonians, possibly also adding Daniel 7:21 and 11:32-35 in reference to the "falling away" that comes first, described as the "stumbling" of the people in chapter 11 and the "prevailing over" of the set-apart ones in chapter 7. But even then there is still no explanation as to where he got the phrase and idea from of "The Man of Lawlessness/Sin" or from where he got this concept of a person restraining the Man of Lawlessness/Sin, holding him back from being revealed. The different men in Isaiah 14 and Ezekiel 28 and Daniel 11 and the Little Horn in Daniel 8 are each definitely different prophecies about completely different people.

Antiochus IV Epiphanes fulfilled Daniel 11, but never fulfilled the Little Horn in Daniel 8, which means the Little Horn in Daniel 8 is a different person from Antiochus in Daniel 11. This leaves only two possibilities about Paul's words in 2 Thessalonians 2, either Paul was throwing together a bunch of fragments from other prophecies that should never have been put together in the first place, because they have no relation to one another, or he was writing a brand new prophecy he had received from Yahuweh/Yehovah that is not found in any other prophecy in Scripture except possibly in Isaiah 14 and Ezekiel 28.

The only way to know for certain which of these possibilities is correct is to see if the words of this prophecy in 2 Thessalonians come true or not, if such a Man of Lawlessness/Sin ever exists or does the things Paul describes, or if Yeshua returns and none of it happens. If it never happens then it means that Paul was writing a teaching/commentary on prophecy, trying to predict how the prophecies will be fulfilled in the future using the imagination of his own mind, which never works. On the other hand, if this is a brand new prophecy that Paul is writing about a Man of Lawlessness/Sin who was never written about in any other prophecy in Scripture (except maybe Isaiah 14), then we will see it happening at some point. One thing for certain is that the "Apostasia," meaning "falling away" or "turning against," is certainly happening among Christians today as they deny Yeshua and turn against him and his words in Scripture, even though they might still call themselves Christians, or give up all following of Yeshua completely to follow the commands of the world culture.

Regardless, the prophecy of the Man of Sin/Lawlessness and the prophecies of the King of Babel and King of Tyre have nothing to do with the prophecy of the Little Horn in Daniel 7 and 8. There is nothing that connects those prophecies of the King of Babel and the King of Tyre with the Little Horn, and they are separate prophecies about different entities and persons in the Time of the End. The only slight similarity between the King of Babel in Isaiah 14 and the Little Horn in Daniel 8 is both of them trying to raise themselves up among the stars or hosts of the heavens, but that single phrase that is not even a complete sentence is the only similarity between them. Otherwise they do entirely different things. The Little Horn is a man or entity that is different from all other men or entities in the prophecies of the Time of the End and the Great Tribulation, not spoken of once in the entire book of Revelation, and not mentioned in the other prophecies in Daniel, in chapters 2 or 9 or 11 through 12. And the Little Horn is in no way connected with Isaiah 14 or Ezekiel 28 or 2 Thessalonians 2.

The majority of the prophecy in Isaiah 14 does not take place until the destruction of Babel after the Great Tribulation in Revelation 18 and Jeremiah 50 – 51. It is about the death of the King of Babel that happens as all of the tribes of Israel return together as one nation through Yeshua the Messiah in Isaiah 49. But there are pieces in the description of the King of Babel in the prophecy that happen before the destruction of Babel that help identify what the King of Babel is. There is a mention of the King of Babel in Jeremiah 50 but no specific mention of any King of Babel in Revelation 18. In Revelation 17 – 18 the city of Babel itself is called a "queen" and "woman" and "prostitute/whore" that all of the kings of the earth prostitute with. If the city of Babel is the "queen" then the king of Babel is certainly those who are trying to join with the queen in prostitution, all of the kings of the earth trying to become king of Babel.

The King of Babel is the one trying to use Babel for his power, to gain power and control through the global city of Babel on the earth today. And we can see today many different literal kings/rulers of nations and governments fighting for control of this global city of Babel that has been built in recent decades, both physically and virtually, especially in the more economically and technologically powerful nations in both the West and East. But there are also many wealthy individuals and entrepreneurs and businessmen who have been fighting to become kings of Babel as well, to prostitute with Babel and become the king and ruler with the queen of Babel. The prophecy of Isaiah 14 is Yahuweh/Yehovah letting us know that the kings who prostitute with Babel in the Time of the End will not be getting away without judgment and destruction upon them as well, at the same time that the "queen" city of Mystery Babel is destroyed.

The environmentalist movement used by many "kings" on the earth, especially through the United Nations, is perfectly described in Isaiah 14:17 and 21, as they are trying to destroy the rural cities and towns and villages to turn the world back into a wilderness, to preserve nature untouched by man, and push all of the people into small, confined spaces in large, centralized cities run by green energy, filling the face of the world with cities of Babel with no people inhabiting the preserved wildernesses around these cities. Environmentalists do not want to live in the wilderness; they want to preserve the wilderness by pushing everyone into cities run by natural energy, making the world filled with cities and removing nations. These "kings" are only those who want to rule Babel as kings that are pushing these agendas (like United Nations Agenda 21).

It is the same old agenda from the original city of Babel in Genesis 11 where the people disobey Yahuweh/Yehovah in his command in Genesis 1 for mankind to be fruitful and multiply, filling all of the earth with people and subduing the earth. The building of a city of Babel is the exact opposite, bringing everyone collectively together to live in a small space together, leaving the world around them an untouched wilderness, empty of people and completely unsubdued. It is preventing humans from ruling over nature and all of the plants and animals, leaving them wild while all of the people are crammed into small city spaces in a world without Yahuweh/Yehovah and without his world of nature he created.

The gold-gatherers (wealthy) and oppressors (bureaucratic governments making rules impossible for anyone to follow), in Isaiah 14:4, are commonplace today, especially in all of the cities of the world and on the virtual global city of the internet. Together as they regulate and try to control the global city of people they hit the people with blow after blow, ruling over the nations with anger and wrath in verse 14:6.

The people of the world are becoming more and more slaves and prisoners in the house of the King of Babel, with the government regulations and oppression around the world making it more and more difficult for people to live in the global city of Babel without completely giving themselves over to the system, to make the system their master. It is harder and harder for independent businesses to run and operate because of increasing regulations, and the kings of Babel in all of the cities of the earth, prostituting themselves with the city of Babel for their power, keep taking more control and regulation, making the people more and more their prisoners trapped in the global system of Babel, slaves to their smart phones and technology in the cities, like electricity, with regulations forcing everyone to have to live to a certain standard of technology, even if they cannot afford it, or be cast out of the system that everyone depends on to survive. This is the way it is becoming in every nation, whether it is a democracy or authoritarian dictatorship. This is done to try to remedy the problem of slums in cities, but instead of fixing things it brings more oppression into the city system, which is based on the corrupted ways of men that cannot fix anything.

And now today people are literally going into the heavens to try to "sit" there, or "dwell/live" there (the Hebrew "eshev" "אֵשֵׁב" meaning "I shall sit" and "I shall dwell" simultaneously), above the stars and above the clouds in space, as is described in Isaiah 14:12-14. The kings of the earth, the people who sit as kings or rulers over the city of Mystery Babel, physically and virtually, are trying to raise themselves up into space above the stars in the heavens to sit there in colonies, such as on the Moon or Mars, and beyond. They really want to be God, to replace Yahuweh/Yehovah as the God of the universe, in control of creation and existence with scientific achievement and technology. This is something new that has not ever been in the history of the world since the creation of the man and the woman, Adam and Chavvah (Eve). And it is the global city of Mystery Babel across the earth that has given men and women the power to be able to go into space above the clouds and try to ascend above the stars of God to dwell there among the planets and moons.

Additionally, through modern technology mankind is able to go into the virtual reality "clouds," to dwell and sit there in the virtual reality cloud on the internet and become gods in their own virtual reality "heavens." A person can create and be in control of any kind of world they want, like gods creating and controlling worlds, except in the virtual reality world that is like a spiritual realm in the heavens outside of our physical realm, except that unlike the spiritual realm, it is only an imaginary simulation world that does not really exist in real life.

Every city on the earth has turned into Babel, and they are all becoming very oppressive places to live, except to those who are willing to be prisoners to the Babel city system, and love being in its system of sin that is running the cities. It is getting harder and harder for Yahuweh/Yehovah's people to survive inside of Mystery Babel anymore, or under the rule of the kings of Babel across the earth. But like the children of Israel leaving Egypt, Yahuweh/Yehovah's people have to leave Babel, to leave this entire world that exists as Babel. It is the whole world this time, not just a single nation Egypt, that Yahwueh/Yehovah's people have to get out of in order to not share in the sins and plagues of Babel that exists across the entire earth. The time of the exodus out of Babel is coming along with the destruction of the queen of Babel and its kings of Babel, in Revelation 18 and Isaiah 48:20-22. Every follower of Yeshua across the world today is working through this leaving of Babel in their own lives, and what this means for them in their relationship with Yeshua.

The only way to know for certain who these "kings" are that prostitute themselves with Babel and make themselves into kings of Babel will be to see their destruction and fall when this prophecy in Isaiah 14 is completely fulfilled in the future, but there are pieces of this prophecy already happening in reality showing that the time of the destruction is coming soon in the future, together with the destruction of Mystery Babel.

The Dragon and the Little Horn are the Only Ones in Prophecy to Rise Up into the Heavens and Cause Stars to Fall Down from the Heavens, but There is Nothing in Scripture About the Little Horn Ever being Worshipped by Anyone, nor that the Little Horn is the Same Entity as the Dragon/Serpent:

Daniel 8:9-11

Revelation 12:3-4, 7-12

Revelation 13:2-4

Word for Word Prophecy Examination of Fulfilled Verses **Daniel 8:9-11** and **Revelation 12:3-4, 7-12** and **Revelation 13:2-4** – The Little Horn in Daniel 8:10 rises up into the heavens and causes some of the stars and host of the heavens to fall to the earth where he tramples them down. In Revelation 12:4 the Dragon draws out 1/3 of the stars in the heavens and then throws them to the earth. This is the only similarity between the Little Horn and the Dragon. Everything else they do is different from one another and only the Dragon is prophesied to be worshipped, along with the Beast Out of the Sea. The Little Horn is never prophesied to be worshipped at any time, nor claim to be a god or the God of Israel Yahuweh/Yehovah. Also, the Dragon is a spiritual being, said to be the serpent of old, haSatan, the Adversary in the garden of Eden in Genesis 3. The Little Horn is described as a man who is a little king, a physical person on the earth. So the Little Horn is his own separate person in prophecy not mentioned in any other prophecies in Scripture outside of Daniel 7 and Daniel 8.

Those Who Lead Many to Righteousness Shine like the Stars:
    Daniel 8:10
    Daniel 12:3

Word for Word Prophecy Examination of Fulfilled and Partially Fulfilled Verses **Daniel 8:10** and **Daniel 12:3** – If the Little Horn is described as a man who is a little king, then what would it mean for the Little Horn to become great, going up to the host of the heavens and then causing some of the stars and some of the host of the heavens to fall back down to earth? There is a clue here in that Daniel uses the word "host" of the heavens together with the word "stars." In Daniel 12:3 the messenger explains that the ones who "lead many to righteousness" are "like the stars forever," revealing that those people who are righteous and leading others to righteousness, Yahuweh/Yehovah's set-apart ones, are represented as the picture of stars in the heavens. The Little Horn in Daniel 8:10 is causing some of those set-apart ones of Yahuweh/Yehovah, some of those who are righteous and pure and lead others to righteousness, to fall down to the earth and be trampled under it. This is the same imagery as Yeshua's warning in Matthew 24 that during the Great Tribulation it is possible for even the Chosen/Elect to be deceived by the false messiahs and false prophets during that time. Here it is the Little Horn who is bringing down some, but not all, of the Chosen/Elect with its deceptions.

The Little Horn Prophecies:
    Daniel 7:7-8, 19-26
    Daniel 8:1-27

Prophecy Fulfillment of Verses **Daniel 7:7-8, 19-26** and **Daniel 8:1-27** – The vision Daniel had in Daniel 8:1-8 is interpreted by the messenger Gavri'el in Daniel 8:15-22. A ram with two horns, one horn bigger than the other, representing the combined forces of (Peres) Persia and (Madai) Media, pushed out their empire towards the north and south, and especially the west through the Babylonian Empire. Then from the west there was a male goat with a single, conspicuous horn between its eyes, representing Yavan (Greece) and the ruler of Greece, Alexander the Great, who attacked the ram with two horns of the Medio-Persian Empire and destroyed it completely. Alexander the Great then created the Greek Empire in place of the Medio-Persian

Empire, but the empire did not last long. And after Alexander the Great died the Greek Empire was divided up among four horns that grew in place of the one horn on the goat, representing the four empire divisions of the Greek Empire made by Alexander's four generals **Cassander**, **Lysimachus**, **Ptolemy I Soter**, and **Seleucus I Nicator**.

1. **Cassander Kingdom** (305 B.C.E. to 297 BC.E.) – became **Antigonid Empire** (306 B.C.E. to 168 B.C.E.) ruling from the capital of Pella, Greece
2. **Lysimachus Kingdom** (306 B.C.E. to 281 B.C.E.) – became **Attalid Empire** (282 B.C.E. to 129 B.C.E.) ruling from the capital of Pergamon/Bergama, Turkey
3. **Ptolemy Kingdom** (305 B.C.E. to 282 B.C.E.) – became **Ptolemy Empire** (305 B.C.E. to 30 B.C.E.) ruling from the capital of Alexandria, Egypt
4. **Seleucid Kingdom** (305 B.C.E. to 281 B.C.E.) – became **Seleucid Empire** (312 B.C.E. to 63 B.C.E.) ruling from the capital of Seleucia, Iraq and later Antioch, Turkey

All of verses 8:1-8 and 8:15-22 fit perfectly with what happened in fulfillment of them with the destruction of the Persian Empire and rise of the Greek Empire in its place. Greece broke apart into four horns or kingdoms made up originally of four of Alexander's generals. This is why the rest of the prophecy about the Little Horn rising up from one of these four horns in Daniel 8:9-14 and 8:23-27 has been such a mystery for over 2,000 years. For during that time scholars and theologians have tried to make Antiochus IV Epiphanes fit as the fulfillment of this Little Horn in Daniel 8 and so far none have succeeded, because of major problems exposed in the records of Antiochus IV Epiphanes in First and Second Maccabees. The Little Horn is definitely supposed to come from one of the four horns of the four broken divisions of the Greek Empire, and it would seem that Antiochus was a Little Horn that sprang up out of the horn of the Seleucid division of the empire. The biggest problem is in the counting of 2,300 evening morning, which is 2,300 literal days of the sun rising and setting 2,300 times and cannot be symbolic of any other frame of time such as years.

There is supposed to be an attack against the foundation of the set-apart place at the Temple Mount, not against the set-apart place itself, and also against the continual, that lasts for a literal 2,300 days which calculates to about 6 years and 3 months. The very first attack that Antiochus made against the set-apart place and continual offerings and sacrifices in Jerusalem is recorded in 1 Maccabees 1:21 where it says that it was in the "one hundred forty and third year" of the Greek Empire. And then later in 1 Maccabees 4:52 it records the year that the continual and the set-apart place were restored in the "one hundred forty and eighth year" of the Greek Empire on the 25th day of the 9th month called Kislev. No matter how one calculates these dates together, the absolute maximum amount of time that a person can stretch this out to is about 5 years and 9 months, but probably closer to just 5 years. It is impossible on any calendar, whether it be the ancient Hebrew or ancient Greek or even Julian/Gregorian calendars, to fit 2,300 days into 5 years and 9 months. So it is impossible for Antiochus to have been the fulfillment of this prophecy of the Little Horn in Daniel 8, and this timing of 2,300 literal days Yahuweh/Yehovah included for the reason to make sure that everyone would know that Antiochus IV Epiphanes was not the fulfillment of this prophecy.

Also, there is no record in the books of Maccabees or in Greek history that the armies of Antiochus ever attacked or did damage to the foundation of the set-apart place on the Temple Mount as is prophesied. And even though Antiochus became great to the south in attacking Egypt, he became exceedingly weak to the east as his empire started falling apart as it was prophesied it would in Daniel 11:44. There is also no record of Antiochus ever being skilled at deceit and intrigues, causing people to fall spiritually or physically through deceptions. He was very good at flatteries and came into power with his flattering tongue, in fulfillment of Daniel 11:21, but there is no record that he was especially good at or even tried to deceive people in any special ways. Also, very importantly, the Little Horn is not a king that rises up to power as the king of one of the Four Horns, ruling over one of the Four Horns, but instead is a tiny little kingdom with an insignificant king that rises up as its own separate kingdom or nation separate from the Four Horns, but in place of where one of the four horns was located. And Antiochus did not rise up and start a separate tiny kingdom that was apart from the Four Horns; he was the ruler of one of the Four Horns.

It is because this prophecy of the Little Horn in Daniel 8 is for the "latter time" at the "Time of the End" as the messenger Gavri'el states, existing as the same Little Horn in Daniel 7 that also is at the Time of the End right before Yahuweh/Yehovah comes to set up his reign on the earth. The prophecies of the Little Horn in Daniel 7 and 8 are for the end and were not fulfilled during the days of the Greek Empire, the bronze hips of the image in Daniel 2 and the Third Beast in Daniel 7. Daniel 8:23 has an interesting key in it though, saying that the Little Horn is a king who "stands up" at the latter time of the rule of the four horns or four kingdoms of the Greek Empire. This indicates that somehow the four kingdoms of the Greek Empire are still around up to the present day, existing all through history up to the Time of the End. Where are the four kingdoms of the Greek Empire today started by Alexander's four generals that divided his empire?

1. **Greece Kingdom/State**: Lasted through the Roman and Islamic Empires to essentially stay the same horn of the Cassander Kingdom up to the present day, with the present day capital at Athens, Greece.
2. **Ottoman Empire** (1299 to 1922): The final and most recent representation of the horn of the Lysimachus Kingdom was the Ottoman Empire, based in western Turkey with its capital and center of power in Constantinople/Istanbul, Turkey, not far away from the Lysimachus capital Lysimachia, Turkey and later capital in Pergamon/Bergama, Turkey when it changed into the Attalid Empire. The nation state of modern Turkey is the closest remnant representation still remaining of the horn of the Lysimachus Kingdom.
3. **Ayyubid Empire** (1171 to 1260): The final and most recent representation of the horn of the Ptolemy Kingdom was the Ayyubid Empire that ruled from Cairo, Egypt as the Sultanate of Egypt, basing its power very close to where the Ptolemy capital was located in Alexandria, Egypt. The modern day nation state of Egypt is all that remains as anything similar to or resembling what once was the horn of the Ptolemy Kingdom.
4. **Abbasid Empire** (750 to 1258): The final and most recent representation of the horn of the Seleucid Kingdom was the Abbasid Empire that ruled and had its power centered in the middle of Iraq, most of the time from the capital Baghdad, Iraq that was built almost upon the exact same site as the original

capital of the Seleucid Kingdom in Seleucia, Iraq. There is really nothing left today in modern times representing the vast and powerful Seleucid Empire/Kingdom horn that stretched across many countries and regions. It is the only one of the four horns that has not survived into any comparable modern nations or states, after the collapse of its final form in the Abbasid Empire.

The locations of the Four Horns of the four divisions of the Greek Empire continued to be centers of power for later empires through history, and even though they were broken up at times, they would form back together again as power centers, continuing the Four Horns. This is a phenomenon that happens with a few other locations on earth through history, but this is a precise prophecy about these particular four horns located in the Middle East area around Israel. All through history the nation of Greece would go through a cycle of being conquered and then gaining independence again to the point that today it still exists as its own independent kingdom/nation with approximately the same borders as the Cassander Horn Kingdom well over 2,000 years ago. This horn of the nation of Greece itself never truly went away or was lost and continued to be influential through history even though it did not have any of its former power.

The Eastern/Byzantine Roman Empire had its center of power located in Constantinople in the same territory location of the Lysimachus Kingdom, and later the Ottoman Empire replaced the Eastern/Byzantine Roman Empire in the exact same location with the same capital changed to the name of Istanbul. This horn of the Four Horns continued to be a very powerful horn used by both the Roman and Islamic Empires as a center of power for some of the time in history, and it continued in power up until the fall of the Ottoman Empire in 1922. Now today the independent and influential kingdom/nation of Turkey is located with its center of power in Ankara, not far from Istanbul and Lysimachia, and still centered within the Lysimachia Kingdom Horn, in the same territory. So this horn also has survived as a place of power and influence up to the present time, still in existence. It is the same with the Ptolemy Horn Kingdom that has survived through history, having great power even in the 13th Century with the Ayyubid Empire, and still its own independent kingdom/nation today as Egypt, with almost the same borders that the Ptolemy Kingdom had.

The really interesting horn though is the horn of the Seleucid Kingdom, because it is the only horn that does not exist anymore today in any kind of comparable form or with its powerful borders it once had. The nation of Iraq today with its capital at Baghdad, located on almost the exact same land of the ancient city of Seleucia that served as the original capital of the Seleucid Empire is among the poorest and least influential nations in the world today, with nowhere near the borders of land as the Seleucid Horn Kingdom. The final true form of the Seleucid Horn was with the Abbasid Empire that existed for hundreds of years up to about the year 1258. It had control of all of the same land as the Seleucid Empire that ruled before it, through central Asia up to India and the northern Middle East. But the thing that was different about the Abbasid Empire is that it also included part of Egypt and North Africa in its territory, as well as the entire Arabian Peninsula.

Since this Seleucid Kingdom Horn is the only one of the four horns not to exist anymore today, after the fall of the Abbasid Empire, perhaps it is the horn that the Little Horn comes out of in Daniel 8:9 as its own separate little kingdom. It is very interesting to look at what Daniel 8:9 actually says in the original Hebrew.

Translations always translate the word written here "hatsevi" as "the Beautiful *Land*" but honest translations will put the word "Land" written here in italics, because the word "Land" does not exist here in the original Hebrew. The translators look at Daniel 11 where the words are written in Hebrew "the Beautiful Land" referring to the nation of Israel and automatically assume that Daniel made a mistake in Daniel 8 and forgot to write the word "Land" there. So they think that they can correct Daniel's error and correct Scripture to say what they think it is supposed to say.

Everyone ignores the grammatical reality of what Daniel wrote when he wrote the word "tsevi" "צְבִי" in Daniel 8 as a noun instead of as an adjective describing a noun. In Daniel 11 there is no doubt that the word "tsevi" means "Beautiful" or "Splendid," because it is being used as an adjective of the word "Land." But as soon as the word "land" is removed, as in Daniel 8, "tsevi" suddenly becomes a noun in the sentence, which means that as a noun it very often has the meaning of "gazelle" instead of "beautiful," as a gazelle is a very beautiful or splendid animal representing beauty in nature. Did Daniel really make a mistake in forgetting to write the word "Land" here? Or did he leave out the word "Land" on purpose in order to change the word "tsevi" into a noun so that it could mean "gazelle." In the Hebrew Daniel 8:9 says, "umin ha'achath mehem yatsa qeren achath mitstse'irah vattigdal yether el hanegev ve'el hammizrach ve'el hatstsevi" " וּמִן הָאַחַת מֵהֶם יָצָא קֶרֶן אַחַת מִצְּעִירָה וַתִּגְדַּל יֶתֶר אֶל הַנֶּגֶב וְאֶל הַמִּזְרָח וְאֶל הַצֶּבִי," literally meaning, "And from the one of them came out one little horn and it became exceedingly great to the south and to the east and to the gazelle."

Daniel says that the Little Horn becomes exceedingly great in a certain direction from the four larger horns, specifically to the south and east or to the south-east of the Four Horns. If we go in the direction of the south-east from the central power locations of each of the Four Horns, to the south-east of Egypt and Greece and western Turkey and Iraq, we come to the southern half of the Arabian Peninsula, especially the eastern horn of the peninsula located along the Persian Gulf. And when we look for "the gazelle" we find a small, little horn/kingdom named the Abu Dhabi Emirate, the name "Abu Dhabi" in Arabic meaning, "Father of Gazelle." Not only is this little kingdom named "Gazelle" but uses the picture of the gazelle as its symbol. The Abu Dhabi Emirate first rose up into existence in the year 1761, by its founder and first king/ruler Sheikh Dhiyab bin Isa Al Nahyan of the Bani Yas Tribe of Arabs located in that area of the Arabian Peninsula. And this Little Horn Kingdom of Abu Dhabi, of "the Gazelle," rose up out of one of the land and territory of one of the Four Horns or Kingdoms, rising up out of the territory of the Abbasid Empire that had control of the Arabian Peninsula within its borders before it became an end to the fourth horn of the Seleucid Kingdom.

The Abu Dhabi Emirate was an insignificant Little Horn Kingdom for 200 years until Dhiyab bin Isa's great-great-great grandson Sheikh Zayed bin Sultan Al Nahyan joined together all of the little emirates in the horn of the Arabian Peninsula into a single nation called the United Arab Emirates and with the help of the oil industry there began to build this tiny little nation of the UAE into a very strong and wealthy nation, under the rule of the Al Nahyan family of Abu Dhabi. And out of this Little Horn Kingdom has come the king that is the Little Horn that has now become exceedingly great, raising up this small, little horn of Abu Dhabi into one of the greatest and strongest centers of power in the world, in fulfillment of Daniel 8:9, Zayed's bin Sultan's son **Sheikh Mohammed bin Zayed Al Nahyan**, the current king/ruler of Abu Dhabi and Third President of the United Arab Emirates.

Bani Yas Tribe

	House of Al Nahyan
5th Great Grandfather	**Isa bin Nahyan Al Nahyan**
4th Great Grandfather	Sheikh **Dhiyab bin Isa Al Nahyan**, King of the Bani Yas (1761-1793) <u>Founder of the Abu Dhabi Emirate and Name in 1761</u>
3rd Great Grandfather	Sheikh **Shakhbut bin Dhiyab Al Nahyan**, King of Abu Dhabi (1793-1816)
2nd Great Grandfather	Sheikh **Khalifa bin Shakhbut Al Nahyan**, King of Abu Dhabi (1833-1845)
Great Grandfather	Sheikh **Zayed bin Khalifa Al Nahyan**, King of Abu Dhabi (1855-1909)
Grandfather	Sheikh **Sultan bin Zayed Al Nahyan**, King of Abu Dhabi (1922-1926)
Father	Sheikh **Zayed bin Sultan Al Nahyan**, King of Abu Dhabi (1966-2004) <u>First President and Founder of the UAE in 1971</u>
	Sheikh <u>**Mohammed bin Zayed Al Nahyan**</u>, King of Abu Dhabi (2022-) Third President of the UAE

Most people do not know about or have heard about Mohammed bin Zayed Al Nahyan, because he is a Little Horn or little king as prophesied. He has been the de facto ruler of the UAE since his brother Sheikh Khalifa bin Zayed Al Nahyan had a stroke in 2014 and had been unable to run the country. After his brother's death in 2022 Mohammed bin Zayed became the king/ruler of Abu Dhabi and Third President of the UAE on May 14, 2022. He has followed in his father's footsteps, making the Little Horn Kingdom of Abu Dhabi and the United Arab Emirates exceedingly great as one of the wealthiest nations in the world. Mohammed bin Zayed is said to possibly be the wealthiest man in the world with access to a sovereign treasury of about $1.3 trillion, with his appearance greater than any of the other horns/kings in the world today, especially the Ten Horns, in fulfillment of Daniel 7:20. Before Mohammed's father Zayed bin Sultan built the UAE, the area was mostly a desert wasteland with tribal nomads living in poverty, but now Abu Dhabi and the United Arab Emirates it formed has become the center of wealth and splendor in the Middle East and rivals any other nation or city in the world in its great appearance of beauty and economic power.

Mohammed bin Zayed is also responsible for building the UAE military into one of the most advanced militaries in the Middle East, second only to Israel, during his time as General of the UAE armed forces, in fulfillment of verses 7:20 and 8:9, making a Little Horn Kingdom and himself as a Little Horn exceedingly great with a greater appearance than the other horns. Bin Zayed had his military training at the Royal Military Academy Sandhurst at Sandhurst, England, graduating from there in April 1979. The tallest structure in the world, the Burj Khalifa, is located in the UAE in Dubai, built in 2010, and the cities of the UAE are among the most technologically advanced and wealthiest cities in the world, bringing in people from nations all over the world to live and work there. The UAE is at the forefront of the Middle Eastern nations in terms of wealth and power and prestige. And Mohammed bin Zayed is the one leading and influencing the Arab nations and the Middle East from the shadows, one of the most important men influencing the world and nations even the size of Russia and China and America, and yet most have never heard of him or do not know anything about him if they have heard his name.

Mohammed bin Zayed has strong power globally, but not by his own power, in fulfillment of verse 8:24, because his power only comes because of his father's creation and unification of the United Arab Emirates, uniting together seven separate emirates into one country giving the nation power it would not have otherwise had. The power is given to him by a group of powers that have come together, making bin Zayed and the UAE stronger than it normally would have been otherwise. He is only stepping into the power that was already built for him by his father Zayed bin Sultan, and the love that the people of the UAE had for the legendary figure of his father Zayed.

The Little Horn has the eyes of a man with a mouth speaking great things in Daniel 7:8 and 20, and with a strong/fierce face, skilled at intrigues and deceit in Daniel 8:23 and 25. He subdues or humbles three of the Ten Horns in Daniel 7:24. The important key here is that later on all of the Ten Horns have to still be around to destroy Babel in Revelation 17 at the very end of the 3.5 years of Great Tribulation, which means that the subduing/humbling/making low of three horns cannot remove them from power, or conquer or defeat them in any way. The Little Horn is using his mouth speaking great things and his eyes with wisdom and knowledge of sight to influence through intrigue and deception of other horns/kings, and other people in general.

Mohammed bin Zayed has already subdued and brought under his influence all of the horns/governments of the major Arab countries including Saudi Arabia, through his influence of the Crown Prince Mohammed bin Salman, and Bahrain and Oman and possibly Qatar. It is well known that Mohammed bin Zayed is the one who has been for years behind the scenes setting the present course that the gulf nations are on at the present time. It was not China who influenced Saudi Arabia into restoring ties with Iran, nor Russia that influenced Saudi to restore ties with Syria. The reason that Saudi Arabia is moving to normalize relations with Iran and Syria is because Mohammed bin Zayed already in 2022 had the UAE normalize and restore relations with those countries as he moves the UAE closer to Russia and China and India ultimately, and brings together the nations of the Middle East in greater unity.

Mohammed bin Zayed is called an "old friend" by Vladimir Putin as they have known each other for decades, and it is bin Zayed who has made the way, even stronger than countries like Turkey and China, for Russia to avoid western sanctions, allowing the use of UAE banks and financial institutions for money transfers between Russia and other countries such as India so that India is able to buy Russian oil and other things like that. And the United States of America is completely powerless to stop Mohammed bin Zayed from helping Russia avoid the sanctions, even though the Biden Administration has tried and failed to convince them. It is because the UAE is too powerful for even America to stop or apply sanctions to without harmful consequences, and no amount of pressure is able to change Mohammed bin Zayed in his plans. It used to be that America and the UAE were close. In years past bin Zayed had convinced America to build him more advanced planes that America had only started in the planning phase but not built yet. He paid the money and the American military built planes for him, so that in the end the UAE ended up with more advanced planes than what the American military had at that time. This is the kind of mouth of influence he has of nations, even giant nations with big government horns like America and Russia.

For many years bin Zayed has been building relations with India and China, and recently in 2023 allowed India to start up their new digital/global currency system through the UAE financial system. Mohammed bin Zayed has been very busy building relations with countries and influencing countries around the world, such as Egypt and Sudan and Morocco, and all through Europe. When the oil crisis came because of western sanctions on Russia, it was the UAE and Mohammed bin Zayed that western countries went to for help, such as Prime Minister Boris Johnson from the United Kingdom and President Emmanuel Macron from France. The Biden administration tried and failed to get bin Zayed to help out America with the oil prices, and then later went to Saudi Arabia as a last resort when they failed with bin Zayed. It is because the Little Horn of Mohammed bin Zayed and the UAE is more powerful and influential in the Arabian portion of the Middle East than any other country or government or individual.

On September 15, 2016 Mohammed bin Zayed visited and met with Pope Francis at the Vatican. It is unknown what they talked about beyond that bin Zayed was strengthening ties with Vatican City to make a closer relationship. Not long after this visit Pope Francis began meeting with Sheikh Ahmed El-Tayeb, Grand Imam of Al-Azhar, the highest authority figure in Sunni Islam. Then Mohammed bin Zayed sent his brother Foreign Minister Abdullah bin Zayed Al Nahyan to the Vatican with an invitation to the Pope to come to Abu Dhabi for a meeting and ceremony with Ahmed El-Tayeb. It was there in Abu Dhabi that Pope Francis and Sheikh Ahmed El-Tayeb, in the presence of Mohammed bin Zayed, signed the *Document on Human Fraternity* or *Abu Dhabi Declaration* on February 4, 2019, for strengthening ties between the three Abrahamic Faiths of Islam, Christianity, and Judaism.

The basic principle laid out in the *Document on Human Fraternity* is that "God" has created the world with a diversity of religions and faiths, and no one should try to convert anyone from one religious faith to another. Everyone should stay the religion that they already are and believe in and have unity across all religions through the diversity of religious freedom: unity through diversity. The Roman Catholic Church had already for many decades been trying to find a way to begin switching over to a system of polyreligion, accepting a diversity of religion and religious freedom and belief within the Catholic Church. Mohammed bin Zayed provided the way they had been looking for.

Out of this signing of the *Document on Human Fraternity*, of bringing all the world together in unity of religion through diversity of religious beliefs, came the declaration of a new United Nations holiday celebrated on February 4 called International Day of Human Fraternity. Construction also began in Abu Dhabi on the Abrahamic Family House, completed and dedicated on February 16, 2023. The Abrahamic Family House is a compound built with three houses of worship co-existing separately but together from each of the three Abrahamic Faiths, including the Imam Al-Tayeb Mosque (named after Ahmed El-Tayeb and representing Islam), St. Francis Church (representing the Roman Catholic Church), and Moses Ben Maimon Synagogue (representing Rabbinic Orthodox Judaism).

Pope Francis began teaching and preaching the Human Fraternity signed in Abu Dhabi and as part of this Human Fraternity visited one of the highest ranking clerics in Shia Islam, Grand Ayatollah Ali Al Sistani on March 6, 2021 at his home in Najaf, Iraq. This was to create closer ties between the Roman Catholic Church and Sunni and Shia Islam together, as part of the *Document on Human Fraternity* of bringing the Abrahamic religions closer together. On that same day Pope Francis also visited the ruins of the city of Ur where Abraham was born and grew up, in continuation of proclaiming the principles of the Human Fraternity that the religions of Islam, Christianity, and Judaism all come from the same root of Abraham and should live together in unity as separate denominations supposedly all following the same God of Abraham. In honor of Pope Francis and Grand Ayatollah Al Sistani meeting, that day of March 6 was declared a holiday in Iraq by the Prime Minister Mustafa Al Kadhimi, called Day of Tolerance and Coexistence. On March 7, 2021 Pope Francis officiated over a mass in Mosul, Iraq at Church Square, where he made prayers specifically for the "fraternity" of all religions in Iraq to be able to live together in peace.

Now through Mohammed bin Zayed, Abu Dhabi has become the symbol of religious tolerance and peaceful co-existence between world religions. Bin Zayed personally saw to it that a Hindu Temple would be built there in Abu Dhabi as well, for the Hindu worshipping population living there. With a mouth of influence speaking great things, Mohammed bin Zayed has convinced and subdued many people, and many kings/horns and religious leaders. Mohammed bin Zayed had been giving advice to President Barak Obama about Syria and other Middle Eastern matters during the time of the Arab Spring, even continuing to talk to him on a regular basis when President Obama was not listening to him. Eventually their relationship deteriorated when Obama went in an opposing direction to bin Zayed, and after President Donald Trump was elected in 2016, Mohammed bin Zayed snubbed a farewell lunch with Obama to meet with Trump's team and Jared Kushner in New York City instead.

It was bin Zayed who initiated relations with the Trump Administration and with Jared Kushner, who he was very involved with during the years of Trump's presidency as they worked on peace deals and political intrigues together. Outwardly it appeared that President Trump was the one who came up with the Abraham Accords, which is the way that Mohammed bin Zayed works, staying in the shadows and letting others take credit for his ideas. But later Joel Rosenberg, who was also closely involved in the Abraham Accords, revealed in his book *Enemies and Allies*[33] that it was actually Mohammed bin Zayed who came up with the idea of the Abraham Accords beginning in December 2019 (very shortly after the signing of the *Document on Human Fraternity*), going beyond the initial proposals of the Trump Administration to something new that even they had not envisioned.

The Abraham Accords became a continuation of Mohammed bin Zayed bringing together the Abrahamic Faiths, this time bringing the Jews and Israel, and especially Prime Minister Benjamin Netanyahu, into the covenant that Pope Francis and Sheikh Ahmed El-Tayeb had signed. *The Abraham Accords Declaration* even used many of the same phraseology and wording as the *Document on Human Fraternity*, saying, "We, the undersigned, recognize the importance of maintaining and strengthening peace in the Middle East and

---

[33] Joel C. Rosenberg, *Enemies and Allies: An Unforgettable Journey Inside the Fast-Moving & Immensely Turbulent Modern Middle East* (Carol Stream, Illinois: Tyndale House Publishers, 2021)

around the world based on mutual understanding and coexistence, as well as the respect for human dignity and freedom, including religious freedom. We encourage efforts to promote interfaith and intercultural dialogue to advance a culture of peace among the three Abrahamic religions and all humanity."

The Abraham Accords were signed in Washington D.C. on September 15, 2020 (in the same location as the signing of the Oslo Accords) by President Donald Trump, Prime Minister Benjamin Netanyahu, Foreign Minister of Bahrain Abdullatif bin Rashid Al Zayani, and Foreign Minister of the UAE Abdullah bin Zayed Al Nahyan. Mohammed bin Zayed could not be there himself because of the ongoing investigation by the United States Government into his possible connections with "Russian collusion" involving the Trump Administration, and also because bin Zayed was still the de facto ruler of the UAE at that time. Once again he stayed in the shadows and the extent of his involvement in the Abraham Accords as the real creator and instigator of them would not have been known without Joel Rosenberg's reporting on it in his book.

Mohammed bin Zayed's brother Abdullah bin Zayed also confirmed the reason why Mohammed went ahead with the Abraham Accords when he did, confirming what Joel Rosenberg reported. In a *Wall Street Journal* article published September 14, 2020[34] Abdullah said that the Abraham Accords were for the central purpose of making progress toward Palestinian statehood and stopping the annexation of the West Bank territories that Prime Minister Netanyahu was about to annex at that time. And that now that Israel would be signing onto the Abraham Accords with the UAE, the UAE (and especially Mohammed bin Zayed and the UAE government) would be able to have more weight and influence on Israel on the issue of Palestinian statehood and progress towards a state of Palestine. They certainly have used that weight and pressure, as evidenced in the case of January 3, 2023 when the UAE requested an emergency Security Council meeting at the United Nations on the issue of Knesset Member Itamar Ben-Gvir visiting the Temple Mount and the status quo of the Temple Mount.

Mohammed bin Zayed in his short rule has subdued/humbled many kings/governments with his mouth and eyes of influence, saying great things and having a great appearance, with wisdom of foresight with his eyes giving advice to kings and governments all over the world, leading them into his plans and goals for the Middle East and the world. He is like a mentor and wise leader among the Gulf States as they follow his lead, especially the king of Saudi Arabia Salman bin Abdulaziz Al Saud and Mohammed bin Salman, who is changing the nation of Saudi Arabia and building his Artificial Intelligence city NEOM at the location of the real Mount Sinai in Saudi Arabia in order to keep up with the UAE and Mohammed bin Zayed bringing religious freedom and great wealth through smart cities that they are already upgrading more and more as with Abu Dhabi and Dubai.

Pope Francis is another "king" or head of state (of the nation of Vatican City) that Mohammed bin Zayed subdued/humbled into the Human Fraternity, influencing over billions of Catholics and Muslims around the world with the philosophy and concept of the *Document of Human Fraternity*. And he subdued Israel and the Israeli government, and multiple kings within the Israeli government during the last few years, into the Human Fraternity with the Abraham Accords. It can be seen that the governments of Bahrain and Morocco

---

[34] "Peace. Shalom. Salaam" by Abdullah bin Zayed Al Nahyan, (*The Wall Street Journal*, September 14, 2020)

and Sudan are three more horns/kings that Mohammed bin Zayed has subdued under his influence with the Abraham Accords (it was Mohammed bin Zayed and the UAE behind the April 2019 coup in Sudan that overthrew the then President Omar Al-Bashir).

And President Donald Trump is another king/ruler Mohammed bin Zayed subdued, as well as more importantly the king/ruler Prime Minister Benjamin Netanyahu, bringing them into a covenant against the God of Israel with the Abraham Accords. It brought the Israeli government into a humbled position more dependent on Mohammed bin Zayed and the UAE, giving him more influence in Israel and preventing Israel from being able to annex land they need for their defense in the West Bank in any land deals that might be made with the Palestinians. Mohammed bin Zayed is certainly a man skilled at deceptions and intrigues, influencing and subduing kings with his mouth and eyes of vision in fulfillment of Daniel 7:8 and 20 and 8:23 and 25, with a strong/fierce face that no one else is able to influence or deter in his set path and plan he is working out.

And this is where the fulfillment of Daniel 7:21 and 25, and Daniel 8:24-25 come into play, as Mohammed bin Zayed is fighting against the set-apart ones, both in Israel and in the Christian world, wearing them down and destroying them spiritually. There were many Christians who actually thought that the Abraham Accords, a covenant turning Israel against the God of Israel, Yahuweh/Yehovah, was a good thing, completely overcome by the deception that Mohammed bin Zayed brought in it. Many of the chosen/elect, many of the set-apart ones who are true believers in Yeshua, saw this covenant taking Israel away from Yahuweh/Yehovah, to rely on the world and the nations around them for their strength and help, was a good thing to happen, to exchange the selling of the souls of Israelis in exchange for peace. Deceptions always look so good; it seems so wonderful for all of the religions of the world to co-exist together in peace and unity, not converting each other and saying that all of the Abrahamic Faiths are really separate denominations of one religion that all worship the same god.

But Yahuweh/Yehovah has always been very jealous for Israel and his covenant, as seen in Jeremiah where Israel gets into big trouble with Yahuweh/Yehovah for whoring into covenants with the other nations around them, allowing and accepting the freedom of religion to worship false gods. Those who are in covenant with the world cannot be in the set-apart covenant with Yahuweh/Yehovah at the same time; those who are in covenant with the nations and with other religions of false worship cannot be simultaneously in covenant with Yahuweh/Yehovah, worshipping him as the one and only God, through his covenant of Yeshua/Salvation.

There were many righteous, set-apart ones, Christians shining like the stars in the heavens who Mohammed bin Zayed threw down to the earth and trampled on the ground with the Abraham Accords, in fulfillment of Daniel 8:10, destroying them spiritually in fulfillment of verse 8:24. And bin Zayed destroyed Israel spiritually as well, taking them farther away from Yahuweh/Yehovah and bringing them into a covenant of accepting the false gods of Islam mixed as false worship in with the worship of the true God of Israel, entering into a covenant of peace with men and nations and breaking the covenant of peace with Yahuweh/Yehovah, making him common instead of set-apart.

Through deceptions and intrigues Mohammed bin Zayed has brought down low many kings and many Christians, believing in what he is doing as good. At this point bin Zayed is completely prevailing over most Christians around the world and also very importantly against Israel. It is only now since bin Zayed has become the proper ruler/king of the UAE that the danger of the Abraham Accords covenant is becoming apparent, as he has restored ties with Israel's enemies Syria and Iran, helping the Gulf States, especially Saudi Arabia, to follow that lead. It is causing peace to come between the Sunni and Shia Muslims in the Middle East again after 12 years of civil war caused by the Arab Spring, freeing up Israel's enemies, especially Iran, to be able to focus on destroying Israel, both Shia and Sunni Muslims together. As Saudi Arabia and the Houthi Rebels negotiate peace in Yemen, Iran is doing exactly that, uniting nations together to focus on war with Israel, as seen in the surprise, combined rocket attacks from Gaza, Lebanon, and Syria during Passover and the Festival of Unleavened Bread in April 2023. Reports came out in Israeli media that the real reason Prime Minister Netanyahu's planned trip to meet with Mohammed bin Zayed in Abu Dhabi in early 2023 was cancelled was because bin Zayed was afraid that Netanyahu might speak against Iran during his trip there.

The full extent of destruction by Mohammed bin Zayed is only beginning to be revealed now, especially the destruction of mighty men, even spiritually mighty men, led astray by his skill at deceiving. But for certain bin Zayed is very prosperous in all that he is doing, in fulfillment of verses 8:24-25, and destroying many people who were at ease, completely unaware of what he was doing and taken into the deceptions. Bin Zayed is the one responsible for setting the course that the Middle East is currently on, coming closer to Russia and China and breaking away from America, and bringing the Middle East closer to Iran through the process in preparation for the instability of the world heading into world war. Whatever happens next with Israel, we will be able to look back and see that Mohammed bin Zayed started it all in motion as the catalyst since about 2019 to 2020. There is the appearance in all of these moves that outwardly bin Zayed's intention is to create a peaceful and stable Middle East, bringing everyone together in unity, but the reality progressing right now is towards a war centered around Israel and the attempt to create a Middle East without the existence of Israel in it anymore.

The Little Horn says things against the Most High and exalts himself up to the Prince of the Host and stands against the Prince of Princes in Daniel 7:25 and Daniel 8:11 and 25. In each of these cases "Most High" and "Prince of the Host" and "Prince of Princes" are referring to Yahuweh/Yehovah. There are of course billions of people through history who have done the same, to try to "be like God" ever since Adam and Eve in the garden. It is what all people naturally do in their rebellion against Yahuweh/Yehovah, to try to be God and stand against him in their lives, and even speak against him in the most extreme cases. Only those submitting in surrender to him and choosing to follow and obey him go through the process of his destruction of their flesh and cleansing to make them able to be free to live in peace without striving to become gods all of the time.

But kings of nations and empires fight against Yahuweh/Yehovah and try to become god in his place on a different level with the power and authority they have. The prophecy concerning the Little Horn is referring to how greatly the Little Horn stands against Yahuweh/Yehovah and tries to raise himself up to a god position of authority and power. And this can be clearly seen in fulfillment with Mohamed bin Zayed in the Human

Fraternity and Abrahamic Family House and Abraham Accords, to place himself in a position of authority in bringing the Abrahamic Religions together in unity under the worship of a same god between them. It is a position of pride causing people to turn toward the worship of a false god, and away from the worship of the one true God Yahuweh/Yehovah, who is set-apart and not like any of the imaginary gods that people have invented in their minds through history.

Bin Zayed is a small king over a small kingdom/nation, and yet from that position of smallness he is still exalting himself to a position of influence and authority over Yahuweh/Yehovah's covenant nation Israel, turning them away from that covenant with Yahuweh/Yehovah more than any other in Israel's modern history. Saying that Yahuweh/Yehovah is the same god as Allah, or that a rejection of Yeshua as Messiah and God is alright, because Yahuweh/Yehovah wants people to be diverse in their religious beliefs and wants people to follow him according to their own ways and desires instead of his commands, this is the epitome deception of speaking words against Yahuweh/Yehovah, the Most High.

Also the fulfillment of Daniel 7:25 can be seen in Mohamed bin Zayed concerning the Little Horn "intending to change appointed times and law" and "wearing out the set-apart ones." The Aramaic wording here literally says that the Little Horn "intends/thinks" to change "appointed times" or "times of appointment." This is referring to calendar dates and specific times made for appointments to do things, which can include festivals such as Yahuweh/Yehovah's festivals, but can also include anything done at certain times. It is all about having control over "when" things happen, and changing when they will happen. This is a phrase that Daniel understood well what it meant, because he uses the same phrasing in Daniel 2:21 in saying that Yahuweh/Yehovah himself "changes the times and appointed times."

Yahuweh/Yehovah is in control of "when" things happen and changes the appointed times of when things will happen. He changes the plans of man and does things according to his timing, changing the times of man and their appointed times, to do things according to his appointments and set dates. The Little Horn intends to change appointed times and law (Yahuweh/Yehovah's statutes in Scripture) but never accomplishes this. We can see with the Abraham Accords and Human Fraternity/Abrahamic Family House that Mohamed bin Zayed certainly has this "intention" to get in control of deciding when things are going to happen for the physical nation of Israel and for Yahuweh/Yehovah's set-apart people who are believers in Yeshua around the world in place of Yahuweh/Yehovah, and deciding the "law" or statute that they will live by. The International Day of Human Fraternity was also the creation of a new holiday or "appointed time" that came as a result of Mohamed bin Zayed's work with creating this Human Fraternity/Abrahamic Family House, intended as a change to a new "appointed time" for everyone to shift over to celebrating among Jews and Christians and Muslims, an appointed time of unity without Yahuweh/Yehovah involved.

The *Document of Human Fraternity* lays out this statute that all people of all religions need to stop trying to convert each other and accept that every person in their own religion is following their path to the same god in their own way, achieving salvation according to their own methods. This is a changing of the "law" or principle/statute that Yahuweh/Yehovah is the only one who forgives sins and brings salvation, through his way that he has chosen, through his son the Passover Lamb Yeshua. This shows very definitively the intention of Mohamed bin Zayed to change law, even though he will not succeed, and his intention to change appointed times of when things will happen by subduing/humbling Israel under his influence, to try to steer them in a different direction from Yahuweh/Yehovah's appointed times of fulfillment of prophecies in Scripture concerning his plan of what he wants to do with Israel.

And the "wearing out" of the set-apart ones in the Aramaic is literally referring to wearing out or wearing down or wearing away of a person. It is like pushing on someone to get them to do something over and over, slowly wearing them down over time until they finally are willing to go along with what the person wants them to do. This again is exactly what Mohamed bin Zayed has been doing with many kings/horns in influencing them, but this did not start toward the set-apart ones until the Abraham Accords. That is the deception that began to bring many true set-apart ones, true believers in Yeshua, into the deception and wearing them down to accept the deception that the covenant with the Abrahamic Faiths coming together in unity was a good thing and a miracle performed by Yahuweh/Yehovah to bring peace to Israel. In reality it is a covenant that will bring the destruction of Israel spiritually and physically.

The wearing down of the set-apart ones is the only part of the Little Horn prophecies that has a specific time frame to it other than the 2,300 evening morning, lasting for a time, times, and half a time. Everything that has happened in connection with Mohamed bin Zayed surrounding the Human Fraternity, Abrahamic Family House, and Abraham Accords is already a fulfillment of these verses in Daniel 7:25 and 8:11 and 25, and there is nothing more that needs to happen to fulfill them further than they already are. From Joel Rosenberg's reports in his book we know that there were even Christians involved in the creating process of the Abraham Accords with bin Zayed.

Daniel 7:8 and 24 describes the Little Horn in subduing/humbling three of the Ten Horns that are three kings that eventually join together in destroying Mystery Babel the Great City. As already discussed previously there are some horns/kings or governments of nations that are currently beginning to hate the global city of Mystery Babel because it takes away their power and control that they have in their own nations to rule as dictators or classic monarchs. The governments/horns of Turkey, Iran, Russia, China, North Korea, Afghanistan, Syria, and Cuba are seven of those governments who are currently trying to cut off from the virtual global city of the internet more and more, as well as beginning to cut off from the physical global city network of Babel that connects the world together economically and culturally, making all nations technology clones of each other.

Some governments that are beginning to lean that direction towards hating Babel are countries like Saudi Arabia, Sudan, Libya, Belarus, Malaysia, Somalia, Honduras, and Venezuela. The only two horns/governments that the locations are known for certain are in Turkey and Iran, and the others cannot be known for certain until after the 3.5 years of Great Tribulation are at an end. One of the Ten Horns that Mohamed bin Zayed has recently subdued is the government of Turkey, initiating contact with the meeting of his brother, UAE National Security Advisor Tahnoun bin Zayed Al Nahyan, and President Recep Tayyip Erdogan in Ankara, Turkey in August 2021. Then Mohammed bin Zayed met with Erdogan in Ankara on November 24, 2021, formally restoring and normalizing relations between the countries. Suddenly after this visit by bin Zayed, Turkey restored and normalized ties with Israel and Egypt, and then on February 14, 2022 Erdogan met with bin Zayed in Abu Dhabi and signed the final formal cooperation agreement between the two countries. This agreement included large sums of money the UAE invested in Turkey and subdued the Turkish government under Mohamed bin Zayed's influence to a great extent, including convincing the Turkish government to restore relations with Israel and Egypt.

This is at least one of the ten horns that has already been subdued by Mohamed bin Zayed, but as to the other two there is no way to know for certain until Mystery Babel is destroyed. Saudi Arabia is a king/horn that Mohamed bin Zayed has subdued, but there is no way to know if it is part of the Ten Horns yet. Sudan is another king/horn he has subdued that might or might not be part of the ten. The government of Russia is another potential horn/king of the Ten Horns in the right position to be part of them, and Mohamed bin Zayed does have influence there, but perhaps not subdued yet. The only other horn known for certain is the government of Iran, which Mohamed bin Zayed might be in process of subduing since the end of 2021.

On December 6, 2021 bin Zayed's brother Tahnoun bin Zayed met with the Iranian President Ebrahim Raishi in Tehran, Iran, to begin restoring ties between the two nations, which has continued to grow since that time. On March 16, 2023 Mohamed bin Zayed met with the Secretary of Iran's Supreme National Security Council Ali Shamkhani in Abu Dhabi as they strengthened and normalized their relationship more. And the peace negotiations between Saudi Arabia and the UAE and Iran are happening now because of Mohamed bin Zayed's instigation and influence as the catalyst bringing it about.

Mohamed bin Zayed and the kingdom of Abu Dhabi are a small Little Horn that has become exceedingly great as the prophecies of Daniel 7 and 8 foretold. Everything in those prophecies is already at a place of fulfillment now, including possibly the part of the three horns out of ten that are subdued. That is the only part that there is no way to know for certain it is fulfilled until after Yeshua returns and Mystery Babel is destroyed, along with the destruction of the power of the Little Horn at the same time. Everything else is already done and finished now at present as the Little Horn prophecies are simply playing out to their conclusion.

The only part of the prophecy that still needs further investigation and examination is the Little Horn Mohamed bin Zayed's connection to Daniel 8:11, with the attack against the foundation of the set-apart place at the Temple Mount from evening to morning June 13-14, 2018. Unfortunately it is all so hidden in the darkness that happens from evening to morning there is no way to see that connection clearly yet. All that we know is that there was a secret meeting between Prime Minister Benjamin Netanyahu and Mohamed bin Zayed at some time during the year 2018 in Abu Dhabi.

The meeting was so secret no one knew about it until after the Abraham Accords were announced, and even the exact date in 2018 is unknown, except that it might have been around the months of September or October. Their meeting had something to do with Mohamed bin Zayed subduing Netanyahu and Israel into the Abraham Accords, but there is nothing known beyond that. Everything surrounding that timeframe of June 2018 and the event of the attack on the foundation of the set-apart place at the Temple Mount in Jerusalem is still, years later, very hidden and secret. But one thing we do know for certain is that the Palestinian people involved in the June 2018 event on the Temple Mount are all of the same Muslim people or "host" as Mohammed bin Zayed and the other Muslim nations of the Middle East, all with the same goal and desire to bring the control of the Temple Mount and the Old City of Jerusalem under Muslim governance and control again.

Section 17. **The Beast Out of the Earth and the Image of the Beast Out of the Sea:**

The Beast Out of the Earth Prophecy:
Revelation 13:11-14

Prophecy Fulfillment of Verses **Revelation 13:11-14** – John provides no details or descriptions at all as to what this Beast Out of the Earth actually looks like in the vision. He only says that it has two horns that are like lamb horns, but as for the rest of the beast/animal itself we have no idea what it was that John saw. The only other detail is that it speaks like a dragon. If this Beast Out of the Earth speaks like "the" Dragon in Revelation 12, which is also the Serpent from the garden in Genesis 3 then we know from Scripture how this Beast Out of the Earth speaks in speaking like the Serpent/Dragon, because we have one single record of the words of the Serpent in Genesis 3:1-5. The Serpent says to the Woman concerning the eating of the tree of the knowledge of good and evil, "You shall surely not die. For God knows that in the day you eat of it your eyes shall be opened and you shall be like God, knowing good and evil."

The Beast Out of the Earth in speaking like a Dragon/Serpent as in Genesis 3 says the same things, that people will not die by gaining knowledge about good and evil things. The Beast Out of the Earth says that the gaining of knowledge only opens people's eyes so that they can "be like God." The Beast Out of the Earth is the pursuit of men (in following the deception of the Dragon/Serpent) to be like gods or to become gods through the gaining of knowledge through science and scientific discovery. And the fact that these are two lamb horns on the Beast Out of the Earth shows the spiritual and religious deception leading people astray with a lamb-like appearance of horns that do not appear to be dangerous, but lead astray with the words of the Dragon/Serpent.

And beasts/animals do not generally rise up out of the earth when they are born. Animals and beasts are born from their mothers, but the things that do rise up out of the earth are the things that man creates and builds out of the materials of the earth. Men and women eating from the tree of the knowledge of good and evil, using science to create technology and give people the power to be like Yahuweh/Yehovah, to be like God and attempt to become gods, building things out of the earth and elements of the earth from the knowledge they gain, is what the Beast Out of the Earth is. And when spiritual and religious deception is added to the pursuit of knowledge of good and evil through science, it is the joining together of science and religion like two horns of power, science and religion. It turns science into a religion of worshipping men and women as gods evolving to a higher life form and worshipping the things that men and women create with their hands and knowledge. It also turns traditional religions into a science based pursuit of knowledge to gain the same thing in science, creating technology and worshipping men and women, and what they create, as gods.

The Beast Out of the Earth is only prophesied about in Revelation; there are no prophecies about this beast anywhere else in Scripture. And it is a beast that is definitely in existence today since the 19th century (1800's) when science and man's pursuit of scientific knowledge began to turn into a religion through the theories of Evolution. Since that time science and religion have become more and more joined together as one, with secularists and atheists using science as their religion and system of faith/belief, while people of all religions around the world, including large numbers in Christianity especially within the Roman Catholic Church, are joining the pursuit of knowledge through science into their religions with great importance.

The Beast Out of the Earth is in its fullness of existence today with religion and science inseparable. It is men and women believing the same lie from the Serpent/Dragon in the garden, that through the pursuit of the knowledge of good and evil mankind can overcome death and have their eyes opened to the ability to become powerful gods. Science today is all about mankind becoming gods or worshipping the things that they create as gods, the things they build out of the materials of the earth through technology. It is deceptive religion in the guise of science and scientific invention, in fulfillment of verse 13:11, which includes the environmentalist movement and the worship of the earth.

The Catholic Church under Pope Francis is at the forefront of this movement of joining together science and religion, and the pursuit of making men and women into gods, right along with all of the rest of the world pushing scientific discovery and man's invention of technologies to create a utopia world. For the first time in history mankind has become truly powerful with its knowledge of good and evil in building technology. One of the main focuses of the Catholic Church through Pope Francis has been environmentalism and how religion should participate in modern science and technology. He has released many speeches and writings about this, and the Catholic Church itself has had many conferences and gatherings over the last few years of professionals in various fields progressing scientific research and technology, that have been all about how to integrate the world of technology more with religion in unification. It is "humanism" which is what the Catholic Church has moved toward greatly in recent years in many teachings and writings as part of "Human Fraternity."

And the Vatican in Vatican City has not been the only ones pushing this joining together of religion and science from the Christian world. Sheikh Mohamed bin Zayed Al Nahyan and the UAE centered in Abu Dhabi and Dubai have also been pushing this same joining of religion and science/technology in Islam. Abu Dhabi and Dubai have been major centers for many years for global environmentalist gatherings and conferences as well, pushing the advancement of man's technology and creating a world where mankind is in perfect control and harmony with the earth like gods evolving to a higher state. All of the religions around the world are part of this movement, craving for the power and wealth/luxury that the science and technology gives to them. The centers of this movement are within the broken up remnant pieces of the Beast Out of the Sea of the two feet of the Roman and Islamic Empires.

The Beast Out of the Earth of man's religion of science and humanism of worshipping men as gods has the same authority around the world as the Beast Out of the Sea in fulfillment of verse 13:12, because it is the beast that gives all of the "miraculous" technology power to the Beast Out of the Sea, in its presence. And the Beast Out of the Earth has created so many "miracles" of science that things that once were considered supernatural only 200 years ago are now commonplace in people's everyday lives. The Beast Out of the Earth causes people to worship the system of the Beast Out of the Sea because it is the Beast Out of the Earth that has created the technology and great signs, in fulfillment of verses 13:12-13, that gives the Beast Out of the Sea the power to exist and authority to function in all of the countries across the world.

The great signs that have come from the Beast Out of the Earth, from men and women pursuing the knowledge of good and evil through science, are all sorts of miraculous technologies from cars and planes, to photography and film, and even the ability to make fire to fall down from the heavens onto the earth right in front of people's eyes. It is so commonplace for the miracle of fire to fall from the heavens today that no one even gives a second thought to it, as explosive and incendiary bombs fall from the sky either from artillery or rockets to missiles and bombs dropped from planes and create fire regularly since the 1800's. And the most impressive fire from the heavens of all is the nuclear bomb that creates a fire so intense nothing can survive in it, and it melts away stone and wood and metal.

There is also the fire of light that comes down from the heavens through satellite signals to create a fire/light on people's smart phone or television or computer screens. Or the fire/light of satellites in orbit around the earth, or satellites burning up in the earth's atmosphere, that look like falling stars. All of this is possible through the Beast Out of the Earth as it causes people to worship the world of man made up of the Beast Out of the Sea, worshipping the Beast Out of the Sea that is mankind's world that he has built for himself. It was the Beast Out of the Earth, the merging of science and religion, that created the "miracle" COVID vaccines that brought the Beast Out of the Sea back to life again from what appeared to be a mortal wound, causing people to worship the Beast Out of the Sea that had appeared to be dead and yet lived again, in fulfillment of verses 13:12-13. For any plagues that Yahuweh/Yehovah sends on the earth, the Beast Out of the Earth has an answer with a miracle technology to stop the effects of the plagues on people being able to recover and continue on with "normal" life.

And because of the amazing signs that the Beast Out of the Earth technology has done for people on the earth, it has caused them to be led astray in fulfillment of verse 13:14, to worship the Beast Out of the Sea, which is the worship of mankind and the world mankind has created, and causing people to fall for the lie that mankind can be like God, can be like Yahuweh/Yehovah, if they only eat the fruit of the knowledge of good and evil by pursuing knowledge through science. The perfect integration today of science with religion, mixing science and religion together into the worship of the Beast out of the Sea (the worship of the world and system of modern man), is already today the deception prophesied that leads people astray into making material, manmade things into idols and gods to be worshipped on a new level not seen before in the past.

The Beast Out of the Earth is already completely fulfilled today as it is now, with nothing more needing to happen to make it any more fulfilled than it is now. There is already a complete global religion in existence today of people worshipping the Beast Out of the Sea in their daily lives since it came back to life in 2021 after COVID, because of the power and technology, signs and wonders, done by the Beast Out of the Earth that allows the Beast Out of the Sea to exist, leading astray everyone to worship the Beast Out of the Sea based upon the equal authority and power from the Beast out of the Earth.

All of the religions of the world have fully integrated themselves into the Beast Out of the Earth of man's creation and pursuit of knowledge through science, and through this it leads astray the people of the world to make the Beast Out of the Sea, made up of the broken up empires of the past integrated into all of the nations of the world through the kings/horns of the world giving their authority for the Beast Out of the Sea to come into their nations, into a thing to be worshipped above Yahuweh/Yehovah. It allows mankind to attain the knowledge of good and evil so that people can truly try now in today's world to be like God, to become gods with great powers of manmade technology or to worship the manmade technology as gods/idols.

The Beasts are Empires that Mankind Makes in Their Own Image and the Cities are the Locations Where the Physical Images of the Empires (Beasts) of Man, and the Images of Man, are Built and Created as Part of the Cities Themselves:

Daniel 2:32-42

Daniel 7:2-7

Historical Examination of Verses **Daniel 2:32-42** and **Daniel 7:2-7** – The Beast Out of the Sea in Revelation 13 is only the final form at Yeshua's Return of what are many beasts through history from the prophecies in Daniel 2 and 7. The Beast Out of the Sea in Revelation 13 is not the only beast in the prophecies in history, and when looking historically at how the other beasts in Daniel were already fulfilled we can see what the images of each of those beasts or empires looked like. This is because every empire in history, even those empires not part of the prophecies in Daniel, all consistently build and form the cities of the empire into the physical, visible images of what that empire looks like.

It is the cities that are the image of the empires through history and it is the cities that are the image of the beasts in Daniel 7. All empires in history destroy and conquer nations and cities, and then rebuild the cities to look the same as each other, with the images of the empire placed all over the cities. Each empire has a distinct look or image that is different from the others, that identifies it, and each city that is under that empire's control can be seen clearly in archaeological digs by finding the images and influence of that empire located in each city.

The Babylonian Empire/Beast built the cities of the empire to be a certain, distinctive image of Babylonian culture. Then the Persians and Medes took over and changed the cities to look like the image of Persia and Media, their culture and many religions combined together. Then the Greeks took over and changed all of the cities to look like the image of the Greek culture and Greek life and Greek religious influence. Then the Romans took over and changed all of the cities to look like Rome, remade into the image of the beast of Rome. Then Islam took over and changed all of the cities to look like the image of the beast of Islam, its culture and religion, making the cities under its control into clones of each other like all of the empires before it.

The people of each nation and culture group create the image of their nation and people in the cities that they build. The cities have a distinctive look as the image of the people who inhabit and make them. The cities are always the places where the image is built and created of each beast, because each beast in prophecy through history is simply a world created by men and women in their own image. And the physical representation of that image is in the cities, because the cities are completely manmade worlds built by man completely separated from Yahuweh/Yehovah's world he created in the beginning in the heavens and earth, in nature.

Even though the "image" in Daniel 2 is not specifically described as being the image of a man, from the description of head, arms, thighs, chest, legs, and toes it is probably the image of a man. This stature image in the dream in Daniel 2 is also a representation of all of the beasts or empires through history, and it is an "image" of all of those empires. Every beast is no more than a world created by man, and each one is made in the image of man. Man is the image of each beast because man creates each beast/empire through history, and it is the cities where those images of man are located on the earth and within each beast/empire. Outside of the cities in the wilderness and rural countryside areas there are no images of man and no images of the beasts, because it is Yahuweh/Yehovah's world that he has created for man to live in, with the man and woman as his image. The cities are the world of man that man has created as his image, as the image of the beasts or worlds that he creates.

The Epitome Image of the Beast Out of the Sea of People is Mystery Babel on the Scarlet Beast Out of the Pit of the Deep, Made by the Sea of People in the Image of the Sea of People; the Cities of the World (Babel) are Made by Man (the Beast Out of the Sea) in the Image of Man (the Beast Out of the Sea), and the Empires (Beasts) through History that are Made by Man Always have Their Power and Image of the Empire (Beast) Centered in the Cities:

Genesis 11:1-9
Isaiah 14:4-22
Jeremiah 50:1 – 51:57
Revelation 11:7
Revelation 13:15, 18
Revelation 17:6-8
Revelation 18:1-24

Word for Word Prophecy Examination of Fulfilled and Partially Fulfilled and Unfulfilled Verses **Isaiah 14:4-22** and **Jeremiah 50:1 – 51:57** and **Revelation 13:15, 18** and **Revelation 17:6-8** and **Revelation 18:1-24** and **Revelation 11:7** with **Genesis 11:1-9** – Mystery Babel is riding on a Scarlet Beast Out of the Pit of the Deep that John describes as almost identical to the Beast Out of the Sea. This is because the Scarlet Beast Out of the Pit is the Image of the Beast Out of the Sea, with Mystery Babel riding on it as part of that Image of the Beast Out of the Sea. Every beast through history has always had the cities within its control made and created into the image of that beast, and Mystery Babel is the Image of the Beast Out of the Sea at the Time of the End. Mystery Babel is the cities of the world and is the physical Image and representation of the final Beast Out of the Sea in Revelation 13 on the earth.

Mystery Babel is what the Beast Out of the Sea looks like as a physical form that people can see in the cities, made by the sea of people in the image of the sea of people, made by man in the image of man's world of the Beast Out of the Sea. Cities are nothing more than people coming together to live in one place and build their lives together in one place. Cities are people, made into the image and desires of those people.

The desires of people's hearts are exposed in a way to be able to see those desires in the cities they build, in the buildings and what those buildings are used for.

Mystery Babel is the "mother of the whores and abominations of the earth" where all abominations and whoring originates from the city of Babel. But what is the real source of abominations on the earth? It is men and women who are the real source of abominations; it is mankind who creates all of the abominations on the earth. Without mankind on the earth there would be no abominations or whoring. Mystery Babel began with Babel in Genesis 11, the beginning of building a city in rebellion against Yahuweh/Yehovah. And once again at the Time of the End mankind creates the final Beast Out of the Sea on the earth into this same image of Babel from Genesis 11, making all of the cities of the earth as Babel. All that Mystery Babel is is a gathering together of people in rebellion against Yahuweh/Yehovah to create a world without him in it. And in creating that world without Yahuweh/Yehovah they are creating a world of abominations, a world that represents the desires of their hearts for those abominations.

Wherever the people who are of the world and belonging to the world are gathered together, they are part of the city of Mystery Babel. And wherever Yahuweh/Yehovah's people, belonging to him, are gathered together, they are part of the city of the New Jerusalem. Wherever people are gathered together in rebellion against Yahuweh/Yehovah anywhere on the earth, they are part of the city of Mystery Babel, and wherever people are gathered together in surrender to the will of Yahuweh/Yehovah anywhere on the earth, they are part of the city of the New Jerusalem. Yahuweh/Yehovah's people who follow him all together make up the city of the New Jerusalem at all times wherever they are on the earth, and all those who are in rebellion against him, who are of the world and have friendship with the world, all together make up the city of Mystery Babel at all times wherever they are on the earth.

Genesis 11 records the beginning of Babel as mankind beginning the creation of cities in rebellion against Yahuweh/Yehovah and the image of themselves. And the prophecies in Isaiah 14 and Jeremiah 50 to 51 and Revelation 17 to 18 explain how that same Babel in Genesis 11 continues on into the very end as the same rebellion, the same global city of people trying to gather together in rebellion against Yahuweh/Yehovah since after the flood, still around all the way to the very end when it is finally destroyed. Eventually at the very end of this world the gathering together of people in rebellion against Yahuweh/Yehovah to create all of the abominations of the earth together in the cities of the world is finally permanently ended.

Mystery Babel in Revelation 17 is the one killing, killing the witnesses of Yeshua, and then the Scarlet Beast Out of the Pit of the Deep is the one killing people, killing the witnesses of Yahuweh/Yehovah in Revelation 11. The Image of the Beast Out of the Sea in Revelation 13 is also the one causing people to be killed who do not worship it. There is no mention about the Beast Out of the Sea or the Beast Out of the Earth ever killing anyone, only the Image of the Beast Out of the Sea and Mystery Babel and the Scarlet Beast Out of the Pit of the Deep, because all three of these entities are describing the same thing. The Scarlet Beast Out of the Pit of the Deep with Mystery Babel sitting upon it is the same thing as the Image of the Beast Out of the Sea. Mystery Babel is the cities of the world, and the cities of the world at the Time of the End are made into the Image and physical representation on the earth of the Beast Out of the Sea, just like every beast/empire before it. Except this time the Image that is being created and made is specifically of Babel, from the city of Babel in the very beginning, uniting all of the world together in rebellion against Yahuweh/Yehovah as one, global city, virtually and physically.

Mystery Babel and the Scarlet Beast Out of the Pit of the Deep are the source of all the killing of the witnesses of Yahuweh/Yehovah and the slain of all the earth in Revelation 11:7 and 17:6 and 18:24. Within the city of Mystery Babel is found the blood of every single prophet and set-apart one and every single person who has ever been killed since the murder of Abel in the beginning. Everyone who has ever been murdered throughout all of time are found to have been killed in the city of Mystery Babel, because the city of Mystery Babel is everywhere on the earth wherever people are gathered together in unrighteousness and rebellion against Yahuweh/Yehovah. And as the source of all of the killing, Mystery Babel on the Scarlet Beast Out of the Pit of the Deep are the epitome physical representation and Image of the Beast Out of the Sea, which is itself a mixing together of all of the beasts of Daniel through history.

The final Beast Out of the Sea in Revelation 13 is a mixing together of all of the cultures and nations and peoples that were part of all of the beasts through history in the Middle East and Europe, as well as from the whole world according to Revelation 13:7. And there is no better Image or visible picture of that final Beast Out of the Sea than the cities of the world represented as Mystery Babel, which is itself a uniting and joining together of all of the peoples of the earth as one, global city in rebellion against Yahuweh/Yehovah as in Genesis 11. The number of the Beast Out of the Sea is the number of mankind, six hundred and sixty and six, because the Beast Out of the Sea, like all of the beasts before it in Daniel 2 and 7, are made by mankind in the image of mankind, creating a world of mankind shown in the picture/image in the cities of mankind, Mystery Babel.

The Image of the Beast Out of the Sea Prophecy:
   Revelation 11:7
   Revelation 13:14-15
   Revelation 14:9-11
   Revelation 17:3, 7-8, 11
   Revelation 20:4

Prophecy Fulfillment of Verses **Revelation 13:14-15** and **Revelation 17:3, 7-8, 11** and **Revelation 11:7** with examination of **Revelation 14:9-11** and **Revelation 20:4** – During the year that the Beast Out of the Sea was shut down from its fatal wound from the COVID 19 pandemic, the Beast Out of the Earth made up of Science and Technology being joined together into Religion said to those living on earth at the time to help in making an Image to the Beast Out of the Sea, in fulfillment of Revelation 13:14. This Image that the people of the world came together to create was the Scarlet Beast Out of the Pit of the Deep with Mystery Babel riding upon it, the global, virtual city of Babel. Everyone rushed to connect through the global Mystery Babel city, the Image of the Beast Out of the Sea, building it up and becoming a connected city again through the internet.

All areas of life, from business to school to entertainment and news switched to remote connecting between everyone from their homes through the internet around the whole world. The city of Mystery Babel is the joining together of people to become a city together, as the Image of themselves and of the desires of their hearts, including abominations against Yahuweh/Yehovah, exactly like in Genesis 11. Mystery Babel is the creation of the Image of man, the image of the people who create it, and Mystery Babel on the Scarlet Beast Out of the Pit of the Deep is the Image of the larger Beast Out of the Sea world system that man creates in its own image. The virtual world of the internet is an entirely man created world made as a city in the image of mankind who has created it together. And it is even filled with the "Images" or photographs and videos of all of the people of the world, virtually showing an image of them that is not really there physically, in fulfillment of Revelation 13:15.

The Beast Out of the Earth of scientific invention of man has created a way for the Image of the Beast Out of the Sea, the global city of Mystery Babel, to become a talking city through the virtual city of the internet. Now the cities of people of the world can be talking images of the physical cities of people. Since the release of *The Jazz Singer* in 1927 talking images have become commonplace as part of normal, everyday life. But first television, and then especially the internet later on in the late 1980's, brought the cities of people to life as the cities themselves being joined together as a virtual city of talking images, with a spirit of life in them in fulfillment of Revelation 13:15.

It was not until during COVID, when the Beast Out of the Earth of man's creation of Science and Technology told everyone to build the Image of the Beast Out of the Sea to stay connected into the virtual global city of Mystery Babel that the true worship of the Image of the Beast Out of the Sea really began. This was when many began to worship the internet and globally connected city of Mystery Babel in its virtual and physical forms as the Image of the Beast Out of the Sea, wanting to do anything to go back to normal life in the Beast and relying on the Beast for provision and security instead of Yahuweh/Yehovah. The people of the world at that time made a clear choice if they did not want the world to end yet and wanted the world of man to continue going on, so that they could continue living in it, like the children of Israel wanting to go back to Egypt or Lot's wife turning to go back into Sodom as it was destroyed. Or people chose that they wanted this world of man, this Beast Out of the Sea and Mystery Babel to end and not come back to life again, but instead to trust Yahuweh/Yehovah for provision in the wilderness and rely on him, following him into his Promised Land in the New Heavens and New Earth.

Not everyone on the internet during that time was worshipping the Image of the Beast Out of the Sea or participating in its building by the people of the world coming together in an attempt to keep the Beast Out of the Sea going after its fatal wound. In the same way that Yahuweh/Yehovah's people still had to be in the midst of Egypt up until a certain time when he brought them out, his people are still inside of Mystery Babel up until his coming in Revelation 18:4 when he calls his people to leave Babel, to leave the world like leaving Egypt and Sodom, to follow him into the wilderness. Yahuweh/Yehovah's people are still in the midst of the Beast Out of the Sea and the Image of the Beast Out of the Sea in Mystery Babel, but in their hearts they do not have to like it or want to be part of it or worship it. The worship of the Image of the Beast Out of the Sea was by all those who wanted the world, wanted the Beast Out of the Sea with all their hearts, to come back again and be part of their lives, rejecting Yahuweh/Yehovah and his world and system, in fulfillment of Revelation 13:15.

Only being in the midst of Mystery Babel as the Image of the Beast Out of the Sea is not enough to be worshipping that Image. It is a matter of what each person has chosen in their heart since the temporary shutdown of the Beast Out of the Sea during COVID, to have friendship with the world as an enemy of Yahuweh/Yehovah (James 4:4) and worship the Beast and its Image as the god of their lives, or to turn away from the Beast and its Image, wanting them to end and to move on to be with Yahuweh/Yehovah in the wilderness and in the New Heavens and New Earth. It is not the act of using the internet that is an act of worship, but the desires of the heart placing the internet of Mystery Babel representing the Image of the Beast Out of the Sea, as a god above Yahuweh/Yehovah, to be more important in a person's life than Yahuweh/Yehovah.

Many began to worship the Beast Out of the Sea and the Image of the Beast Out of the Sea (Mystery Babel) as the most important thing in their lives during the COVID global shutdown, and those who did not worship it, who did not worship the global, connected city of Mystery Babel in both its physical and virtual forms were and are being "caused" to be killed by the global city of Mystery Babel. It does not say in Revelation 13 that the Image of the Beast Out of the Sea kills those who refuse to worship it, but instead indirectly "causes" them to be killed. Anyone, especially those living in the physical cities of the world, the cities of Mystery Babel, who refused to make the global city of Mystery Babel, the Image of the Beast Out of the Sea, as their dependency of survival during the COVID lockdowns and restrictions, worshipping it, were pushed out and isolated from society by Mystery Babel, the Image of the Beast Out of the Sea. This led to the Image of the Beast Out of the Sea causing people indirectly to be killed around the world who were cut off from resources and necessities for surviving within the cities.

Those in the wilderness and in remote areas mostly went on with life as normal because they did not have to worry about the restrictions and lockdowns in the cities that are the Images of the Beast Out of the Sea, Mystery Babel, or especially the virtual city of Mystery Babel in the internet. But anyone living within the physical cities of Mystery Babel around the world who refused to worship the Image of the Beast Out of the Sea, relying on it to be able to go back to "normal" life within the Beast Out of the Sea like before, were cut out of the city societies, making it difficult for them to survive, especially in countries that were really extreme like China and parts of Australia and Europe, or in Israel or Hawaii and parts of California.

The Scarlet Beast Out of the Pit of the Deep that is also part of Mystery Babel as the Image of the Beast Out of the Sea is the same thing as the Beast Out of the Sea, except that it is a copy, image representation of it that is more visible as part of the cities of the world. It is covered in names of blasphemy against Yahuweh/Yehovah and part of the abominations of Mystery Babel, the abominations of mankind centered in the cities of the world built by man. But this Scarlet Beast Out of the Pit of the Deep was in existence in the past before the days of John, and then did not exist anymore during the days of John according to Revelation 17:8, and then comes back again during the Time of the End for its destruction. It is the true, original Babel in Genesis 11 that has been gone for thousands of years in its true, original, pure form of a global city connecting everyone together as one city of people. Only within the last few decades has Mystery Babel been able to come back again in its true form going beyond borders to join the world together again as one beyond the language barriers that Yahuweh/Yehovah created in Genesis 11, in fulfillment of Revelation 17:8.

The Scarlet Beast Out of the Pit of the Deep, according to Revelation 17:11, is an eighth head attached onto the Beast Out of the Sea that is of the seven heads. The Scarlet Beast Out of the Pit of the Deep and Mystery Babel also were almost shutdown and lost during the COVID pandemic, because the cities became more and more cut off from one another, and nobody knew if this new SARS virus variant (called SARS-CoV-2) would continue to mutate to a point that the world would be shut down indefinitely until a vaccine was made many years in the future. It was only the global city of the internet that kept it going and brought it back to life again alongside the Beast Out of the Sea, so that people marveled at and worshipped the Scarlet Beast Out of the Pit of the Deep at the same time, as the Image of the Beast, in fulfillment of Revelation 17:8.

But the Scarlet Beast Out of the Pit of the Deep, with Mystery Babel upon it, upon the seven heads, is also an eighth head, and of the seven. This is because as an eighth head it finally brought all of the other seven heads together as a foundation under Mystery Babel, the other seven heads from the previous beasts as already discussed earlier with their foundations of making the modern world run from medical and education systems to technology and transportation and travel. It is the bringing together of all of these seven heads that are seven mountains into the eighth head of the Image of the Beast Out of the Sea, the talking images of the city of Mystery Babel through computers and internet, that has brought back Mystery Babel from Genesis 11 into existence once again, in fulfillment of Revelation 17:8 and 11. And now there is a stronger dependency on Mystery Babel, through the virtual Babel of the internet and interconnected physical cities as the Image of the Beast Out of the Sea, than ever before since COVID, making and building the Image of the Beast Out of the Sea into something stronger and greater since then that people are required to use more than ever before in order to survive within the Beast Out of the Sea and the cities of Mystery Babel.

With the smartphones available today, everyone is constantly online, spending all of their time worshipping the idol/image of the internet that man has created with his hands, bringing to life the Image of the Beast Out of the Sea represented in the physical cities of the world, into a virtual, living city with spirit in it. And all of the cities of the world are becoming clones of one another, being turned into "smart" cities of technology, making people completely dependent on the technology to survive within those cities or be indirectly caused to be killed trying to survive in them without the technology. The physical cities of the world themselves are being worshipped by people today along with the virtual global city, like Lot's wife worshipping the city of Sodom (Luke 17:32), refusing to leave them and go with Yahuweh/Yehovah into the wilderness. Everyone is making their choices if they love and worship the cities of mankind, the cities of Babel across the world, or if they want to leave the cities of Babel and go with Yahuweh/Yehovah into the wilderness as the woman going into the wilderness, to be part of Yahuweh/Yehovah's city of the New Jerusalem.

Everything concerning the prophecies of the Image of the Beast Out of the Sea and the Scarlet Beast Out of the Pit of the Deep with Mystery Babel are already in fulfillment today, including the worship of the Image of the Beast Out of the Sea that has been ongoing since 2020. There is nothing more and nothing new that needs to happen to make these prophecies be more fulfilled than they already are right now at the present time. Yahuweh/Yehovah temporarily shut down the whole world with his COVID plague he sent on the earth so that everyone would be able to make a clear choice if they want the world or want him, ahead of his permanently shutting down the world and ending it at his coming.

1 – People create their own worlds that are separate from and in rebellion against Yahuweh/Yehovah and when these worlds that people create are in the form of empires, they are talked about in Scripture as beasts or animals.

2 – The images for these beasts or empires through history have been made and created in the cities of each of those beasts, with not only images like statues and pictures being involved, but both the physical construction and cultural society of those cities are made into the images portraying the beasts or empires. Everything in the cities of each empire is transformed to create the image of what that empire world or beast world looks like in the physical realm.

3 – In the same way that the beasts or empires through history created images of that world of each beast with its cities, Mystery Babel on the Scarlet Beast Out of the Pit of the Deep is the image of the world that the Beast Out of the Sea has created in its cities on the earth.

4 – The physical cities themselves of the earth are going through a transformation process of becoming exact clones of one another, each becoming the image of the Beast Out of the Sea represented as Mystery Babel on the Scarlet Beast Out of the Pit of the Deep. Every city on earth is transforming into the world of Mystery Babel, the world that represents the image of the world of the Beast Out of the Sea in the tangible realm of reality where it can be seen and worshipped.

5 – In this final Beast Out of the Sea in Revelation 13, it is the first of all of the beasts in prophecy since the days of the building of the tower and city of Babel in Genesis 11 to go to an extra extreme beyond the physical cities, succeeding in building a global city through the virtual city of the internet, creating the internet into the ultimate image and city of the Beast Out of the Sea. The internet has become the global city of Mystery Babel that is the epitome image of the Beast Out of the Sea, the epitome of the people of the earth gathering together in rebellion against Yahuweh/Yehovah into a global city of rebellion if they choose to use the infrastructure of the internet highway for that purpose. And people are able to choose to worship the image of the Beast Out of the Sea, to worship the global city of Mystery Babel online, if they want to, lifting up man's created world of the Beast Out of the Sea, in the image of Mystery Babel, above Yahuweh/Yehovah.

6 – Anyone who does not worship the image of the Beast Out of the Sea in its physical cities or online virtual city of Mystery Babel today, by trying to cut off from using the internet or from the dependency of using the physical systems of the city of electricity and plumbing and bureaucracy codes are indirectly caused to be killed by the Image of the Beast Out of the Sea, Mystery Babel, without a way to survive independently from Mystery Babel.

Section 18. **The Mark of the Beast Out of the Sea:**

The Ancient and Modern Hebrew Word for "Mark" is "Tav" תו; An Exact Literal Translation of the Greek of Revelation 13:16-17 Reveals Greater Depth to the Only Prophecy in Scripture About the Mark

Ezekiel 9:1-7

Revelation 13:16-17

Word for Word Examination of Verses **Ezekiel 9:1-7** and **Revelation 13:16-17** – One of the only examples where the Hebrew word for "Mark" is used in Scripture is in Ezekiel 9:1-7, where a man in white linen is instructed to "mark" the foreheads of those in the city of Jerusalem who are sad about the abominations being done there. This Hebrew word used for "Mark" is Tav תו, and there is no doubt about the meaning of this Hebrew word Tav, that it means in its noun form a "Mark." This Hebrew word Tav is the most comparable and alike to the Greek word Charagma χάραγμα used in Revelation 13:16-17, Charagma meaning a mark in terms of an etching or engraving created into a mark symbol, or a badge or stamp form of a mark. Modern Hebrew translations of Revelation from the last 150 years consistently translate this Greek word Charagma as the Hebrew word Tav.

On the following pages Revelation 13:16-17 has been laid out word by word in an exact, literal English translation of the Greek, and it reveals some very interesting things about this prophecy that are not shown in most standard translations. The Greek word Agorasai ἀγοράσαι actually means "go to market" and according to all sources that explain the meaning of this Greek word, it always means "go to market" in every context and never means only the word "buy" by itself alone except in the sense of "buy at market." It only ever has the meaning of buying from a physical location marketplace, but it really means "go to market." And the Greek word Echon ἔχων that is usually translated as "have" or "possess" really literally means "hold," especially in the context of talking about a right hand that holds the Mark. So what Revelation 13:17 really says is, "and that not any person is able <u>to go to market</u> or to trade if not that one is <u>holding</u> the mark, the name of the beast, or the number of the name of it."

Anyone can see this for themselves in the side by side comparison with the Greek on the following pages, that in the context no one is able to go to market or to trade and barter as a seller unless they are "holding" the Mark or the name of the Beast Out of the Sea or the number of its name in their right hand or upon their forehead. The mark is something that is held upon the right hand or upon the forehead, and it keeps people from being able to enter into the physical locations of marketplaces and businesses unless this Mark is held upon the hand to get into them, for both people who want to buy things or to sell things.

*... **and it causes all, the small and the great (big), and the wealthy and the poor, and the free and the slave, that it should give to them a badge/stamp/mark upon the hand of them the right or upon the forehead (amid-face) of them, and that not any person is able to go to market (to purchase at market) or to trade/sell (to barter as a merchant) if not that one is holding the badge/stamp/mark, the name of the beast, or the number of the name of it.** Revelation 13:16-17*

Revelation 13:16-17
Strong's Greek Concordance Literal Translation

καὶ	ποιεῖ	πάντας,	τοὺς
and	**it causes**	**all,**	**the**
2532. καί kaí, kahee; appar. a prim. particle, having a copulative and sometimes also a cumulative force; and, also, even, so, then, too, etc.; often used in connection (or composition) with other particles or small words:—and, also, both, but, even, for, if, indeed, likewise, moreover, or, so, that, then, therefore, when, yea, yet.	4160. ποιέω poiéō, poy-eh'-o; appar. a prol. form of an obsol. prim.; to make or do (in a very wide application, more or less direct):—abide, + agree, appoint, × avenge, + band together, be, bear, + bewray, bring (forth), cast out, cause, commit, + content, continue, deal, + without any delay, (would) do (-ing), execute, exercise, fulfil, gain, give, have, hold, × journeying, keep, + lay wait, + lighten the ship, make, × mean, + none of these things move me, observe, ordain, perform, provide, + have purged, purpose, put, + raising up, × secure, shew, × shoot out, spend, take, tarry, + transgress the law, work, yield. Comp. 4238.	3956. πᾶς pas, pas; includ. all the forms of declension; appar. a prim. word; all, any, every, the whole:—all (manner of means), alway (-s), any (one), × daily, + ever, every (one, way), as many as, + no (-thing), × throughly, whatsoever, whole, whosoever.	3588. ὁ ho, ho; includ. the fem. ἡ hē, hay; and the neut. τό tó, tó, in all their inflections; the def. article: the (sometimes to be supplied, at others omitted in English idiom):—the, this, that, one, he, she, it, etc.

μικροὺς	καὶ	τοὺς	μεγάλους,
small	**and**	**the**	**great (big),**
3398. μικρός mikrós, mik-ros'; includ. the comp. μικρότερος mikróteros, mik-rot'-er-os; appar. a prim. word; small (in size, quantity, number or fig.) dignity):—least, less, little, small.	2532. καί kaí, kahee; appar. a prim. particle, having a copulative and sometimes also a cumulative force; and, also, even, so, then, too, etc.; often used in connection (or composition) with other particles or small words:—and, also, both, but, even, for, if, indeed, likewise, moreover, or, so, that, then, therefore, when, yea, yet.	3588. ὁ ho, ho; includ. the fem. ἡ hē, hay; and the neut. τό tó, tó, in all their inflections; the def. article: the (sometimes to be supplied, at others omitted in English idiom):—the, this, that, one, he, she, it, etc.	3173. μέγας mégas, meg'-as [includ. the prol. forms, fem. μεγάλη megálē, plur. μεγάλοι megáloi, etc.; comp. also 3176, 3187]; big (lit. or fig., in a very wide application):—(+ fear) exceedingly, great (-est), high, large, loud, mighty, + (be) sore (afraid), strong, × to years.

καὶ	τοὺς	πλουσίους	καὶ
and	**the**	**wealthy**	**and**
2532. καί kaí, kahee; appar. a prim. particle, having a copulative and sometimes also a cumulative force; and, also, even, so, then, too, etc.; often used in connection (or composition) with other particles or small words:—and, also, both, but, even, for, if, indeed, likewise, moreover, or, so, that, then, therefore, when, yea, yet.	3588. ὁ ho, ho; includ. the fem. ἡ hē, hay; and the neut. τό tó, tó, in all their inflections; the def. article: the (sometimes to be supplied, at others omitted in English idiom):—the, this, that, one, he, she, it, etc.	4145. πλούσιος ploúsios, ploo'-see-os; from 4149; wealthy; fig. abounding with:—rich.	2532. καί kaí, kahee; appar. a prim. particle, having a copulative and sometimes also a cumulative force; and, also, even, so, then, too, etc.; often used in connection (or composition) with other particles or small words:—and, also, both, but, even, for, if, indeed, likewise, moreover, or, so, that, then, therefore, when, yea, yet.

τοὺς	πτωχούς,	καὶ	τοὺς
the	**poor,**	**and**	**the**
3588. ὁ ho, ho; includ. the fem. ἡ hē, hay; and the neut. τό tó, tó, in all their inflections; the def. article: the (sometimes to be supplied, at others omitted in English idiom):—the, this, that, one, he, she, it, etc.	4434. πτωχός ptōchós, pto-khos'; from πτώσσω ptōssō (to crouch); akin to 4422 and the alt. of 4098); a beggar (as cringing), i.e. pauper (strictly denoting absolute or public mendicancy, although also used in a qualified or relative sense; whereas 3993 prop. means only straitened circumstances in private), lit. (often as noun) or fig. (distressed):—beggar (-ly), poor.	2532. καί kaí, kahee; appar. a prim. particle, having a copulative and sometimes also a cumulative force; and, also, even, so, then, too, etc.; often used in connection (or composition) with other particles or small words:—and, also, both, but, even, for, if, indeed, likewise, moreover, or, so, that, then, therefore, when, yea, yet.	3588. ὁ ho, ho; includ. the fem. ἡ hē, hay; and the neut. τό tó, tó, in all their inflections; the def. article: the (sometimes to be supplied, at others omitted in English idiom):—the, this, that, one, he, she, it, etc.

ἐλευθέρους	καὶ	τοὺς	δούλους,
free	**and**	**the**	**slave,**
1658. ἐλεύθερος eleútheros, el-yoo'-ther-os; prob. from the alt. of 2064; unrestrained (to go at pleasure), i.e. (as a citizen) not a slave (whether freeborn or manumitted), or (gen.) exempt (from obligation or liability):—free (man, woman), at liberty.	2532. καί kaí, kahee; appar. a prim. particle, having a copulative and sometimes also a cumulative force; and, also, even, so, then, too, etc.; often used in connection (or composition) with other particles or small words:—and, also, both, but, even, for, if, indeed, likewise, moreover, or, so, that, then, therefore, when, yea, yet.	3588. ὁ ho, ho; includ. the fem. ἡ hē, hay; and the neut. τό tó, tó, in all their inflections; the def. article: the (sometimes to be supplied, at others omitted in English idiom):—the, this, that, one, he, she, it, etc.	1401. δοῦλος doûlos, doo'-los; from 1210; a slave (lit. or fig., invol. or vol.; frequently therefore in a qualified sense of subjection or subserviency):—bond (-man), servant.

ἵνα	δῶσιν	αὐτοῖς	χάραγμα
that	**it should give**	**to them**	**a badge/stamp/mark**
2443. ἵνα hína, hin'-ah; prob. from the same as the former part of 1438 (through the demonstrative idea; comp. 2588); in order that (denoting the purpose or the result):—albeit, because, to the intent (that), lest, so as, (so) that, (for) to. Comp. 3363.	1325. δίδωμι dídōmi, did'-o-mee; a prol. verb (which is used as an altern. in most of the tenses); to give (used in a very wide application, prop. or by impl., lit. or fig.; greatly modified by the connection):—adventure, bestow, bring forth, commit, deliver (up), give, grant, hinder, make, minister, number, offer, have power, put, receive, set, shew, smite (+ with the hand), strike (+ with the palm of the hand), suffer, take, utter, yield.	846. αὐτός autós, ow-tos'; from the particle αὖ au [perh. akin to the base of 109 through the idea of a baffling wind] (backward); the reflex. pron. self, used (alone or in the comp. 1438) of the third pers., and (with the prop. pers. pron.) of the other persons:—her, it (-self), one, the other, (mine) own, said, ([self-], the) same, ([him-, my-, thy-]) self, [your-] selves, she, that, their (-s), them ([-selves]), there [-at, -by, -in, -into, -of, -on, -with], they, (these) things, this (man), those, together, very, which. Comp. 848.	5480. χάραγμα cháragma, khar'-ag-mah; from the same as 5482; a scratch or etching, i.e. stamp (as a badge of servitude), or sculptured figure (statue):—graven, mark.

ἐπὶ	τῆς	χειρὸς	αὐτῶν
upon	**the**	**hand**	**of them**
1909. ἐπί epi, ep-ee'; a prim. prep. prop. mean. superimposition (of time, place, order, etc.), as a relation of distribution [with the gen.], i.e. over, upon, etc.; of rest (with the dat.) at, on, etc.; of direction (with the acc.) towards, upon, etc.:—about (the times), above, after, against, among, as long as (touching), at, beside, X have charge of, (be-, [where-]) fore, in (a place, as much as, the time of, -to), (because) of, (up-) on (behalf of), over, (by, for) the space of, through (-out), (un-) to (-ward), with. In compounds it retains essentially the same import, at, upon, etc. (lit. or fig.).	3588. ὁ ho, ho; includ. the fem. ἡ hē, hay; and the neut. τό to, to, in all their inflections; the def. article; the (sometimes to be supplied, at others omitted in English idiom):—the, this, that, one, he, she, it, etc.	5495. χείρ cheir, khire; perh. from the base of 5494 in the sense of its congener the base of 5490 (through the idea of hollowness for grasping); the hand (lit. or fig. [power]; espec. [by Heb.] a means or instrument):—hand.	846. αὐτός autos, ow-tos'; from the particle αὖ au [perh. akin to the base of 109 through the idea of a baffling wind] (backward); the reflex. pron. self, used (alone or in the comp. 1438) of the third pers., and (with the prop. pers. pron.) of the other persons:—her, it (-self), one, the other, (mine) own, said, ([self-], the) same, ([him-, my-, thy-]) self, [your-] selves, she, that, their (-s), them ([-selves]), there [-at, -by, -in, -into, -of, -on, -with], they, (these) things, this (man), those, together, very, which. Comp. 848.

τῆς	δεξιᾶς	ἢ	ἐπὶ
the	**right**	**or**	**upon**
3588. ὁ ho, ho; includ. the fem. ἡ hē, hay; and the neut. τό to, to, in all their inflections; the def. article; the (sometimes to be supplied, at others omitted in English idiom):—the, this, that, one, he, she, it, etc.	1188. δεξιός dexios, dex-ee-os'; from 1209; the right side or (fem.) hand (as that which usually takes):—right (hand, side).	2228. ἤ ē, ay; a prim. particle of distinction between two connected terms; disjunctive, or; comparative, than:—and, but (either), (n-) either, except it be, (n-) or (else), rather, save, than, that, what, yea. Often used in connection with other particles. Comp. especially 2235, 2260, 2273.	1909. ἐπί epi, ep-ee'; a prim. prep. prop. mean. superimposition (of time, place, order, etc.), as a relation of distribution [with the gen.], i.e. over, upon, etc.; of rest (with the dat.) at, on, etc.; of direction (with the acc.) towards, upon, etc.:—about (the times), above, after, against, among, as long as (touching), at, beside, X have charge of, (be-, [where-]) fore, in (a place, as much as, the time of, -to), (because) of, (up-) on (behalf of), over, (by, for) the space of, through (-out), (un-) to (-ward), with. In compounds it retains essentially the same import, at, upon, etc. (lit. or fig.).

τὸ	μέτωπον	αὐτῶν,	καὶ
the	**forehead (amid-face)**	**of them,**	**and**
3588. ὁ ho, ho; includ. the fem. ἡ hē, hay; and the neut. τό to, to, in all their inflections; the def. article; the (sometimes to be supplied, at others omitted in English idiom):—the, this, that, one, he, she, it, etc.	3359. μέτωπον metōpon, met'-o-pon; from 3326 and ὤψ ōps (the face); the forehead (as opposite the countenance):—forehead.	846. αὐτός autos, ow-tos'; from the particle αὖ au [perh. akin to the base of 109 through the idea of a baffling wind] (backward); the reflex. pron. self, used (alone or in the comp. 1438) of the third pers., and (with the prop. pers. pron.) of the other persons:—her, it (-self), one, the other, (mine) own, said, ([self-], the) same, ([him-, my-, thy-]) self, [your-] selves, she, that, their (-s), them ([-selves]), there [-at, -by, -in, -into, -of, -on, -with], they, (these) things, this (man), those, together, very, which. Comp. 848.	2532. καί kai, kahee; appar. a prim. particle, having a copulative and sometimes also a cumulative force; and, also, even, so, then, too, etc.; often used in connection (or composition) with other particles or small words:—and, also, both, but, even, for, if, indeed, likewise, moreover, or, so, that, then, therefore, when, yea, yet.

ἵνα	μὴ	τις	δύνηται
that	**not**	**any person**	**is able**
2443. ἵνα hina, hin'-ah; prob. from the same as the former part of 1438 (through the demonstrative idea, 3588); in order that (denoting the purpose or the result):—albeit, because, to the intent (that), lest, so as, (so) that, (for) to. Comp. 3363.	3361. μή mē, may; a prim. particle of qualified negation (whereas 3756 expresses an absolute denial); (adv.) not, (conj.) lest; also (as interrog. implying a neg. answer [whereas 3756 expects an affirm. one]) whether:—any, but (that), X forbear, + God forbid, + lack, lest, neither, never, no (X wise in), none, nor, [can-] not, nothing, that not, un [-taken], without. Often used in compounds in substantially the same relations. See also 3362, 3363, 3364, 3372, 3373, 3375, 3378.	5100. τὶς tis, tis; an enclit. indef. pron.; some or any person or object:—a (kind of), any (man, thing, thing at all), certain (thing), divers, he (every) man, one (X thing), ought, + partly, some (man, -body, -thing, -what), (+ that no) thing, what (-soever), X wherewith, whom [-soever], whose ([-soever]).	1410. δύναμαι dunamai, doo'-nam-ahee; of uncert. affin.; to be able or possible:—be able, can (do, + -not), could, may, might, be possible, be of power.

ἀγοράσαι	ἢ	πωλῆσαι	εἰ
to go to market (to purchase at market)	**or**	**to trade/sell (to barter as a merchant)**	**if**
59. ἀγοράζω agorazō, ag-or-ad'-zo; from 58; prop. to go to market, i.e. (by impl.) to purchase; spec. to redeem:—buy, redeem.	2228. ἤ ē, ay; a prim. particle of distinction between two connected terms; disjunctive, or; comparative, than:—and, but (either), (n-) either, except it be, (n-) or (else), rather, save, than, that, what, yea. Often used in connection with other particles. Comp. especially 2235, 2260, 2273.	4453. πωλέω pōleō, po-leh'-o; prob. ultimately from πέλομαι pelomai (to be busy, to trade); to barter (as a pedlar), i.e. to sell:—sell, whatever is sold.	1487. εἰ ei, i; a prim. particle of conditionality; if, whether, that, etc.:—forasmuch as, if, that, ([al-]) though, whether. Often used in connection or composition with other particles, espec. as in 1489, 1490, 1499, 1508, 1509, 1512, 1513, 1536, 1537. See also 1437.

μὴ	ὁ	ἔχων	τὸ
not	**that one**	**is holding**	**the**
3361. μή mē, may; a prim. particle of qualified negation (whereas 3756 expresses an absolute denial); (adv.) not, (conj.) lest; also (as interrog. implying a neg. answer [whereas 3756 expects an affirm. one]) whether:—any, but (that), X forbear, + God forbid, + lack, lest, neither, never, no (X wise in), none, nor, [can-] not, nothing, that not, un [-taken], without. Often used in compounds in substantially the same relations. See also 3362, 3363, 3364, 3372, 3373, 3375, 3378.	3588. ὁ ho, ho; includ. the fem. ἡ hē, hay; and the neut. τό to, to, in all their inflections; the def. article; the (sometimes to be supplied, at others omitted in English idiom):—the, this, that, one, he, she, it, etc.	2192. ἔχω echō, ekh'-o (includ. an alt. form σχέω scheō, skheh'-o; used in certain tenses only); a prim. verb; to hold (used in very various applications, lit. or fig., direct or remote; such as possession, ability, contiguity, relation or condition):—be (able, X hold, possessed with), accompany, + begin to amend, can (+ -not), X conceive, count, diseased, do, + eat, + enjoy, + fear, following, have, hold, keep, + lack, + go to law, lie, + must needs, + of necessity, + need, next, + recover, + reign, + rest, return, X sick, take for, + tremble, + uncircumcised, use.	3588. ὁ ho, ho; includ. the fem. ἡ hē, hay; and the neut. τό to, to, in all their inflections; the def. article; the (sometimes to be supplied, at others omitted in English idiom):—the, this, that, one, he, she, it, etc.

χάραγμα **badge/stamp/mark,**	τὸ **the**	ὄνομα **name**	τοῦ **of the**
θηρίου **beast,**	ἢ **or**	τὸν **the**	ἀριθμὸν **number**
τοῦ **of the**	ὀνόματος **name**	αὐτοῦ. **of it.**	

... and it causes all, the small and the great (big), and the wealthy and the poor, and the free and the slave, that it should give to them a badge/stamp/mark upon the hand of them the right or upon the forehead (amid-face) of them, and that not any person is able to go to market (to purchase at market) or to trade/sell (to barter as a merchant) if not that one is holding the badge/stamp/mark, the name of the beast, or the number of the name of it. Revelation 13:16-17

The Ancient and Modern Hebrew Word for Calculate is "Chashav" חשב and the Modern Hebrew Word for Computer, "Machshev" מחשב, Comes from the Root "Chashav":

Revelation 13:18

Word for Word Examination of Verses **Revelation 13:18** – In Revelation 13:18 John says that the number of the Beast Out of the Sea has to be calculated. The Greek word used here for "Calculate" is "Psephisato" ψηφισάτω, which also means "Compute." The comparable ancient Hebrew word for the Greek here is "Chashav" חשב, which means the same thing, to "Calculate" or "Compute." In modern Hebrew today this word Chashav has been used for the Hebrew word for Computer, by following the ancient Hebrew grammar rules and adding the letter Mem to the beginning of the word, turning it into the noun "Machshev" מחשב, meaning "Computer." It is the same principle as in the English language when taking the verb "Compute" and adding an "er" to the end of it, changing it into the noun "Computer."

In both the Greek and Hebrew it can be clearly seen that the number of the Beast Out of the Sea has to be calculated or computed, giving a clear reference to a device that calculates or computes like a calculator or computer. The number of the Beast Out of the Sea, the number six hundred and sixty-six, is able to be computed and calculated using a computer or a calculating device.

The Hebrew Letter Numerals for the Numbers 600 and 60 and 6 are Final Mem ם and Samek ס and Vav ו from Ancient Times, at Least as Far Back as When the Book of Revelation was Written in about 90 C.E.; Computer Binary Code is a Repetition of the Western Arabic Numeral Numbers 0 and 1 Over and Over Again in Different Orders:

Revelation 13:18

Word for Word Examination of Verses **Revelation 13:18** – The two oldest surviving fragments of copies of Revelation 13:18 are both from the late 3rd century C.E., about 200 years after Revelation was written. Both of these Greek manuscripts write the number of the Beast Out of the Sea using Greek letter numerals, which means that they use the Greek letters as each representing numeral numbers. The oldest of the two, Papyrus 115, has the scribal error of writing the number as six hundred sixteen, or as the three letter numerals 600 and 10 and 6 instead of six hundred sixty-six.[35] But the second oldest, Papyrus 47, has the correct number and writes the number of the Beast Out of the Sea in Greek Majuscule (Uppercase) letters as the three Greek numerals "Chi" X and "Xi" Ξ and "Stigma" (Final Sigma) C.[36] In the text of the manuscript itself it looks like this: X Ξ C.

Prior to the 10th century C.E. all Greek manuscript copies of the New Testament were written in these Greek Majuscule letters, either as shown above as letter numerals or, as in the case of the Codex Sinaiticus, spelled out completely in words, writing the numbers 600 and 60 and 6 as six hundred sixty-six in Greek wording.[37] Then beginning in the 10th Century C.E. all of the manuscript copies of the New Testament in Greek switched to Miniscule (Lowercase) letters, and writing out the number of the Beast Out of the Sea in Greek letter numerals became "Chi" χ and "Xi" ξ and "Stigma" (Final Sigma) ς, looking like this: χ ξ ς.

By the 1st century C.E. when John wrote the book of Revelation, sometime around the year 90 C.E., the Hebrew language had almost entirely switched over to what is known as Hebrew Square script, and it has remained essentially unchanged for 2,000 years since that time up till now in Israel today where modern Hebrew is used. The exact same Hebrew Square script is still in use today as in the time of John, and that Hebrew Square script is based upon the same script that the ancient Aramaic language was written in hundreds of years before that, known as Royal or Imperial Aramaic. This form of Hebrew Square script that came from ancient Aramaic had extra forms of the letters added into it (known as "Finals") that are written differently at the end of a word for the purpose of adding in enough letters to be able to use the Hebrew (or Aramaic) Alephbet as letter numerals also.

When writing the number of the Beast Out of the Sea in Revelation 13:18 as Hebrew letter numerals from the 1st century C.E., the three letters "Final Mem" ם and "Samek" ס and "Vav" ו are used, which when read from right to left would look like this, in both the 1st century C.E. at the time of John and today: ו ס ם. On the following page are examples of how these three letters were written from an example of the Dead Sea Scrolls fragment 11Q5 from about the year 50 C.E. to the Aleppo Codex in the 10th century C.E., and through the Middle Ages, including examples of the Hebrew cursive scripts and Modern Hebrew computer fonts.

---

[35] *Revelation* (circa 275 C.E. copy) Papyrus 115 [P. Oxy. LXVI 4499]; Ashmolean Museum of Art and Archaeology, Oxford.
[36] *Revelation* (3rd Century C.E. copy) Papyrus 47 [P. Chester Beatty III]; Chester Beatty Library, Dublin.
[37] *Codex Sinaiticus* (4th Century C.E. copy) Add. Ms. 43725; British Library, London. [Some pages in other libraries as well]

1st Century C.E. Square Hebrew

Dead Sea Scrolls Fragment Psalms 11Q5 circa 30-50 C.E. (from Psalms 125)

Final Mem	Samek	Vav
ס – 600	ס – 60	ו – 6

10th Century C.E. Square Hebrew

Aleppo Codex circa 920 C.E. (from 2 Samuel 22)

Final Mem	Samek	Vav
ם – 600	ס – 60	ו – 6

Middle Ages Square Hebrew

Final Mem	Samek	Vav
ם – 600 (Spain)	ס – 60 (Spain)	ו – 6 (Spain)
ם – 600 (Germany)	ס – 60 (Germany)	ו – 6 (Germany)

Late Middle Ages Cursive Hebrew

Final Mem	Samek	Vav
○ – 600 (Spain)	℘ – 60 (Spain)	ʃ – 6 (Spain)
○ – 600 (Middle East/Asia)	℘ – 60 (Middle East/Asia)	ו – 6 (Middle East/Asia)
ᴗ – 600 (Italy)	○ – 60 (Italy)	ʃ – 6 (Italy)
℘ – 600 (Germany)	○ – 60 (Germany)	ʔ – 6 (Germany)

Modern Square Hebrew Fonts

Final Mem	Samek	Vav
ם – 600	ס – 60	ו – 6
ם – 600	ס – 60	ו – 6
ם – 600	ס – 60	ו – 6
ם – 600	ס – 60	ו – 6
ם – 600	ס – 60	ו – 6
ם – 600	ס – 60	ו – 6

It can be seen through the last 2,000 years of history that the Hebrew letters "Final Mem" ם and "Samek" ס since the time of the writing of Revelation have looked almost identical to one another, sometimes being used interchangeably in different areas of the world, switching them around between Jews writing them in Italy versus Spain or Germany or Asia. And these two Hebrew letters of Final Mem and Samek are also the only two Hebrew letters since the 1st century C.E. that have looked like the modern Arabic Numeral zero 0.

The Hebrew letter "Vav" ו has been almost completely unchanged during the last 2,000 years and is the only Hebrew letter during that time since the writing of the book of Revelation that has looked like the Arabic Numeral one 1. John says in Revelation 13:18 that the number of the Beast Out of the Sea has to be calculated or computed to find the complete number six hundred sixty-six, and when computing these three numbers in Hebrew letter numerals into a computer binary code, it becomes clear that the binary code itself is a repetition of these three Hebrew letter numerals six hundred (Final Mem) and sixty (Samek) and six (Vav) repeated over and over again, with the ability to use Final Mem or Samek (600 or 60) interchangeably for the Arabic Numeral 0 and using the Vav (6) for the Arabic Numeral 1, like this: 1 – ו | 0 – ס | 0 – ם

Many forget that the number of the Beast Out of the Sea is not three sixes in a row, it is not 6 6 6. The number of the Beast Out of the Sea is the three numbers 600 and 60 and 6, and when using the Hebrew letter numerals that John would have known and been familiar with when he wrote the book of Revelation, the modern computer binary code calculates to these three numbers 600 and 60 and 6 used over and over in continuous repetition. And QR codes are very simply the same computer binary code of zeros 0 and ones 1 made into a visible picture that a computer can read and calculate through a photographic lens, being able to read the information stored in the Quick Reference (QR) Code. Computer binary code itself is made up of the number of the Beast Out of the Sea, six hundred sixty-six, in both Ancient and Modern Hebrew letter numerals at its very core and foundation.

Solomon Who Asked for Wisdom Received Six Hundred Sixty-Six Talents of Gold Yearly:

1 Kings 10:14

Revelation 13:18

Word for Word Examination of Verses **1 Kings 10:14** and **Revelation 13:18** – Solomon, who asked Yahuweh/Yehovah for wisdom, according to 1 Kings 10 received six hundred sixty-six talents of gold as his yearly income. Then in Revelation 13:18 John once again mentions the word "wisdom" and the number "six hundred sixty-six" once again. The connection here is very simply showing that the number of the Beast Out of the Sea and its Mark are interconnected with economy and money and wealth. Like Solomon who asked for wisdom and then became very wealthy and corrupted and turned completely away from Yahuweh/Yehovah at the end of his life, with no record of him repenting and turning back ever, the number of the Beast Out of the Sea and the Mark are also connected with people turning to wealth and the world and away from Yahuweh/Yehovah.

The Mark is the outward sign of a person's choice for the world and wealth and power like Solomon, becoming corrupted with the world like Solomon to the point of losing Yahuweh/Yehovah in the end as Revelation 14 explains. Using the number of the Beast Out of the Sea and the Mark to gain entry to the marketplace for buying and selling there is a love of the world and danger leading toward the end of losing eternal life like Solomon may have lost his life because of his unrepentance. It is nothing to play around with or toy with. It is better to live like John the Immerser in the wilderness, who Yeshua himself calls the greatest person born of a woman who ever lived (Matthew 11:11).

The Mark of the Beast Out of the Sea Prophecies:
Revelation 13:16-18
Revelation 14:9-11
Revelation 20:4

Prophecy Fulfillment of Verses **Revelation 13:16-18** with examination of **Revelation 14:9-11** and **Revelation 20:4** – There are four major myths already earlier discussed about the Mark of the Beast Out of the Sea. The first and biggest myth is the myth of the Anti-Christ which is not found anywhere in prophecy, and especially not in the book of Revelation. Anyone can see for themselves that there is no Anti-Christ mentioned in Revelation 13 in connection with the Mark of the Beast Out of the Sea. John is very clear in his letters that Anti-Christs or Anti-Messiahs are former Christians who have left the body of believers to start their own religious sects that give false teachings about who Yeshua was, either that he was only a man and not the Messiah, or that Yeshua was the Messiah and did not come as a man. There is no mention or description of any person fitting John's definition of an Anti-Christ mentioned as being involved in any way with the Beast Out of the Sea or the Mark.

The second myth is the myth that there is a man whose name calculates to the number six hundred sixty-six. Anyone who reads Revelation 13 will see that there is no prophecy there about any man's name calculating to the number six hundred sixty-six or that anyone is supposed to calculate the name of any man. John very clearly says that the number of the Beast Out of the Sea is "the number of man" or "the number of a man," not the number of the <u>name</u> of any man, and makes no prophecy or indication that there is the name of any man involved at all. There is no prophecy anywhere in Scripture that says that we are supposed to calculate the name of any person and there is nowhere in Revelation that says that the number of the name of the Beast Out of the Sea is the name of a man. And as already shown at the beginning of the book, when looking at the way that John wrote this prophecy in the Greek he wrote it in such a way as to indicate that the correct understanding of the words is "the number of man" and not "the number of a man" as it is often translated.

The third myth as already discussed is that people get their heads chopped off for refusing to take the Mark. Anyone can read Revelation for themselves and see that there is nowhere that John prophesies about people getting their heads cut off for refusing the Mark. The only reason that John gives in Revelation 20:4 for believers in Yeshua getting their heads cut off is because of their witness of Yeshua and the Word of Yahuweh/Yehovah. This is the only reason and there is no other reason prophesied for believers being beheaded, which has certainly been happening and already fulfilled in recent years. There is nothing in the prophecies about the Mark of anyone being forced against their will to take the Mark. The only consequence for not taking it is purely and only economic, being shut out from going to market or being able to sell things as a vendor or trader out on the streets or in the marketplace.

The fourth myth is that there is a religious act of worship or allegiance to a cult religious group run by an Anti-Christ involved in taking the Mark, which is not true according to Scripture. Anyone can read the verses about the Mark for themselves and they will see that there is no one mention of anyone making an allegiance to a cult or religious group involved in the prophecy about the Mark. It is purely economic and the only consequence for not taking the Mark is the inability to go to the physical marketplace to trade and barter and buy and sell. There is nothing in the prophecy about anyone making any kind of outward religious act of worship in connection with the Mark. There is no prophecy in Revelation or Scripture about people taking the Mark being required to take any kind of oath of allegiance to anyone or anything or to be involved in any kind of religious organization or outward religious acts of worship. The idea that the Mark is connected with joining a cult religious group is a fiction that came from the imaginations of people's minds over the years, especially within the last 100 years, and is only a myth.

If the above imaginations of people's minds had been fulfilled then everyone would have recognized their imaginations being fulfilled right away, but instead the words of the prophecy about the Mark were fulfilled and nobody was ready for the prophecy itself to be fulfilled instead of their imaginations. If it were not for all of the above listed myths then every Christian believer in Yeshua in the world who had read the book of Revelation would be saying that the Mark of the Beast Out of the Sea has already happened and been fulfilled. Everyone is busy looking for the name of a man on the earth to calculate to the number six hundred sixty-six when there is no prophecy in Scripture about calculating the number of the name of any particular man, and everyone is watching for an Anti-Christ person to start a religious cult that requires the worshippers to take the Mark, instead of watching for a purely economic Mark that simply prevents people from going to market to buy things or sell things.

The Mark of the Beast Out of the Sea began in China in February 2020, not connected in any way with vaccines, and in fact China never nationally connected the Mark with vaccines at any time during its use. In February 2020 China began a mandatory use of the QR (Quick Reference) Code for all Chinese citizens or foreigners coming into the country. The QR code is basic computer binary code that, as has already been explained, contains the Hebrew letter numerals for 600 and 60 and 6 repeated over and over again in the digits 0 and 1, put into a two dimensional image that computers can read through a camera lens or picture. There is no other way to describe this two dimension image other than as a Mark, a Mark made by man with the number of man, six hundred sixty-six, at its core foundation.

This means that a person using this QR code is using not only the Mark of the Beast Out of the Sea, but also simultaneously the number of the name of the Beast Out of the Sea, the calculated/computed number six hundred sixty-six, in fulfillment of Revelation 13:17-18. And not only that, but in the QR code binary code every name and every word calculates to the number of the name of the Beast Out of the Sea, repeating the numbers 600 and 60 and 6 over and over again in every name that is recorded in that QR code image.

And because of the use of smart phones, this Mark became very convenient to use during the COVID pandemic plague. A person makes the Mark appear on the screen of their smart phone when using it, and as they hold the smart phone upon their hand, they are also clearly holding the Mark upon their hand, in fulfillment of Revelation 13:16-17 where a person has to literally "hold" the Mark "upon their right hand." Because most people (70% to 95%) are right handed they naturally hold their smart phone containing the Mark upon their hand, in their right hand most of the time. And the machines for reading the QR code Mark are made for right handed people, so that left handed people have to hold the Mark on their smart phone upon their right hand also in order to use the machines. But according to Revelation 14:9 either hand is fine to use for the mark, because John says, "or upon his hand," making no distinction about right or left hand. So a person can still hold the Mark upon their left hand or their right hand and still fulfill the prophecy of the Mark.

Anyone can look for themselves at the many videos and photos and images made from the years of COVID and see that the people using the Mark of the Beast Out of the Sea all held the Mark upon their hands, exactly as John describes in Revelation, fulfilling the prophecy word for word. John also writes that people can "hold" the Mark "upon their foreheads," and everyone constantly holds their smart phones, containing the Mark, up to their ears on the side of their forehead to talk on the phone or held up to their forehead in front of their face to take selfies and photographs. So everyone with the smart phones, containing the Mark on their phone, is constantly holding the Mark not only upon their hand, but also upon their forehead as well, in fulfillment of Revelation 13:16-17.

Where the Mark began in China, the Chinese government mandated that everyone in the country was required to hold this QR code Mark, in their possession, and shown upon their hand, in order to "go to market" or "purchase at market" or to be able to sell as a trader in the marketplace, in exact fulfillment of Revelation 13:16-17. No one was allowed into physical market places such as shops and stores of any kind, or places of business, or places to buy services such as restaurants and entertainment venues, or grocery stores or malls, or schools and places of education. Only those who were holding the Mark of the Beast Out of the Sea, which was also simultaneously the number of the name of the Beast Out of the Sea in the foundational binary code of the Mark, were allowed to go to market and to buy at market, or to be able to have their business open to sell their goods.

And every single person in China was required to be holding in possession of this Mark, from the lowliest to the highest in the nation, no matter whether they were poor or rich, or a free person or an employee/slave of the Communist government system in China. No one in China from any area of society or level of hierarchy in power and government were able to go to market to buy or to sell from their business unless they have the Mark of the Beast Out of the Sea, simultaneously being the number of the name of the Beast Out of the Sea, in fulfillment of Revelation 13:16-17. In China and a few other countries the Mark was so extreme that it was impossible for anyone to live in the cities without one. There were reports in the news of a man in China who was a wanted criminal trying to live on the streets without the Mark, and found it impossible to the point of facing starvation. In the end he turned himself in at a local police station to go to jail, and the prisons have turned out to be the only safe place from the Mark in China during its many years of use up to the present, other than the wilderness or miracles from Yahuweh/Yehovah.

China was only the place where the fulfillment of the prophecy of the Mark began. There were many other nations that the Mark spread to after February 2020, and in many of those nations they also allowed a person to hold a printed certificate with the QR code Mark printed on it and the name of the Beast with its number instead of just using the Mark alone as with the smart phones. The printed certificates were often Marks of the Beast Out of the Sea used for international travel to be able to gain access to going to the market and doing business in the economy and marketplace of other nations while traveling. These certificates were also used by people who did not have smart phones and generally contained the name of the person and the name of the nation that is joining together as part of the Beast Out of the Sea.

The beasts in Daniel through history have all had names like Babylon or Persia or Greece or Rome or Islam, but the final Beast Out of the Sea is made up of all of these previous beasts with all of their names and more added of all of the nations in the final beast. By carrying the name of the nation and its Mark of the Beast out of the Sea that it has implemented, a person was able to use the name of their nation as part of the international system of the Beast Out of the Sea to still be able to use their Mark in other countries across borders, using the name of the Beast Out of the Sea made up the names of many nations in league and unity together in the international system that have decided to be part of the Beast out of the Sea, in fulfillment of Revelation 13:17. The name of each person's individual country bore the authority backing up their Mark to be used in and accepted by other nations within the Beast Out of the Sea, because the names of each of those nations are parts of the total sum name and authority of the complete Beast Out of the Sea.

In the spring of 2020 the Mark began to be enforced in Moscow, Russia, once again having nothing to do with vaccines. It was done quietly with nothing ever officially being reported in any news media. It was only because people living in Moscow at that time reported on it in social media and through uploaded videos on the internet that there was even any way to know about it happening. Only those who had a QR code Mark held upon their hand were able to access the marketplace in many types of shops or to be able to go to work as employees. [It is interesting to note that the Ancient Hebrew word for servant/slave/worker is now used in Modern Hebrew to refer to employees, so that employees being required to take the Mark in order to go to work are also a part of the fulfillment of Revelation 13:16 of "slaves" having to take the Mark too.] The Mark lasted for a few months in Moscow during the spring of 2020 and then was not heard about anymore until they tried to bring it back again in late 2021 in connection with vaccines and was rejected by the majority of the population. But the Moscow population already had the opportunity to take the Mark before the vaccines were in existence, so it did not matter, because they had already all made their choices.

From there Singapore began to use the Mark in the fall of 2020, requiring everyone on every level of society to take it in order to access the physical marketplace, in order to go to market and buy things at all levels of business, or to sell or work in business. Even the homeless in Singapore were required to take the Mark, which shows just how much Revelation 13:16 was fulfilled with every level of society being given the Mark. Most nations also required children to receive the Mark in order to access public businesses and venues, but did not require the children to be vaccinated, such as Israel did.

Saudi Arabia was one of the most extreme in implementing the Mark, beginning around the late fall of 2020, once again not linked to vaccinations in any way. In Saudi Arabia people were not allowed to go anywhere in public without holding the Mark upon their hand in order to get access to any marketplace or business or educational building, including grocery stores as in China. And Saudi Arabia continued to be one of the most extreme with the Mark even after they linked vaccinations to it in late 2021. But everywhere around the world those who took the Mark were never forced to get vaccinated. There was always a choice of recovering from COVID or PCR testing included, because the Mark had nothing to do with vaccinations. It was all about making a choice for the Beast Out of the Sea world of mankind instead of Yahuweh/Yehovah.

England also started their Mark around the same time as Saudi Arabia in about November 2020. There were only a few reports in British news media about how people were unable to go shopping, to go to market to buy things, unless they had a QR code Mark that they carried with them showing a negative PCR test. Eventually England upgraded this QR code Mark to the NHS QR code Mark that added the extra choice of vaccines, and then Scotland and Wales and Northern Ireland created their own NHS Marks, Wales and Scotland being much more extreme in their restrictions to buying and selling in the marketplace than England.

But it was Israel adopting the Mark of the Beast Out of the Sea beginning on February 21, 2021 that convince the rest of the world that they needed the Mark too. It was Israel that led the way with their success at beating Yahuweh/Yehovah's COVID plague with the Mark of the Beast Out of the Sea that made them the poster child of the Mark convincing the rest of the world that they needed it too. In Israel the Mark was called Tav Yaroq תו ירוק, which literally translates as "Green Mark." In Israel they even called the QR code a "Mark" literally. Native Hebrew speakers at the time would constantly stumble over trying to say Tav Yaroq in English in the news and social media, because in English everyone called it the "Green Passport," but the Hebrew word Tav does not mean passport or pass in either ancient or modern Hebrew. It means "Mark" or "Label" but never passport, which caused native Hebrew speakers to stumble over the words Green Passport all the time, because they all knew that it was not called a passport. The sellers in Israel had to have the Tav Sagol תו סגול that literally means "Purple Mark."

In Israel the restrictions started light and eventually progressed to every area of public life, including restricting access to all public places of business: shops, stores, malls, public entertainment venues, restaurants, hair salons, swimming and recreation buildings, schools, colleges, universities, synagogues and public places of worship, all public transportation, and medical buildings except emergency hospitals and pharmacies. Grocery stores were the only thing exempt, but every single other area of the marketplace was restricted to only those holding the Mark of the Beast Out of the Sea upon their hands or foreheads with their smart phones, or certificates, in fulfillment of Revelation 13:16-17. And every person at every level of society from rich or poor, and slave (employee) or free, and from the highest to lowest levels of society were required to take the Mark to access the economy of the marketplace, to go to market to buy. Even every member of the Israel government took the Mark, including Prime Minister Benjamin Netanyahu releasing a video of himself showing his Mark of the Beast Out of the Sea that he was holding upon his hand, in fulfillment of Revelation 13:16.

Later on Israel changed the name of its Mark from "Green Mark" to haTav haSameach התו השמח, which literally means, "The Mark of Rejoicing" or "The Mark of Joyfulness." In English it was generally called "The Happy Pass," but the Hebrew word Tav does not mean "Pass" and the Hebrew word Sameach does not mean "Happy," even though this word is often used inaccurately in modern English translation for the purpose of helping English speakers better understand what is being said in Hebrew phrases sometimes. Israel even began rejoicing in the Mark, as an act of joy about the Mark of the Beast Out of the Sea, which is much like worship.

If it had not been for Israel the rest of the world probably would not have taken the Mark, except for those few countries that had already started using it in 2020. But Israel convinced the European Union and other countries around the world to follow along and implement the Mark too. In total there were all together about 56 nations, states, or cities around the world that implemented the Mark of the Beast out of the Sea during the years 2020 to 2022, as can be seen on the following chart. They had different levels of restrictions, some more extreme than others, but all of them restricted access in some form to being able to buy at the marketplace or sell goods as a trader, or to buy marketplace services from entertainment and sports venues and public transportation. Many of them additionally prevented people from accessing places of education or worship unless they had the Mark as well. But vaccines were never forced on anyone as part of the Mark in any of these countries except in rare cases like Austria.

Nation, State, or City	*Mark Implemented*	*Level of Restriction*	*Population in 2021*
1. **Israel**	21 February 2021	Extreme	8,789,000
2. **China**	February 2020	Extreme	1,451,768,000 *Includes Hong Kong*
3. **Moscow, Russia** *Possibly Other Cities*	Spring 2020	Medium	53,344,000
4. **Singapore**	Fall 2020	Extreme	5,896,000
5. **Saudi Arabia**	Fall 2020	Extreme	35,340,000
6. **England**	November 2020	Medium	56,530,000
7. **Eastern Australia** (Queensland, New South Wales, Victoria)	November 2020 *First in New South Wales*	Extreme	19,731,000
8. **Chile**	May 2021	Extreme	19,212,000
9. **United Arab Emirates**	15 June 2021	Extreme	9,991,000
European Union	----------------	----------------	----------------
10. **Austria**	1 July 2021	Extreme	9,043,000
11. **Belgium**	1 July 2021	Medium	11,632,000
12. **Bulgaria**	1 July 2021	Medium	6,896,000
13. **Croatia**	1 July 2021	Medium	4,081,000
14. **Cyprus**	1 July 2021	Medium	1,215,000
15. **Czech Republic**	1 July 2021	Medium	10,724,000
16. **Denmark**	February 2021	Extreme	5,813,000
17. **Estonia**	1 July 2021	Medium	1,325,000
18. **Finland**	1 July 2021	Medium	5,548,000
19. **France**	19 April 2021	Extreme	65,426,000
20. **Germany**	1 July 2021	Medium	83,900,000
21. **Greece**	May 2021	Extreme	10,370,000
22. **Hungary**	1 July 2021	Medium	9,634,000
23. **Ireland**	1 July 2021	Medium	4,982,000
24. **Italy**	1 July 2021	Medium	60,367,000
25. **Latvia**	1 July 2021	Medium	1,866,000
26. **Lithuania**	1 July 2021	Medium	2,689,000
27. **Luxembourg**	1 July 2021	Medium	634,000
28. **Malta**	1 July 2021	Medium	442,000
29. **Netherlands**	1 July 2021	Medium	17,173,000
30. **Poland**	1 July 2021	Medium	37,797,000
31. **Portugal**	1 July 2021	Medium	10,167,000

32. **Romania**	1 July 2021	Medium	19,127,000
33. **Slovakia**	1 July 2021	Medium	5,460,000
34. **Slovenia**	1 July 2021	Medium	2,078,000
35. **Spain**	1 July 2021	Medium	46,745,000
36. **Sweden**	1 July 2021	Medium	10,160,000
----------------	----------------	----------------	----------------
37. **Indonesia**	23 August 2021	Medium	276,361,000
38. **Kurdistan Region, Iraq**	August 2021	Minimal	5,000,000
39. **Azerbaijan**	1 September 2021	Extreme	10,223,000
40. **Switzerland**	September 2021	Medium	8,715,000
41. **South West Nigeria** (Edo and Ondo)	September 2021	Minimal	9,500,000
42. **Vatican City**	1 October 2021	Extreme	812
43. **Scotland**	1 October 2021	Extreme	5,480,000
44. **Wales**	11 October 2021	Extreme	3,105,000
45. **Northern Ireland**	13 December 2021	Medium	1,905,000
46. **Morocco**	21 October 2021	Extreme	37,344,000
47. **Taiwan**	25 October 2021	Medium	23,855,000
48. **Canada**	October 2021	Medium – Nationally Extreme – Quebec	38,067,000
49. **New Zealand**	29 November 2021	Extreme	4,860,000
50. **Lebanon**	Fall 2021	Medium	6,769,000
51. **Vietnam**	20 December 2021	Medium	98,168,000
United States of America	----------------	----------------	----------------
52. **New York State**	2 April 2021	Minimal – Statewide Extreme – New York City	19,835,000
53. **California State**	June 2021	Minimal – Statewide Medium – Los Angeles County Extreme – San Francisco	39,237,000
54. **Hawaii State**	10 September 2021	Minimal – Statewide Extreme – Honolulu City/County and Maui County	1,441,000
55. **New Orleans, Louisiana**	16 August 2021	Medium	998,000
56. **Chicago, Illinois**	December 2021	Medium	8,877,000
			Total = 2,705,635,812 ⅓ of Mankind

The total amount of population of the earth that came under restrictions of the Mark of the Beast out of the Sea in some form is about 2.7 billion people, which is 1/3 of the total population of the earth of about 7.9 billion to 8 billion people from the year 2021 to the present. This is 1/3 of mankind who lived in places where the Mark of the Beast Out of the Sea was available to anyone at any time who wanted it. Added to this are hundreds of millions or even a billion or two more people who potentially traveled into those areas at the time when the Mark was available and could choose to take the Mark as well. But it was 1/3 of mankind that had the Mark implemented where they lived.

And it was once again the Beast Out of the Earth compelling or causing people to take the Mark during the years it has been in use around the world since 2020, with the excuse that the Mark is for science to bring the global Beast Out of the Sea economy back to life again from the deadly wound, in fulfillment of Revelation 13:16. It was the technology and mankind's worship of technology as an idol that provided the way for the Mark to be able to happen in the first place, and then the base argument used for the Mark in all of the nations that implemented it was that everybody has to follow what "science" says to do about the COVID SARS virus variant pandemic. And the Mark was part of a scientific way of getting back to normal and getting the Beast Out of the Sea back to life again, only letting people not infected with the virus or vaccinated against it to be out in public places, scientifically preventing the spread of the virus by keeping track of infected and uninfected with a Mark.

And two of the main centers as already discussed for bringing together science and religion in the Beast Out of the Earth, Vatican City and the United Arab Emirates, were two of the strictest places in implementing the Mark of the Beast Out of the Sea. Everybody either living in or visiting those two nations were absolutely required to have the Mark at every level of society, to gain access to anything at all in those nations. This was by order of Pope Francis and the then de-facto ruler of the UAE, Mohammed bin Zayed Al Nahyan.

Out of the population of 2.7 billion people who were living in areas with the Mark being used, this included hundreds of millions of Christians living in those areas who had the potential chance of receiving the Mark. Unfortunately there are very few reports of Christians refusing the Mark in these places, but there are reports of Christians who Yahuweh/Yehovah supernaturally intervened for them to not have to receive the QR code Mark, even though they did not recognize it as the Mark. They still did not want to take it and Yahuweh/Yehovah made a way for them to continue working in places like Greece even though the Mark was required by law in their countries. It was mostly just a few Messianic Jews in Israel that recognized the Mark, and unfortunately the reports are that about half of the Messianic Jewish congregations of believers in Yeshua took the Mark of the Beast Out of the Sea. From the numbers of Israelis who were vaccinated, it is estimated that at least about six million to seven million Jewish and Arab Israelis potentially took the Mark of the Beast Out of the Sea, which in 2021 was almost the entire eight million population of the country.

This has put Israel in the worst spiritual situation it has ever been in in its entire history as a nation, even rivalling the really bad situation they were in when they were destroyed by the Babylonian and Assyrian Empires. But this is exactly what Yahuweh/Yehovah prophesied in Daniel 12:1 and Matthew 24:21, that the nation of Israel and all of the believers in Yeshua who are grafted into Israel would be in a unique time of Great Tribulation, a unique kind of spiritual tribulation putting Israel into the most dire situation it has ever been in in its history. And now we see that almost the entire nation of Israel has rejected Yahuweh/Yehovah and chosen the Beast Out of the Sea instead, the world. And many Christians went right along with Israel saying that this particular Mark was alright to take, because it did not happen according to their imaginations of the Mark. They were saying that it is OK to play with eternal fire and sulphur, potentially losing eternal life by taking this Mark.

But Yahuweh/Yehovah warns exactly the opposite that believers in Yeshua should not take any Mark at any time in history for the purpose of accessing the marketplace to buy and sell for any reason, no matter if a person thinks it is the Mark or not. If it fulfills every exact word of the prophecies of the Mark of the Beast Out of the Sea without anything missing, then it should not be touched, but everyone made their choices if they wanted the world or if they wanted Yahuweh/Yehovah. And this is the very first time in all of the thousands of years of recorded history that a Mark has ever been used upon people's hands and foreheads to give them access to go to market to buy and sell. And yet there is hardly anyone even talking about this historic event, that this has happened for the first time in thousands of years of earth history. In the past marks have been used on pieces of paper to control economies, but never a mark actually upon a person's hand as has just happened since 2020.

So far there have not been any reports about any of the hundreds of millions of Christians in China refusing the Mark. There probably were some, but so far there are no public reports in international languages that have come out about it. There were reports of Christians who went to China in 2020 and received the Mark of the Beast Out of the Sea there so that they could work as missionaries in China. Yahuweh/Yehovah exposed the hearts of many and showed how most Christians today around the world do not really listen to him and obey him, that they are doing what they want to do out of their own agendas.

The word that Yahuweh/Yehovah spoke through David Damien on December 29, 2018 at the sealing of the 144,000 turned out to be true, that Yahuweh/Yehovah needed to seal his people upon their foreheads ahead of time to protect them from the chip that was coming (that would contain the Mark of the Beast Out of the Sea). Only it turned out to be a chip that was upon people's hands in their smart phones containing the Mark instead of a chip inside of the hand, but Yahuweh/Yehovah had to seal his people ahead of time to protect them, because he knew that almost none of the Christians or Jewish people in Israel were going to recognize the Mark when it came. Almost all of Israel is lost now, and there are hardly any Christians who even care. Most of them deny that it ever even happened. And potentially hundreds of millions of Christians have been lost, and most Christians just ignore it as though reality is not there. There is no mourning or sadness or repentance, only a continuing on of "normal" life denying reality, which is exactly what Yeshua prophesied would happen in Matthew 22 where those who are invited to the wedding are too busy doing their "normal" everyday lives at the end of the Great Tribulation to be able to go.

Since 2020 there are many Christian ministries that began using the Mark of the Beast Out of the Sea, the QR codes, for donations to their ministries, which is once again money transactions and economy as is prophesied in Revelation 13:16-18 and is very borderline, big-time playing with fire. Instead of staying away from any Mark that is ever used for economic reasons and restrictions to the marketplace for buying and selling, they are inviting the Mark of the Beast Out of the Sea right into their ministries and lives, choosing the world and money and wealth over Yahuweh/Yehovah. Whenever a person scans that QR code, that Mark appears upon their hand as they are donating money to that ministry, very borderline to what is described in Revelation 13. It shows the deceiving of even the chosen (elect) happening as Yeshua prophesied would happen in the Great Tribulation, in Matthew 24 and Mark 13.

The Mark has not gone away even today in the present. Now people are embracing using it without having to have any government mandates. Businesses like Amazon through Whole Foods are on their own, without the government, doing trials of restricting people from entering their market without a Mark upon their right hand to be able to get in and shop in America in 2023. Since COVID the QR code Mark has become very popular around the world, boosting its use by large percentages. China has simply switched over its Mark of the Beast Out of the Sea to control the population completely unrelated to COVID now.

The world has already made its choices regarding the Mark of the Beast Out of the Sea. Even in countries where the Mark was not implemented, the people in those countries made their choices if they wanted it in their country or not. In polls about half of Americans wanted President Joseph Biden to nationally enforce the QR code Mark of the Beast Out of the Sea in America. Unfortunately the majority of the protests against the Mark around the world, which were extremely small, were based entirely on political reasons that had nothing to do with the spiritual reasons for not taking the Mark. But at least people were still making choices in their hearts and deciding before Yeshua returns at the end of the Great Tribulation if they want him or the world, if they want life or death as in Genesis 3.

Every part of this prophecy of the Mark of the Beast Out of the Sea has already been fulfilled in exact detail and there is nothing more or nothing new that needs to happen to make the prophecy more fulfilled. The events that have happened are already a complete fulfillment of the prophecy as it stands and everyone has already made their choices in the desires of their hearts if they want the Mark or not. This means that this prophecy never has to be fulfilled again in the future, and anyone wanting to wait for a better fulfillment more to their liking of how they want the prophecy to be fulfilled in their imagination might have a long wait. The Rabbis have been waiting for 2,000 years for Yahuweh/Yehovah to send them a Messiah that fulfills the prophecies in Scripture according to the way they want them to be fulfilled, and they are still waiting with no new Messiah come yet.

We can see now why Yahuweh/Yehovah included the prophecy about the Mark of the Beast Out of the Sea included in Revelation, because the nation of Israel would be one of the places where people would be in the greatest danger of receiving it. All of the prophecies in Scripture are Israel centered, because that land belongs to Yahuweh/Yehovah for his covenant. There were also other nations around the world that tried and had plans to implement the Mark in their countries too, such as in Ukraine, South Africa, South Korea, and Japan. But they failed to ever get the system of using the Mark up running internally within their own borders inside of their countries. The reason the Mark failed in Ukraine was because the corruption in the government there is so bad, most of the QR code Marks given out to international travelers were faked by government agents in exchange for money and bribes, so they never actually used it inside of their country.

Section 19. **The Deceiving of the Elect (the Chosen) and Their Refining:**

The Anti-Christs (Anti-Messiahs), of which there are No Prophecies, are Most Likely Among the False Prophets that Lead Astray and Deceive Even the Elect (the Chosen) During the Great Tribulation Trouble, Even Coming in the Name of Yeshua/Jesus:

Matthew 24:4-5

1 John 2:18-25; 4:1-5

2 John 1:7

Word for Word Examination of Verses **Matthew 24:4-5** and **1 John 2:18-25; 4:1-5** and **2 John 1:7** – As already discussed John gives no prophecies about the Anti-Christs in his teaching and description of what Anti-Christs are in 1 and 2 John. He only says that these Anti-Christs that are around in his day will continue to be around in the future, and that they are a sign that the last days of the last 2,000 years began in the 1st century C.E. John lays out very simply in three short sections the criteria of what an Anti-Christ is:

1. They go out from "us" (the Apostles or Body of Believers in Yeshua) and refuse to stay with "us" (the Apostles or Body of Believers in Yeshua), at one time part of the body of believers who leave to create their own Christian denominations and sects based on beliefs about Yeshua not found in Scripture.
2. They deny that Yeshua is the Messiah, denying that he is the Son of the Father and thereby denying both the Son and the Father Yahuweh/Yehovah.
3. Any spirit or person that does not confess Yeshua came in the flesh, in a physical body as a man, and leads others astray with this falsehood is the spirit of the Anti-Christ or the Anti-Christ, even if they still say that Yeshua is the Messiah.

From this criteria list giving the definition of an Anti-Christ we can see that Anti-Christs are not false messiahs. Anti-Christs do not claim to be a messiah, nor do they claim to be the Messiah Yeshua. They are false prophets and false teachers claiming to be followers of Yeshua, but lead people astray with false teachings about who Yeshua is as the Messiah. They create their own, separate Christian sects or denominations and lead astray Christians into following a false Jesus/Yeshua that contradicts the record in Scripture of the truth of who Yeshua really is.

There are many examples of such people through history who fit the definition of Anti-Christs, and there are many people and organizations in history who have been called Anti-Christs, but who do not fit John's description at all. According to Yeshua in Matthew 24 and Mark 13 it is not until the Great Tribulation that the Anti-Christs, as a part of the false prophets, are able together with the false messiahs to lead astray even the chosen/elect. It is one of the clear signs that Yeshua gives of the Great Tribulation, that the false prophets and false messiahs are able to deceive even the chosen/elect, which includes the Anti-Christs as part of that sign, when we see the Anti-Christs for the first time in 2,000 years are also able to deceive even the chosen/elect, where they were unable to do so before.

The Serpent in the Garden was the Original False Prophet, Deceiving the Man and Woman to Eat from the Fruit of the Knowledge of Good and Evil so that They could be Like God, Like Yahuweh/Yehovah:

Genesis 3:1-19

Examination of Verses **Genesis 3:1-19** – The very first false prophet leading men and women astray was the Serpent in the garden of Eden. The Serpent was a false prophet because he prophesied a false future to Adam and Chavvah (Eve) as to what would happen to them after they ate the fruit of the knowledge of good and evil. He prophesied that they would not die, which turned out to be a false prophecy, because they both died eventually. Moses also records in Genesis 3 the root of all deception, the root reason why a person is able to be deceived. The reason that Chavvah (Eve) believed the lie of the Serpent that she would not really die if she ate the fruit of the knowledge of good and evil is because she "desired" the fruit.

It is only when we "want" or "desire" something that we are able to be deceived, because then we are willing to believe anything in order to get that thing that we desire. The opposite of this is surrendering and letting go of the desire to Yahuweh/Yehovah for his "desire" or "will" to be done instead (Matthew 6:9-13; Luke 22:40-42). In the Great Tribulation when even the chosen/elect are deceived, it is no different from the root of how everyone is always deceived through time, it is because they desire something that they want to have and are willing to believe the deceptions in order to get the thing they want. And this root of desire that causes a person to stumble into deception all comes from simple pride, in thinking that we are smarter than Yahuweh/Yehovah and no better what is a good thing to desire for ourselves than he does.

Yahuweh/Yehovah Empowers the False Prophets and False Spirits with the Power to do Signs and Wonders in Order to Test the Hearts of His People; Those Who Fail the Test are Deceived by the Great Delusions of haSatan (the Adversary) and the Anti-Christ (Anti-Messiah) Spirits:

Deuteronomy 13:1-5

Isaiah 30:27-28

2 Thessalonians 2:9-12

1 John 4:1-6

Revelation 12:9

Word for Word Examination of Verses **Deuteronomy 13:1-5** and **Isaiah 30:27-28** and **2 Thessalonians 2:9-12** and **1 John 4:1-6** and **Revelation 12:9** – When a false prophet gives a true prophecy that comes true, but then entices people away from Yahuweh/Yehovah into deceptions, it is because Yahuweh/Yehovah is using that false prophet with prophecies that come true in order to test the hearts of his people, if they truly love him or not. This is what Moses explains in Deuteronomy 13, that Yahuweh/Yehovah empowers and uses false prophets and false messiahs to test the hearts of his followers, to find out if they love him or not, if they truly want to follow him or not.

Isaiah gives a prophecy from Yahuweh/Yehovah about this same concept, prophesying about his coming at the Time of the End when Yahuweh/Yehovah tests the hearts of all of the people on the earth in all of the nations with a "sieve of falsehood" and a "misleading bridle." This prophecy can be seen in fulfillment today as Yahuweh/Yehovah shakes all of the nations violently in his sieve, using the great deceptions in the world to test everyone's hearts to see if they truly want him or not. He is allowing the misleading of the bridle on the mouths of the people on the earth to turn them away into deceptions so that everyone on the earth can see their own hearts clearly and visibly as to whom they really want to serve and follow, the world or Yahuweh/Yehovah.

Paul continues this same concept in 2 Thessalonians, that only those who receive a love of the truth, a love of Yahuweh/Yehovah who is the truth, are able to be saved from the great delusions of haSatan, the Adversary. And Paul continues the same concept from Deuteronomy 13 that it is Yahuweh/Yehovah who sends the delusions from the false prophets and false messiahs, so that those who love unrighteousness and evil will believe the lies of the false prophets. Yahuweh/Yehovah empowers the false prophets with signs and wonders to convince people to believe and follow their lies. It is so that the hearts of the people can be tested with a true and real test as to whether or not they love the truth or love unrighteousness more, and when they choose wickedness and evil, then they can be righteously judged with true judgment based upon their deeds and actions that they themselves freely chose as they were sifted through the sieve of lies.

John explains in 1 John that it is simple to be able to tell who has received the Spirit of Truth, the Spirit of Yahuweh/Yehovah, or the spirit of the delusion, by listening to them speak. Anyone with worldly speech, speaking as those in the world speak, with an audience of worldly people listening to them, has received a spirit of delusion. They do not listen to those who speak of Yahuweh/Yehovah, but those who are of Yahuweh/Yehovah, know him and listen when anyone is speaking of him.

Yahuweh/Yehovah is the Only One Who Saves Us from Deceptions and Lies When We Cry Out to Him in Humility:
Psalms 43:1-5

Word for Word Examination of Verses **Psalms 43:1-5** – In the end it is impossible for any man or woman to save themselves from deceptions and delusions, because the flesh is weak and always has a weakness for one deception or another to believe it. Nobody can save themselves from the strong deceptions and delusions that come on the earth and look so good on the outside and are always smarter than we think we are. Yahuweh/Yehovah is the only one who can save anyone from deception and keep them safe from believing in lies. Only those who cry out to Yahuweh/Yehovah to send his truth and exposing light to lead them to Yahuweh/Yehovah's dwelling place on his mountain are able to be saved from falsehood, because only Yahuweh/Yehovah is smart enough to save anyone from their follies.

The harder we try in our flesh to save ourselves from lies, the greater danger we are in of being deceived, because then we become filled up with pride that we can save ourselves from deceptions and do not have to rely on Yahuweh/Yehovah to save us. The pride gets us in the end and causes us to fall into worse deceptions and delusions. In a person's striving to protect themselves from lies they build walls around themselves, thinking they can protect themselves, but instead they cause themselves to slowly wither and die without any ability to grow into greater and clearer truth. They stop in their growth and get stuck in believing the mixture of truth and lies they have accepted, unwilling to learn and grow and discover the lies they are still holding onto that they need to get rid of and the greater understanding of truth that they need to move forward to. They trap themselves in their own delusions (a delusion being a lie that a person believes and holds onto even when shown irrefutable evidence of the truth) because they want to be in control of their own life. And if they would only let go of the control, giving it over to Yahuweh/Yehovah to show them the truth, then they could be free of the deceptions they have trapped themselves into.

John the Immerser, the Greatest Man to have Ever been Born of Women, versus Solomon, the Wisest Man to have Ever Lived, Who Turned Away from Yahuweh/Yehovah in Complete Rebellion Against Him, Leading the Whole Nation of Israel Astray into Deceptions:

1 Kings 2:12 – 11:43

Matthew 3:1-14

Matthew 11:1-15

Word for Word Examination of Verses **1 Kings 2:12 – 11:43** and **Matthew 3:1-14** and **Matthew 11:1-15** – Solomon has given us the example of his life recorded primarily in 1 Kings as to why it is never a good idea to ask Yahuweh/Yehovah for wisdom. Solomon in all of his wisdom became extremely wealthy and powerful among the nations, and then filled with pride in thinking that he could fulfill his every desire and have anything he wanted. It was this pride and eating the fruit from the tree of the knowledge of good and evil that he desired, satisfying his desires and taking anything he wanted, that turned his heart completely away from Yahuweh/Yehovah. In the end he became the first king of Israel to bring the worship of false gods into the nation. There is no record that he ever repented and turned back to Yahuweh/Yehovah ever again after turning away from him to worship other gods, the gods of his foreign wives.

John the Immerser was exactly the opposite of Solomon in every way. John lived in the wilderness as a hobo and bum without a job or a house, living off the land as a wild man without owning any property. Solomon on the other hand had achieved the pinnacle of worldly greatness with the equivalent of the highest degrees of education and wisdom, and the position of the richest man on earth while being a king ruling a country at the same time. Solomon was a world celebrity loved by not only his own nation, but also by nations and kings all around him coming to hear him. By the world's standards no man or woman can achieve a position of greatness any higher than Solomon with wit and wisdom and wealth and vast amounts of property and hundreds of wives and probably hundreds or thousands of children as well.

And yet Yeshua said that it was his cousin John the Immerser who is the greatest person to have ever lived born of a woman. John gave up everything, even his life, to follow Yahuweh/Yehovah, including giving up the entire world. Solomon gained the whole world and lost Yahuweh/Yehovah, giving up nothing at all to follow him. There is no record that Solomon ever repented and very probably will not enter into eternal life at the resurrection. Solomon went right into all of the deceptions, falling into the worship of false gods and being completely turned away from Yahuweh/Yehovah, because he did not surrender his own desires to

Yahuweh/Yehovah for Yahuweh/Yehovah's much better desires of righteousness and justice. And so his pride in thinking he knew better than Yahuweh/Yehovah caused him to fall into the same lies that Chavvah (Eve) and Adam believed from the Serpent in the beginning.

John the Immerser, even though he had his doubts and uncertainties about Yeshua while he was in prison, did not fall for the deceptions and delusions of the world as Solomon did and was kept safe in Yahuweh/Yehovah. Complete surrender and trust in Yahuweh/Yehovah is the only place of safety from the lies and delusions; letting go of all control to let him be in complete control as the only one who is able to save. He gets us through his tests and sifting of deceptions he sends to the world, to save us through to the other side to be completely free in the truth afterwards, no lies able to hold us prisoner anymore.

The Believers in Yeshua and Elect (Chosen) in the Time of the End Who Love the World and have Friendship with the World are in the Most Danger of being Deceived and Losing Their Lives in the Great Tribulation:
Matthew 6:24-34
Matthew 16:24-27
Matthew 22:1-14   Luke 14:15-24
James 4:4 – 5:11
1 John 2:15-17

Word for Word Examination of Verses **Matthew 6:24-34** and **Matthew 16:24-27** and **Matthew 22:1-14** and **Luke 14:15-24** and **James 4:4 – 5:11** and **1 John 2:15-17** – In Matthew 6 Yeshua explains how a person cannot serve both God (El) and the world at the same time. In the original Hebrew Gospel of Matthew, in Yeshua's original Hebrew words, he actually says the word "world," not Mammon as it says in the Greek translation of Matthew. Matthew 6:24 in the Hebrew says, "In that time Yeshua said to His disciples, 'No man is able to serve two masters, unless he hates the one and loves the other, or he honors the one and despises the other. You are not able to serve El and the world.'"[38] If the world is our master that we love, then we cannot serve and love Yahuweh/Yehovah at the same time. And if we are serving Yahuweh/Yehovah as our master then we will hate the world and be unable to serve it.

It is for this very reason of being unable to serve two masters, both Yahuweh/Yehovah and the world at the same time, that Yeshua says to not worry about our lives or tomorrow, and not to worry about our provision of food and clothing and shelter. Yahuweh/Yehovah will provide us with all of the things that we need if we will serve him and seek his righteousness. We do not need to live in fear, going to the world in Egypt and Sodom and Mystery Babel for our provision and master, because Yahuweh/Yehovah will provide for us in the wilderness, like John the Immerser. Yeshua continues to talk about this same concept in Matthew 16 and 22, which is also recorded in Luke 14, that what good does it do for a man to gain the whole world, just to lose their eternal life in the end. And in the parable of the wedding, all of the believers in Yeshua, the Christians

---

[38] " בעת ההיא אמר יש״ו לתלמידיו לא יוכל איש לעבוד לשני אדונים כי אם האחד ישנא והא(חד) יאהב או לאחד יכבד ולאחד יבזה לא תוכלו לעבוד האל והעולם" *Even Bochan*, Shem Tov (1696 C.E. copy) Add. Ms. 26964; British Library, London.

around the world at the Time of the End, who are invited to the wedding are too busy chasing after all of their dreams in the world to go to the wedding when it is time.

Jacob continues the same concepts from Yeshua's teachings about the world in James 4, where he is in complete agreement with what Yeshua said in Matthew 6. Friendship with the world (a love of the world as your master) means being an enemy of Yahuweh/Yehovah (hating Yahuweh/Yehovah as your master). It is impossible to serve both Yahuweh/Yehovah and the world, to have them both as masters at the same time. Each person has to choose one or the other, friendship with Yahuweh/Yehovah, which means being an enemy of the world, or friendship with the world, which means being an enemy of Yahuweh/Yehovah.

And John continues this exact same concept also in 1 John 2, saying that no one should love the world at all, because if a person does love the world it means that the love of Yahuweh/Yehovah is not in them. The world will pass away, but those who do the will and desire of Yahuweh/Yehovah will never pass away. Jacob (in James 4 and 5) connects the love of the world and friendship with the world to the last days. He prophesies about all those in the last days who have laid up wealth and treasure, becoming rich in their love of the world. But all the wealth and riches will pass away and rot, and all that work of amassing the wealth will have been for nothing.

The warnings are all through Scripture to beware of following after and trying to gain the world with its pleasures and wealth, because it corrupts people's hearts and causes them to lose their lives in Yahuweh/Yehovah as Solomon lost his. It puts believers in Yeshua in danger of loving the world and making the world their friend and master, following after the Beast Out of the Sea and its Image and Mark that are of the world. It causes Christians to reject the invitation to go to the wedding because they are too busy with building their ministries and amassing wealth to live luxurious lives in the world system with private jets and mansions and fancy jewelry. Those are all things that pass away and will be destroyed one day; none of them are eternal or have any importance in eternity. The real treasure to seek after is Yahuweh/Yehovah himself and eternal life with him. He is priceless and it is worth giving up everything of the world here on earth to rush to the wedding to be with Yahuweh/Yehovah in eternity.

The deceptions and delusions always begin with desires of the heart, wanting something so badly we are willing to believe anything to get it, in our pride of thinking we know better than Yahuweh/Yehovah who created us. And the world is all about taking everything for ourselves that we want and making all our dreams come true, creating the perfect trap for any believer in Yeshua who is wanting to get all of those things of the world, wealth and power and prestige and fame. The deceptions of the false prophets and false messiahs in the Great Tribulation become extra dangerous to anyone who has friendship with or a love of the world.

Yeshua Said that There Would Always be Deceptions and Lies Mixed in with the Truth Among the Believers Until He Returns and Ends the World, but the Deceptions of the Great Tribulation are Unique in that Even the Elect (the Chosen) are Able to be Deceived for a Time, Times, and Half a Time, Which is Why the Time has to be Shortened:

Matthew 13:18-43

Matthew 24:22-24

Prophecy Fulfillment of Verses **Matthew 13:18-43** and **Matthew 24:22-24** – In the parable of the wheat and weeds that Yeshua uses to explain about the last days, he reveals the concept that from that time during his day until his return there will be good and bad mixed together in the field. There will be true believers in Yeshua and false believers who do not really want eternal life with Yeshua mixed together side by side for all of this time. It also means at the same time that there would be truth and lies mixed together among the congregations and body of believers in Yeshua until he returns, and that he would leave it that way until his coming when he sorts out all of the truth and lies for everybody and makes it all clear.

And this has certainly been the case for the last 2,000 years, as every congregation and denomination has some truth in it and some errors and lies. All of the different congregations and denominations have fought each other in the last 2,000 years saying that their group is the pure group that has only the truth and no errors or lies mixed in whatsoever, but the reality is that every single one of them have held doctrines that are anti-Scripture and against the Words of Yahuweh/Yehovah in Scripture in one form or another. Not one has ever been absolutely pure without some errors and lies mixed into their teachings and doctrinal beliefs. They all have adopted some things that do not line up with the Word of Yahuweh/Yehovah and are in error. And this has all been exactly as Yeshua has promised and prophesied it would be in the Matthew 13 parable.

But if Yeshua promised that there would always be some errors mixed in with the truth that all believers, even all of the "wheat" through history, would believe in, then what is he talking about in the time of the Great Tribulation when even the chosen/elect can be deceived? He promised that even the chosen/elect "wheat" would have some weeds of error mixed in among them that they believe in some false things, but in the past these are things that are not salvation issues. The errors that are mixed in with the truth that most Christians have believed through the last 2,000 years have not been errors that would cause a person to lose their salvation and eternal life with Yahuweh/Yehovah, and Yeshua says that he would leave weeds or tares among the body of believers until he returns to straighten everything out for everybody and burn away the errors along with the people who have been false believers, turning Christianity into a manmade religion based on how they want it to be.

What Yeshua is talking about during the Great Tribulation is not simple doctrinal errors in beliefs that have been around among all believers for 2,000 years and are unimportant for a person's salvation into eternal life. He is giving a much more serious warning about the false prophets and false messiahs in the Great Tribulation Trouble Distress, who are able to actually deceive Christians into false beliefs that cause them to turn away from Yahuweh/Yehovah and lose eternal life. They are not making Christians believe in little, unimportant doctrinal errors, but come with deceptions that even the chosen/elect are able to believe and fall into the trap of, that causes them to fall away from Yahuweh/Yehovah completely in the falling away. This is why Yeshua says that those days are reduced and shortened for the sake of the chosen/elect, because otherwise all flesh would not be saved, no flesh would still be saved at the end.

The Prophecies of the Great Tribulation Trouble Deceptions, which are able to Deceive Even the Elect (the Chosen):

Matthew 24:21-26   Mark 13:19-23

Revelation 13:11-18

Prophecy Fulfillment of Verses **Matthew 24:21-26** and **Mark 13:19-23** and **Revelation 13:11-18** – Everyone has made the assumption from Yeshua's words in Matthew 24 about the Great Tribulation that he was talking about physical tribulation. But the reality is that Yeshua does not make any mention at all about physical tribulation when he is describing specifically the time frame of the Great Tribulation. Before the Great Tribulation he describes physical tribulations and troubles of various kinds, such as war and earthquakes. But then after the Great Tribulation begins with the setting up of the Disgusting Idol Abomination, the only description he gives of the Great Tribulation is that there will be false prophets and false messiahs with deceptions so great it is possible for even the chosen/elect to be deceived. Spiritual tribulation is the only kind of tribulation that Yeshua describes during the Great Tribulation, not physical tribulation.

And the Disgusting Idol (Abomination) Desolating itself is also something that does not cause physical tribulation, it causes spiritual tribulation through spiritual deception. That is what abominations and disgusting objects of idolatry are all about, spiritual tribulation through spiritual deception. The false prophets and false messiahs are not causing persecution or physical tribulation to the chosen/elect in the Great Tribulation. They are not killing the chosen/elect, they are only deceiving them with powerful deceptions that Yeshua says to run from and not listen to them or believe them.

What we are watching today is the fulfillment of the type of spiritual tribulation trouble that Yeshua describes, with spiritual deceptions across Christianity and the body of believers in Yeshua around the world. Large numbers of Christians around the world since 2020 and the COVID pandemic have believed the deceptions of the Beast Out of the Earth and Beast Out of the Sea, going right into the love of the world and friendship with the world, into worshipping the Beast and its Image and either taking its Mark or saying that it is alright for people to take its Mark, or the Little Horn deceptions, as has already been earlier discussed. Even the chosen/elect have been deceived into many of these things already in the same way that the Pharisees and many of the Jewish people rejected Yeshua when he was on the earth, because they elevated their imaginations of the prophecies in Scripture above the words actually written in the prophecies. But there are also other deeper deceptions within the body of believers today beyond just the things happening with the Beasts.

The world has reached a state today with virtual media where no one can tell what is real and what is fake imagination anymore. There is great confusion within the congregations and body of believers around the world, being swayed one way and another way, nobody knowing what to believe anymore or what is true anymore. The whole world, including the whole body of followers of Yeshua are in a huge mess and in desperate need of Yahuweh/Yehovah to come and take over the rule of the earth, shepherding and teaching everyone directly to set everything straight again with clarity to the dividing line between truth and lies/imagination.

It is not like the older simpler days when Christians argued over unimportant doctrinal errors that had nothing to do with salvation, sometimes even going to war and killing each other over these unimportant differences. These are real deceptions that are causing people to leave their faith in Yeshua completely, leaving Christianity to follow after the modern religion of the culture or to follow a host of fake Jesuses/Yeshuas that look so close to the real thing that even the chosen/elect are being deceived by them. There are too many crazy and insane deceptions that people are believing around the world today to be able to list them all, because the deceptions are all tailor made to fit the desires of the hearts of each person who is trying to get what they want. But these are some examples of deceptions today that did not exist prior to the late 20th century in the highly deceptive form they are in now:

1. BE JESUS; BE LIKE JESUS; WHAT WOULD JESUS DO Deception: This deception started out innocently in the 1990's as a simple question that each person should ask themselves, "What Would Jesus Do?" in different circumstances and then copy and imitate him, based upon verses about imitating Messiah in 1 Corinthians 11:1 and imitating God in the same way a child imitates their parents. But it began to take Paul's words out of context and started to morph into focusing on Yeshua/Jesus as just a man, separate from being the God of Israel, Yahuweh/Yehovah. It began to turn into imitating Jesus to the point of becoming Jesus, or a Jesus, misrepresenting Paul's words to be "conformed to the image of His Son" in Romans 8:29.

There is nowhere in Scripture that says we should "Be Jesus" or even "Be Like Jesus," but it is a very subtle deception, because today everybody thinks that they need to be like Jesus on the earth and to become a Jesus on the earth. It switches over that fine line very rapidly into people thinking of Jesus as being just a man like other people, and anyone can imitate him and become him, to become an actual Jesus. Then from there it does not take much for a person to start thinking that they can "Be God" or "Be Like God," since Jesus is God himself, not just a man. And the only one in Scripture who says to "Be Like God" is the Serpent in Genesis 3, deceiving the man and the woman in the garden.

This is a deception that is only recently in the last few years becoming prevalent and tricking many people into thinking that they can become like gods, to become like Yahuweh/Yehovah, with the power like a god inside of them to Be God. Saying, "Be Like Jesus," is the same thing as saying, "Be Like God," because Yeshua/Jesus is God. But the focusing on the humanness of Yeshua/Jesus turning him into just a man, forgetting that he is the creator of the heavens and earth and Yahuweh/Yehovah the God of Abraham, Isaac, and Jacob, causes people to slip into the subtle deception where they begin to think they can become another Jesus, another God, too. And when people start thinking of themselves as being Jesuses or gods, they start to worship themselves as gods and lose Yahuweh/Yehovah in the process.

2. WEALTH AND PROSPERITY JESUS Deception: This deception started out innocently based on teachings in Scripture on the blessings of Yahuweh/Yehovah in the 1970's and 80's. But today it has turned into a belief system that if a person is not extremely wealthy and living according to the way the world tells us

to live in order to be happy, then it means that person does not have enough faith in Yeshua and they are not a true Christian. It has led people astray into living according to how the world tells people to live for happiness, instead of how Yahuweh/Yehovah says to live in Scripture to find true joy according to his standard of living. Yeshua explains this in Matthew 11:11 that there is no one born of women greater than John the Immerser, who lived completely dependent upon Yahuweh/Yehovah for all of his needs, with no dependency on the world or any of the wealth or prosperity of the world, separated from the world in the wilderness.

And this turning people to the wealth and prosperity of the world, exactly opposite of John the Immerser, has made the Wealth and Prosperity Gospel into a deception that turns people's hearts away from Yahuweh/Yehovah and living life according to his example of being set-apart and separated from the world, to total love and friendship with the world. This is exactly the deception that Jacob wrote the warning prophecy about in his letter in James 5, that those going after wealth and prosperity will find that they have nothing in the end when it all passes away. And Yeshua warns over and over again in the Good News that it is hard for rich and wealthy people to enter into eternal life in the reign of the heavens.

And yet today Yeshua's words are ignored and it has become a requirement for a believer in Yeshua to be showered with lots of riches and wealth as "blessings" of Yahuweh/Yehovah, or else there is something wrong with them and they are not a true Christian. It is really the exact opposite, because Yeshua says in parables and teachings all over the place, again and again, that it is a curse to have lots of wealth and riches beyond a person's basic needs, not a blessing, because it prevents the person from being able to enter into eternal life as they are holding onto and loving the world.

3. JESUS AND SATAN EQUAL-OPPOSING GODS OF GOOD AND EVIL Deception: This deception has been around for a very long time, but it is only recently that it has turned into a form that even the chosen/elect are falling for sometimes. It is very subtle, because the teaching throws out the book of Job as a part of Scripture and says that only good things come from Yeshua/Jesus, from God, and he will never allow anything bad to happen to anybody ever at any time, or cause anything bad to happen to anybody ever at any time. The teaching says that all bad things only come from haSatan, the Adversary, and whenever anything bad happens to someone then it can only be haSatan doing it.

This creates the position where Yeshua/Jesus is not powerful enough to prevent or stop haSatan from doing bad things to people, which means that he cannot be God over haSatan anymore. It elevates haSatan up to the position of equal power and strength as another god beside Yahuweh/Yehovah, able to do bad and evil things to people that are outside of the will and desire of Yahuweh/Yehovah. The only way that Yahuweh/Yehovah can be God is because everything that happens is happening because it is part of his will to either cause it to happen, or allow another person to cause it to happen. Otherwise he is no longer God.

The idea that there is a powerful god force for good and that is equal to an opposing and powerful god force for evil comes from the Pagan and polytheist religions around the world and is not found anywhere in Scripture. Instead Yahuweh/Yehovah says that he is the one who created evil and bad things into existence in Isaiah 45:5-7. It is because he is God and even though he is good, evil was only able to come into existence through his creating it into existence. Evil is not able to exist on its own strength and power and haSatan and the fallen messengers have no power as gods at all, only the power that Yahuweh/Yehovah gives to them and allows them to have. And Yahuweh/Yehovah himself brings "evil" or bad or destructive things upon people in his kindness and mercy of judgement and justice, over and over again through Scripture, or allows evil to be done to his righteous servants as part of the way he set things up in this world.

Saying that only good comes from Yahuweh/Yehovah and nothing bad ever comes from him, elevating haSatan as a god force that is equally as strong as Yahuweh/Yehovah, able to overcome him and defeat him to cause bad things to happen outside of the will and desire of Yahuweh/Yehovah, creates a system of worshipping haSatan as a god, along with many other gods like the Pagans do. And then it turns people's hearts away from the true God Yahuweh/Yehovah, to worship other gods and lose Yahuweh/Yehovah completely in the end if they do not get turned around again. Not everything bad that happens comes from Yahuweh/Yehovah, but he still allows those bad things to happen, when he could have stopped them and chooses not to, in order to bring about greater good from them in the end.

4. POLITICIAN JESUS Deception: It is a wonderful thing to have a righteous and good person ruling over a nation and its government. But Yeshua/Jesus is the only one perfectly righteous and worthy of ruling as king over any people or nation. All men and women will always fail, and it is Yeshua/Jesus who is the one who places every man and woman into their position of power to rule over the nations of the world. Every single person who has ever ruled over nations from the beginning of man creating governments over themselves has been placed there by Yahuweh/Yehovah, even the ones elected by the people, according to Daniel 4. Yahuweh/Yehovah never makes a mistake as to who he puts in to power in each nation, to bring good or evil upon the nation according to the hearts of the people, and he removes them as he decides to remove them.

The deception that has come is that Yeshua/Jesus needs Christians and believers on the earth to put in the correct politician to rule over a nation, because he is not strong enough or powerful enough to put into power the man or woman he has chosen. And it has caused people to be distracted into thinking that a powerful man or woman leading their nation is what they need to save them from having to go through bad things and hardships, because Yeshua/Jesus is not powerful enough to know when we need to go through good things or bad things in our lives, and protect us accordingly. Then it turns people's hearts away from wanting Yeshua/Jesus to come and rule and reign as the only king over the earth who is worthy to rule, and instead wanting to put all of their faith and trust in a fallible politician to reign over them.

This turns people's hearts away from Yahuweh/Yehovah to the world, focusing on the world instead of on him, and wanting this world to be heaven on earth instead of the New Heavens and New Earth. This is what made so many stumble and fall over President Donald Trump, wanting this world to be made into heaven, instead of wanting to leave this world to go be with Yahuweh/Yehovah in the New Heavens and New Earth. And anyone who goes back to listen to all of the prophecies given by the prophets at that time will find an interesting pattern. Consistently, right down the line, every single false prophet that gave a false prophecy that Donald Trump would be re-elected President of the United States of America in that election of 2020 also said in their exact same prophecy about Trump that Yeshua/Jesus will <u>not</u> be returning in the next 5 years or the next 10 years or the next 20 years or the next 25 years or the next 30 years or the next 50 years. Each of them gave a different amount of years between 5 and 50, most of them saying 10 years.

This should have been a big wake up to everybody, because when Donald Trump did not win the election those prophecies were exposed as false. And it became the very first time in the recorded history of the last 2,000 years that the false prophets were prophesying that Yeshua will <u>not</u> be returning in a certain time frame. Before in the past the false prophets were always exposed when they prophesied Yeshua's return at a certain time frame, but this time the false prophets were the ones prophesying that Yeshua will <u>not</u> be returning in a certain time frame, during the years 2020 to 2025, or the years 2020 to 2030, or the years 2020 to 2050, or the years 2020 to 2070, something that has never been seen before in the history of the world. Thankfully a few of the people who gave false prophecies at that time repented of what they did and really turned around their lives, but there were not many who repented unfortunately. And there were many of the chosen/elect deceived.

5. LOVER OF SIN JESUS Deception: The entering into covenant with Yeshua/Jesus is a wonderful thing, with a beautiful and incredible and incredibly painful process of being cleaned and washed of sin, made into a new and restored creation. Unfortunately within the last couple decades a new belief system has come into the body of believers that the real reason Yeshua/Jesus came and died in the crucifixion as the Passover Lamb sacrifice for sin is so that Christians can be set free from having to obey Yahuweh/Yehovah's commands and words in Scripture and are able to sin and live a life of rebellion with a love of the world and a love of their own flesh as much as they want to and still be able to enter into eternal life.

The whole point of the covenant that Yahuweh/Yehovah set up for people to enter into with him is so that they can make a choice if they want to live life according to his way of living, living set-apart together with him, or if they want to live life their own rebellious way as the world lives and would rather go to their second death in the lake of fire, where they get what they want, to not be with him in eternal life. But the teaching and belief system that a person can continue to sin and do whatever they want, rejecting the wonderful process of getting cleaned up from the sin over time and receiving a heart of love that wants to obey and do Yahuweh/Yehovah's commands in his Torah in fulfillment of Ezekiel 36 and Jeremiah 31, causes people to turn their hearts away from Yahuweh/Yehovah into loving the world and choosing the world instead of him. It leads people astray into the deceptions of the world very rapidly and easily, causing Christians to reject the wedding invitation when it comes.

6. BUILDER OF THE KINGDOM OF MAN JESUS Deception: This belief and teaching has been around for a very long time, well over 1,000 years, but only recently since about the 1990's or 2000's has turned into a deception that causes people to go astray. It is all about building a powerful religious kingdom for man to rule over on earth, but saying that the kingdom being built is for Yeshua/Jesus, even though it really is not for him, because he already has his own kingdom and reign that he is building separately. It puts all of the focus onto building physical buildings on the earth that will one day pass away, and building spiritually and financially successful ministries that follow the business models of the world to make their ministry culturally popular, turning people's hearts to the world and away from Yahuweh/Yehovah.

It is all about building spreading the Good News of Yeshua/Jesus for the purpose of creating a global religious system run by man, conquering the earth and making everybody and everything good on the earth like heaven. It is all about taking over the governments of nations to be run by Christians, and all of the businesses to be run by Christians, converting the whole world into Christians following the Christian religion that man has created separate from Scripture. Then when the whole world is Christian, following Christian-Judeo values, it will end all wars and bad things that happen, and the world will become a Christian empire ruled by man in the name of Yeshua/Jesus, but not ruled by him.

The deception is that it looks on the outside like Christians are building the Kingdom of God on earth, bringing the earth under his rule and dominion, but it is really not the reign of Yeshua/Jesus that is being brought. It is really the reign of fallible man with manmade religion taking control of the earth for their own rule and their own will to be done. But it is done in the guise of the Great Commission to bring the Good News to all the world. Yeshua never said anything about teaching and proclaiming the Good News across all the earth for the purpose of making the entire world Christian. It was only for the purpose of being a witness about him to all the nations, so that at the Time of the End everyone could make an honest choice for or against him. He never said anything about conquering nations and turning everybody into Christians, or making regions all Christian through revivals.

This deception once again causes believers in Yeshua to focus on the world and building the world that will pass away in fire as Isaiah prophesied and Peter referred to, instead of focusing on Yahuweh/Yehovah and his will, wanting him to come and rule over the earth. And it causes believers in Yeshua to become so busy building the religious Christian Kingdom of Man on earth, that they are too busy to accept the invitation to the wedding when it comes from the King.

During 2020 Yahuweh/Yehovah shut down the churches around the world with his COVID plague, especially the ones that are organizational in populated areas outside of rural and wilderness areas. (Those living in persecuted countries where they are not allowed to go to church were the safest from the abominations.) This was his kindness and mercy to warn and prepare his people in the churches to get out before March 2021 when the abominations of spiritual deceptions would set up among the religious institutions of the churches around the world. Those who listened and removed themselves from churches and religious institutions during that time were kept much safer from the abominations that began to be set up in the midst of Christianity worldwide.

Those who did not listen to Yahuweh/Yehovah and went back to church in the spring of 2021, or never stopped going to church, went straight into all of the various abominations of spiritual deceptions. And the reason for this is not because of the act itself of gathering together, because there is nothing wrong with the gathering of the believers together. The reason that going back specifically to the Church or the Synagogue gatherings again has become an open door to the spiritual deceptions and abominations causing desolation is because of the container or religious system that the Christians and believers in Yeshua are gathering inside of. It is the Church and Synagogue container, the Church and Synagogue religious system, that is the old corrupted container and system that anyone who remains in it is in very grave danger of the abominations causing desolation and deception in it.

It was alright before in the past when the wheat and the tares had to remain together for a while inside of the corrupted container of the Church and Synagogue, but now since COVID in 2020 Yahuweh/Yehovah is removing his people out of the old, corrupted container of the manmade religious systems of the Church and Synagogue, and anyone staying in that old religious system will fall for the abominations and spiritual deceptions of those abominations that have permeated the churches and synagogues of the believers today. It is not the act of gathering together that is wrong, but the gathering together inside of the corrupted, abomination filled religious system of the Church and Synagogue that has now become wrong and rebellion against Yahuweh/Yehovah since 2020.

Yahuweh/Yehovah removed himself as the continual, already discussed, that had been among the body of believers within the churches around the world, using the manmade religious structures of the churches in Christianity for the last 1,800 to 1,900 years to interact with people. But that time of using manmade Christian religion structure had come to an end, and he removed himself, as the continual, to move on into the new container (wineskin) of his family/nation/house of Israel, from all of the twelve tribes of Israel and gentile nations, who have entered into his Yeshua covenant with him. At the same time the abominations in the churches in recent years reached a new point where it had gone way beyond only error and mistake in belief that has nothing to do with salvation, but into the realm of true deceptions and abominations causing people to worship deceptive false gods in the old container of the churches, among even the chosen/elect.

This meant that Yahuweh/Yehovah has to remove himself from those places where the people have chosen to worship false gods and perform false worship. The abominations come in as Yahuweh/Yehovah removes himself out as already discussed from the example of Ezekiel 8. There have always been many abominations done in some churches or parts of Christianity since the Roman Empire tried to take over the control of the church at the Council of Nicaea in 325 C.E. But this was all part of the mixing of the weeds and wheat together in Matthew 13 that Yeshua promised would happen until his return and many in the midst of these things have still found eternal life with Yeshua as wheat in the midst of all of the weeds. Now the abominations of spiritual deceptions are overtaking all of the churches and places where Christians gather, even among the chosen/elect.

By removing everyone out of the churches for a year, it caused a clear moment of choice for each believer, to be able to see the abominations clearly if they wanted to, after seeing the opposite outside of the religious institutions of the churches. The great acceleration since the reopening of churches in 2021 of the acceptance of homosexuality and Lesbian, Gay, Bisexual, Transsexual, Queer, etc. lifestyles as being condoned and supported by Jesus/Yeshua is only one of the obvious twistings of truth into an abomination lie. For some countries like Australia and New Zealand, and to some extent Israel and a few other countries, people were required to take the Mark of the Beast Out of the Sea in 2021 in order to be able to go back to church again, which is a major abomination or spiritual deception they were accepting.

And many churches brought the Mark right into their ministries, completely deceived and taken in by it, even though they were using it in the same way as the Mark in commerce situations around the world. There were many pastors who said during that time that it is alright for Christians to get vaccinated for the purpose of receiving the QR codes if they need to use them to travel in countries that are enforcing them by law, the QR codes that happened at that time being a perfect word for word fulfillment of the Mark of the Beast Out of the Sea. Even many pastors, in fighting so hard to keep their churches open in 2020 to 2021, have also been completely taken in by the abominations and spiritual deceptions in the churches.

The big day that most Christians started coming back to church around the world in 2021 was for Easter Sunday, with big events done by many churches celebrating coming back again. Throughout that year more and more churches began coming back to life, or the churches that never closed began celebrating the overcoming of Yahuweh/Yehovah's plague without any of them having had to repent and change their lives. Some went to the Beast Out of the Sea and Beast Out of the Earth celebrating being saved by man and the Beast systems without having to go to Yahuweh/Yehovah and rely upon him at all. In most of the churches a big but subtle change could be seen in the way they conducted church, turning the services into purely entertainment performances for a religious and pious experience to entice people to come back to church again. A very clear shift with their worship and teachings into a worldly performance could be seen, bringing in the abominations of the world to get people to come to church again or gather in big church events again.

The churches under the spiritual deception that true Christians cannot have anything bad happen to them ever, or else there is something wrong with them as Christians, had to try to explain why such a bad thing would happen to shut down all of the churches around the world as with COVID. And so they had to go even deeper into the abominations of spiritual deception to try to explain it away and get people to continue listening to the wealth and prosperity gospel. One thing that could be seen very clearly was that Yahuweh/Yehovah was not there in the midst of the people in the churches anymore. He was the one really big thing missing, creating a giant empty hole in the congregations of people. There was still the religious church experience that people were used to, but there was no Yahuweh/Yehovah there in it anymore. And no one realized that the false messiahs coming in the name of Jesus could simply be characters of Jesus (not the actors themselves but just the Jesus characters) portrayed fictionally on television and internet, deceiving even "The Chosen" into following a Jesus that promotes the message to "Be Like Jesus" or to "Be Jesus/Be God," among other common deceptions today.

We are living in the days of the fulfillment of Yeshua's prophecy about the Great Tribulation, that even the chosen/elect would be able to be deceived. Those deceptions are all over the place now today, leading astray even the most ardent and on-fire believers, because the deceptions feed into that ardency to distract with the world and take the believer's focus away from Yahuweh/Yehovah. The deceptions make people want to stay in the old container (wineskin) and keep building this world, instead of wanting to leave the old here in this world to move on to the new container that Yahuweh/Yehovah has been preparing since the creation of the heavens and the earth in the beginning, the eternal container of his nation/family/house of people in the New Heavens and New Earth. But most Christians will have to see the spiritual deceptions for themselves, trusting in Yahuweh/Yehovah, because the deceptions and delusions are so strong and so subtle right now, portraying a false lamb as the one who takes away sin as happened in Israel in 2021, no one can see the deceptions without Yahuweh/Yehovah's help.

The Prophecies of the Refining of the Elect/Chosen in the Great Tribulation Trouble:

Daniel 12:1, 10

Revelation 3:10

Revelation 7:9-17

Prophecy Fulfillment of Verses **Daniel 12:1, 10** and **Revelation 3:10** and **Revelation 7:9-17** – The Great Tribulation is for the believer and the Wrath is for the unbeliever. The Great Tribulation is not for the unbelievers to experience or go through; it is for the believers only, in the same way that the Wrath is only for the unbelievers to go through and not the believers. In Daniel 12 Yahuweh/Yehovah reveals that the Great Tribulation Trouble upon Israel, all of his people who are his followers, at the Time of the End results in many being cleansed, refined, and made white.

This same concept from Daniel is prophesied again even more specifically that those whose robes are washed clean and white in the blood of the Lamb are the ones coming out of the Great Tribulation. The purpose of the Great Tribulation is for the cleansing and the making white in righteousness of the set-apart ones, the believers and followers of the Lamb Yeshua. The Great Tribulation is specifically for those who are followers of the Lamb Yeshua for them to be washed clean and white through the Great Tribulation, and not for the unbelievers who have chosen to not be made clean by Yeshua. Those who reject the cleansing of the Great Tribulation have chosen to go through the Wrath of Yahuweh/Yehovah that comes later on at his coming.

In Revelation 3 Yeshua says that those who guard his Word of endurance are saved from the one hour of trial that comes upon the whole world, which is different from the Great Tribulation or the Wrath, because it is a trial for the whole world, not for any specific group. This trial is the testing that Yahuweh/Yehovah does for people all through history so that everyone can make clear choices in the trial if they want Yahuweh/Yehovah or not; if they want life or death. But that test for people to choose life or death has to come in a very short span of time during the Great Tribulation for everybody all at once, so that everyone can make that final decision before Yahuweh/Yehovah comes to rule the earth and set up his reign. Those who have already made a clear choice for Yahuweh/Yehovah, guarding that Word of endurance to stay with him through anything that comes, are guarded (not saved) from the hour of trial on the whole world, being kept safe in the midst of it.

The Great Tribulation that Yeshua prophesies about in Matthew 24 and Mark 13, which he only describes as spiritual tribulation, not physical tribulation, is a good thing. Daniel 12 and Revelation 7 reveal the reason why Yahuweh/Yehovah has set it up that way to put his people through the Great Tribulation at the end, so that they will be washed clean and made white of all of the sin and be ready for his coming to be able to enter into eternal life with him. It is a great hope as we watch the chosen/elect being deceived in Great Spiritual Tribulation, because it is humbling everyone, cleansing them and washing them, getting their wedding garments made white and ready for the wedding and marriage covenant that is coming. It is also separating the sheep from the goats, the wheat from the weeds, as we enter into the final harvest of the earth, the final harvest that harvests both the good and bad simultaneously together.

The Great Spiritual Tribulation bringing a crisis of faith and a shaking of their houses they have built on sand is causing those who are the true remnant to stop their lives and the destructive direction they were going toward, toward loving the world, to instead become more set-apart with Yahuweh/Yehovah and isolated from the world. It was simple pride that the Christians around the world thought that they could get out of going through the Great Tribulation by already being perfect and clean and white, but these recent years since 2020 has exposed that there are really no Christians on the earth today who are clean enough and made white enough yet to be ready to be caught up into the air to be with Yeshua at his coming and go to the wedding. As Yeshua says in the parable in Matthew 22 that those who do not have clean and white wedding garments will not go into the wedding and into eternal life in covenant with him.

And so that is why Yahuweh/Yehovah has to take all of the Christians around the world today through the Great Tribulation now in order for them to be made white and clean enough to be able to get into the wedding, when they would not have been able to otherwise and might have lost their eternal lives. The Great Spiritual Tribulation that Yahuweh/Yehovah has brought upon the body of believers around the world today is his kindness to cleanse and purify them through fire, making them clean and white, washed in the blood of the Lamb, truly saved and repentant. It is Yahuweh/Yehovah's Great Spiritual Tribulation that is saving his remnant from death, not destroying them, in the end. We are watching the process of the fulfillment of these prophecies happening right now in the time we are living in, with many being cleansed and refined in fire around the world.

The Set-Apart Ones (the Elect/Chosen) have to be Worn Out and Overcome for a Time, Times, and Half a Time During the Great Tribulation Trouble:
    Daniel 7:20-22, 24-25
    Daniel 8:10-13
    Daniel 12:7
    Revelation 12:10-11
    Revelation 13:5-7
    Revelation 15:2-4
    Revelation 17:12-14

Prophecy Fulfillment of Verses **Daniel 7:20-22, 24-25** and **Daniel 8:10-13** and **Daniel 12:7** and **Revelation 12:10-11** and **Revelation 13:5-7** and **Revelation 15:2-4** and **Revelation 17:12-14** – The same concept as the cleansing of the chosen/elect, the set-apart ones, is continued in another way with their being overcome and worn out. Already Christians around the world, the true believers and remnant, are becoming cleaner and more set-apart, more isolated, from the world, because of this overcoming and being worn out. Many believers are going through great sickness and disease, chronic illnesses and strokes, that are weakening their bodies and flesh, helping them to separate from the world and stay isolated with Yahuweh/Yehovah, focused on him. For others it is being put in prison that is cutting them off and setting them apart from the world, to be alone with Yahuweh/Yehovah and focused on him. Yahuweh/Yehovah has many different ways of cutting his people off from the world, to make them set-apart with him, including allowing the world systems with the Beast Out of the Sea, the Beast Out of the Earth, Mystery Babel and the Image of the Beast Out of the Sea, and the Little Horn and Ten Horns, to overcome and defeat his people, forcing them out of society into isolation in the wilderness with him, like with John the Immerser.

Yahuweh/Yehovah's people have to be overcome as part of the Great Spiritual Tribulation, overcome spiritually and by the deceptions of the world, totally spiritually destroyed, so that Yahuweh/Yehovah can separate them from the world, make them clean, and take them out of the old container of manmade religion in the Churches to go into his new container of Israel in the New Heavens and New Earth. Yahuweh/Yehovah's true remnant of believers have to be made dead in the grave for a Time, Times, and Half a Time, for 3 ½ years, in the same way that Yeshua was in the grave for 3 days and 3 nights.

As already shown earlier, for the most part the set-apart ones are currently completely overcome and defeated by the Beast Out of the Sea and its Image and its Mark and the number of its name, deceived into thinking that what is in existence today is only a precursor or preparation of what is to come in the future and denying that it already exists right now, to the point of even supporting the Beast Out of the Sea in some cases by supporting the use of its Mark or other systems already mentioned in previous sections. And many of the set-apart ones are completely taken in by Mohammed bin Zayed and the Abraham Accords and the Abrahamic Family House and the Document of Human Fraternity, not even acknowledging what has really happened with any of it and calling it good in some cases. All of that has already been discussed, but in the end the Lamb Yeshua is the one who truly overcomes and defeats all of the Beast Out of the Sea and Ten Horns and Little Horn. None of it has any power except for what Yeshua allows it to have, and eventually at the appointed time he ends it all, along with the whole world of man.

But in many cases the overcoming that the set-apart ones are experiencing around the world today is actually Yahuweh/Yehovah protecting them from the Beast and all of its parts, and from loving the world and being friends with the world. The ones he is taking out of ministry through prison or disease or chronic illness or scandal, or even taking them home through death, are the ones he is protecting and the ones who have been kept the safest from all of the deceptions through the last few years. According to Revelation 12 and 15, those who in the end do overcome the Dragon and the Beast Out of the Sea and its Image and its Mark and the number of its Name, are those who hold to the Word of their witness of Yeshua and do not love their lives unto death.

The ones overcoming right now, even if they do not recognize that the Beast Out of the Sea and its Mark and its Image are already here overcoming everyone, are those who stay close to Yahuweh/Yehovah and do not love their lives here in this world, but are ready to die to hold onto their set-apart life with Yahuweh/Yehovah that is separate from the world. There are some who are still overcoming the Dragon and Beast in the midst of being overcome by them, by overcoming in their personal lives with the simple choices of standing with Yahuweh/Yehovah and separating from the world no matter what. The body of believers in Yeshua during the Great Tribulation is not the strongest generation of Christians that has ever lived, it is the weakest and most overcome generation of followers of Yahuweh/Yehovah that has ever lived, like the condition of the body of Yeshua today.

The body of believers is in a greater mess today than at any other time in history, with so many contradicting beliefs and so much confusion that nobody knows what to believe, or who to trust, or what is real or fake anymore. And the culture has completely overcome the congregations like a tsunami, overtaking and eating away at everyone's faith in Yeshua and the Word of Yahuweh/Yehovah in Scripture that has been almost completely thrown out now. Even in Texas where the state legislature tried and failed to bring back the Ten Words or Ten Commands into schools, they have completely changed around the words in the commands, compromising the original words so that the words would only apply to Christians and not apply to people of other religions, so that people of other religions such as the Atheist religion would not be offended by thinking that they have to obey the Ten Commands too. Christianity has already been defeated and overcome, compromised with the world in prostitution and whoring, with very few Christians who believe in Scripture as the Word of Yahuweh/Yehovah anymore. It is only in isolated, wilderness areas or areas of great persecution that the believers in Yeshua are still doing well spiritually, set-apart and separated from the world as those who are in illness or prison or being pushed out of society and church.

Section 20. **The Shepherds (Pastors/Religious Leaders) Removed to Make Way for Only One Shepherd, Yeshua, to Shepherd His People:**

The End Time Shepherd Prophecies, When the Earthly Shepherds (Pastors/Religious Leaders) of Men are Removed to Make Way for Yeshua, the Messiah Descendant of David, to Shepherd His People and the Nations, at His Return:

Ezekiel 34:1-31

Micah 5:1-4

Zechariah 10:2-5

Psalms 2:1-12

Matthew 25:31-46

Revelation 12:1-6

Revelation 19:11-15

Word for Word Prophecy Examination of Partially Fulfilled, Fulfilled, and Unfulfilled Verses **Ezekiel 34:1-31** and **Micah 5:1-4** and **Zechariah 10:2-5** and **Psalms 2:1-12** and **Matthew 25:31-46** and **Revelation 12:1-6** and **Revelation 19:11-15** – Ezekiel 34 and Zechariah 10 are the two prophecies about the Time of the End when the shepherds (pastors) are removed and judged in preparation for Yeshua's coming to the be one and only shepherd of his followers. Micah 5, Psalms 2, and Revelation 12 and 19 referencing Psalms 2 are the prophecies about Yeshua, as the Messiah, will shepherd his followers and nation of people, as well as shepherding all of the nations of the earth with a rod of iron as ruler over the earth. And Matthew 25 is Yeshua telling the parable about his separating the sheep and the goats, which he references from the prophecy in Ezekiel 34.

The Micah, Psalms and Revelation prophecies, together with the parable prophecy of Matthew 25, will not be fulfilled until Yeshua returns and becomes the one and only shepherd over all of his nation Israel, including his gentile followers who are grafted into Israel, as the Messiah descendant of David. These prophecies simply show and explain the reasoning in Ezekiel 34 as to why Yeshua is removing all of the shepherds (pastors and rabbis and religious leaders) of the earth in preparation for his coming to be the only shepherd over his flock of people. The fulfillment of Zechariah 10:2-4 has already been at the beginning of this book that talks specifically about the shepherds of Yehudah, of only the Rabbis and religious leaders over the Jewish people, at the Time of the End in the time of the latter rain. But Ezekiel 34 is different, because it deals with all of the shepherds of the nation of Israel, including the gentiles who have been grafted into Israel (Romans 11), meaning all of the shepherds or religious leaders of all of the followers of Yeshua in the earth. Yeshua has to remove all of them from positions over his flock of his followers in order to prepare the way for his becoming the only shepherd who will ever again be over his flock for all eternity.

For those who do not already know, the word "Pastor" means "Shepherd" originally. When the word "pastor" was first applied to religious leaders they were purposely being called "shepherds." Everywhere that the word "shepherd" is used in Scripture to refer to a leader, it is talking about a spiritual leader, including in

Ezekiel 34. According to Ezekiel 34:31 Yahuweh/Yehovah makes sure that everyone understands clearly the flock and sheep he is referring to in the prophecy are "men" or "people." And the shepherds are the men or people who are religious leaders leading his flock in the Time of the End at his coming when he separates the sheep and the goats (in Ezekiel 34:17-22 and Matthew 25:31-32). When we look at the shepherds today, not only the Rabbis among the Orthodox Jewish communities, but also all of the religious leaders in Christianity including Rabbis, Pastors, Bishops, Priests, Chaplains, Vicars, Deacons, Preachers, and Presbyters, the very large majority fit the description of Ezekiel 34.

There are still small numbers of Christian shepherds who are doing their job faithfully as Yahuweh/Yehovah has called them, but most of the shepherds, the religious leaders who hold specific titles and office, across all Christian denominations globally today are only feeding themselves and not the sheep, in fulfillment of Ezekiel 34:2-3. Most of the shepherds today are only concerned with building up themselves and their own image and status in the world and society. They are eating all of the fat from the choice of the sheep, taking their wool to wear, but not feeding the flock at all. They are taking in large amounts of tithes and offerings and donations, becoming very rich and wealthy and fattened, taking all of the choice provision from the sheep. And in exchange they feed the sheep nothing at all, only giving them false teachings that have no basis in Scripture, twisting the Scriptures and leading astray the sheep, in fulfillment of Ezekiel 34:3. They give the sheep only errors and withhold the truth, so that the sheep have no food or sustenance at all from the Word of Yahuweh/Yehovah.

Most of the shepherds today do not help those in need, they do not help the weak to strengthen them again or heal the sick or bind up the wounds of the broken, or go out to seek the lost and straying sheep out in the world. They stay in their buildings and tell everyone to come to church, but they do not go outside of their churches to help the strayed sheep who are outside of the church or unable to go to church. Those that are sick and weak they leave to die outside of the church, because they are unwilling to go help them if they are not inside of the pasture of the church building, in fulfillment of Ezekiel 34:4. And they do not go out to help those who have strayed and are lost out in the world, because they only want sheep coming in to them to bring in more money and prestige, in fulfillment of Ezekiel 34:4.

The shepherds rule over the sheep by being strong and harsh against them, condemning the sheep for not coming to church to keep them in their jobs as shepherds, but refusing to go out and help the sheep in their daily lives, in fulfillment of Ezekiel 34:4. And because of the shepherds taking all of the food for themselves and leaving nothing for the sheep, it has caused the sheep to be scattered out into the world, being forced to have to stay outside of the pastures of the assembly places in the churches, where the sheep have been devoured as food for the living creatures of the field, in fulfillment of Ezekiel 34:5. The sheep have been scattered all over because of the shepherds who have not taken care of them, but instead have only taken care of their own selves, with no one going out searching for Yahuweh/Yehovah's wandering sheep, in fulfillment of Ezekiel 34:6.

It is because of this, in Ezekiel 34:7-9, that Yahuweh/Yehovah is against the shepherds, all of the religious leaders in Christianity, who have all been grafted into Israel. It is not only the Rabbis in Orthodox Judaism that Yahuweh/Yehovah is talking about here, but all believers in Yeshua who have become part of Israel through his covenant. And during the COVID-19 plague that Yahuweh/Yehovah brought upon the world, beginning in 2020, he began to deal with the shepherds and to separate the shepherds from his sheep, beginning the deliverance of his sheep from the devouring mouths of the shepherds in Christianity, in fulfillment of Ezekiel 34:10. The plague caused churches to be shut down and people stopped going to the churches and the shepherds ruling the churches, being separated from the shepherds. There were many shepherds who died of COVID in the plague, trying to keep their churches open and running, but it was because Yeshua was beginning to remove the shepherds from being the ones feeding his sheep, the ones who were really devouring his sheep, to prepare for himself as the descendant of David to be their one and only shepherd, in Ezekiel 34:23. During 2020 and 2021 Yahuweh/Yehovah began taking the sheep away from the shepherds and removing the shepherds from over the sheep by isolating them from each other, as he prophesied he would be doing at the time of his coming in Ezekiel 34:10.

Not all of the shepherds of the churches around the world are in rebellion against Yahuweh/Yehovah and not all of them are being judged, but they all still have to step down and remove themselves from the positions of spiritual leaders in these days in preparation for Yeshua to be their "one" shepherd and only one. Since 2020 Yahuweh/Yehovah has been dealing with the shepherds and going through the process of removing them from his sheep in fulfillment of Ezekiel 34:10, exposing scandals and sin in their lives that they do not repent of, or dealing with their churches and organizations by using betrayers or divisions within the organization to shake up the church or ministry. (The scandal at the International House of Prayer in Kansas City is a prime example of Yahuweh/Yehovah removing and dealing with the shepherds right now for their devouring of the sheep.) And it is a good sign when Yahuweh/Yehovah is dealing with a church or ministry and its people like that, because it means that there is hope of them being saved out of the trap of the love of the world and the spiritual deception abominations they are in.

The first part of this prophecy in Ezekiel 34 is in fulfillment now as it needs to be in preparation for the rest of the chapter, and the other prophecies about Yeshua coming as the shepherd, to be fulfilled later on at his coming. The shepherds who are refusing to submit and surrender to Yahuweh/Yehovah, refusing to let go their control over Yahuweh/Yehovah's sheep and to step out of the way to make way for the "one" and only shepherd Yeshua, will be forcefully removed by him as Ezekiel 34:10 is in process of being fulfilled today. And then Yahuweh/Yehovah himself will be the shepherd seeking out his own sheep and delivering them in the day of clouds and thick darkness, the day of his coming, in Ezekiel 34:11-12

Section 21. **The Final Great Harvest of All the Earth and Yahuweh/Yehovah Pouring Out His Spirit on All Flesh:**

The Final End Time Revival During the Great Tribulation is Yahuweh/Yehovah's Destruction of the Church (the Old Temple), as He Leaves the Old Container Corrupted by Manmade Religion to Build the New Container of His Nation of People Who will Inhabit the New Heavens and New Earth [in the Same Way He Left the Old Temple Container and Called Out His People to Come with Him into the New Container When He Came as Yeshua; in the Same Way He Called His People Out of Egypt to Follow Him into the Wilderness When He Came on Mount Sinai; in the Same Way He Called Abraham Out of His Land Away from His Family to Wander Without a Home and be Made into a Great Nation]:

Genesis 12:1 – 25:10

Exodus 3:1 – 20:18

Ezekiel 34:1-31

Hosea 2:13-23

Zechariah 10:1-3

Matthew 9:15-17   Mark 2:19-22

Matthew 13:24-58

Matthew 22:1-14   Luke 14:15-24

Matthew 25:31-46

Acts 1:1 – 2:47

Revelation 19:1-10

Examination of Verses **Genesis 12:1 – 25:10** and **Exodus 3:1 – 20:18** and **Ezekiel 34:1-31** and **Hosea 2:13-23** and **Zechariah 10:1-3** and **Matthew 9:15-17** and **Mark 2:19-22** and **Matthew 13:24-58** and **Matthew 22:1-14** and **Luke 14:15-24** and **Matthew 25:31-46** and **Acts 1:1 – 2:47** and **Revelation 19:1-10** – Each time that Yahuweh/Yehovah makes another step in his covenant with mankind on the earth, there is always a leaving behind of the old ways of man to come into greater completeness in Yahuweh/Yehovah's ways. Yahuweh/Yehovah's calling out of Abraham from his family and from his homeland in Ur Kasdim to become a nation meant leaving the old container and systems of the world of man that Abraham was used to.

Abraham was not the only one on earth at that time who worshipped and followed the God Yahuweh/Yehovah, when Yahuweh/Yehovah called him out from the world to begin a covenant nation as the first Ivri or Hebrew. There were many others who worshipped the Most High God Yahuweh/Yehovah, including apparently an entire town in what was then Kena'an (Canaan), called Shalem, in Genesis 14. This town Shalem later became the city of Yerushalayim (Jerusalem), and the king of Shalem, named Malki Tsedeq, meaning King of Righteousness, was also simultaneously the high priest and king of Shalem. This Malki Tsedeq (Melchizedek) gave a blessing to Abraham after Abraham's victory in battle, and then Abraham gave Malki Tsedeq a tenth of all the spoils.

Abraham was a gentile like all the other gentiles of the nations at that time, but he had to leave the old ways, including leaving the old ways that he knew of for worshipping and following Yahuweh/Yehovah, to enter into covenant with Yahuweh/Yehovah. And then everything changed from that point onward as Abraham entered into the new covenant that Yahuweh/Yehovah began, and the covenant grew with Isaac and Jacob and the twelve sons that became the twelve tribes of Israel. Many of Abraham's other descendants from his other children not through the covenant of Isaac continued to know and worship and follow Yahuweh/Yehovah, as we know from the time that Moses spent in Midyan among his cousins there at Mount Sinai in Arabia, where the nation of Midyan was located at that time. But eventually the worship and following of Yahuweh/Yehovah outside of the covenant nation of Israel became corrupted and lost, so that by only a few hundred years later the nation of Israel was the only place that the true worship of Yahuweh/Yehovah could be found on earth. Anyone wanting to truly worship Yahuweh/Yehovah and know him without the corruption had to become citizens of Israel, in the new container, which many gentiles did according to the record of Exodus through Deuteronomy.

But Yahuweh/Yehovah did not stop with Abraham, because then came Moses and the giving of the Torah on Mount Sinai, the next step of the covenant. Everyone wanting to have true, uncorrupted worship of Yahuweh/Yehovah in true obedience of following him had to step out of the old container again of the world of man to enter into the new container of the next building stage of Yahuweh/Yehovah's covenant. It was not a leaving of the old covenant with Abraham to start a brand new covenant with Moses. It was a continuation of the covenant with Abraham. Later when Yeshua came to the earth as the Messiah and Lamb offering for sin, Yahuweh/Yehovah made the next stage of his covenant. And once again everyone had to leave the old container of the world of man and its commands of men, to enter into the new container and new covenant stage of Yahuweh/Yehovah. It was not a leaving of the old covenant with Abraham or the old covenant with Moses, but a continuation of those two previous covenant pieces, building on another third stage to the covenant.

At Yahuweh/Yehovah's next coming to end the world of man and rule over the earth he is bringing the fourth piece of the covenant to put in place, the fourth stage with the marriage covenant to him. Once again everyone will have to leave the old container of the ways and world of man, to enter into the new covenant and new container of the complete covenant with Yahuweh/Yehovah. Nobody will be leaving the old covenants with Abraham or with Moses or with Yeshua; they will only be leaving the old container of man's corruption and the world of man, to enter into the fullness of Yahuweh/Yehovah's covenant.

Abraham and his family and descendants through Isaac had to leave the world to become Ivri or Hebrew, made set-apart and separated from the world, and entering into the first state of the covenant with Yahuweh/Yehovah. And then Yahuweh/Yehovah destroyed the old container of the world system of man with the destruction of the cities of Sedom, 'Amorah, Admah, and Tsevoyim. Abraham had to leave the old container of the world systems of the cities, such as Ur Kasdim and Charan, to live in the new container of the first stage of Yahuweh/Yehovah's covenant. Next he called out Abraham's descendants through Jacob and the twelve tribes of Israel to leave the world where they were living in Mitsrayim (Egypt) and enter into the new container of the first and second stages of the covenant combined together. And he destroyed the old container of the world system of man in Mitsrayim (Egypt).

After that Yahuweh/Yehovah called out all peoples of all nations to leave the old container of the world systems in each of their nations and old religious systems and enter into the new container of all of the first three stages of the covenant combined together. And in order to preserve his set-apart and clean pictures in his covenant of animal sacrifices and the way that the nation of Israel should be operated according to his Torah, he destroyed the Second Temple and the nation of Judah and Israel at that time, removing them from the land, so that the corruption of their old container of manmade religion in Orthodox Judaism would not be corrupting and destroying his set-apart shadow pictures in his Torah and the observances of duties in the Temple set-apart place. This essentially destroyed the old container systems of man and the world that man had brought as corruption into Yahuweh/Yehovah's set-apart covenant.

This is the way that Yahuweh/Yehovah has always done things as each of the previous stages of his covenant, and it is no surprise that he will do the same thing again now. Abraham and the world was becoming corrupted in their ways in the old container religious systems of man that they had known, and Yahuweh/Yehovah pulled Abraham out to begin the new container of his set-apart covenant. In the same way Israel once again became corrupted with manmade religious systems in Egypt, and they had to be pulled out of the old container of corruption to be restored back into the covenant again at Mount Sinai. And many gentiles were pulled out with them according to the record of Exodus, entering into the new and restored covenant with them, as Yahuweh/Yehovah built the next stage.

Yahuweh/Yehovah again pulled out the Jews who were believers in Yeshua out of the old corrupted container of manmade religion in Judaism to be restored back into the new covenant again, with the next stage built on through Yeshua. And once again Yahuweh/Yehovah began pulling many more gentiles into his covenant along with Israel and the Jewish people. It is no surprise then that since Yahuweh/Yehovah does this every time that he is building on the next stage of the covenant, making it restored and new again, that he destroys the old container that has become corrupted with the world, this time destroying the Churches and Synagogues in the same way he destroyed the Second Temple.

Yahuweh/Yehovah says himself that he never wanted a physical temple built on the earth, as previously discussed, because he is more interested in building the covenant house and nation of his people rather than physical buildings on the earth. As he comes again he will be bringing his people out of the world systems again, out of Mystery Babel this time as already discussed, to take them into the wilderness again to enter into his newly restored covenant with the fourth and final stage built onto it. And he will be destroying the old containers behind, but this time it is the entire world that will be destroyed, including the entire world system of Mystery Babel like he destroyed Egypt, and the entire religious systems of man that have corrupted his covenant in the Churches and Synagogues in Christianity and Judaism, like he destroyed the Second Temple.

And this is the revival and awakening that Yahuweh/Yehovah has promised and prophesied to do all throughout Scripture. It is part of his character and who he is, thankfully, to destroy the old and corrupted containers of man in his kindness and love and mercy, and bringing everyone out into the restored and set-apart and pure container that he makes new again. The revivals that happen at the times of his coming to make the different stages of his covenant in history are always revivals that destroy the old containers and bring everyone into the restored and made new containers.

The revival with Abraham was small consisting of only a family, but it still brought destruction to the old and restoration into the made new. The revival with the nation of Israel out of Egypt became substantially bigger, as the old was destroyed that they had been in, and everything was restored and made new again. Then the revival got even bigger including all the nations all over the world as Yahuweh/Yehovah destroyed the old and brought everyone into the restored and made new again container. This time the revival includes the resurrection of the dead, bringing in all of the righteous who made the choice to enter into Yahuweh/Yehovah's covenant from the creation of the world into the final stage and renewal of the covenant at his coming. Everyone through time who has entered into his covenant of eternal life will all be part of the final revival and harvest of the earth, as the wheat all enter into eternal life and the restored covenant of Yahuweh/Yehovah, made complete.

But all of the old container of the Churches and Synagogues and manmade religious institutions all have to be destroyed so that not one stone of them will be left upon another as with the Second Temple. The revival at the Festival of Weeks (Pentecost) brought lots of destruction of the old as Yahuweh/Yehovah restored and built everything like new again. The same thing has to happen now with this revival on the earth at the end, with all of the old systems and old physical buildings being brought down and destroyed as Yahuweh/Yehovah pours out his Spirit on all flesh. Wherever there are churches and colleges and universities being shut down and closing as the people all leave them to follow Yahuweh/Yehovah into the wilderness and renewal of his covenant, into his family/nation/house/city of people, of Israel, that is where the true revival and awakening is happening from the latter rain outpouring of his Spirit.

That is the true, final outpouring revival and awakening of Yahuweh/Yehovah's Spirit, bringing down and destroying the old container of the Churches and Synagogues and man's corrupted religious systems, setting everyone free once again as in the past to be able to go out to the wilderness to worship him there in fullness and completeness of covenant at his coming. The true final revival is the separating of the wheat from the weeds as Yahuweh/Yehovah cleans up his house in justice and righteousness and truth in Matthew 13. We can see this clearly in Zechariah 10 that his pouring out the revival rain of Yahuweh/Yehovah's Spirit is linked together with his cleaning house and bringing judgement on the shepherds. Ezekiel 34 is the same way showing how in the final harvest, as in the parable of the wheat and weeds, Yahuweh/Yehovah is dealing with the shepherds in judgement, and at the same time separating and judging between the sheep.

The revivals at the times of Yahuweh/Yehovah's coming through history, building his covenant, always involve judgement and destruction. At the very end it is the judgement of all the earth and all who have ever lived since the creation of the heavens and the earth, harvesting both the wheat and the weeds at the same time out of the earth. It is no surprise then that Yahuweh/Yehovah has not changed and is doing the same thing now as he shakes up and brings down all of the Churches and Synagogues of the world, to save the congregations of peoples belonging to him into the wilderness with him for his marriage covenant at the end. It is the whole world that has to be ended as in the days of Noah and the global flood, in order to go on to the new in the New Heavens and the New Earth. All those who let go of and leave the old will be safe in the new, but those who try to hold onto and stay in the old will go down with it as Yahuweh/Yehovah mercifully destroys it and ends it so that no one can be deceived anymore in the future. Yahuweh/Yehovah does not want to have to destroy any of the people in the churches and synagogues, but if they refuse to leave as he is asking them to, they will be destroyed in the midst of Mystery Babel/Sodom/Egypt/The Second Temple as he brings it all down.

The Prophecies of the Final Great Harvest of the Earth and Outpouring of Yahuweh/Yehovah's Spirit on All Flesh:
    Isaiah 63:1-6
    Ezekiel 34:17-25
    Hosea 6:1-3   Psalms 90:4
    Joel 2:21-31
    Joel 3:1-14
    Zechariah 10:1
    Matthew 13:24-58
    Matthew 25:31-46
    Revelation 14:14-20

Word for Word Prophecy Examination of Partially Fulfilled, Fulfilled, and Unfulfilled Verses **Isaiah 63:1-6** and **Ezekiel 34:17-25** and **Hosea 6:1-3** and **Psalms 90:4** and **Joel 2:21-31** and **Joel 3:1-14** and **Zechariah 10:1** and **Matthew 13:24-58** and **Matthew 25:31-46** and **Revelation 14:14-20** – The prophecies in Isaiah 63, Ezekiel 34, Joel 3, Matthew 13, Matthew 25, and Revelation 14 are all about the same event of the final harvesting of the earth that Yahuweh/Yehovah does when he comes to end this world and reign over the earth. Each of these prophecies use different figurative, parable examples to explain how Yahuweh/Yehovah is harvesting the people of the earth. On one side there is the wheat that is being harvested, described in the parable of Matthew 13 and in Revelation 14 and Joel 3 where the Son of Adam (Yeshua) and the messengers are harvesting out the wheat of the earth with the sickles.

The wheat are the righteous and those who have entered into covenant with Yeshua through his sin sacrifice. The wheat in Matthew 13 and Revelation 14 are the same thing as the sheep in Matthew 25 and Ezekiel 34, where the sheep are separated out at the end by the Righteous Judge, Yeshua, setting apart his people from the world into eternal life. On the other side, being separated out to their second death in the lake of fire, are the weeds in Matthew 13, and the goats or rams in Matthew 25 and Ezekiel 34, and the grapes in Isaiah 63 and Joel 3 and Revelation 14. The weeds are taken away from the wheat to be thrown into the fire, and the goats are taken away from the sheep into eternal repulsion, and the grapes are trodden by Yahuweh/Yehovah in his winepress of wrath, utterly destroyed.

This is the final harvest, revival, outpouring, awakening that Yahuweh/Yehovah has promised and prophesied that he will bring at the end of the Great Tribulation, bringing in the last of those on the earth who want eternal life with him in his covenant, and bringing death to those who want death apart from him. But everyone is being taken away and ripped up out of where they are. The wheat are getting cut down just as much as the weeds and grapes; it is only the destination of where they are each carried to that is different, the wheat to eternal life and the weeds and grapes to eternal/second death in the lake of fire. These particular prophecies in Isaiah 63, Ezekiel 34, Joel 3, Matthew 13, Matthew 25, and Revelation 14 cannot be completely fulfilled until after Yeshua has already come, but they can begin in the process of fulfillment before he has arrived in the dark clouds in thunder and lightning.

The key consistency in these prophecies is that everyone, both the righteous and the wicked, no matter their destination, are being cut away from and pulled up by their roots, so that they have no more roots or foundation in this earth and this world anymore. Yahuweh/Yehovah is taking away all foundation and stability in the earth, shaking everything so that people do not have any safety or security or stability in their lives in this world anymore. It is the preparation for everyone to be taken up out of the earth eventually, to eternal life in the New Heavens and New Earth or eternal death in the lake of fire, and this is what can be seen on the earth today, growing stronger and stronger during the last century. Everyone and everything is being shaken across the earth as everyone is being pulled up and cut up out of their roots on the earth without any stability or foundation here to stand on.

Everyone is falling over in weakness and instability in the transition of getting ready to be removed from one place and taken to another place, unable to stay standing on the certainty and foundation of this world that was once there for people to have stability and assurance in. It used to be in the past few thousand years there were certain things that people could count on with the way the world worked and nature's cycles, but the world is changing so rapidly today with technology and culture as the world is falling apart into uncertainty about the future, the only firm foundation left is the rock of Yahuweh/Yehovah to be able to stay standing on. There is no foundation in the world and no way to keep roots in the ground of this world to stay held up on anymore. The condition of the world today is the way it should be for the fulfillment of these prophecies about the wheat and weeds and grapes and sheep and goats to be in process of fulfillment in preparation for the fullness of their fulfillment when Yeshua comes.

The other key part is that the wheat and weeds/grapes, and the sheep and goats, are being separated from each other by Yahuweh/Yehovah. This means that they cannot be near each other or in each other's lives anymore, which means that they cannot be going to church together anymore. This is why Yahuweh/Yehovah has to be shaking and bringing down all of the churches, separating out the people in the churches so that the wheat are being taken out one way and the weeds are being removed the other way, divided and separated away from each other. This is why Yahuweh/Yehovah has to destroy the old, corrupted container of the churches and synagogues, taking his people out of the churches and synagogues, set-apart and separated from the world and from the weeds and goats.

This can also be seen to be happening since Yahuweh/Yehovah's COVID plague he brought upon the world, beginning the process of isolating and separating everyone from each other, setting apart his people out of the world and out of the churches where they cannot be with the weeds that are there anymore. The two cannot mix or stay together anymore like in the past when it was alright for the weeds and wheat to be going to church together with the mixture of truth and errors in the teachings during the last 1,900 years. It is not okay anymore, as Yahuweh/Yehovah is pulling out his people into the wilderness to set them apart and separate them from the world, and the world be separated from his people as well as he gets the world out of them. Yahuweh/Yehovah is emptying the churches and synagogues of the people as worldwide fewer and fewer people are going to church, both wheat and weeds leaving the churches, because they have to be separated from each other. And that separation and division between them is the revival that Yahuweh/Yehovah promised would come at the end.

Hosea 6, Joel 2, and Zechariah 10 are the three primary prophecies about the latter rain and how Yahuweh/Yehovah pours himself out as rain at the Time of the End right before his coming to the earth in tangible form. In Hosea 6, Hosea prophesies about Yahuweh/Yehovah coming like the latter rain at the end of two days, on the third day. Psalms 90 explains how one day is the same as one thousand years to Yahuweh/Yehovah, explaining the timing of this prophecy in Hosea 6. In the same way that Yeshua was raised from the dead on the third day, after three days and three nights in the grave, he will raise his people back to life on the third day, reviving them at the end of two days.

As already extensively shown in *Calculating the Last Seven*, the earliest possible date for Yeshua's death and resurrection would be in the year 28 C.E. and the very latest possible date for his death and resurrection would be in the year 32 C.E., and no later than the year 32 C.E. (since there is no record anywhere in Scripture to suggest that Yeshua's ministry lasted longer than a maximum of about 2 to 2 ½ years).[39] If we

---

[39] The 3 ½ year ministry of Yeshua is a myth and fiction created by Eusebius in his book *Demonstratio Evangelica* published in about the year 311 C.E. Eusebius provides no sources or evidence for his mythical 3 ½ year ministry of Yeshua, only saying that a person has to be "attentive" in reading the book of John to find his imaginary 3 ½ year ministry that he made up. In the original myth, Eusebius claims that the approximate 40 days when Yeshua is showing himself to his disciples after his resurrection equaled another 3 ½ years, in order to make a complete 7 years (or one week of Daniel's seventy weeks) from the start of Yeshua's ministry to his ascension 40 days after his resurrection. Eusebius does not make it clear if he believed that the 40 days were actually a literal 3 ½ years that Yeshua was on the earth after his resurrection, or if the 40 days somehow magically transformed into a symbolic 3 ½ years, but either way he was only making up these dates from his own imagination, not having anything to do with reality. The truth is that in the book of John with the three Passovers recorded, there is no record in Scripture for Yeshua's ministry lasting more than about 2 or 2 ½ years at the very most.

Eusebius wrote, "Now the whole period of our Saviour's Teaching and working of Miracles is said to have been three-and-a-half years, which is half a week. John the Evangelist, in his Gospel, makes this clear to the attentive. One week of years therefore would be represented by the whole period of His association with the Apostles, both the time before His Passion, and the time after His Resurrection. For it is written that before His Passion He shewed Himself for the space of three-and-a-half years to His disciples and also to those who were not His disciples : while by teaching and miracles He revealed the powers of His Godhead to all equally whether Greeks or Jews. But after His Resurrection He was most likely with His disciples a period equal to the years, being seen of them forty days, and eating with them, and speaking of the things pertaining to the Kingdom of God, as the Acts of the Apostles tells us. So that this would be the prophet's week of years, during which He 'confirmed a covenant with many,' confirming that is to say the new Covenant of the Gospel Preaching." W. J. Ferrar, *The Proof of the Gospel being the Demonstratio Evangelica of Eusebius of Caesarea, Vol. II* (London: The Macmillan Company, 1920) pgs. 135-136

In his *Ecclesiastical History* in about 325 C.E. Eusebius admitted that the first three Gospels only record about a one year ministry for Yeshua, and he tried to figure out a way to use John's Gospel to force Yeshua's ministry to last longer than a year, ultimately to the 3 ½ years that he wanted and made up from his imagination. "Matthew also having first proclaimed the gospel in Hebrew, when on the point of going also to other nations, committed it to writing in his native tongue, and thus supplied the want of his presence to them, by his writings. But after Mark and Luke had already published their gospels, they say, that John, who during all this time was proclaiming the gospel without writing, at length proceeded to write it on the following occasion. The three gospels previously written, having been distributed among all, and also handed to him, they say that he admitted them, giving his testimony to their truth; but that there was only wanting in the narrative the account of the things done by Christ, among the first of his deeds, and at the commencement of the gospel. And this was the truth. For it is evident that the other three evangelists only wrote the deeds of our Lord for one year after the imprisonment of John the Baptist, and intimated this in the very beginning of their

count two days or 2,000 years from Yeshua's death and resurrection we arrive at the years 2028 C.E. to 2032 C.E. and no earlier or later than this range of years. The prophecy in Hosea 6 says that Yahuweh/Yehovah will revive us, all of his people Israel, at the end of or after two days, after 2,000 years, with him pouring out himself like the latter rain. There is no question that we are currently living at the end of the two days or 2,000 years when the reviving or revivaling happens as Yahuweh/Yehovah prophesied it would come, and the time of the latter rain has already begun since on December 28, 2017, in fulfillment of Zechariah 10:1 as already earlier discussed.

We are in the time of the latter rain outpouring of Yahuweh/Yehovah coming like the rain onto the earth, but it is coming as he prophesied it would, by cutting down and pulling up everyone out of their roots, both the wheat and weeds, in harvest. It is a revival of literal judgement in the literal sense of the word, judging between sheep and sheep, between sheep and goats, between wheat and weeds or grapes, by separating them out from each other, some to eternal life and others to eternal second death in the lake of fire. The set-apart ones are being pulled away from and separated from the world, being made clean in Great Tribulation, while the rest of the world is being uprooted right along with the believers in Yeshua, without any stable or reliable ground to stand on in this world anymore. The harvesting revival of the Time of the End, at the end of the two days or 2,000 years, is just as painful for the wheat as it is for the weeds, as they get cut down and violently pulled up out of their comfortable and predictable world they have been living in on this earth, to be taken away to be with Yahuweh/Yehovah in eternal life. He is the only sure foundation rock to still be able to stand on and be in peace and contentment in through the shaking transition time, that is just as difficult to go through as the Israelites being violently ripped out of their homes and livelihoods in Egypt to go into the wilderness.

Sarah was the original "woman" who birthed the nation, Isaac, at the beginning of Yahuweh/Yehovah's covenant nation. Then that nation descended from Isaac was born again as Israel, into the physical land of Israel, with the Torah and Moses. Next Miryam (Mary) was the "woman" who birthed the nation, Yeshua, bringing in the Gentile nations into Yahuweh/Yehovah's covenant nation. The final stage is what we are in now, as Yahuweh/Yehovah births that nation from Yeshua to be born again, through the first-fruits of the 144,000, into a whole and complete nation that will enter into the physical land of the New Heavens and New Earth, to live as a nation of people together there, the nation Israel made up of all of the twelve tribes of Israel together with the gentiles who have entered into the covenant and become part of the twelve tribes. This is prophesied in Ezekiel 47:22-23 where Yahuweh/Yehovah says that even Gentiles (sojourning strangers) will receive land among the twelve tribes of Israel in the New Heavens and New Earth and the New Jerusalem, and become native born Israelis with the same inheritance in the same Yeshua covenant as the natural born descendants of the twelve tribes of Israel. John uses these descriptions from Ezekiel 47 and 48 to describe the New Jerusalem in Revelation 21 and 22, so that we know this prophecy in Ezekiel 47 is talking about the New Heavens and New Earth.

---

history." Rev. C. F. Cruse, A. M., *The Ecclesiastical History of Eusebius Pamphilus* (New York: Swords, Stanford, & Co., 1833) pg. 108

This is the latter rain outpouring of Yahuweh/Yehovah at the end of the two days or 2,000 years, the destroying of the old container and the reviving of his people into the new container, being born again as the complete and whole nation of Israel, with descendants who have entered into covenant with Yeshua from all of the twelve tribes of Israel, together with all of the Gentiles of the nations who are in covenant with Yeshua. This is what is prophesied in Isaiah 49 and Jeremiah 31, that Yeshua would gather natural, literal descendants from all of the twelve tribes of Israel together to him at his coming, to become one nation Israel in covenant with him, with all of the Gentile believers being grafted into his covenant nation Israel in fulfillment of Isaiah 56 and Ezekiel 47. Every believer in Yeshua becomes part of the new covenant of Yahuweh/Yehovah that is with his nation Israel, every believer becoming part of his covenant nation Israel.

The real revival, latter rain outpouring of Yahuweh/Yehovah's Spirit is happening in fulfillment of Joel 2, upon all flesh. This means that the real revival is happening with the individuals in their daily lives, who are not in groups or in special, physical locations. It is on all flesh, meaning that there is no particular place or event that a person has to go to in order to be part of the revival, and no particular person that they have to go and see or listen to. The prophecy of Joel 2 of Yahuweh/Yehovah pouring out his Spirit on all flesh is a prophecy that has never been fulfilled in all of history before this time we are living in now. It was spoken of by Peter in Acts, but anyone who reads the New Testament will see that there is not one person who ever prophesies with a dream or vision, except for the Apostle John in the book of Revelation. There is no record that even any of the other Apostles ever once prophesied with a dream or vision in the New Testament, let alone people from all walks of life from the lowliest slaves, or people of all ages from the youngest to the oldest.

This prophecy was never fulfilled in the New Testament, and there is no record going back through the last 2,000 years of any time in history where people of all ages, from children to the aged, including the average workers/employees or slaves, having dreams and visions and then prophesying about those dreams and visions on a mass scale of thousands and thousands all across the earth. There began to be a little bit of prophesying with dreams and visions in the late 19th century, in the last 150 years, but not on a very large scale, and certainly not among all levels of society including the average person on the street. All through the last 150 years this prophesying with dreams and visions has slowly increased, especially in the 1980's and 90's.

But it has only been since about 2010 that there suddenly started to be more and more people from all levels of society and all ages from children to seniors that began prophesying with dreams and visions publicly on a large scale. And then after 2017, and again after 2020, this began increasing more and more into thousands and tens of thousands of people having dreams and visions about Yeshua's soon return and prophesying about it. The scale of dreams and visions that people are having, and then sharing publicly, proclaiming and prophesying, these dreams and visions through the internet in fulfillment of Joel 2:28-29, is something that has never before been seen in the recorded history of the world. There has never been a time like this at any time in history where there are thousands and thousands, possibly hundreds of thousands and millions, of people who are prophesying with dreams and visions they have had of Yeshua's return and the Great Tribulation.

Since 2015 private individuals and news organizations have been recording eye witness video of the moon turned to a blood red color and the sun completely darkened from smoked filled skies in the massive wild fires across the continents of Australia, North America, Europe, and Asia. It also includes video of lots of pillars of smoke caused by fire tornadoes across these continents. Many cities have been so darkened by the smoke that they are turned almost to night in the middle of the day, as the sun is turned to darkness, and others outside of the cities see the moon turned to blood at night, from the atmospheric conditions of the smoke changing the color of the moon to a true blood red color. Even the city of London itself was on fire in 2022, something not seen since The Blitz in World War II, and Israel has been on fire with wildfires as well in recent years. This is at least a partial fulfillment of the signs that are seen in the heavens in Joel 2:30-31, but it is not the fullness of fulfillment yet, which comes with the Sixth Seal, discussed later on. But it is still a sign that this prophecy of Joel 2 with Yahuweh/Yehovah pouring out his Spirit on all flesh is in process of fulfillment now, as we are in the time of the latter rain in Zechariah 10.

The Matthew 25:1-13 parable of the ten virgins is all about containers, specifically containers of oil that provide light. The five foolish virgins only brought their lamps with them, but no containers of oil, while the five wise virgins brought their lamps, plus extra containers filled with the oil of Yahuweh/Yehovah. The wise virgins had containers of oil and the foolish virgins did not have containers. It is because the final revival, harvest, awakening of Yahuweh/Yehovah pouring out his Spirit is the same as he always does, removing his people from and then destroying the old container or wineskin, moving them into the new container or wineskin. The five wise virgins moved into the new container where the oil of Yahuweh/Yehovah is located, and the five foolish virgins stayed in the old container that Yahuweh/Yehovah had removed and destroyed. The old container is gone, and the five foolish virgins, not wanting to move into the new container where the oil of Yahuweh/Yehovah is located, were left with no container and no oil at all, no Yahuweh/Yehovah in their lives.

Wherever the churches are being shut down and lie empty and vacant, wherever the religious institutions and colleges and universities shut their doors and are permanently closed down, these are the places where the true revival is happening as the people in them are all leaving the old container of the churches and synagogues to enter into the new container of Yahuweh/Yehovah's complete and whole nation of Israel that will inhabit the New Heavens and New Earth. As everyone goes out from the old container where there is no more oil of Yahuweh/Yehovah inhabiting it, especially no more oil of the Two Witnesses of his Word, the wise virgins will go into the new container where the oil of Yahuweh/Yehovah is moved to, where there is still a source of oil from him in his unified nation in the wilderness heading to his coming at Mount Sinai.

As Yahuweh/Yehovah is removing and tearing down the old container of the churches and Christian religious institutions, there is no more oil available from him in that old container. And everyone trying to stay in that old container are having to race to wherever it sounds like there might be some oil, to see if they can buy oil from whatever physical location that sounds like or appears to be having a revival. But Yahuweh/Yehovah's revival is in the new container, not confined to any physical location where a group of people are gathered together. It is right there with each individual person in their daily lives if they are willing to enter into the new container where the oil is located.

There is a famine of the oil and Word of Yahuweh/Yehovah on the land, across the world, where nobody can get oil in the old container that they had relied upon for nearly 2,000 years. Now the new container has all of the oil and is there ready for anyone who will enter into it, into his nation/house/family/city of Israel and the New Jerusalem. From Matthew 25 and Joel 2 we can see that it is simultaneously a famine of the oil of the Spirit and Word of Yahuweh/Yehovah (in the old container) as he pours out his oil of his Spirit and Word on all flesh (in the new container). The old container passes away, because it was based upon man's corruptions of Yahuweh/Yehovah's Word, which Yeshua promised would happen in the parable of Matthew 13 of the wheat and weeds. But the final revival is the separating and removing of both the wheat and weeds from the old corrupted container. Both the wheat and the weeds have to all leave the churches and synagogues and Christian religious institutions to be ready for Yahuweh/Yehovah's coming and to be birthed as a nation of people into the New Heavens and New Earth. Since the COVID plague Yahuweh/Yehovah has started the process of emptying out and destroying the old container of the churches exactly as would be expected for the final revival in the Great Tribulation. Everything is in place and in process for the prophecies of the final harvest to be in the midst of fulfillment now, even if they cannot be completely fulfilled until after Yahuweh/Yehovah comes at the end of the Great Tribulation.

Harvest Outpouring of Yahuweh/Yehovah's Spirit Simultaneous with the Great Delusions and Falling Away (Turning Against):

Matthew 22:1-14   Luke 14:15-24

Word for Word Prophecy Examination of Partially Fulfilled Verses **Matthew 22:1-14** and **Luke 14:15-24** – The parable of the wedding in Matthew 22, repeated in a similar form in Luke 14, is the example of how the paradox of the final harvest, revival, awakening, outpouring of Yahuweh/Yehovah's Spirit on all flesh takes place. At the same time that the falling away is taking place, and the Christians who were invited to the wedding are refusing to come, walking away from the covenant with Yahuweh/Yehovah and eternal life, there are others on the streets who are coming into the covenant with Yeshua and into eternal life. These two things are happening simultaneously, as we can see today, as many Christians are falling away or turning against their faith in Yeshua, refusing to come to the wedding because they are too busy with the things of the world.

Even as many Christians around the world are leaving their faith and walking away from eternal life, there is a harvest of many others on the streets and in everyday life who are leaving the world and believing in Yeshua. But not all those who are believing in and accepting the covenant with Yeshua in the revival of the Time of the End will enter into eternal life, because some will decide that they do not want to be cleaned up of their sin by Yeshua, to have clean wedding robes of righteousness, and will ultimately be thrown out into the darkness. Because it is a revival of separating out the sheep and goats, wheat and weeds, from each other, it is a revival of Christians falling away and losing their eternal lives and salvation by their own choices, just as much as bringing in the harvest of wheat of people gaining eternal life and salvation by accepting the covenant of Yeshua.

And we can see these two things happening simultaneously today as Yeshua described in the Matthew 22 and Luke 14 parable. And we can see that as the Christians who were invited to come to the wedding refuse to come because they are too busy with the things of the world such as marriage and careers, running businesses or running fields of Christian ministry trying to bring in the harvest in their own flesh, the old container they have been in of their cities, in their lives and their churches, is destroyed by Yahuweh/Yehovah and burned to the ground. They were too busy at the very end of the Great Tribulation with building churches and growing churches, building ministries and growing ministries, building careers and growing businesses, to come to the wedding.

This could be seen as part of the process of fulfillment of these verses during the COVID plague when Christians all over the world were telling Yahuweh/Yehovah that he could not return yet or start the Great Tribulation yet, because they were still too busy doing their plans and ministries on the earth to go to the wedding yet. Everyone still wanted to finish their plans they had of what they wanted to do in their own flesh for the Kingdom, and did not want to be going to any wedding or having Yeshua return at such an inconvenient time in the history of the world. There are many today leaving their faith in Yeshua at the same time that many are coming into faith in Yeshua, simultaneously as Yeshua said would happen at the time of his coming in Matthew 22 and Luke 14.

Egypt, Israel, and Syria become a Highway Together at the Time of the End When Yahuweh/Yehovah Comes in the Clouds, with a Revival of Believers in Yeshua (the Savior) Among Those Three Nations:

Isaiah 19:2-16, 20, 23-25

Prophecy Fulfillment of Verses **Isaiah 19:2-16, 20, 23-25** – From the first verse of this prophecy we know that this is a prophecy about Yahuweh/Yehovah's coming in the clouds, riding on a swift cloud, at the Time of the End. Verse 1 of this prophecy cannot be completely fulfilled until Yahuweh/Yehovah has tangibly come at the end of the Great Tribulation, but most of the rest of this prophecy is able to be fulfilled beforehand.

In 2011 the nation of Egypt erupted into a civil war of Egyptian against Egyptian, fighting against one another, against their brothers and their neighbors, as part of the Arab Spring, in fulfillment of verses 19:2-3. They lost all counsel and did not know what to do anymore in the civil war and revolution that had begun, as they did not know where to turn to or how to fix their government. In the chaos of the people of Egypt seeking their idols and trying to find what to do to fix their nation, they voted in the Muslim Brotherhood to rule over them in 2012.

During the years 2012 to 2013 the Muslim Brotherhood were very cruel masters and a dictator government worse than the one they had had before it, in fulfillment of verse 19:4. The Muslim Brotherhood were rounding up people off the streets, both Muslims and Christians, to horrifically torture them, leaving their victims near death or sometimes killing them. Yahuweh/Yehovah first brought the nation into a civil war of Egyptians fighting each other, then brought them a cruel master with the Muslim Brotherhood, which they themselves democratically elected into government, exactly as described in the first parts of this prophecy.

This created an even greater uprising by the Egyptian people than before, to overthrow the Muslim Brotherhood government in more civil war and bring in a military led government in 2013.

Then beginning in 2015 through 2019 there was a severe drought in Egypt, causing the waters of the sea to fail and the rivers to become a wasteland and dried up, in fulfillment of verses 19:5-8. The drought was very bad and the Nile River almost completely dried up at one point, making it difficult for the farmers and fishermen exactly as described in the prophecy of 19:7-8, with the plants withering and dying. The Egyptian economy had suffered badly from the continuous blows from the 2008 Great Recession to the civil war and revolution and dictatorship of the Muslim Brotherhood from 2011 to 2013. So the Egyptian economy by that time in 2015 to 2021 was experiencing a depression, causing the merchants such as fabric makers, to become ashamed in hard times in fulfillment of verse 19:9. And the wage workers were grieved in poverty from the foundation of the economy being crushed in fulfillment of verses 19:10 and 15, especially the tourism economy greatly suffering many blows, the final one being the COVID pandemic in 2020 to 2021. The Egyptian people did not have enough work for everyone in the economic depression, making life very difficult in the country.

And all of the princes and wise ones in Egypt became fools without any sense, deceived and leading the nation astray during the years 2011 to 2021, in fulfillment of verses 19:11-14. The Egyptian government and its Pharoaohs/Rulers since 2011 have been completely incapable of solving and fixing Egypt's problems as a nation in turmoil, especially during the years 2011 to 2021. Throughout 2011 to 2021 the people of Egypt have been living in fear and trembling for one reason and another, because of the hand of Yahuweh/Yehovah upon the nation and what he has been doing in their midst, in fulfillment of verse 19:16.

By 2020 with the start of the COVID plague some in Egypt began to cry out to Yahuweh/Yehovah for a Savior, for Yeshua, in partial fulfillment of verse 19:20. At the time of Isaiah, the word and concept of "internet" did not exist yet, so how would Yahuweh/Yehovah give a prophecy through Isaiah about something that he had no understanding. A comparable word to use at that time that Isaiah would understand would be to use the word "highway." Today we not only have physical highways to travel on to visit with other people, but we can now visit with them using audio and video that is sent across the internet highway, which is commonly called a highway by people around the world, traveling on the internet highway to speak with one another and gather. The internet highway is only a piece of infrastructure like any physical highway that someone might travel on, and is in itself not evil, only the worship of it as a virtual city of Mystery Babel to join together in rebellion against Yahuweh/Yehovah.

At the beginning of the COVID plague many believers in Yeshua began gathering together on the internet highway, including many believers from countries all over the world. David Damien (an Egyptian from Egypt) and Asher Intrater (a Jew from Israel), together with hundreds of other believers from Egypt, Israel, and Syria gathered together on the internet highway in fulfillment of verses 19:23-25, becoming one in Yeshua, during a series of previously unplanned online events beginning with *Passover – Holy Alignment* on April 7, 2020, then *The Unveiling* on May 14, 2020, finishing with the culmination of *The Outpouring* on May 28, 2020. Believers in Yeshua physically located in or descended from the nations of Egypt and Israel and Syria gathered together in unity on the internet highway, creating a continuous and whole highway between the believers in these three nations. This was the first time in known, recorded history that Christians from these three nations came together in unity and repentance and forgiveness after the hundreds and hundreds of years of hatred and division between each other.

If they had gathered together in a physical location they would not have been on a highway and this would not have been the fulfillment of the prophecy, but because they gathered together on the internet highway, they became the fulfillment of the highway connecting the three nations together in verses 19:23-25, bringing together the three nations of believers in Yeshua in unity as a continuous highway between them, without the division anymore. Through Yeshua, the Savior, in verse 19:20 Egyptians are now able to become his people, and Syrians the work of his hand, unified as one with his inheritance of the nation of Israel, to become one nation of people together under Yeshua. After nearly 2,000 years this finally is coming into being in fulfillment of verses 19:23-25, as Yahuweh/Yehovah forms all of his people in his covenant with him into one nation and one house and one city and one family of people. It is actually happening now in real life where there once was division with all of the followers of Yeshua scattered among the nations all across the earth; true unity in righteousness and in the covenant of Yeshua instead of counterfeit unity among false religions in the Beast Out of the Earth and the Beast Out of the Sea.

The only parts left to be fulfilled in their fullness in this prophecy of Isaiah 19 are verses 1, 17-19, and 21-22. Everything else has happened, and the rest of this prophecy does not have any requirement to be fulfilled before Yeshua returns.

Section 22. **The Days of Noah and Lot and the Great Tribulation Trouble for a Time, Times, and Half a Time:**

References to the Days of Noah and Lot Prophecies:
Genesis 6:1 – 9:17
Genesis 19:1-26

Word for Word Examination of Verses **Genesis 6:1 – 9:17** and **Genesis 19:1-26** – Yeshua likens his coming as the Son of Adam at the Time of the End to the days of Noah and the days of Lot. Both the days of Noah and Lot have in common a day of destruction that comes upon the people of the earth unexpectedly and suddenly, taking everyone by surprise except for the few righteous who are left. And both are times of judgment when Yahuweh/Yehovah is ending the corruption and evil taking place, because there is no longer a chance for any of the people to turn around in repentance and be saved.

During the days of Noah there was great wickedness being done by men, with the thoughts of their hearts being only continual evil. There was also corruption on the earth and violence, and there were the Nephilim, which means "Fallen Ones," that came from the marriages between sons of God and daughters of men. But of all of these things taking place before the flood, not one of them is a unique or special thing that was happening only during the days of Noah before the flood. Since the flood there has always been great wickedness on the earth, and there has always been men doing only continuous evil, and there has always been corruption and violence all over the earth.

Even the Nephilim are not unique to the time before the flood, because Moses records that the sons of God and daughters of men continued to marry and have Nephilim children even after the flood, in Genesis 6:4 and Numbers 13:33. It does not matter even what anyone believes about who the Nephilim are, according to Moses the Nephilim (whoever or whatever they are) have always continued to be on the earth after the flood and are not unique or special to the time of Noah before the flood.

If all the things happening before the flood continued to happen as a part of normal life after the flood, then why did Yahuweh/Yehovah grieve about making man and have to destroy all of mankind at that time? What was the unique thing at that time that made it impossible for humanity to continue on the earth and required its complete destruction with the end of the world? The unique thing at that time was the same reason that Yahuweh/Yehovah always brings total judgment destruction to a group of people or city or nation at any time throughout history. The corruption and violence and great wickedness and continual evil thoughts were filled up full, to a complete fullness where there was nowhere left on the earth to find an absence of these things. The earth was full of all of these things, and all flesh was completely filled with these things, meaning that Yahuweh/Yehovah had to destroy and end it all, with nothing left to save except a few remaining righteous.

It was the same in the days of Lot, with the destruction of the cities of Sodom and Gomorrah, and all the cities of the plain except Zoar. The cities had reached the fullness of corruption and violence and great wickedness and continual evil thoughts, requiring the cities to be destroyed, with only Lot and two of his daughters saved from the judgment. Yahuweh/Yehovah explains this concept in his prophecy to Abraham in Genesis 15:16 where he explains that the descendants of Abraham have to wait as sojourners in the nations for 400 years, and cannot take the land of Canaan as their own yet, until the wickedness of the inhabitants, the Amorites, is complete.

When the wickedness and evil is at its point of fullness and completeness, with nowhere left to go to find an absence of the wickedness and corruption and violence and continual evil thoughts, then Yahuweh/Yehovah brings the judgment and end of that nation or city or even the entire world if it is the entire world that has reached that point. He did not allow Israel to take the land of the Amorites until the Amorites had reached the completeness of their wickedness. Also, Lot and his family had become so corrupted by the overpowering corruption in Sodom that none of them even wanted to leave by the time that Yahuweh/Yehovah brought the judgment, and Lot lost his wife and more than one daughter in the city because they loved the city of Sodom (Mystery Babel) more than their own lives.

From the days of Noah and Lot there are two main points that can be seen about those days. In both cases the great wickedness and corruption and violence and continual evil thoughts had reached a point of fullness, with every space and person in the place of judgment completely full of these things. And the second thing that happened in both cases was that the day of the destruction came upon the people completely by surprise without any warning signs that their world was about to end, even up to the very day in the moment right before their world ended forever.

Even up to the very day of the destruction everyone continued on with their normal, everyday lives as though their world was going to go on forever, with no signs of ending, and then suddenly in a moment everything changed and everyone was dead, except for a small remnant of righteous saved by Yahuweh/Yehovah, whom he prepared and got ready in time so that they would be saved (even if it was reluctantly on the part of Lot). And one of the main reasons why it was such a surprise is that the destruction coming on them in both cases was something new and unbelievable that had never happened before.

In the case of the global flood, according to Genesis 2:5-6 it had never rained on the earth before, so it was inconceivable that rain could fall from the sky and water could rush up from under the earth and flood the whole world. Likewise, it was inconceivable that fire could rain down from the sky to destroy Sodom and Gomorrah, because fire had never come down from the sky before, so why would anyone believe such a crazy thing would happen. When the future destruction is coming in an inconceivable form, it always comes as a shock and surprise, because no one has experienced it before it happens, meaning there is no warning sign to precede the coming destruction for the very reason that it is something that has never happened before.

The Days of Noah and Lot Prophecies:
Matthew 24:37-39
Luke 17:26-32

Prophecy Fulfillment of Verses **Matthew 24:37-39** and **Luke 17:26-32** – The emphasis that Yeshua places on the comparison between the days of Noah and the days of Lot with his coming at the end of the Great Tribulation is that everyone on the earth on the day of his coming will be living normal life with no signs that the world is about to end or that Yeshua is about to come. As Yeshua says, everyone will be eating and drinking and having families, buying and selling and planting and building, up to the very day of his coming. And then his coming and his judgment he brings with his coming will be a complete surprise to everyone on the earth except the righteous who he prepared ahead of time and were ready for his coming.

This is his coming "after the tribulation/trouble of those days" when the Great Tribulation is ended, that everyone is living normal life and his coming is a complete surprise to the general world, because his coming will be something new that has never happened before on the earth. This means there are no signs that can happen ahead of time that tell people from experience that Yeshua is about to come in the clouds, in exactly the same way that no one had experienced water raining down from the heavens or fire raining down from the heavens before in the days of Noah and Lot. No one knew that it was possible at that time for the whole world to be flooded, or for entire cities to be almost instantly consumed by fire and sulphur falling on top of them from the sky. In the same way there will be nothing happening on earth before Yeshua's coming, even up to right before he comes on the very day of his coming, that will let anyone know that he is about to come.

It will not seem possible for him to be coming on the day that he comes; people like Noah and his family or Lot have to simply decide to believe Yeshua when he says that he is about to come, even though there is no proof of his coming to end the world even up to the day of his coming at the very end of the Great Tribulation. This is Yeshua's warning about the days of Noah and Lot, that even the signs that happen before his coming (in Matthew 24 and Mark 13 and Luke 21) are only able to let people know that he is near to coming, but do not give any proof about the day or timing of when he is about to come (discussed in greater detail further on).

Every day now since the flood normal life has continued in the way Yeshua describes normal life will be happening on the day of his coming at the end of the Great Tribulation, which means that every day is a day that looks like the day of Yeshua's coming. Yeshua is warning that the day itself of his coming at the end of the Great Tribulation will have nothing special or unique about it to be able to tell that it is the day of his coming until he has already come in thick, dark clouds at the sound of the shophar. But the important thing that people have missed or not paid attention to in past generations is what the days of Noah and Lot really mean concerning the judgment of Yahuweh/Yehovah. The issue is not the existence of evil on the earth, because that has always been on the earth. The corruption and violence and great wickedness and continual evil thoughts of men that were on the earth before the flood have always been on the earth in every generation, and looking at history every generation has had the same wickedness on the earth that was before the flood. But the real question that each generation has missed and should be asking is whether or not that wickedness is full, completely filling the whole earth and all flesh on the earth, to the point that there is no flesh that is uncorrupted or saved.

Going back through thousands of years of recorded history to the time since the flood, even though there has always been great evil done on the earth by men and women to one another, there has also always been places on the earth with moral codes and rule of law where some righteousness or integrity can be found. The earth in the past has not been completely filled up full of evil and wickedness and violence toward one another, but the trend through the last few thousand years has been toward the earth filling up fuller and fuller through each generation. The morality and codes of civility toward one another in societies have been slowly eroded away, and by the late 1800's to early 1900's it has certainly become harder and harder to find a place on the earth where there is no corruption and violence and great wickedness. The Pilgrims (and later many other Christian groups of Europe) were able to escape the morally decaying Europe in 1620 by coming to the New World. But now that world in America is filled with more corruption and violence in people's everyday lives than the Europe that the Pilgrims left behind 400 years ago. Even just 400 years ago or 300 years ago or 200 years ago there were many place still left on the earth where people could escape to in wildernesses to find communities without much corruption or violence or great wickedness or continual evil thoughts. But now today where is there left to go to find a place on the earth that is not completely filled with corruption or violence or great wickedness or people thinking evil thoughts continuously? Even children and ordinary, average people on the streets commit mass murder against one another as a part of normal, everyday life on the earth today.

The only places on the earth today that are not completely full of corruption and violence and great wickedness and continual evil thoughts are in the places where there are no people at all, in the wildernesses, and there are almost no wildernesses left for people to live in where they can stay isolated and uncorrupted by the outside world, because of modern technology that has joined everyone together into a single city of Mystery Babel. Mystery Babel, the Great Mother of all the whoring and abominations on the earth, is infiltrated everywhere inside of everyone's homes and businesses and work places. There is nowhere left on the earth to escape it without complete cutting off from all contact with people and technology, living like John the Immerser/Baptist in the wilderness without any family, except going another step beyond with no people contact allowed whatsoever. The child education and housing laws of most governments around the world today do not allow for a family with children to be raised outside of Mystery Babel in an uncorrupted wilderness environment.

And with the continuous barrage of evil thinking from the internet and television today, it is possible for people to sit and think about evil and doing evil continuously, every waking moment, if they want to (or forced against their will if they do not want to), with a think tank of evil thoughts coming from billions of people all together at the same time, to think of evil that a person would normally never even imagine in generations past. Sin and immorality today is being normalized as a part of normal, everyday life across the whole world at the same time, no longer done in secret or shunned by society as in the past.

Comparing the world today with past generations, this generation and the generations in the last 100 years are certainly exponentially fuller of the corruption and violence and great wickedness than any other generation that has been on the earth since the time of the flood. And if the world has to get much fuller of evil than it already is right now, it will be spilling over out into space and the universe, because there are few places left on the earth that can hold the evil anymore. It is at the bursting point where it is pouring out of every pour and crack on the earth, pouring out of people, overflowing, and hopefully the wickedness will not have to get much fuller than it already is now before Yeshua returns, or there will not be any uncorrupted, saved flesh on the earth left anywhere.

Today's world in the last few decades has become the perfect environment for Yeshua's coming, during days like Noah and Lot, with the earth completely filled full with great wickedness. The evil being done on the earth today has always been on the earth before, but now the earth is full of it, with righteousness and integrity rapidly disappearing no matter what anyone has done in the last few decades to try to slow it down or turn it around. And that is the very sign itself of fullness of evil, when it cannot be turned around anymore, because there is no repentance anymore. Yahuweh/Yehovah had to bring the flood in Noah's day and the fire and sulphur in Lot's day to destroy and kill everyone at once because of the hardness of the hearts of the people and their refusal of repentance. It was because there was no more repentance and no chance for the kind of repentance as in Nineveh that the destruction had to come. Yahuweh/Yehovah sent Jonah to Nineveh to preach to them repentance because there was a chance of repentance, but he did not send Noah to preach to the world or Abraham to preach to Sodom and Gomorrah, because the corruption and wickedness was full with no longer any chance of repentance.

No matter how hard people have tried in the last 40 years around the world to preach repentance and change things back around, there has been no repentance and no change. Since the time of the flood the world has certainly been moving closer and closer to being filled up full of evil like in the days of Noah, but it has only been in the last 150 years that it has exponentially accelerated towards where we are today with a global fullness of great wickedness not seen since the days of Noah. The world has only become fuller and fuller of great wickedness without a single nation to turn around in repentance back to Yahuweh/Yehovah or morality and righteousness for at least 40 years since the 1980's. The world is full and completely hardened in rebellion against repentance, which means that it is ready to come to an end like in the days of Noah and the days of Lot.

The Great Tribulation Trouble Prophecies for a Time, Times, and Half a Time, and a Day – *Dealing with the Myth that the Day of Yahuweh/Yehovah Begins at the Beginning of a 7 Year or 3.5 Year Tribulation Period of Time, and Includes the Great Tribulation Period of 3.5 Years Before He has Come*:

Isaiah 2:10-22; 13:1-22; 26:16-21; 34:1-17; 63:1-6

Jeremiah 25:15-38; 30:1 – 31:14

Daniel 7:9-25; 12:1-13

Joel 2:32 – 3:21

Obadiah 1:1-21

Zephaniah 1:1 – 3:20

Zechariah 14:1-15

Psalms 2:1-12

Matthew 24:15-31   Mark 13:14-27   Luke 17:24-37

1 Thessalonians 4:13 – 5:10

Revelation 6:12-17; 7:9-17; 11:1-19; 12:1 – 13:18; 14:14-20; 16:12-16; 19:11-21

Word for Word Prophecy Examination of Partially Fulfilled, Fulfilled, and Unfulfilled Verses **Isaiah 2:10-22; 13:1-22; 26:16-21; 34:1-17; 63:1-6** and **Jeremiah 25:15-38; 30:1 – 31:14** and **Daniel 12:1-13** and **Joel 2:32 – 3:21** and **Obadiah 1:1-21** and **Zephaniah 1:1 – 3:20** and **Zechariah 14:1-15** and **Psalms 2:1-12** and **Matthew 24:15-31** and **Mark 13:14-27** and **Luke 17:24-37** and **1 Thessalonians 4:13 – 5:10** and **Revelation 6:12-17; 7:9-17; 11:1-19; 12:1 – 13:18; 14:14-20; 16:12-16; 19:11-21** – Throughout the Tanak (Old Testament) prophets there is a reoccurring phrase that many of them use multiple times, called, "The Day of Yahuweh/Yehovah." Not one of them in the original Hebrew ever once uses the phrase "Day of the Lord" or "Day of the Master" or "Day of the Messiah," only, "The Day of Yahuweh/Yehovah." And this "Day of Yahuweh/Yehovah" is described in great detail in many prophecies in the Tanak (Old Testament) as a day when the Sun, Moon, and Stars are darkened in Isaiah 13 and Joel 3; a day when the heavens and the earth are shaken in Isaiah 13 and Joel 3; a day of the sounding of the shophar in Zephaniah 1; a day of all the nations of the world gathered together for battle against Yahuweh/Yehovah in Isaiah 13 and Joel 3 and Zechariah 14 and Zephaniah 3; a day of thick and dark clouds causing the earth to be darkened in Zephaniah 1 and Zechariah 14; a day of tribulation trouble that is the wrath of Yahuweh/Yehovah poured out as judgment on the unrighteous, but that Jacob is saved from, in Isaiah 13 and Isaiah 26 and Isaiah 34 and Jeremiah 25 and Jeremiah 30 and Joel 3 and Zephaniah 1 – 3 and Zechariah 14; a day when everyone on the earth, both men and women, are experiencing the labor pains of giving birth in Isaiah 26 and Jeremiah 30; and a day when all of the nations of the earth are destroyed and every living person on the earth who does not belong to Yahuweh/Yehovah is killed like with the global flood in Isaiah 13 and Jeremiah 25 and Jeremiah 30 and Joel 3 and Zephaniah 1 – 2 and Zechariah 14.

In Matthew 24 and Mark 13 Yeshua prophesies about this same Day of Yahuweh/Yehovah that is described many times in prophecy, and then very precisely connects with his own coming as the Son of Adam in the clouds from Daniel 7. In Matthew 24 and Mark 13 Yeshua brings together the darkening of the sun, moon, and stars from Isaiah and Joel, and the shaking of the heavens and the earth from Isaiah and Joel, and the sounding of the shophar from Zephaniah, and the dark, thick clouds and darkening of the earth from Zephaniah and Zechariah, combined with all of the families of the earth mourning from Zechariah 12 and the lightnings and thunderings and dark clouds and sounding shophar from Exodus 19.

Yeshua takes the pieces from all of the prophecies about "The Day of Yahuweh/Yehovah" and brings them together into a complete prophecy describing the Day of his coming as the Son of Adam. But at the same time he says that this Day of his coming, this Day that is the same Day as the Day of Yahuweh/Yehovah prophesied throughout Scripture, happens "after the tribulation/trouble of those days." Yeshua very clearly sets out the timing of the tribulation/trouble of the Day of Yahuweh/Yehovah as being after the Great Tribulation that Yeshua had just described earlier, from Daniel 12, which lasts for 1,290 days plus 45 days after the Disgusting Idol (Abomination). He separates out these two events in prophecies as being separate and different from one another. First there is the Great Tribulation/Trouble that happens before he comes, described in Daniel 12 that lasts for about 3.5 years, then there is the Day of Yahuweh/Yehovah Tribulation/Trouble of his wrath that happens on the Day of Yeshua's coming in the clouds, after the Great Tribulation is all over and done.

Prophecies Specifically Describing the Tribulation Trouble of the Time, Times, and Half a Time
Lasts for 3.5 Years Before the
Coming of Yahuweh/Yehovah

Daniel 7:19-25
Daniel 12:1-13
Matthew 24:15-26
Mark 13:14-23
Revelation 7:9-17
Revelation 11:1-11
Revelation 12:1 – 13:18

Prophecies Specifically Describing the Tribulation Trouble of the Day of Yahuweh/Yehovah
Lasts for a "Day" During the "Day"
of the Coming of Yahuweh/Yehovah

Isaiah 2:10-22
Isaiah 13:1-22
Isaiah 26:16-21
Isaiah 34:1-17
Isaiah 63:1-6
Jeremiah 25:15-38
Jeremiah 30:1 – 31:14
Daniel 7:9-18
Joel 2:32 – 3:21
Obadiah 1:1-21
Zephaniah 1:1 – 3:20

Zechariah 14:1-15
Psalms 2:1-12
Matthew 24:27-31
Mark 13:24-27
Luke 17:24-37
1 Thessalonians 4:13 – 5:10
Revelation 6:12-17
Revelation 11:15-19
Revelation 14:14-20
Revelation 16:12-16
Revelation 19:11-21

When all of the prophecies are laid out according to how Yeshua says that they happen, it becomes really clear that there are two distinctly different times and types of tribulation/trouble at the Time of the End. First comes the 3.5 years of Great Tribulation that in Daniel and Matthew/Mark and Revelation is described as a time of spiritual tribulation that is specifically only for the believers in Yeshua to go through, for their refining and preparation to be made clean and righteous for Yahuweh/Yehovah's coming. These verses are listed on the left in the previous chart, and anyone can see for themselves that it is only Yahuweh/Yehovah's own people, his set-apart ones, who go through that Great Tribulation, which is described as a unique kind of spiritual tribulation of deceptions and being overcome spiritually on the earth by the world, etc. The rest of the world of unrighteous, non-believers does not experience the Great Tribulation, because it is only for the refining of the believers.

Then after that time of the Great Tribulation for the believers in Yeshua and Israel, the non-believers and unrighteous experience the Day of Yahuweh/Yehovah tribulation of his wrath, on the day of his coming in the clouds. The believers are gathered up together by the messengers and "Jacob" is saved out of this day of tribulation/trouble of the wrath of Yahuweh/Yehovah. The believers in Yeshua do not experience "The Day of Yahuweh/Yehovah Tribulation/Trouble" on the Day of Yeshua's coming in the clouds, because that tribulation/trouble wrath is only for the non-believer. And the non-believer does not experience "The Great Tribulation/Trouble" that comes before Yeshua's coming in the clouds, because that tribulation/trouble is the love of Yahuweh/Yehovah to get his people made ready and clean for his coming, so that they are not thrown out into the lake of fire at his coming. "The Great Tribulation/Trouble" is Yahuweh/Yehovah's love for his people, to save them from "The Day of Yahuweh/Yehovah Tribulation/Trouble" that is his wrath that comes later, on the Day of his coming after the Great Tribulation is ended.

If Yeshua so clearly teaches and explains that the Day of Yahuweh/Yehovah does not come until the day of his coming at the very end of the Great Tribulation, after the Great Tribulation is over, then where does the myth come from that the Day of Yahuweh/Yehovah happens during the 3.5 years of Great Tribulation instead of afterward like Yeshua says? The myth comes from two primary verses in Revelation. The first one of these verses is in Revelation 1:10 when John says literally, "I came to be in the Spirit on the Lord's day." Christians and scholars have argued for many hundreds of years what this phrase "the Lord's day" actually means, but the myth that the Day of Yahuweh/Yehovah happening during the Great Tribulation instead of afterward like Yeshua says comes from the interpretation that this phrase "the Lord's day" should instead say and mean "the day of Yahuweh/Yehovah." If John is saying that he was taken in the Spirit "on the day of Yahuweh/Yehovah" then it could be interpreted to mean that the entire vision revelation of John in the entire book of John is referring to "The Day of Yahuweh/Yehovah."

The other interpretation that people have placed on this phrase "the Lord's day" is that it should instead say and mean "the first day of the week" representing the day of Yeshua's resurrection or "the Sabbath day" representing the weekly Sabbath, either on Saturday or Sunday. But when looking at the textual evidence from the Greek phrase written here and comparing it with other similar Greek phrases in other books of the New Testament, together with old Aramaic and Hebrew translations, and other Christian writings from the same time period, anyone can see for themselves that both of these interpretations of John's words of "the Lord's day" are incorrect and have no textual or historical evidence to back them up.

The Master's Day versus The Day of Yahuweh/Yehovah and The Day of the Master

1 Thessalonians 5:2 – *written circa 51 C.E.*

   Greek: heymera Kuriou | ἡμέρα Κυριου

     English Translation: **day of Lord**

2 Thessalonians 2:2 – *written circa 51 C.E.*

   Greek (Manuscript Variation 1): heymera tou Kuriou | ἡμέρα τοῦ Κυρίου [40]

     English Translation: **day of the Lord**

   Greek (Manuscript Variation 2): heymera tou Christou | ἡμέρα τοῦ Χριστοῦ [41]

     English Translation: **day of the Christ**

Revelation 1:10 – *written circa 90 C.E.*

   Greek: en tey kuriakey heymera | ἐν τῇ κυριακῇ ἡμέρᾳ

     English Translation: **on the lord's day** (or) **on the lordly day**

   Syriac Aramaic (Translation): beyaoma dechadbeshaba | ܒܝܘܡܐ ܕܚܕܒܫܒܐ [42]

     English Translation: **on the first day of the week**

   Hebrew (Possible Translation): bayom adoniyi | בַּיּוֹם אֲדֹנָיִי [43]

     English Translation: **on the Masterly day**

   Hebrew (Known for Certain Translation): beyom echad beshabbath | בְּיוֹם אֶחָד בְּשַׁבָּת [44]

     English Translation: **on first day, on Sabbath**

   Hebrew (Modern Translations): beyom ha'adon | בְּיוֹם הָאָדוֹן

     English Translation: **on day of the Master**

The Didache: Chapter 14 – *written late 1st century C.E.*

   Greek: Kata kuriakeyn de Kuriou sunachthentes klasate arton | Κατὰ κυριακὴν δὲ Κυρίου συναχθέντες κλάσατε ἄρτον [45]

     English Translation (Possibility 1): **According to lord's, also Lord, assemble yourselves and break bread**

     English Translation (Possibility 2): **Every lord's, also Lord, assemble yourselves and break bread**

Epistle of Ignatius to the Magnesians: Chapter 9 – *written circa 110 C.E.*

   Greek: meyketi sabbatisontes, alla kata kuriakeyn sontes | μηκέτι σαββατίζοντες, ἀλλὰ κατὰ κυριακὴν ζῶντες

     English Translation: **no longer Sabbath living, but according to lord's living**

---

[40] Every manuscript of 2 Thessalonians 2 that is not of the *Byzantine/Majority Text* or *Codex Claromontanus*

[41] *Byzantine/Majority Text* consisting of the majority of surviving manuscript copies of the Greek New Testament, and *Codex Claromontanus: D₂; 06* (circa 550 C.E. copy) Gr. 107; Bibliotheque Nationale de France, Paris.

[42] John Gwynn, *The Apocalypse of St. John in a Syriac Version Hitherto Unknown* (Grafton Street, Dublin: Hodges, Figges, and Co., 1897) [From a manuscript of the book of Revelation in Syriac dated from about the 9th to 12th century C.E.]

[43] *Revelation of St. John in a Hebrew Version* (17th century C.E. copy) Sloane Ms. 237; British Library, London.

[44] Domenico Gerosolimitano, *The New Testament Translated from Syriac, Greek, Latin, and Arabic into the Hebrew Language: Volume 2* (1617 C.E.) Neofiti. 33; Biblioteca Apostolica Vaticana, Vatican City.

[45] Roswell D. Hitchcock and Francis Brown, *Teaching of the Twelve Apostles [The Didache]* (New York: Charles Scribner's Sons, 1884) Chapter XIV, pg. 24

The two biggest problems for understanding the phrase "the Lord's day" is that in the Greek language of the New Testament the word for "lord," which is "Kurios Κυρίος," can have two different meanings. The primary meaning of Kurios is "lord" or "master," but there is also no doubt that sometimes this word is used in the Greek language of the New Testament in place of the name of Yahuweh/Yehovah. We know for certain that this replacement of the name of Yahuweh/Yehovah with the Greek word Kurios in various different grammatical spelling forms happened in the Greek New Testament, because of the many places in the New Testament that quote from the Hebrew Tanak (Old Testament) and replace the name of Yahuweh/Yehovah in those quotes with the various forms of Kurios, such as in Acts 2:21; 2:25; 2:34; 3:22; 4:26; 7:30; 7:33; 7:37; 7:49, etc.

Therefore there are some places in the New Testament that Kurios means "master" and there are other places that it is written in place of where the name of Yahuweh/Yehovah should be. In 1 Thessalonians 5:2 there is no doubt that the phrase that Paul is writing is "day of Yahuweh/Yehovah" because this Greek phrase "heymera Kuriou" is what is found in the Greek Septuagint translation of the Old Testament (in the copies that the early gentile Christians used) in the verses that say "day of Yahuweh/Yehovah" in the Hebrew. There is some question about what Paul was writing in 2 Thessalonians 2:2 because half of the old Greek manuscripts have written there the phrase "heymera tou Christou," meaning, "day of the Christ" or "day of the Messiah," and the other half have the phrase "heymera tou Kuriou," meaning, "day of the Lord" or "day of the Master." Since the definite article "the" is used here in the phrase "day of the Lord," different from "day of Lord" found in 1 Thessalonians 5:2, it probably does not indicate that the name of Yahuweh/Yehovah is written here, but instead has the meaning of "master."

Paul often referred to the day of Yeshua's coming with many different phrases in his letters, including "the day of Yahuweh/Yehovah" or "the day of the Master Yeshua" or "the day of Messiah Yeshua" or "the day of Messiah" or sometimes simply as "The Day." So it does not matter which phrase is the original here in 2 Thessalonians, whether it be "day of the Master" or "day of the Messiah," because to Paul they both have the exact same meaning, referring to the day of Yeshua's coming on "the day of Yahuweh/Yehovah." But from these variations of phrases in 1 Thessalonians and the different manuscripts of 2 Thessalonians we can see how phrases referring to the coming of Yeshua were used in the 1st century C.E. like "the day of Yahuweh/Yehovah" and "the day of the Master" or "the day of the Messiah."

In Revelation 1:10 there is a completely different phrase that is written there in the Greek, as "tey kuriakey heymera," meaning, "the Lord's day," instead of "heymera Kuriou" or "heymera tou Kuriou." If John is referring to "the day of Yahuweh/Yehovah" or "the day of the Master" or "the day of the Messiah," then why would he not have simply said those phrases or used these common phrases already in use at that time in Christianity for the day of Yeshua's coming. If John was talking about the day of Yeshua's coming, then he would have simply used those common phrases that were already in use that everyone already understood. By using the phrasing "the Lord's day" it is in order to distinguish this phrase so that people will not think that he is talking about the actual day of Yeshua's return, and then be confused into thinking that he is saying that Yeshua has already returned on that day that Yeshua appeared to John in the vision. That appearance by

Yeshua in the vision was not the day of Yeshua's actual coming in the future, so John writes "the Lord's day" instead.

The next question is what does "Lord" mean here to John in his writing? Is he writing "on the Master's day" or is he writing "on Yahuweh/Yehovah's day." Because the definite article "the" is present here it is more likely that he is writing "on the Master's day" referring to Yeshua as "the Master." And this is backed up by Hebrew translations from the Greek. The 17th century C.E. manuscript that contains a possible Hebrew translation of the first two chapters of Revelation writes in the name of Yahuweh/Yehovah in the complete Hebrew letters Yod Hey Vav Hey יְהֹוָה in places where the Greek only has "Lord," such as in Revelation 1:8. But in this manuscript, even though it uses the name of Yahuweh/Yehovah, in Revelation 1:10 it has written there "bayom adoniyi," meaning, "on the Masterly day." This is certainly an interesting and unusual reading of this verse, maybe in an attempt to try to match the Hebrew with the strange Greek wording written in the verse, but it shows the point that the meaning here of "Lord" in this verse is "Master" instead of the name of Yahuweh/Yehovah.

Most modern Hebrew translation done since the 1800's that also input the name of Yahuweh/Yehovah in place of the Greek word "lord" in places like Revelation 1:8, also use a similar wording here of "beyom haadon," meaning, "on day of the Master." And this wording of "on day of the Master" also illustrates the point that the meaning here is "Master" instead of the name of Yahuweh/Yehovah.

Using the phrase "on the Master's day" means that John is trying to avoid using the traditional phrases about the day of Yeshua's coming. If he meant to say "the day of Yahuweh/Yehovah" then he would have said it, and if he meant to say "the day of the Master" or "the day of the Messiah" then he would have said it, but he did not. He is still trying to communicate an important day that is a special day belonging to Yeshua though. This is where the other interpretation comes in that perhaps it is referring to the day of Yeshua's resurrection on the first day of the week (even though it clearly says in the Gospels that the women arriving at the tomb before sunrise on the 1st day of the week discovered that Yeshua had already risen before the 1st day of the week), or perhaps it refers to the day of the Sabbath, either on the first day of the week or the seventh day of the week.

One of the oldest, or possibly the oldest, manuscript of the book of Revelation in Syriac Aramaic is the one recorded by John Gwynn in his book *The Apocalypse of St. John in a Syriac Version Hitherto Unknown*, from sometime during the 9th to 12th centuries. The congregations of believers in the East who used Aramaic scriptures instead of Greek did not accept the book of Revelation as Scripture for many hundreds of years, which is why most agree beyond any doubt that any Aramaic versions of Revelation are translations from Greek, since the Aramaic speaking Christians did not preserve the book of Revelation until the 9th century or later. Also John Gwynn believed that he had found the Greek textual copy of Revelation that the Aramaic manuscript he was working with had come from. This Aramaic manuscript, as well as the official Peshitta Aramaic copy of the New Testament used by the Christians in the East for over a thousand years, translates this Greek phrase "on the Lord's day" as "on the first day of the week."

Domenico Gerosolimitano in the year 1617 also made a Hebrew translation of the New Testament from four different languages at once, from Syriac Aramaic and Greek and Latin and Arabic manuscripts of the

New Testament simultaneously. And he translated this phrase into Hebrew as "on first day, on Sabbath." These two translations show how the Greek phrase "on the Lord's day" cannot refer to the first day of the week or the Sabbath day, because if John had meant to say "on the first day of the week" then he would have written "on the first day of the week" as is found in the Aramaic. And if he had meant to say "on the first day, on Sabbath" he would have written "on the first day, on Sabbath," because it makes more sense and is very clear. The phrase "on the Master's day" is an ambiguous, confusing phrase, and if you were to mean to say "on the first day of the week" then you would just write that, because there is no confusion in the statement anymore.

Many hundreds of years later this phrase "on the Master's day" came to have the meaning of "the first day of the week Sabbath," and that is why translators added that interpretation to his words written here. But that was only their later interpretation, and they changed John's words to mean what they wanted those words to mean. But there is nowhere in all of Scripture that the Sabbath day or the first day of the week are called "the Master's day" or "the day of the Master" or "Yeshua's day" or even "Yahuweh/Yehovah's day." So the translators in the Aramaic and in the case of Gerosolimitano into his Hebrew translation had to change the words "the Master's day" entirely in order to make them mean "first day of the week" or "Sabbath." If the phrase "the Master's day" really was referring to the first day of the week or the Sabbath then they would have had no reason to change the words at all; they could have left the phrase exactly as it was and everyone would have known instantly what that phrase meant. The fact that the translators had to try to change it shows how the phrase "the Masters day" as it is written in the Greek does not make any sense and it is a mystery which no one for at least the last 1,000 years has known the truth of what it really means.

Because within Scripture itself there is no answer to the true meaning of this phrase "the Master's day," many have tried looking at other early Christian and Church Father writings that were written close to the same time period as Revelation around the year 90 C.E. But this too brings no answers when looking at the original Greek words those writings were written in. The English translations of those writings unfortunately fool people into thinking that the early Christians were writing about a "Lord's day" using the exact same phrase that John used in Revelation for "Lord's day." But the reality is that not one of the early Christian writings in the 1st and 2nd centuries C.E. uses this phrase "Master's day" or "Lord's day."

The oldest source used to try to explain this phrase is the apocrypha book known as The Didache, written close to the same time as the book of Revelation at the end of the 1st century. Most translations of this work, at the beginning Chapter 14, add in the word "day" even though it does not exist there in the sentence. What the sentence says at its beginning in the Greek, as shown in the earlier chart, uses the same word "Lord's" or "kuriakeyn" as the word "kuriakey" in Revelation 1:10, but anyone can see for themselves that the Greek word for "day," which is "heymera," does not exist there in the sentence. There are two main possible meanings for this sentence in Greek: either it means "According to lord's, also Lord, assemble yourselves and break bread," or it means "Every lord's, also Lord, assemble yourselves and break bread." It could mean that according to a "lord's" something Christians are supposed to gather together to break bread, or it could mean that regularly at every "lord's" something Christians are supposed to gather together to break bread. Either way this sentence has nothing to do with "the Master's day" that John talks about. If the writer of this apocrypha work meant to say the phrase "Lord's day" then he would have said the phrase "Lord's day," but instead he wrote the phrase "Lord's also Lord."

It is the same in the case of the letter that Ignatius wrote to the Magnesians around the year 110 C.E., shortly after the book of Revelation was written. Most translations make it sound like Ignatius is talking about a "Lord's day," but as can be seen from the Greek of his letter in Chapter 9 (shown in the earlier chart) what he really is saying is that Christians should not keep the Sabbath at all anymore, on any day of the week, which is the same thing that most of the Church Fathers wrote in the 2nd to 4th centuries C.E. Again he uses the Greek word "kuriakeyn," but the word "heymera" for "day" does not exist in the sentence with it. And he writes literally, "no longer Sabbath living, but according to lord's living." He says that Christians should no longer be doing "Sabbath living," but instead be doing "Lord's living," which could mean many different things, but the one thing for certain that it does not have anything to do with is a "Lord's day."

This letter written by Ignatius also has nothing to do with the phrase of "the Master's day" that John writes about in Revelation, and has no relevance in explaining what John meant with his phrase. If Ignatius meant to say "Lord's day" then he would have said "Lord's day," but instead he wrote the phrase "Lord's living," which has nothing to do with any particular day of the week or year. "Lord's living" can be done anytime of any day without any restrictions to it. These two writings are only two of the earliest examples, but it is the same with all of the other early Christian writings from the 1st and 2nd centuries C.E. Every one of them that supposedly talks about a "Lord's day" in translations, when reading them in the original Greek do not say anything about a "Lord's day," or even about keeping a Sabbath or a celebration on any particular day called a "Lord's day." That was something made up around a thousand years later in translations of the early Christian writings and of Scripture itself, to make the words mean what Christians in the middle ages and later ages interpreted them to mean, according to their own modern Christian religious practices that did not exist in the 1st and 2nd centuries.

At this point there is no historical manuscript or record that has been found from the 1st and 2nd centuries that can explain what John's words about "the Master's day" mean. The term meant something to John that he understood what it meant, and the seven assemblies in Asia he sent the book of Revelation to would have also understood what he was talking about. He was making a special connection with the fact that Yeshua appeared to him on the same day that was a special day belonging to Yeshua. What that day was we can only speculate until more information can be discovered and brought out into the open from ancient manuscripts and writings from that time, or the discovery of other older manuscripts of the book of Revelation itself that could give a clue about its meaning. All that we know for certain is that there is no evidence that this phrase "the Master's day" has anything to do with the Sabbath or the first day of the week, or the day itself in the future of Yeshua's coming on the Day of Yahuweh/Yehovah. There is no evidence that John is claiming from this verse that his entire vision, including the time of the Great Tribulation before Yeshua returns, is part of "the day of Yahuweh/Yehovah" in prophecy.

The second place in Revelation that the myth about the Day of Yahuweh/Yehovah happening before the day of Yeshua's return comes from is in 6:15-17. After the Sixth Seal is opened, the events of the Sixth Seal cause the kings, great ones, rich, commanders, mighty, and every slave and every free person to hide in the caves and in the rocks of the mountains. This list includes every single person on the entire earth are all hiding, and while they are hiding they say that they want the rocks to fall on them and hide them from the wrath of the Lamb, "because the great day of His wrath has come." There is no doubt whatsoever that all of the people of the earth who are hiding in the ground and in the mountains are saying at this time that "The Day of Yahuweh/Yehovah" has come, when comparing these words with the other prophecies already mentioned concerning the Day of Yahuweh/Yehovah. But there is nothing that John has written here about the Sixth Seal that says the Sixth Seal has to happen before the very end of the Great Tribulation time period. And there is nothing that John has written here that says that all of the Sixth Seal has to happen at once after it has been opened, nothing preventing it from happening over a period of time with the last part of the Sixth Seal taking place at the time of Yeshua's coming.

And in fact John himself in the way he has written the book of Revelation supports the fact that this part of the Sixth Seal, with everyone on the earth hiding from the Lamb, actually happens at the "day" of the Lamb Yeshua's coming when the Great Tribulation is already over and done. Because all of these exact same people mentioned in Revelation 6:15-17 John writes about again in Revelation 19:17-18, except that all of these same kings, commanders, mighty, and every slave and free and small and great person on the earth who were once hiding from the Lamb are now all dead corpses, killed by the Lamb Yeshua in judgment. At first they are all running and hiding from Yeshua in Revelation 6, afraid that he is about to kill them in his wrath, and then in the next instant in Revelation 19 they are all dead.

There cannot be a very large gap of time in between the events of the Sixth Seal and Yeshua's return, especially concerning the last part of the Sixth Seal. There cannot be a span of time of more than hours, or a day or two, in between the people of the earth hiding in Revelation 6 and then all of them dead in Revelation 19, because in Revelation 6:15-17 Yeshua has already returned and all of the people of the earth can see him and "the face of the One" on the throne. That is why they are trying to hide, because they can see the face of Yahuweh/Yehovah in the heavens and are trying to hide, like Adam and Eve in the garden after they ate the fruit of the knowledge of good and evil, so that he cannot see them. So there is nothing in what John has written about the Sixth Seal that the last part of it has to happen before Yeshua has already returned. The other parts of it could begin happening within a few months or weeks before his coming on the Day of Yahuweh/Yehovah, but there is no requirement that the part of the people hiding from the face of Yahuweh/Yehovah and from the wrath of the Lamb have to be doing so on any day other than the actual day of his coming at the end of the 3.5 years of Great Tribulation.

It is important to understand that the 3.5 years of Great Tribulation are not the Day of Yahuweh/Yehovah, and that the Day of Yahuweh/Yehovah does not begin until the day of Yeshua's coming as the Son of Adam in the dark and thick clouds, on a day of great darkness when the sun and moon and stars are all darkened without any light coming from them. Because anyone who does not understand this will experience Yeshua and the Day of Yahuweh/Yehovah coming upon them as a thief in the night, thinking from the myths about the Great Tribulation that all normal, everyday life stops in the terrible, wrath tribulation of Yahuweh/Yehovah's judgment for a full 3.5 or 7 years, and then it will be easy to see that the world is ending and Yeshua is returning at any moment. And experiencing Yeshua returning as a thief in the night on a day at the end of the 3.5 years of Great Tribulation when, according to Yeshua, everyone will be going on with their normal, everyday lives as though the world will never end, is not a good thing for anybody to experience.

The Coming of the Son of Adam (Yeshua) as a Surprise, as a Thief in the Night, to the All the World, Including to the Wicked and to the Unrighteous and Unfaithful Servants, at the End of the Great Tribulation, but Not as a Surprise or as a Thief in the Night to the Righteous and Faithful Servants – *Dealing with the Myth that Yeshua Comes as a Thief in the Night to Everyone, Even to the Righteous and Faithful Servants Who are Awake and Sons of the Day, because, According to the Myth, the True Followers of Yeshua are Really the Same as the Unrighteous and Unfaithful Servants Who are Sons of the Night and Darkness, Who are Asleep and Do Not Know the Day or the Hour of the Day of Yahuweh/Yehovah or of the Return of Their Master Yeshua, so that that Day Overtakes Them as a Thief in the Night and Together with the Wicked They are Thrown Out into the Darkness Where There is Weeping and Gnashing of Teeth*:

Genesis 7:1-12
Exodus 19:9-20; 24:1-18; 34:1-10
Leviticus 23:23-25
Matthew 24:29-51   Mark 13:24-37   Luke 17:24-37   Luke 21:34-36
Matthew 25:1-13
1 Thessalonians 5:1-10
2 Peter 3:10-15
Revelation 3:3
Revelation 16:15

Word for Word Prophecy Examination of Partially Fulfilled, Fulfilled, and Unfulfilled Verses **Genesis 7:1-12** and **Exodus 19:9-20; 24:1-18; 34:1-10** and **Leviticus 23:23-25** and **Matthew 24:29-51** and **Mark 13:24-37** and **Luke 17:24-37** and **Luke 21:34-36** and **Matthew 25:1-13** and **1 Thessalonians 5:1-10** and **2 Peter 3:10-15** and **Revelation 3:3** and **Revelation 16:15** – Yeshua warns that his coming will be like the days of Noah and Lot, with everyone living normal, everyday life even up to the very day of his coming at the end of the Great Tribulation (after the tribulation/trouble of those days). In the same way that everyone was eating and drinking and marrying and having children and planting and building and buying and selling even on the very day that the destruction came to the entire earth or to Sodom and Gomorrah, at the end of the Great Tribulation everyone will be living out normal, everyday life even up to the very day that Yeshua comes. These are Yeshua's own words in Matthew and Mark and Luke, his warning that his coming at the end of the Great Tribulation will be a surprise to all those who are destroyed in his judgment on that day, because life will look so normal up to the day of his coming it will appear that the world is continuing on as it always has and will never end.

Yeshua explains the reason that his coming will be such a surprise to anyone not listening to him and obeying him as Noah and his family or Abraham and then later Lot (reluctantly), is because he will be coming like a thief in the night. Yeshua was the first to use this analogy in Matthew 24, explaining that if a person were to know the day and time (day and hour) that a thief were to break into their home, then they would have been watching for the thief and prevented the thief from breaking in. Yeshua will come like that thief, unexpectedly by surprise to all those who do not know the day or time when he is coming, to steal the earth away from them, ending the world of mankind on the earth. And he explains that the only ones who will be taken by surprise by his coming, because in Matthew 24:50 they do not know the day or the time of his coming, are the wicked and unrighteous and unfaithful servants. This includes those Christians or servants who are unfaithful to Yahuweh/Yehovah and because of their unfaithfulness to Yeshua he comes on a day and at a time they do not know or expect.

Later Yeshua again talks about his coming like a thief in the night in Revelation 3 and 16. In Revelation 3 he warns his followers who are asleep that they need to wake up and know the exact time of his coming, or else he will come to them as a thief in the night at a time they do not know. And from Matthew 24:50 Yeshua has already explained that those who experience Yeshua coming as a thief in the night at a time they do not know will be cut in half and appointed to be with the hypocrites where there is weeping and gnashing of teeth. From Revelation 16:15 we also know that those who experience Yeshua coming as a thief in the night will, because they have fallen asleep, have to walk naked and everyone see their shame that Yeshua came to them as a surprise, without their knowing ahead of time that he was coming. This is Yeshua's warning about his coming as a thief in the night, as a surprise, at the end of the Great Tribulation.

Paul and Peter both make the same warning about Yeshua coming as a thief in the night, by warning about the day of Yeshua's coming on the Day of Yahuweh/Yehovah as a thief in the night. When the Day of Yahuweh/Yehovah comes at the end of the Great Tribulation, it will come as a thief in the night, with sudden destruction at a time when everyone is living out their normal, everyday lives in the midst of peace and safety and the end of the Great Tribulation. And Paul makes the same warning as Yeshua, that that day of Yeshua's coming should not come as a thief in the night to any true believer and follower of Yeshua, who is a son of the light and the day. That day of Yeshua's coming on the Day of Yahuweh/Yehovah at the end of the Great Tribulation should only come as a thief in the night to those who will be destroyed in the wrath of Yahuweh/Yehovah on that day. And those who are true followers of Yeshua will be saved from the wrath of that day of his coming, but only if his coming to them is <u>not</u> like a thief in the night and is <u>not</u> a surprise to them.

The question then is that if Yeshua says that he is coming as a thief in the night, on a day when everyone is living out their normal, everyday lives, at the very end of the Great Tribulation, how is it that in spite of all of the signs preceding his coming, no one but the righteous are able to recognize and be ready for his coming? In Matthew 24:32-33 Yeshua explains that from the signs as with the parable of the fig tree, we can "know when He is near to the gates." But in Matthew 24:36 he explains that from these signs as with the fig tree "none know … that day or that time." [46] The signs that precede his coming only tell people he is near, but do not reveal or give proof for the day and the time (hour) of his coming. Even though there are many signs

---

[46] See Appendix: Hebrew Matthew Chapter 24

listed that happen before his coming in Luke 21:25-28, none of those signs give any proof about when Yeshua is actually going to come.

Yeshua says that there will be signs in the sun and moon and stars before he comes, but there are always signs happening in the sun and moon and stars in every generation, and these signs are nothing special or unique that would prove to anyone that Yeshua is actually about to come. And most reject the signs that happen anyways, as most have rejected or now forgotten about the signs in the sun, moon, and stars that have been happening over the last decade. On the earth there is the sign of anxiety among the nations, which has been growing with greater and greater anxiety for the last 100 years through World War I and World War II and many pandemics and economic troubles. The nations are in great anxiety this year of 2023 as the world leaders meet in the United Nations, greater anxiety than there has been since World War II and the creation of Israel. But this is nothing new and it is not a sign of proof that Yeshua is actually going to return now.

There is also the roaring of the sea (of people) prophesied from Isaiah 17:12-14 and people in great fear of what might happen on the earth in the future. They are all in perplexity and bewilderment about what is happening with the sea of people rising up in madness and violence around the world and bewilderment about the future. This certainly describes the days the world has been living in for the last 200 years, and especially the world today, but the sign itself is "perplexity" at the present and "fear" of an unknown and uncertain future. The sign itself shows that no one is able to figure out or understand what is happening or what is going one, and no knows what will happen in the future, in other words saying that at the time of Yeshua's coming no one can figure out that Yeshua is returning or that Yeshua is about to come in the future. They do not know that Yeshua is about to return in the future, which is why they are filled with fear about an unknown future, and they do not know that the current signs of the times in the present they are living in show that Yeshua is about to return in the future, because they are in perplexity about what is happening in the present. No one on the earth during the Great Tribulation before Yeshua returns is able to figure out from the signs in the present that Yeshua is about to return, and because of this they are in fear from not knowing about Yeshua's coming in their future.

The signs that happen before Yeshua's coming are no signs at all for the unrighteous and wicked and the unfaithful servants, and even for the righteous they are no proof for when Yeshua is returning. It was the same during the days of Noah and Lot, in which the signs they had were no proof that destruction would actually come to them. In the days of Noah the only sign that people had of a coming flood (because there had been no rain on the earth yet and no experience of flooding or water falling from the sky) was that Noah was building a giant boat to fit a lot of animals into. But that sign was no proof that the flood would actually come, because people build boats, even big boats, all of the time and the act of building a boat does not cause a flood to happen.

The only sign that the people in Sodom had that their city was about to be destroyed was two strangers coming into town and then a sudden experience of blindness on the people who tried to homosexually attack them. That experience, as miraculous as it was, was certainly no proof that fire was about to fall from the heavens and kill them all. Strangers walking into towns and strange events happening are no sign that the world is about to end for the people of a certain city. In the same way, the signs that Yeshua gives that will happen before his coming are also signs that, even though they might be strange and cause people to be bewildered, still happen as part of normal, everyday life and are not in any way proof that he is about to come. Therefore none of the signs that precede Yeshua's coming at the end of the Great Tribulation are proof of his coming, which means that he still comes as a thief in the night, by surprise, in the same way the destruction of the flood and of the fire came in the days of Noah and Lot.

Then of course we might ask about all of the prophecies being fulfilled during the 3.5 years of Great Tribulation. Would not all of those prophecies being fulfilled be a sign, especially to the Christians around the world, that would cause people to see and recognize that Yeshua is about to return, so that his coming is no longer a surprise like a thief in the night? But the reality is that the majority of people living during the times when prophecies are being fulfilled reject those fulfillments, and either rebel against them and try to change them or deny that they are even happening. This includes even the vast majority of Yahuweh/Yehovah's own people who are in covenant with him or who say they believe in him and follow him. Even Abraham and Sarah at first rejected Yahuweh/Yehovah's way of fulfilling his prophecy to them about a son, Isaac, being miraculously born to them, and tried to make the prophecy happen in their own way, resulting in the birth of Ishmael. Later they accepted Yahuweh/Yehovah's fulfillment of the prophecy in their son Isaac, but at first they tried to make the prophecy be fulfilled in their own way.

Joseph's brothers not only rejected any fulfillment of the prophecies that Yahuweh/Yehovah had given to him in dreams, but rejected the prophecies themselves as false. And through this rejection of the prophecies they tried to prevent the prophecies from ever being fulfilled by selling Joseph into slavery. But their act of rejecting Yahuweh/Yehovah's prophecies and trying to stop them from happening actually are what then made the prophecies happen and be fulfilled, propelling Joseph into the right place at the right time for Yahuweh/Yehovah to place him into the second most powerful position of authority in the most powerful nation in the world at that time.

When Yahuweh/Yehovah began using Moses to fulfill his prophecy he had given to Abraham in Genesis 15 by bringing the children of Israel out of bondage in Egypt, and judging that nation Egypt before taking Israel to the land he had promised to them in Canaan, the children of Israel fought Yahuweh/Yehovah all the way through. Every step of the way they were rebelling against him and rejecting his fulfillment of the prophecies to try to make them happen their own way, either by going back to Egypt and becoming a nation there instead in their old homes, or by building an Egyptian golden calf idol to worship as a god, or by refusing to enter and fight for the promised land in Canaan. In the end Yahuweh/Yehovah refused to let any of the generations of Israel above age 19 to enter the land and made them all die slowly in the wilderness for 38 years. They missed out on seeing the end fulfillment of the prophecies entirely, because they so thoroughly rejected Yahuweh/Yehovah's way of fulfilling the prophecies, and tried to make the prophecies happen their own way instead. Only two men from all those generations were allowed to see the final fulfillment of the prophecies and the completion of Yahuweh/Yehovah's promise, entering into the land and becoming their own, free nation.

And then Yahuweh/Yehovah gave many prophecies for hundreds of years through prophets like Isaiah and Jeremiah and Daniel and Zechariah about a coming Messiah. But when the Messiah finally came and the prophecies were being fulfilled, once again the vast majority of the people rejected the Messiah and the fulfillments of the prophecies completely. Some just ignored that it was happening at all, but there were some among the Pharisees who went even further like Joseph's brothers and tried to stop the prophecies from being fulfilled at all, after they found that they could not change Yahuweh/Yehovah's prophecy fulfillments to the way they wanted them to be by manipulating Yeshua and making him be the Messiah that they wanted to have. That is when they killed the promised and prophesied Messiah, and in so doing actually caused the prophecies to be fulfilled in the same way that Joseph's brothers caused Yahuweh/Yehovah's prophecies to be fulfilled by trying to prevent them from ever being fulfilled.

During the time of Noah, the entire world rejected the prophecy that Yahuweh/Yehovah had given to Noah and his family that a flood was coming to destroy the whole world. The only ones we know of for certain, from what is recorded in Genesis, who accepted Yahuweh/Yehovah's prophecy were Noah and his immediate family who prepared and were ready for it. All through recorded history in most of the cases where Yahuweh/Yehovah brings about a fulfillment of his prophecies, the vast majority of the people alive during that time of the fulfillment reject his fulfillment and try to manipulate and control the fulfillment to happen according to the way they want the prophecies to be fulfilled. [This is especially so in the times when Yahuweh/Yehovah has prophesied judgment and destruction on a city, like Jerusalem, or a nation, like Israel.] Later on some turn around in repentance and then accept Yahuweh/Yehovah's fulfillments of his prophecies, but even then most who live through and experience the fulfillments of prophecies never accept Yahuweh/Yehovah's way that he does the prophecies and try to control the prophecies, to change them into the way they want them or prevent them from happening at all.

Therefore fulfillments of prophecies during the Great Tribulation are no sign at all either that Yeshua is about to come at the end of the Great Tribulation, because the vast majority of people, including most of Yahuweh/Yehovah's own people, which now includes his own Christian followers, just like every time in the past, will reject those fulfillments and either deny that they are happening, or try to control and change them by manipulating Yahuweh/Yehovah to do things a different way, like the children of Israel with all of their tantrums in the wilderness. It is the way that people always are when dealing with Yahuweh/Yehovah, even the majority of his own people, wanting their own way because they think that they can do the prophecies better than Yahuweh/Yehovah can. Even the prophecies being fulfilled are no proof to people that Yeshua is about to return as a thief in the night, because the time of the Great Tribulation is no different from any other time in history when most alive during that time reject that the prophecies are even happening.

Yahuweh/Yehovah's prophecies are always fulfilled as a part of normal, everyday life, which is inconceivable when people have already imagined his prophecies happening in epic ways that stop all normal life from being able to happen. But a crazy thing about people is that there is nothing more precious to them than making sure they can carry on with their normal, everyday lives no matter what happens. Even two world wars in half a century were unable to stop people from going on with their normal, everyday lives around the world. Even in the midst of the battles during the wars they were unable to stop the civilians from living their normal, everyday lives for more than a few days or months at a time at the very most. And no pandemic through world history, except momentarily the COVID-19 pandemic, succeeded in stopping the world from going on with their normal, everyday lives right through every second of the pandemic amid great numbers of dead. When the atom bombs were dropped on Hiroshima and Nagasaki, the entire world, and even the entire rest of the nation of Japan, went on with their normal, everyday lives as though nothing had happened. Everyone focuses on the massive destruction the bombs caused within the cities, but no one talks about how outside of the blast areas, outside of the small radiation zones where the death and cancer took place, everybody went on with life as usual, as just another day to live through, even within Japan itself.

Not even nuclear weapons have been able to succeed in stopping people from living their normal, everyday lives around the world. One of the big news reports that the reporters were so impressed about after the recent earthquake in Turkey in 2023 that killed tens of thousands was how everybody in the destroyed cities went right back to living their normal, everyday lives as though nothing had happened within only a couple of days after the earthquakes, running their businesses and going about their normal lives again. It is no wonder that Yeshua warns that on the day of his coming at the end of the Great Tribulation everyone will be living out normal, everyday life as though the world is going to go on forever, not expecting him to come at any moment.

It is for all of these types of reasons that Yeshua warns that he will be coming like a thief in the night at the end of the 3.5 years of Great Tribulation. It is part of Yahuweh/Yehovah's plan to come stealthily at the end of the Great Tribulation, and the purpose of the Great Tribulation is specifically only for those who are in covenant with him, for his own followers and chosen, in order to get them clean and ready for him to come, prepared to marry him at the wedding. It is part of Yahuweh/Yehovah's plan to come as a total surprise to all of the world, with only those who are listening to him and truly following him in covenant with him knowing ahead of time that he is coming, having already prepared themselves ahead of time with their container of oil and their clean, white wedding garments of righteousness.

In Matthew 24:43-44 Yeshua explains in a parable about how his coming will be like a thief, and in this parable he explains how it is impossible to be able to watch for the coming of a thief to a house unless the person living there in the house first knows the day and the time when that thief is coming. Yeshua says that if the person had known the exact time when the thief would come to break into his house, he would have been able to watch for the thief and not allow him to break in. But because a person does not know the exact time and day when a thief is coming, then they are no longer able to watch for the thief's coming. In the same way the only way that a person can watch for Yeshua's coming like a thief in the night is if they first know the day and time when he is coming, or else it is impossible to be able to even obey Yeshua's command to watch for his coming.

No matter how much a person might watch over their property, hiring security guards and surveillance systems to watch for the coming thief, the coming of the thief will always be a surprise that will catch the watchers off guard unless they first know the exact day and time when the thief is coming to watch for him. It is the same with a defending army in wartime waiting and watching for an attack to come from the enemy. No matter how much that defending army watches day and night for the coming attack, the attack will always come as a surprise unless the defender can learn the day and time of the attack ahead of time. Then they can watch and be ready for the attack, preventing the attacker from being able to surprise them.

It is the same in all cases in real life when waiting for a visitor to come. The only way to watch for them and not be surprised by their coming is to know the day and time and year when they will come. Otherwise if the day and time and year of their coming is not known, then their arrival will always be a surprise and those waiting for their guest to arrive will not be ready or prepared for their guest no matter how much watching they did day after day. Yeshua is explaining in Matthew 24 in the various parables about the days of Noah and the thief coming and the return of the master to his house that watching for someone to come is useless and does no good without first knowing the day and time they will be coming, in order to be ready and watching on that day. And every single time that Yeshua explains this concept, whether it be in Matthew or Mark or Luke or Revelation, it is always the unfaithful servants, the unrighteous and wicked, who experience Yeshua coming on a day and a time that they do not know ahead of time. Never once does Yeshua come on a day and at a time that the righteous and faithful servants do not already know.

Yeshua first says that the signs of his coming only warn when he is near to coming, but cannot warn a person of the day and time when he is coming, so that a person who recognizes that he is near to coming could still experience his coming on a day and at a time they do not know. And if that happens, then they are in big trouble, because those who experience Yeshua coming on a day and at a time they do not know are not prepared and ready for him to come and do not enter into the wedding covenant of eternal life.

And this is why Yeshua says that the day of his coming at the end of the Great Tribulation as a thief in the night will be like the days of Noah, because the day of the flood only came as a thief in the night, as a surprise, to the entire world at that time, except for Noah himself and his family. The day of the flood was no surprise to Noah, because in Genesis 6:3 Yahuweh/Yehovah had already revealed to Noah ahead of time the exact year that the flood would come, in 120 years. Then 20 years later he revealed to Noah the plan of how to prepare for the flood and survive through it, by building a very large boat for his family and the animals. Then after another 100 years had gone by, for a total of 120 years, in Genesis 7:1-4 and 10-11 Yahuweh/Yehovah revealed to Noah the exact day and date that the flood would come, in exactly 7 days on the 17th day of the 2nd month, so that Noah would have time to prepare for the flood by getting all of the animals into the ark in time before the flood came.

And Yeshua said that the day of his coming will be the same as the day that the flood came, when it came as a surprise to everyone, except to the righteous like Noah who knew ahead of time directly from Yahuweh/Yehovah the exact day of its coming. The only way that Yeshua can be telling the truth here in this prophecy, that his coming will be like the days of Noah, is if Yahuweh/Yehovah, the Father, tells the righteous on the earth the exact day of his coming ahead of time as he did for Noah, however many days ahead of time that are needed for his people to be able to prepare and then watch for his coming. Just because no one throughout history has known the day or the hour of the coming of the Son of Adam, there is nothing in Yeshua's words that says that Yahuweh/Yehovah is not allowed to tell the day of his coming to the righteous right before he comes the same way that he told Noah the day that the flood would come (and the way that he told Moses the day of his coming in three days on Mount Sinai discussed in a couple paragraphs). The point of what Yeshua is saying in Matthew 24:36 and afterward is that no man or messenger (angel) has the power to figure out or reveal the day of Yeshua's coming, but Yahuweh/Yehovah is God and will do whatever he wants to do with revealing the days of future events that his people need to be prepared for, especially if it means saving his people from the day of his coming overtaking them as a thief in the night and the danger that they do not enter into eternal life, because they are not prepared for his coming.

If he does not tell the righteous ahead of time the exact day of his coming as he did for Noah in the flood, then Yeshua becomes a false prophet for saying that his coming will be the same as the day of the coming of the flood in the days of Noah. Yeshua's coming can only be like the days of Noah if the righteous know ahead of time the exact day Yeshua is coming as Noah knew ahead of time the exact day of the coming of the flood. This is good news that Yeshua says that his people will be told ahead of time the day of his coming so that they will be able to obey him in his instruction to watch for his coming. Because as Yeshua explains there is no way to be able to watch and be prepared for his coming like a thief unless we can know at least a few days ahead of time what day and time that coming will be.

But his revealing to his set-apart ones, his chosen, the day and time of his coming is for a very specific purpose, so that they can prepare and get ready for his coming in the same way that Noah needed time to prepare and get ready for the flood to come. Also, Yeshua describes his coming word for word to be exactly the same as his coming in Exodus 19. In Matthew 24 and Mark 13 Yeshua describes his coming in the darkened sky of clouds in the exact same way he came in the dark clouds above Mount Sinai in Exodus 19, and he comes with the sound of a shophar in the exact same way that he came with the sounding of the shophar as he came down upon Mount Sinai. And there is lightning and thunder when he came onto Mount Sinai in the same way there is lightning and thunder when he comes in the clouds as the Son of Adam at his return.

In Exodus 24 Moses writes that the seventy elders actually ate and drank with Yahuweh/Yehovah on Mount Sinai and they even saw him and did not die. And then in Exodus 34 Moses describes Yahuweh/Yehovah passing before him in enough of a physical form that he could see him well enough to be able to run over to him and bow down to him. When Yahuweh/Yehovah came down on Mount Sinai it was him actually coming down to walk upon the earth, upon Mount Sinai, and was a true coming of Yahuweh/Yehovah to the earth to be with and dwell with mankind for a short time. Yahuweh/Yehovah himself even says that this was one of his "comings" to the earth when he says to Moses in Exodus 19:9 "look, I come to you in the thick cloud."

In this coming of Yahuweh/Yehovah to the earth, on Mount Sinai in the cloud, which Yeshua describes in Matthew 24 and Mark 13 as being exactly the same as his coming in the future, Yahuweh/Yehovah tells Moses and the people the exact day of his coming ahead of time, on the third day. They also knew the exact day of Yahuweh/Yehovah's coming ahead of time by 3 days, because he told them when he was coming. And the reason he told them the exact day of his coming is so that they could prepare and get ready for his coming, all of them dressed in clean white garments, the garments that are the righteousness of the set-apart ones washed in the blood of the Lamb as in Revelation 7 and 19. Then Yahuweh/Yehovah created a festival called the Day of Trumpets, or the Day of Blowing the Alarm, to commemorate this day of his coming in the clouds every year on the 1st day of the 7th month in Leviticus 23:23-25.

Yeshua comes as a thief in the night by surprise to the world, because there are no signs of proof that prove to anybody ahead of time during the 3.5 years of Great Tribulation that he is actually coming. But he does not come as a thief in the night by surprise to the set-apart ones, his chosen, because Yahuweh/Yehovah tells them ahead of time the day that he will be coming in the same way that he told Noah the day the flood would be coming and he told the people at Mount Sinai ahead of time the exact day he would be coming in the clouds. And in both cases with Noah and the flood and the people waiting at Mount Sinai for Yahuweh/Yehovah's coming in the clouds there were no signs of proof that happened ahead of time to be able to know for certain that the flood would actually come or that he would actually come. In both cases Noah and Moses and the people with them had to simply believe Yahuweh/Yehovah and take him at his word that the flood would come on a certain day or that he would come on a certain day.

And in both cases there was no one prophesying or giving prophecies about the day that the flood would come or that Yahuweh/Yehovah himself would come. There was no prophesying happening about that day; Yahuweh/Yehovah simply told his set-apart ones the exact day, and then they are all so busy preparing for the day there is no time for prophesying or even caring about prophesying the day of his coming. Because everyone has to be ready and prepared for the appointed day that Yahuweh/Yehovah has decided and if they are not prepared by that day then they will be lost and destroyed, either in the flood or for not being clean in the presence of a perfectly righteous God. Yahuweh/Yehovah understands that it is impossible to watch for his coming as a thief if we do not know the day and time he is coming, and that is why he will give his set-apart ones warning, however many days ahead of time that are needed, to prepare and get ready, so that that day, the Day of Yahuweh/Yehovah, does not overtake them as a thief in the night and they walk in shame as they are cut in two and thrown out with the hypocrites to where there is weeping and gnashing of teeth, banging on the gate to be let into the wedding feast because of being unprepared and gone at the market at the time the bridegroom comes.

Section 23. **The Roaring Sea of People:**

References to the Roaring Sea of People Prophecies:
   Daniel 7:2-3
   Revelation 13:1
   Revelation 17:1, 15

Word for Word Prophecy Examination of Fulfilled Verses **Daniel 7:2-3** and **Revelation 13:1** and **Revelation 17:1, 15** – In Revelation 17:15 the messenger explains how waters are a picture and a symbol of people, especially crowds and groupings of people come together. This gives the understanding in both Daniel 7 and Revelation 13 and 17 about how people are represented as many waters, or like a sea or ocean. This can be seen in reality when large crowds of people come together they look exactly like a moving sea or ocean or rivers of water, flowing together.

The Roaring Sea of People Prophecies; the Sea of People Receded into Their Homes Like a Tsunami Causing the Ocean to Recede from the Beach, Before Pouring Out in Wave After Wave Like a Tsunami Covering the Earth with a Roaring Sea:
   Isaiah 17:12-14
   Luke 21:25-26

Prophecy Fulfillment of Verses **Isaiah 17:12-14** and **Luke 21:25-26** – There is another prophecy about people being like many waters or like the seas in Isaiah 17, but this prophecy is rarely spoken of. In the Hebrew of this prophecy in Isaiah 17:12-14 it reads, "Woe to the roar of many peoples, like the roar of the seas roaring, and crashing of gathered peoples (nations) like the crashing of mighty waters making a crashing. Gathered peoples (nations) shall rush like the crashing of many waters. But he shall rebuke it and it shall flee far away, and be chased like the chaff of the mountains before the wind, and like a whirlwind before a wind storm (hurricane). Toward the time of evening, and look, terror. Before morning it is no more. This is the portion of those plundering us, and the lot for those robbing us." [47] Then in the Greek of Luke 21:25 Yeshua says, "in perplexity, the roaring sound of the sea and tossing." [48]

The words here match in the Hebrew of Isaiah 17 and the Greek of Luke 21, where the people are making the roaring sound like the sound of the sea in both places, and then the Hebrew word for "crash," "שָׁאוֹן" "sha'on," describes the same definition as the Greek word "σάλος" "salos," meaning tossing or rolling. They both are describing the destructive and violent force of waves of water as in a storm or on a rough day at sea when the waves are stronger and louder than normal. And in both cases the Hebrew and Greek words are describing the waves as they are crashing onto shore and tossing about with destructive and violent force.

---

[47] הוֹי הֲמוֹן עַמִּים רַבִּים כַּהֲמוֹת יַמִּים יֶהֱמָיוּן וּשְׁאוֹן לְאֻמִּים כִּשְׁאוֹן מַיִם כַּבִּירִים יִשָּׁאוּן לְאֻמִּים כִּשְׁאוֹן מַיִם רַבִּים יִשָּׁאוּן וְגָעַר בּוֹ וְנָס מִמֶּרְחָק וְרֻדַּף כְּמֹץ הָרִים לִפְנֵי רוּחַ וּכְגַלְגַּל לִפְנֵי סוּפָה לְעֵת עֶרֶב וְהִנֵּה בַלָּהָה בְּטֶרֶם בֹּקֶר אֵינֶנּוּ זֶה חֵלֶק שׁוֹסֵינוּ וְגוֹרָל לְבֹזְזֵינוּ

[48] ἐν ἀπορίᾳ ἤχους θαλάσσης καὶ σάλου

It does not matter whether Yeshua is describing Isaiah 17 in Luke 21 as one of the prophecy signs of his coming, or if he is describing literal seas and water. Isaiah 17 still is a clear prophecy on its own describing when the peoples of the world, including nations or gatherings of peoples, are like a roaring sea that has crashing and rolling waves, causing mass destruction like a mob. But if Yeshua is describing these verses of prophecy in Isaiah 17:12-14 as one of the signs that happens before his coming as a warning about his coming, then it is a prophecy that needs to be fulfilled during or before the 3.5 years of Great Tribulation.

There are several key important elements of this prophecy in Isaiah 17. First are the descriptions of peoples and groups of peoples coming together and acting like the waves of sea, in their sound of roaring and their destructive motion of crashing. The word used here in the Hebrew for "nations," "le'om לְאֹם," is not the traditional word for nations. It more literally means "peoples," but in the specific sense of peoples who are gathered together as in a community or nation. Second is the way that the people are described moving like a sea of destructive waves. The people are rushing like waves and then crashing against things destructively as they come, but in many waves, or "many waters," wave after wave. This is the perfect description of a sea of waves like a tsunami, with wave after wave methodically coming into shore doing more and more damage from the previous wave, one crashing wave after another. One of the key features of a tsunami or tidal wave is that first all of the water recedes away and disappears from the shore entirely for a considerable length of time, then slowly small waves begin to pour in, with bigger waves behind those, and even bigger waves behind those, with wave after wave causing the water levels to rise faster and faster, one wave after another crashing onto the land and bringing more and more destructive force with it.

The third part of this prophecy is that the people come crashing in waves like many waters primarily beginning at evening, sometime shortly before evening and sunset, but then they are gone by morning because of being rebuked. The "he" that is doing the rebuking is not specified in the prophecy. The "he" referred to earlier in chapter 17 in verses 8-9 is "man" or "mankind," and then later it switches to talking about Israel in the second person as "you" in verses 10-11. "Elohim" or "God" is referred to in those verses also, but there is no way to know for certain if the "he" is referring to "God" or "mankind" by the time that we reach verses 12-14. Or perhaps the prophecy Isaiah is writing is referring to another "he" entirely that is not talked about anywhere in the prophecy. The important thing is that the people are rebuked and then they scatter like chaff being blown around in the wind off of the mountains or like little whirlwinds that are being chased by a larger hurricane. The Hebrew word here for "wind storm" or "hurricane," is the feminine noun form "suphah סוּפָה," and comes from the masculine noun form "suph סוּף," which means "reeds" and is also the name of the Red Sea in Hebrew, literally the Sea of Reeds. This indicates that "suphah" specifically refers to whirlwind types of storms at sea like hurricanes or typhoons. The people come together before sunset, then are like a sea of destructive waves at night, then are chased away by a more powerful force and scattered, until by morning they are gone again.

The final key element of this prophecy is that the people who are acting like a destructive sea or tsunami of waves are plundering and robbing people, looting at the same time as they go along like a violent sea of waves bringing destruction to everything in their path. When all of these parts of the prophecy come together we see a clear picture of fulfillment. First, exactly like a tsunami, the people around the world receded and went into their homes at the beginning of the COVID-19 plague in February and March 2020, like at the beginning of a tsunami of people. First all of the waves of people recede and disappear, leaving the streets and public places empty and desolate, like the sea disappears from the shore, leaving it empty of water.

Then the sea of people around the world started getting more and more agitated with the COVID-19 lockdowns, with small numbers of protesters starting to come out into the streets in April and May 2020 like small waves, usually beginning their protests in the afternoons and evenings a few hours before sunset. The initial small waves were not very destructive and they were chased away and scattered by the stronger police forces before morning, before sunrise, rebuked by governments and most of the people who wanted to stay safe. But the waves of people began to slowly build, until much larger waves of people began pouring out into the streets, especially beginning during the protests of May 27-29, 2020 that brought in protests against racist police brutality together with other protest movements against the lockdowns. These protests started turning into riots with the tsunami waves of the sea of people causing major damage to many cities, beginning in the United States, and later in cities in Europe and South America, and much later countries like South Africa.

Cities on every continent began experiencing the tsunami waves of people pouring out in protests and riots, with some nations experiencing much worse damage than others. One of the key features of the riots that swept cities across the world in 2020 and 2021 (and continuing today) was the plundering and robbing and looting of businesses, and in some cases homes, and almost always the worst parts of the rioting and looting, that came like violent, stormy, crashing waves, like a rushing sea of people, was in the evening in the hours before sunset and through the night. Almost always the people were chased away and scattered by police and locally formed vigilante groups before the morning. And I am sure that the people who were caught up in the midst of the rioting and looting as they would see it coming and forming together at evening time would feel terror as Isaiah describes in the prophecy.

But those who were participating in the robbing and plundering, and the rioting that was like tsunami waves of people bringing destruction to cities and leaving communities in ruin, were usually rebuked by the wider population, even by many of the protesters themselves who were trying to protest peacefully. And eventually they would be chased away and scattered by the stronger hurricane forces of police and military, even if it took them many nights in a row of fighting with protesters to remove them from the streets and return them back to normal. Sometimes it was many weeks or months of nights in a row of scattering the protesters, or being overcome for a time as in Minneapolis, but eventually after 2 years the tsunami of people protesting for many different reasons subsided, after mass destruction was caused by their crashing waves of rioting and plundering and robbing in the evening and at night. These events during the years of 2020 to the present perfectly fulfill this prophecy in Isaiah 17:12-14, and also, if Yeshua in Luke 21 was talking about this prophecy in Isaiah 17, it perfectly fulfills the sign he talks about of the perplexity and bewilderment of people at the roaring sea of people, and the rolling and crashing of their waves.

Of course rioting and what Isaiah describes in chapter 17 is nothing new on the earth and has been around for possibly thousands of years. But the rioting that has taken place around the world since the late 1700's with the French Revolution has been growing in intensity and frequency. The key important thing that is different about Yahuweh/Yehovah's prophecy in Isaiah 17 is that it is focused on looting and destructive violence of property, with no mention of mass murder and killing as has taken place in most riots in history. What is described in Isaiah 17 specifically refers to rioting that is focused on looting instead of killing, which the recent riots fulfill perfectly, but the majority of riots through history do not, because most riots in history are focused on killing certain people or people groups with looting as a secondary result of mass murder. Also, there are no other riots in history that have first had a time of everyone on the earth receding away and disappearing from the streets, leaving them empty and desolate like a tsunami, before pouring out in crashing waves upon the cities with mass destruction of property and buildings.

The other thing about past riots in history is that the rioters are usually organized political groups that eventually win against the larger hurricanes and take over the governments in revolutions, or are supported by corrupt, stronger governments backing them as with the Nazi riots against the Jews in Germany, which is the opposite described by Isaiah in chapter 17. What Isaiah describes in Yahuweh/Yehovah's prophecy in Isaiah 17 is something that is extremely rare on the earth, and if Yeshua was talking about this prophecy in Luke 21, then we have witnessed the fulfillment of this sign and prophecy that happens shortly before Yeshua's return during these riot events in 2020 to the present.

Section 24. **The Covenant with Death and the Grave:**

At the Time of Yahuweh/Yehovah's Coming at the Time of the End, to Make His Tabernacle/Booth Dwelling Place with Men and Rule Over and Restore Jerusalem, Right Before He Comes the Nation of Israel and the City of Jerusalem have Turned so Far Away from Yahuweh/Yehovah in Rebellion and Sin Against Him that He has to Destroy the Nation of Israel and City of Jerusalem in Judgment Again (While Judging All the Nations at the Same Time):

Isaiah 3:1 – 4:6

Joel 2:32 – 3:21

Zechariah 14:1-21

Word for Word Prophecy Examination of Partially Fulfilled and Unfulfilled Verses **Isaiah 3:1 – 4:6** and **Joel 2:32 – 3:21** and **Zechariah 14:1-21** – At the time of Yahuweh/Yehovah's coming, on the Day of Yahuweh/Yehovah, in Joel 2 to 3 and Zechariah 12 to 14, he gathers together all of the nations of the earth to judge them in battle at Jerusalem. But in the midst of Yahuweh/Yehovah's judgment upon the nations for how they have treated the Jewish people over thousands of years and how they have divided up his land in Israel and in the city of Jerusalem as prophesied in Joel, at the same time in Zechariah there is prophesied one last partial destruction of the city of Jerusalem, with horrible judgments on the Jewish people living there. In the prophecy in Zechariah the question is then left open that if Yahuweh/Yehovah is judging the nations and bringing the final justice upon everyone on the earth, why does Yahuweh/Yehovah allow one more final, horrible judgment and destruction on the city of Jerusalem? This question is not answered in Zechariah, or in Joel, which both explain that after that moment of Yahuweh/Yehovah's coming to rule the earth and end the nations of the world on the Day of Yahuweh/Yehovah, Jerusalem will not be destroyed ever again after that, because the remnant left in the city are only the true, set-apart followers of Yahuweh/Yehovah in covenant with him.

The answer to this question is found in the prophecy of Isaiah 3 and 4, in which Yahuweh/Yehovah very clearly says is a prophecy about the day of his coming, the exact same day prophesied about in Joel 2 to 3 and Zechariah 12 to 14. This is a prophecy, in Isaiah 4:2, that is about the Branch of Yahuweh/Yehovah, the Messiah. And in the same verse Yahuweh/Yehovah talks about the "escaped ones" of Israel, in the same way in Joel 2:32 that there is an "escape" in Jerusalem for those Yahuweh/Yehovah has called. And there is a remnant of set-apart ones left in Jerusalem in Isaiah 4:3 in the same way that there is a remnant left in Jerusalem in Joel 3:17 and Zechariah 14:2. Then in Isaiah 4:5-6 there is a cloud of smoke in the day and a fire by night over every inhabited house in Jerusalem, in the same way that Yahuweh/Yehovah was a cloud in the day and a fire at night guiding the children of Israel through the wilderness as they were living in tents.

This event in the wilderness of living in tents and following the cloud and the fire of Yahuweh/Yehovah was commemorated by Yahuweh/Yehovah in the Festival of Booths or Sukkoth סֻכּוֹת to be celebrated every year from the 15th to the 21st days of the 7th month. And right here in Isaiah 4:6 Yahuweh/Yehovah prophesies that there will be a sukkah סֻכָּה or booth as a place of refuge and shelter for everyone to live in, in fulfillment of the Festival of Sukkoth of living in booths. In Zechariah 14:16-19 Yahuweh/Yehovah also prophesies about the fulfillment of his Festival of Sukkoth at his coming, as he will be requiring all peoples of all nations to come to Jerusalem to celebrate and live in booths when he reigns over the earth.

The prophecy of Isaiah chapters 3 and 4 is a prophecy about the same exact time and day of Yahuweh/Yehovah's coming on the Day of Yahuweh/Yehovah, when part of the city of Jerusalem is destroyed in judgment. But in Isaiah 3 Yahuweh/Yehovah explains why Jerusalem is partially destroyed again, one last time in judgment, because the city of Jerusalem and the nation of the Jewish people in the land of Israel at the time of his coming have once again become so corrupted and filled with sin that they have to experience the judgment of destruction one last time when he comes. Yahuweh/Yehovah's prophetic description of what the city of Jerusalem and nation of Judah of the Jewish people in Israel looks like at his coming is exactly how Jerusalem and the Jewish people of Judah in Israel look today.

The nation of Israel, including Jerusalem, have become like Sedom as Yahuweh/Yehovah prophesied they would in Isaiah 3:8-9, with all of the sin done openly. Homosexuality is only one of the sins of Sedom that they did openly; there were many more sins of violence and many sins that were not recorded in Genesis. But the point that is made in this prophecy in Isaiah 3 is that sin is done openly in Jerusalem and across Israel, which the world has witnessed over the last two decades with homosexual pride parades done not only in Tel Aviv and other cities in Israel, but openly in the streets of Jerusalem as well. The sins of the nation of Israel are done openly, with the people declaring their sin out in public. And the nation has turned more and more against Yahuweh/Yehovah, with their tongues and their actions, provoking Yahuweh/Yehovah with their fallen state and stumbling of sin.

And many daughters of Zion in Israel today literally walk with arrogance in seducing ways and dress, wearing fancy jewelry and trying to seduce with eyes and appearance, in fulfillment of Isaiah 3:16-23. But these verses at the same time are happening in a symbolic way representing the whole nation, as the nation of Israel has taken on the world, trying to look seductive to the nations of the world in order to bring in mankind's systems of immorality with Mystery Babel and the Beast Out of the Sea and the Beast Out of the Earth. Israel tries to woo and seduce worldly business and technology to come into the nation and make the nation wealthy and covered in fine jewelry all over it. Also they are trying to seduce the nations to join in peace and normalization deals with them, so that Israel can be just another nation filled with sin and immorality like every other nation on the earth, no longer set-apart to Yahuweh/Yehovah.

And there is a definite problem in Israel of the poor being plundered and crushed, as in Isaiah 3:14-15, with great difficulty for the poor to survive the extremely high cost of living and housing. It is for all of these such things in Isaiah 3 that Yahuweh/Yehovah prophesies why he has to bring his judgment on the nation of Israel and the city of Jerusalem one more time when he comes, to remove all of the sin and make his nation completely clean and spotless of sin for him to dwell with for eternity. All those of his people who remain have to be washed clean, in Isaiah 4:4, through the spirit of judgment and burning fire, washed in the blood of the Branch of Yahuweh/Yehovah, the Lamb Yeshua and in his new covenant of Jeremiah 31.

The parts of this Isaiah 3 to 4 prophecy that need to be in process of fulfillment before Yahuweh/Yehovah comes are all in place and position now for Yahuweh/Yehovah to bring his prophesied judgments of Isaiah 3 on Jerusalem and Israel, while at the same time judging all of the nations of the world with them. Everything that needs to have happened and be in place for the prophecy of Isaiah 3 and 4 is in place and ready for Yahuweh/Yehovah to come at his appointed time. Already there is the conflict happening in Israel today between young and old, men against men and against each other's neighbors, and against one another at different statuses of society, as described in Isaiah 3:5 with the judicial and political conflicts in Israel of continuous elections since 2019. And it is moving closer and closer to the point where nobody will want to be a chief or person in a leadership or government position anymore, because of not wanting to take responsibility for the mess that the government and nation is in, as described in Isaiah 3:6-7.

The Covenant with Death and the Grave Prophecy:
Isaiah 28:1-22

Prophecy Fulfillment and Partial Prophecy Fulfillment of Verses **Isaiah 28:1-22** – This prophecy beginning with Ephrayim and then talking about the nation of Judah and the covenant with death that the leaders of Jerusalem enter into was actually already fulfilled at the time of Isaiah. And we would say today that this prophecy is finished and fulfilled and done with if it were not for two major parts of the prophecy that did not happen, the main one being in Isaiah 28:22 (which is also mentioned in Isaiah 10:16-34).

The prophecy begins with Yahuweh/Yehovah prophesying about the northern tribes of Israel that make up a separate nation from Judah at that time, poetically called by the name of the tribe of Ephrayim. The northern division of Israel at that time had completely turned away from Yahuweh/Yehovah and he calls them drunkards. In verses 28:1-8 the prophecy is all about the pride of northern Israel and their straying away from Yahuweh/Yehovah in drunkenness, including their priests and prophets gone astray in strong drink. And their capital of Samaria (called Shomron in Hebrew) is poetically described by its location on the head elevated on high ground above the surrounding fertile valleys, with vineyards of drunkenness all around.

All of these earlier verses were already fulfilled at the time of Isaiah, as northern Israel was a fading flower and the nation of Assyria (called Ashshur in Hebrew) came into the nation "like a rainstorm of hail and a destroying storm, like a flood of mighty waters overflowing," in fulfillment of verse 28:2. Assyria destroyed the nation like a storm that came over it, and they came from Yahuweh/Yehovah, because he is the one who brought them to destroy the nation of northern Israel in judgment, according to verse 28:2. Because of the filth of the vomit from the drunkenness of Ephrayim, of northern Israel, the nation had to be cleaned up and taken into exile. And we know that "the strong and mighty one" that Yahuweh/Yehovah is referring to here as the one belonging to him that he brings to destroy Ephrayim is the Assyrian Empire at that time, because of the prophecy in Isaiah 8:7-8 that describes the king of Assyria as the "strong and mighty" flood waters that would come not only to the northern Israel kingdom of Shomron and Ephrayim, but also pass through the southern kingdom of Judah (called Yehudah in Hebrew).

Ephrayim was destroyed by the Assyrians as prophesied, and then later the Assyrians came flooding into the southern nation of Judah like a storm of hail and a flood of waters in fulfillment of Isaiah 28:17-19. They came like terrorist attacks, passing through day by day, and eventually besieging the walled cities, including Jerusalem itself. The beds for people to sleep on at night became too short with not enough blanket to wrap in, in fulfillment of verse 28:20, because of the hardships of the Assyrian army attacking and pillaging and besieging across the land, preventing people from being able to sleep comfortably at night and have all of their needs met. And the reason that Yahuweh/Yehovah brought and allowed the Assyrian army to attack the nation of Judah also is because of the "covenant with death" and the vision with She'ol that the leadership and government in Jerusalem had made at that time.

We know about what this covenant is from Isaiah 30:1-3 where Yahuweh/Yehovah prophesies about those of Judah relying upon Egypt as their place of refuge, instead of relying on Yahuweh/Yehovah. And in 2 Kings 18:19-23 we discover that the leaders of Jerusalem, either with or without the support of King Hezekiah, had entered into a covenant with Egypt and the Pharaoh of Egypt, trusting in them for military aid to help Judah defend against Assyria. But Yahuweh/Yehovah says in Isaiah 28:14-15 that these rulers in Jerusalem (possibly including Hezekiah or possibly not) were scoffers and scorners against Yahuweh/Yehovah in this covenant they had made with Egypt. And he says that this covenant with Egypt is really a covenant with death, and a vision of She'ol, which in Hebrew refers to the place of the dead after they have died. He says that it is death for Judah to trust in Egypt to save them, and that instead of making Egypt their refuge in Isaiah 30:2 they have really made lying their refuge in Isaiah 28:15. Yahuweh/Yehovah was saying that Egypt and Pharaoh at that time were liars when they made the covenant with Israel, because they never intended to help or aid Judah, or to fulfill their part of the covenant.

And this prophecy was fulfilled in Isaiah 28:15 and 17-19 when the Assyrians came like a storm of hail and overflowing water, like an overflowing scourge, sweeping away and exposing the lies of Egypt. As we know from 2 Kings 18 and 19 Egypt never came to aid Judah and abandoned the nation to their death. The covenant with Egypt turned out to be a covenant with the death of the nation of Judah. Yahuweh/Yehovah used the overflowing scourge of the Assyrian army to annul that covenant with death that the government of Jerusalem had made with Egypt, and instead, as recorded in 2 Kings 18 and 19, Yahuweh/Yehovah is the one who supernaturally spared Judah from destruction. Yahuweh/Yehovah's own messenger came in the night and killed most of the Assyrian army that was besieging Jerusalem, and then later the king of Assyria, Sennacherib, was murdered by his own sons.

Those who trusted in Yahuweh/Yehovah as their precious corner-stone and stone of their foundation in Jerusalem were saved, and the city was saved, in fulfillment of Isaiah 28:16. We know that this foundation corner-stone, tried and precious, is referring to Yahuweh/Yehovah himself because of Isaiah 8:14-15 where Yahuweh/Yehovah is spoken of as the set-apart place for people, but at the same time a stumbling stone for both nations of Israel, Ephrayim and Judah, and for Jerusalem, for those who do not fear him. Also 1 Kings 5:17 refers to the foundation of the set-apart place of Yahuweh/Yehovah, when the First Temple was built that was still standing at the time of Isaiah. And the foundation was laid with "precious stones" as with the precious cornerstone foundation in Isaiah 28:16. Yahuweh/Yehovah himself is the set-apart place and

Temple, the cornerstone foundation for people to trust in and stand on without falling, or to stumble on and fall on if they do not trust in him. This concept is reaffirmed in 1 Peter 2:4-8 in referring to Yeshua as this precious and living corner-stone of Zion in Jerusalem.

We would say at this point now that this prophecy in Isaiah 28 concerning the covenant with death is already completely fulfilled, and there is no need for it to be fulfilled again, except for one problem in Isaiah 28:22 in which Yahuweh/Yehovah warns the scoffers, the scoffing rulers of Jerusalem in Isaiah 28:14, about their scoffing, because he has decreed that the entire earth be destroyed. Anyone can see for themselves that this part of the prophecy in Isaiah 28:22 did not happen at that time. The entire earth was not destroyed at that time when the rulers of Jerusalem were scoffing. And the whole reason why Yahuweh/Yehovah gives to the rulers in Jerusalem not to scoff is because the earth is going to be destroyed in their lifetime. If the earth was not going to be destroyed in their lifetime, then the destruction of the entire earth becomes irrelevant to the rulers of Jerusalem, if they are not alive to see it and experience it.

Isaiah 10:16-34 reveals more prophetic details about this prophecy in Isaiah 28:22. This section of prophecy in Isaiah 10 is about Yahuweh/Yehovah's final coming, to make an end of all the earth and to return a remnant of Jacob, referring to the entirety of the nation of Israel with all of its 12 tribes, back to him. This is a prophecy about his coming as fire burning away and cleansing everything, as well as the Light of the nation of Israel. The time of his coming is the time of his destruction of all the earth, and mixed in with this prophecy about his coming at the Time of the End, he says that "therefore" Jerusalem, in 10:24-25, does not need to fear Assyria who has struck them. Yahuweh/Yehovah says he will use this time of his displeasure on Judah to eventually destroy Assyria.

There is a mixing together of the prophecies fulfilled at that time about Assyria and Jerusalem and Egypt in Isaiah 10, with unfulfilled prophecies about Yahuweh/Yehovah's coming at the Time of the End when he carries out the destruction that he has decided and decreed for all the earth. In Isaiah 28:22 Yahuweh/Yehovah does the same thing, mixing them together, showing there is still a part of the covenant with death in Isaiah 28:14-22 that was not fulfilled at the time of Isaiah, which explains why the nations of Assyria and Egypt are never once mentioned by name, nor any nations mentioned by name specifically except for Jerusalem. Also, the part of the prophecy in Isaiah 28:16-17 about Yahuweh/Yehovah being the precious cornerstone and foundation of Zion, of Jerusalem, was not finished and completed at the time of Isaiah either, because only decades later after Isaiah the city of Jerusalem turned so far away from Yahuweh/Yehovah as their set-apart place and foundation that he had to destroy the city and the First Temple with Nebuchadnezzar's army. And then the city had to be destroyed again, together with the Second Temple by the Roman army about 500 years after that, lying in a state of decay for over 1,900 years even after Yeshua came and the city of Jerusalem rejected him as their precious corner-stone foundation and stumbled over him instead.

The part of the prophecy in Isaiah 28:16-17 is an unfinished part of the prophecy that has been through a process of 3,000 years that will only be completed when Yeshua comes to rule over the earth from Jerusalem at the Time of the End. Since this prophecy has elements to it from Yahuweh/Yehovah's coming at the end of this world, there is part of it that still has to happen before he returns. There is no requirement for his annulment of Jerusalem's covenant with death to happen before he returns, because he can annul it with the final war that takes place at his coming, with the armies of the nations that gather together against Jerusalem prophesied throughout Scripture as already discussed with the Isaiah 3 to 4 prophecy. The only part that has to happen again in some form is the part about the covenant with death itself, made by the scoffers of the government of Jerusalem who have to be alive still at the time of his coming to destroy all of the earth in Isaiah 28:22 in order for the destruction of all the earth to be relevant to them.

And we can see today that the government rulers at Jerusalem have once again entered into another covenant with death like the one that Jerusalem entered into at the time of Isaiah with Egypt. Out of fear of war with Iran and its allies surrounding Israel in Lebanon and Syria and the Gaza Strip and the West Bank and Yemen and Iraq and to some extent in Jordan and Turkey, Israel has entered into a covenant with the United Arab Emirates, called the Abraham Accords, put together by Sheikh Mohammed bin Zayed. And this covenant signed on September 15, 2020 also includes the nations of Bahrain, Morocco, and Sudan, with President Joseph Biden during this year of 2023 pushing hard to get Saudi Arabia included into that covenant. Once again there is the promise of peace and stability, as a covenant with Arab nations that will help strengthen Israel in the Middle East to stand up against Iran and Israel's other enemies. Prime Minister Benjamin Netanyahu was even willing to give up Israeli land in the West Bank in exchange for peace and normalization ties with the Arab nations, but it is once again a covenant with death for the nation of Israel.

The Abraham Accords is once again another covenant where the apparent refuge and place of safety in the United Arab Emirates and other Arab nations is all a lie. When the nations of the earth gather together against Jerusalem to destroy Israel at the Time of the End, they will not help Israel in the same way that Egypt never helped Judah against the Assyrians. They will turn against Israel and leave the nation to die along with all the other nations of the earth. The covenant with death and the vision with She'ol, the place of the dead, is already in place, lulling Israel into a false security thinking that they can normalize ties and relationships with the nations around them in friendship. It is giving a false confidence and false hope, a false hiding place of refuge trusting in man instead of in Yahuweh/Yehovah to save them and help them, causing the nation to turn away from Yahwueh/Yehovah as their foundation and precious corner-stone.

But Yahuweh/Yehovah will annul this covenant with death and the surviving remnant of the nation of Israel will see with their own eyes that there is no true refuge except in Yahuweh/Yehovah alone. Ironically it has been the Palestinians who have been the only ones saving Israel from entering into this covenant with death with the nations around them sooner. If it had not been for the Palestinians refusing every single two state solution with Israel that has been proposed over the last few decades, and then violently attacking Israel constantly through the years, making it impossible for Israel to enter into any kind of peace with them, then this covenant with death in the Abraham Accords would have happened long ago and Israel would have been very rapidly on its path to death and destruction, living completely unprepared for war in peace and safety. But the Palestinians have been Yahuweh/Yehovah's rainstorm of hail and overflowing scourge on the land of Israel all these years, preventing them from entering into the covenant with death until now, at the appointed time.

Everything is in place now with this prophecy for it to be finally finished and completed in its fulfillment with Yahuweh/Yehovah's coming to Jerusalem and his destruction of all the earth. Hamas carried out its surprise attack and abhorrent massacre as an operation they called "Al-Aqsa <u>Flood</u>" on October 7, 2023, on the 21st day of the 7th month, on the seventh day of the Festival of Booths or Sukkot, which was the 22nd day of the 7th month on the eighth day of the festival on the modern Jewish Calendar that no longer keeps the Scriptural Calendar of beginning months with the sighting of the new moon. This started what Prime Minister Benjamin Netanyahu termed Israel's "Second War for Independence," and also began Yahuweh/Yehovah's process of annulling Israel's covenant with death in the Abraham Accords, with the overflowing scourge or flood that comes literally at "morning" like Hamas did and passes through by day and night in fulfillment of Isaiah 28:17-20. The Assyrians at the time of Isaiah were just as brutal as the Hamas terrorists today.

Section 25. **The Sixth through Seventh Seals and the First through Fourth Trumpets:**

References to the Sixth Seal Prophecy:
  Isaiah 2:1-22
  Isaiah 34:1-17
  Hosea 10:8
  Joel 2:28-31
  Zephaniah 1:1 – 3:20
  Malachi 3:1-6
  Matthew 24:27-31   Mark 13:24-27

Word for Word Prophecy Examination of Fulfilled, Partially Fulfilled, and Unfulfilled Verses **Isaiah 2:1-22** and **Isaiah 34:1-17** and **Hosea 10:8** and **Joel 2:28-31** and **Zephaniah 1:1 – 3:20** and **Malachi 3:1-6** and **Matthew 24:27-31** and **Mark 13:24-27** – John references from and quotes from these seven primary prophecies in Isaiah, Hosea, Joel, Zephaniah, Malachi, Matthew, and Mark as he describes and hears the words of the people in his vision of Yeshua opening the Sixth Seal. In John's description of all of the various people of the earth hiding in caves and rocks in Revelation 6:15-16 he uses the same wording as in Isaiah 2:19-21, and both of these prophecies are about the time at the end of the Great Tribulation at Yahuweh/Yehovah's coming. For the part of the vision in Revelation 6:13-14 when John is describing the stars of the heavens falling to the earth like a fig tree dropping its unripe figs as the heavens depart like a double scrolled book being rolled, he is using the same wording from Isaiah 34:4 where the "host" or "stars" of the heavens fading away like fig leaves fading on a fig tree, and the heavens are rolled like a double scrolled book. And once again both of these prophecies are about the time of Yeshua's coming at the end of the Great Tribulation, according to Yeshua in Matthew 24:29. The reference of the stars falling from the heavens is very specifically referencing Yeshua's words in Matthew 24:29 and Mark 13:25

The words that John hears all of the people of the earth say in his vision in Revelation 6:16, asking for the mountains and rocks to fall on them and hide them, come from Hosea 10:8. But the prophecy in Hosea 10:8 is already fulfilled and instead has only the northern kingdom of the ten northern tribes of Israel saying to the mountains and hills to fall on them and hide them, and as far as is known this prophecy has nothing to do with the Time of the End nor the Great Tribulation nor the coming of Yahuweh/Yehovah. In Revelation 6:12 John partially uses the words of Joel 2:31 where the moon is turned to blood, but instead of the sun being turned into darkness, he describes the sun turning black with sackcloth covering over it. The sun description is similar but not exactly the same. Both of these prophecies concerning the moon turning to blood and the sun appearing to be darkened by a sackcloth substance are about the time right before Yahuweh/Yehovah comes, right before the end of the Great Tribulation.

Lastly, the words that John hears the people say in Revelation 6:17 are referencing the prophecy in Zephaniah 1:14-15, combining "the great day" of Yahuweh/Yehovah in verse 14 with the description of that day as a "day of wrath" in verse 15. Together they become the great day of Yahuweh/Yehovah's wrath. Then the words that the people say at the very end of Revelation 6:17 come from Malachi 3:2, partially quoting from this verse that says, "who is able to stand when He appears?" This prophecy in Malachi is referring to the day of the coming of "the Master" or "Messenger of the covenant," which are referring to the coming of the Messiah Yeshua to his Temple. All three of these prophecies in Zephaniah and Malachi and Revelation are referring to the day of Yeshua's coming, the day of the coming of the Lamb with wrath at the end of the Great Tribulation, after the Great Tribulation is ended.

This single part of John's vision when Yeshua opens that Sixth Seal has more word for word or paraphrasing references to prophecies in Scripture, especially in the Tanak or Old Testament, than any other part of John's vision in Revelation. There are even a few more references beyond these seven shown, but these seven are the most important ones for understanding the Sixth Seal.

References to the Seventh Seal Prophecy:
Exodus 19:1 – 24:11
Leviticus 16:1-34
Matthew 24:27-31

Word for Word Prophecy Examination of Unfulfilled Verses **Matthew 24:27-31** with Examination of **Exodus 19:1 – 24:11** and **Leviticus 16:1-34** – The main part of the Seventh Seal prophecy is the messenger who is standing before the golden altar at Yahuweh/Yehovah's throne, with a golden censer containing incense and the prayers of the set-apart ones. And then the smoke of the incense and prayers goes up from the fire on the altar before Yahuweh/Yehovah. This ceremony or ritual is part of the service of the High Priest that must be done every year before the ark of the covenant (the throne of Yahuweh/Yehovah on earth) on the Day of Atonement or Yom Kippur. It is recorded in Leviticus 16:12-13 that Yahuweh/Yehovah commanded for the High Priest on the Day of Atonement to bring a censer filled with the burning coals of the fire of the altar, and carry incense with him in his hands into the Most Set-Apart Place where the ark of the covenant is located. And then the High Priest puts the incense onto the fire of the censer and covers the lid of atonement (the lid of the ark of the covenant) with a cloud of incense.

This account in Leviticus 16 of the instruction for the High Priest on the Day of Atonement is almost word for word the same thing that the messenger does when the Seventh Seal is opened, taking the incense in a censer of fire, and causing the incense to fill the air (like a cloud) over the throne of Yahuweh/Yehovah (the ark of the covenant). The only difference is that the prayers of the set-apart ones are included in with this incense, and then the fire that the messenger takes from the altar and places in the censer (in the same way the High Priest is commanded to take the coals of the fire from the altar on the Day of Atonement and place in the censer that is taken into the ark of the covenant) are thrown down to the earth.

Thus there is a very clear picture connection that John sees in his vision of the Seventh Seal with the Day of Atonement or Yom Kippur that is observed every year on the 10th day of the 7th month. Then after the messenger throws the censer filled with fire from the altar down to the earth, there are noises, thunders, lightnings, and earthquakes, and the preparing of the sounding of trumpets, referencing the day that Yahuweh/Yehovah came in the clouds at Mount Sinai in Exodus 19:16-19, and commemorated every year on the 1st day of the 7th month on the Day of Trumpets, or literally "the Day of Sounding the Alarm." This same reference to the coming of Yahuweh/Yehovah in the clouds in Exodus 19 with the thunders, lightnings, the trembling of the earth shaking on Mount Sinai, and the sounding of the shophar or trumpets, with the "noise" of the "voice" of Yahuweh/Yehovah and the "voice" or "noise" of the shophar, is repeated in Revelation in the Seventh Trumpet and the Seventh Bowl of Wrath. This same event of Yahuweh/Yehovah's coming in Exodus 19 is referenced by Yeshua in Matthew 24 as the description of the day of his coming at the end of the Great Tribulation, with the lightning referenced specifically as the description of how he will come as the Son of Adam.

References to the First through Second Trumpet Prophecies:
Exodus 7:14-25
Exodus 9:18-35
Isaiah 2:1-22
Ezekiel 38:1 – 39:21

Word for Word Prophecy Examination of Unfulfilled Verses **Isaiah 2:1-22** and **Ezekiel 38:1 – 39:21** with Examination of **Exodus 7:14-25** and **Exodus 9:18-35** – The events of the First and Second Trumpet prophecies that John sees in his vision are primarily references from Exodus and Isaiah. The seas or oceans of the world turning to blood and killing the creatures and fish in the sea in the Second Trumpet are a reference to the plague in Egypt of the water turned to blood in Exodus 7:17-18, that killed all of the fish in the rivers of Egypt. This plague is started in the Second Trumpet with only 1/3 of the seas and oceans turned to blood, killing only 1/3 of the creatures of the sea, but this event of the Second Trumpet does not end until all of the seas are turned to blood and all of the fish and creatures of the sea are dead in the Second Bowl of Wrath later on in Revelation.

The hail that falls to the earth, bringing with it fire that starts large wildfires destroying 1/3 of the trees and grass, in the First Trumpet in Revelation is a reference to the plague of hail and fire in Egypt in Exodus 9:23-24, where the plague of hail is described by Moses as having continuous fire flashing through the hail. There is no record by John about his visions in Revelation of this particular plague ever being completed are finished with the trees and grass burning up, but there is a lot more hail that comes later on in the Seventh Trumpet and Seventh Bowl of Wrath.

There is no record in Exodus of the hail and fire in Egypt causing wildfires like described in the First Trumpet in Revelation, but the part of the trees being burned down comes from Isaiah 2:12-13 where Yahuweh/Yehovah says he has a day coming (at the day of his coming) to bring down all of the things that are high and proud, cutting them down low and humbling them. This includes bringing down the trees such as the cedars of Lebanon and the oaks of Bashan, as with the fire bringing down the trees in the First Trumpet. And then in the Second Trumpet 1/3 of the ships of the sea are destroyed in the same way that

Yahuweh/Yehovah says in Isaiah 2:16 that he will be bringing down and destroying all of the ships of Tarshish and all of the beautiful, proud ships and sea going vessels.

Ezekiel is only slightly referenced with the blood that is mixed with the hail and fire in the First Trumpet in Revelation, from Ezekiel 38:22. It is one of the plagues of destruction that Yahuweh/Yehovah brings upon the armies of Gog of the land of Magog, raining down hail that is mixed with fire and sulphur upon them, together with judging Gog and his armies with blood.

References to the Third Trumpet Prophecy:
Jeremiah 9:15-16
Jeremiah 23:15-40

Word for Word Examination of Verses **Jeremiah 9:15-16** and **Jeremiah 23:15-40** – What John saw in the vision of the Third Trumpet is what Yahuweh/Yehovah prophesied for the people of Israel and the prophets of Israel when the Babylonians destroyed the nation and Jerusalem and carried away Judah into exile. In Jeremiah 9:15 and 23:15 Yahuweh/Yehovah says that he will make them eat bitter wormwood and drink poisoned water, which was fulfilled probably both literally and symbolically/poetically simultaneously at that time. The judgment they received at that time was like eating bitter wormwood and drinking poisoned water, but during the sieges, especially in Jerusalem, and in the destruction of the towns and villages of the nation there were probably people who literally drank poisoned water that was bitter like wormwood.

In the Third Trumpet prophecy it is entirely literal with a burning star falling on 1/3 of the rivers and fountains of water on the earth, causing many people to die from drinking the poisoned, wormwood bitter waters. These two Jeremiah prophecies were already fulfilled in the past, at the time of Jeremiah, and are not prophecies about the coming of Yahuweh/Yehovah or the Time of the End. But the principle in these two prophecies is connected by John's vision of the Third Trumpet into the Time of the End.

References to the Fourth Trumpet Prophecy:
Isaiah 13:1-22
Joel 1:1 – 3:21
Matthew 24:27-31   Mark 13:24-27

Word for Word Prophecy Examination of Unfulfilled Verses **Isaiah 13:1-22** and **Joel 1:1 – 3:21** and **Matthew 24:27-31** and **Mark 13:24-27** – The prophecies of Isaiah 13:10 and Joel 3:15 are about the sun and moon and stars becoming completely darkened all of the way during the Day of Yahuweh/Yehovah. As already discussed, Yeshua connects these prophecies of the Day of Yahuweh/Yehovah as being the same day as his coming at the end of the 3.5 years of Great Tribulation in Matthew 24:29 and Mark 13:24-25. The only difference is that Yeshua describes the stars being darkened by falling from the heavens, instead of simply saying that they are darkened by disappearing as in Isaiah 13 and Isaiah 34 and Joel 3.

There is also one other time in prophecy, in Joel 2:10-11, where the sun and moon and stars are darkened at another time in connection with the Day of Yahuweh/Yehovah, but from Joel 2:1 we discover that at that time in Joel chapters 1 and 2 the day of Yahuweh/Yehovah is only near to coming in the future, but has not yet arrived. In John's vision of the Fourth Trumpet the sun and moon and stars are darkened as in these other prophecies, but only by 1/3 of each, as well as only 1/3 of the day and 1/3 of the night. This means that the Fourth Trumpet, while referencing all of these other prophecies about the sun and moon and stars being darkened, is not at the complete fullness of those prophecies yet. It is still only in process of being partially darkened at the time of the Fourth Trumpet, on its way to eventually be fully darkened in the future, but not yet there at that moment of the sounding of the Fourth Trumpet.

The Sixth through Seventh Seal and the First through Fourth Trumpet Prophecies:
    Revelation 6:12-17
    Revelation 8:1-12

Word for Word Prophecy Examination of Unfulfilled Verses **Revelation 6:12-17** and **Revelation 8:1-12** – Out of all of the prophecies of Seals and Trumpets and Bowls in John's vision in Revelation, the Sixth Seal is the linchpin moment that brings together all of the other parts of the Seals and Trumpets and Bowls into order. The very important moment in the Fifth Seal is when those who have been killed for their witness and testimony of Yeshua and the Word of Yahuweh/Yehovah are told to "rest for a little while longer" before their blood can be "judged" and "avenged." The question then is, when is it that their blood is both judged and avenged, because they have to wait for a little while, for a length of time of resting, from the Fifth Seal to whenever this judging and avenging takes place. A length of time of resting has to happen before that judging and avenging can be fulfilled and completed.

This "judging" and "avenging" of the "blood" of those who bear witness to Yeshua and the Word of Yahuweh/Yehovah is a reference to a much larger prophecy of vengeance that Yahuweh/Yehovah has promised for all of his servants and prophets and set-apart ones who have been slain throughout all of time. In the song of Moses in Deuteronomy 32:43 Moses talks about Yahuweh/Yehovah avenging the blood of his servants and bringing vengeance upon his adversaries. This is part of who Yahuweh/Yehovah is to avenge and bring vengeance for the blood spilled of his servants, his set-apart ones. And this is why in Joel 3:21 Yahuweh/Yehovah prophesies that in the Day of Yahuweh/Yehovah, at the day of his coming to take over control of the earth, he will avenge all of the blood that he has not yet avenged.

It is this prophecy in Joel 3:21 that John sees referred to in his vision of the Fifth Seal, when Yahuweh/Yehovah avenges the blood of his servants that have not yet been avenged on the day of his coming at the end of the 3.5 years of Great Tribulation. In Isaiah 26:19-21 Yahuweh/Yehovah makes the same prophecy, at the end of the Great Tribulation, at the time of the resurrection, he will uncover all of the blood and murdered people on the earth so that none of it is hidden any longer and it is finally dealt with. In Isaiah 34:1-8 and Isaiah 63:3-4 Yahuweh/Yehovah prophesies about a day of vengeance, in a year of recompense of his redeemed, when he finishes out his vengeance in his heart on the earth.

In both of these prophecies in Isaiah 34 and 63 Yahuweh/Yehovah explains that this is the time of his wrath, and from Revelation 11:18 and Revelation 14:19-20 and Zephaniah 1:14-15 and 2:2-3 we know that this day of his wrath is the day of his coming, the Day of Yahuweh/Yehovah, that happens at the end of the Great Tribulation. This avenging of the blood of those killed for their witness in the Fifth Seal is very specifically said to be fulfilled in John's vision during the Third Bowl of Wrath in Revelation 16:5-6. The day of wrath of Yahuweh/Yehovah avenging the blood of his set-apart ones and prophets is also part of the destruction of the city of Mystery Babel in Jeremiah 51:6-11 and Jeremiah 51:49 and Revelation 16:19 and Revelation 18:20-24 and Revelation 19:2. In these prophecies Yahuweh/Yehovah through the destruction of Mystery Babel also avenges the blood of every single person who has ever been murdered throughout the entire history of the world.

All of these prophecies together show that the Day of Yahuweh/Yehovah, the day of his coming to take over the rule of the earth, is the same day of his wrath, and is the same day of his vengeance, when he avenges the blood of those who have not yet been avenged. And it is the same day of the destruction of Mystery Babel, which is also destroyed as part of his day of vengeance and avenging the blood of his servants (in Revelation 19:2 in fulfillment of the Song of Moses in Deuteronomy 32:43). The day of Yahuweh/Yehovah's judgment of the earth is the same day of his vengeance is the same day of his avenging is the same day of his wrath is the same day of his coming to rule the earth as king from Jerusalem is the same day that is called "The Day of Yahuweh/Yehovah."

Therefore we know the answer to the Fifth Seal as to when the Master will avenge the blood of his servants and set-apart ones and prophets who were martyred for their witness to him, when he comes on the Day of Yahuweh/Yehovah at the end of the 3.5 years of Great Tribulation. In the book of Revelation this avenging of the blood of Yahuweh/Yehovah's servants, the set-apart ones and the prophets and all those who were killed for their witness of Yeshua and the Word of Yahuweh/Yehovah happens during the wrath of Yahuweh/Yehovah of the Seventh Trumpet, and during the turning of all the water to blood in the Third Bowl, and the destruction of the city of Mystery Babel in the Seventh Bowl. So we know for certain that there is a span of time of resting for a little while in between the Fifth Seal in Revelation 6:10-11 and the Seventh Trumpet through all of the Seven Bowls in Revelation 11:5-19 and Revelation 16:1-21. There is no doubt at all that the Seventh Trumpet and all of the Seven Bowls in John's vision are altogether describing the time of the Day of Yahuweh/Yehovah at Yeshua's coming in the clouds at the end of the 3.5 years of Great Tribulation, to end this world and reign from Jerusalem.

But there is still another prophecy in Revelation that John saw very specifically as being the Day of Yahuweh/Yehovah, the day of his wrath and vengeance when he avenges the blood of all those not yet avenged on the day of his coming at the end of the 3.5 years of Great Tribulation, and that prophecy is the Sixth Seal in Revelation 6:12-17 that takes place right after the martyrs in the Fifth Seal are told to rest a little while longer before the avenging of their blood takes place. This is why the Sixth Seal is the linchpin part of the prophecy of the Seals and Trumpets and Bowls in Revelation, because of the superficial appearance of its being completely out of place in the proper chronological order of events. The following chart illustrates how much the Sixth Seal really does fit into place correctly with the rest of the chronology of Revelation, bringing together multiple layers of events that are all happening simultaneously, but still in chronological order as they all happen together at the same time.

Patterns in the Seals, Trumpets, and Bowls from the 5th Seal to the 7th Bowl

	Event Series 1:	Event Series 2:	Event Series 3:	Event Series 4:
Event Series 1:	**1st – 4th Seals** (Rev. 6:1-8) – *The First Four Seals have No Correlation with Any Other Seals, Trumpets, or Bowls*			
Event Series 2:	**5th Seal** (Rev. 6:9-11) – Those Slain for the Word of God and Witness They Held Ask How Long Until He Judges and Avenges Their Blood; Told to Rest a Little While Longer **6th Seal** (Rev. 6:12-15) – Stars of the Heaven Fell to Earth	**3rd Trumpet** (Rev. 8:10-11) – A Great Star from the Heaven Named Wormwood Fell Upon the Rivers and Fountains of Water One Third of the Rivers and Fountains of Water Turned Bitter	**3rd Bowl** (Rev. 16:4-7) – YHWH has Judged Those Who Shed the Blood of the Set-Apart Ones and Prophets by Giving Them Blood to Drink Rivers and Fountains of Water became Blood	**Destruction of Babel** (Rev. 19:1-2) – YHWH has Judged the Great Whore and Avenged the Blood of His Servants Poured Out at Her Hand
Event Series 3:	**6th Seal** (Rev. 6:12-15) – Sun became Black as Sackcloth Moon became as Blood Stars of the Heaven Fell to Earth	**4th Trumpet** (Rev. 8:12) – One Third of Sun Darkened One Third of Moon Darkened One Third of Stars Darkened	**4th Bowl** (Rev. 16:8-9) – Sun Burned Men with Fire/Heat	
Event Series 4:	**6th Seal** (Rev. 6:12-15) – Sun became Black as Sackcloth Stars of the Heaven Fell to Earth	**5th Trumpet/1st Woe** (Rev. 9:1-12) – Sun Darkened, Also the Air, from the Smoke of the Pit A Star from the Heaven that had Fallen to Earth Opened the Pit of the Deep	**5th Bowl** (Rev. 10-11) – Kingdom of the Beast became Darkened	
Event Series 5:	**6th Seal** (Rev. 6:12-15) – Great Earthquake Kings, Great Ones, Rich, Commanders, Mighty, Every Slave and Every Free Hide in the Caves and in the Rocks of the Mountains They Say to the Mountains and Rocks to Hide Them from the Wrath of the Lamb, because the Great Day of His Wrath has Come	**6th Trumpet/2nd Woe** (Rev. 9:13-21; 11:13-14) – Great Earthquake (Causing a Tenth of the City to Fall) Four Messengers Bound at the Great River Euphrates Released to Kill One Third of Mankind with Armies of Horsemen Numbering Two Hundred Million	**6th Bowl** (Rev. 16:12-16) Water of the Great River Euphrates Dried Up to Prepare the Way of the Kings from the Rising of the Sun, and the Entire World, to Gather Them to the Battle of the Great Day of God the Almighty They are Gathered to the Battle of the Great Day of God the Almighty, to the Place Called Har Megiddon	**Battle of Armies from 6th Bowl** (Rev. 19:11-21) – Birds Gather to Eat the Flesh of Kings, Commanders, Mighty, Horses and Horse Riders, Every Slave and Free, Small and Great The One on the White Horse, Called 'The Word of God,' Treads the Winepress of the Fierceness and Wrath of God Almighty
Event Series 6:	**6th Seal** (Rev. 6:12-15) – Every Mountain and Island Moved Out of Place **7th Seal** (Rev. 8:1-6) – Noises Thunders Lightnings Earthquake **1st Trumpet** (Rev. 8:7) – Hail and Fire Mixed with Blood	**7th Trumpet/3rd Woe** (Rev. 11:15-19) – Voices Thunders Lightnings Earthquake Great Hail	**7th Bowl** (Rev. 16:17-21) – Every Island Fled Away and the Mountains were Not Found Noises Thunders Lightnings Great Earthquake (Causing the Great City to be Divided into Three Parts and the Cities of the Nations to Fall) Great Hail	
Event Series 7:	**1st Trumpet** (Rev. 8:7) – One Third of Trees and Green Grass Burned Up	**5th Trumpet/1st Woe** (Rev. 9:1-12) – Locusts Out of the Pit of the Deep Not Allowed to Harm the Grass or Plants or Trees		
Event Series 8:		**1st Bowl** (Rev. 16:2) – Evil Sore Came Upon Those with the Mark or Worshipping Image	**5th Bowl** (Rev. 16:10-11) – They Blasphemed the God of the Heaven for Their Pains and Sores	
Event Series 9:	**2nd Trumpet** (Rev. 8:8-9) – One Third of Sea became Blood and One Third of Living Creatures in the Sea Died	**2nd Bowl** (Rev. 16:3) – Sea became Blood and Every Living Creature in the Sea Died		

In the Sixth Seal the people are trying to hide from the face of Yahuweh/Yehovah on his throne, because he has come, and are trying to escape from the great day of the wrath of the Lamb, which is the great day of the wrath of Yahuweh/Yehovah in Zephaniah 1:14-15. As already shown, the day of the wrath of Yahuweh/Yehovah is the day that he avenges the blood of all those who have yet been avenged, including those from the Fifth Seal who are waiting for that vengeance to be carried out. And the stars falling from the heavens with the heavens rolling out like a double scrolled book in the Sixth Seal specifically comes from the prophecy of Isaiah 34, which is also a prophecy about the day of the vengeance of Yahuweh/Yehovah when he avenges the blood of those not yet avenged. It also links together specifically in Isaiah 34 that the wrath of Yahuweh/Yehovah is the same day as the vengeance of Yahuweh/Yehovah, so that once again here we see that the Sixth Seal is the day when Yahuweh/Yehovah avenges the blood of those slain that are referred to in the Fifth Seal.

Every mountain and island moving out of place in the Sixth Seal is also connected with every mountain and island completely disappearing in the Seventh Bowl, which is also the destruction of Mystery Babel and Yahuweh/Yehovah's avenging of the blood of his servants from the Fifth Seal. Almost every part of the Sixth Seal is intricately connected into the prophecies in Scripture that are specifically about Yahuweh/Yehovah avenging the blood of those whose blood has not yet been avenged, on the day of his wrath, on the Day of Yahuweh/Yehovah, on the day of Yeshua's coming in the clouds at the end of the 3.5 years of Great Tribulation, during the Seventh Trumpet in Revelation 11:15-19. The only part of the Sixth Seal that is required to happen before Yeshua's coming on the Day of Yahuweh/Yehovah at the end of the 3.5 years of Great Tribulation is the part of the moon turning to blood from Joel 2:28-31, which happens "before" the "Great and Terrible Day of Yahuweh/Yehovah."

This shows two things clearly, the first being that if the Sixth Seal is also the Day of Yahuweh/Yehovah when he avenges the blood of those not yet avenged like the Seventh Trumpet and all of the Seven Bowls of Wrath, then it means that there has to be a considerable span of time of resting and waiting in between the opening of the Fifth Seal and the opening of the Sixth Seal. The second is that part of the Sixth Seal has to happen before Yeshua comes at the end of the 3.5 years of Great Tribulation, and part has to happen during the day of and after Yeshua comes at the end of the 3.5 years of Great Tribulation.

As already shown in the previous chart the Sixth Seal is connected into every series of the following seals, trumpets, and bowls that come after it, except for the Second Trumpet, First Bowl, and Second Bowl. This is because in the chronological order of the seals, trumpets, and bowls of Revelation, the opening of the Sixth Seal is the catalyst moment that sets off all of the rest of the seals, trumpets, and bowls, from the Seventh Seal through all of the Seven Trumpets and all of the Seven Bowls, causing them all to happen simultaneously together, each one continuing together with the rest as they are set off one by one, like rows and rows of dominoes each set off at different times but continuing on together until they all crash at once into one, single conclusion at the end. They are all in chronological order in the traditional way that everyone has always seen, but at the same time they are in chronological order of specifically mentioned events that go on simultaneously together.

Traditional Vertical Linear Chronological Order Recorded In Revelation:

(1) 6th Seal
  (2) 7th Seal
    (3) 1st Trumpet
      (4) 2nd Trumpet
        (5) 3rd Trumpet
          (6) 4th Trumpet
            (7) 5th Trumpet/1st Woe
              (8) 6th Trumpet/2nd Woe
                (9) 7th Trumpet/3rd Woe
                  (10) 1st Bowl
                    (11) 2nd Bowl
                      (12) 3rd Bowl
                        (13) 4th Bowl
                          (14) 5th Bowl
                            (15) 6th Bowl
                              (16) 7th Bowl

Additional Simultaneous Horizontal Linear Chronological Order Recorded in Revelation:

(1) 6th Seal	(5) 3rd Trumpet	(12) 3rd Bowl	[Destruction of Babel / Promise of 5th Seal Accomplished]		
(1) 6th Seal	(6) 4th Trumpet	(13) 4th Bowl			
(1) 6th Seal	(7) 5th Trumpet/ 1st Woe	(14) 5th Bowl			
(1) 6th Seal	(8) 6th Trumpet/ 2nd Woe	(15) 6th Bowl	[Battle of Armies Gathered at 6th Bowl]		
(1) 6th Seal	(2) 7th Seal	(3) 1st Trumpet	(9) 7th Trumpet/ 3rd Woe	(16) 7th Bowl	
(1) 6th Seal	*(2) 7th Seal*	*(3) 1st Trumpet*	*(7) 5th Trumpet/ 1st Woe*		
(1) 6th Seal	*(2) 7th Seal*	*(3) 1st Trumpet*	*(9) 7th Trumpet/ 3rd Woe*	*(10) 1st Bowl*	*(14) 5th Bowl*
(1) 6th Seal	*(2) 7th Seal*	*(3) 1st Trumpet*	*(4) 2nd Trumpet*	*(11) 2nd Bowl*	

    A progression of simultaneous events can be seen beginning with the opening of the Sixth Seal, where the sun is darkened and the moon turns to blood, then they become normal again but are darkened 1/3 of the way, then the sun becomes completely darkened again from the smoke of the pit, then hot and bright again, burning men with fire, and then completely darkened again with darkness over the kingdom of the Beast Out of the Sea. The stars fall from the heavens, and then continue to fall from the heavens in the third trumpet and fifth trumpet while at the same time being up in the sky as 1/3 of them darkened.

    There is a great earthquake in the Sixth Seal that continues into the Sixth Trumpet which is also the Second Woe, and all of the people who are hiding in the caves and rocks in the Sixth Seal are then gathering for battle at the Euphrates River and then Har Megiddon, after the four messengers are first released at the

Euphrates River in the Sixth Trumpet, resulting in first 1/3 of mankind dead, and then all of mankind dead when Yeshua rides down to earth on the white horse to do battle with the gathered armies, killing all of the people who were hiding during the Sixth Seal. When the events of the Sixth Seal with the mountains and islands being moved out of place are combined with the chronological order of the Seventh Seal of the noises and thunderings and lightnings and earthquake and hail of the First Trumpet, those same events of the noises/voices and thunderings and lightnings and hail continue on through the Seventh Trumpet and the Seventh Bowl.

From the Sixth Seal onwards everything in the rest of the seals, trumpets, and bowls are a continuous series of groupings of events that happen simultaneously together, over the top of each other, continuing on one from the other as a stream of non-stop hail storms and lightnings and thunderings, and great earthquakes with aftershocks (including from the Sixth Seal and Sixth Trumpet) that first destroy 1/10 of the city and then completely destroy all of the cities of the earth. Every mountain and island begins to move out of place in the Sixth Seal and then they finish moving out of place and disappear entirely in the Seventh Bowl, because they are a continuous, unending chain of events that do not stop until all of them are completed at the very end in Revelation 19 when Yeshua has come to the earth and has destroyed all of the nations with no person left alive on the earth, neither slave nor free, nor small nor great.

The Second Trumpet and Second Bowl with the sea turning to blood and the creatures of the sea dying, starting out with 1/3 of them and finishing with all of them, is a continuous, non-stop event. The 1/3 of the rivers and fountains of water turning bitter poisonous, and then all of them to blood in the Third Trumpet and Third Bowl are a continuous, non-stop event together. All of the events beginning with the Sixth Seal onward through the Seventh Seal and Seven Trumpets and Seven Bowls are continuous events that do not stop once they have begun with the opening of the Sixth Seal, no matter how long that amount of time takes for them to finish at the Seventh Bowl. Each of the Seals and Trumpets and Bowls are snapshots in time of many events happening together at the same time in tandem, seeing frozen moments in time of each series of events as they progress together toward their simultaneous conclusion.

As the oceans are slowly turning to blood, killing all of the creatures in the sea, first at 1/3 then growing in greater and greater fractions until all of the sea is blood, the star is falling on 1/3 of the rivers of the earth, first turning them to poisonous wormwood, then all of the rivers into blood. And as all of the seas and the rivers and waters of the earth are slowly turning into blood, at the exact same time the sun is being darkened then brightening again to 1/3 darkness, then darkening again, then brightening again, then darkening again, as the moon is first turned to blood, then brightened to 1/3 darkness, then darkened again. And some of the stars are falling to the heavens, while 1/3 of the others in the sky are being darkened, and then later completely darkened, all at the same time as everything happening with the sun and moon and the seas and rivers are turning to blood. And while all of these things are taking place every island and mountain on the earth is moved out of place and then continues moving out of place until all of them are completely gone in the end. And at the same time as all of the mountains and islands are fading away, while the seas and the rivers are turning to blood and the sun and moon and stars are being darkened and lightened or falling to varying degrees, there is hail and fire falling with blood that then turns into great hail that no longer has fire in it, but becomes very heavy and large.

And while all of the hail is happening, with the sun and moon and stars going crazy, and the seas and the rivers turning to blood with all of the creatures in the sea dying, and the ships in the sea being destroyed, and the islands and mountains disappearing little by little, there are earthquakes and aftershocks of earthquakes and then even greater earthquakes, first only destroying 1/10 of the city, then all of the cities of the earth to be completely destroyed. And then in the midst of all of the hail and the seas and rivers turning to blood and the creatures of the sea dying together with the ships being destroyed and the islands and mountains disappearing and the earthquakes destroying every city on earth, in the midst of all of this there is massive wildfires that destroy 1/3 of the grass and trees, which then suddenly stops as the grass and trees are no longer allowed to be harmed, with the coming of the army of locusts that goes out to harm men but not kill them.

And in the midst of the army of locusts, and the hail, and the rivers and seas turning to blood, and the creatures of the seas dying, and the mountains and islands disappearing, and the sun and moon and stars going crazy with being darkened by different forms of either clouds or smoke or other atmospheric conditions of lightnings and thunderings of dark clouds and storms, and all of the cities of the earth being eventually destroyed by earthquakes, everybody on the earth is hiding from the coming of the Lamb Yeshua with his wrath, then start gathering together from the entire world to come to Jerusalem and Israel, first meeting at the River Euphrates, for the final war that begins with 1/3 of mankind killed, but eventually, as Yeshua comes down to the earth on the white horse to enter into the war himself, leads to all of mankind lying dead as corpses for the birds to eat. And in the midst of all of this there are the boils that come on the people who received the Mark or worshipped the Beast Out of the Sea. All of these things from the Sixth Seal to the Seventh Bowl are continuous chronological order events that are happening simultaneously together, only finished when Yeshua has arrived on the earth and has ended this world.

The myth was created by Christians over the years that the events of the Sixth Seal through the Sixth Trumpet could start to happen 7 years or 3.5 years before Yeshua's coming at the Seventh Trumpet, at the end of the 3.5 years of Great Tribulation. But the reality that John records in his vision in Revelation is that as soon as the Sixth Seal is opened, starting the chain of events of all of the other trumpets and bowls, it starts an extinction level event of the earth which no one would be able to survive through for more than a few months at the very most. And Yeshua's own words in Matthew 24 and Luke 17 expose this myth about the Sixth Seal through Sixth Trumpet events happening many years before Yeshua returns, because he says that on the day of his coming, after the Great Tribulation, everyone will be eating and drinking and being fruitful and multiplying and planting and building and buying and selling. If the earth extinction level event that begins with the Sixth Seal has already started 7 years or 3.5 years before Yeshua has come, then there will not be anyone left eating or drinking or having children or building or buying and selling or growing food when he comes, because they will all be dead or in a survival situation of being almost dead every day. Yeshua's words in Matthew 24 and Luke 17 become false and in error, especially his words about coming as a thief in the night at the end of the Great Tribulation, unless the events of the Sixth Seal through Sixth Trumpet do not happen until the very end of the Great Tribulation at the same time as the Seventh Trumpet of his coming.

There is no way to predict how these events from the Sixth Seal and Seventh Seal through all of the Seven Trumpets and Seven Bowls will happen, or the timing of how they will all happen together, but it is clear from what John has recorded of his vision that there is no requirement for any of these prophecy events from the Sixth Seal through all of the Seven Trumpets and Seven Bowls to have to happen before the very end of the 3.5 years of Great Tribulation. And all of the evidence of them shows that after the Sixth Seal is opened there is very little time left to when Yeshua comes at the end of the 3.5 years of Great Tribulation. It is a matter of only months or days until he comes at that point, when those events begin to happen. And any of them that do happen before Yeshua returns have to happen in such a way that they do not disturb or stop people from eating and drinking and being fruitful and multiplying and planting and building and buying and selling up to the very day that he comes at the end of the 3.5 years of Great Tribulation.

The events of the Sixth Seal are not happening yet in any kind of fullness that is visible on the earth, which means that the Sixth Seal is probably not open yet. But when the Sixth Seal does open and we begin seeing the events of the Sixth Seal start to happen in some way, we can know that we are living at the time of the very end of the 3.5 years of Great Tribulation, in the final months or days of the Great Tribulation. The Sixth Seal is the very last and final prophecy to watch for its fulfillment right before Yeshua returns, and when we see it we can know that there is almost no time left to his coming, and the Great Tribulation is almost over. The moon turned to blood part of the Sixth Seal prophecy from Joel 2:30-31 is the only part that has to happen before Yeshua returns on the Day of Yahuweh/Yehovah, and most of the rest of the Sixth Seal is required to have to happen after Yeshua returns at the end of the Great Tribulation. This means that after the Joel 2:30-31 prophecy reaches its final and complete fulfillment in the opening of the Sixth Seal, with the sun turned to darkness and the moon to blood in the heavens, and blood, fire, and pillars of smoke on the earth, Yeshua's return will finally at that moment become "imminent" for the first time in the last 2,000 years of world history.

Appendix: Blood Moons

As a note on the moon turned to blood and the sun turned to darkness in the prophecy of Joel 2:30-31 connected with the Sixth Seal in Revelation 6:12: There was a big commotion in the years 2014 to 2015 about the sign in the sun and moon and stars of the "Blood Moon Tetrad" consisting of four total lunar eclipses that turned the moon to a blood red color four times during those two years. And each of those four times were on dates of Yahuweh/Yehovah's Festivals that he created to be celebrated in the spring and in the fall.

The first total lunar eclipse was on the 15th day of the 1st month on the first day of the Feast of Unleavened bread during the night of April 14-15, 2014. The second total lunar eclipse was on the 12th day of the 7th month during the night of October 7-8, 2014, two days after the Day of Atonement or Yom Kippur and three days before the first day of the Feast of Booths or Tabernacles. [On the modern Jewish calendar that does not keep Yahuweh/Yehovah's Scriptural/Biblical calendar of starting the month at the sighting of the New Moon in Israel it was during the Feast of Booths.] The third total lunar eclipse was on the 14th day of the 1st month on the day of Passover during the night of April 3-4, 2015. And the fourth total lunar eclipse was on the 14th day of the 7th month during the night of September 27-28, 2015, one day before the first day of the Feast of Booths. [On the modern Jewish calendar that does not keep Yahuweh/Yehovah's Scriptural/Biblical calendar of starting the month at the sighting of the New Moon in Israel it was during the Feast of Booths.] There was also a total solar eclipse that turned the sun to darkness in the middle of these Blood Moons that was visible in Israel on March 20, 2015 on the 28th day of the 12th month, two days before the start of the new year or Rosh haShanah in the spring.

When no rapture happened during those years and nothing of major significance appeared to happen, everyone discarded the signs in the sun, moon, and stars that Yeshua said in Luke 21 would happen before his coming, throwing out these total lunar eclipses that happened in the midst of Yahuweh/Yehovah's major feast days during the years 2014 to 2015. There is no way to know yet at this point whether or not that Blood Moon Tetrad in 2014 to 2015 with the total solar eclipse in the middle between them had anything to do with the prophecy of the moon turning to blood and sun to darkness in Joel and Revelation, but now looking back we can see that there were several major events that happened at that time in connection with those signs in the heavens that did not look important then, but now can be seen to be the catalyst events that completely changed the world forever for us today.

1 – The first event was the Fifty Day War between Israel and Hamas in Gaza from July 8 to August 26, 2014, which included a ground war operation by Israel inside of the Gaza Strip. This was the first time that Hamas tried to make a ground incursion or invasion inside of Israel and the first time that Israel found out about Hamas's tunnels and their desire to invade Israel. There were many in the Israeli government and military at that time who wanted to destroy and end the Hamas organization at that time, including Likud member Danny Danon. It was the last time that Israel was inside of the Gaza Strip with a significant ground force and their last chance when there was a strong will among Israelis to take out Hamas. The Israeli public at that time were more ready than they had ever been to go into Gaza and remove Hamas from power and existence in the Gaza strip. Avigdor Lieberman, head of the Yisrael Beiteinu Party in Israel, was a key ally and partner in a coalition government with Prime Minister Benjamin Netanyahu and the Likud Party at that time. He was ready and pushing to go into Gaza and remove Hamas from power, but it was the decision by Prime Minister Benjamin Netanyahu and others in the government and military at that time to stop the operation with only destruction of the tunnels while leaving Hamas in power that was the catalyst moment that led to the massacre of Israeli civilians on October 7, 2023, on the 21st day of the 7th month, the seventh day of the Feast of Booths according to the sighting of the new moon in Israel, and on the eighth day of the festival, on the day of the Feast of Conclusion or Feast of Atsereth (Assembly) using the modern Jewish calendar.

The choices of the Israeli government at that time to not finish Hamas when they had the opportunity, deciding to place Israeli popularity in the world above the security of its citizens, was the catalyst moment that led to the October 7, 2023 massacre of Holocaust proportions and subsequent war that became the first time in 50 years since the Yom Kippur War that Israel officially made a declaration of war. It was also the catalyst moment that led to Israel's current "Second War for Independence" beginning on October 7, 2023, because it was the first time that Hamas began its attempts and attacks to invade Israel, continually trying to get through the border until they succeeded on October 7. And this 2023 Second War for Independence beginning on October 7 is the most serious war that Israel has been in since the Yom Kippur War in 1973 that is pulling in nations from all over the world, drawing them closer into a world war, because of the horrific atrocities carried out by Hamas terrorists in Israel. The Fifty Day War in Gaza and Israel in 2014 was the beginning moment that led to the horrors of October 7, 2023 and subsequent war that is helping to create a world war.

Interestingly, Prime Minister Ariel Sharon died on January 11, 2014 only a few months before the first of the Blood Moons in the Tetrad, and Ariel Sharon is the one who was responsible for signing the order for Israel to pull out of Gaza to begin with, allowing Hamas to come into power and become a threat to Israel in the first place in 2005. He had been in a coma for 9 years before he died and his very last act as Prime Minister before going into the coma was to sign over Israeli owned land in Gaza over to the Palestinians and hand Gaza over to Palestinian rule, working in league with President George W. Bush of the United States of America.

2 – Also during the Blood Moon Tetrads in the year 2014, there was the 5 Day Revolution of Ukraine during February 18-23, 2014 to overthrow the corrupt dictatorship in the country. And this in turn led to Russia's invasion and annexation of Crimea from February 20 to March 26, 2014, and the counter revolution forming the Donetsk People's Republic on April 7, 2014 and the Luhansk People's Republic on April 27, 2014. These moments of revolution and counter revolution and invasion and annexation that happened during the beginning of the Blood Moon Tetrads became the catalyst moment that led to the Russia-Ukraine War that started on February 24, 2022, which is drawing all of the nations in the world into a world war that threatens to become a nuclear world war. The war also displaced over 100,000 Jews who left Ukraine since 2014 and since then a Jewish President has now come into power in Ukraine, Volodymyr Zelensky, tying in a lot of Jewish connections with the Russia-Ukraine War and the Blood Moon Tetrad.

These are two very significant catalyst moments where the decisions and actions of people in 2014 concerning Ukraine and Israel both created catalyst moments that would cause both of these events in Ukraine and Israel to explode exponentially in 2022 and 2023. And now both of these nations of Ukraine and Israel are in ongoing wars and conflicts that are happening simultaneously together, both together pulling in the nations of the world around them into a greater and greater world war. Even just one of these two events on their own have the potential to create a nuclear world war, but the catalyst moments for both of these conflicts between Ukraine and Russia and between Israel and Iran through its proxies like Hamas happened together during the Blood Moon Tetrad in 2014. Now they are both escalating together in tandem in 2022 and 2023, with two areas of war drawing the world together into a world war at the same time, perhaps even a nuclear world war.

Now with the advantage of looking back we can see the very clear warning taking place during the Blood Moon Tetrad, and there could be even more events that happened at that time that were the beginning of greater things that are happening now or will be happening shortly in the future, but for certain we now know of at least two in which the decisions and actions made in connection with Israel and Ukraine at that time set the course to allow these even bigger, more catastrophic and apocalyptic events, to happen now that have the potential of at the very least changing the world or at the most ending the world. Maybe the Blood Moon Tetrad of 2014 and 2015 had nothing to do with the blood moon prophecies in Joel and Revelation, but we can see now that they were a warning sign in the heavens about significant events taking place at that time that would lead to bigger things to come in the future that would see the beginning of atrocities and wars in 2022 and 2023 on a scale not seen since World War II and the Holocaust. It is certainly not every day that events happen like those that took place in 2014 that become catalyst moments for causing world wars.

Appendix: Conclusion

The Reality is that the Words of the Prophecies are being Fulfilled Instead of the Myths About the Prophecies: If we are brutally honest with ourselves looking at the events unfolding in the last 80 years, and especially those in the last 10 years, the events taking place are fulfilling all of the words of the prophecies concerning the Time of the End and Yeshua's Return. The only things that are not being fulfilled right now are the myths and imaginations and legends and theories and interpretations and doctrines and commentaries and fictions and fantasies and desires of those prophecies. This is simply reality that the events of recent years and recent decades are all fulfilling the prophecies of the Time of the End word for word as they are written. The prophecies are in the midst of fulfillment now in the present; the events of the present are the fulfillment of the exact words of the prophecies now and are not a precursor or preparation to a future fulfillment of the prophecies. The prophecies concerning the time of the Great Tribulation and the events leading up to it are already in fulfillment now and are no longer future events that are coming at some point later on. Now in the present is the fulfillment and they will continue to be fulfilled into the future. But we are no longer waiting for their fulfillment to come at an unknown time in the future; the fulfillment is now in the present.

There was no way to even include all of the prophecies being fulfilled, or thoroughly write about all of the fulfillments happening in the prophecies that are included in this book, because the book would have been too long for anyone to be able to read. There are many other important prophetic events connected with all of the prophecies happening that were too numerous to include in this book and it would take many volumes of books to cover everything that is going on. But when looking at the most essential prophecies that have to be fulfilled before Yeshua Returns, every single one of them is in process of happening now with events all taking place together simultaneously in the right places and right times, fulfilling the words of every one of these essential prophecies.

If the myths about the prophecies were being fulfilled instead of the words of the prophecies then everyone would be recognizing the prophecies happening. But it is the natural thing that humans do, creating imaginary, make believe about things that they want to learn about and understand, and there is nothing wrong with that as long as the myths and fictions created are not believed in as though they were reality. Each time since the creation of the world that Yahuweh/Yehovah gives prophecies about future events connected with his future plans, he gives greater numbers of prophecies about what he will do and greater lengths of time in between when the prophecies are fulfilled. This makes each time of fulfillment of his prophecies harder to recognize instead of easier, because there is more time and more material for humans to do what they are good at, creating myths and fictions.

None of that would be bad as long as those myths are not raised up as doctrines in higher authority than the words that are actually written in prophecy, and unfortunately this time, this is the first time to have the extra confusion of entire fictional novels and films and television series about the prophecies of the Time of the End. There is a whole genre of fiction that has been created now in recent history that is like the Science Fiction or Fantasy or Historical Fiction genres, except that it is Eschatology Fiction. There is nothing wrong with them as long as people do not believe that the prophecies will actually be fulfilled in those imaginary ways, but when people take novels and fictional films as doctrine concerning the fulfillments of prophecy they will be very disappointed when reality never turns out like fantasy.

But the myths are easier for people to process and think about, and are more dramatic and romantic, than the reality of what is actually written in the prophecies. It has come to the point now, just like during the days of Yeshua, that the myths are taught in place of reading the words that are actually written in the prophecies. And now we are watching things play out exactly the same way as every other time in history when the reality of the prophecies is different from the myths and imaginations and interpretations that were taught about them, exactly the same as the Pharisees who created myths and legends about the prophecies of the Messiah that they raised up in higher authority than the actual words written in the prophecies. <u>Now is the time to be set free of the myths and not fall into the same trap as the Pharisees and Sadducees and Essenes and other religious groups at the time of Yeshua who followed their myths and fictions about prophecy instead of the words that are written and the reality of fulfillment of those words right before their own eyes.</u>

The Reality is that All of the Prophecies Concerning the Time of the Great Tribulation that are Required to Happen Before Yeshua Returns are Either Already Fulfilled and Finished or are in Process of being Fulfilled Now and are Almost Finished, which Means that Either We are Already Living in the 3.5 Years of Great Tribulation Now or the 3.5 Years of Great Tribulation is About to Begin Imminently at Any Moment: All of the prophecies required to happen or begin to happen before Yeshua returns are all fulfilled or in process of fulfillment according to the words that are written in those prophecies. The only truthful conclusion that we can come to if we are going to accept reality wholly and completely without any imagination is that either we are already living in the 3.5 years of Great Tribulation now, or the prophecies being fulfilled now are going to carry over and continue into an imminent beginning of the 3.5 years of Great Tribulation that could start at any moment. This is the reality that we are living in now, if we throw out all imagination and make believe about the prophecies and only focus on the reality of the words that are written.

Looking back through history there is no other time when there are a series of events happening simultaneously in a very short period of time that fulfill all of the prophecies precisely word for word of the time before Yeshua's return as this time now. Anyone can look back through history and try to find another time when Israel is in existence as a nation at the same time that there is a Mark required upon the hand (not only on a piece of paper but upon the literal hand or forehead) in order to be able to go to the marketplace to buy and to sell. While at the same time the Witness of the Word of Yahuweh/Yehovah in his commands and Torah is being completely removed from all of society in every place around the world, and the world is so full of corruption and violence that people no longer try to hide their sins, but instead parade their sins and glorify them in public, even things like torture and rape and murder. And at the same time there is a Babel system that brings together the entire world as a single city in rebellion against Yahuweh/Yehovah with technology like the internet, and simultaneously, at the same time, the Good News is taught and available to every person in every nation across the entire earth, from one end to the other, who wants to hear it. When else in history is there another time when there are a series of dozens of events taking place together in a short period of time that all fulfill the words of the prophecies of the Time of the End all together at once.

The only major prophecy left to happen is the opening of the Sixth Seal, and completion of all of the prophecies at Yeshua's Return and his gathering of all of the nations together for a World War III or nuclear world war event, centered around Jerusalem and the destruction of Mystery Babel (by the Ten Horns) and the destruction of the Beast Out of the Sea, which includes the destruction of every city and every nation on earth. The world war that takes place at the end of the 3.5 years of Great Tribulation as a result of the opening of the Sixth Seal, together with Yahuweh/Yehovah's coming to Jerusalem to destroy the armies that he has gathered to fight there at Jerusalem, are the only significant things left to happen now in the prophecies. Everything else has had an event or precise sign in the real world showing its fulfillment since Israel became a nation in 1948. There is not one single precursor event taking place right now, only the actual fulfillments of all of the prophecies in real life. <u>There is not a lot of time left to Yeshua's Return and the end of the 3.5 years of Great Tribulation, and as soon as the Sixth Seal is opened there is no time left to his coming.</u>

The whole purpose of Yahuweh/Yehovah giving his prophecies in Scripture is in order to know him more deeply and intimately, and for those who know Yahuweh/Yehovah they will be able to see his fingerprints in all of these events and fulfillments happening. The way things are happening now is the way that he always does things, using a single event like his COVID plague to fulfill and ignite the fulfillment of many multiple prophecies all happening at once together. This is how the prophecies happened with Yeshua in a very short amount of time, layer upon layer of prophecy over one another, and this is how he took the children of Israel out of Egypt with a mighty hand, with a lot of things happening in a very short period of time, waiting for hundreds of years until a single moment in time to suddenly accomplish all of his words and promises in prophecy all at once in an instant.

And when Yahuweh/Yehovah comes we will finally no longer care about how he will fulfill his prophecies and do his plan of ending this world and creating a new heavens and new earth, because we will be with him and he will do his prophecies any way he wants to and no one will care how he does it. The prophecies in Scripture are different from his instructions and commands and requirements of righteousness, because the prophecies are his thoughts and plans of the future. And he tells us in Isaiah 55 that we cannot figure out his thinking and planning on our own, and he will accomplish and do his prophecies and promises in spite of our not having any understanding of what he is doing. He has to be the one to tell us and explain to us what the prophecies mean and what he is doing with his prophecies, because we cannot know unless he tells us directly and helps us to understand.

And he does not always tell us until after he has already finished and accomplished his prophecies, when they are all done. Then when they are already fulfilled or in the midst of fulfillment, they become very easy to understand and comprehend. This is because before the prophecies are fulfilled we are wanting the prophecies to be fulfilled according to our own will, wanting our own will to be done on the earth and interpreting the prophecy to be the way we think Yahuweh/Yehovah should fulfill his prophecies. But after Yahuweh/Yehovah's will has already been done when the prophecy is all finished and over, then we can see that his will is better than our own will, and we want Yahuweh/Yehovah's will instead of our own.

The Reality is that There are a Number of the Prevalent Prophecy Myths Taught and Believed Today that are Actually Prophesied in Scripture to Never Happen: There are a lot of myths about prophecies that people are watching for to happen in the future, which are never prophesied to happen anywhere in Scripture. But there are some of these myths that the prophecies in Scripture actually prophesy about very clearly that these myths will <u>not</u> happen. Some of the myths we do not need to worry about or be concerned about ever happening, because Yahuweh/Yehovah clearly says in the prophecies about the Time of the End and his coming that they are <u>not</u> going happen.

1. The Anti-Christ/Anti-Messiah Myth Everyone is Watching for that is Prophesied to Never Happen: There is no doubt or controversy that there have been in the past and always will continue to be in the present and future anti-christs or anti-messiahs until Yeshua returns, as John teaches about in his first and second letters (1 John and 2 John). These anti-christs or anti-messiahs that John talks about are a type of people that are always around in the fallen world we live in like the false prophets and false messiahs. Moses warns about the false prophets that would be coming to the nation of Israel in their future in Deuteronomy, which are not very different from the warnings of the anti-christs that John talks about in 1 John and 2 John. And Yeshua warned more than once about the coming of false messiahs and false prophets in the same way that Moses warned about the false prophets as well, and how to watch out for them in order to not fall into their deceptions. There is nothing particularly special about false prophets and false messiahs and anti-messiahs or anti-christs, except that they come as deceivers all through history and will continue to come until Yahuweh/Yehovah makes his permanent dwelling among men.

Unfortunately through the years Christians began to create a mythical, superhuman, supervillain Anti-Christ, borrowing bits and pieces from different prophecies in Scripture to eventually create a fictional character that is not prophesied about in Scripture. From passages in the Talmud it appears that the myth about a supervillain false messiah (called by the name of Anti-Christ by Christians later on) originated from the Pharisees. One of the earliest Christian records of the Christian version of the Anti-Christ myth is from the writings of Irenaeus in his *Against Heresies, Book 5* in Chapter 30, written in about 174-189 C.E. Since that time there have been many more Anti-Christ myths created to the point that now there are many different versions of the Anti-Christ myth that different Christians have believed in through history and today. There are too many Anti-Christ myths to go through them all, but one prevalent part of the Anti-Christ myth that has been around since the time of Irenaeus in the 2nd century C.E. is that the Anti-Christ will be the Little Horn prophesied in Daniel 7 and Daniel 8 and that the Anti-Christ will become a dictator king or ruler over the final beast empire, taking over from all of the other rulers as the sole and only ruler in total and absolute control of a resurrected empire brought back to life again.

There are many different versions of this myth of the Anti-Christ being like a Caesar or Emperor of a resurrected Roman Empire, or a Pope of a resurrected Roman Catholic Empire, or a Kaliph of a resurrected Islamic Empire, or a dictator style President of a powerful nation like the United States of America, or a Fuhrer over a Nazi style Reich. The myth is still essentially the same in all of its different versions that the Anti-Christ rises up like a Little Horn in a position of total power and control, either religiously or politically or both, as the sole and only power ruling over the final Fourth Beast or Beast Out of the Sea Empire in

Daniel and Revelation. And it is this part of the myth that we can know for certain will never happen, because in both Daniel and Revelation this is prophesied to never happen. Such a supervillain dictator with absolute power over a religious or political system that rules over the entire world, or a region of the world, is prophesied to never happen during the Time of the End and the Great Tribulation when Yahuweh/Yehovah comes to set up his reign on the earth after crushing all of the empires and reigns of man.

Daniel 2:41-44 prophesies that at the time of the coming of Yahuweh/Yehovah's kingdom to reign over the earth in place of man's kingdoms, the final kingdom empire in existence is broken apart into pieces and remains that way all the way to the end, with no one able to bring it together into an empire ever again. In Daniel 7:7-8 and 19-28, as well as in Revelation 13:1-3 and Revelation 17:1-18, this final kingdom empire is again pictured as being broken up and in fragments among many nations and many kingdoms and many governments with many different rulers over it. It is made very clear in Daniel 7 that the Little Horn never succeeds in getting control over the empire, nor is ever in any position of any significant power, with at least ten other kings and kingdoms reigning throughout all the way to the end. None of the Ten Horns are ever removed from power or conquered by the Little Horn or any other king all the way to the very end where in Revelation 17 they are all still in power to be able to destroy Mystery Babel.

In Daniel 2 and Daniel 7 and Revelation 13 and Revelation 17 it is made clear in several different ways that the reign of the final beast or final empire is divided up among many different rulers and kings and governments, never to be united under the rule of a single supervillain dictator ever again. The feet and toes of the statue image in Daniel 2 are broken up between iron and clay all the way to the end, never to be united under the rule of a single Anti-Christ person ever again. And in Daniel 7 the reign is divided up among many kings, among many horns, with Ten Horns and an eleventh Little Horn, which never succeed in conquering one another or getting control over one another. In Revelation 13 the Beast Out of the Sea is made up of Seven Heads and Ten Horns, and fragmented pieces of all of the previous empires in history since the time of Daniel. This is once again showing a fragmented and divided empire with many different rulers over it, made up of pieces of many different nations and cultures and languages that are divided against each other from within the kingdom empire. And in Revelation 17 the Ten Horns that are ten kings give their power temporarily to the Beast Out of the Sea, but never are removed from their positions as heads of government and are never conquered. And they never give their power to the Little Horn at any time, or to any single man to be a dictator emperor over a united empire.

Therefore we can know for certain that the Anti-Christ myth of an all-powerful, supervillain dictator rising up into total power and control, conquering nations and creating an empire of any size will never happen, because Yahuweh/Yehovah has prophesied in Scripture that it will never happen. We can know this with as great of certainty as we know that he is coming to set up his reign and end all of the reigns of mankind in this world. So we can relax and not worry about having to watch for an Anti-Christ dictator to take over the world or to take over an empire, because it will never happen.

The Little Horn in Daniel 7 and 8 is prophesied to be only great in a certain direction or small area of the Middle East, to the south and to the east and to the "Gazelle" or "Beautiful/Splendid," while the Beast Out of the Sea is prophesied to have authority over every tribe, tongue, and nation. This means that the Little Horn and the Beast Out of the Sea cannot be the same person or entity, because the Little Horn is only regionally great with influence in a small area of the world and the Beast Out of the Sea is great with influence across the entire earth. The Little Horn is only able to subdue (not even conquer) only three of the Ten Horns, while the Beast Out of the Sea is able to get all Ten Horns to give their power and authority to it willingly without having to do any military conquest at all. This means that once again the Little Horn and the Beast Out of the Sea cannot be the same person or entity, because the Little Horn only has small influence and power over Three Horns, failing to conquer or have any influence at all over the other Seven Horns, while the Beast Out of the Sea has big influence and power over all Ten Horns.

The Little Horn is only one small cog in the greater machinery of the Beast Out of the Sea, with the Beast Out of the Sea having power and control over the Little Horn and all of the Ten Horns, and even having authority and influence throughout every nation and tribe on earth beyond its borders. The Little Horn is a small power that is under the greater power of the Beast Out of the Sea, as is the case with all Ten Horns and many nations and peoples beyond them. The Little Horn cannot be the same entity as the Beast Out of the Sea, and neither of these can be the same entities as the Ten Horns or the Seven Heads. Each are different entities all joined together into the same system, each playing their role in a larger conglomeration of many separate parts trying to work together, or fight against each other, toward a common goal of power.

The reality in the prophecies in Scripture is much more complex than the Anti-Christ myth that tries to simplify them into a classic hero/villain novel. As already discussed throughout the book, in reality there are the many anti-christs that John talks about in his letters, but these anti-christs are separate from and have nothing to do with the prophecies of the Beast Out of the Sea with Ten Horns and a Little Horn and Seven Heads and fragments of Four Beasts consisting of Two Feet and Ten Toes that are fragmented clay and iron mixed together, or the Beast Out of the Earth with Two Horns, or the Image of the Beast Out of the Sea, or the Scarlet Beast Out of the Pit of the Deep with Ten Horns and Seven Heads plus an Eighth Head carrying the prostitute Queen of Mystery Babel, or the Dragon with Seven Heads and Ten Horns, or Abaddon the Messenger Out of the Pit of the Deep, or the King of Babel. All of these many different entities in prophecy were combined together into one, single supervillain person called "The Anti-Christ" ruling over a single organization or government, but in reality all of these entities are separate and different people and groups of people in different organizations and governments and nations. There is no prophecy in Scripture that says that any of these entities have anything to do with the anti-christs or anti-messiahs that John talks about in his letters.

And there is no connection that Paul makes to any of the previously mentioned entities in Daniel and Revelation and his Man of Lawlessness/Sin in 2 Thessalonians, as already discussed. He never says anything about this Man of Lawlessness/Sin having anything to do with the prophecies of Daniel 2 or Daniel 7, and the things that he says the Man of Lawlessness/Sin will do are not prophesied in any prophecies anywhere else in Scripture to happen. As already earlier discussed, his prophecy in 2 Thessalonians is a unique prophecy not found anywhere else in Scripture and not prophesied to happen anywhere else in Scripture.

<u>Unfortunately everyone is watching for "The Anti-Christ" supervillain myth to come, which will never happen as a fulfillment of any prophecies, because it is not in prophecy. So we can relax and rest in the words</u>

of Yahuweh/Yehovah that are written down in Scripture and know that at least this one prophecy myth about "The Anti-Christ" is one myth that will never happen. There will be no Anti-Christ who makes a 7 year peace covenant with Israel, and there will be no Anti-Christ that is worshipped as a god who requires a Mark be taken by people in allegiance and worship to him, and there will be no Anti-Christ who rules as a dictator or god over a regional or global empire. And there will never be a One World Government or New World Order Government that rules over the world or a region of the world with absolute power as a dictator government, because Yahuweh/Yehovah has prophesied in Daniel 2 and Daniel 7 and Revelation 13 and Revelation 17 that it will never succeed and never come into existence before he comes and destroys all of the governments of mankind.

2. The Temple/Tabernacle Myth Everyone is Watching for that Ignores the Will and Heart of Yahuweh/Yehovah in His Prophecies: Yahuweh/Yehovah has no desire for, and has never had any desire for, a physical building to be standing on the Temple Mount for him to sit in and dwell in. His desire has always been to make his people into his Temple dwelling place, sitting as king in the Temple of his people. It is man who is always trying to build a physical house for Yahuweh/Yehovah to be trapped inside of that house, so that they only have to be with him when they go to that physical house and they can keep him shut out of their lives for all of the rest of the time when they are not inside of that physical house or temple. But Yahuweh/Yehovah's goal has always been to make his people his dwelling place and house, so that he is dwelling with every person every moment of every day and night, never separated for a single second, as in a marriage covenant. And that way we are always with him at all times, inside or outside, or anywhere in any place.

If a physical Third Temple were ever built on the Temple Mount it would have no consequence or significance to Yahuweh/Yehovah's plans and goals. It would be a worthless building of no value that would pass away and be destroyed along with the rest of the Temples that have stood there before it, because Yahuweh/Yehovah would never be dwelling there in that place. He has no desire for temples or physical buildings to be living in as he says in 2 Samuel 7 and Isaiah 66:1-2, quoted in Acts 7:47-49, and in Revelation 21:22. A Third Temple or even a Second Tabernacle Tent on the Temple Mount would never be a set-apart place, because Yahuweh/Yehovah's goal is to make his people into his House and Tabernacle dwelling place, into his set-apart place to live in, to make his Tabernacle with men as he says in Revelation 21:2-3.

He is living with his people, rebuilding his people into his set-apart place to live in, in fulfillment of Amos 9:11-15, which means he has no reason to ever build a physical temple building ever again for all eternity. There is no way to know for certain at this point with available textual evidence if the original word written in Amos 9:12 is the nation "Edom" "אדום" as it says in the Hebrew Masoretic text we have available today or if it originally said "Adam" "אדם," meaning "mankind," as it is quoted to say in Acts 15:17. The difference in ancient Hebrew before vowel pointing is only a single letter Vav ו between "Edom" and "Adam," and the fact that in the Greek of Acts 15:17 it says "mankind" instead of the nation of "Edom" indicates that in the 1st century C.E. at the time of the book of Acts there were at least some copies of Amos that had "mankind" or "Adam" written in them in Hebrew in place of "Edom." But either way the Booth of David that is prophesied to be rebuilt in Amos 9 is the rebuilding of the people and nation of Israel through the Messiah, and bringing in the nations or gentiles of the world into that nation Israel through the Messiah, descended of David. It is the people and the nations, not a physical, temporary building or tent that can be destroyed and torn down again, as confirmed in Revelation 7:13-15 as the people dwell with Yahuweh/Yehovah as a tent, like the Booth of David in Amos 9. Isaiah 56 also confirms this, as Yahuweh/Yehovah brings in the nations or gentiles into his House of Prayer, making the nations and peoples of the earth, joined together with Israelis, into his house and dwelling place.

When Yahuweh/Yehovah came to walk the earth in the physical body as a man, that physical body he lived in on the earth as Yeshua he called a temple in John 2:13-22. And from that Paul expands the concept and understanding of how Yahuweh/Yehovah wants his people to become the "body" that he dwells in, in 1 Corinthians 3:16-17. It is the people, the worshippers of Yahuweh/Yehovah, who are measured as the temple in Revelation 11:1-2, because at the time of Yahuweh/Yehovah's coming it is his people he has made into his Temple or Tabernacle dwelling place instead of having a physical temple to dwell in.

Unfortunately everyone is watching for a Third Temple or a Second Tabernacle/Tent structure to be built with daily sacrifices resuming to create the conditions for a Disgusting Idol (Abomination) Desolating, which will never happen as a fulfillment of any prophecies, because, as already discussed throughout the book, the rebuilding of a Temple or the resuming of daily animal sacrifices is not prophesied to happen anywhere in end-time prophecy as a prerequisite for the Disgusting Idol (Abomination) Desolating to take place. And Yahuweh/Yehovah has no desire for building more physical temples when he has his people to dwell in as his Temple now. It is his people from all the nations, including Israel, that he is making into his set-apart place to dwell in, and since he already has his set-apart place that is almost finished and built now with his people, he has no need to build another physical set-apart place again for a Disgusting Idol (Abomination) Desolating to be placed inside of it. His own people are already his set-apart place and they each have to decide if they are going to set up any unclean abominations into that set-apart place of themselves or not.

Therefore we can relax in knowing from the word of Yahuweh/Yehovah in Scripture that no Third Temple or Second Tabernacle Tent built on the Temple Mount or anywhere else is required or needed as a set-apart place for Yeshua to be able to return, because such a physical Temple or Tabernacle place can never again be his true set-apart place. His set-apart place is with his people now and that is never going to change again for all eternity. The prophecy myth that Yahuweh/Yehovah wants a Third Temple or Second Tabernacle Tent prophecy is another myth that we can know for certain will never happen. We can know with absolute certainty that Yahuweh/Yehovah will never build another physical building or physical tent structure on the Temple Mount or in Jerusalem for a set-apart place, because he does not want one and has no need for one. Any Third Temple or Second Tabernacle Tent that might be built in Jerusalem or on the Temple Mount will be built by man for the desires and purposes of man and not by Yahuweh/Yehovah. Yahuweh/Yehovah does not want a house of stone or tent of leather; he wants a house and tent of people.

3. The Two Witnesses Myth Everyone is Watching for that is Prophesied to Never Happen: As already previously shown, John writes specifically in the prophecy and description of the Two Witnesses being "the Two Lampstands" in Revelation 11:4-6 that the Two Witnesses can only be referring to God himself, and cannot ever be men because men can never be God. The "Two Lampstands," which are referring to the lampstands or menorahs in Revelation 4:5 and 5:6 and Zechariah 4:1-14, are clearly representing the seven eyes of Yahuweh/Yehovah, which are the seven Spirits of Yahuweh/Yehovah, and can only be Yahuweh/Yehovah himself. No man or woman or messenger (angel) or spiritual being can be the seven eyes and seven Spirits of Yahuweh/Yehovah, only he himself can be his own eyes and his own Spirits.

Additionally, the Two Witnesses have the authority to bring any plague on the earth at any time that they themselves "wish" or "determine" to bring a plague on the wicked. Only God has the authority to bring plagues on anyone he "wishes" or "determines" to judge with plagues. Only God, only Yahuweh/Yehovah himself, has the authority to "determine" when a person or a city or a nation deserves or needs to have the judgment of plagues brought down upon them, and only God himself has the authority to "wish" to bring a plague of judgment upon people and then carry out that wish. Luke 9:54-56 is an example why Yahuweh/Yehovah does not give the authority of a god to men and why he does not give men authority to bring down plagues whenever they wish or determine to do so.

The Two Witnesses can only be God himself, Yahuweh/Yehovah himself, and his attributes and things that make up who he is, such as his words, because only God can be the Two Lampstands in Zechariah 4 and Revelation 4 and 5 and only God has the authority to bring plagues whenever he wishes upon men. Unfortunately the myth was created very early on in the early days of Christianity that the Two Witnesses are men, especially men who have come back to life from the dead like Moses or Elijah or Enoch, but even men who come back from the dead cannot be gods or take the place of Yahuweh/Yehovah as God and creator of the universe. This created a myth where the Two Witnesses are two men that Yahuweh/Yehovah brings back from the dead and recreates them into demi-gods with the same and equal powers and authority of Yahuweh/Yehovah himself, performing superhuman and magical feats like mini-gods right out of fictional Pagan mythologies.

The myth makes for an exciting and dramatic story like would be found in a novel or romantic hero versus villain tale, but the reality of the prophecy in Scripture is that this is Yahuweh/Yehovah alone, as always, who has the power of God. He alone is God and there are no others beside him, and he never gives men and women the power and authority of gods, even though men and women try to take his place and gain his power as gods. In Luke 9:54 we can see that the Apostle John was one of those who Yeshua rebuked for wanting to have the kind of power of the Two Witnesses in Revelation 11 to call down fire whenever he wanted to like Elijah, to destroy the Shomron (Samaritan) village in judgment for rejecting Yeshua. But of course Elijah never once made fire come down from the heavens; it was always Yahuweh/Yehovah who did that. John knew exactly what he was writing about with the Two Witnesses in Revelation 11, knowing all the time that he was not writing about two physical men doing the very thing that he had already been rebuked by Yeshua for wanting to have the power to do himself.

Men also fall short of the perfect righteousness and perfect foresight of Yahuweh/Yehovah, which is why while Moses and Elijah were alive, Yahuweh/Yehovah never even allowed them to possess the authority that the Two Witnesses have in Revelation 11, to bring down any kind of plague they wanted whenever they wished or to kill their enemies with fire coming out of their mouths or to be the eyes of Yahuweh/Yehovah himself with the sight of gods being able to see everyone and everything, including the thoughts in the hearts of men, and being able to see everything that has happened in the past and everything that will happen in the future. No men can possess the seven eyes of Yahuweh/Yehovah, of Yeshua the seven eyed Lamb in Revelation 5.

<u>Unfortunately everyone is watching for two human men to be the Two Witnesses shooting fire from their mouths and calling down plagues on the earth, which will never happen as a fulfillment of any prophecies, because Yahuweh/Yehovah has actually prophesied in Revelation 11 that it will never happen and the Two Witnesses will never be human men or women. This is another myth that we can know with absolute certainty from the words of Yahuweh/Yehovah prophesied in Scripture that will never happen; there will never be two men or two women acting as the Two Witnesses.</u> There are all of the believers in Yeshua who act as Yahuweh/Yehovah's witnesses, often in pairs of two, but the Two Witnesses in Revelation 11 will not be men.

The three myths about the Anti-Christ, the Third Temple, and the Two Witnesses are among the oldest of all of the myths created about prophecy in Scripture, which is why they are the hardest for people to let go of. They are so ingrained as a part of prophecy teaching and thinking that it is hard for people to even think that thought that these three myths might not ever happen, because of them never being prophesied to happen anywhere in Scripture. <u>It is okay to no longer rely upon these three myths and no longer depend upon them happening as signs before Yeshua's return.</u> The myths about these three things are not Scripturally based and have no guarantee or certainty anywhere in the written words of Yahuweh/Yehovah to ever happen. It is better to rely upon the Word of Yahuweh/Yehovah and Yahuweh/Yehovah himself instead of putting all your faith into a certain scenario of how the prophecies might be fulfilled. These three myths are built on shaky, sandy ground that has no foundation in the words and prophecies of Yahuweh/Yehovah in Scripture.

The Final Thing Left to Do is Get Ready and Prepare for Yeshua's Coming with Washed and Clean Wedding Garments, Leaving the Old Container of this World of Mystery Babel to Enter into the New Container of His – One Stick (Restored Nation Israel Made Up of All of the Tribes) – One City and Bride (New Jerusalem) – One House of Prayer and One Tabernacle Tent Booth (Made Up of Peoples from All Nations Grafted into the Restored Nation Israel) – One New Man Body (Made Up of Jews and Gentiles Become One Restored Family Nation Israel Through Messiah):

<u>Watch in Order to Prepare</u>: The interesting thing about Yeshua's words in Matthew 24:37 – 25:13 and Mark 13:33-37 (and later repeated in the same theme in Revelation 3:2-3) is that Yeshua warns his followers to watch for his coming so that they can become prepared for his coming. He does not say to always be prepared for his coming at all times so that a person has no need to watch for his coming anymore. He says that a person needs to watch for his coming, so that they can then become prepared for his coming only after they know that he is coming. Yeshua says clearly that there is no way to prepare for his coming except by watching for his coming first, and only when we know for certain that he is coming are we then able to get prepared for his coming.

There is a special preparation for his coming that only the generation living at the time of his coming is able to do. This is a different preparation than always being prepared to die and meet Yeshua every day like the previous generations of the last 2,000 years. There is a preparation for Yeshua's coming that can only be made by those who are alive at the time of his coming, who have watched for his coming and know he is about to come. In Matthew 24 to 25 and Mark 13 Yeshua does not specifically say what that special preparation is that can only be made after we have seen he is coming through watching, because he uses parables as symbols of the ways to prepare. One preparation is to know ahead of time when Yeshua is coming so that he does not come as a thief in the night (Matthew 24:43-44), and another preparation is to be a trustworthy servant living in obedience to our master Yahuweh/Yehovah (Matthew 24:45-51). A third preparation is to have extra oil stored up in our containers in order to survive through the delay of Yeshua's coming (Matthew 25:1-13).

Revelation 3 is much more specific, with Yeshua warning to repent as a result of our watching and to make sure that our works done before him are complete before he comes. Also, we must wake up before he arrives and know when he is coming so that he does not come to us as a thief in the night or we will be in big trouble when he arrives, possibly missing out on eternal life. Yeshua says a similar thing in Mark 13 where we have to watch for his coming so that we can be awake and not asleep at the time of his coming. But all of these preparations in Matthew 24 to 25 and Mark 13 and Revelation 3 are really all summed up in the preparations for the Marriage of the Lamb, when we will call Yahuweh/Yehovah, "Ishi" or "My Husband" (Hosea 2:16-20).

There is no other generation that has to prepare to go to the Marriage Supper of the Lamb except for the final generation that is alive at that time. The other generations who came before and already died will already be prepared in the resurrection, but the preparing for the Marriage of the Lamb is a unique preparation that only those who are alive at the time of Yeshua's coming have to get ready for at that time when they know he is about to come. The only other generation in all of world history that has had to go through a similar time of preparation is when the children of Israel left Egypt to enter into the shadow picture of marriage to Yahuweh/Yehovah in the wilderness at Mount Sinai.

<u>Prepare for the Wedding Covenant of the Lamb by Leaving Mystery Babel (the World)</u>: One of the most important preparations that the generation alive at Yeshua's Return has to make is the preparation of leaving Mystery Babel in Revelation 18:5 and Jeremiah 51:6-9. Leaving Mystery Babel is only a symbol for leaving the entire system and world of mankind on the earth, called "the World" in James 4:1-4 and 1 John 2:1-17. No other generation in world history has had to actually leave the world system of Mystery Babel except for the generation of Israel that left Egypt and followed Moses into the wilderness. At the time of Yeshua's Return a believer has to literally and physically be ready to leave or already in process of leaving Mystery Babel with all of its manmade systems that are in rebellion against Yahuweh/Yehovah in the same way as leaving Egypt.

A person has to have no love of the world and absolutely no friendship with the world when Yeshua returns, or else they will find themselves an enemy of Yeshua at his coming instead of a friend. In 2 Peter 3:5-10 the whole world will be burned up and destroyed at Yeshua's coming and there cannot be any holding onto even a tiny piece of the world at that point if we do not want to be like the wife of Lot who turned to look back and was destroyed with Sodom (Mystery Babel) in judgment (Luke 17:32). We have to be able to leave everything behind at his coming, taking nothing with us, in Luke 17:31, with nothing of the world holding us back from following Yeshua into the New Heavens and New Earth. In Matthew 22:1-14 there are many Christians invited to the wedding feast, but they are so in love with the world and Mystery Babel that they refuse to leave the world behind in order to enter into the Marriage Covenant with the Lamb. They were too busy working their fields and running their businesses, and in Luke 14:20 too busy getting married, to go to the wedding supper and go into eternal life into the Marriage Covenant with Yahuweh/Yehovah. It is vitally important at the time of Yeshua's Return that every believer be ready for his coming by being enemies with Mystery Babel and the world, leaving them behind and getting them out of their lives in order to have nothing holding them back from going to the wedding when the invitation comes.

Prepare for the Wedding Covenant of the Lamb with Clean Wedding Clothes: Preparing for the wedding and marriage of the Lamb is a unique time in world history. Only one other generation had to prepare for the wedding of the Lamb, the wedding to Yahuweh/Yehovah, in the shadow picture of the wedding made by the children of Israel at Mount Sinai accepting Yahuweh/Yehovah's covenant. In Exodus 19:9-18 all of Israel as a nation had to prepare for the wedding by getting their white garments completely spotless and perfectly clean without blemish to enter into covenant with Yahuweh/Yehovah at Mount Sinai. They were given 3 days to get their clean and white wedding clothes ready for Yahuweh/Yehovah's coming in the clouds at the sound of the shophar or trumpet on Mount Sinai.

This was the rehearsal and shadow picture of the marriage to Yahuweh/Yehovah at his coming again in the clouds, with Yeshua giving the same requirement again for his coming. In Matthew 22:1-14 once again Yeshua says that the wedding garments are required in order to enter into the marriage covenant and eternal life with him. The explanation of these clean and white wedding garments is in Revelation 7:9-17, where we find out that the clean and white garments represent being washed clean from sin in the blood of the Lamb. And again in Revelation 19:7-9 John explains that the clean and white garments are the righteousness of the set-apart ones. It is also in Revelation 19 that we discover that this is the way that the bride of the Lamb prepares herself, with these clean and white wedding garments, being washed clean of sin and unrighteousness. And it is the Great Tribulation in Revelation 7 that is the process that helps the bride get her garments washed and ready for the wedding.

Preparing for the wedding of the Lamb is a unique preparation that only the generation alive at the time of Yeshua's Return has to prepare for. And there is no way to prepare for the wedding unless we watch for Yeshua's coming and know that he is coming, because the preparation for the wedding with the clean and white wedding clothes can only be made during the 3.5 years of Great Tribulation. Without the Great Tribulation it is impossible for the bride to get herself prepared and ready for the wedding. This is why Yeshua says to watch and know when he is coming, because the preparation for his coming, the preparation for the wedding with the wedding clothes, can only be made during the 3.5 years of Great Tribulation right before he comes.

In Matthew 22:34-40 Yeshua explains what the two greatest commands are in the Torah covenant of Yahuweh/Yehovah, which are the foundation of all of the other commands. The greatest command is in Deuteronomy 6:5 to love Yahuweh/Yehovah, and the second greatest command is in Leviticus 19:18 to love our neighbor. These are the two greatest commands, because they deal with the two most important relationships in order to be able to live life. The greatest and most important relationship is the one with Yahuweh/Yehovah, to have a right relationship with him in his covenant, obeying him and his commands out of love for him. But the other part of that covenant with Yahuweh/Yehovah is that we also have to be able to love one another, to love the other people he has created too, and be able to get along with them in love. This means that in the preparation for the wedding covenant, there are two different parts to the preparation of getting the clean and white wedding clothes on. There is the one side that is preparing and getting washed clean for your own individual relationship with Yahuweh/Yehovah, but there is also the other side of preparing and getting clean in order to come together as one family nation corporately with all of Yahuweh/Yehovah's people in covenant with him, to be one bride together with love for all of our neighbors as we together become one with Yahuweh/Yehovah in his covenant nation.

Prepare for the Wedding Covenant of the Lamb with Clean Wedding Clothes Individually: The greatest command in the Torah in Deuteronomy 6:4-8 has to do with the individual relationship that every person has with Yahuweh/Yehovah. This is the primary most important preparation for the wedding that each believer makes, to make sure that they are individually cleaned up in the blood of Yeshua, with the spotlessly clean and white wedding clothes. This is what Yeshua talks about in Matthew 22:11-14 when there is one of the guests who does not have any wedding clothes on at the wedding feast. That man is thrown out into the darkness and does not enter into eternal life, because he did not prepare his individual relationship with Yahuweh/Yehovah, going through the process of being made clean and pure from his sin. He did not set himself apart and become individually separated from the world and sin and rebellion of the flesh in order to be in a set-apart relationship with Yahuweh/Yehovah, knowing him personally.

In Genesis 3:8-24 every individual on earth became cut off from the tree of life, from Yahuweh/Yehovah. The goal then became for every person through history since Adam and Chavvah (Eve) to make a choice between life and death, between Yahuweh/Yehovah and the world of rebellion against him. That is why Yahuweh/Yehovah set up the process over thousands of years of putting in place a covenant, as in John 3:16-21, to bring people back into set-apart relationship with him and be able to be restored into eternal life with him. All those who have individually prepared themselves with the clean wedding clothes of righteousness, true righteousness that comes from Yahuweh/Yehovah and not from manmade religion and legalistic oral laws of church tradition, in Revelation 22:1-3 and 12-17 get to have access to the tree of life again as it was in the Garden of Eden.

Prepare for the Wedding Covenant of the Lamb with Clean Wedding Clothes Corporately: The individual preparation of getting dressed in the clean and white wedding clothes before Yeshua returns is talked about often in Christianity and most believers understand and know about it already. The part that is never talked about, because it is much harder to do and no believers really want to do it is the part of getting ready for the wedding in our clean wedding clothes corporately as a body. This is the part of the second greatest command in the Torah in Leviticus 19:18 to love our neighbor as ourselves, dealing with the relationship of all those who are followers of Yeshua in his nation and body of believers. This is in Revelation 19:7-9, where John writes that the "bride" has prepared herself for the Marriage of the Lamb. The bride as the entire body of believers have all prepared themselves together corporately for the wedding feast by getting cleaned up of all division and hatred toward one another in the body. This means everyone restoring their relationships with everyone else in the body, everyone loving one another and forgiving one another, in order that every individual may be forgiven by Yahuweh/Yehovah and enter into eternal life. In Matthew 18:21-35 Yeshua says that a person who does not forgive those who have debts and trespasses against them will not be forgiven by Yahuweh/Yehovah of their own sins and debts against him, which is a very serious matter that can prevent a person from entering into eternal life without forgiveness of their own sins, because they refused to forgive the sins that others committed against them.

In the beginning in the Garden of Eden Yahuweh/Yehovah did not start off creating a religion, but instead started his creation of man and woman in his image by creating a family. He created the man and the woman and told them to be fruitful and multiply, beginning mankind as a family that would grow continuously and exponentially into a larger, potentially never ending, family. He created mankind to all be one, single family together, but when Adam and Chavvah (Eve) broke covenant with Yahuweh/Yehovah and chose death instead of life for the family, he had to then act to make a way for people in the family of mankind to have a choice to return to life again if they wanted it.

Then in Genesis 12:1-3 Yahuweh/Yehovah started again with Abraham, and once again Yahuweh/Yehovah did not create a religion. Instead he once again created a family through Abraham's son Isaac, starting a nation instead of a religion. The only difference this time from Adam and Chavvah, was that Abraham and Sarah would be the beginning of a set-apart nation and set-apart family in covenant with him, separated and divided from the rest of the world, but unified within. Yahuweh/Yehovah did not command Abraham to go and make converts to enter into the covenant with Abraham, bringing in people from all over to become a religious organization together. Instead he had Abraham start a family with Sarah through their son Isaac, to create a nation or family of people as his set-apart container or house. This same family house Yahuweh/Yehovah continued with Isaac's son Jacob in Genesis 32:24-32 and Genesis 35:9-15. The word "house" itself in Hebrew also has the meaning of "family" as it does in many languages in genealogical terms. The word "house" in Hebrew is the Hebrew word for family, as with the phrases "House of Israel" or "House of David" or "House of Jacob." The house that Yahuweh/Yehovah has always been interested in building has always been a family instead of a physical Temple made of physical stones.

Throughout Genesis it can be seen clearly that the concept of a nation is simply a family. In the genealogies after the Flood and the Tower of Babel, the descendants of Noah broke apart into divided families or divided nations, each nation their own genealogical family that was still related to the other nations or families on the earth. A nation is nothing more than a family, and Yahuweh/Yehovah created his nation Israel through the covenant with Abraham and Sarah, and their son Isaac, to be a set-apart family that is separated from all other nations. It is still related to all the other nations biologically, but it is separated out from them into covenant with Yahuweh/Yehovah.

Yahuweh/Yehovah continued to build and grow his set-apart nation or family through Moses and the time in the wilderness, preparing them to enter into the land of Israel and become a nation with their own land, separated and divided from the nations around them. Once again with Moses Yahuweh/Yehovah did not start or create a religion, instead in Exodus 19:1-6 and Leviticus 20:26 he continues to create a set-apart nation that would be in covenant with him, separated from the rest of the world to belong to him as his possession. It is once again a set-apart family that he is creating, with the seal on the forehead of the high priest in Exodus 28:36-38 to be all about set-apartness unto Yahuweh/Yehovah, but this time he begins to bring in people from other nations into his set-apart covenant family. This can be seen very clearly in Leviticus 19:33-34 where Yahuweh/Yehovah commands that the strangers, the gentiles of other nations, who live among the children of Israel "to love as you love yourself" as in the second greatest command in Leviticus 19:18. But there is also the addition to this that they are to become as native born Israelis, to become part of the set-apart family as citizens of Yahuweh/Yehovah's set-apart nation Israel in covenant with him. And when they become as native born Israelis, they no longer are foreigners and the command to not marry foreign wives no longer applies to gentile strangers who are considered to be native born citizens.

Always from the beginning Yahuweh/Yehovah was creating a set-apart nation in covenant with him that others from the nations all around the earth could enter into as native born citizens, and this goal never changed throughout prophecy in Isaiah 56:1-12, Ezekiel 47:22, Zechariah 2:10-13, and Zechariah 14:16-21. In Isaiah 56 Yahuweh/Yehovah prophesies about his House of Prayer being a house or family made up of people in covenant with him, obeying his Sabbaths and his Torah, from all nations of the earth as citizens of his set-apart nation family Israel. In Ezekiel 47 Yahuweh/Yehovah prophesies about gentiles from the nations becoming native born citizens of his set-apart and covenant nation Israel. In Zechariah 2 he actually prophesies about gentiles from the nation being joined to him personally into his set-apart and covenant nation Israel.

Yahuweh/Yehovah's original goal of making a set-apart nation family as the container or house or vehicle to be able to restore relationship and dwell together with mankind again has never changed in thousands of years. When Yeshua came as the Messiah and Passover Lamb sacrifice for sin it was only a continuation of the same nation as always that Yahuweh/Yehovah has always been building. He never did away with anything from the past, he continued to grow and complete the same nation and covenant that had always been in place before. And once again he did not create a religion when Yeshua came, instead he continued to create his people into a set-apart nation family in covenant with him as Paul and Peter write about in Romans 11:1-36 and 1 Peter 2:9-10. The gentiles are only grafted into the existing set-apart nation Israel, with some of the natural branches of natural born Israelis or Jews being broken off because of their decision to reject and not be part of Yahuweh/Yehovah's covenant nation Israel.

Nothing changed with Yahuweh/Yehovah's set-apart nation when Yeshua came and the gentiles who accept Yahuweh/Yehovah's covenant through Yeshua can still decide to leave and be broken off again from the covenant nation. And there are not multiple nations either. The gentiles do not get to be in a separate nation from the Jews and natural born Israelis. All believers in Yeshua and everyone who accepts Yahuweh/Yehovah's covenant all have to be in one, single, set-apart, family nation together, in Yahuweh/Yehovah's eternal nation Israel together, as one people. There is no division into separate and different nations. Peter quoting from Exodus and Isaiah clearly says that all believers in Yeshua have to be part of the same set-apart nation Israel that Yahuweh/Yehovah has been building since Abraham and Moses. It is the same set-apart nation Israel as always, and the gentiles do not get to be part of their own separate nation that is divided from the Jews and the natural born Israelis of the twelve tribes of Israel, nor do they get to take over the nation Israel and turn it into their own manmade Church/Synagogue religion using imaginary replacement theology that does not exist in Scripture in an attempt to prevent Jews who are believers in Yeshua and natural born Israelis of the twelve tribes who are believers in Yeshua from being in the nation.

This preparation in Revelation 19 by the entire bride, the entire body-nation-family, to get ready with clean and white wedding garments for the marriage to the Lamb, is a preparation that cannot be made at any other time in history except for right before Yeshua returns. This is a preparation that can only be made through watching for him to come and then through the watching recognizing and knowing when he is coming, in order to get ready during the 3.5 years of Great Tribulation. According to Revelation 7 the only time in which it is possible to get ready as a body and bride together with the white and clean wedding garments is during the 3.5 years of Great Tribulation. The Great Tribulation is itself the time that allows the set-apart ones to be given the white and clean wedding robes that are washed in the blood of the Lamb, and at no other time in history before those 3.5 years of Great Tribulation is it possible for the body of believers together to be able to prepare as a single bride in oneness to get cleaned up as a body of people ready for the wedding. All believers have to come together as one family nation with only one shepherd and king, Yahuweh/Yehovah, ruling over it, with everyone united as one together in unity, one in Yahuweh/Yehovah and Yeshua in the same way that Yahuweh/Yehovah and Yeshua are one in John 17. And the only way that that unity is possible according to John 17:14 is when everyone in the body of believers has become set-apart and separated from the world, not of the world and the ways of the world, made clean from sin together as a body and nation.

All of the believers in Yeshua have to leave the old corrupted container or wineskin of the Church and Synagogue, that also includes everything and every part of this world, to enter into the new container or new wineskin of the set-apart nation of Yahuweh/Yehovah, which is the same nation that he has always been building from the beginning and has never stopped building since the beginning. Yahuweh/Yehovah has never changed (Malachi 3:6) and his plan and covenant are the same now as always from the beginning.

Old Container or Wineskin to Leave	New Container or Wineskin to Enter Into
1. ***The Days of Abraham and Lot*** – Leaving Every City on Earth (Sodom and Mystery Babel): Genesis 12:1-4; Genesis 18:1 – 19:38; Deuteronomy 12:13-18; Isaiah 48:20-22; Jeremiah 50:1 – 51:64; Matthew 22:1-7; Luke 17:28-32; Revelation 16:19; Revelation 18:1-24	1. ***The New Jerusalem*** (One City and Bride): Isaiah 60:1-22; Isaiah 62:1-12; Ezekiel 48:30-35; Revelation 19:6-9; Revelation 21:2 – 22:5
2. ***The Days of Moses*** – Leaving Every Nation on Earth (Egypt and the Beast Out of the Sea): Exodus 6:28 – 24:18; Jeremiah 25:15-33; Joel 3:1-21; Zechariah 12:9 – 13:6; Zechariah 14:1-21; Revelation 19:17 – 20:3	2. ***The Restored Israel*** (One Nation and Stick): Isaiah 60:1-22; Jeremiah 30:1 – 31:34; Ezekiel 37:15-28; Ezekiel 47:1 – 48:29; Zechariah 2:10-13; Zechariah 14:16-19; 1 Peter 2:9-10; Revelation 7:3-8; Revelation 21:10-21
3. ***The Days of Yeshua*** – Leaving Every Temple on Earth (The Second Temple and the Beast Out of the Earth, Including All Religious Organizations and Denominations and Churches and Synagogues): Jeremiah 25:34-38; Ezekiel 34:1-31; Zechariah 10:1-3; Matthew 9:16-17; Matthew 13:24-50; Matthew 24:1-3; Matthew 25:1-13; Matthew 25:31-46	3. ***The House of Prayer and Booth of David*** (One Body and New Man): Isaiah 16:5; Isaiah 56:1-12; Ezekiel 40:1 – 46:24; Hosea 6:1-3; Amos 9:11-15; John 2:13-22; Romans 11:1-36; 1 Corinthians 12:1-31; Ephesians 1:3 – 3:7; Colossians 1:9 – 3:17; Hebrews 9:11-12; Revelation 7:9-17; Revelation 21:3; Revelation 21:22-24
4. ***The Days of Noah*** – Leaving Everything of This World on Earth (All of the World of Mankind and the Earth Itself): Genesis 6:1 – 8:22; Isaiah 24:1-23; Matthew 10:34-37; Matthew 12:30-33; Matthew 22:1-14; Matthew 24:37-39; Luke 14:16-33; Luke 17:26-27; John 15:9-20; James 4:1-4; 1 John 2:1-17; 2 Peter 3:5-10	4. ***The New Heavens and New Earth*** (One as Yahuweh/Yehovah and Yeshua are One): Isaiah 65:17-25; Zechariah 2:10-13; John 17:11-26; Revelation 21:1 – 22:5

As in the days of Abraham and Lot all followers of Yeshua have to leave the city of Sodom or Mystery Babel, which includes leaving every city on earth this time, to go into the new container of the New Jerusalem. As in the days of Moses all followers of Yeshua have to leave the nation of Egypt or the Beast Out of the Sea, which includes leaving every nation on earth this time, to go into the new container of the Restored Israel. As in the days of Yeshua all followers of Yeshua have to leave the physical Temple or Church and Synagogue, which includes every temple, every physical religious building like a Church or Synagogue, to go into the new container of the House of Prayer and Booth of David made up of the people of

Yahuweh/Yehovah only without any physical building in existence (Revelation 21:22-24). As in the days of Noah all followers of Yeshua have to leave the entire earth as it is all destroyed in fire, including absolutely everything of this world of man in rebellion against Yahuweh/Yehovah, to go into the New Heavens and New Earth.

In order to prepare corporately as one people, every believer has to be in process of leaving every city on earth to become one city and bride, the New Jerusalem. Ever believer has to be in process of leaving every nation on earth to become one nation and stick, the Restored Israel. Every believer has to be in process of leaving every temple on earth, every church and every synagogue and every religious organization or institution, to become one body and new man, the House of Prayer and Booth of David. And every believer has to be in process of leaving everything of this world on the earth, including the entire earth itself, to become one as Yahuweh/Yehovah and Yeshua are One, the New Heavens and New Earth with the Heavens and the Earth joined together as one (Yahuweh/Yehovah in the heavens and mankind on the earth joined together and dwelling as one). This is the final major preparation of the bride that still has to happen as far as the believers are willing to obey in order to be ready for the wedding when Yeshua returns.

<u>The Real Latter Rain Revival is the Leaving of and Destruction of the World and of the Old Container of the Church and Synagogue to Enter into the New Container of the City – Bride – Nation – Family – Body – House – New Man of Yahuweh/Yehovah Who are One as He is One</u>: No one likes to talk about what the real latter rain revival is at the Time of the End right before Yeshua returns. The real, final revival that is prophesied to take place in Zechariah 10:1-3 and Ezekiel 34:1-31 and Jeremiah 25:34-38 is Yahuweh/Yehovah's wrath and judgment on the shepherds as he completely removes them all out of their positions of authority and power in preparation for his coming. It is the destruction and removal of the shepherds (all religious and spiritual leaders in positions of authority over the sheep) that is one of the primary signs that the final latter rain revival is taking place. The only way that there can be only one shepherd over Yahuweh/Yehovah's flock as prophesied in Ezekiel 34:23 is if all other shepherds have been removed, not only all rabbis in Judaism but also all pastors and rabbis and bishops and priests and spiritual fathers and spiritual mothers in Christianity too, no matter how anyone wants to interpret the meaning of Israel in the Ezekiel 34 prophecy. The number 1 means the number 1, not more than 1, and the only way there can be only one shepherd, Yahuweh/Yehovah's servant David, at the end is if all other shepherds have been removed without exception.

The reason for this removal of the shepherds is because they bring division to his body and nation of believers, preventing everyone from following God who is one, Yahuweh/Yehovah, as their only leader, king, and shepherd. There can only be one leader if there is ever to be unity in the body, and that one leader can only ever be the creator of the heavens and the earth, the God of Abraham, Isaac, and Jacob. The removal of the shepherds is only one part of the leaving of the old container of the Church and Synagogue to enter into the new container of Yahuweh/Yehovah's restored nation and family Israel, made up of people from all of the nations of the earth joined together with descendants from all twelve tribes of Israel. This is the true and final latter rain revival on the earth, as Yahuweh/Yehovah restores his people and brings them together as one people and one nation and one family in fulfillment of John 17.

All of the old container things of this world have to be left behind, as already shown in the many prophecies in the previous chart, including the old container of the Church and Synagogue of the physical Temple buildings on the earth in order to enter into the new container where the people themselves are the House of Yahuweh/Yehovah's dwelling place, his House of Prayer that is for all nations made up of his people instead of a physical building. This is shown in the Matthew 13 parable of wheat and tares, when the Master, Yeshua, lets them stay together, lets the corrupt container of the Church and Synagogue continue, until the end when he harvests all of the wheat and tares out of the Church and Synagogue. Then he promises to remove all of the wheat out of and then destroy in fire the old, corrupt container of the Church and Synagogue system of manmade religion on this earth, harvesting all of the wheat into the new container of his nation family of people unified together as one.

All old container institutions and organizations have to pass away and all of those who decide to follow Yeshua will have to leave the old container and follow him into the new, leaving Sodom and Egypt and the Temple and the entire World to become the new container of the people themselves as the container dwelling place of Yahuweh/Yehovah. In both Matthew 24 and Luke 17 Yeshua is very clear about being able to leave everything behind throughout the Great Tribulation and at the time of his coming at the end of the Great Tribulation, in order to not be like Lot's wife. This is repeated again in the Matthew 22 parable, this warning that we have to be able to stop and leave behind everything of this entire world, everything of the old container including all ministry work and Church/Synagogue work, in order to go to the wedding and into the new container.

It is very important to Yahuweh/Yehovah that everyone who wants to be with him in eternal life is also able to get along with the others who want to be with him too, without hurting each other all of the time. This is why through history Yahuweh/Yehovah has done this continuous process of bringing his people into a more and more complete covenant with him, cleaning house by destroying the old, corrupted containers of manmade religion that come in and try to take over his covenant nation, restoring the container of his nation into a clean and new container. The preparation for the Marriage of the Lamb at this fourth coming, when he is completing his covenant in its entirety, will be the last time that his bride, his body and nation and family of believers, have to get cleaned up with their clean wedding clothes, because this time everyone will stay clean and never get dirty in sin again. It will finally all be finished and complete.

The new and restored container of Yahuweh/Yehovah's family nation is where the real revival is at, because it is the place of real and true repentance as the bride gets herself cleaned up of sin in the blood of the Lamb and ready for his coming and the marriage covenant. There has to be true repentance among the believers and followers of Yeshua themselves this time as we all have to repent together and get clean corporately as a body and nation and family. Since Yahuweh/Yehovah's COVID plague in 2020 he has been exposing among his body across the world that in most countries the believers are saying with their mouths that they repent, but in their hearts and deeds and actions they are refusing to repent and get cleaned up of their sin. They continue in their sin with only lip service repentance, especially among the shepherds. This is why there is no revival except in countries where Christians are persecuted such as across the Middle East and southern Asia.

Revival in itself is very simply repentance, with nothing more added on beyond that and has nothing to do with miracles. Miracles are things that believers should be experiencing as part of their ordinary, everyday lives as they interact with Yahuweh/Yehovah personally with him as individuals. Revival is only about repentance and Yahuweh/Yehovah has been exposing that there is no repentance among the Christians in the world today, as they continue on in their sin, refusing to change. Yahuweh/Yehovah has left the old container of the Church and Synagogue, as there is no more oil in that old container that he is now destroying and bringing down stone by stone, brick by brick, piece by piece. There are only store bought oil revivals (discussed earlier in the book from Matthew 25) that are now happening in the old container, where there is no lasting or true repentance taking place of a changed life. But in the new container of Yahuweh/Yehovah's people all becoming one bride and house and city and nation and family and body and new man there is true repentance and true revival among those who see that Yahuweh/Yehovah is coming and are preparing for the wedding by focusing on getting clean with white wedding clothes of righteousness instead of spending time on running ministries and sitting in churches listening to shepherds give another teaching that once again leads to no repentance whatsoever, week after week.

Yahuweh/Yehovah's entire focus from now on is just permanently ending this world and getting his people ready as one nation family to go with him to the New Heavens and New Earth. Anyone continuing in the old container, trying to continue doing what they have always been doing, what Christianity has always continued to do for 2,000 years, while ignoring or rejecting what Yahuweh/Yehovah is doing, will miss out on his revival and will miss out on getting to be close with him at this Time of the End of the world.

Each New Container of Each New Covenant Does Not Do Away with the Old Covenant, but Instead Brings It into Greater Completion: Since the beginning of Yahuweh/Yehovah's covenant through Abraham, Isaac, and Jacob, he has been building his covenant and nation container of Israel step by step. As with any house, it takes time to build a house container to make a dwelling place for Yahuweh/Yehovah to dwell in with his people. Before construction on the house can even begin, first the tools to make the house have to be built and constructed. Then every individual piece of materials has to be formed and made to fit with all of the other pieces, using the tools to craft each individual piece of the house so that it can then be built together. The foundation of the house also has to be made firm and strong if the house is going to survive and continue to stand.

In the same way Yahuweh/Yehovah has had to do a process of steps over the last 4,000 years since the time of Abraham in order to build his people into a house where everyone can live together as a family without hurting each other and killing each other and without any division in the house of people that would cause it to fall and collapse. That is why he has had to build his covenant and house of people piece by piece over a long process, first building the tools themselves to form the people of the house so that they can fit together with each other and hold strong together without falling apart. And he has also had to build a strong foundation to the house of people so that the people can live together for eternity without falling down and collapsing into division and war against each other.

Yahuweh/Yehovah began the process with Abraham, with the initial part of the covenant in Genesis 15:1-21 and Genesis 17:1-27. The next part of the covenant, built onto the previous part with Abraham, came with Moses and the Torah. Moses says in Deuteronomy 5:1-5 that the covenant of the Torah that Yahuweh/Yehovah had given to Moses and the children of Israel at Chorev was a brand new covenant that had not been given to Abraham, Isaac, and Jacob or any of their other fathers before them. Even though this covenant of the Torah was a brand new covenant that Yahuweh/Yehovah made with his nation Israel, it did not do away with the old covenant with Abraham. It only made the covenant more complete. Then when Yeshua came he put in place a brand new covenant again in Matthew 26:26-28, in fulfillment of the prophecy in Jeremiah 31:31-34. And once again this brand new covenant that Yeshua made specifically with the nation of Israel according to Jeremiah 31 did not do away with the old portions of the covenant that came through Abraham and Moses, because this brand new covenant in Jeremiah 31 Yahuweh/Yehovah says is the same old Torah covenant he gave through Moses, except that this time his Torah is written on our hearts instead of on stone and sheep skin.

Yeshua reaffirms this concept in Matthew 5:17-20 that the brand new covenant that he came to put in place does not do away with the previous Torah covenant with Moses, it only makes that covenant more complete, building another piece of the house of Yahuweh/Yehovah's people and nation Israel. In the same way that the Torah covenant that came through Moses was a brand new covenant that Yahuweh/Yehovah had not made with any of the fathers of the children of Israel that had come before, the Lamb covenant through Yeshua was also a brand new covenant that Yahuweh/Yehovah had not made with any of the fathers of the children of Israel before them. And as each new part of the covenant is built onto the house, making Yahuweh/Yehovah's set-apart nation Israel more and more complete, each new part of the covenant does not tear down or do away with the old parts of the covenant that came before it, or else the house of Yahuweh/Yehovah's family nation of people would be torn down and destroyed.

The covenant through Abraham and through Moses and through Yeshua is only complete in all of its parts brought together as one, none of them doing away with any previous parts of the covenant. Now as Yeshua returns there is the marriage of the Lamb to his bride, his set-apart nation of people, to put in place the final piece of the covenant, making the entire covenant complete with the marriage to the Lamb, turning the bride into the wife of the Lamb in Revelation 21:9. And once again this final piece of the covenant does not do away with any of the previous parts of the covenant through Abraham and Moses and Yeshua, but instead will make it all finally finished and complete, a finished house with all of Yahuweh/Yehovah's people living together with him in unity without any more division, as everyone lives in righteousness without any more sin to cause harm to one another.

<u>Unity with Yahuweh/Yehovah Requires Division and Enmity Against the World, and Unity in His Set-Apart Nation and Body Also Requires Division and Enmity Against the World</u>: Since the beginning when Yahuweh/Yehovah created the heavens and the earth, everything on this earth has been about the choice

between life and death, the tree of life or the tree of the knowledge of good and evil. This choice in its simplest form can be seen throughout Scripture and the history of the world as a choice each person makes between wanting to be god themselves, in complete control and power to have their own will be done, or to surrender to Yahuweh/Yehovah to let him be God and let him be in control and power to submit to his will being done instead. The tree of life and the choice of life is to choose to let Yahuweh/Yehovah be himself, which is God in control of everything as the head and leader, to let him determine what is good and what is evil; and the tree of the knowledge of good and evil is the choice of death, the choice to try to be our own god in control as the head and leader of our own lives and the lives of others, determining for ourselves what we say is good or evil.

The tree of the knowledge of good and evil is nothing more than people trying to be gods with total power and control all to themselves, determining for themselves what they say is good and what they say is evil, making up their own rules on what they want to be a good thing or evil thing for themselves and for others. It is a total rejection of Yahuweh/Yehovah's ways of living, of what Yahuweh/Yehovah as God says is good and is evil. This fight that each person goes through in their own lives has continued throughout time, with each person deciding if they are going to stubbornly go with their own will all of the time according to what they say is good or is evil for themselves, or if they will surrender to the will of Yahuweh/Yehovah and what he says is good or is evil for them. And the end goal for Yahuweh/Yehovah, for the choice of eternal life with Yahuweh/Yehovah, is always total and complete surrender to him and his covenant and his ways in his Torah instruction in the end, even when what he says is good or is evil is different from how we as humans think it should be. The goal is humility and surrender, instead of the pride of thinking we know better than God himself as to what is good and what is evil in our attempts to be gods in rebellion against him.

Throughout history the majority always choose the tree of the knowledge of good and evil, wanting to be gods and determine for themselves what is good or evil. The majority always want their own imperfect will to be done their way and refuse to surrender and change to the perfect will of Yahuweh/Yehovah. The majority always want the world and the system of mankind in the world that consists of all of the individual wills of all of the people fighting against each other until the most powerful rise above the rest and force their will on everyone else, until another defeats them and takes their place.

At the time of Abraham the majority chose to not follow Yahuweh/Yehovah and wanted the world instead, as with Lot who chose to live in the evil city of Sodom in Genesis 13:5-13 instead of in the wilderness like Abraham. At the time of Moses the majority of the children of Israel chose to live in Egypt instead of in the wilderness and instead of fighting to take the land of Kena'an to become the nation of Israel in Numbers 13:1 – 14:45 and in Psalms 78:1-55. They continually grumbled against and fought against Yahuweh/Yehovah in every way at every possible moment, fighting against his will so that they could have their own wills be done. They wanted to determine what was good and what was evil for themselves, believing Egypt to be good and becoming a nation in the land of Israel to be evil, and continually trying to convince Yahuweh/Yehovah to do things their way because they believed they knew better than him what was best for them. In the end Yahuweh/Yehovah killed them all in the wilderness and let the next generation of their children be the ones to become the nation of Israel living in their own land instead.

Again when Yeshua came the majority of the people on earth rejected him, including the majority of Israel once again. Yeshua in many examples spoke of their rebellion and rejection of him, such as in Matthew 11:20-24 and Matthew 17:17. Always and every time in history the majority reject Yahuweh/Yehovah as God and reject his covenant of eternal life in order to try to be gods of their own lives, eating from the tree of the knowledge of good and evil. It was not only at the time of Yeshua that the majority on earth, including the majority of Yahuweh/Yehovah's nation Israel, have rejected his covenant and chosen not to follow him. It is at every time through history the majority always rejects him and his covenant and what he is doing on the earth. That is the fight that has been ongoing for thousands of years and the goal is absolute surrender and humility to accept the person of who Yahuweh/Yehovah is as God and to accept his covenant exactly according to his way without any changes. The only way to do this is to turn in repentance away from our own rebellious ways that Yahuweh/Yehovah says are evil or sin and to turn away from the world of mankind that is in rebellion against Yahuweh/Yehovah to be set apart from it.

This is why there are numerous verses in Scripture that deal with choosing to serve Yahuweh/Yehovah as our Master instead of the world and becoming separated and divided from the world in order to be joined together with Yahuweh/Yehovah. In James 4:1-4 it is very clear, to be a friend of the world is to be an enemy of Yahuweh/Yehovah and to be in unity with the world is to be divided and separated from Yahuweh/Yehovah (James 4:1-4). There can be no unity with Yahuweh/Yehovah if there is unity with the world, and there can be no unity with the world if there is unity with Yahuweh/Yehovah. Yahuweh/Yehovah's goal from the beginning has always been to create a nation that is set-apart and separated from the world that has unity with him and among themselves but complete separation from the world. Anyone in his nation who tries to have unity with the world separates themselves and becomes divided against the body and nation of Yahuweh/Yehovah's people. Yahuweh/Yehovah's goal is unity in him with his nation that is set-apart from and divided against the world, having no fellowship or unity with the world, and only fellowship and unity with him among his nation family that is separated and divided from the world.

This can be seen very clearly in Matthew 10:34-37 where Yeshua says that he came, not to bring peace but division, to create division between people to the point of even dividing up families against each other as enemies. This is because when there is fellowship and unity with Yeshua, there can only be division against those who choose the world and choose to live in rebellion against Yeshua. This is further explained by Yeshua in Matthew 12:30-33 where he explains that anyone who is not for him as friend is against him as an enemy. There is no neutrality when it comes to Yeshua and there is no such thing as a civilian or bystander. Everyone is either a friend of Yahuweh/Yehovah or an enemy of Yahuweh/Yehovah and there is no middle ground in between, which means that anyone who becomes a friend of the world has automatically made themselves an enemy against Yahuweh/Yehovah, bringing division as an enemy against his body as well.

This concept is repeated by Yeshua again in John 17:11-26 where Yeshua talks about his will for all of his body of people to become one in unity, but the only way this is possible is if his people are not of the world and are hated by the world. Also in John 15:9-20 the only way to love one another and have the love of Yeshua is to be hated by the world and not of it. We are to be set apart from the world as enemies who are divided against each other. We are still to love our enemies, to love the people in the world without loving the world itself, doing no evil against them even though they hate us, but there can be no unity or fellowship with anyone in the world who is an enemy of Yahuweh/Yehovah in rebellion against him. Anyone who loves the world does not have the love of Yahuweh/Yehovah in them, as in 1 John 2:1-17, and anyone who has the love of Yahuweh/Yehovah in them has no love for the world and its rebellion against Yahuweh/Yehovah.

The key to having the unity in the body of believers in John 17 is division from the world and total surrender to the will of Yahuweh/Yehovah and his ways in his covenant. When a person is set-apart to Yahuweh/Yehovah, divided from the world and in complete surrender and submission to him, then unity is automatic between his people. There is only division when everyone is trying to be gods themselves, controlling each other and trying to determine what is good or evil for themselves, creating their own manmade religions and denominations. Yahuweh/Yehovah has allowed this mixture of the world in the midst of his people for this time of waiting for his return, as in the parable of Matthew 13:24-50, but at the end at his return he separates and divides everyone in his body, dividing his followers away from the world and those who love the world, to make them set-apart and clean in preparation for his coming in Matthew 22:1-14 and Luke 14:16-33.

Every believer in Yeshua at the Time of the End has to separate from the world and have no love of the world in order to enter into eternal life. This is true throughout all of time, but at the end when Yeshua returns it is very urgent right before he comes because people do not have their whole lives to make their decision in to separate from the world and surrender to him completely as they go through the aging and dying process. It is suddenly in a moment, all at once, everyone has to be able to leave the things of the world and their loves of the world, as in the Matthew 22 and Luke 14 parable, in order to go with Yeshua when he comes and not miss out on eternal life if they do not have their wedding clothes on and ready as in Revelation 7:9-15 and Revelation 19:7-9 and the shadow picture of Exodus 19:3-24.

We can see everything happening again the same way as it has always happened before with the large majority rejecting what Yahuweh/Yehovah is doing, wanting to be gods to have their own will to be done instead their way. There is no surprise in this because it is the way things always are on this earth with most wanting to eat from the tree of the knowledge of good and evil to be in control of Yahuweh/Yehovah's body and nation and house of people and to be in control of the earth in general. We are in a time of delay, when Yeshua has delayed his coming like Samuel delaying his coming to do the sacrifice in 1 Samuel 15. In the same way as at that time, because of Yahuweh/Yehovah's delay the people are scattering and leaving the churches and Christianity and the world is falling apart into a mess. And like Saul who was losing his power and control over the people and was filled with fear that he would not be able to defeat the enemy that was coming against him in battle, Christians are wanting to rise up and take back control of the earth and the house of Yahuweh/Yehovah's people.

Christians want to have power and control again to defeat the enemy that is coming against them strongly and they are afraid of being defeated by the enemy spiritually, but Yeshua is not coming and intervening like he is supposed to be doing. He has delayed to come and take back the earth spiritually, so Christians all across the world instead of waiting patiently for Yeshua to return are doing the sacrifice themselves in various ways by trying to restore the body (the Church and Synagogue) spiritually to make it clean and pure again instead of waiting for Yeshua to come as the already finished Lamb sacrifice that makes it all clean and pure again. And they are trying to get the Orthodox Jews in Israel to do physical animal sacrifices started again before Yeshua (before Samuel) has come, instead of waiting for Yeshua to return and be the already finished Lamb sacrifice that takes away everyone's sins. Everyone can tell that Yeshua is supposed to be coming now and doing something, that the prophecies are needing to be fulfilled or something needs to happen with an intervention before the world is completely lost, but Yeshua is delaying and not coming, and he is not intervening to save the Christians and save Christianity as a whole. Instead it continues to fall apart and be destroyed more and more, without any revivals to save it like everyone thought would happen right now.

This is because Yahuweh/Yehovah's goal is different from the goals of men and women, from the goals of Christianity as it is today. Yahuweh/Yehovah's goal is to get all of his people completely surrendered to him and his will, and then to get them completely cleaned up and separated and divided from the world in order to join together all of his people into perfect unity. This means that he has to bring down and destroy anything that is causing division within his body of people, and he is testing his people to see who will wait for him in surrender to let him do things his way, or who will try to be gods themselves going forward in their own flesh to try to save the day themselves in their own way and will. Everyone talks about wanting unity among the body of believers in Yeshua, but when we examine through prophecies in Scripture what it takes to actually achieve that unity it can be seen why the majority are always wanting to rebel against Yahuweh/Yehovah like the children of Israel in the wilderness, because it means giving up having things done the way we think is best to let Yahuweh/Yehovah have his complete and perfect way as God.

We have to remember that Yahuweh/Yehovah's goal has never been to have a unified bride and body of followers only, but specifically to have a unified bride of followers who are unified in cleanness and purity from sin and from the world. The goal has always been for a nation bride of people who are set-apart and divided from the world, made clean in the blood of the Lamb Yeshua to be able to walk in and live in his ways of perfect righteousness as a nation of priests to the other nations. That is why the old corrupt and sin filled container of the Church and Synagogue system cannot continue on into the new container of the purified and unified bride that is prepared and ready for Yeshua's Return.

The things that are preventing unity and causing division among the body of believers, which are preventing the bride from preparing for Yeshua's coming:

1. <u>Ministry Organizations and People in Ministry and Spiritual Leadership Positions</u> (Ministers, Pastors, Spiritual Leaders, Shepherds) – Anyone in a position of spiritual authority or leadership as a shepherd trying to lead Yahuweh/Yehovah's sheep cause division among the sheep by making the sheep follow different shepherds in different directions. This is why Yahuweh/Yehovah has prophesied and promised in Ezekiel 34:1-31 that he will remove all shepherds, remove everyone from ministry and positions of spiritual authority, so that his sheep can become one in following only him as their one shepherd. No one gets to be in ministry or in a position of ministry anymore at Yahuweh/Yehovah's coming. This does not mean that everyone has to stop serving others and doing good to one another when people are in need as in Matthew 25:31-46. No one

needs a ministry to be able to do the words of Yeshua in Matthew 25 of feeding the hungry, giving water to the thirsty, clothing the naked, and visiting those sick and in prison. Individuals can do these things on their own without any ministry, or even groups of individuals getting together can do this without any ministry involved.

It was alright for people to have ministries and run ministries in the past during the time when Yahuweh/Yehovah was allowing the wheat and weeds (tares) to live together in the Church and Synagogue system. That time has now changed during the last few decades as Yahuweh/Yehovah has been calling everyone to leave ministry and live a life of obedience to him with everyone as sheep following only him as their shepherd, removing all shepherds and all ministries from position. And the start of COVID in 2020 was the cut-off time when it was time for everyone to shut down their ministries and leave ministry entirely, interacting together with the body as individuals who are all sheep together with no one in positions of authority over anyone else and no ministry organizations to run with money. It was 2020 that became the cut-off point when it turned into disobedience to continue running ministries and trying to stay in positions of ministry. There were a few through the years who listened to Yahuweh/Yehovah and have been slowly transitioning to shut down their ministries and leave positions of ministry, who have avoided the pain of having Yahuweh/Yehovah bring down their ministries and remove them from ministry positions, but those who have stayed have had to go through very painful experiences with broken relationships as Yahuweh/Yehovah has in his mercy forced them out of ministry to save them from the judgment that comes on the shepherds later at his coming.

2. <u>The Church and Synagogue</u> (Physical Buildings, Institutions, Religious Systems, Denominations) – In Matthew 13:24-50 Yeshua has prophesied and promised that at the Time of the End at his coming he will be removing all of the wheat and weeds (tares) from the world, from the Church and Synagogue system that the followers of Yeshua have been living in for the last 2,000 years. And in Revelation 21:22 he has promised that there will be no more physical temples as his goal to make only himself and his people dwelling together in unity into the only Temple in existence. The churches and synagogues, both the physical buildings and the manmade religious systems that run those buildings such as denominations and non-denominations and religious institutions, are dividing Yahuweh/Yehovah's body and bride against one another. The only way there can be unity is if everyone leaves all of the denominations, all of the physical churches and synagogues, in the world, leaving behind the practice of every denomination to only follow Yeshua himself directly without any manmade organization of legalism in the way.

Yahuweh/Yehovah allowed the Church and Synagogue system of denominations and religious organizations with physical temples all over the world causing his people to be divided as enemies against one another by the physical and intellectual and spiritual walls of the churches and synagogues, but COVID in 2020 was the cut-off point when it became disobedience to continue keeping the churches and synagogues open instead of shutting them down. And Yahuweh/Yehovah in his love and mercy will destroy and bring down every single one of these temples in these churches and synagogues, until there are no more physical building temples ever again. For nearly 2,000 years Christians have worshipped buildings as temples, trying to build bigger and more beautiful buildings to house bigger congregations, each church and synagogue growing their own little kingdoms to their own glory and power, the glory of man and worship of man. As Yahuweh/Yehovah comes he will destroy and bring down every church and every ministry and every religious institution, including schools and colleges and universities and every ministry of every kind that has to be run as an organization with people in authority giving paychecks to other people. Yahuweh/Yehovah allowed it in the past, but now the only way that his people can come together as one bride in unity, washed clean from all of the corruption in the old Church and Synagogue container, is to destroy the old Temple of the Church and Synagogue that is tearing his family apart and bring everyone out of it into unity in him.

3. <u>Unwillingness to Accept that the End Time Prophecies are in Fulfillment Now in the Present</u> – Any rejection by anyone that the prophecies of Yeshua's Return are in fulfillment now in the present brings division to the body, because if the prophecies are not being fulfilled right now in the present then there is no reason for the bride to prepare for his coming now in the present. And if there is no reason for the bride to prepare now then there is no reason to shut down and stop all ministry and there is no reason to shut down and stop all churches and synagogues and Christian institutions and denominations around the world. It is only in recognizing that we are in the fulfillment of the prophecies now in the present that there is any reason for the bride and family of Yahuweh/Yehovah to obey him and come together in unity, leaving all of the old container behind of this world. Those who reject that we are in the process of Yeshua's return right now in the present have to fight against those who want to obey Yahuweh/Yehovah and shut down all ministries and churches and synagogues and denominations and non-denominations, causing division among the body.

This can be seen in the Matthew 22:1-14 parable where those Christians who are invited to the wedding of the king reject his invitation, because they do not accept that the prophecies are in fulfillment in the present time and that Yeshua's Return is in the present. They reject that he is returning and find the things of the world more important, to keep the world going and running as normal and fight against Yahuweh/Yehovah shutting down everything of the world, including all ministries and organizations and building in churches and synagogues. As Yeshua prophesied in Matthew 24:48-51, there are many Christians (many of his servants) who will beat and attack other Christians (other servants) because Yeshua has delayed in returning and they refuse to believe that the time of his return has come. They refuse to recognize that the prophecies of Yeshua's Return are happening in the present, and because of it they attack the Christians who are recognizing it and bring division to Yahuweh/Yehovah's body and family and bride.

4. <u>Love of the City of Mystery Babel and Friendship with the World</u> – There can be no unity with both Yahuweh/Yehovah and the world at the same time, as already discussed. In order to have the John 17 unity among Yahuweh/Yehovah's family nation of people, his city and bride that is prepared for his coming, there has to be division and separation from the rest of the world as Yeshua says he has brought in Matthew 10:34-37 and Matthew 12:30-33 and John 15:9-20. Jacob (James) in James 4:1-4 repeats this same concept and John repeats it in 1 John 2:1-17. In order to have fellowship and unity among the bride and body and family of believers in Yeshua, there has to be a separation from and division against the world. There can be absolutely no unity with other religions in the world and no friendship or fellowship with those who are not for Yeshua, but against him as enemies. As soon as any Christian has any friendship or fellowship with the

world and those in other religions then they have divided themselves against Yahuweh/Yehovah and against his body, making it impossible to be in the set-apart fellowship within Yahuweh/Yehovah's set-apart family.

If any believer in Yeshua is like Lot's wife and refuses to leave Sodom, to leave the global city of Mystery Babel and all of the things of this world that it represents, then they have brought division to Yahuweh/Yehovah's body and family, without any way to have fellowship together anymore. Anyone who is a friend of the world is an enemy of Yahuweh/Yehovah and his family, his bride, causing the fellowship to be broken. In Revelation 18:5 Yahuweh/Yehovah says for his people to come out of the city of Mystery Babel, because at the time of his coming his people are living inside of the city of Mystery Babel. If none of his people were living in the city of Mystery Babel then there would be no reason for him to tell his people to come out, but we are all inside of Mystery Babel in this world now as Mystery Babel has taken over everywhere across the entire earth. The only way that there can be unity in Yahuweh/Yehovah's bride is for his people to leave Mystery Babel, to leave the city where the people of the world have come together in unity in their rebellion against Yahuweh/Yehovah, and be divided from them into the city of the New Jerusalem (the bride) where everyone has come together in unity of submission to the will of Yahuweh/Yehovah on earth.

5. <u>Unwillingness to be Servants of One Another, Trying to be in Positions of Authority and Control Instead</u> – In Matthew 20:20-28 Yeshua says that those who are great in his kingdom and reign, in his family and nation, are those who serve one another. And he makes it really clear that this is the opposite system of the world's system of mankind where rulers in positions of authority are considered great. He makes it very clear that anyone who is in a position of political or spiritual authority is not in the position of a servant, but is instead in the position that is opposite of a servant. As soon as a person is a shepherd or rabbi/teacher/pastor in a position of authority in a ministry or church or synagogue organization, then that person is in the position that is exactly opposite of where Yeshua says to be as a servant.

Those who are in positions of spiritual authority are not servants and are not serving others in that position; they are leaders in a place of power over others, controlling others and telling them what to do or what to think or what to believe. If they were servants then they would be taking orders, not giving them, and as soon as there is anyone in a position of control over others, then there is division among the body. The only way there can be unity is if everyone is following the command of only one person, Yahuweh/Yehovah himself. Everyone should be serving one another, only taking orders from Yahuweh/Yehovah directly and not giving orders to one another. Everyone in the body should be helping each other and going through the difficulties and joys together as a family, with no one trying to control anyone else or have any kind of power over anyone else. Mentoring and edifying one another can be done without controlling each other with positions of authority.

In Luke 10:38-42 Yeshua never condemns Martha for being a servant, serving others. He tells her that she should stop being worried and troubled. The actual problem that Martha has in Luke 10:38-42 is not that she is working and doing things in her serving others, but that she has gotten herself distracted with worry so that she is no longer listening to Yeshua as Mary is listening to him. And then she tries to control Mary and tell Mary what to do through Yeshua's authority. She tries to take Yeshua's authority and twist it around so that she can make Mary do what she wants her to do, to help her. The real problem and issue that Martha had was that she was filled with worry, distracting her from Yeshua, which then caused her to try to control other people around her and put herself into a position of authority as a god over them in place of Yeshua. It was not rest from work or rest from serving that was Martha's problem, but instead Yeshua focused on her worry as her problem and that she needed to be like Mary in her resting from her worrying so that she would no longer be distracted and could hear Yeshua too. The goal is to prioritize listening to Yeshua and his word first, obeying his words and commands, and then doing whatever serving he says to do without having any worry or distraction from him in our doing of things.

It was as soon as Martha tried to put herself into a position of authority and control over Mary, trying to be god over Mary in place of Yeshua, that she brought division between herself and Mary. Yeshua was then able to prevent that division, but Jacob (James) and John did the same thing in Matthew 20. As soon as they tried to put themselves into positions of power and authority over the other disciples they brought division to the body and family. The only way there can be unity among the body is if everyone humbles themselves into positions of servants obeying only Yahuweh/Yehovah as their only authority, and no longer trying to be in positions of authority and control over one another. As soon as anyone tries to control anyone else in the body, in the family nation, then they bring division as everyone has to fight for their positions of control and power over everyone else and it becomes the world's system of the pyramid of hierarchy with one in power at the top and degrees of power delegated to different positions of power going down through to the lowliest people at the bottom who have no power at all. Instead Yeshua says that there is no one in his body who has any positions of authority and control over one another, and he himself is right there as a servant with us, serving one another instead of controlling one another.

These are all of the things that Yahuweh/Yehovah has to deal with in order for his bride to be purified and cleansed in the fire, and brought together in unity as one family nation. All of the things of this world and of the old container he has to shut down and end and destroy, breaking down everything that is causing division among his bride, his city New Jerusalem that has prepared herself for his coming. In the end not one person will be left in ministry, not one church or synagogue or religious building will be left standing, not one denomination or Christian organization will be left in operation, not one molecule of the dirt and garbage of the world will be left on anyone's white and clean wedding clothes, and everyone in his body will have finally decided to submit to Yahuweh/Yehovah's will to be done on the earth instead of their own wills. Then there will at last be the John 17 unity that Yeshua prayed for.

Appendix: Seventy Sevens

As already discussed in *Calculating the Last Seven*, the prophecy of 70 Sevens given to Daniel in Daniel 9:24-27 began its fulfillment when Yeshua came the first time. As discussed in the book, we know from ancient records that without any doubt Artaxerxes I gave the first command to rebuild the city of Jerusalem in the year 458 B.C.E. The ancient Hebrew calendar new year begins in the spring and if we count 69 Sevens of years, or 483 years, from the Hebrew calendar year of the spring of 458 B.C.E. to the spring of 457 B.C.E. we arrive at the date of spring 26 C.E. to spring 27 C.E. According to the record of John 2:19-20 Yeshua's ministry began in the 46th year of the reconstruction of the Second Temple, which dates the start of his ministry to the winter of 27 C.E., just a couple months before the new year of the next year began in the spring at Passover of 27 C.E. Yeshua's ministry began exactly 69 sevens of years or 483 years from the command by Artaxerxes I to rebuild Jerusalem in 458 B.C.E.

But at that time there was never a fulfillment of the final 7 years or 1 Seven in years. The records in the gospels show that Yeshua's ministry could not have lasted for more than 2.5 years at the very most and all of the early church fathers agree that his ministry lasted for about 1 year. As already discussed in this current book, Eusebius was the one almost 300 years later who invented the myth that Yeshua's ministry lasted for 3.5 years, and in his original myth he actually claimed that Yeshua's ministry lasted for a full 7 years, continuing on for another 3.5 years somehow in between his resurrection and ascension. This myth was later changed into creating a fictional 3.5 years between Yeshua's ascension and the martyrdom of Stephen, 3.5 years which are not recorded anywhere in Scripture or in any records at all from the 1st century C.E. or the hundreds of years after that. Instead Yeshua fulfilled the 70 sevens prophecy by his ministry lasting for a literal 70 weeks or about 1 year, and in the middle of the literal week on a Wednesday, on the 4th day of the week, he was crucified and rose again on the Sabbath day on the 7th day of the week on Saturday, since the women going to the tomb early in the morning on the 1st day of the week discovered an empty tomb and found out that he had already risen before the 1st day of the week.[49]

Yeshua never fulfilled the final 1 Seven of years of the 70 Sevens of years that had begun with the command to rebuild Jerusalem in 458 B.C.E., only 483 years or 69 sevens of years of the prophecy. He only fulfilled the complete 70 Sevens, including the final 1 Seven, as a literal 70 Weeks or 490 days without finishing the years. This means that the final 1 Seven or 7 Years of the 70 Sevens of 490 years still has to be fulfilled, which also means that the final part of the 70 Sevens prophecy in the verse of Daniel 9:24 has yet to be finished and completed. We then have to ask the question if there is another time in history after Yeshua's ministry began in 27 C.E. that there was a command given to rebuild Jerusalem. And in the records of history there are only two other times since that date that there has been a command given to rebuild Jerusalem, first by Suleiman I within a few years before the date of 1534 C.E., then second by the Ministerial Committee for Economic Affairs on September 8, 1968. There were no other commands given in history to rebuild Jerusalem except for commands that were right away afterward reversed before any construction began, with the order given to destroy Jerusalem in place of rebuilding it. These are the only two true commands given to

---

[49] Michael John Rood, *The Chronological Gospels* (Fort Mill, South Carolina: Aviv Moon Publishing, 2013)

rebuild Jerusalem since Yeshua's death and resurrection. Jerusalem would be rebuilt sometimes in the midst of getting destroyed through those years, but there is no record of any command ever being given to rebuild the city or its wall until Suleiman I.

As already discussed in Calculating the Last Seven the exact date that Suleiman I gave his command to rebuild Jerusalem is unknown; we only know from the surviving dates on the fountains built in the city by Suleiman that it was before the year 1536, and no later than the year 1535 at the very latest. The Daniel prophecy of sevens is broken up into three parts, with one part being 62 Sevens or 434 years, another part being 7 Sevens or 49 years, and a third part being 1 Seven or 7 years. If we count 62 sevens or 434 years backward from the year 1968 we arrive at the year 1534. If we count forward 7 Sevens or 49 years from 1968 we arrive at the year 2017, which makes a completion of 69 Sevens of years from 1534, very close to the most likely date that Suleiman I gave his command to rebuild Jerusalem. Even if Suleiman gave his command to rebuild Jerusalem in 1535 then the counting of 69 sevens cannot begin any later than this date of 1535 at the very latest. This means that the completion of 70 Sevens of years or 490 years from the command to rebuild Jerusalem has to be completed in either the year 2024 or no later than the year 2025 at the very latest.

Whether we like it or not, whether we want to accept it or not, during the years 2024 to 2025 we are entering a time of the completion of the fulfillment of the prophecy of Daniel's 70 Sevens, and a fulfillment specifically of Daniel 9:24. It would be wonderful if Daniel 9:24 is a prophecy about the coming of the Messiah and Yeshua's return during the years 2024 to 2025, but if we actually read the words written in the prophecy there is nothing about the Messiah coming or Yeshua's Return at the completion of Daniel's 70 Sevens. That is an interpretation and theory that has been added onto the words written in Scripture, but there is no promise that we get to see Yeshua's Return at the completion of the 70 Sevens or even at the completion of the final 1 Seven of years or 7 years in Daniel 9:27. Whether we like it or not this prophecy of Daniel 9:24 will be in its time of fulfillment and will be either completely fulfilled or begin to be fulfilled in the years 2024 to 2025, whatever that means and whatever that will look like.

We have to wait and see after the prophecy is fulfilled to understand its fulfillment. This prophecy will eventually have something to do with Yeshua's Return at some point in the future, but there is nothing in the prophecy itself that promises that Yeshua will return during the 490th year when the full Seventy Sevens of years are completed. It would be nice if it did, but it does not. It would be wonderful if he does return, but there is no promise in the prophecy that he has to return right away at that date when this prophecy is fulfilled in the years 2024 to 2025. There is not even anything in the prophecy of 70 Sevens that says that this prophecy has to be connected with the 3.5 years of Great Tribulation; that connection was made by men in their interpretations and theories hundreds of years later after Yeshua's death and resurrection. This prophecy of Daniel 70 Sevens might have nothing to do with the 3.5 years of Great Tribulation prophesied later in Daniel and in Revelation. It is time for everyone to humble themselves and no longer stumble in pride in thinking that we have the prophecies all figured out and that all of our myths we have created about the prophecies of Yeshua's Return will happen the way we say they will. We are now in the years 2024 to 2025 at the time of the completion of 70 Sevens from the command to rebuild Jerusalem given by Suleiman I and the fulfillment of Daniel 9:24, that is reality and there is no changing that reality. It is our myths and interpretations and theories and imaginations of the prophecies that have to change; the Christian world has turned into the Pharisees of Yeshua's day who could not give up their myths about the prophecies as the prophecies were fulfilled right in front of their eyes.

It is interesting to note that there is only one World War that is prophesied about in Scripture, and that is the World War that happens at the end of the 3.5 years of Great Tribulation in Isaiah 13:1-22, Joel 3:1-21, Zephaniah 3:1-20, Zechariah 12:9 – 14:21, Revelation 8:13 – 9:21, Revelation 11:13-14, and Revelation 16:12-16. [Remember that Revelation 8:13 clearly without any mistake says that the 5th through 7th Trumpets are the Three Woes, meaning that the 6th Trumpet does not happen until the time of the Second Woe in Revelation 11:13-14 at the very end of the Great Tribulation when Yeshua returns. Placing any world wars at any other time in prophecy than at the end of the 3.5 years of Great Tribulation is only based upon theory and interpretation and conjecture and imagination, because there are no prophecies about a World War happening at any other time in the End Time events.] This gathering of all of the nations of the earth by Yahuweh/Yehovah at the very end of the 3.5 years of Great Tribulation, right before he comes and during in the midst of his coming, is the only World War that is prophesied about in all of Scripture and is the only World War that involves Israel in the prophecies. As we watch the nations gather together into a World War in Israel this year in 2023 and into 2024 we can know that no matter where we are in the timing of the End Time prophecies, the end of the 3.5 years of Great Tribulation is not far away with the fulfillment of the World War prophesied about during Yeshua's Return already starting to happen now.

The Counting of Seventy Sevens or 490 Years from the command to rebuild Jerusalem and its wall by Suleiman I in 1534 to 1535 is completed in the year **2024** or **2025**.

The Counting of 2,300 Evening Morning (Literal Days) from June 14, 2018 connected with the Transgression Desolating discussed in Chapter 7 is completed on **September 30, 2024**.

The Counting of 1,290 Days from March 24, 2021 connected with the Disgusting Idol (Abomination) Desolating discussed in Chapter 9 is completed on **October 4, 2024**, which will probably be within 24 hours of the Day of Trumpets.

The Counting of 42 Months (42 Literal Cycles of the Moon) from April 23, 2021 connected with the Nations (Gentiles) Trampling Jerusalem discussed in Chapter 10 is completed on approximately **September 14, 2024**.

The Counting of 1,260 Days from March 29, 2021 connected with the Woman in the Wilderness discussed in Chapter 12 is completed on **September 9, 2024**.

More understanding and discovery are still needed for the countings of days and months connected with the Two Witnesses and the Blaspheming of the Beast Out of the Sea in Chapters 11 and 13. The difficulty with understanding the timing of the 42 months of blaspheming by the Beast Out of the Sea, which is made up of the broken nation remnants of the Babylonian, Persian, Greek, Roman, and Islamic Empires in Europe, the Middle East, North Africa, and Central Asia, is that there has been a process of growing blaspheming against Yahuweh/Yehovah over many years in those regions. The really serious blaspheming against

Yahuweh/Yehovah, the God of Israel, did not really begin in the Muslim nations until after the fall of the Ottoman Empire and subsequent rise of fanatical Islamic groups in the 20th century.

The holiday of International Blasphemy Rights Day was created on September 30, 2009 for protecting the rights of anyone to blaspheme the god of any religion, including the God of Israel, Yahuweh/Yehovah. Up until the year 2008 most of the nations in Europe had anti-blasphemy laws making it illegal to blaspheme Yahuweh/Yehovah and his Name and his tent as in the prophecy of Revelation 13. But since 2008 almost every nation in Europe has now repealed those laws making it legal to blaspheme Yahuweh/Yehovah almost anywhere on the continent as of 2021, which in turn as of 2021 has made it legal for most living in the remnants of the the Beast Out of the Sea in Europe and West Asia and North Africa to blaspheme Yahuweh/Yehovah without fear. The fact that these anti-blasphemy laws have been repealed now also shows the movement that has happened since about 2008 in the culture of Europe, with the culture and people and governments of the nations of Europe now indifferent towards or even supportive of blasphemy against Yahuweh/Yehovah, where for 1,500 years before that blasphemy was mostly illegal in Europe and frowned upon by the culture and people.

France has led the way in Europe with their repeal of their anti-blasphemy laws against Yahuweh/Yehovah and Christianity happening in 1881. Sweden repealed their anti-blasphemy laws against Yahuweh/Yehovah and Christianity in 1970. England and Wales repealed theirs in 2008, The Netherlands in 2014, Iceland and Norway in 2015, Alsace-Moselle, France and Malta and Italy in 2016, Denmark in 2017, Germany and Finland and Greece in 2019, Ireland in 2020, with Scotland finishing the sequence of repealing on April 23, 2021. Spain is in process of repealing their borderline anti-blasphemy law that was not completely repealed in 1988, leaving Northern Ireland and Poland as the only two countries left in Europe since 2021 who still have anti-blasphemy laws against Yahuweh/Yehovah officially in their law codes and enforceable.

There is no doubt that since 2008 to 2009 we have been living in a time of a shifting in history unlike any time before for over 1,500 years when the global culture from the Beast Out of the Sea of people has changed to allowing and encouraging blasphemy against Yahuweh/Yehovah. There is also no doubt that at least since the spring of 2021, when that shift came into its fullness, we have been living in the timeframe of the fulfillment of the blaspheming of Revelation 13:5-6 as everyone in the global culture has now changed around to allowing blaspheming, and even wanting to protect it as a right. Many hate speech laws in many countries now protect the right for a person to blaspheme against Yahuweh/Yehovah and Christianity, while preventing Christians from speaking against immorality without breaking the law. We are in the time of the fulfillment of the prophecy, but more information is still needed for pinpointing an exact date for starting the counting of the 42 months of blaspheming. As of the spring of 2021, anywhere that anyone goes throughout the Beast Out of the Sea in the broken remnant nations of Europe and North Africa and West Asia a person is now able to legally blaspheme against Yahuweh/Yehovah, except in Northern Ireland and Poland.

Appendix: Hebrew Matthew Chapter 24

Translated from a Copy of the Original Hebrew Preserved by Messianic Jews in the Middle Ages and Unintentionally Saved in an Imperfect State by Orthodox Jews in the Shem Tov Copy He Included in His 14th Century Book *Even Bochan*

Manuscript Copies Used:

A *Even Bochan*, Shem Tov (16th to 17th century C.E. copy) Ms. Or. 4766; Bibliotheek der Rijksuniversiteit, Leiden.

B *Even Bochan*, Shem Tov (16th to 17th century C.E. copy) Ms. Michael 119; Bodleian Library, Oxford.

D *Even Bochan*, Shem Tov (17th century C.E. copy) Ms. 2426; Library of the Jewish Theological Seminary, New York. https://primo-tc-na01.hosted.exlibrisgroup.com/permalink/f/1jhdiph/JTS_DIGITOOL231918

E *Even Bochan*, Shem Tov (17th century C.E. copy) Ms. 2279; Library of the Jewish Theological Seminary, New York. https://primo-tc-na01.hosted.exlibrisgroup.com/permalink/f/1jhdiph/JTS_DIGITOOL239401

F *Even Bochan*, Shem Tov (16th to 17th century C.E. copy) Ms. 2209; Library of the Jewish Theological Seminary, New York.
https://primo-tc-na01.hosted.exlibrisgroup.com/permalink/f/1jhdiph/JTS_DIGITOOL231561

G *Even Bochan*, Shem Tov (16th to 17th century C.E. copy) Ms. 2234; Library of the Jewish Theological Seminary, New York.
https://primo-tc-na01.hosted.exlibrisgroup.com/permalink/f/1jhdiph/JTS_DIGITOOL231599

H *Even Bochan*, Shem Tov (16th to 17th century C.E. copy) Ms. Michael 137; Bodleian Library, Oxford.

J *Even Bochan*, Shem Tov (16th century C.E. copy) Vat. Ebr. 101; Biblioteca Apostolica Vaticana, Vatican City. https://digi.vatlib.it/view/MSS_Vat.ebr.101

K *Even Bochan*, Shem Tov (16th century C.E. copy) Plut. 2.17; Biblioteca Medicea Laurenziana, Florence.
http://mss.bmlonline.it/s.aspx?Id=AWODj2lhI1A4r7GxL9f3&c=Lapis%20discernens#/oro/277

L *Even Bochan*, Shem Tov (16th century C.E. copy) Ms. 3099; Casanatense Library, Rome.
https://web.nli.org.il/sites/NLI/English/digitallibrary/pages/viewer.aspx?&presentorid=MANUSCRIPTS&docid=PNX_MANUSCRIPTS000085622-1#|FL60257435

M *Even Bochan*, Shem Tov (1578 C.E. copy) F 46891(8); Biblioteka Uniwersytecka w Wrocławiu, Warsaw.
http://www.manuscriptorium.com/apps/index.php?direct=record&pid=set031101set1196#search

O *Even Bochan*, Shem Tov (17th century C.E. copy) Cod. Parm. 2259; Palatina Library, Parma.
https://web.nli.org.il/sites/NLI/English/digitallibrary/pages/viewer.aspx?&presentorid=MANUSCRIPTS&docid=PNX_MANUSCRIPTS000078680-1#|FL14611785

P *Even Bochan*, Shem Tov (17th century C.E. copy) Ms. Guenzberg 58; Russian State Library, Moscow.
https://web.nli.org.il/sites/NLI/English/digitallibrary/pages/viewer.aspx?&presentorid=MANUSCRIPTS&docid=PNX_MANUSCRIPTS000085639-1#|FL61655700

Manuscript L has been used for the base text.

Manuscript Families for Chapter 24: Degree of Assimilation to the Greek Translation of Matthew

Least Assimilation	Medium Assimilation	Medium Assimilation	Most Assimilation	Medium Assimilation	Most Assimilation
(L)	(B)	(H, O, P)	(A, J, K, M)	(E, F)	(D, G)

Fragmentary Manuscripts:

H = 24:20, 27-28, 34-35

O = 24:20, 27, 29, 34-35

P = 24:20, 27, 29, 34-35

English Translation

24. ₁ And it came to be when Yeshua went out from the set-apart place, and when He was walking, His disciples drew near to show Him the buildings of the set-apart place.

₂ And He said, "You see all these? Truly I say to you that all shall be destroyed, and no stone upon a stone shall be left there."

₃ And in His sitting on the Mount of Olives opposite the set-apart place, Kepha and Yochanan and Anderai asked Him in secret,[50] "When shall all these be, and what is the sign that it shall be when all of these related matters come to be;[51] or when shall they begin, and when is the end of the world and your coming?"

₄ And Yeshua answered them, "Beware lest *any* man leads you astray,

₅ for many shall come in My Name, saying, 'I am he, the messiah,' and they shall lead you astray.

₆ And you, when you hear of wars and the joining of armies, beware lest you are vain, for all this is destined in future to come, but the time is not yet of the end.

₇ And nation shall rise[52] against nation,[53] and reign against reign, and many troubles shall come to be, and grievous hunger, and earthquakes in places.[54]

₈ All these are the beginning of pains.

₉ Then they shall imprison you to persecute *you*, and they shall kill you, and you shall become a disgrace to all the peoples over My Name.[55]

₁₀ And then many shall be agitated, and those in fright shall be treacherous, and they shall be angry among themselves.

₁₁ And prophets of falsehood shall arise and lead astray the many.

₁₂ And when wickedness is great, the love of many shall lose intensity.

₁₃ But whoever waits until the end shall be saved.

₁₄ And this Good News shall be taught in all the ends of the earth[56] for a witness about Me across all the nations. And then the end comes,[57]

₁₅ and this is the disgusting idol desolating,[58] the one spoken of by the mouth of Dani'el the prophet standing on the set-apart place (and let the one reading understand).

₁₆ Then whoever is in Yehudah, let them flee to the mountains.

₁₇ And whoever is upon the house, let him not run down to grab *any* set thing from his house.

₁₈ And whoever is in the field, let him not go back to grab his shirt.

₁₉ Woe to the pregnant and nursing women in those days.

₂₀ Pray to El that your flight shall not be on the day of Shabbath.[59]

---

[50] Mark 13:3
[51] Mark 13:4
[52] 'shall rise' according to ABDEFGJKM; spelling error in L
[53] 'nation' according to ABDEFGJKM; missing from L by scribal error
[54] Mark 13:8
[55] 'My Name' according to ABDEFGJKM; L has 'His Name' written here in place of "My Name," and there is not enough evidence to know for certain which is the more original and correct reading, since 'His Name' could be referring to the Name of יהוה YHWH.
[56] Psalms 98:3
[57] Daniel 8:17, 19; Daniel 11:27
[58] Daniel 11:31; Daniel 12:11

₂₁ For then shall be great trouble⁶⁰ which has not been from the creation of the world until now, and the like shall not be. ⁶¹

₂₂ And unless those days are reduced, all flesh would not be saved; but for the sake of the chosen those days⁶² shall be reduced.

₂₃ And in that same time, if a man says to you, 'Look, the messiah is here or there,' you do not believe him.

₂₄ For false messiahs and prophets of falsehood shall arise, and they shall give signs and great miracles in relation, that if it is possible for it to be, they shall come with deceptions against the chosen.

₂₆ And then if ⁶³ they say to you, 'Look, he is in the wilderness,' you do not go out, and, 'Look, he is in the rooms,' you do not believe it.

₂₅ See, I have told you before it has come to be." ⁶⁴

₂₇ Again Yeshua said to them, to His disciples, "As the lightning goes forth in from the east and is seen in from the west, so shall it be in the coming belonging to the Son of Adam.

₂₈ In whatever place that there shall be the decomposing body, there the eagles shall be gathered.⁶⁵

₂₉ And in that time, after the trouble of those days, the sun shall darken and the moon shall not shine forth its light, and the stars shall fall from the heavens,⁶⁶ and the strength of the heavens shall be shaken.⁶⁷

₃₀ And then shall appear the sign in the heavens belonging to the Son of Adam, and all of the families of the ground shall weep⁶⁸ and shall see the Son of Adam in the dark clouds of the heavens⁶⁹ with a large army and with a terrifying appearance.

₃₁ And He shall send His messengers with a shophar and with a great voice⁷⁰ to gather His chosen from the four winds of the heavens,⁷¹ from one end of the heavens unto the other end.⁷²

₃₂ From the fig tree learn the parable: when you see its branches and leaves sprouting you know when *the summer is near.*

₃₃ *So you also, when you see all these, know*⁷³ He is near to the gates.⁷⁴ ⁷⁵

---

⁵⁹ 'on the day of Shabbath' according to BEFHOP; M has 'on the day of Shabbath in winter' through the process of assimilation to the Greek; L has 'in shame' in place of 'on the day of Shabbath' and there is not enough evidence to know for certain if it is a scribal copyist spelling error or perhaps does preserve a more original reading.

⁶⁰ L flips the words 'great trouble' out of the normal Hebrew grammatical order; not flipped in ABDEFGJKM

⁶¹ Jeremiah 30:7; Daniel 12:1

⁶² L adds the word 'days' twice by scribal error; second word 'days' not in ABDEFGJKM

⁶³ 'And then if' according to AJKM; L has spelling error 'and if those'

⁶⁴ All manuscripts have verse 26 before verse 25, which is the more logical order of continuous thought for Yeshua to complete the concept he is teaching before moving on.

⁶⁵ Ezekiel 39:17

⁶⁶ Isaiah 13:10; Isaiah 34:4; Ezekiel 32:7; Joel 2:10; Joel 3:15

⁶⁷ Isaiah 13:13; Joel 3:16

⁶⁸ Zechariah 12:10-12

⁶⁹ Exodus 19:9; Daniel 7:13

⁷⁰ Exodus 19:16, 19; Isaiah 27:13; Psalms 47:5; Psalms 98:6

⁷¹ Daniel 7:2

⁷² Deuteronomy 4:32

⁷³ The words *'the summer is near. So you also, when you see all these, know'* are missing from all of the available manuscripts by scribal error, based on the textual evidence that the word 'near' is written twice in verses 32-33, and the scribe's eye strayed to the second word 'near' in verse 33, missing all of the words in between the two words 'near' in 32 and 'near' in 33.

⁷⁴ 'to the gates' according to ABDEFGJKM; missing from L by scribal error

⁷⁵ Ezekiel 44:1-2

₃₄ Truly I say to you, that generation shall not pass until that all these things have come to be done.

₃₅ And the heavens and the earth shall pass away,[76]

₃₆ but of that[77] day and of that time there are none who know, nor do the messengers of the heavens, but the Father only."

₃₇ Again Yeshua said to His disciples, "As in the days of Noach, so it shall be in the coming belonging to the Son of Adam.

₃₈ As it was before the flood, they were eating and drinking and being fruitful and multiplying[78] until the day that Noach entered into the ark.[79]

₃₉ And they did not know until the flood came upon them and destroyed them; so it shall be in the coming belonging to the Son of Adam.

₄₀ Then if there comes to be two ploughing in a certain field, the one righteous and the other evil, the one shall be seized and the other shall be left.

₄₁ And two women shall be grinding in a certain mill; the one shall be seized and the other shall be left. And this shall be because the messengers during the end of the world shall be taking away the stumbling blocks from the world,[80] and they shall separate the good from the evil." [81] [82]

₄₂ Then Yeshua said to His disciples, "Therefore watch with Me, because you do not know at that time what time your Master comes.

₄₃ This you do know: If he had known at that time what time the thief was coming, he would have watched and not left him to break into his house.

₄₄ So you should become ready, because you do not know at that time what time the Son of Adam shall be destined in future to come.

₄₅ What do you think of the trustworthy and wise servant whose master positions him over his children to give them to eat in its due time?

₄₆ Happy is that servant whose master finds him so doing in his coming.

₄₇ Truly I say to you that he shall give him position over his goods.

₄₈ But if it shall be that servant is evil and says in his heart, 'My master is delaying to come,' [83]

₄₉ and he begins to beat the servants of his master, and eats and drinks with the gluttons.

₅₀ And his master comes on a day that he does not wait for, and in a time that he does not know;

₅₁ and he shall break him apart and place his allotment with the hypocrites. There shall be weeping and gnashing of teeth."

---

[76] Psalms 102:25-26
[77] 'that' according to ABDEFGJKM; missing from L by scribal error
[78] Genesis 1:28
[79] Genesis 7:7
[80] Isaiah 57:14; Zephaniah 1:3; Matthew 13:40-41
[81] 'and they shall separate the good from the evil' according to ABDEFGJKM; missing from L by scribal error
[82] Matthew 13:49
[83] Exodus 32:1

24.

1. ויהי כאשר יצא ישו מן המקדש וכשהיה הולך נגשו תלמידיו להראותו בניני המקדש
2. ויאמר תראו כל אלה אמן אני אומר לכם שהכל יהרס ולא ישאר שם אבן על אבן
3. ובשבתו על הר הזתים נגד המקדש שאלו לו פיטרוש ויוחנן ואנדריאה בסתר מתי יהיה כל אלה ומה האות שיהיה כשיהיו כל אלה העניינ׳(ם) או כשיתחילו ומתי יהיה תכלית העולם וביאתך
4. ויען להם ישו השמרו פן יתעה אתכם איש
5. שרבים יבאו בשמי לאמר אני הוא המשיח ויתעו אתכם
6. ואתם כאשר תשמעו המלחמות וחברת הצבאות השמרו פן תהבלו שכל זה עתיד לבא אבל עדיין אין התכלית
7. ויקם גוי וממלכה על ממלכה ויהיו מהומות רבות ורעב כבד ורעש במקומות
8. כל אלה תחילת המכאובות
9. אז ימסרו אתכם לצרות ויהרגו אתכם ותהיו לחרפה לכל העמים על שמו
10. ואז ירגזו רבים ויבגדו הם באים ויתקצפו ביניהם
11. ויקומו נביאי השקר ויטעו את הרבים
12. וכאשר תרבה הרשעות תפוג אהבת רבים
13. ואשר יחכה עד התכלי׳(ת) יושע
14. ותדרש בשורה [לעז אוונג״יליין] זאת בכל אפסי ארץ לעדו׳(ת) עלי על כל הגוים ואז תבא התכלית
15. [זה אנט״קרישטוש] וזהו שקוץ שומם האמור על פי דניאל הנביא עומד במקום קדוש והקורא יבין
16. אז אשר ביודא ינוסו להרים
17. ואשר על הבית לא ירד לקחת שום דבר מביתו
18. ואשר בשדה לא ישוב לקחת כתנתו
19. הוי לנשי׳(ם) הרות ולמניקות בימים ההם
20. התפללו לאל שלא תהיה מנוסתכם בשבת
21. שאז תהיה גדולה צרה אשר לא נהיתה מבריאת העולם עד עתה וכמוה לא תהיה
22. ולולי היות הימים ההם מעטים לא יושע כל בשר רק בעבור הנבחרים ימעטו הימים ההם
23. ובאותו הזמן אם יאמר איש לכם הנה המשיח לכאן או לשם לא תאמינו
24. שיקומו משיחי שקרים ונביאי השקר ויתנו אותות ומופתי׳(ם) גדולים בעניין שאם יוכל להיות יבאו בטעות עם הנבחרים

26. ואם הם יאמרו לכם הנו במדבר אל תצאו והנו בחדרים אל תאמינו

25. הנני אומרו לכם קודם היותו

27. עוד אמר להם ישו לתלמידיו כמו שהברק יוצא במזרח ונראה במערב כן תהיה ביאתו של בן אדם

28. באיזה מקום שיהיה הגויה שם יתחברו הנשרים

29. ובאותה שעה אחרי צרת הימים ההם יחשך השמש והירח לא יגיה אורו והככבים יפלו מהשמים וחיל השמים יתנודד

30. ואז יראה האות של בן אדם בשמים ויבכו כל המשפחות האדמה ויראו את בן האדם בעובי השמים בחיל רב ובצורה נוראה

31. וישלח מלאכיו בשופר ובקול גדול לאסוף את נבחריו מארבע רוחות השמים מקצה השמים עד קצותם

32. מעץ התאנה תלמדו המשל כאשר תראו ענפיה ועלים צומחים תדעו כי

33. קרוב הוא

34. אמן אני אומר לכם שלא יעבור זה הדור עד שכל אלה הדברי׳(ם) יהיו עשויים

35. והשמים והארץ יעברו

36. ומהיום ומהעת ההיא אין מי שיודע ולא מלאכי השמים אלא האב בלבד

37. עוד אמר ישו לתלמידיו כאשר בימי נח כן תהיה ביאתו של בן אדם

38. כאשר היו קודם המבול אוכלים ושותים ופרים ורבים עד יום שבא נח בתיבה

39. ולא ידעו עד שבא המבול עליהם וישחיתם כן תהיה ביאתו של בן אדם

40. אז אם יהיו שנים חורשי׳(ם) בשדה אחד האחד צדיק ואחד רשע האחת ילכד והאחת יעזב

41. ושתים נשים טוחנות בטחון אחד האחת תלכד והאחת תעזב וזה יהיה שהמלאכי׳(ם) בתכלית העולם יסירו המכשולים מהעולם

42. אז אמר ישו לתלמידיו לזאת שמרו עמי שלא תדעו איזו שעה אדוניכם בא

43. זאת תדעו אם היה יודע איזה שעה הגנב בא ישמור ולא יעזוב לחתור ביתו

44. כן אתם תהיו נכונים שלא תדעו איזו שעה בן אדם עתיד לבא

45. מה אתם חושבים מהעבד הנאמן והחכם ששם אותו אדוניו על טפיו לתת אכלם בעתו

46. אשרי העבד ההוא שימצאהו אדוניו בבואו עושה כן

47. אמן אני אומר לכם שעל טובו ישימהו

48. ואם יהי׳(ה) העבד ההוא רע ויאמר בלבו אדוני מתמהמה לבא

49. ויתחיל להכות עבדי אדוניו ויאכל וישתה עם הזוללי'(ם)

50. ובא אדוניו ביום אשר לא יחכה ובעת אשר לא ידע

51. ויפרדיהו וישים חלקו עם החנפי'(ם) שם יהיה בכי וחרוק שנים

All differences between the other available Manuscripts with Manuscript L

24:1 בנין הבית והמקדש G | בניני המקדש [בניני EF | את add G [להראותו | מהמקדש [מן המקדש G

24:2 ויאמר [ואומר EF, add להם G | שם] omit J | [שהכל omit A

24:3 AGJK [פיטרוש [פיטרו | A [לו | omit M | שאלו [שאלו DG add בית [נגד AJKM | בהר [על הר M ובשבת [ובשבתו | ABDGJKM או [העניינים [הענינים M ואנדריאו [ואנדריו K, אנדריב J, אנדראוס G, אנדריאס EF, ואנדריאה A וביאתה [ובאתך F [מתי ונומתי EF לו add [כשיתחילו omit G [כשיתחילו

24:4 EF אתכם [לכם EF add לכם [השמרו

24:5 AJM את הרבים [אתכם ויטעו [ויתעו | omit A [הוא KM [יבואו

24:6 ABDEFGJKM עדיין [ועדיין K [לבא ולבוא GM תבהלו [ותבהלו

24:7 ABDEFGJKM על גוי add גוי | ABDEFGJKM ויקום [ויקם

24:8 omit A [המכאובות ABDEFGJKM תחלת [תחילת

24:9 ABDEFGJKM שמי [שמו M חרפה [לחרפה BDG יאסרו [ימסרו

24:10 F ויתקפצו [ויתקצפו ADEGJKM בהם [באים EF ירגשו [ירגזו K יהרגו add [ואז

24:11 G שקר [השקר

24:13 M את [עד

24:14 omit D [אפסי omit M, K אונגליו EF אואנגילו BDG, אוונגילי AJ, אונגילין [ולעז B, omit M | בלעז G [בא G העם [הגוים omit A [על ABDEFGJK הארץ [ארץ

24:15 J, אנטקרישט EF, אנטקריסטו BDG, אנטקרישטוש AK, אנטקרישט [אנטקריסטו EF והוא [AKM זהו M אנטקריטו (separated note in JK) omit BD [הנביא EF בדניאל [על פי דניאל

24:16 AEFJKM ביהודה [ביודא G ואז [אז

24:17 D לקח G, omit EF לקרות [לקחת

24:18 M קמתו [כתנתו

24:19 EF ולמנקות [ולמניקות ABDEFGJKM להרות [הרות omit ABDEFGJKM לנשים | אוי EF, הוא M [והוי

24:20 BEFHOP, בסתו ובשבת AK, בסתו ביום השבת [בשבת ובשבת G omit [לאל K תהיה [ותהיה F התפלל [והתפללו M ביום השבת בסתיו J, בסתיו ובשבת DG

24:21 M ועד [עד ABDFG מבראת [מבריאת EF שלא [אשר לא ABDEFGJKM צרה גדולה [גדולה צרה

24:22 omit ABDEFGJKM [הימים² D יושיע [ויושיע F מועטים [מעטים omit EF [הם¹ J ולא [ולולא A, ולילא [ולולי omit M [הם²

24:23 omit G [או לשם M לשם או לכאן [לכאן או לשם omit DG [לכאן M לכם איש [איש לכם M זמן [הזמן

357

24:24 את וְעִם AJKM | יביאו ויבאו AJKM | בְּעִנְיַן בענין ABDEFGJKM | ונבאי ונביאי ABDG | רבים וְשִׁקְרִים ABDGJKM, אות EF

24:26 וְהִנְנוּ EF | הננו A, וְהִנּוּ | תצאו EF | הם omit BDEFG | הם AJKM | ואז אם וְאִם הם

24:25 היותו] omit AJ

24:27 להם] omit AJM | ממזרח בְּמִזְרָח BG | של בן אדם BDGH, שלבן האדם JKM | של בן האדם

24:28 שתהיה וְשִׁיהִיָה AJM

24:29 מן השמים וּמֵהַשָּׁמַיִם EF | והכוכבים וְהַכּוֹכָבִים KMO | הם] omit M | הם] omit D | צרת 24:29

24:30 בעבי וּבְעוּבִי ABDEFGJKM | המשפחות וְהַמִּשְׁפָּחוֹת ABDEFGJKM | האדם וְאָדָם ABDEFGJKM | שלבן של בן BDG | ABDEFGJKM | וחיל וְבָחֵל M

24:31 ומארבע מִדּ׳ EFM | השמים¹] omit AEFKM | עד וְעַד EFM

24:32 (all manuscripts missing part of 32-33 by scribal error)

24:33 הוא] add לשערים ABDGJKM, add לשעירים EF

24:34 אלה] אלו ADEFGKOP, omit B | H ואלה הדברים | האלו H נעשים עשוים ABDG, H עשויים וְעֲשֻׂיִּים

24:36 ומהיום] add ההוא ABDEFGJKM | שידע וְיוֹדֵעַ EF | האב] האב E with marginal correction

24:37 האדם וְאָדָם ABDEFGJKM | של בן ABDG | שלבן בימינו וביאתו DG

24:38 לתיבה וּבְתֵיבָה M | פרים וּפָרִים A

24:39 האדם וְאָדָם ABDEFGJKM | J והשחיתם וַיִּשְׁחִיתֵם EF | המבול וְהַמַּבּוּל

24:40 והב׳ וְהָאֶחָד ADGJK, EF, וְהָאַחַת הָא׳ EF | ADGM, הָאַחַת וְהָאֶחָד KM, וְהָאַחַת EF, הָא׳ וְאֶחָד EF, בְּ׳ שנים M וְהָאָח׳

24:41 ויהיה M והאחרת K, וְהָאַחַת EF א׳, ABDJK וְאַחַת אַחַת M שְׁהֵן add נשים EF וּבְ׳, DG ושתים

24:42 אדוניכם וַאֲדוֹנֵיכֶם K אדוניכם בא] omit J (scribal error) | שעה אדוניכם ABDG בא וְאָז] איזו G שמעו וְשִׁמְרוּ בא אדוניכם G

24:43 הגנב ABDEFGM איזה] וְאֵיזוֹ AM אדון הבית add יודע] ויודע omit J (scribal error) | זאת תדעו אם היה יודע איזה D לחבור וְלַחְתֹּר M יבא וְיָבֹא AJ, יבא M השעה שהגנב וְשָׁעָה

24:44 בא BG עתיד לבא FGJ | האדם וְאָדָם EF | תהיו וְהָיוּ

24:45 להם A add לתת] omit G | והחכם EF הנאמן וְנֶאֱמָן

24:46 שתצווהו וְשֶׁצִּיוָּהוּ DG

24:47 טפיו וְטוּבוֹ D

24:48 DG ובא B, לבוא וְלָבֹא M הוא add אדוני] A, omit EF העב וְהָעֶבֶד

24:50 יבא וְיָבֹא AJKM

24:51 שינים וְשָׁנִים ABDEGM | שנים BDEFGKM ויפרידו AJ, ויפחדהו וְיִפְרִידֵהוּ

Scribal Error Notes

Matthew 24:20 – The progression of assimilation to the Greek in verse 20 from the available manuscripts (from manuscript J to manuscript M to manuscript B) leans more heavily as evidence in the direction toward ביום השבת 'on the day of Shabbath' being the original words written here; and בבשת 'in shame' is probably a scribal error in Manuscript L. But more evidence needs to be found in more manuscript copies to know for certain. Manuscript M demonstrates how the scribes gradually changed the original Hebrew words toward reading as a translation from the Greek. 'On Shabbath' בשבת and 'in shame' בבשת are spelled almost the same in Hebrew, with only the letters beyth ב and shin ש in reverse positions.

Manuscript L = התפללו לאל שלא תהיה מנוסתכם בבשת
Pray to El that your flight shall not be in shame. = Manuscript L

Manuscript B = התפללו לאל שלא תהיה מנוסתכם ביום השבת
Pray to El that your flight shall not be on the day of Shabbath. = Manuscript B

Manuscript M = התפללו לאל שלא תהיה מנוסתכם ביום השבת בסתיו
Pray to El that your flight shall not be on the day of Shabbath in winter. = Manuscript M

Manuscript J = התפללו לאל שלא תהיה מנוסתכם בסתיו ובשבת
Pray to El that your flight shall not be in winter and on Shabbath. = Manuscript J

Matthew 24:32-33 – All manuscripts have same error as J in 42-43 of the scribe seeing the word קרוב 'near' written twice in verses 32-33 and leaving out all of the original words in between. Unfortunately because all manuscripts leave out these words by scribal error, the original words in the missing gap in 32-33 are lost at present.

Manuscript L plus correction from ABDGJKM = מעץ התאנה תלמדו המשל כאשר תראו ענפיה ועלים צומחים תדעו כי (קרוב) --- קרוב הוא לשערים

Matthew 24:42-43 – Manuscript J has scribal error where Hebrew words איזו שעה are written twice (with this spelling in most manuscripts) in verses 42 and 43, causing the scribe's eye to stray and leave out the words שעה אדוניכם בא זאת תדעו אם היה יודע איזו in between.

Manuscript L = אז אמר ישו לתלמידיו לזאת שמרו עמי שלא תדעו איזו שעה אדוניכם בא זאת תדעו אם היה יודע איזה שעה הגנב בא ישמור ולא יעזוב לחתור ביתו

Manuscript J = אז אמר ישו לתלמידיו לזאת שמרו עמי שלא תדעו איזו שעה --- הגנב בא ישמור ולא יעזוב לחתור ביתו

www.ingramcontent.com/pod-product-compliance
Lightning Source LLC
Chambersburg PA
CBHW060418010526
44118CB00017B/2260